Agatha Christie

McFarland Companions to Mystery Fiction

Agatha Christie

*A Companion
to the Mystery Fiction*

J.C. BERNTHAL

McFarland Companions to Mystery Fiction, 12
Series Editor Elizabeth Foxwell

McFarland & Company, Inc., Publishers
Jefferson, North Carolina

ISBN (print) 978-1-4766-7620-3
ISBN (ebook) 978-1-4766-4715-9

Library of Congress and British Library
cataloguing data are available

Library of Congress Control Number 2022029935

On the cover: inset Agatha Christie arriving at the Schiphol Airport
in Amsterdam, 1964 (Dutch National Archives);
illustration of Hercule Poirot (Shutterstock/ Alexander Sorokopud)

Printed in the United States of America

*McFarland & Company, Inc., Publishers
Box 611, Jefferson, North Carolina 28640
www.mcfarlandpub.com*

Table of Contents

Acknowledgments

This book is a lot longer than initially planned, and a full list of acknowledgments would likely double its size again. This project consolidates a decade of research activity that started when I began my PhD at the University of Exeter, so first and foremost I wish to acknowledge my supervisors Vike Martina Plock, Jana Funke, and Lisa Downing. The direction of Agatha Christie scholarship has been fundamentally changed, enhanced, and democratized by the international Agatha Christie conferences, and I wish to thank all delegates, but especially my co-organizers over the years: Mia Dormer, Sarah Martin, Mark Aldridge, and Stefano Serafini.

I wish also to thank Rebecca Mills and Mary Anna Evans, collaborators on different projects, whose insights into close-reading and context have been hugely influential on the systematic approach this text takes. I am especially grateful to Professor Evans for alerting me to materials within the *Ellery Queen Mystery Magazine* archive at Columbia University and Tina Hodgkinson for more insights into the Miller family tree and the Christies' London life than it is possible to mention.

The following archives and their excellent archivists have been especially helpful over the years: the Agatha Christie Family Archive, the British Library, the British Newspaper Archive, Columbia University's Archival Collections, the Imperial War Museum in London, the Mass Observation Archive, the University of Bristol Special Collections, the University of Exeter Special Collections, and the University of Tasmania Special and Rare Collections. At the University of Tasmania, I wish especially to thank Heather Excell, who kindly and insightfully solved the mystery of the 1932 play *Roads of Memory*, unearthing this "lost" Christie play from the Fuller papers.

Other individuals who have been especially helpful and insightful include Mathew and Lucy Prichard, the late Tom Adams, John Curran, Jared Cade, Lucy Worsley, and Tony Medawar. On the personal side, I wish to thank my spouse Alan Bernthal-Hooker. Thank you also to my preternaturally patient editor, Elizabeth Foxwell, whose work on this manuscript has been incredible. Finally, I would like to thank my grandfather, Gerald Pinner, who passed away shortly after the first draft of this manuscript was completed. He introduced me to Agatha Christie and instilled in me the value of reading for pleasure.

Preface

Agatha Christie would be confused by this book. She was firmly of the opinion that detective fiction should be enjoyed, not studied. She once told a postgraduate student, writing a dissertation on her plays, that any heavy analysis of her plots would simply spoil the fun. When I started studying Christie, I came across this attitude from several quarters, especially in the British media, although resistance to the idea of taking mysteries seriously has lessened considerably in recent years.

Like many readers, I discovered Christie at a young age, as my first "adult" author. The books—not just the puzzles—stuck with me, and it never occurred to me that I would not want to find out more. As I entered academia, I noticed a bizarrely dismissive attitude to Christie and popular writers in general; it was as if popularity precluded intellectual value. I was discouraged from writing my undergraduate dissertation on Christie and told that, if I wanted to write about a woman writer, there was mileage yet in Virginia Woolf. I wrote the dissertation I wanted to write, and the academic who made that remark even picked up their first Christie novel and became an admirer.

There remains a certain cliché about Christie: the image of the vicarage tea party, abstract and artificial, removed from real life's grim realities. The story goes that, in Agatha Christie Land, a corpse is not real but a pretext for a puzzle. Two-dimensional characters pepper her pages, more concerned with the intricacies of a railway timetable than the horrors of murder. At the end of the book, order is restored, and all the characters have tea, in a blissful haze of faux–Edwardiana. This kind of view of Christie and her work was not helped by the kind of scholarship that existed at that time: generally light, deliberately so, and often not even bothering to engage with the texts but written in general terms, allusive, and from memory.

Attitudes to Christie are changing. This is thanks in large part to screen adaptations in the 2010s, which, unlike the nostalgic, highly conservative television productions of the 1980s and 1990s, emphasize darker, more psychologically astute aspects of Christie's plots. Christie is continuously being rediscovered and re-evaluated. But through all the years of critical neglect and critical reclamation, she has remained intensely, unbelievably popular. The statistics and accolades are widely known and much touted. Outsold only by the Bible and Shakespeare, translated into every major language, Christie is more than a popular author. She is an institution, as embedded in the literary landscape as *The Mousetrap* (her play, which opened in 1952 and is still running) is in the West End of London.

I was fortunate enough to enter the conversations with my first monograph and edited volume on Christie as the tide was starting to change. In fact, *The Ageless Agatha Christie*, which I edited and published with McFarland in 2015, was the first ever edited collection on Christie printed by an academic press. It is remarkable that it took so long, given Christie's ubiquity. The tide has not stopped, though, and now there is a sea of excellent analysis around the academic world. It is, clearly, time to get some of the material in order.

It is time for a companion that will serve researchers, students, and enthusiasts who want to dig into this remarkable body of creative work, and need to know where to look. While several Christie companions exist, these tend to describe the key works or characters, and to date no volume has catalogued Christie's *entire* published oeuvre, let alone her many unpublished or lesser-known works. That is the aim of this volume: to set out what Christie wrote and when, and what she wrote *about*. There are several resources, including poems, articles, and interviews, that have been critically completely untapped. Some are mentioned here for the first time.

Writing this book has felt at times like a Herculean labor. The original plan, to cover every single character ever mentioned as well as every single title and adaptation, had to be abandoned. The book would have ended up beating *The Complete Miss Marple* as the longest book in the world if every character had their own entry. Instead, I have listed all characters in published works and included entries on major and recurring ones. As with any emerging field of scholarship, I also found that new things kept emerging all the time. I would like to draw attention here to the archival research of Mark Aldridge and Marco Amici, both of whom have uncovered "forgotten" material in their projects for Christie's British and Italian publishers. A less pleasant obstacle has been the COVID-19 pandemic, which has made archival visits and face-to-face interviews impossible. However, I have been lucky enough to have a decade of research in these archives and well-established relationships in the world of Christie to draw upon.

Over a century after her first novel was published, nearly half a century after her death, and entering the eighth decade of *The Mousetrap*'s West End run, Agatha Christie has no serious contender for the title "Queen of Crime." Her sales continue to grow, as screen adaptations, video games, and interest in her life and work abound year on year. It is my earnest hope that the present companion will serve all generations of scholars as well as fans and casual readers who want to dig a little deeper and uncover new connections, angles, or ideas in this remarkable author's vast body of work.

Organization
of the Companion

This companion is designed to aid anyone with an interest in Dame Agatha Christie. Enthusiasts, students, journalists, and readers alike can find useful material within these pages, including exhaustive details about Christie's entire published output, unpublished materials—some discussed for the first time—media adaptations from around the world, and the key points of her life and career. In addition, the companion provides overviews of key debates and the most significant themes and avenues of scholarship.

Entries cover novels; short stories; collaborative writing; scripts; poetry and music; memoirs; articles; interviews; letters; and third-party adaptations for stage, screen, and radio plus themes, characters, fictional locations, real people and events, and more. All entries are arranged alphabetically. Not all of Christie's creations—which number in the thousands—are discussed in detail, but all who appear in published works are named, and there are separate entries for each significant/distinctive or recurring character, plus every name that is used more than once.

This project is based on a lifetime of personal, scholarly, and professional interest in Christie and three years of intensive archival research. As a result, I believe it to be the most thorough Agatha Christie research aid in existence, equally valuable for new and longtime Christie fans as well as seasoned academics.

Agatha Christie:
A Brief Biography

The world's bestselling and most influential novelist was born Agatha Mary Clarissa Miller to a British-Irish mother and an American father on 15 September 1890. She was raised in Torquay, on the west coast of England. She adored her father, Frederick Miller, who died when she was 10, and was affectionate toward her mother, Clarissa "Clara" Miller, who was often nervous and experimented with several of the more esoteric brands of Christianity. Clara decided that girls should not learn to read, so Agatha was largely homeschooled and made to play in the garden, unlike her older sister, Margaret "Madge" Watts, who published several stories and became a West End playwright. Nonetheless, Agatha taught herself to read and write at a young age.

As a teenager and young woman, Agatha was attractive to men and briefly became engaged before breaking it off to marry Colonel Archibald Christie, a reserve pilot with the Royal Air Force. Their daughter, Rosalind, was born in 1919. Christie also wrote stories, poetry, and music, and had some ambition of being an opera singer, for which her voice was not suited. Some of her composition such as "One Hour with Thee" survive. During World War I, she wrote her first crime novel, *The Mysterious Affair at Styles*, which was rejected by several publishers before it was optioned by John Lane of The Bodley Head. The novel introduces her Belgian detective—the diminutive, idiosyncratic Hercule Poirot—based on the refugees with whom she worked as a Voluntary Aid Detachment (VAD) nurse and apothecary assistant during the war and makes significant use of her medical training and knowledge of poisons.

The book was a success, and before long, Christie was writing one a year, rapidly becoming one of the highest-regarded writers in the busy field of crime fiction. The year 1926 brought both positive and negative developments. Christie had by now acquired an agent, Edmund Cork, who negotiated a new, preferential contract with William Collins and son: the Collins/Christie relationship continues to this day and was instrumental in spawning the genre-defining Collins Crime Club imprint, whereas Christie's contract with Lane and The Bodley Head led in a roundabout way to the creation of Penguin Books. *The Murder of Roger Ackroyd*, published by Collins in 1926, became an international *cause célèbre*, thrusting its author into household name status. With its then-unguessable twist ending, *The Murder of Roger Ackroyd* has come to typify the Golden Age of crime fiction. It would soon inspire the first major stage adaptation of Christie's work, *Alibi*, and significant film, television, and radio adaptations.

However, the heights of success were tempered. Christie's mother died in April 1926, which caused the author considerable distress. In August, she suffered a severe depression and went to Scotland to recover. When she returned, Archie announced that he had been having an affair and wanted a divorce so he could marry his mistress. Struggling to raise Rosalind, deal with her marital issues, grieve for her mother, and balance a career writing one novel and dozens of stories a year, Christie saw her mental health deteriorate significantly toward the end of the year. In December 1926, she left her home in Berkshire, and her car was found abandoned.

The disappearance caused an international media sensation, with journalists following the action on an hour-by-hour basis and thousands involved in searches, including major writers such as Dorothy L. Sayers and Sir Arthur Conan Doyle. Others published their opinions, claiming that the missing novelist was either staging her disappearance as a publicity stunt or that her husband had killed her. She was found after 11 days, staying at a health spa in Harrogate under a name similar to that of her husband's mistress. It was announced but not universally believed that she had suffered from a form of amnesia, and Christie rarely discussed the incident in subsequent years. Two years later, the Christies' divorce was finalized.

Christie continued writing, introducing another enduring detective in 1927. Elderly spinster Jane Marple made her first unobtrusive appearance in a set of short stories, which became *The Thirteen Problems*, before making her novelistic debut in *The Murder at the Vicarage* in 1930. The character was well-received as a new kind of detective, and before long, Christie was regretting that her two most successful creations, Monsieur Poirot and Miss Marple, had been introduced as elderly people, when she would likely have to keep writing about them for many years to come.

For her own mental health, Christie treated herself in 1928 to a trip on the Orient Express and travelled to Ur, where she met archaeologists led by Leonard Woolley. When she returned the next year, she met Woolley's assistant, Max Mallowan. She enjoyed an unusual courtship with this much younger man, and they married in September 1930. Subsequently, Christie joined her husband on most of his digs, becoming actively involved in archaeology and drawing inspiration for several novels and a personality-filled memoir, *Come, Tell Me How You Live*.

The 1930s form the most typical decade of Golden Age crime fiction and the decade in which Christie reached the peak of productivity, producing up to six books in any given year. She published under the Christie name but also wrote under a pseudonym, Mary Westmacott, to produce psychological novels without crime, exploring often personal themes and ideas. Some of her most iconic titles were published in the 1930s, including *Murder on the Orient Express*, *Death on the Nile*, and—at the end of the decade—*And Then There Were None*, which has become the world's second best-selling novel of any kind (after Charles Dickens's *A Tale of Two Cities*) and likely the most heavily adapted.

During World War II, Christie returned to volunteer medical work while lending her holiday home, Greenway House, to the U.S. military and maintained her prolific publication schedule. She had always written plays, and one, *Black Coffee*, had been staged in 1930, but now she started considering writing seriously for the West End. Unsatisfied with several third-party adaptations of her work, she turned *And Then There Were None* into a play, which was well-received despite an early closing when its venue, St. James's Theatre, was bombed and gained a Broadway production. It launched a secondary career for Christie and established her as the most successful female playwright in history.

The most famous of Christie's plays, *The Mousetrap*, opened in the West End in 1952 and has enjoyed the world's longest continuous run, outrunning its competitors by several decades. It even changed venues in 1972 without skipping a performance, and the curtain only went down in March 2020 when the COVID-19 pandemic forced London to close its theaters. It reopened in May 2021. The play has become a quintessential feature of London itself, as recognizable as Queen Elizabeth II (who has reigned a little longer than its run), and an essential tourist attraction as well as a domestic one. It has come to typify a sense of nostalgia often linked to Christie's work.

In 1950, Christie was elected a fellow of the Royal Society of Literature. Six years later, after some debate among officials over whether to grant her a damehood, she was appointed a Commander of the Order of the British Empire (CBE). The University of Exeter awarded her an honorary doctorate in literature in 1961, and in 1969 she became Lady Mallowan when her husband

Agatha Christie arrives at Schiphol Airport in Amsterdam, 17 September 1964. Photo by Joop van Bilson. Anefo, Dutch National Archives.

was knighted for services to archaeology. In 1971, she was awarded a damehood, becoming Lady Mallowan (or Dame Agatha) in her own right.

Her health deteriorated, and, by 1974, she was no longer capable of producing a novel. Short stories were published in lieu of her annual novel that year and, the next year, a novel that had been saved for posthumous publication, *Curtain*, in which Poirot dies, was published. The public reaction was immense, and the detective received a unique front-page obituary—really more a retrospective on his creator's career—in the *New York Times*. Christie died at Winterbrook House, after a short bout with pneumonia, on 12 January 1976. West End theaters dimmed their lights in her honor. She was buried at St. Mary's Church, Cholsey, and her gravestone is inscribed with favored lines from Edmund Spenser's *The Faerie Queene*: "Sleepe after toyle, / Port after stormie seas, / Ease after warre, / Death after life / Does greatly please" (Spenser 107).

A Career Chronology

September 1890: Agatha Mary Clarissa Miller is born in Torquay.

July 1901: Agatha Miller first publishes in a local newspaper.

November 1901: Father Frederick Miller dies.

1908: Agatha Miller's first musical publication, "One Hour with Thee," appears.

October 1912: Meets and begins dating Archie Christie.

July 1914: Outbreak of World War I.

December 1914: Agatha Miller and Archie Christie marry in Torquay.

1918: *The Mysterious Affair at Styles* is accepted for publication.

November 1918: World War I concludes.

August 1919: Rosalind, the Christies' only child, is born.

May 1920: *The Mysterious Affair at Styles* is serialized, introducing Hercule Poirot.

October 1920: *The Mysterious Affair at Styles* is published in book form.

January 1922: The Christies take part in the British Empire Exhibition tour.

April 1926: Christie's mother, Clara Miller, dies.

June 1926: *The Murder of Roger Ackroyd* is published, catapulting its creator to international celebrity.

December 1926: Christie disappears for 11 days, prompting a major media event.

1928: After a divorce from Archie, Christie meets Max Mallowan.

May 1928: Michael Morton's *Alibi*, the first play based on a Christie novel, opens.

July 1928: The first Christie movie, *The Passing of Mr. Quinn*, is released in the United Kingdom.

1930: Christie cofounds the Detection Club with other mystery writers.

April 1930: Christie's first novel under the pseudonym Mary Westmacott, *Giant's Bread*, is published.

September 1930: Christie and Mallowan marry in Edinburgh.

October 1930: *The Murder at the Vicarage*, the first Miss Marple novel, is published.

December 1930: *Black Coffee* becomes Christie's first original play to receive a West End run.

September 1939: World War II is declared; Christie will volunteer at University College Hospital, London.

November 1939: *And Then There Were None*, the bestselling crime novel in history, is published.

May 1941: Christie's London home, 58 Sheffield Terrace, is bombed.

September 1945: World War II ends.

May 1947: The BBC airs a special play written for Queen Mary's 80th birthday, *Three Blind Mice*, which will become *The Mousetrap*.

April 1949: Following a successful secret career as Mary Westmacott, Christie faces the exposure of her true identity.

June 1950: A blaze of publicity and juggled figures mark *A Murder Is Announced* as Christie's 50th book.

November 1952: *The Mousetrap* opens in London's West End.

1955: Christie is named a Grand Master by Mystery Writers of America and wins the Edgar Award in the Best Play category for *Witness for the Prosecution*.

January 1956: Christie is appointed a Commander of the Order of the British Empire.

December 1957: Billy Wilder's *Witness for the Prosecution*, based on the play, opens in cinemas; Christie begins her term as president of the Detection Club.

April 1958: *The Mousetrap* becomes the longest-running show in the West End; soon after, it becomes the longest-running show in the world.

January 1969: Max Mallowan is knighted.

1971: UNESCO declares Christie the world's most-translated author and bestselling novelist, outsold only by the Bible and William Shakespeare.

January 1971: Christie is created a Dame Commander of the British Empire (DBE).

November 1974: Sidney Lumet's *Murder on the Orient Express*, based on the novel, is released to international success, becoming the highest-grossing film of the decade and winning an Academy Award. Christie's last public appearance is at the premiere.

September 1975: *Curtain: Poirot's Last Case* is published.

January 1976: Christie dies in Wallingford.

November 1977: Christie's autobiography is published posthumously.

1978: Christie's autobiography is nominated for an Edgar Award in the Best Critical/Biographical Work category.

December 1983: BBC television begins airing its influential series, *Miss Marple*.

January 1989: ITV begins airing its influential series, *Agatha Christie's Poirot*.

November 2002: *The Mousetrap* marks its unprecedented golden jubilee.

October 2004: Rosalind Hicks dies; control of Agatha Christie Ltd. passes to Hicks's son, Mathew Prichard.

December 2015: The BBC's *And Then There Were None* contributes to a public reevaluation of Christie as a dark, psychological novelist.

November 2017: Kenneth Branagh's *Murder on the Orient Express,* the first cinematic treatment of Christie since 1988, is released.

March 2020: *The Mousetrap* closes in London due to COVID-19 after a nearly 68-year run.

May 2021: *The Mousetrap* reopens in London.

Christie's Works
in Alphabetical Order

"The AA Alphabet for 1915" (collaborative poem, unpublished)

The ABC Murders (novel, November 1935)

Absent in the Spring (novel, August 1944)

"Accident" (story, September 1929; alternative titles: "Test for Murder," "The Uncrossed Path")

"The Actress" (story, May 1923; alternative title: "A Trap for the Unwary")

"The Adventure of Johnnie Waverly" (story, October 1923; alternative titles: "At the Stroke of Twelve," "The Kidnapping of Johnnie Waverly")

"The Adventure of the Cheap Flat" (story, May 1923; alternative title: "Poirot Indulges a Whim")

"The Adventure of the Christmas Pudding" (novella, October 1960; alternative title: "The Theft of the Royal Ruby")

The Adventure of the Christmas Pudding (short story collection, October 1960; alternative title: *The Adventure of the Christmas Pudding and a Selection of Entrees*)

"The Adventure of the Clapham Cook" (story, November 1923; alternative title: "Find the Cook")

"The Adventure of the Dartmoor Bungalow" (story, January 1924; alternative title: "The Importance of a Leg of Mutton")

"The Adventure of the Egyptian Tomb" (story, September 1923; alternative titles: "The Egyptian Tomb," "The Next Victim")

"The Adventure of the Italian Nobleman" (story, October 1923; alternative title: "The Regent's Court Murder")

"The Adventure of the Peroxide Blonde" (story, February 1924)

"The Adventure of the Sinister Stranger" (story, October 1924; alternative title: "The Case of the Sinister Stranger")

"The Adventure of the 'Western Star'" (story, April 1923; alternative title: "Poirot Puts a Finger in the Pie")

"The Affair at the Bungalow" (story, May 1930)

"The Affair at the Victory Ball" (story, March 1923; alternative title: "The Six China Figures")

After the Funeral (novel, January 1953; alternative titles: *Funerals Are Fatal; Murder at the Gallop*)

"Agatha Christie's Mystery Potatoes" (recipe, July 1940)

Akhnaton (play, May 1973; alternative title: *Akhnaton and Nefertiti*)

"The Ambassador's Boots" (story, November 1924; alternative title: "The Matter of the Ambassador's Boots")

And Then There Were None (novel, June 1939; alternative titles: *Ten Little Indians, Ten Little N-----s*)

And Then There Were None (play, September 1943; alternative titles: *Ten Little Indians, Ten Little N-----s*)

"The Apples of Hesperides" (story, May 1940; alternative title: "The Poison Cup")

Appointment with Death (novel, August 1937; alternative title: *Date with Death*)

Appointment with Death (play, January 1945)

"The Arcadian Deer" (story, May 1940; alternative title "Vanishing Lady")

At Bertram's Hotel (novel, November 1965)

"At the Bells and Motley" (story, November 1925; alternative titles: "The Disappearance of Captain Harwell," "A Man of Magic")

9

"The Augean Stables" (story, March 1940)

An Autobiography (memoir, November 1977)

"The Baited Trap" (story, February 1924)

"The Ballad of the Flint" (poem, January 1925)

"Ballad of the Maytime" (poem, January 1925)

"Beatrice Passes" (poem, January 1925)

"Beauty" (poem, October 1973)

"Behind the Screen" (collaborative novella, June 1930)

"Being So Very Wilful" (story, unpublished)

"The Bells of Brittany" (poem, January 1925)

"Best of the Year" (review, January 1952)

The Big Four (novel, January 1927)

The Big Four (short story collection, December 2016; alternative title: *The Man Who Was Number Four: Further Adventures of M. Poirot*)

"The Bird with the Broken Wing" (story, April 1930)

Black Coffee (play, December 1930; alternative title: *After Dinner*)

Bleak House (screenplay, unpublished)

"Blindman's Buff" (story, November 1924; alternative title: "Blind Man's Buff")

"The Bloodstained Pavement" (story, March 1928; alternative titles: "The Blood-Stained Pavement"; "Drip! Drip!"; "Miss Marple and the Wicked World")

"The Blue Geranium" (story, December 1929)

The Body in the Library (novel, May 1941)

The Burden (novel, November 1956)

Butter in a Lordly Dish (radio play, January 1948)

By the Pricking of My Thumbs (novel, November 1968)

"The Call of Wings" (story, October 1933)

"Calvary" (poem, October 1973)

"The Capture of Cerberus" (story, March 1947; alternative titles: "Hercule Poirot in Hell"; "Meet Me in Hell!")

"The Capture of Cerberus" (story, August 2009)

Cards on the Table (novel, May 1936)

A Caribbean Mystery (novel, November 1964)

"The Case of the Caretaker" (story, January 1942)

"The Case of the Caretaker's Wife" (story, September 2011)

"The Case of the City Clerk" (story, August 1932; alternative title: "The £10 Adventure")

"The Case of the Discontented Husband" (story, August 1932; alternative title: "His Lady's Affair")

"The Case of the Discontented Soldier" (story, August 1932; alternative title: "Adventure by Request")

"The Case of the Distressed Lady" (story, August 1932; alternative titles: "The Cat and the Chestnut"; "Faked!")

"The Case of the Middle-Aged Wife" (story, October 1932; alternative title: "The Woman Concerned")

"The Case of the Missing Lady" (story, October 1924)

"The Case of the Missing Will" (story, October 1923; alternative titles: "Sporting Challenge," "Where There's a Will")

"The Case of the Perfect Maid" (story, April 1942; alternative titles: "The Perfect Maid," "The Servant Problem")

"The Case of the Rich Woman" (story, August 1932; alternative title: "The Rich Woman Who Wanted Only to Be Happy")

Cat Among the Pigeons (novel, September 1959)

"The Chess Problem" (story, February 1924; alternative titles: "A Chess Problem," "A Game of Chess")

"The Chocolate Box" (story, May 1923; alternative titles: "The Clue of the Chocolate Box," "The Time Hercule Poirot Failed")

"A Choice" (poem, October 1973)

"The Choice" (story, unpublished)

"Christmas Adventure" (story, December 1923)

"A Christmas Tragedy" (story, January 1930; alternative titles: "The Hat and the Alibi"; "Never Two without Three")

"Cleopatra as the Dark Lady" (letter, February 1973)

"The Clergyman's Daughter" (story, December 1923; alternative titles: "The First Wish"; "The Red House")

"The Clock Stopped" (story opening, Autumn 1949)

The Clocks (novel, November 1963)

The Clutching Hand (play, unpublished)

"Columbine's Song" (poem, January 1925)

Come, Tell Me How You Live (memoir, November 1946)

"The Coming of Mr. Quin" (story, March 1924; alternative title: "The Passing of Mr. Quinn")

"The Companion" (story, February 1930; alternative title: "The Resurrection of Amy Durrant")

The Conqueror (play, unpublished)

"The Cornish Mystery" (story, November 23)

"Count Ferson to the Queen" (poem, October 1973)

"The Crackler" (story, November 1924; alternative titles: "The Affair of the Forged Notes," "The Case of the Forged Notes")

"The Crag in the Dolomites" (story, March 1924)

"The Cretan Bull" (story, September 1939; alternative titles: "The Case of the Family Taint"; "Midnight Madness")

"The Crime Passionnel" (article, February 1930)

Crooked House (novel, October 1948)

"Ctesiphon" (poem, October 1973)

Curtain (novel, September 1975; alternative title: *Curtain: Poirot's Last Case*)

"Dark Sheila" (poem, 1919)

"Dartmoor" (poem, October 1973)

A Daughter's a Daughter (novel, November 1952)

A Daughter's a Daughter (play, July 1956)

"The Dead Harlequin" (story, March 1929; alternative title: "The Man in the Empty Chair")

Dead Man's Folly (novel, July 1956)

"Dead Man's Mirror" (novella, March 1937)

"Death by Drowning" (story, November 1931; alternative title: "Village Tragedy")

Death Comes as the End (novel, October 1944)

Death in the Clouds (novel, February 1935; alternative title: *Death in the Air*)

"Death on the Nile" (story, April 1933)

Death on the Nile (novel, May 1937)

Destination Unknown (novel, September 1954; alternative title: *So Many Steps to Death*)

"Detective Writers in England" (article, December 2008)

"The Disappearance of Mr. Davenheim" (story, March 1923; alternative titles: "Hercule Poirot, Armchair Detective"; "Mr. Davenby Disappears")

"Does Woman's Instinct Make Her a Good Detective?" (article, May 1928)

"The Double Clue" (story, December 1923)

"Double Sin" (story, September 1928; alternative title: "By Road or Rail")

Double Sin (short story collection, 1961; alternative title: *Double Sin and Other Stories*)

"Down in the Wood" (poem, January 1925)

"The Dream" (story, October 1937; alternative title: "The Three Strange Points")

"The Dream Spinners" (poem, January 1925)

"The Dressmaker's Doll" (story, December 1958)

"Drugs and Detective Stories" (article, 1941)

Dumb Witness (novel, July 1937; alternative title: *Poirot Loses a Client*)

"The Dying Chinaman" (story, March 1924)

"Easter, 1918" (poem, January 1925)

"The Edge" (story, February 1927)

Elephants Can Remember (novel, November 1972)

"Elizabeth of England" (poem, January 1925)

"Enchantment" (poem, October 1973)

Endless Night (novel, October 1967)

"The Erymanthian Boar" (story, May 1940; alternative title: "Murder Mountain")

Eugenia and Eugenics (play, unpublished)

Evil Under the Sun (novel, December 1940)

"The Face of Helen" (story, April 1927)

"A Fairy in the Flat" (story, September 1924; alternative titles: "Blunt's Brilliant Detectives"; "The Affair of the Pink Pearl"; "Publicity")

Fiddlers Five (play, 1971; alternative titles: *Fiddle de Dee*; *Fiddlers All*; *This Mortal Coil*; *Sixpence Off*)

Fiddlers Three (play, August 1972)

"Finessing the King" (story, October 1924)

Five Little Pigs (novel, September 1941; alternative title: *Murder in Retrospect*)

The Floating Admiral (collaborative novel, December 1931)

"The Flock of Geryon" (story, May 1940; alternative title: "Weird Monster")

"Four and Twenty Blackbirds" (story, November 1940; alternative title: "Poirot and the Regular Customer")

4.50 from Paddington (novel, October 1957; alternative titles: *Eyewitness to Murder*, *Murder She Said*, *What Mrs. McGillicuddy Saw!*)

"The Four Suspects" (story, April 1930; alternative title: "Some Day They Will Get Me")

"The Fourth Man" (story, December 1925)

"From a Grown-up to a Child" (poem, October 1973)

"A Fruitful Sunday" (story, August 1928)

"The Gate of Baghdad" (story, April 1933; alternative titles: "At the Gate of Baghdad," "The Gate of Death")

"The Gentleman Dressed in Newspaper" (story, October 1924)

Giant's Bread (novel, April 1930)

"The Gipsy" (story, October 1933; alternative title: "The Gypsy")

"The Girdle of Hippolyta" (story, September 1939; alternative titles: "The Case of the Missing Schoolgirl," "The Disappearance of Winnie King")

"The Girl in the Train" (story, February 1924)

Go Back for Murder (play, March 1960)

"Gold, Frankincense and Myrrh" (poem, October 1965)

"The Golden Ball" (story, August 1929; alternative title: "Playing the Innocent")

The Golden Ball (short story collection, 1971; alternative title: *The Golden Ball and Other Stories*)

The Grand Tour (collected correspondence, November 2012)

"The Green Gate" (story, unpublished)

"Greenshaw's Folly" (novella, December 1956)

"A Greeting" (poem, October 1965)

Hallowe'en Party (novel, November 1969)

"The Harlequin Tea Set" (story, November 1971)

The Harlequin Tea Set (short story collection, April 1997; alternative title: *The Harlequin Tea Set and Other Stories*)

"Harlequin's Lane" (story, May 1927)

"Harlequin's Song" (poem, before 1919)

"Have Ye Walked in the Wood Today?" (poem, unpublished)

"Have You Got Everything You Want?" (story, April 1933; alternative titles: "Express to Stamboul," "On the Orient Express")

"Hawthorn Trees" (poem, October 1973)

"Her Own Story of Her Disappearance" (interview as article, February 1928)

"The Herb of Death" (story, March 1930; alternative title: "Foxglove in the Sage")

"Hercule Poirot and the Greenshore Folly" (novella, September 2014; alternative title: "The Greenshore Folly")

"Hercule Poirot: Fiction's Greatest Detective" (article, January 1938; alternative title: "How I Created Hercule Poirot")

Hercule Poirot's Christmas (novel, November 1938; alternative titles: *A Holiday for Murder, Murder at Christmas, Murder for Christmas*)

"Heritage" (poem, January 1925)

Hickory Dickory Dock (novel, May 1955; alternative title: *Hickory Dickory Death*)

The Hollow (novel, May 1946; alternative titles: *Murder After Hours; The Outraged Heart*)

The Hollow (play, February 1951; alternative title: *The Suspects*)

"The Horses of Diomedes" (story, June 1940; alternative title: "The Case of the Drug Peddler")

The Hound of Death (short story collection, October 1933; alternative title: *The Hound of Death and Other Stories*)

"The Hound of Death" (story, October 1933)

"The House at Shiraz" (story, April 1933; alternative titles: "At the House in Shiraz," "The Dream House of Shiraz")

"The House of Beauty" (story, unpublished)

"The House of Dreams" (story, January 1926)

"The House of Lurking Death" (story, November 1924)

"How Does Your Garden Grow?" (story, August 1935)

"How I Became a Writer" (article, August 1938)

"Hymn to Ra" (poem, January 1925)

"I Wore My New Canary Suit" (poem, October 1973)

"The Idol House of Astarte" (story, January 1928; alternative titles: "The Solving Six and the Evil Hour"; "The 'Supernatural' Murder")

"In a Dispensary" (poem, January 1925)

"In a Glass Darkly" (story, December 1934)

"In Baghdad" (poem, October 1973)

"In the Cool of the Evening" (story, November 1965)

"In the Market Place" (story, unpublished)

"The Incident of the Dog's Ball" (story, September 2009)

"The Incredible Theft" (novella, March 1937)

"Ingots of Gold" (story, February 1928; alternative titles: "The Solving Six and the Evil Hour," "The 'Supernatural' Murder")

"An Island" (poem, October 1973)

"The Island" (story, November 1965)

"Islot of Brittany" (poem, October 1973)

"Jane in Search of a Job" (story, August 1924)

"Jenny by the Sky" (poem, October 1965)

"The Jewel Robbery at the Grand Metropolitan" (story, March 1923; alternative titles: "The Curious Disappearance of the Opalsen Pearls," "The Jewel Robbery at the 'Grand Metropolitan,'" "The Theft of the Opalsen Pearls")

"The Kidnapped Prime Minister" (story, April 1923)

"The King of Clubs" (story, March 1923; alternative titles: "The Adventure of the King of Clubs," "Beware the King of Clubs")

The Labours of Hercules (short story collection, September 1947)

"The Lady on the Stairs" (story, January 1924)

"Lament of the Tortured Lover" (poem, October 1973)

"The Lamp" (story, October 1933)

"The Last Days of Nimrud" (poem, unpublished)

"The Last Séance" (story, March 1927; alternative titles: "The Stolen Ghost," "The Woman Who Stole a Ghost")

The Last Séance (short story collection, October 2019; alternative title: *The Last Séance: Tales of the Supernatural*)

The Last Séance (play, unpublished)

"The Last Song of Columbine" (poem, January 1925)

"The Lemesurier Inheritance" (story, December 1923)

"The Lernean Hydra" (story, September 1939; alternative titles: "The Hydra of Lernea, or the Case of the Gossipers"; "Invisible Enemy")

"A Letter from Agatha Christie" (letter, October 1968)

"A Letter to my Publisher" (fictional letter, April 1936)

Letter to "Woman's Day" (letter, unpublished)

The Lie (play, August 2020; alternative title: *The Sister-in-Law*)

"The Listerdale Mystery" (story, December 1925; alternative title: "The Benevolent Butler")

The Listerdale Mystery (short story collection, June 1934)

"A Little Cowslip" (poem, unpublished)

"The Lonely God" (story, July 1926)

Lord Edgware Dies (novel, March 1933; alternative title: *Thirteen at Dinner*)

"The Lost Mine" (story, November 1923)

"The Love Detectives" (story, December 1926; alternative title: "At the Crossroads")

"Love Passes" (poem, January 1925)

"Magnolia Blossom" (story, March 1926)

"The Man from the Sea" (story, October 1929)

The Man in the Brown Suit (novel, November 1923; alternative titles: *Anna the Adventuress, Anne the Adventurous*)

"The Man in the Mist" (story, December 1924)

"The Man Who Knew" (story, September 2011)

"The Man Who Was Number Sixteen" (story, December 1924)

"The Manhood of Edward Robinson" (story, December 1924; alternative titles: "The Day of His Dreams"; "Romance and a Red Runabout")

"Manx Gold" (story, May 1930)

"Margery Allingham: A Tribute" (obituary, 1966)

"The Market Basing Mystery" (story, October 1923)

Marmalade Moon (play, unpublished)

"The Million Dollar Bond Robbery" (story, May 1923)

The Mirror Crack'd from Side to Side (novel, November 1962. Alternative title: *The Mirror Crack'd*)

"Miss Marple Tells a Story" (monologue/ story, May 1934; alternative title: "Behind Closed Doors")

Miss Marple's Final Cases (short story collection, October 1979; alternative titles: *Miss Marple's Final Cases and Two Other Stories; Miss Marple's 6 Final Cases and 2 Other Stories*)

Miss Perry (play, unpublished)

"Mr. Eastwood's Adventure" (story, August 1924; alternative titles: "The Mystery of the Second Cucumber," "The Mystery of the Spanish Shawl")

"Motive v. Opportunity" (story, April 1928; alternative title: "Where's the Catch?")

The Mousetrap (play, October 1952)

The Moving Finger (novel, March 1942; alternative title: *The Case of the Moving Finger*)

Mrs. McGinty's Dead (novel, October 1951; alternative title: *Blood Will Tell*)

The Murder at the Vicarage (novel, August 1930)

Murder in Mesopotamia (novel, November 1935; alternative title: *No Other Love*)

"Murder in the Mews" (novella, December 1936; alternative title: "Good Night for a Murder")

Murder in the Mews (short story collection, March 1937; alternative titles: *Dead Man's Mirror; Murder in the Mews: 4 Poirot Stories*)

Murder in the Studio (radio script collection, 2019; alternative title: *Murder on Air*)

A Murder Is Announced (novel, February 1950)

Murder Is Easy (novel, November 1938; alternative title: *Easy to Kill*)

The Murder of Roger Ackroyd (novel, July 1925; alternative title: *Who Killed Ackroyd?*)

The Murder on the Links (novel, December 1922; alternative title: *The Girl with Anxious Eyes*)

Murder on the Nile (play, January 1944; alternative titles: *Hidden Horizon; Moon on the Nile*)

Murder on the Orient Express (novel, September 1933; alternative title: *Murder in the Calais Coach*)

"My Flower Garden" (poem, October 1973)

The Mysterious Affair at Styles (novel, February 1920; alternative title: *Mystery at Styles*)

The Mysterious Mr. Quin (short story collection, April 1930)

"The Mystery of Hunter's Lodge" (story, May 1923 alternative title: "Investigation by Telegram")

"The Mystery of the Baghdad Chest" (story, January 1932)

"The Mystery of the Blue Jar" (story, July 1924)

The Mystery of the Blue Train (novel, February 1928)

"The Mystery of the Spanish Chest" (story, September 1960)

N or M? (Novel, March 1941)

"The Naughty Donkey" (story, November 1965)

"The Nemean Lion" (story, November 1939; alternative title: "The Case of the Kidnapped Pekingese")

Nemesis (novel, September 1971)

New Moon (play, unpublished)

"Next to a Dog" (story, September 1929)

"The Nile" (poem, October 1973)

Nimrud Book of Dreams (poetry collection, unpublished)

"Nursery Rhyme of Nimrud" (poem, unpublished)

"Ode to Christopher Columbus" (poem, unpublished)

"One Hour with Thee" (waltz, 1908)

One, Two, Buckle My Shoe (novel, August 1940; alternative titles: *An Overdose of Death, The Patriotic Murders*)

"The Oracle at Delphi" (story, April 1933)

Ordeal by Innocence (novel, September 1958; alternative title: *The Innocent*)

The Pale Horse (novel, September 1961)

"A Palm Tree in Egypt" (poem, January 1925; alternative title: "A Palm Tree in the Desert")

Parker Pyne Investigates (short story collection, November 1934; alternative title: *Mr. Parker Pyne, Detective*)

Partners in Crime (short story collection, September 1929)

Passenger to Frankfurt (novel, September 1970)

"The Pearl of Price" (story, April 1933; alternative titles: "Once a Thief," "The Pearl")

Peril at End House (novel, June 1931)

Personal Call (radio play, May 1954)

"Philomel Cottage" (story, November 1924; alternative title: "A Stranger Walked In")

"Picnic 1960" (poem, October 1973)

"Pierette Dancing on the Moon" (poem, January 1925)

"Pierrot Grown Old" (poem, January 1925)

"Pierrot's Song by the Hearth" (poem, January 1925)

"Pierrot's Song to the Moon" (poem, January 1925)

"The Plymouth Express" (story, April 1923; alternative titles: "The Girl in Electric Blue," "The Mystery of the Plymouth

Express," "The Plymouth Express Affair")

A Pocket Full of Rye (novel, September 1953)

Poems (poetry collection, October 1973)

"Poirot and the Regatta Mystery" (story, June 1936)

Poirot Investigates (short story collection, March 1924)

Poirot Knows the Murderer (short story collection, March 1946)

Poirot Lends a Hand (short story collection, March 1946)

Poirot on Holiday (short story collection, November 1943)

Poirot's Early Cases (short story collection, September 1974)

Postern of Fate (novel, October 1973)

"A Pot of Tea" (story, September 1924; alternative title: "Publicity")

"The Princess Sings" (poem, January 1925)

"Problem at Pollensa Bay" (story, November 1935; alternative title: "Siren Business")

Problem at Pollensa Bay (short story collection, November 1991; alternative title: *Problem at Pollensa Bay and Other Stories*)

"Problem at Sea" (story, February 1936; alternative titles: "Poirot and the Crime in Cabin 66"; "Crime in Cabin 66"; "The Quickness of the Hand")

"Progression" (poem, January 1925)

"Promotion in the Highest" (story, November 1965)

"Pulcinella" (poem, January 1925)

"Racial Musings" (poem, October 1973)

"The Radium Thieves" (story, January 1924)

"The Rajah's Emerald" (story, July 1926)

"The Red House" (story, December 1923; alternative titles: "The Clergyman's Daughter"; "The First Wish")

"The Red Signal" (story, June 24)

The Regatta Mystery (short story collection, April 1939)

"The Regatta Mystery" (story, April 1939)

"Remembrance" (poem, October 1973)

"The Road of Dreams" (poem, January 1925)

The Road of Dreams (poetry collection, January 1925)

The Rose and the Yew Tree (novel, November 1948)

Rule of Three (play-set, December 1962)

Sad Cypress (novel, November 1939)

"The Saints of God" (poem, October 1965)

"Sanctuary" (story, October 1954; alternative titles: "The Man on the Chancel Steps," "Murder at the Vicarage")

"The Scoop" (collaborative novella, January 1931)

"The Sculptor" (poem, October 1973)

"The Second Gong" (story, July 1932)

The Secret Adversary (novel, August 1921)

The Secret of Chimneys (novel, June 1925)

The Secret of Chimneys (play, late 1940s; alternative title: *Chimneys*)

The Seven Dials Mystery (novel, January 1929)

"The Shadow on the Glass" (story, October 1924; alternative title: "Jealousy Is the Devil")

"The Sign in the Sky" (story, July 1925; alternative title: "A Sign in the Sky")

"Sing a Song of Sixpence" (story, December 1929)

"Sir Allen Lane: A Flair for Success" (obituary, July 1970; alternative title: "Enter Allen Lane and the Penguins")

The Sittaford Mystery (novel, March 1931; alternative title: *The Murder at Hazelmoor*)

Sleeping Murder (novel, July 1976)

Snow upon the Desert (novel, unpublished)

Someone at the Window (play, unpublished)

"S.O.S." (story, February 1926)

"The Soul of the Croupier" (story, November 1926)

Sparkling Cyanide (novel, July 1944; alternative title: *Remembered Death*)

Spider's Web (play, September 1954)

"Spring" (poem, January 1925)

"Star Over Bethlehem" (story, December 1946)

Star Over Bethlehem (short story/poetry collection, November 1965; alternative title: *Star Over Bethlehem and Other Stories*)

"The Strange Case of Sir Arthur Carmichael" (story, October 1933)

"Strange Jest" (story, November 1931; alternative title: "A Case of Buried Treasure")

The Stranger (play, January 2020)

"Stronger than Death" (story, unpublished)

"The Stymphalean Birds" (story, September 1939; alternative titles: "The Case of the Vulture Women," "Vulture Women")

"The Submarine Plans" (story, November

1923; alternative title: "The Shadow in the Night")

"The Sunningdale Mystery" (story, October 1924; alternative title: "The Sunninghill Mystery")

"Swan Song" (story, September 1926)

Taken at the Flood (novel, March 1948; alternative title: *There Is a Tide*)

"Tape-Measure Murder" (story, February 1942; alternative titles: "The Case of the Retired Jeweller," "Village Murder")

Teddy Bear (play, unpublished)

Ten Years (play, unpublished)

"The Terrible Catastrophe" (story, March 1924)

"There Where My Lover Lies" (poem, January 1925)

They Came to Baghdad (novel, March 1951)

They Do It with Mirrors (novel, April 1952; alternative title: *Murder with Mirrors*)

Third Girl (novel, November 1966)

"The Third-Floor Flat" (story, January 1929; alternative title: "In the Third Floor Flat")

The Thirteen Problems (short story collection, June 1932; alternative titles: *Miss Marple and the Thirteen Problems*; *The Tuesday Club Murders*)

Three Act Tragedy (novel, June 1934; alternative title: *Murder in Three Acts*)

Three Blind Mice (radio play, October 1947)

"Three Blind Mice" (novella, May 1948)

Three Blind Mice (short story collection, 1950; alternative title: *Three Blind Mice and Other Stories*)

"The Thumb Mark of St. Peter" (story, May 1928; alternative title: "Ask and You Shall Receive")

The Times Anthology of Detective Stories (coedited short story collection, 1972)

"To a Beautiful Old Lady" (poem, January 1925)

"To a Cedar Tree" (poem, October 1973)

"To M.E.L.M. in Absence" (poem, October 1973)

Towards Zero (novel, May 1944; alternative title: *Come and Be Hanged!*)

Towards Zero (play, 1945)

Towards Zero (collaborative play, September 1956)

"The Tragedy at Marsdon Manor" (story, April 1923; alternative titles: "Hercule Poirot, Insurance Investigator"; "The Marsdon Manor Tragedy"; "The Mystery at Marsdon Manor")

"The Tragic Family of Croydon" (article, August 1929)

"The Trams" (poem, July 1901)

"Triangle at Rhodes" (novella, May 1936; alternative titles: "Before It's Too Late," "Double Alibi," "Poirot and the Triangle at Rhodes")

"The Tuesday Night Club" (story, December 1927; alternative titles: "The Solving Six," "The Tuesday Club Murders")

"The Unbreakable Alibi" (story, December 1928; alternative title: "Alibi")

"The Under Dog" (story, April 1926)

The Under Dog (short story collection, 1951; alternative title: *The Under Dog and Other Stories*)

"Undine" (poem, October 1973)

"The Unexpected Guest" (story, January 1924)

The Unexpected Guest (play, August 1956)

Unfinished Portrait (novel, March 1934)

"The Veiled Lady" (story, October 1923; alternative titles: "The Case of the Veiled Lady"; "The Chinese Puzzle Box")

Verdict (February 1958)

Vision (novella/novel, unpublished)

"The Voice in the Dark" (story, December 1926)

"A Wandering Tune" (poem, October 1973)

"The War Bride" (story, unpublished)

"Wasps' Nest" (story, November 1928; alternative title: "Worst of All")

The Wasp's Nest (screenplay, June 1937)

"The Water Bus" (story, November 1965)

"The Water Flows" (poem, October 1973)

"What I Would Do if I Were Starving" (article, July 1931)

"What Is Love?" (poem, October 1973)

What We Did in the Great War (collaborative anthology, unpublished)

"While the Light Lasts" (story, April 1924)

While the Light Lasts (short story collection, August 1997; alternative title: *While the Light Lasts and Other Stories*)

Why Didn't They Ask Evans? (novel, November 1933; alternative title: *The Boomerang Clue*)

"The Wife of the Kenite" (story, September 1922)

"Wild Roses" (poem, October 1973)

"Wireless" (story, December 1925; alternative title: "Where There's a Will")

"Witch Hazel" (story, unpublished)

"Within a Wall" (story, October 1925)

"The Witness for the Prosecution" (story, January 1925; alternative title: "Traitor Hands")

The Witness for the Prosecution (short story collection, 1948)

Witness for the Prosecution (play, September 1953)

"World Hymn, 1914" (poem, 1919; alternative title: "World Hymn")

"The World's End" (story, November 1926; alternative title: "World's End")

"A Wreath for Christmas" (poem, October 1973)

"Yellow Iris" (story, July 1937; alternative title: "Hercule Poirot and the Sixth Chair"; "There's Nothing Like Love")

The Yellow Iris (radio play, October 1937; alternative title: *Yellow Iris*)

"The Yellow Jasmine Mystery" (story, February 1924)

"Young Morning" (poem, January 1925)

The Young Students (operetta, unpublished)

Christie's Works in Order of First Publication/Performance

"The Trams" (poem, July 1901)

"One Hour with Thee" (waltz, 1908)

"Harlequin's Song" (poem, before 1919)

"Dark Sheila" (poem, 1919)

"World Hymn, 1914" (poem, 1919; alternative title: "World Hymn")

The Mysterious Affair at Styles (novel, February 1920; alternative title: *Mystery at Styles*)

The Secret Adversary (novel, August 1921)

"The Wife of the Kenite" (story, September 1922)

The Murder on the Links (novel, December 1922; alternative title: *The Girl with Anxious Eyes*)

"The Affair at the Victory Ball" (story, March 1923; alternative title: "The Six China Figures")

"The Disappearance of Mr. Davenheim" (story, March 1923; alternative titles: "Hercule Poirot, Armchair Detective"; "Mr. Davenby Disappears")

"The Jewel Robbery at the Grand Metropolitan" (story, March 1923; alternative titles: "The Curious Disappearance of the Opalsen Pearls"; "The Jewel Robbery at the 'Grand Metropolitan'"; "The Theft of the Opalsen Pearls")

"The King of Clubs" (story, March 1923; alternative titles: "The Adventure of the King of Clubs'" "Beware the King of Clubs")

"The Adventure of the 'Western Star'" (story, April 1923; alternative title: "Poirot Puts a Finger in the Pie")

"The Kidnapped Prime Minister" (story, April 1923)

"The Plymouth Express" (story, April 1923; alternative titles: "The Girl in Electric Blue"; "The Mystery of the Plymouth Express"; "The Plymouth Express Affair")

"The Tragedy at Marsdon Manor" (story, April 1923; alternative titles: "Hercule Poirot, Insurance Investigator"; "The Marsdon Manor Tragedy"; "The Mystery at Marsdon Manor")

"The Actress" (story, May 1923; alternative title: "A Trap for the Unwary")

"The Adventure of the Cheap Flat" (story, May 1923; alternative title: "Poirot Indulges a Whim")

"The Chocolate Box" (story, May 1923; alternative titles: "The Clue of the Chocolate Box"; "The Time Hercule Poirot Failed")

"The Million Dollar Bond Robbery" (story, May 1923)

"The Mystery of Hunter's Lodge" (story, May 1923; alternative title: "Investigation by Telegram")

"The Adventure of the Egyptian Tomb" (story, September 1923; alternative titles: "The Egyptian Tomb"; "The Next Victim")

"The Adventure of Johnnie Waverly" (story, October 1923; alternative titles: "At the Stroke of Twelve"; "The Kidnapping of Johnnie Waverly")

"The Adventure of the Italian Nobleman" (story, October 1923; alternative title: "The Regent's Court Murder")

"The Case of the Missing Will" (story, October 1923; alternative titles: "Sporting Challenge"; "Where There's a Will")

"The Market Basing Mystery" (story, October 1923)

"The Veiled Lady" (story, October 1923; alternative titles: "The Case of the Veiled Lady"; "The Chinese Puzzle Box")

"The Adventure of the Clapham Cook" (story, November 1923; alternative title: "Find the Cook")

"The Cornish Mystery" (story, November 1923)

"The Lost Mine" (story, November 1923)

The Man in the Brown Suit (novel, November 1923; alternative titles: *Anna the Adventuress*; *Anne the Adventurous*)

"The Submarine Plans" (story, November 1923; alternative title: "The Shadow in the Night")

"Christmas Adventure" (story, December 1923)

"The Clergyman's Daughter" (story, December 1923; alternative titles: "The First Wish"; "The Red House")

"The Double Clue" (story, December 1923)

"The Lemesurier Inheritance" (story, December 1923)

"The Red House" (story, December 1923; alternative titles: "The First Wish"; "The Clergyman's Daughter")

"The Adventure of the Dartmoor Bungalow" (story, January 1924; alternative title: "The Importance of a Leg of Mutton")

"The Lady on the Stairs" (story, January 1924)

"The Radium Thieves" (story, January 1924)

"The Unexpected Guest" (story, January 1924)

"The Adventure of the Peroxide Blonde" (story, February 1924)

"The Baited Trap" (story, February 1924)

"The Chess Problem" (story, February 1924; alternative titles: "A Chess Problem"; "A Game of Chess")

"The Girl in the Train" (story, February 1924)

"The Yellow Jasmine Mystery" (story, February 1924)

"The Coming of Mr. Quin" (story, March 1924; alternative title: "The Passing of Mr. Quinn")

"The Crag in the Dolomites" (story, March 1924)

"The Dying Chinaman" (story, March 1924)

Poirot Investigates (short story collection, March 1924)

"The Terrible Catastrophe" (story, March 1924)

"While the Light Lasts" (story, April 1924)

"The Red Signal" (story, June 1924)

"The Mystery of the Blue Jar" (story, July 1924)

"Jane in Search of a Job" (story, August 1924)

"Mr. Eastwood's Adventure" (story, August 1924; alternative titles: "The Mystery of the Second Cucumber"; "The Mystery of the Spanish Shawl")

"A Fairy in the Flat" (story, September 1924; alternative titles: "Blunt's Brilliant Detectives"; "The Affair of the Pink Pearl"; "Publicity")

"A Pot of Tea" (story, September 1924; alternative title: "Publicity")

"The Adventure of the Sinister Stranger" (story, October 1924; alternative title: "The Case of the Sinister Stranger")

"The Case of the Missing Lady" (story, October 1924)

"Finessing the King" (story, October 1924)

"The Gentleman Dressed in Newspaper" (story, October 1924)

"The Shadow on the Glass" (story, October 1924; alternative title: "Jealousy Is the Devil")

"The Sunningdale Mystery" (story, October 1924; alternative title: "The Sunninghill Mystery")

"The Ambassador's Boots" (story, November 1924; alternative title: "The Matter of the Ambassador's Boots")

"Blindman's Buff" (story, November 1924; alternative title: "Blind Man's Buff")

"The Crackler" (story, November 1924; alternative titles: "The Affair of the Forged Notes"; "The Case of the Forged Notes")

"Philomel Cottage" (story, November 1924; alternative title: "A Stranger Walked In")

"The Man in the Mist" (story, December 1924)

"The Man Who Was Number Sixteen" (story, December 1924)

"The Manhood of Edward Robinson" (story, December 1924; alternative titles: "The Day of His Dreams"; "Romance and a Red Runabout")

"The House of Lurking Death" (story, November 1924)

"The Ballad of the Flint" (poem, January 1925)

"Ballad of the Maytime" (poem, January 1925)

"Beatrice Passes" (poem, January 1925)

"The Bells of Brittany" (poem, January 1925)

"Columbine's Song" (poem, January 1925)

"Down in the Wood" (poem, January 1925)

"The Dream Spinners" (poem, January 1925)

"Easter, 1918" (poem, January 1925)

"Elizabeth of England" (poem, January 1925)

"Heritage" (poem, January 1925)

"Hymn to Ra" (poem, January 1925)

"In a Dispensary" (poem, January 1925)

"The Last Song of Columbine" (poem, January 1925)

"Love Passes" (poem, January 1925)

"A Palm Tree in Egypt" (poem, January 1925; alternative title: "A Palm Tree in the Desert")

"Pierette Dancing on the Moon" (poem, January 1925)

"Pierrot Grown Old" (poem, January 1925)

"Pierrot's Song by the Hearth" (poem, January 1925)

"Pierrot's Song to the Moon" (poem, January 1925)

"The Princess Sings" (poem, January 1925)

"Progression" (poem, January 1925)

"Pulcinella" (poem, January 1925)

"The Road of Dreams" (poem, January 1925)

The Road of Dreams (poetry collection, January 1925)

"Spring" (poem, January 1925)

"There Where My Lover Lies" (poem, January 1925)

"To a Beautiful Old Lady" (poem, January 1925)

"The Witness for the Prosecution" (story, January 1925; alternative title: "Traitor Hands")

"Young Morning" (poem, January 1925)

The Secret of Chimneys (novel, June 1925)

The Murder of Roger Ackroyd (novel, July 1925; alternative title: *Who Killed Ackroyd?*)

"The Sign in the Sky" (story, July 1925; alternative title: "A Sign in the Sky")

"Within a Wall" (story, October 1925)

"At the Bells and Motley" (story, November 1925; alternative titles: "The Disappearance of Captain Harwell"; "A Man of Magic")

"The Fourth Man" (story, December 1925)

"The Listerdale Mystery" (story, December 1925; alternative title: "The Benevolent Butler")

"Wireless" (story, December 1925; alternative title: "Where There's a Will")

"The House of Dreams" (story, January 1926)

"S.O.S." (story, February 1926)

"Magnolia Blossom" (story, March 1926)

"The Under Dog" (story, April 1926)

"The Lonely God" (story, July 1926)

"The Rajah's Emerald" (story, July 1926)

"Swan Song" (story, September 1926)

"The Soul of the Croupier" (story, November 1926)

"The World's End" (story, November 1926; alternative title: "World's End")

"The Love Detectives" (story, December 1926; alternative title: "At the Crossroads")

"The Voice in the Dark" (story, December 1926)

The Big Four (novel, January 1927)

"The Edge" (story, February 1927)

"The Last Séance" (story, March 1927; alternative titles: "The Stolen Ghost"; "The Woman Who Stole a Ghost")

"The Face of Helen" (story, April 1927)

"Harlequin's Lane" (story, May 1927)

"The Tuesday Night Club" (story, December 1927; alternative titles: "The Solving Six"; "The Tuesday Club Murders")

"The Idol House of Astarte" (story, January 1928; alternative titles: "The Solving Six and the Evil Hour"; "The 'Supernatural' Murder")

"Her Own Story of Her Disappearance" (interview as article, February 1928)

"Ingots of Gold" (story, February 1928; alternative titles: "Miss Marple and the Golden Galleon"; "The Solving Six and the Golden Grave")

The Mystery of the Blue Train (novel, February 1928)

"The Bloodstained Pavement" (story, March 1928; alternative titles: "The Blood-Stained Pavement"; "Drip! Drip!"; "Miss Marple and the Wicked World")

"Motive v. Opportunity" (story, April 1928; alternative title: "Where's the Catch?")

"Does Woman's Instinct Make Her a Good Detective?" (article, May 1928)

"The Thumb Mark of St. Peter" (story, May 1928; alternative title: "Ask and You Shall Receive")

"A Fruitful Sunday" (story, August 1928)

"Double Sin" (story, September 1928; alternative title: "By Road or Rail")

"Wasps' Nest" (story, November 1928; alternative title: "Worst of All")

"The Unbreakable Alibi" (story, December 1928; alternative title: "Alibi")

The Seven Dials Mystery (novel, January 1929)

"The Third-Floor Flat" (story, January 1929; alternative title: "In the Third Floor Flat")

"The Dead Harlequin" (story, March 1929; alternative title: "The Man in the Empty Chair")

"The Golden Ball" (story, August 1929; alternative title: "Playing the Innocent")

"The Tragic Family of Croydon" (article, August 1929)

"Accident" (story, September 1929; alternative titles: "Test for Murder"; "The Uncrossed Path")

"Next to a Dog" (story, September 1929)

Partners in Crime (short story collection, September 1929)

"The Man from the Sea" (story, October 1929)

"The Blue Geranium" (story, December 1929)

"Sing a Song of Sixpence" (story, December 1929)

"A Christmas Tragedy" (story, January 1930; alternative titles: "The Hat and the Alibi"; "Never Two without Three")

"The Companion" (story, February 1930; alternative title: "The Resurrection of Amy Durrant")

"The Crime Passionnel" (article, February 1930)

"The Herb of Death" (story, March 1930 alternative title: "Foxglove in the Sage")

"The Bird with the Broken Wing" (story, April 1930)

"The Four Suspects" (story, April 1930; alternative title: "Some Day They Will Get Me")

Giant's Bread (novel, April 1930)

The Mysterious Mr. Quin (short story collection, April 1930)

"The Affair at the Bungalow" (story, May 1930)

"Manx Gold" (story, May 1930)

"Behind the Screen" (collaborative novella, June 1930)

The Murder at the Vicarage (novel, August 1930)

Black Coffee (play, December 1930; alternative title: *After Dinner*)

"The Scoop" (collaborative novella, January 1931)

The Sittaford Mystery (novel, March 1931; alternative title: *The Murder at Hazelmoor*)

Peril at End House (novel, June 1931)

"What I Would Do If I Were Starving" (article, July 1931)

"Death by Drowning" (story, November 1931; alternative title: "Village Tragedy")

"Strange Jest" (story, November 1931; alternative title: "A Case of Buried Treasure")

The Floating Admiral (collaborative novel, December 1931)

"The Mystery of the Baghdad Chest" (story, January 1932)

The Thirteen Problems (short story collection, June 1932; alternative titles: *Miss Marple and the Thirteen Problems*; *The Tuesday Club Murders*)

"The Second Gong" (story, July 1932)

"The Case of the City Clerk" (story, August 1932; alternative title: "The £10 Adventure")

"The Case of the Discontented Husband" (story, August 1932; alternative title: "His Lady's Affair")

"The Case of the Discontented Soldier" (story, August 1932; alternative title: "Adventure by Request")

"The Case of the Distressed Lady" (story, August 1932; alternative titles: "The Cat and the Chestnut"; "Faked!")

"The Case of the Rich Woman" (story, August 1932; alternative title: "The Rich Woman Who Wanted Only to Be Happy")

"The Case of the Middle-Aged Wife" (story, October 1932; alternative title: "The Woman Concerned")

Lord Edgware Dies (novel, March 1933; alternative title: *Thirteen at Dinner*)

"Death on the Nile" (story, April 1933)

"The Gate of Baghdad" (story, April 1933; alternative titles: "At the Gate of Baghdad"; "The Gate of Death")

"Have You Got Everything You Want?" (story, April 1933; alternative titles: "Express to Stamboul"; "On the Orient Express")

"The House at Shiraz" (story, April 1933; alternative titles: "At the House in Shiraz"; "The Dream House of Shiraz")

"The Oracle at Delphi" (story, April 1933)

"The Pearl of Price" (story, April 1933; alternative titles: "Once a Thief"; "The Pearl")

Murder on the Orient Express (novel, September 1933; alternative title: *Murder in the Calais Coach*)

"The Call of Wings" (story, October 1933)

"The Gipsy" (story, October 1933; alternative title: "The Gypsy")

The Hound of Death (short story collection, October 1933)

"The Hound of Death" (story, October 1933)

"The Lamp" (story, October 1933)

"The Strange Case of Sir Arthur Carmichael" (story, October 1933)

Why Didn't They Ask Evans? (novel, November 1933; alternative title: *The Boomerang Clue*)

Unfinished Portrait (novel, March 1934)

"Miss Marple Tells a Story" (monologue/story, May 1934; alternative title: "Behind Closed Doors")

The Listerdale Mystery (short story collection, June 1934)

Three Act Tragedy (novel, June 1934; alternative title: *Murder in Three Acts*)

Parker Pyne Investigates (short story collection, November 1934; alternative title: *Mr. Parker Pyne, Detective*)

"In a Glass Darkly" (story, December 1934)

Death in the Clouds (novel, February 1935; alternative title: *Death in the Air*)

"How Does Your Garden Grow?" (story, August 1935)

The ABC Murders (novel, November 1935)

Murder in Mesopotamia (novel, November 1935; alternative title: *No Other Love*)

"Problem at Pollensa Bay" (story, November 1935; alternative title: "Siren Business")

"Problem at Sea" (story, February 1936; alternative titles: "Poirot and the Crime in Cabin 66"; "Crime in Cabin 66"; "The Quickness of the Hand")

"A Letter to My Publisher" (fictional letter, April 1936)

Cards on the Table (novel, May 1936)

"Triangle at Rhodes" (novella, May 1936; alternative titles: "Before It's Too Late"; "Double Alibi"; "Poirot and the Triangle at Rhodes")

"Poirot and the Regatta Mystery" (story, June 1936)

"Murder in the Mews" (novella, December 1936; alternative title: "Good Night for a Murder")

"Dead Man's Mirror" (novella, March 1937; alternative title: "Hercule Poirot and the Broken Mirror")

"The Incredible Theft" (novella, March 1937)

Murder in the Mews (short story collection, March 1937; alternative titles: *Dead Man's Mirror*; *Murder in the Mews: 4 Poirot Stories*)

Death on the Nile (novel, May 1937)

The Wasp's Nest (screenplay, June 1937)

Dumb Witness (novel, July 1937; alternative title: *Poirot Loses a Client*)

"Yellow Iris" (story, July 1937; alternative title: "Hercule Poirot and the Sixth Chair"; "There's Nothing Like Love")

Appointment with Death (novel, August 1937; alternative title: *Date with Death*)

"The Dream" (story, October 1937; alternative title: "The Three Strange Points")

The Yellow Iris (radio play, October 1937; alternative title: *Yellow Iris*)

"Hercule Poirot: Fiction's Greatest Detective" (article, January 1938; alternative title: "How I Created Hercule Poirot")

"How I Became a Writer" (article, August 1938)

Hercule Poirot's Christmas (novel, November 1938; alternative titles: *A Holiday for Murder*; *Murder at Christmas*; *Murder for Christmas*)

Murder Is Easy (novel, November 1938; alternative title: *Easy to Kill*)

The Regatta Mystery (short story collection, April 1939).

"The Regatta Mystery" (story, April 1939)

And Then There Were None (novel, June 1939; alternative title: *Ten Little Indians, Ten Little N-----s*)

"The Cretan Bull" (story, September 1939; alternative titles: "The Case of the Family Taint"; "Midnight Madness")

"The Girdle of Hippolyta" (story, September 1939; alternative titles: "The Case of the Missing Schoolgirl"; "The Disappearance of Winnie King")

"The Lernean Hydra" (story, September 1939; alternative titles: "The Hydra of Lernea, or the Case of the Gossipers"; "Invisible Enemy")

"The Nemean Lion" (story, November 1939; alternative title: "The Case of the Kidnapped Pekingese")

Sad Cypress (novel, November 1939)

"The Stymphalean Birds" (story, September 1939; alternative titles: "The Case of the Vulture Women"; "Vulture Women")

"The Augean Stables" (story, March 1940)

"The Apples of Hesperides" (story, May 1940; alternative title: "The Poison Cup")

"The Arcadian Deer" (story, May 1940; alternative title: "Vanishing Lady")

"The Erymanthian Boar" (story, May 1940; alternative title: "The Murder Mountain")

"Flock of Geryon" (story, May 1940; alternative title: "Weird Monster")

"The Horses of Diomedes" (story, June 1940; alternative title: "The Case of the Drug Peddler")

"Agatha Christie's Mystery Potatoes" (recipe, July 1940)

One, Two, Buckle My Shoe (novel, August 1940; alternative titles: *An Overdose of Death*; *The Patriotic Murders*)

"Four and Twenty Blackbirds" (story, November 1940; alternative title: "Poirot and the Regular Customer")

Evil Under the Sun (novel, December 1940)

"Drugs and Detective Stories" (article, 1941)

N or M? (novel, March 1941)

The Body in the Library (novel, May 1941)

Five Little Pigs (novel, September 1941; alternative title: *Murder in Retrospect*)

"The Case of the Caretaker" (story, January 1942)

"Tape-Measure Murder" (story, February 1942; alternative titles: "The Case of the Retired Jeweller"; "Village Murder")

The Moving Finger (novel, March 1942 alternative title: *The Case of the Moving Finger*)

"The Case of the Perfect Maid" (story, April 1942; alternative titles: "The Perfect Maid"; "The Servant Problem")

And Then There Were None (play, September 1943; alternative titles: *Ten Little Indians*; *Ten Little N-----s*)

Poirot on Holiday (short story collection, November 1943)

Murder on the Nile (play, January 1944; alternative titles: *Hidden Horizon*; *Moon on the Nile*)

Towards Zero (novel, May 1944; alternative title: *Come and Be Hanged!*)

Sparkling Cyanide (novel, July 1944; alternative title: *Remembered Death*)

Absent in the Spring (novel, August 1944)

Death Comes as the End (novel, October 1944)

Towards Zero (play, 1945)

Appointment with Death (play, January 1945)

Poirot Knows the Murderer (short story collection, March 1946)

Poirot Lends a Hand (short story collection, March 1946)

The Hollow (novel, May 1946; alternative titles: *Murder after Hours*; *The Outraged Heart*)

Come, Tell Me How You Live (memoir, November 1946)

"Star Over Bethlehem" (story, December 1946)

"The Capture of Cerberus" (story, March 1947; alternative titles: "Hercule Poirot in Hell"; "Meet Me in Hell!")

The Labours of Hercules (short story collection, September 1947)

Three Blind Mice (radio play, October 1947)

The Witness for the Prosecution (short story collection, 1948)

Butter in a Lordly Dish (radio play, January 1948)

Taken at the Flood (novel, March 1948; alternative title: *There Is a Tide*)

"Three Blind Mice" (novella, May 1948)

Crooked House (novel, October 1948)

The Rose and the Yew Tree (novel, November 1948)

"The Clock Stopped" (story opening, Autumn 1949)

The Secret of Chimneys (play, late 1940s; alternative title: *Chimneys*)

Three Blind Mice (short story collection, 1950; alternative title: *Three Blind Mice and Other Stories*)

A Murder Is Announced (novel, February 1950)

The Under Dog (short story collection, 1951; alternative title: *The Under Dog and Other Stories*)

The Hollow (play, February 1951)

They Came to Baghdad (novel, March 1951)

Mrs. McGinty's Dead (novel, October 1951; alternative title: *Blood Will Tell*)

"Best of the Year" (review, January 1952)

They Do It with Mirrors (novel, April 1952; alternative title: *Murder with Mirrors*)

The Mousetrap (play, October 1952)

A Daughter's a Daughter (novel, November 1952)

After the Funeral (novel, January 1953; alternative title: *Funerals Are Fatal*; *Murder at the Gallop*)

A Pocket Full of Rye (novel, September 1953)

Witness for the Prosecution (play, September 1953)

Personal Call (radio play, May 1954)

Destination Unknown (novel, September 1954; alternative title: *So Many Steps to Death*)

Spider's Web (play, September 1954)

"Sanctuary" (story, October 1954; alternative titles: "The Man on the Chancel Steps"; "Murder at the Vicarage")

Hickory Dickory Dock (novel, May 1955; alternative title: *Hickory Dickory Death*)

A Daughter's a Daughter (play, July 1956)

Dead Man's Folly (novel, July 1956)

The Unexpected Guest (play, August 1956)

Towards Zero (collaborative play, September 1956)

The Burden (novel, November 1956)

"Greenshaw's Folly" (novella, December 1956)

4.50 from Paddington (novel, October 1957; alternative titles: *Eyewitness to Murder*; *Murder She Said*; *What Mrs. McGillicuddy Saw!*)

Verdict (February 1958)

Ordeal by Innocence (novel, September 1958; alternative title: *The Innocent*)

"The Dressmaker's Doll" (story, December 1958)

Cat Among the Pigeons (novel, September 1959)

Go Back for Murder (play, March 1960)

"The Mystery of the Spanish Chest" (story, September 1960)

"The Adventure of the Christmas Pudding" (novella, October 1960; alternative title: "The Theft of the Royal Ruby")

The Adventure of the Christmas Pudding (short story collection, October 1960; alternative title: *The Adventure of the Christmas Pudding and a Selection of Entrees*)

Double Sin (short story collection, 1961; alternative title: *Double Sin and Other Stories*)

The Pale Horse (novel, September 1961)

The Mirror Crack'd from Side to Side (novel, November 1962; alternative title: *The Mirror Crack'd*)

Rule of Three (play-set, December 1962)

The Clocks (novel, November 1963)

A Caribbean Mystery (novel, November 1964)

"The Water Bus" (story, November 1965)

"Gold, Frankincense and Myrrh" (poem, October 1965)

"A Greeting" (poem, October 1965)

"Jenny by the Sky" (poem, October 1965)

"The Saints of God" (poem, October 1965)

At Bertram's Hotel (novel, November 1965)

"In the Cool of the Evening" (story, November 1965)

"The Island" (story, November 1965)

"The Naughty Donkey" (story, November 1965)

"Promotion in the Highest" (story, November 1965)

Star Over Bethlehem (short story/poetry collection, November 1965; alternative title: *Star Over Bethlehem and Other Stories*)

"Margery Allingham: A Tribute" (obituary, 1966)

Third Girl (novel, November 1966)

Endless Night (novel, October 1967)

"A Letter from Agatha Christie" (letter, October 1968)

By the Pricking of My Thumbs (novel, November 1968)

Hallowe'en Party (novel, November 1969)

"Sir Allen Lane: A Flair for Success" (obituary, July 1970; alternative title: "Enter Allen Lane and the Penguins")

Passenger to Frankfurt (novel, September 1970)

Fiddlers Five (play, 1971; alternative titles: *Fiddle de Dee*; *Fiddlers All*; *This Mortal Coil*; *Sixpence Off*)

The Golden Ball (short story collection, 1971; alternative title: *The Golden Ball and Other Stories*)

Nemesis (novel, September 1971)

"The Harlequin Tea Set" (story, November 1971)

The Times Anthology of Detective Stories (coedited short-story collection, 1972)

Fiddlers Three (play, August 1972)

Elephants Can Remember (novel, November 1972)

"Cleopatra as the Dark Lady" (letter, February 1973)

Akhnaton (play, May 1973; alternative title: *Akhnaton and Nefertiti*)

"Beauty" (poem, October 1973)

"Calvary" (poem, October 1973)

"A Choice" (poem, October 1973)

"Count Ferson to the Queen" (poem, October 1973)

"Ctesiphon" (poem, October 1973)

"Dartmoor" (poem, October 1973)

"Enchantment" (poem, October 1973)

"From a Grown-up to a Child" (poem, October 1973)

"I Wore My New Canary Suit" (poem, October 1973)

"In Baghdad" (poem, October 1973)

"An Island" (poem, October 1973)

"Islot of Brittany" (poem, October 1973)

"Lament of the Tortured Lover" (poem, October 1973)

"My Flower Garden" (poem, October 1973)

"The Nile" (poem, October 1973)

"Picnic 1960" (poem, October 1973)

Poems (poetry collection, October 1973)

Postern of Fate (novel, October 1973)

"Racial Musings" (poem, October 1973)

"Remembrance" (poem, October 1973)

"The Sculptor" (poem, October 1973)

"To a Cedar Tree" (poem, October 1973)

"To M.E.L.M. in Absence" (poem, October 1973)

"Undine" (poem, October 1973)

"A Wandering Tune" (poem, October 1973)

"The Water Flows" (poem, October 1973)

"What Is Love?" (poem, October 1973)

"Wild Roses" (poem, October 1973)

"A Wreath for Christmas" (poem, October 1973)

"Hawthorn Trees" (poem, October 1973)

Poirot's Early Cases (short story collection, September 1974)

Curtain (novel, September 1975; alternative title: *Curtain: Poirot's Last Case*)

Sleeping Murder (novel, July 1976)

An Autobiography (memoir, November 1977)

Miss Marple's Final Cases (short story collection, October 1979; alternative titles: *Miss Marple's Final Cases and Two Other Stories*; *Miss Marple's 6 Final Cases and 2 Other Stories*)

Problem at Pollensa Bay (short story collection, November 1991; alternative title: *Problem at Pollensa Bay and Other Stories*)

The Harlequin Tea Set (short story collection, April 1997; alternative title: *The Harlequin Tea Set and Other Stories*)

While the Light Lasts (short story collection, August 1997; alternative title: *While the Light Lasts and Other Stories*)

"Detective Writers in England" (article, December 2008)

"The Capture of Cerberus" (story, August 2009)

"The Incident of the Dog's Ball" (story, September 2009)

"The Case of the Caretaker's Wife" (story, September 2011)

"The Man Who Knew" (story, September 2011)

The Grand Tour (collected correspondence, November 2012)

"Hercule Poirot and the Greenshore Folly" (novella, September 2014; alternative title: "The Greenshore Folly")

The Big Four (short story collection, December 2016; alternative title: *The Man Who Was Number Four: Further Adventures of M. Poirot*)

Murder in the Studio (radio script collection, 2019; alternative title: *Murder on Air*)

The Last Séance (short story collection, October 2019; alternative title: *The Last Séance: Tales of the Supernatural*)

The Stranger (play, January 2020)

The Lie (play, August 2020; alternative title: *The Sister-in-Law*)

"The AA Alphabet for 1915" (collaborative poem, unpublished)

"Being So Very Wilful" (story, unpublished)

Bleak House (screenplay, unpublished)

"The Choice" (story, unpublished)

The Clutching Hand (play, unpublished)

The Conqueror (play, unpublished)

Eugenia and Eugenics (play, unpublished)

"The Green Gate" (story, unpublished)
"Have Ye Walked in the Wood Today?" (poem, unpublished)
"The House of Beauty" (story, unpublished)
"In the Market Place" (story, unpublished)
"The Last Days of Nimrud" (poem, unpublished)
The Last Séance (play, unpublished)
Letter to "Woman's Day" (letter, unpublished)
"A Little Cowslip" (poem, unpublished)
Marmalade Moon (play, unpublished)
Miss Perry (play, unpublished)
New Moon (play, unpublished)
Nimrud Book of Dreams (poetry collection, unpublished)

"Nursery Rhyme of Nimrud" (poem, unpublished)
"Ode to Christopher Columbus" (poem, unpublished)
Snow upon the Desert (novel, unpublished)
Someone at the Window (play, unpublished)
"Stronger than Death" (story, unpublished)
Teddy Bear (play, unpublished)
Ten Years (play, unpublished)
Vision (novella/novel, unpublished)
"The War Bride" (story, unpublished)
What We Did in the Great War (collaborative anthology, unpublished)
"Witch Hazel" (story, unpublished)
The Young Students (operetta, unpublished)

List of Abbreviations

Abbreviation	Christie/Westmacott Work
AA	*An Autobiography*
ABC	*The ABC Murders*
ABH	*At Bertram's Hotel*
ACH	*The Agatha Christie Hour*
ACM	*A Caribbean Mystery*
ACP	*The Adventure of the Christmas Pudding and a Selection of Entrées*
ADD	*A Daughter's a Daughter*
AIS	*Absent in the Spring*
AMIA	*A Murder Is Announced*
ATF	*After the Funeral*
ATTWN	*And Then There Were None*
AWD	*Appointment with Death*
BC	*Black Coffee*
BIL	*The Body in the Library*
BPT	*By the Pricking of My Thumbs*
C	*Curtain: Poirot's Last Case*
CAP	*Cat Among the Pigeons*
CCW	"The Case of the Caretaker's Wife"
CDL	"Cleopatra as the Dark Lady"
CH	*Crooked House*
COT	*Cards on the Table*
CTMHYL	*Come, Tell Me How You Live*
DCE	*Death Comes as the End*
DDS	"Drugs and Detective Stories"
DITC	*Death in the Clouds*
DMF	*Dead Man's Folly*
DOTN	*Death on the Nile*
DU	*Destination Unknown*

Abbreviation	*Christie/Westmacott Work*
DWE	"Detective Writers in England"
DWI	"Does a Woman's Instinct Make Her a Good Detective?"
ECM	*Elephants Can Remember*
EN	*Endless Night*
FLP	*Five Little Pigs*
450FP	*4.50 from Paddington*
GB	*Giant's Bread*
HDD	*Hickory Dickory Dock*
HOD	*The Hound of Death and Other Stories*
HOS	"Mrs. Agatha Christie: Her Own Story of Her Disappearance"
HP	*Hallowe'en Party*
HPC	*Hercule Poirot's Christmas*
LED	*Lord Edgware Dies*
LOH	*The Labours of Hercules*
LP	"A Letter to My Publisher"
MAS	*The Mysterious Affair at Styles*
MA-T	"Margery Allingham—A Tribute"
MAV	*The Murder at the Vicarage*
MBS	*The Man in the Brown Suit*
MBT	*The Mystery of the Blue Train*
MIE	*Murder Is Easy*
MIM	*Murder in Mesopotamia*
MITM	*Murder in the Mews*
MITS	*Murder in the Studio*
MMD	*Mrs. McGinty's Dead*
MMFC	*Miss Marple's 6 Final Cases and 2 Other Stories*
MMQ	*The Mysterious Mr. Quin*
MOE	*Murder on the Orient Express*
MOL	*The Murder on the Links*
MOTN	*Murder on the Nile*
MRA	*The Murder of Roger Ackroyd*
N	*Nemesis*
NOM	*N or M?*
OBI	*Ordeal by Innocence*
12BMS	*One, Two, Buckle My Shoe*
P	*Poems*
PEC	*Poirot's Early Cases*

Abbreviation	*Christie/Westmacott Work*
PEH	*Peril at End House*
PFR	*A Pocket Full of Rye*
PI	*Poirot Investigates*
PIC	*Partners in Crime*
POF	*Postern of Fate*
PPB	*Problem at Pollensa Bay and Other Stories*
PPI	*Parker Pyne Investigates*
PRM	"Poirot and the Regatta Mystery"
PTF	*Passenger to Frankfurt: An Extravaganza*
RYT	*The Rose and the Yew Tree*
SAL	"Sir Allen Lane: A Flair for Success"
SBS	*The Scoop & Behind the Screen*
SdC	*Sad Cypress*
SM	*Sleeping Murder*
SOC	*The Secret of Chimneys*
SOC-P	*The Secret of Chimneys* (play)
SpC	*Sparkling Cyanide*
SW	*Spider's Web*
SOB	*Star Over Bethlehem and Other Stories*
TATF	*Taken at the Flood*
TB	*The Burden*
TBF	*The Big Four*
TC	*The Clocks*
TCS	"The Clock Stopped"
TCTB	*They Came to Baghdad*
TDM	*They Do It with Mirrors*
TFA	*The Floating Admiral*
TFC	"The Tragedy Family of Croydon"
TG	*Third Girl*
TGF	*Hercule Poirot and the Greenshore Folly*
TGT	*The Grand Tour: Letters and Photographs from the British Empire Expedition*
TH	*The Hollow*
3AT	*Three Act Tragedy*
3BM	*Three Blind Mice and Other Stories*
TLM	*The Listerdale Mystery*
TLS	*The Last Séance: Tales of the Supernatural*

Abbreviation	Christie/Westmacott Work
TMC	*The Mirror Crack'd from Side to Side*
TMF	*The Moving Finger*
TMT	*The Mousetrap and Other Plays*
TPH	*The Pale Horse*
TSA	*The Secret Adversary*
TSM	*The Sittaford Mystery*
TTP	*The Thirteen Problems*
TZ	*Towards Zero*
UP	*Unfinished Portrait*
WDE	*Why Didn't They Ask Evans?*
WLL	*While the Light Lasts and Other Stories*
WWS	"What I Would Do If I Were Starving"

The Companion

"The AA Alphabet for 1915" (poem)

Letters and documents survive from the early married days of Agatha and Archie Christie. They show a great deal of playfulness—effortless on her part and manufactured on his. "The AA Alphabet for 1915" is an example of an ostensibly collaborative effort, of which the wife was clearly the architect. "AA" stands for "Archie and Agatha," although biographer Janet Morgan points out that it also stands for "Ack Ack, as the anti-aircraft guns were called" (68).

The Christies' marriage was a hasty wartime one, and as they were still relative strangers, activities like these would have bonded them tremendously and helped them explore their relationship. The poem consists of 26 rhyming couplets following the "A Is for..." formula. References to war are light: "K is for Kaiser, of Kultur the King! / (Indirectly the cause of a new wedding ring!)" (qtd. in Morgan 68). Domestic conflict, too, is minimized and seen as a strengthening part of the marriage: "Q is for Quarrels that end so 'demurely' / Each apology binds them together securely!" (qtd. in L. Thompson 179).

The opening and closing couplets have a strong sense of Tommy and Tuppence Beresford, and could be used as evidence for this young marriage, and future projections on what might have been, being the model for that pair:

A is for Angel, by nature(?) and name
And also for Archibald, spouse of the same.
...
Z for the Zest of that wonderful pair
The Archibald Christies, who make their bow
  here! [qtd. in L. Thompson 100]

The poem is housed in the Christie Family Archive.

See also **Christie, Colonel Archibald "Archie"**

Aarons, Joseph

Joseph Aarons is a theater agent who helps Hercule Poirot navigate theatrical circles in *The Big Four*, "Double Sin," *The Murder on the Links*, and *The Mystery of the Blue Train*.

Aatagara. See **Indian-Language Adaptations**

The ABC Murders (computer game). See **Games**

The ABC Murders (DS game). See **Games**

The ABC Murders (novel)

The twist in *The ABC Murders* is rather obvious today. However, when Christie wrote it, this was not the case. A classic serial killer novel, it features Hercule Poirot, who receives letters signed "A.B.C.," boasting of murders to be committed. The first is in Andover, the second in Bexhill, and so on. Moreover, the victims have alliterative names—Alice Asher, Betty Barnard, and Carmichael Clarke—and an ABC railway guide has been found by each body. Occasionally, Captain Hastings's narrative breaks off, and the reader learns about a traveling salesman, the highly nervy and unstable Alexander Bonaparte Cust, who is visiting each of these towns.

Few readers today would suspect Cust of being the culprit; most would rightly assume that another character will turn out to be ABC. However, in 1936, when the novel was published, serial killer stories looked very different. For example, Philip

MacDonald's *Murder Gone Mad* (1931) similarly features a serial killer whose crimes appear unconnected; the point is that his motive is a lust for killing, and the tension lies in the fact that nobody is safe. The mystery, therefore, is *how* to track him down. *The ABC Murders* plays on the expectation that this will be the tone, when Poirot worries about "[t]he sanity of a city full of men against the insanity of one man," urging Hastings to consider "the long continued success of Jack the Ripper" (64). Christie turns this on its head when Poirot reveals that the random murders are a smoke screen to hide one deliberate crime.

Looked at from that angle, it is easy to solve. Of the four victims in the towns of Andover, Bexhill, Churston, and Doncaster, only one is rich, and sure enough, the heir to his fortune is the killer. The murder has been hidden in an apparently mad pattern. This idea has been linked to G.K. Chesterton's war-conscious short story, "The Sign of the Broken Sword," in which a dead body is hidden on a battlefield where it will not be noticed (Edwards, "Plotting" 189). However, the idea of hiding a motivated murder amid several unmotivated ones seems to be new. As usual for Poirot in the mid–1930s, he solves the case but has only circumstantial evidence, so he invents some—in this case, as in *Death in the Clouds*, a fingerprint—to trap the murderer into a confession.

Christie was tiring (again) of Captain Hastings by 1936, excluding him from as many Poirot novels as those in which he appeared. The narrative, moving between the first and third person, illustrates a frustration with writing in his limited voice. She would only include him in two more novels, one of which would not be published until 1975. However, his sportsman's banter is in full swing here, as he clashes with Poirot over what is and is not playing the game. Poirot has the last word on this when he tells the murderer that the crime was "not an English crime at all—not above-board—not *sporting*" (*ABC* 248, emphasis in original). Perhaps he has outgrown his need for Hastings now. Nonetheless, the novel ends, echoing that of *The Mysterious Affair at Styles*, with Poirot telling Hastings: "we

went hunting once more, did we not? *Vive le sport*" (252).

When *The ABC Murders* was serialized in the *Daily Express* in 1935, it ran alongside a column of "Readers' Guesses," with some demonstrating an extraordinary level of familiarity with the ABC railway guide. In 1936, Collins published the book in the United Kingdom, and Dodd, Mead published it in the United States. It has proven a novel that has influenced several murder plots on page and screen. Notable examples, both of which work characters reading *The ABC Murders* into their plots, include Elizabeth Linington's *Greenmask!* (1964) and Peter Swanson's *Rules for Perfect Murders* (2020).

The book has also inspired two video games; two graphic novels; three radio plays; one movie; and five television adaptations in English, French, and Japanese.

Characters: Anderson, Colonel; **Ascher, Alice, and Franz**; Ball, Mr.; **Barnard, Elizabeth ("Betty")**; **Barnard, Megan**; Barnard, Mr. and Mrs.; Capstick, Nurse; **Clarke, Franklin**; **Clarke, Lady Charlotte**; **Clarke, Sir Carmichael**; Crome, Inspector; **Cust, Alexander Bonaparte**; Deveril; Downes, Roger; Drower, Mary; Earlsfield, George; Fowler, Edie and Mrs.; **Fraser, Donald ("Don")**; **Grey, Thora**; Hartigan, Tom; **Hastings, Captain Arthur**; Higley, Milly; **Jameson, Inspector**; **Japp, Chief Inspector James**; Jerome, Colonel; Kelsey, Inspector; Kerr, Dr.; Leadbetter, Mr.; Marbury family; Partridge, James; **Poirot, Hercule**; **Rice, Inspector**; Roe, Miss; Sir Lionel; Thompson, Dr.

See also: ***Agasa Kurisuti no Meitantei Powaro to Māpuru***; ***Agatha Christie's Poirot***; **BBC Television Adaptations since 2015**; **CBS Radio Adaptations**; **Games**; ***Hercule Poirot*** **(BBC radio series)**; ***Meitantei Akafuji Takashi***; **MGM Films**; ***Les Petits Meurtres d'Agatha Christie***; **True Crime**

The ABC Murders (television adaptation). See **BBC Television Adaptations since 2015**

ABC Satsujin-jiken. See ***Meitantei Akafuji Takashi***

Abdul

Christie created four Abduls, all of whom are presented in subordinate relationships to White men. In *The Sittaford Mystery* (1931), Abdul is in service to Captain Wyatt. In *Appointment with Death* (1938), Abdul is an unflatteringly-drawn servant who discovers Mrs. Boynton's body. In "The Horses of Diomedes" (1940), Abdul is the servant of an Indian Army officer, General Grant—although the general, and presumably the servant, turn out to be bogus. In *They Came to Baghdad* (1951), Abdul is a friend of Henry Carmichael, a fictionalized Lawrence of Arabia. As Christie saw more of Western Asia and became more worldly, she became more comfortable presenting characters from other cultures as individuals, as the fourth Abdul shows.

Abdullah

In *Murder in Mesopotamia*, Abdullah is a servant boy who washes pots on the dig. In *They Came to Baghdad,* Abdullah works in the Foreign Office with Mr. Dakin.

Abenteuer GmbH, Die (Adventures Inc.; film)

Die Abenteuer GmbH (Adventures Inc.), the second Christie screen adaptation, was a German silent film based on *The Secret Adversary.* Humorlessly faithful to the plot, the one-hour film makes some small adjustments such as Europeanizing the characters so American Jane Finn becomes Jannette Finné, and Brits Tommy and Tuppence become Pierre and Lucienne, and changing the sinking of the *Lusitania* to the sinking of a fictional ship, the *Herculine.* The biggest departure from the novel is the ending, which closes with the capture of the villain rather than the central characters declaring their love. The film is difficult but not impossible to view today, mirroring its relatively limited impact outside of Germany at the time it was made. It caused no stir upon its release in early 1929 but received good reviews.

With a screenplay by Jane Bess and directed by Fred Sauer, the film starred Eve Gray as Lucienne (based on Tuppence Cowley) and Carlo Aldini as Pierre (i.e., Tommy Beresford) with Elfriede Borodin as Janette (i.e., Jane Finn), and Hilda Bayley as Rita.

See also: *The Passing of Mr. Quinn* (film and novel); *The Secret Adversary* (novel)

Abercrombie Forgery Case

Like Sir Arthur Conan Doyle's Sherlock Holmes, Hercule Poirot occasionally refers to unchronicled past cases. However, this is much rarer with Poirot than with Holmes. Conan Doyle would often write out an idea he had mentioned (for example, "The Adventure of the Second Cucumber"), but Christie did not do this. "The Abercrombie Forgery Case," mentioned in *The Mysterious Affair at Styles* and "A Letter to My Publisher," occurred in 1904 in Brussels and is the case that features the meeting of Poirot and Inspector James Japp. Although it is a matter of time, to date no subsequent author has tried to re-create the case as a narrative.

See also: **"A Letter to My Publisher"**; *The Mysterious Affair at Styles*

Abernethie, Helen

In *After the Funeral*, Helen Abernethie's keen observation puts her in danger. She is the widow of Leo Abernethie and sister to the late Richard Abernethie.

Abernethie, Maude, and Timothy

A younger brother to the late Richard Abernethie in *After the Funeral*, Timothy is a middle-aged hypochondriac. Maude is his extremely loyal wife, who indulges his constant, and entirely self-perpetuated, ill-health.

Abernethie, Richard

Richard Abernethie is a wealthy elderly man, the oldest of six siblings, whose funeral marks the beginning of the action in *After the Funeral.* Although he died of natural causes, much of the investigation centers on a belief that he was murdered. Richard's son, Mortimer Abernethie, died of polio six months before Richard's death.

Absent in the Spring

The third novel under Christie's Mary Westmacott pseudonym, *Absent in the Spring* is almost entirely composed of its protagonist's inner thoughts. This was the last Westmacott novel published by Collins (in 1944) and the last one before the author's true identity became public knowledge. It was published in the United States by

Farrar & Rinehart in the same year. Written over three days without food or sleep, and Christie considered it her "proudest joy": "it was written with integrity, with sincerity, and it was written as I wanted to write it" (*AA* 500). The idea had been "building up" for six or seven years (499) and after the writing of this, which Christie considered "an imperative," nothing about the manuscript had to be changed for publication (500). It is not an innovative novel—the central character begins by assessing her reflection in the mirror, a tired device by 1945—but it is an accomplished work of modernist introspection.

The "strait-laced" Joan Scudamore (*AIS* 603) is returning to England after visiting her daughter in Iraq. After meeting Blanche Haggard, a hedonistic friend from her school days, she congratulates herself on her own superiority as a wife and mother: Blanche looks her age, has married multiple times, and gossips freely, including about an affair Joan's daughter is rumored to have had. Readers begin to suspect that Joan is not as in control of her life as she thinks, when she brushes these comments off and recalls how happy her husband Rodney was to see her off on the original journal.

The train is delayed by flooding, and Joan is forced to stay at a rest house in Tell Abu Hamid. As boredom sets in, she starts thinking about her life, and thoughts of the vivacious, happy Blanche set in. She realizes that her daughter Barbara Wray was not in fact happy to see her in Iraq and that Barbara has been desperately unhappy, even suicidal, lacking a support network as her marriage fell apart, because Joan refuses to talk about unpleasant things. She realizes that Rodney is being stifled by her. Recalling how she felt when bullied by a self-righteous and censorious schoolmistress, she realizes that she is not an asset to her family, but an obstruction. When she returns home, Joan vows to her husband to change. She is grateful that she is no longer alone. While welcoming her back, Rodney thinks: "You are alone, and you always will be. But, please God, you'll never know it" (755).

As Merja Makinen points out in one of the few scholarly readings of the Mary Westmacott books, when Joan judges other women for superficial things, it reflects poorly on her: the other women "are shown to be failures neither as mothers nor as wives but depicted as vibrant and generous. It is Joan who is presented as 'blood-less' and 'a prig'" (*Investigating* 106). Makinen concludes that "[t]he novel gradually and unerringly unpacks the emptiness of a 'circumscribed' domesticity lived to fit social conventions" (107).

Critically, the book has been praised; it is probably the best-known of the Westmacott texts. However, it has not been studied in any particular depth, partly because it is rarely consulted except by nonfiction writers, and these tend to box it into a life-writing category as well. Osborne calls it "an emotional autobiography" (203). Gillian Gill and Laura Thompson have similarly mined it for autobiographical details.

However, there are stirrings of critical interest in the text beyond attempts to read it as a memoir, which are certainly easier with the two first Westmacott novels. Makinen has called it "an astonishingly accomplished modernist masterpiece of a woman's self-delusion of happy respectability" and, instead of encouraging life-writing readings, has urged further scholarship into the presentation of key themes such as "sheltered childhoods that damage an adults' ability to cope with vicissitude, the damage inflicted by possessive love, and the inability to know how life can transform others, linked to the inalienable difficulties of knowing oneself" ("Hidden").

For a novel generally considered "a *tour de force*" (Osborne 203), and compared by author Dorothy B. Hughes to the enormously successful *Brief Encounter* (qtd. in Osborne 204), dramatizations have been a surprisingly long time coming. The book was adapted into a 45-minute radio play, as part of a short series of lesser-known Christies, in 2020. Starring Harriet Walter and directed by Catherine Bailey, it was broadcast on BBC Radio 4 on 31 August 2020.

Characters: Averil; Callaway, Michael; Gargill, Rupert; Gilby, Miss; **Haggard, Blanche;** Hohenbach Salm, Princess Sasha; **Randolph, Myrna; Reid, Major; Scudamore, Joan; Scudamore, Rodney;**

Scudamore, Tony; **Sherston, Captain Charles, and Leslie; Wray, Barbara, and William**

See also: *An Autobiography*; BBC Radio Adaptations; Westmacott, Mary

"Accident" (story; alternative titles: "Test for Murder"; "The Uncrossed Path")

Almost an inversion of "Philomel Cottage," "Accident" features Inspector Evans, a retired C.I.D. man, who realizes that the new wife of an absent-minded chemistry professor once got away with murder. When Evans recognizes Margaret Merrowdene as Margaret Andrews, whose first husband died of arsenical poisoning, he worries for George Merrowdene. He arranges a meeting with Margaret to confront her. However, it emerges that she has poisoned his tea—she was plotting to kill him, not her husband, all along.

This story may have its roots in the many sensational narratives on convicted murderer Florence Maybrick. Either way, it is a vivid sketch. It was first published in the *Sunday Dispatch* in 1929 and has appeared in the United Kingdom in *The Listerdale Mystery* (1934) and in the United States in *The Witness for the Prosecution* (1948). In 1939, it was dramatized by Margery Vosper as a one-act play, *Tea for Three*, which has been performed occasionally by repertory companies.

Characters: Anthony, Mr.; Evans, Inspector; Haydock, Captain; Merrowdene, George; Merrowdene, Margaret; **Zara**

See also: *The Listerdale Mystery* (story collection); "Philomel Cottage"; *Tea for Three*; *Witness for the Prosecution* (story collection)

Ackroyd, Flora

In *The Murder of Roger Ackroyd*, Flora Ackroyd is the victim's petite, beautiful niece who takes on a kind of wallflower role but is revealed to have hidden depths of passion and desperation: she is engaged to Ralph Paton but in love with Major Blunt and steals £40 from her dead uncle's drawer.

Ackroyd, Roger

Roger Ackroyd is the victim in *The Murder of Roger Ackroyd* and the first of Christie's victims to be a self-made millionaire as opposed to a hereditary one. Although he is a sympathetic character and better treated by Christie than the ridiculous Lord Whitfield in *Murder Is Easy*, he is nonetheless mocked as trying too hard: he is "more impossibly like a country squire than any country squire could really be" (7). In the stage adaptation, *Alibi*, he was turned into a baronet.

"The Actress" (alternative title: "A Trap for the Unwary")

In this breezy short story, Jake Levitt decides to blackmail an actress, whom he recognizes as an old acquaintance with a new identity. However, the actress, Olga Stormer, ropes in her understudy to stage a murder scene and scare Levitt off. Disguised as maid, she congratulates herself on being a true actress. This is a neat vignette, which includes a typically dramatic murder set-up and plays on the idea, long-running in Christie's works, that full attention is never paid to the servants. It also celebrates female agency and, surprisingly for an early Christie story, judges the man harshly while celebrating the resourcefulness of a woman, despite her unsavory past. It was first published in *The Novel Magazine* in 1923 and, in 1990, was included in a commemorative booklet to mark Christie's centenary. In 1997, it was collected in *While the Light Lasts* in the United Kingdom and *The Harlequin Tea Set* in the United States.

Characters: Danahan, Syd (Danny); Levitt, Jake; Ryan, Margaret; Stormer, Olga; Taylor, Nancy

See also: *Evil under the Sun* (novel); *The Harlequin Tea Set* (story collection); Theatricality; *While the Light Lasts* (story collection)

Adams, Carlotta

Carlotta Adams is a character in *Lord Edgware Dies*, inspired by—but not based on—the American actor and impressionist Ruth Draper (1884–1956), whom Christie greatly admired. It is never in question that Carlotta impersonated Lady Edgware on the night of the murder, but when and why she did so is initially unclear. One of Christie's most likable victims, she opens the novel with a performance, setting the scene for a highly theatrical novel. By the end, she has emerged as more real than many of the people she imitates—Lady Edgware, for example, is a highly artificial person who exists as no more than the sum of her affectations. Christie had previously developed a character inspired by Ruth Draper: Aspasia Glen in "The Dead Harlequin."

Adams, Tom (1926–2019)

Originally from Providence, Rhode Island, Tom Adams provided the most distinctive and best-known illustrations for Christie's fiction. The grandson of Thomas Adams, the urban planner and adviser to Herbert Hoover and Franklin D. Roosevelt, he came from a Scottish family and was raised in Britain. He studied at Cambridge University and served in the Royal Navy before training as an artist at the Chelsea School of Art and Goldsmith's College, London before beginning a career in the 1950s.

Adams's first success as an illustrator came with a cover for John Fowles' *The Collector,* and a productive working relationship led to covers for further Fowles titles. These much-admired covers in turn led to a "trial" with Fontana, the paperback imprint of Collins, to design a cover for *A Murder Is Announced.* The result was a success, and Adams was commissioned to produce paintings for almost all the Christie fictional works for Fontana. Others in the series mimicked Adams's style, and the paintings were reused in several editions with slightly altered designs, as well as in international publications—not always matched with the same title. In a separate commission for Pocket Books in the United States, he created larger paintings, detailing a scene from each text.

The oil paintings are detailed, combining realism with symbolism or surrealism, and each serves two purposes: as an arresting work of art in its own right and as a clue to the mystery or, in some cases, what happens in the story. For example, a thornless rose features on a lost-love-themed design for *Sad Cypress*, both an element of the overall evocation and a clue: the murderer in that book claims to prick her finger on a rose, which is thornless. Fowles described Adams's strength as the presentation of "obliquity that ... constitutes a lure" and a strategic combination, as in Christie, "of the banal and the exotic" (8). However, like Christie, Adams tended to shy away from analysis of his work. When Christie scholar John Curran suggested that a snake on the cover of *Ordeal by Innocence* symbolized the centrality of the family home, Viper's Point, in the novel, Adams responded: "There is no more significance in the snake than the obvious one—this cover is essentially 'innocence versus evil'" (Adams and Curran 116).

Adams prints and originals have become popular with art collectors and more so with collectors of Christie memorabilia, which is a growing community. By 1980, when Adams published his first art book, comprising Christie covers, eight of the originals could no longer be traced and several images had to be sourced from private collections. By 2015, with the second book, which followed a series of exhibitions, around half had to be privately sourced. By the 1980s, fashions had changed enough for new, less illustrated Christie covers to be used.

However, Adams continued to provide illustrations for adjacent works such as Charles Osborne's *The Life and Crimes of Agatha Christie* (1980), Randal Toye's *The Agatha Christie Who's Who* (1980), and Julian Symons' *The Great Detectives* (1981). In 2014, he produced "The Mystery of Agatha Christie," a lifescape montage painting not dissimilar to works he had produced under commission depicting Benjamin Britten, President Tubman of Liberia, and Enid Blyton, and illustrated the newly released *Hercule Poirot and the Greenshore Folly.* In 2016, with the revival of interest in his work, Adams provided new illustrations for a special two-volume edition of *The Mysterious Affair at Styles* and *Curtain*, neither of which he had illustrated before.

Aside from Christie, Fowles, and lifescape work, Adams had an extensive career. His covers adorned works by such novelists as Raymond Chandler, Eric Ambler, and Sue Grafton. He painted album sleeves for musicians such as Lou Reed, Kokomo, and illustrated advertising campaigns for the likes of Bell's Whiskey and the BBC.

Adams illustrated covers for the following Christie titles, some up to three times, with additional expanded gallery illustrations for some: *The ABC Murders; The Adventure of the Christmas Pudding; After the Funeral; Appointment with Death; At Bertram's Hotel; The Big Four; The Body in the Library; By the Pricking of My Thumbs; Cards on the Table; A Caribbean Mystery; Cat Among the Pigeons; The Clocks; Crooked House; Curtain; Dead Man's Folly; Death Comes as the End; Death in the Clouds; Death on the Nile; Destination Unknown; Elephants Can Remember; Endless Night; Evil under the Sun; Five Little Pigs; 4.50 from Paddington; Hallowe'en Party; Hercule Poirot and the Greenshore Folly; Hickory Dickory Dock; The Hollow; The Hound of Death; The Labours of Hercules; Lord Edgware Dies; The Man in the Brown Suit; The Mirror Crack'd from Side to Side; Miss Marple's Final Cases; The Moving Finger; Mrs. McGinty's Dead; The Murder at the Vicarage; A Murder Is Announced; Murder Is Easy; The Murder of Roger Ackroyd; The Mysterious Affair at Styles; The Mysterious Mr. Quin; The Mystery of the Blue Train; N or M?; Nemesis; One, Two, Buckle My Shoe; Ordeal by Innocence; The Pale Horse; Parker Pyne Investigates; Passenger to Frankfurt; A Pocket Full of Rye; Poirot's Early Cases; Postern of Fate; Sad Cypress; The Seven Dials Mystery; The Sittaford Mystery; Sparkling Cyanide; Taken at the Flood; They Do It with Mirrors; Three-Act Tragedy; Towards Zero;* and *Why Didn't They Ask Evans?*.

See also: *A Murder Is Announced;* **Continuation Fiction**

Addison, Tom

Tom Addison is an elderly, longtime friend of Mr. Satterthwaite's who is a stroke survivor and is in poor health in "The Harlequin Tea Set." His colorblindness, revealed in mismatched footwear, becomes a clue to a murder plot.

Aduthathu. See **Indian-Language Adaptations**

"Adventure by Request." See **"The Case of the Discontented Soldier"**

"The Adventure of Johnnie Waverly" (story; alternative titles: "At the Stroke of Twelve"; "The Kidnapping of Johnnie Waverly")

"The Adventure of Johnnie Waverly" is an early Poirot story, first published in *The Sketch* (10 October 1923). It would not be anthologized until 1950 in the United States (in *Three Blind Mice*) and 1974 in the United Kingdom (*Poirot's Early Cases*).

Poirot and Hastings are asked to investigate the kidnapping of three-year-old Johnnie Waverly from Waverly Court, his home in Surrey. Prior to the kidnapping, the parents had received anonymous letters alerting them to the kidnapping, but the police had not helped to prevent it. At Waverly Court, Poirot uncovers a priest hole and, with it and a reset clock, explains how the kidnapping took place despite precautions. Ultimately, he implicates the boy's father, who confesses to staging the kidnapping for financial gain. Poirot chastises Mr. Waverly as if he is a disobedient child: "Your name is an old and honoured one. Do not jeopardise it again" (*PEC* 66).

The story has been filmed twice: for television, as part of the first series of *Agatha Christie's Poirot* (broadcast on ITV, 2 January 1989) and in the 12th series of *Les Petits Meurtres d'Agatha Christie* (broadcast on France 2 on 26 August 2016). It was dramatized for German radio in 2006, as part of *Krimi-Sommer mit Hercule Poirot* (Crime Summer for Hercule Poirot) for SWR.

Characters: Collins, Miss; Dakers, Dr.; **Hastings, Captain Arthur; McNeil, Inspector; Poirot, Hercule; Tredwell; Waverly, Ada, and Marcus;** Waverly, Johnnie; Withers, Jessie

See also: *Agatha Christie's Poirot; Krimi-Sommer mit Hercule Poirot; Les Petits Meurtres d'Agatha Christie; Poirot's Early Cases; Three Blind Mice* (story collection)

"The Adventure of the Cheap Flat" (story; alternative title: "Poirot Indulges a Whim")

"The Adventure of the Cheap Flat," an early Hercule Poirot short story, distinguishes itself at the outset with Captain Hastings telling the reader that it did not stem from a big fact like "murder or robbery" but from "apparently trivial incidents" spiraling out (*PI* 69). Poirot tells Hastings of a young couple, the Robinsons, who have rented a "beautifully furnished" flat in the "[b]ig handsome building" of Montagu Mansions in high-end Knightsbridge (70–71). They have rented it very cheap without a deposit and are trying to find the catch.

The detectives learn that other couples were rejected by the landlords before the Robinsons were offered the flat. Due in part to Hastings's weakness for auburn-haired women (he notices extensive details about Mrs. Robinson but dismisses her husband as "quite a nice fellow—nothing startling" [76]) and in part to an uncharacteristic excursion in a coal lift, Poirot solves the case. He identifies a criminal network akin to the mafia, which is chasing the flat's owner, who has stolen naval documents. She was looking for a family called Robinson to live in the flat, because the criminal gang knows her under that name. Poirot brings Inspector Japp to the flat to arrest the parties involved, and Poirot recovers the documents from the lining of a velvet telephone cover.

The story was first published in *The Sketch* on 9 May 1923. It appeared in book form in the United Kingdom in *Poirot Investigates* (Collins, 1924) and in the United States in the Dodd, Mead edition in 1925. Dramatizations were aired as part of *Agatha Christie's Poirot* on ITV on 18 April 1990, and as part of *Agasa Kurisutī no Meitantei Powaro to Māpuru* on NHK on 18 July 2004.

Characters: Burton, Mr.; Ferguson, Elsie; Ferguson, Mr.; Hardt, Elsa; **Hastings, Captain Arthur**; **Japp, Inspector James**; Parker, Gerald; **Poirot, Hercule**; Robinson, John; Robinson, Stella; Valdarno, Luigi

See also: *Agasa Kurisutī noMeitantei Powaro to Māpuru*; *Agatha Christie's Poirot*; *Poirot Investigates*; **Robinson, Mr.**

"The Adventure of the Christmas Pudding" (novella; alternative title: "The Theft of the Royal Ruby")

A heavily expanded version of "Christmas Adventure" (1923), "The Adventure of the Christmas Pudding" makes concerted efforts to update the setting. Although the idea of a traditional family Christmas is simply a backdrop to the original story, the tension between modernity and nostalgia is at the forefront in the novella. The plot remains the same: Poirot is to stay at a country house over Christmas to recover a ruby that has been stolen from a foreign prince. During his stay, a group of young people plans a mock-murder as a joke. However, Poirot proclaims the crime a real one and uses the confusion to flush out the thief. The house's owner is now not just old but "absolutely lives in the past" and rejects Poirot's presence as "a foreigner" (*ACP* 19), whereas his wife, although more indulgent, is "upright as a ramrod," "ridiculous" in contemporary surroundings, and frequently compares "the coffee bar set" to the young "[i]n my young day" (19, 20). Poirot even accuses the servant, who has warned him of imminent danger, of watching "too many sensational films [… o]r perhaps it is the television" (58); in the original, he says she has read "too many novelettes" ("Christmas Adventure" 109).

"The Adventure of the Christmas Pudding" was published as the first "main course" in the book of the same name (1960) in the United Kingdom. In the United States, it was edited slightly into "The Theft of the Royal Ruby," appearing in two installments (25 September and 2 October 1960) in *This Week*, a magazine supplement of *the* [Washington, D.C.] *Sunday Star*, before it was included in the collection *Double Sin and Other Stories* (1961). It was filmed under its U.S. title as part of *Agatha Christie's Poirot*, broadcast on ITV on 24 February 1991. An animated version was broadcast on NHK on 5 and 12 December 2004 as part of *Agasa Kurisutī no Meitantei Powaro to Māpuru*. BBC Radio 4 also aired a dramatization, with John Moffatt as Poirot, on Christmas Day 2004.

Characters: Ali, Prince; **Bates, Annie**; Bridget; Hodgkins; Jesmond, Mr.; Lacey, Colin; Lacey, Colonel Horace; Lacey, Emmeline; Lacey, Sarah; Lee-Wortley, Desmond; Lee-Wortley, Miss; Michael; Middleton, Diana; Moreambe, Edwina; Peverell; **Poirot, Hercule**; Ross, Mrs.; Tibbitts; Welwyn, David

See also: *Agasa Kurisutī no Meitantei*

Powaro to Māpuru; *Agatha Christie's Poirot*; *Hercule Poirot* (BBC radio series); "Christmas Adventure"

The Adventure of the Christmas Pudding (story collection; alternative title: *The Adventure of the Christmas Pudding and a Selection of Entrées*)

A collection of short stories published in the United Kingdom in 1960, *The Adventure of the Christmas Pudding* was designed to be a Christmas book and is unusual because Christie made substantial changes to the early magazine stories—most of the contents—that appear in it. The most notable changes are to "The Adventure of the Christmas Pudding" (original version: "Christmas Adventure") and "The Mystery of the Spanish Chest" (original: "The Mystery of the Baghdad Chest"), which are both heavily expanded, with action updated so that they take place in 1960, not 1923 like the originals.

The volume also features "The Under Dog," "Four and Twenty Blackbirds," and "The Dream," all early Poirot stories appearing with minor alterations. The final entry is a Miss Marple story, "Greenshaw's Folly." Christie provided an introduction, explaining to readers that it was a festive book to be enjoyed, not criticized.

See "**The Dream**"; "**Four and Twenty Blackbirds**"; "**Greenshaw's Folly**"; "**The Under Dog**"

"The Adventure of the Clapham Cook" (story; alternative title: "Find the Cook")

The short story "The Adventure of the Clapham Cook" establishes Hercule Poirot as a detective who follows his conscience beyond following paychecks. It was first published in the second series of Poirot stories in *The Sketch*, in November 1923, at a time when Christie was writing in the Sherlock Holmes mold, and shows the detective stepping out of the shadow of his predecessor, as he becomes a more rounded character.

Perusing morning newspapers, Captain Hastings tries and fails to interest Poirot in some sensational, high-stakes cases, because they are not "of national importance" (26). However, when the forceful Mrs. Todd bustles into his flat and asks him

to investigate her missing cook, Eliza Dunn, he agrees. "This case," he suggests, "will be a novelty" (*PEC* 27). Poirot learns that the Todd household has a connection to one of the cases he read about in the papers—that of an absconding bank clerk—and places an advertisement in a newspaper for Eliza Dunn to come forward. She does so and is surprised to hear that anyone is looking for her. She wrote her resignation from service after coming into an inheritance, but the letter was never received. Poirot uncovers a conspiracy whereby the lodger of the Todds got Eliza out of the way purely so that he could steal her luggage trunk, to hide a body—that of the missing bank clerk. Poirot does not cash Mrs. Todd's humble fee, one guinea, but displays it on the wall, as a reminder of "one of the most interesting of my cases" (38).

The story was first collected in Dorothy L. Sayers's anthology for Gollancz, *The Second Omnibus of Crime, Mystery and Horror* (1932), and appeared in the U.S. collection *The Under Dog* (1951) and the U.K. collection *Poirot's Early Cases* (1974). A BBC radio adaptation was broadcast in 1956 and a television adaptation aired in 1989 on ITV as the first episode of *Agatha Christie's Poirot*. The story is also the basis for a two-part episode of *Agasa Kurisutī no Meitantei Powaro to Māpuru* (2005).

Characters: **Annie**; Crotchet, Mr.; Davis, Mr.; Dunn, Eliza; Emmott, Jane; **Hastings, Captain Arthur**; **Japp, Inspector James**; Leech, Eliza; Paterson, Carter; **Poirot, Hercule**; Simpson, Mr.; Todd, Mr.; Todd, Mrs.; Wintergreen, Henry

See also: *Agasa Kurisutī no Meitantei Powaro to Māpuru*; *Agatha Christie's Poirot*; **BBC Radio Adaptations**; *Poirot's Early Cases*; *The Under Dog* (story collection)

"The Adventure of the Dartmoor Bungalow" (alternative title: "The Importance of a Leg of Mutton"). See *The Big Four* (novel)

"The Adventure of the Egyptian Tomb" (alternative titles: "The Egyptian Tomb," "The Next Victim")

"The Adventure of the Egyptian Tomb" is a short story in which Poirot investigates what seems to be an ancient curse. An Egyptologist's widow asks Poirot to look into two deaths within two weeks following the excavation of the tomb of Pharaoh Men-her-Ra. Poirot does so and reveals that a murderer exploited fears about a curse. At the same time, a key clue to what happened is the fact that Poirot realizes a statement everyone has taken as metaphorical was meant literally.

This story capitalizes on media sensations around the discovery and excavation of the tomb of Tutankhamen in 1922–23, and stories of a curse killing off members of the team. It also mentions the Mena House Hotel, where Christie had previously stayed, although it predates her significant interest in archaeology.

It was published in *The Sketch* in May 1923 and appeared the next year in the collection *Poirot Investigates*. There have been television adaptations as part of *Agatha Christie's Poirot* (1993) and *Agasa Kurisutī no Meitantei Powaro to Māpuru* (2004), and a dinner party game adaptation, *The Pyramids of Giza*, in 2002.

Characters: Ames, Dr.; Bleiner, Rupert; Bleibner, Mr.; Harper, Mr.; Hassan; **Hastings, Captain Arthur**; **Poirot, Hercule**; Schneider, Mr.; Tosswill, Dr.; Willard, Lady; Willard, Sir Guy; Willard, Sir John

See also: *Agatha Christie's Poirot*; **Archaeology**; **Curses**; *Poirot Investigates*

"The Adventure of the Italian Nobleman" (story; alternative title: "The Regent's Court Murder")

"The Adventure of the Italian Nobleman" is an early Hercule Poirot story, in which Poirot, Hastings, and Japp investigate when a sleazy Italian count is murdered. There is an obvious suspect in Count Foscatini's death; Signor Paolo, whom he was blackmailing, was said to have met him for dinner, and the remnants of two meals have been found at the crime scene. However, Poirot ascertains that Foscatini's valet-butler, Graves, murdered him for the blackmail money and then ate both meals.

This is one of many examples of Christie exposing British prejudice against other nationalities in her early fiction. As in "The Adventure of the 'Western Star,'" suspicion immediately centers on a non–English character, despite evidence to the contrary, when in fact the English criminal is exploiting the relevant prejudice. The story was first published in *The Sketch* in October 1923 and collected in *Poirot Investigates* the following year. It was filmed as an episode of *Agatha Christie's Poirot* in 1993.

Characters: Ascani, Paolo; Foscatini, Count; **Graves, Mr.**; **Hastings, Captain Arthur**; Hawker, Dr.; **Japp, Inspector James**; **Poirot, Hercule**; Rider, Miss.

See also: "The Adventure of the 'Western Star'"; *Agatha Christie's Poirot*; *Poirot Investigates*

"The Adventure of the King of Clubs." See "The King of Clubs"

"The Adventure of the Peroxide Blonde." See *The Big Four* (novel)

"The Adventure of the Sinister Stranger" (alternative title: "The Case of the Sinister Stranger"). See *Partners in Crime* (short story collection)

"The Adventure of the 'Western Star,'" (story; alternative title: "Poirot Puts a Finger in the Pie")

In this early story, the fabulous jewel in single quotation marks proves not to exist. Poirot and Hastings are consulted by the American film star Mary Marvell, who tells him she has received letters from a Chinese man, threatening to steal her diamond, the Western Star, and return it to its home: the right eye of an ancient idol. Society gossip has it that there are two stones originating in this idol: the Western Star, owned by Marvell, and the Eastern Star, owned by Lady Yardly.

Lady Yardly visits Hastings who tells her this story, and she leads him to believe that she too has received letters. However, Lord Yardly reveals the next day that the story of the stone's origins is false—the Eastern Star comes from India. He is planning to sell it, to his wife's chagrin. Within two days, both Lady Yardly and Mary Marvell claim that their stones have been stolen by a Chinese man or men. However, Poirot deduces that Marvell's husband, a film star who is also Lady Yardly's lover, planned the whole thing. There never was a Western Star: he stole the Eastern Star, so that he could claim insurance and retain the diamond with a spectacular narrative.

A theme of this story—which plays with the genre's roots in Wilkie Collins's *The Moonstone*—is imperialism. Western jewelry has its roots in colonization, looting, and the exploitation of labor, although this is not dwelt upon. Instead, a Chinese man who never existed is scapegoated under the trappings of superstition. There is also a clash between new money—the film star—and old money—the aristocrat, whose lineage is given as Poirot looks her up. Both, it turns out, share a diamond, and at the heart of the trouble is the same handsome cad

Despite its early place in the canon, "The Adventure of the 'Western Star'" references two previous works. Mary Marvell was directed to Poirot by Lord Cronshaw ("The Affair at the Victory Ball") and Lady Yardly by Mary Cavendish (*The Mysterious Affair at Styles*). The story was published in *The Sketch* in 1923 and collected in *Poirot Investigates* in 1924. It was televised as part of *Agatha Christie's Poirot* in 1990.

Characters: **Beltane, Hon./Lord Eustace (6th Lord Cronshaw)**; **Cavendish, Mary**; Cotteril, Baron; **Hastings, Captain Arthur**; Hoffberg, Mr.; Marvell, Mary; Mullings; **Poirot, Hercule**; Rolf, Gregory B.; Stopperton, Hon. Maud; Yardly, Lady; Yardly, Lord.

See also *Agatha Christie's Poirot*; **Class**; *Poirot Investigates*

"The Affair at the Bungalow." See *The Thirteen Problems*

"The Affair at the Victory Ball" (story; alternative title: **"The Six China Figures"**)

The first published Hercule Poirot short story, "The Affair at the Victory Ball" appeared in *The Sketch* on 7 March 1923. Quickly in her career, Christie became well-known among publishers and editors for insisting on control over what was published under her name. This story, however, was heavily edited for publication—perhaps the experience informed Christie's later attitude. The original typescript, housed in the Christie Family Archive, has a slightly different structure than the published version, includes two features that

were removed, and show Christie finding her feet as a mystery writer. One is a foreword by Captain Arthur Hastings, introducing Poirot and himself (recalling details that had appeared in *The Mysterious Affair at Styles* [1920]). The other is a "sign" placed at the point in the story where the reader has all the evidence to solve the puzzle. Christie planned for this to be included in each of the *Sketch* stories, but it featured in none. Many years later, Christie would try to insert a similar moment into a play, including her own recorded voice. It was then, similarly, a failure.

The story shows Christie's interest in the *Commedia dell'arte*, as the crime takes place at a masquerade ball where characters are dressed as Harlequin, Columbine, and other such figures. Poirot is asked by Inspector Japp to investigate the death of Lord Cronshaw, who was stopped in costume at the Victory Ball. During the investigation, Poirot encounters another murder and learns about cocaine addiction and the secret high-society world of hard drug dealing. He identifies the murderer, a respectable figure, who is secretly a cocaine-dealer.

In 1951, "The Affair at the Victory Ball" was anthologized in the United States in *The Under Dog*. It was published in *Poirot's Early Cases* (1974) in the United Kingdom. A television adaptation was broadcast as part of *Agatha Christie's Poirot* on ITV on 3 March 1991.

Characters: **Beltane, Hon./Lord Eustace (6th Lord Cronshaw)**; Courtenay, Coco; Cronshaw, Lord (5th Viscount); Davidson, Chris; Davidson, Mrs.; Digby, Captain; **Hastings, Captain Arthur**; **Japp, Inspector James**; Mallaby, Mrs.; **Poirot, Hercule**

See also: *Agatha Christie's Poirot*; **Commedia dell'arte**; *Poirot's Early Cases*; *The Under Dog* (story collection)

"The Affair of the Forged Notes." See "The Crackler"

"The Affair of the Pink Pearl" (alternative titles: "Blunt's Brilliant Detectives"; "A Fairy in the Flat"; "Publicity"). See *Partners in Crime* (story collection)

Afflick, Dorothy, and Jackie

In *Sleeping Murder*, Jackie Afflick is

a suspected boyfriend of the deceased Helen Kennedy/Halliday. He now owns a tour coach business and is married to Dorothy.

After Dinner. See ***Black Coffee***

After the Funeral **(novel; alternative titles: *Funerals Are Fatal; Murder at the Gallop*)**

A typical 1950s Christie novel, *After the Funeral* concerns a sprawling family, a quarrel over inheritance in a changing world, the late arrival of Hercule Poirot into the action, and classic misdirection around key evidence. It also features one of Christie's more psychologically nuanced murderers.

At the funeral of Richard Abernethie, his flamboyant sister, Cora Lansquenet, is heard to say that he was murdered. Later, she herself is discovered dead. Called in by the solicitor Mr. Entwhistle, Hercule Poirot investigates the extended family—a collection of unpleasant theatrical types and grasping hypochondriacs—trying to work out who would have a motive to kill Richard and then silence Cora. Poirot uncovers several family secrets before finally fixing the blame on Cora's companion, Miss Gilchrist. Richard died naturally. Miss Gilchrist disguised herself as Cora and attended the funeral, where she uttered the words before returning home and killing the real Cora. The aim of the deception was to convince everyone that Richard was the *true* victim, so Cora's death would not be examined in any detail. The motive is to inherit a valuable painting so that Miss Gilchrist can sell it and launch a teashop. The clue is her memory of a wax flower bouquet at the house—something she could only have seen if she had been present at the funeral.

After the Funeral is fundamentally conservative. Attempts to adapt modernity to conservatism are rewarded, whereas attempts to adapt tradition to modernity are punished. When Miss Gilchrist, the "fluffy" eternal spinster, wants to open a teashop, she is punished by falling into the narrative role of murderer. She is declared insane and is due to spend the rest of her life in a mental hospital, where her plans, which can never be realized, become more elaborate,

following the progress of twentieth-century capitalism: she now has "elaborate plans to open a chain of tea-shops" but maintains her old-fashioned "gracious[ness]" (192)—and this idea of "a *lady-like* murderer" is presented as uncanny and "horrible" (189, emphasis in original). On the other hand, the ruthlessly ambitious actress Susan Banks is praised by Poirot for planning "to leave the stage and just be a mother"—Poirot says this is "[a] *rôle* that will suit you admirably" (190).

Nonetheless, the conservatism is self-aware. It is the most unpleasant character who criticizes the "mealy-mouthed socialist" government for the shortage of servants, forcing his wife "to work herself to a shadow" (52)—without ever considering doing some housework or getting a job. His equally unpleasant wife is the one who assumes, with wild and comic inaccuracy, that the murderer must be a "neurotic arty" "adolescent" (49). It is the unchecked conservative assumption that an "old maid" like Miss Gilchrist must be dreaming of a husband (98) that blinds people to the true reasons for her actions. When people do suspect her, fleetingly, of killing Cora, they always fix on "quarrels or resentments" or "animosity arising between women," generally over men (26, 88). Miss Gilchrist's breakdown and confession toward the end of the novel makes, for moments only, "the tea-shop that would never be … more real than the Victorian solidity of the drawing-room at Enderby" (189).

Christie's own family informs some of the family dynamic in this novel. Small quirks remembered by relatives become increasingly significant (one is a clue to the impersonation). The habit of Miss Gilchrist's aunt to refuse to eat anything but boiled eggs is one shared by Christie's grandmother, whereas the cook in Christie's childhood home refused to reveal her age on a census, as does the domestic helper Janet in this novel. When sketching the characters in her notebook, Christie based "Mr. Dent" (who became Richard Abernethie) on her brother-in-law, James Watts (Curran, *Making* 286). Another element of Christie's personal network is a passing reference to "Hubert … the producer" of theatrical flops (102)—likely referring to Christie's own producer, Hubert Gregg, about whom she thought more highly than he did of her.

The book was published first in the United States as *Funerals Are Fatal*. It was serialized in the *Chicago Tribune* from 20 January to 14 March 1953 and published by Dodd, Mead in March 1953. In the United Kingdom, it appeared as *After the Funeral*, serialized (abridged) in *John Bull* from 21 March to 2 May 1953 and published by Collins 16 days later. In many ways—not least the psychology of the motive and the domestic clue of wax flowers—the story feels more like a Miss Marple one than a Poirot one. It could easily have been made to accommodate Miss Marple's one-time-assistant Lucy Eylesbarrow, for example. Indeed, the first dramatization, MGM's *Murder at the Gallop* (1963) replaced Poirot with Marple, played by Margaret Rutherford. A BBC Radio 4 dramatization with John Moffat as Poirot was broadcast on 28 August 1999. An episode of *Agatha Christie's Poirot* based on the novel appeared on ITV 1 on 26 March 2006. This episode was also turned into an interactive DVD game.

Characters: **Abernethie, Helen**; Abernethie, historic family members (Cornelius, Coralie, Leo, Pamela); **Abernethie, Maude, and Timothy, Abernethie, Richard; Banks, Gregory and Susan**; Barton, Dr.; **Crossfield, George**; Dainton, Sorrel; **Entwhistle, Miss, and Mr.; George(s); Gilchrist, Miss; Goby, Mr.**; Guthrie, Alexander; Jacks, Mrs.; **Janet**; Jones, Mrs.; Lanscombe; **Lansquenet, Cora; Lansquenet, Pierre**; Larraby, Dr.; Lewis, Oscar; Marjorie; Morton, Inspector; Panter, Mrs.; Parrott, James; Parwell, Superintendent; **Poirot, Hercule**; Proctor, Dr.; Rosenheim, Mr.; **Shane, Michael, and Rosamund**

See also: *Agatha Christie's Poirot*; **Games**; *Hercule Poirot* (**BBC radio series**); **MGM Films; Nostalgia; Theatricality**

Afternoon at the Seaside. See *Rule of Three*

Agasa Kurisutī no Meitantei Powaro to Māpuru (**animated series; alternative title**: *Agatha Christie's Great Detectives Poirot and Marple*)

In the early 2000s, Agatha Christie Ltd. sought to rebrand in an effort to appeal to young audiences. Part of this involved an animated series in Japan (anime). The program ran for 39 episodes in 2004 and 2005, adapting several short stories and some novels that featured Hercule Poirot (voiced by Koutarou Satomi) or Miss Marple (voiced by Karou Yachigusa). The detectives do not meet in these episodes, but they know of one another, and they are united by the presence of a new character, Maybelle West (Mayasa Kato).

Maybelle is the 16-year-old daughter of Raymond West who spends her time between St. Mary Mead with her great-aunt, Jane Marple, and London, where she lives with Miss Lemon and is training to be Hercule Poirot's assistant. She is accompanied by another new character, a duck called Oliver. Poirot's companion, Captain Hastings, also features as a regular character. For obvious reasons, the Japanese series replaces Inspector Japp with a new character, Inspector Sharpe (although a character of this name does appear in *Hickory Dickory Dock*).

Although all action is relocated to a non-specific 1930s England, and Maybelle and Oliver are inserted into the action, the stories are generally faithful. However, occasionally translated idioms that become important to the plot are replaced. For example, in "Strange Jest," the clue of a dying man tapping his eye refers in English to an expression, "all my eye" (meaning "nonsense"); here, it refers to a stamp that features a winking figure.

The series was made for the NHK network, with music by Toshiyuki Watanabi, and opening and closing themes by Tatsuro Yamashita. The score is somewhat reminiscent of John Williams's Oscar-winning theme for *Schindler's List* (1990). Three of the novel adaptations—*The ABC Murders*, *4.50 from Paddington*, and *Death in the Clouds*—were also released as Manga books.

The following stories and novels were adapted (episode number[s] and broadcast date[s] in parentheses): "The Jewel Robbery at the Grand Metropolitan" (ep. 1, 4 July 2004), "The Adventure of the Cheap

Flat" (ep. 2, 18 July 2004), "Strange Jest" (ep. 3, 25 July 2004), "The Case of the Perfect Maid" (ep. 4, 1 August 2004), *The ABC Murders* (ep. 5–8, 8–25 August 2004), "The Kidnapped Prime Minister" (ep. 9–10, 5–12 September 2004), "The Adventure of the Egyptian Tomb" (ep. 11–12, 19–26 September 2004), "Tape-Measure Murder" (ep. 13, 3 October 2004), "Ingots of Gold" (ep. 14, 10 October 2004), "The Blue Geranium" (ep. 15, 17 October 2004), *Peril at End House* (ep. 16–18, 14–28 November 2004), "The Adventure of the Christmas Pudding" (ep. 19–20, 5–12 December 2004), *4.50 from Paddington* (ep. 21–24, 9–30 January 2005), "The Plymouth Express" (ep. 25–26, 6–13 February 2005), "Motive versus Opportunity" (ep. 27, 20 February 2005), "The Adventure of the Clapham Cook" (ep. 28–29, 27 February–6 March 2005), *Sleeping Murder* (ep. 30–33, 13 March–4 April 2005), "Four and Twenty Blackbirds" (34, 10 April 2005), "The Disappearance of Mr. Davenheim" (35, 17 April 2005), and *Death in the Clouds* (36–39, 24 April–15 May 2005).

See also **Marple, Jane**; *Meitantei Akafuji Takashi*; **Poirot, Hercule**

Agatha (film). See **Fictional Portrayals of Agatha Christie**

Agatha (musical). See **Fictional Portrayals of Agatha Christie**

Agatha (Tynan). See **Fictional Portrayals of Agatha Christie**

Agatha & Alfred (Campoy). See **Fictional Portrayals of Agatha Christie**

Agatha and the Truth of Murder. See **Fictional Portrayals of Agatha Christie**

Agatha Awards

Malice Domestic is an annual U.S. convention of fans and writers of traditional mysteries. Its annual awards ceremony, established in 1989, is known as the Agatha Awards. To be eligible for an Agatha Award, the work in question must be considered "cozy" (meaning it usually has an amateur detective, relative sexlessness, and bloodlessness—but this is more a general principle than a strict rule). The name comes from Christie, widely perceived as the supreme purveyor of cozy mysteries. There are six

categories: Best Novel, Best First Mystery, Best Historical Novel, Best Short Story, Best Nonfiction, and Best Children's/Young Adult Mystery.

Notable winners have included Rhys Bowen, John Curran, Carolyn Hart, Jacqueline Winspear, Jeff Abbott, Louise Penny, Elizabeth Peters, and Laura Lippman. Occasional special awards, the Lifetime Achievement Award and the Poirot Award, are presented, respectively, to mystery writers with distinguished careers and those outside of writing who have contributed to the traditional mystery. Lifetime Achievement Award recipients include Emma Lathen and Tony Hillerman, and recipients of the Poirot include Angela Lansbury and David Suchet.

See also: **Agatha Christie Award**

Agatha Christie: A Life in Pictures. See **Fictional Portrayals of Agatha Christie**

Agatha Christie Award

The Agatha Christie Award is a Japanese literary prize, established in 2010 and presented annually to authors of unpublished crime novels.

See also: **Agatha Awards**

The Agatha Christie Hour (television series; anthology)

This is the title of a television series and an accompanying anthology of short stories, both released in 1982. The series was produced by Thames Television, a production company of ITV, which had already broadcast several Christie adaptations produced by LWT. This 10-part series was based on lesser-known short stories in a range of genres. It was marketed as a showcase of Christie's "great range" (*ACH* blurb) and illustrates the extent to which Christie's name, beyond those of her creations, had become a recognizable media brand by the 1980s. It also forms a part of ITV's strategy to acquire the rights to either Poirot or Miss Marple for television. Ultimately, it would acquire the rights to Poirot toward the end of the decade and to Miss Marple in the twenty-first century.

The episodes were produced by Pat Sandys, who had worked on the LWT productions *The Seven Dials Mystery* and *Why*

Didn't They Ask Evans? With stagey 1920s sets and recognizable guest stars, it enjoyed modest success and has been even better received in export to the United States. The only detective featured is J. Parker Pyne (Maurice Denham), who has otherwise only appeared in radio adaptations. However, his companions Miss Lemon (Angela Easterling) and Ariadne Oliver (Lally Bowers), who would become famous in their own rights in Poirot stories, make their screen debuts in "The Case of the Middle-Aged Wife" and "The Case of the Discontented Soldier."

The tie-in book, published by Collins, features the first U.K. appearance in book form of "Magnolia Blossom," which was later collected in *Problem at Pollensa Bay*. Stories adapted include (broadcast date in brackets): "The Case of the Middle-Aged Wife" (7 September 1982); "In a Glass, Darkly" (14 September 1982); "The Girl in the Train" (21 September 1982); "The Fourth Man" (28 September 1982); "The Case of the Discontented Soldier" (5 October 1982); "Magnolia Blossom" (12 October 1982); "The Mystery of the Blue Jar" (19 October 1982); "The Red Signal" (2 November 1982); "Jane in Search of a Job" (9 November 1982); and "The Manhood of Edward Robinson" (16 November 1982).

See also: **LWT Adaptations; Parker Pyne, J.**

The Agatha Christie Indult

This is an informal name given to an indult signed by Pope Paul VI in 1971, granting Roman Catholic churches in Britain permission to conduct Mass in the traditional Latin. Christie was among high-profile signatories to a petition to the church to reconsider plans to replace the Tridentine Mass rite with a pared-down English version. Petitioners, which also included Iris Murdoch and Nancy Mitford, claimed that the old rite had inspired innumerable artistic and cultural achievements, and should not be dismissed. The name "Agatha Christie Indult" suggests that Christie's name is most closely aligned with the idea of keeping tradition and ceremony—although, unlike some other signatories, Christie was firmly and devotedly a member of the Church of England.

See also: **Christianity**

Agatha Christie Investigates (Joseph). See **Fictional Portrayals of Agatha Christie**

Agatha Christie Ltd.

This business was established by Christie in 1955 in an effort to control income tax. It is now the official presence of her literary estate, managing rights around her work and controlling her media brand. From Christie's death until 2004, it was chaired by Christie's daughter, Rosalind Hicks. Christie's grandson, Mathew Prichard, chaired from 2004 to 2014, and since then it has been chaired and managed by Christie's great-grandson James Prichard. Agatha Christie Ltd. (ACL) is known for its tight hold on copyright and its protectiveness of Christie's media image. The family ownership has been directly responsible for several invasive or exploitative media productions about the woman herself failing to take off.

There are numerous arms and offshoots of ACL, including the Agatha Christie Family Archive, where many unpublished materials are housed; Agatha Christie Productions, which produces media adaptations; and short-lived ventures such as the Agatha Christie Theatre Company, established with Bill Kenwright Productions Ltd, and the Agatha Christie Society, an official fan club from 1993 to 2004. Only 36 percent of ownership is now in the family: the remaining 64 percent is owned by RLJ Entertainment.

See also: **Hicks, Rosalind; Prichard, James; Prichard, Mathew**

"Agatha Christie on Mystery Fiction." See **"Agatha Christie's Algebra"**

"Agatha Christie Writes Animated Algebra." See **"Agatha Christie's Algebra"**

"Agatha Christie's Algebra" (alternative titles: **"The Algebra of Agatha Christie," "Agatha Christie on Mystery Fiction," "Agatha Christie Writes Animated Algebra"**)

It was rare for Christie to grant interviews. One that has been widely quoted was with Francis Wyndham for the *Sunday Times* in 1966 (reprinted in the *Washington Post*). In this, Wyndham famously refers to Christie's plotting as "animated algebra" (E5): the idea is that these books are foremost and substantially puzzles, with everything else mere ornamentation. In the interview, Christie promotes this view, describing herself as "a perfect sausage machine" churning out "a Christie for Christmas" (E5) without much consideration. Glossing the creative process considerably, she describes writing "over the unattractive winter months" (E5) to deliver the next book by March and enjoying the rest of the year without writing. She reflects on fan mail and presents herself as an unambitious, conservative housewife who happens to have stumbled into success. Her remarks are a mix of modesty (she calls *The Mousetrap* "a nice little play" E5) and traditionalism ("Men have much better brains than women, don't you think?" E5), whereas Wyndham completes the scene of vanished Edwardian demureness, describing a "housemaid" entering the room with "sponge cake and Earl Grey" (E5).

The interview is calculated to present an image of internationally marketable, unthreateningly conservative English homeliness. Unsurprisingly, via the Associated Press, it was widely reprinted around the world.

See also: "**Genteel Queen of Crime**"; "**'Queen of Crime' Is a Gentlewoman**"

Agatha Christie's Criminal Games. See *Les Petits Meurtres d'Agatha Christie*

Agatha Christie's Great Detectives Poirot and Marple. See *Agasa Kurisutī no Meitantei Powaro to Māpuru*

Agatha Christie's Little Murders. See *Les Petits Meurtres d'Agatha Christie*

Agatha Christie's Marple **(television series)**
In 2002, media company Chorion announced that it had acquired the broadcast rights for Christie's fiction, as well as that of Enid Blyton and several other authors. It was also announced that there would be a new series of Miss Marple mysteries broadcast on ITV. The promised program, *Agatha Christie's Marple*, ran from 2004 to 2013 and has divided viewers. The tone is deliberately different from that of *Agatha Christie's Poirot*, although both series are unrepentantly nostalgic.

Just as *Poirot* is set in the 1930s, the action of *Marple* is transposed to the 1950s. However, throughout the 2000s and 2010s, the two series shared creative teams, including writers, directors, and many cast members.

Marple deviates significantly from its source material. Most notably, not all the episodes are based on Marple novels (there are only 12 of these, and there are 23 two-hour episodes). One is based on a short story and 10 on non–Marple novels, with the detective inserted into the action. The screenplays, too, rarely resemble their sources, emphasizing comedy, nostalgia, and slapstick. The early episodes give Marple a backstory, involving a married lover killed in World War I, but this element was quickly abandoned. Geraldine McEwan played Miss Marple in the first three series, before the role was taken over by Julia McKenzie, who had previously taken over the role of Ariadne Oliver from Stephanie Cole in the BBC radio adaptations.

Although it never advertised itself as such, the series is a conscious rewriting of the BBC series, which ran from 1984 to 1992, so they have almost equivalent time-spans, 20 years apart. Both series began with striking adaptations of *The Body in the Library*, although the ITV version made a mission statement, by changing the solution to pin the crime on lesbian lovers. Homosexuality, played for shock value more than anything, recurs in this series. Publicity materials emphasize that there is no social commentary here—it is about dressing up, pretty frocks, and frolics. For instance, promoting *The Moving Finger*, guest star Una Stubbs highlighted "that pantomime instinct" ("*The Moving Finger*: Behind the Scenes" 308), and Amanda Holden, in *4.50 from Paddington*, famously employs an accent that started out as a joke. In these materials, Miss Marple was described as "quite flirtatious" ("*The Murder at the Vicarage*: Behind the Scenes" 392).

Conservative commentators were outraged, with the *Daily Telegraph* initially branding the series "Miss Calculation" and "No Modern Marple." However, after the first series, the program evolved to emphasize export appeal: nostalgic visions of English greenery in that period Margaret Thatcher called a "golden age of suburbia"

(Bernthal, *Queering* 215). Cast interviews to promote the second series tended not to use words like "flirtatious," relying instead on words like "cozy" and "British." When McKenzie replaced McEwan, she donned a costume that bore a striking resemblance to Joan Hickson's from the BBC series and did very little to give Miss Marple a personality. This appealed some of the more conservative fans. However, the liberties taken with the plots did not.

The series ran out of steam by 2013, and the last episode broadcast, *Endless Night*, attracted low audience numbers. Besides, by this point, Agatha Christie Ltd. was finalizing a deal with the BBC, so the days of the ITV series were already numbered. Now that almost two decades have passed since its premiere, fans' memories of the series seem to have softened, and it is sometimes held up as "proper Christie" by viewers unhappy with more recent dramatizations. It has a broad audience in the United States and around the world, and is still repeated almost daily on British television.

Episodes include adaptations of the following (original U.K. broadcast dates in parentheses). Season 1 included *The Body in the Library* (12 December 2004), *The Murder at the Vicarage* (19 December 2004), *4.50 from Paddington* (26 December 2004), and *A Murder Is Announced* (2 January 2005). Season 2 included *Sleeping Murder* (5 February 2006), *The Moving Finger* (12 February 2006), *By the Pricking of My Thumbs* (19 February 2006; the first episode based on a non–Miss Marple novel), and *The Sittaford Mystery* (30 April 2006).

The U.K. dates and broadcast orders are mentioned here, although seasons 3–5 were broadcast in a different sequence and aired in the United States before their U.K. broadcasts. Season 3 included *At Bertram's Hotel* (23 September 2007), *Ordeal by Innocence* (30 September 2007), *Towards Zero* (3 August 2008), and *Nemesis* (1 January 2009). Following a cast change in which Julia McKenzie assumed the role of Miss Marple, season 4 included *A Pocket Full of Rye* (6 September 2009), *Murder Is Easy* (13 June 2009), *They Do It with Mirrors* (1 January 2010), and *Why Didn't They Ask Evans?* (15 June 2011).

Season 5 was broadcast between the last two episodes of season 4, making any catalog inconsistent. This included *The Pale Horse* (30 August 2010), *The Secret of Chimneys* (27 December 2010), "The Blue Geranium" (19 December 2010; the first episode based on a short story), and *The Mirror Crack'd from Side to Side* (2 January 2011). The final season, like the final season of *Agatha Christie's Poirot*, aired in 2013. It included *A Caribbean Mystery* (16 June 2013) "Greenshaw's Folly" (23 June 2013), and *Endless Night* (19 December 2013).

See also **Agatha Christie Ltd.**; *Agatha Christie's Marple*; **Marple, Jane**; *Miss Marple* **(television series)**

Agatha Christie's Miss Marple. See *Miss Marple* **(television series)**

"Agatha Christie's Mystery Potatoes" (recipe)

Walter Holz's *A Kitchen Goes to War* was published in 1940, to help the war effort. It includes ration-conscious recipes from 150 famous people—some more famous than others—including Agatha Christie. Her contribution, sensationally titled "Mystery Potatoes," is a recipe that makes use of long-life ingredients such as potatoes (which, as readers of "The Red House" know, can last for years if correctly stored), tinned mackerel, and margarine. This recipe, and the fact that Christie contributed it, show that, by 1940, she was taking the issue of rationing and food shortage far more seriously than in 1931 when she was commissioned to write "What I Would Do if I Were Starving" for *Britannia and Eve*, and replied that she would cook.

See also: **War**; **"What I Would Do if I Were Starving"**

Agatha Christie's Poirot (television series)

The television series *Agatha Christie's Poirot* ran for 25 years (1989–2014). It has become more effective than any other series—more, perhaps, than the texts themselves—in shaping public perceptions of Agatha Christie. Following Christie's death, her estate was initially hostile to bringing Hercule Poirot to the small screen. Only reluctantly had the BBC been commissioned to make *Miss Marple* in the

1980s, and the results had been a runaway success. Early in that process, Christie's daughter Rosalind Hicks suggested a Poirot series to *Miss Marple* producer Guy Slater, but he was not interested. Meanwhile, LWT (part of British broadcaster ITV) had been trying to obtain the rights to Poirot for some time—this is how the company ended up making the Tommy and Tuppence series *Partners in Crime* (1982), which was "indifferently received" (Aldridge, *Screen* 243). LWT entered discussions with the Christie estate in the mid–1980s, and Brian Eastman was brought on board to produce a series.

Just as Christie modeled her early Poirot stories on the Sherlock Holmes formula, the producers of *Agatha Christie's Poirot* planned at the outset to re-create the homely dynamic of Granada's *Sherlock Holmes* series with Jeremy Brett. To this end, it was decided early on that Poirot and three companions—Captain Hastings, Inspector Japp, and Miss Lemon—would recur in most or all episodes. It is generally agreed that Rosalind Hicks chose David Suchet for the title role: some accounts say that she had seen him in *Thirteen at Dinner* (1985), where he played Japp to Peter Ustinov's Poirot, and others cite his leading role in the BBC's *Blott on the Landscape* (1985).

Suchet was cast in 1988, the year filming began and the year before the first broadcast. The program was then known as *Hercule Poirot's Casebook*, which became the title of a tie-in short story collection. At this stage, episodes were to be—as with *Sherlock Holmes*—one hour each (including commercials) and based on short stories. Soon, two-hour specials based on novels began to appear, and by 1995 these had taken over. The first episode filmed was the first one broadcast: "The Adventure of the Clapham Cook," one that shows Poirot's interest in human nature and domestic matters as his client is a woman of little social standing. For exteriors of Poirot's modernist flat block, Whitehaven Mansions, producers used Florin Court in London. A few shots of the private property "in character" were filmed in 1988 and used throughout the next decade or so. After the first hiatus in the 1990s, elements of Poirot's office interior—and his costume—were donated to the Torquay Museum, which has become an informal Christie museum. Christopher Gunning provided music for the series.

Inspector Japp is played by Philip Jackson as a friendly cockney idiot. Captain Hastings is played by Hugh Fraser as a Bertie Wooster–esque everyman. Fraser famously refused to wear a moustache or smoke, as the character in the books does, creating a more likable image for late-twentieth-century audiences. It is highly unlikely that a toothbrush moustache such as that of Hastings (and Adolf Hitler) would ever have been considered. Miss Lemon, a character much amplified for the screen, is played by Pauline Moran, who brings her own interests in spirituality and mysticism to the role. The Felicity Lemon of the series is a maternal secretary who can read tarot cards and has been known to conduct a séance. To capitalize on the sense of comfort and nostalgia desired by the producers, an early decision was made to set nearly every episode in 1936, although Christie wrote about Poirot from the 1910s to the 1970s. As Eastman observed, the move gave the series "a strong visual identity" with a nostalgic, modernist backdrop (qtd. in Haining, *Celebration* 54). It also taps into willful nostalgia for interwar Britain, where things appear to have been simpler (as well as more visually appealing), and the impending war, with its impending loss of innocence, was some years away.

Notwithstanding these changes, the tone of early episodes was so consistent—and so in line with a nostalgic view of Christie, crying out for international export, that the word "authentic" was widely used by critics, viewers, and those involved in the show. Suchet, in particular, has stressed from the outset that his is an "authentic" portrayal of Poirot, grounded in the words of Christie herself. Previous performances, he concluded, were inadequate: Poirot was "quite different" to the larger-than-life characters portrayed by Peter Ustinov, Albert Finney, and Ian Holm: "more elusive, more pedantic, and most of all more human than the person I'd seen on the screen" (Suchet and Wansell 19). Suchet has discussed his process extensively: this has included making extensive longhand notes on every Poirot novel and story, perfecting the accent by listening to Belgian radio, and—to capture Poirot's "mincing gait"—inserting a coin between his buttocks (Haining, *Celebration* 17). A much-quoted governing principle behind his portrayal was reportedly advise from Hicks: Poirot should be laughed *with*, not *at*.

In 1997, LWT conceded that it was not planning to make any more episodes of *Poirot*, and the final one—an adaptation of *Dumb Witness* (1937)—which had been held back, was broadcast that year. Although the series was a hit in the ratings, an international success, and critically praised, it was deemed too expensive to continue producing. ITV returned to Christie the same year with a modernized—and cheap—production of *The Pale Horse* (1961) and the Christie estate looked more broadly at "modern" Christies: this would culminate in the U.S. *Murder on the Orient Express* (2001) and the British *Sparkling Cyanide* (2004), both of which were poorly received.

Poirot returned at the turn of the century, with two new episodes broadcast in 2001, aping the formulae of the past. The first dramatization, *The Murder of Roger Ackroyd,* was an interesting choice. It could have worked well as a "reboot" episode, as the shock factor of the assistant being the murderer could have been played up, with Dr. Sheppard (Oliver Ford-Davis) presented as a potential replacement for Captain Hastings. However, Clive Exton's screenplay seeks to capitalize on the idea of the narrator-as-murderer by framing the episode with the killer's "journal," which Poirot reads in police storage. The presence of Inspector Japp also undermines any suggestion of a new direction. The episode was poorly received. Three more episodes followed, all running to formula and with modest success despite wide publicity. The series went on another hiatus.

It was relaunched and rebranded in 2004, in a deliberate move away from the cozy formulae of the past. The setting had now shifted to 1937—indicating an intent to confront the emergence of World War II, and indeed the final episode, *Curtain* (2014), is set at its outset in 1939. The series had now become darker and more intense. There is here a deliberate contrast to *Agatha Christie's Marple* (2004–13), ITV's other Christie series then emerging in a blaze of campery and 1950s kitsch. The old-hand screenwriters—Anthony Horowitz, Clive Exton, and Douglas Watkinson—were replaced by more modern names such as Mark Gatiss, Nick Dear, and Kevin Elyot, who also worked on *Marple*. Thematically, the series focused on "edgy" themes such as inserting homosexuality into several plots and—at the insistence of Suchet, now an executive producer—Poirot's religious faith, which had barely featured in the series thus far. Hastings, Lemon, and Japp would no longer feature to present Poirot as a lone, troubled man.

Another part of the second rebrand included a cinematic style of filming and a change in music. Gone is the upbeat Art Deco opening sequence, with its magazine origin vibes, to be replaced with moody opening sequences. The second "new" episode—*Death on the Nile* (2004)—opens with a sex scene amid a storm. These episodes also name their guest stars at the beginning, something the series had not done up to that point. Part of this is because now high-caliber stars such as Zoë Wanamaker and Emily Blunt were making guest appearances, whereas the older episodes had invested more of their budgets into sets and costumes. Nonetheless, the series had by this point garnered a reputation for "nurturing" actors who would later become household names, such as Christopher Ecclestone, Polly Walker, Russell Tovey, and Francis Barber. The series also nurtured a popular conservative mystery screenwriter-cum-novelist, Anthony Horowitz.

The final series is retrospective and exists more as a bookend to the program than a set of adaptations. Indeed, the plots of *The Big Four* and *The Labours of Hercules* (2013) bear no relationship to those of their source materials. Hastings, Japp, and Lemon are brought in to the former, which teases the forthcoming death of Poirot. The episode therefore becomes more about that "big four" than the group they are investigating. The series also becomes overtly political—albeit neoliberal and superficial—as it discusses the rise of fascism. The final episode, *Curtain*, was filmed second-last, because it was considered too dispiriting to wrap up production with Poirot's death. Instead, the penultimate episode, *Dead Man's Folly*, was filmed last—with great fanfare, in Christie's holiday home, Greenway, which was the inspiration for that book's setting.

The series has become an institution, earning several accolades, continuous replays around the world, and a knighthood for its star. It typifies the nostalgic, conservative view of Christie that has held sway for many years. The series has won four BAFTAs, with 11 more nominations and an Edgar Award, and been nominated for an Emmy. Ratings dipped over time: the first episode reached more than 11 million viewers, while the final series averaged a still respectable 5.36 million.

As the series progressed, Suchet became increasingly vocal about his desire to star in adaptations of every Poirot text. The series is almost exhaustive, although some short stories have not been adapted for it. In all but one case—that of "The Lemesurier Inheritance"—this is because they are either alternative versions of adapted stories (for example, "The Second Gong" became "Dead Man's Mirror" and "The Submarine Plans" became "The Incredible Theft"). The play *Black Coffee* has also not been adapted for the series, although Suchet starred in a staged reading in Cheltenham shortly after the *Poirot*'s initial run. Suchet has teased in the past about a willingness to film Sophie Hannah's continuation novels, although at the time of writing there are no plans for this. He has similarly expressed willingness to star as Poirot in a cinematic film and has critiqued his on-screen successors Kenneth Branagh and John Malkovich, as have his fans. Suchet, like many of his admirers, believes his performance is the definitive one, and the actor has appointed himself "The custodian of Dame Agatha's creation" (Suchet and Wansell 91).

A full list of episodes and original broadcast dates on ITV (or ITV1) follows. Season 1 (in 1989) included "The Adventure of the Clapham Cook" (8 January), "Murder in the Mews" (15 January), "The Adventure of Johnnie Waverly" (22 January), "Four and Twenty Blackbirds" (29 January), "The Third Floor Flat" (5 February), "Triangle at Rhodes" (12 February), "Problem at Sea" (19 February), "The Incredible Theft" (6 February), "The King of Clubs" (12 March), and "The Dream" (19 March).

Season 2 (in 1990) kicked off with a feature-length episode, *Peril at End House* (7 January), followed by "The Veiled Lady" (14 January), "The Lost Mine" (21 January), "The Cornish Mystery" (28 January), "The Disappearance of Mr. Davenheim" (4 February), "Double Sin" (11 February), "The Adventure of the Cheap Flat" (18 February), "The Kidnapped Prime Minister" (25 February), and "The Adventure of the Western Star" (4 March).

Following a feature-length special, *The Mysterious Affair at Styles* (16 September 1990), season 3 (in 1991) included: "How Does Your Garden Grow?" (6 January), "The Million Dollar Bond Robbery" (13 January), "The Plymouth Express" (20 January), "Wasps' Nest" (27 January), "The Tragedy at Marsdon Manor" (3 February), "The Double Clue" (10 February), "The Mystery of the Spanish Chest" (17 February), "The Theft of the Royal Ruby" (24 February), and "The Affair at the Victory Ball" (3 March).

Season 4 (in 1992) included three feature-length episodes: *The ABC Murders* (5 January), *Death in the Clouds* (12 January), and *One, Two, Buckle My Shoe* (19 January). Season 5 (in 1993) returned for the last time to 52-minute episodes (one hour with commercials): "The Adventure of the Egyptian Tomb" (17 January), "The Under Dog" (24 January), "Yellow Iris" (31 January), "The Case of the Missing Will" (7 February), "The Adventure of the Italian Nobleman" (14 February), "The Chocolate Box" (21 February), "Dead Man's Mirror" (28 February), and "The Jewel Robbery at the Grand Metropolitan" (7 March).

All subsequent episodes are feature-length and, with one exception, based on novels. Season 6 included *Hercule Poirot's Christmas* (1 January 1995), *Hickory Dickory Dock* (12 February 1995), *Murder on the Links* (2 February 1996), and *Dumb Witness*

(9 February 1996). After a hiatus, season 7 aired in 2000, with *The Murder of Roger Ackroyd* (2 January) and *Lord Edgware Dies* (19 February). Season 8 included *Evil Under the Sun* (20 April 2001) and *Murder in Mesopotamia* (2 June 2002).

A rebranding effort resulted in a new look for season 9, which included *Five Little Pigs* (14 December 2003), *Sad Cypress* (26 December 2003), *Death on the Nile* (12 April 2004), and *The Hollow* (26 April 2004). Season 10 (in 2006) included *The Mystery of the Blue Train* (1 January), *Cards on the Table* (19 March), *After the Funeral* (26 March), and *Taken at the Flood* (2 April). Season 11 featured *Mrs. McGinty's Dead* (14 September 2008), *Cat Among the Pigeons* (21 September 2008), *Third Girl* (28 September 2008), and *Appointment with Death* (25 December 2009).

There were two more seasons. Season 12 included *Three Act Tragedy* (3 January 2010), *Hallowe'en Party* (27 October 2010), *Murder on the Orient Express* (25 December 2010), and *The Clocks* (26 December 2011). The final season was broadcast in 2013: *Elephants Can Remember* (9 June), *The Big Four* (23 October), *Dead Man's Folly* (30 October), *The Labours of Hercules* (6 November; this was based on a story collection rather than a novel or story), and *Curtain* (13 November).

See also: **Agatha Christie Ltd.**; *Agatha Christie's Marple*; **Suchet, Sir David**; **Poirot, Hercule**

Agatha Christie's Sven Hjerson (television series)

The idea of a television series based on Sven Hjerson, a detective created by Agatha Christie's fictional alter ego Ariadne Oliver, was first proposed by producer Basi Akpabio in 2016. In 2017, TV4 and B-Reel Films pitched a proposal to Agatha Christie Ltd. The project was announced in 2021, to air on Swedish and German television in August that year. The aim was initially to tap into the then-heightened success of Scandinavian crime drama on the global stage. The idea was to create a program with global export potential, combining the two distinct audiences who flock to Scandinavian noir and anything bearing Christie's name.

The series is set in the modern day and is about Hjerson in name only. The character created by Mrs. Oliver does not appear in this program, but another Hjerson—a celebrity detective, accompanied by a young female television producer—is a new creation. The series was originally to be set in Sweden, until it was pointed out that Mrs. Oliver's detective is Finnish. The province of Åland—culturally Swedish but politically Finnish—was proposed as a dramatically rich alternative to Sweden. Filming commenced in Åland in December 2020.

Episodes as planned are either loosely based on novels or stories or are original narratives sometimes inspired by true crime. Hjerson is played by Johan Rheborg, and Klara Sandberg (his assistant) is played by Hanna Alström. The lead series writer is Patrik Gyllström.

See also: **Hjerson, Sven**

Ah Ling

In *The Big Four*, Ah Ling is Mr. Paynter's servant. Inspector Japp suspects that he is involved in Paynter's murder, mainly because he is Chinese, but Hercule Poirot supposes and proves his innocence.

Akhnaton (play; alternative title: *Akhnaton and Nefertiti*)

Written around the same time as *Death on the Nile*, *Akhnaton* is a three-act play set in ancient Egypt. It concerns the pharaoh Akhnaton and his mission to convert Egypt to monotheism. With three acts and an epilogue, the action spans 83 years around two millennia BCE. It calls for a minimum of 25 actors and several sets.

Christie prepared a script around 1937 and sent it on spec to the distinguished stage actor John Gielgud, hoping he might like to stage it. Viewing it as dauntingly lavish (and likely not very commercial), Gielgud politely declined. The play was largely forgotten until 1973 when Collins published it. The first production was staged in New York in 1979 under the title *Akhnaton and Nefertiti*.

There is general consensus from biographers and commentators that this rarely performed piece is emotionally powerful. Julius Green, the authority on most of Christie's theatrical work, has noted that

Adelaide Phillpotts, daughter of Christie's early mentor Eden Phillpotts, wrote her own *Akhnaton* play around the same time. Both *Akhnatons* share remarkable similarities, including some almost identical dialogue, which Green catalogs. He attributes this to both authors working from the same source material: Arthur Weigall's *The Life and Times of Akhnaton, Pharaoh of Egypt* (1910).

Characters: Ahnaton; Ay; Bek; Horemheb; Nefertiti; Nezzemut; Para; Ptahmose; Tutankhaton; Tyi, Queen

See also **Archaeology**; *Death Comes as the End*; **Phillpotts, Eden**

Akhnaton and Nefertiti. See *Akhnaton*

Akibombo, Mr.

The character of Mr. Akibombo is an example of well-meaning White ignorance. Christie wrote *Hickory Dickory Dock* in the mid–1950s, partly in response to editors' requests that she diversify her characters. Times were changing, and her books were acquiring a reputation for being middle-class and middlebrow as well as geared to middle-aged white readers. *Hickory Dickory Dock*, set in a youth hostel, features an international array of young people. One of these, who receives more airtime than other characters who are not English or American, is Mr. Akibombo, who is shown to be a kind and caring character. However, he also speaks in broken English with extraordinary naïveté and is often laughed at—by other students and the police. He tries to help the police, but his ideas of how to help are "not modern" or realistic (75). As an effort to address charges of racism, the creation of Mr. Akibombo cannot be viewed as an overwhelming success.

"The Algebra of Agatha Christie." See "Agatha Christie's Algebra"

Alfrege, Madame

The owner of a dress shop in *The Hollow*, Madame Alfrege is drawn along anti-Semitic lines as a "vitriolic little Jewess" and "a Whitechapel Jewess with dyed hair and a voice like a corncrake" (126, 127). She speaks with a lisp and is paranoid. This portrayal has been toned down in recent editions and as early as 1948 was the subject of a complaint from the Council Against Intolerance in America.

Alibi (film). See **Twickenham Studios Films**

Alibi (play; alternative title: *The Fatal Alibi*)

The first dramatization of an Agatha Christie novel, *Alibi* (known in the United States as *The Fatal Alibi*) was based on *The Murder of Roger Ackroyd* (1926) and staged at the Prince of Wales Theatre in London on 15 May 1928, running for 250 performances. A Broadway production ran in 1932. The play was adapted by Michael Morton in consultation with Christie, but she was not generally pleased with the result.

Christie "much disliked" Morton's original suggestion, "to take about twenty years off Poirot's age, call him Beau Poirot and have lots of girls in love with him" (*AA* 434), something she later satirized extensively in *Mrs. McGinty's Dead*, through Robin Upwood making similar suggestions for adapting Ariadne Oliver's Sven Hjerson for the stage. Christie turned to Gerald du Maurier for support, and in the end a compromise was reached. The character of gossipy spinster Caroline Shepherd was replaced with a young, pretty love interest, Caryl.

Charles Laughton played Poirot in both the West End and Broadway productions. Although Christie may not have liked *Alibi*, audiences did. The response was helped by tremendous publicity, with large photographic multi-page spreads in newspapers and magazines. It was quickly filmed: Poirot made his screen debut in the 1930 Twickenham Studios film *Alibi*. The BBC Home Service broadcast a radio version in 1944.

See also: **BBC Radio Adaptations**; *Mrs. McGinty's Dead*; *The Murder of Roger Ackroyd*

"Alibi" (story). See "The Unbreakable Alibi"

Alice

Alice is the name given to two devoted maids: that of Katherine Grey in *The Mystery of the Blue Train* and that of Tommy and Tuppence Beresford in *Partners in Crime*.

Allen, Barbara

Barbara Allen is a beautiful woman whose suicide following blackmail is disguised as murder in "Murder in the Mews." Her name evokes the Scottish ballad "The Death of Barbara Allen" about a beautiful woman whose guilt over an old romance leads to her death.

Allerton, Major

Major Allerton is a profligate womanizer, estranged from his Catholic wife, in *Curtain*. Manipulated by Stephen Norton, Captain Hastings tries to poison Allerton, convinced that he is corrupting Judith Hastings.

Allerton, Mrs., and Tim

Mrs. Allerton is a gossipy mother and Tim is her son in *Death on the Nile*. They are distantly related to Joanna Southwood, with whom Tim is involved in jewelry substitution and theft. Mrs. Allerton is pleased and relieved when Tim settles down with Rosalie Otterbourne.

The Alphabet Murders. See **MGM Films**

"The Ambassador's Boots" (alternate title: **"The Matter of the Ambassador's Boots"**). See *Partners in Crime* (story collection)

Amy

Amy is a Christian name often given to servants, retailers, or deceased aunts in the Christie canon. There are Amys without surnames, all of whom are maids, in *The Sittaford Mystery, Mrs. McGinty's Dead*, and *The Mirror Crack'd from Side to Side*.

And Then There Were None (board game). See **Games**

And Then There Were None (computer game). See **Games**

And Then There Were None (novel; alternative title: *Ten Little Indians, Ten Little N-----s)*

To summarize the enormous influence of *And Then There Were None* is an impossible task. The best-selling novel of the twentieth century and the bestselling mystery novel of all time, *And Then There Were None* was voted the "world's favourite Christie" in a 2015 poll conducted by Agatha Christie Ltd.

and has established a trope in popular culture. It tells the story of 10 strangers, lured to an island for a weekend by a host known as U.N. Owen ("unknown"), only to hear a voice on a gramophone record accuse each in turn of having committed murder. Accordingly, they are sentenced to death.

One by one, they die, and each death bears a resemblance to a line from a Victorian counting song, now known as "Ten Little Soldier Boys":

Ten Little Soldier Boys went out to dine; one choked his little self and then there were nine. (Anthony Marston chokes on an after-dinner cocktail.)

Nine Little Soldier Boys stayed up very late; one overslept himself and then there were eight. (Ethel Rogers overdoses on a sleeping draught.)

Eight Little Soldier Boys traveling in Devon; one said he'd stay there and then there were seven. (General MacArthur is battered to death while waiting for his dead wife to emerge from the sea.)

Seven Little Soldier Boys chopping up sticks; one chopped himself in halves and then there were six. (Thomas Rogers is axed to death while chopping wood)

Six Little Soldier Boys playing with a hive; a bumblebee stung one and then there were five. (Emily Brent is poisoned via a syringe.)

Five Little Soldier Boys going in for law; one got in chancery and then there were four. (Sir Lawrence Wargrave is shot, then dressed in a scarlet shower curtain and a white skein of wool.)

Four Little Soldier Boys going out to sea; a red herring swallowed one and then there were three. (Dr. Armstrong is drowned, and when his body is not discovered, he is suspected.)

Three Little Soldier Boys walking in the zoo; a big bear hugged one and then there were two. (William Blore is crushed by a bear-shaped statue.)

Two Little Soldier Boys sitting in the sun; one got frizzled up and then there was one. (During a heated argument on the beach, Philip Lombard is shot.)

One Little Soldier Boy left all alone; he went and hanged himself and then there were none. (Consumed with guilt and psychologically manipulated, Vera Claythorne hangs herself.)

The murderer is, they realize, one of them. There is no detective, and the killer is not caught; indeed, everyone on the island dies, and readers learn the truth via a letter in a bottle. U.N. Owen is, it transpires, Sir Lawrence Wargrave, a judge among the guests, and apparently the sixth victim. He was fueled by a sense of justice: the other members of the party had been responsible for at least one death, much gossiped about but unable to be avenged under the law. They died in order of culpability: so, the first to go is a playboy who simply lacked the empathy to realize he had done anything wrong in running over two children, whereas the last is a governess who, seeking financial gain, had deliberately allowed a child in her care to die.

According to Christie, she wrote the book as a challenge: "it was so difficult to do that the idea fascinated me. Ten people had to die without it becoming ridiculous" (*AA* 471). However, the novel represents more than a technical challenge. As Samantha Walton writes, "*And Then There Were None* exemplifies the possible use of the crime novel as a medium in which to negotiate concerns over legal justice" (19). Like *Murder on the Orient Express*, it exposes the limits of legal justice, but it goes further. Written and published on the eve of World War II, it challenges notions of modernity, civility, and British security.

The island setting is not a creepy gothic one but a home-away-from-home for British tourists: indeed, it is widely thought to be based on Burgh Island, off the coast of Devon. The house is not a decaying castle but a modern, clean mansion, and the brightness of the walls, the impossibility for an external enemy to be hiding, is configured as its most sinister aspect. This goes back to one of Christie's favorite Bible quotes, on which she reflects extensively in *Unfinished Portrait*: "For it was not an enemy that reproached me; then I could have borne it: neither was it he that hated me that did magnify himself against me; then I would have hid myself from him. But it was thou, a man mine equal, my guide, and mine acquaintance" (Psalm 55:22–23, KJV).

During the novel, an "us and them" narrative—the guests persist in believing U.N. Owen is an external agent—breaks down, just as any justification of war against a foreign power will eventually break down. A link to colonization is implicit: the book, like the rhyme that structures it, was originally called *Ten Little N-----s*.

This title has always been problematic, although some conservative scholars deny the fact, attributing controversies to political correctness in the twenty-first century. Indeed, the book's original serialization in the *Evening Post* (1939) and the first U.S. edition (1940), as well as the first feature film adaptation (1945), all used the title *And Then There Were None*, and in the 1950s the book, stage play, and some screen versions started calling it *Ten Little Indians*. The island has variously been called "N----r Island," "Indian Island," and "Soldier Island" in different editions of the text. There have been public protests about the original title, including when a West End revival of the play was mounted in 1960, forcing a change in nomenclature; as recently as 2020, publishers of the French edition faced sufficient online criticism to apologize and adapt.

Given the novel's fame, it is inevitable that various sources for the idea have been claimed. The most compelling possibility is a 1930 novel, *The Invisible Host*, by the married Gwen Bristol and Bruce Manning, which became a 1930 Broadway play by Owen Davis and a 1934 film by Roy William Neill, both titled *The Ninth Guest*. In this story, eight strangers are summoned to a penthouse where a disembodied voice announces that they have all wronged him and will die during their stay (the ninth guest is Death). One by one, they die, eventually realizing that the murderer is one of them. Critics tend to doubt that Christie was familiar with the Bristol and Manning work; as author Bill Pronzini states, "Authors of her stature do not look elsewhere for inspiration" (188).

The Christie novel is by far a bigger influence than any other crime text on popular culture. There have been more than 20 authorized screen adaptations and countless unlicensed ones, including two works of pornography (see **And Then There Were None, Screen Adaptations of**). In addition, the story has been the subject of parodies

Publicity still from *Ten Little Indians* with Elke Sommer as Vera Clyde and Oliver Reed as Hugh Lombard. Embassy Pictures, 1974.

and pastiches (see **Pastiche and Parody**). As an instant sensation, the book was popular worldwide and during World War II, prisoners of war interned at Buchenwald during the Holocaust staged a makeshift dramatization—a testament to the novel's topicality, entertainment value, and reach.

Christie herself dramatized the book for the stage in 1942, following two years of requests from third parties. It opened in 1943 and, notably, Christie changed the ending to a romantic one, where two innocent characters survive and fall in love: historically, film adaptations have used this ending. A new version by Kevin Elyot, staged in London in 2005, includes all 10 characters dying on stage, although the "original" ending has been included in some performances of Christie's script since 1944. The BBC has aired two radio dramatizations: one in 1947 and one in 2010. There have also been three official games based on the book: a Cluedo-style board game by Ideal in 1968, a Spanish version by Peká Editorial in 2014, and a computer game by the Adventure

Company in 2005; the last includes a playable new solution and includes that of the book as a bonus feature. In addition, a graphic novel was released in 2009.

Characters: **Armstrong, Dr. Edward; Blore, William;** Brady, Jennifer; Brent, **Emily; Claythorne, Vera**; Clees, Louisa; Combes; John and Lucy; Culmington, Lady Constance; Dyer, Johnnie; **Hamilton, Cyril Ogilvie, and Hugo;** Landor, James; Leggard, Spoof; Legge, Sir Thomas; **Lombard, Captain Philip; MacArthur, General John;** MacArthur, Leslie; Maine, Inspector; **Marston, Anthony (Tony);** Morris, Isaac; Narracott, Fred; **Owen, U.N.;** Richmond, Lieutenant Arthur; Robson, Elmer; **Rogers, Ethel, and Thomas; Seton, Edward;** Taylor, Beatrice; Turl, Gabrielle; **Wargrave, Sir Laurence**

See also: ***And Then There Were None* (1943 play);** ***And Then There Were None* (2005 play);** ***And Then There Were None,* Screen Adaptations of; BBC Radio Adaptations; Games; Nursery Rhymes; Pastiche and Parody**

And Then There Were None, Screen Adaptations of

And Then There Were None is one of the most dramatized novels of all time and certainly the most dramatized of Christie's. The island setting and the action-packed promise that all (or most) of the characters will die makes it irresistible to filmmakers. Although there is some confusion over whether the book or the play of the same name—or indeed other films—have inspired certain screen adaptations, for the purpose of this entry, they will all be treated as one. Moreover, this entry only considers "official" adaptations, which state their source material outright and hold the necessary copyrights. There are too many screen productions that use the key ideas of *And Then There Were None* to consider here. Even using only credited versions, the 1939 novel has been brought to the screen multiple times in every subsequent decade except the 1990s.

The first was a 1945 movie, directed by René Clair and boasting a cast of veteran players, including Barry Fitzgerald as Judge Quincannon (Wargrave), Walter Huston as Dr. Armstrong, June Duprez as Vera Claythorne, Judith Anderson as Emily Brent, and C. Aubrey Smith as General Mandrake (MacArthur in the book, McKenzie in the play). Dudley Nichols's screenplay is notably bloodless—most corpses "appear" off-screen—and makes minor adjustments to the characters to suit an international cast, something each subsequent cinema version would take to a new extent.

The BBC broadcast a live television adaptation of the play on 20 August 1949. There were some technical issues—not least, the camera rolled too long after a death scene and Arthur Wontner, as General McKenzie, strolled off screen after he was declared murdered. Hearing about this, Christie was relieved to have missed it, as she had been traveling (see Aldridge, *Screen* 47–48). In April 1955, Italian broadcaster RAI aired a theatrical production from the previous year, directed by Alessandro Brissoni and starring Paolo Carlini as Lombard and Niela de Micheli as Claythorne. The illustrious Augusto Mastratoni played Wargrave.

"Bylo 10 Murzynków," an episode of *Television Theatre*, was a live Polish broadcast of the stage play in translation. Directed by Józef Słotwiński, later dubbed "the Polish Hitchcock," it aired on TVP in 1956. The next year, on 16 February, a Brazilian version was broadcast, part of the anthology series *Teledrama*, which had already aired a version of *The Mousetrap*. Another Brazilian version would follow on 28 October 1963, this time as part of *Grande Teatro Tupi*.

A decade after the BBC's version, rival British station ITV aired its own take on the play as part of its long-running and sometimes cutting-edge series *Play of the Week*. The relevant episode starring Felix Aylmer as the judge aired on 13 January 1959. Just five days later, American audiences saw their own version on NBC, featuring Nina Foch as Vera Claythorne, Kenneth Haigh as Philip Lombard, and Barry Jones as Justice Wargrave. Prints of this production survive, making it the earliest extant television version of the novel or play.

In 1965, there were two cinematic adaptations: *Gumnaam*, a Bollywood musical (see **Indian-Language Adaptations**) and *Ten Little Indians* in the United Kingdom. The U.K. film was produced by radio producer Harry Alan Towers, who would go on to remake it twice. This, however, is a remake of the 1945 film: the screenplay, written by Towers under his pseudonym Peter Welbeck, is, in places, word-for-word Dudley Nichols's 1945 script. However, maintaining a contemporary setting, action has been moved for no apparent reason to the Swiss Alps. The cast featured some heavyweights, including Hugh O'Brian as Hugh Lombard (Philip Lombard in the book/play) and Shirley Eaton, two years from a young retirement, as Ann Clyde (Vera Claythorne in the play/book). Wilfrid Hyde-White and Stanley Holloway, who had appeared together in *My Fair Lady* the previous year, played the judge and the policeman respectively. The voice on the tape (an attempt to update the gramophone record of previous versions) was provided, uncredited, by Christopher Lee.

This film, poorly received at the time, has undergone something of a reevaluation in public consciousness, partly because

Towers' subsequent efforts were so unanimously panned. Modern critics tend to see it as the superior one of the three: for example, one cites several elements (a white cat, the judge's final line, and Blore spying on Lombard in the bathroom)—all, incidentally, taken from the René Clair version—as evidence of decent engagement with 1960s culture (Aldridge, *Screen* 114). In reality, it was a cheaply made film without pretensions to longevity. The director, George Pollock, had worked on the widely panned Miss Marple films of MGM. One unique feature, however, was the inclusion of a "Mystery Minute," similar to a feature imposed by Christie in her stage production *Rule of Three*. Shortly before the murderer's identity is revealed, the action halted for 60 seconds while each murder was recapped, so the audience could discuss who might have committed them.

On 5 July 1969, *Zehn Kleine Negerlein* was broadcast on German television—the second of four Christie plays broadcast with minimal adaptations for the screen, and the last in black and white. A French version of the play was broadcast on screen the next year. 1970 also saw the first Tamil version, *Nadu Iravil*, in India. In English, Harry Alan Towers made his second effort in 1974, seeking to capitalize on the publicity generated by *Murder on the Orient Express*, also released that year. This new version used the same screenplay as the 1965 version, with very minor adjustments, and featured a bizarrely-cast set of illustrious actors, including Elke Sommer, Oliver Reed, Richard Attenborough, and Herbert Lom. This one was set in an Iranian desert and is broadly considered one of the worst Christie films of all time. The *New York Times* reviewed it with the words, "Global Disaster in Iran" (qtd. in Tennenbaum 148).

A Russian adaptation, *Desyat Negrityat* (1987), is the only cinematic adaptation to use the novel's ending—that is, all the characters die. It is also significantly more visceral than other versions: the first death involves a character falling facedown into shards of glass. Towers' final version, released two years later, is the first cinematic adaptation that claims to be based on the play rather than the novel—although,

as with Towers's previous films, its primary source material seems to be the 1945 movie script. This time, it is set on an African safari and the cast—including Frank Stallone, Donald Pleasence, Warren Berlinger, and Moira Lister—is more international than ever. Herbert Lom—who played the doctor in the 1974 version—appears as the general.

One fact normally missed by viewers is that it is, in theory, the first English-language adaptation of *And Then There Were None* set in the 1930s. The fact is largely missed because the production team itself seems to forget on numerous occasions that the action is not taking place in the 1980s. With a confusing tone, somewhere between low-budget suspense and high camp, not helped by a tinny soundtrack based on Noel Coward's "Mad Dogs and Englishmen," the film was a commercial and critical failure. It was also the last official adaptation of *And Then There Were None* for 26 years, although numerous films used the premise to varying degrees. The interceding years also included a computer game, a graphic novel, a new stage version, and a radio adaptation.

There were two Indian adaptations in the 2010s, which became controversial because they were so similar: Thakkali Srinivasan's Tamil thriller *Aduthathu* (2011) and K.M. Chaitanya's Kannada thriller *Aatagara* (2015). Over Christmas 2015, the BBC broadcast its highly regarded three-part miniseries adaptation (see **BBC Television Adaptations since 2015**). There was a Japanese mini-series, *Soshite Daremo Inakunatta*, in 2017, which included a detective investigating the deaths on the island, rather undermining a central premise of the story. In 2020, *Ils Étaient Dix*, a contemporary version with a youthful slasher feel set on a Caribbean island, aired on French television. Directed by Pascal Laugier, this six-parter drooped on virtual platforms in its entirety on 16 July 2020. It evokes successful French series such as *Le Chalet* (2018, itself clearly inspired by *And Then There Were None*) and U.S. series such as *Lost* (2004–10).

See also: ***And Then There Were None*** **(1943 play)**; ***And Then There Were None*** **(novel)**; **Pastiche and Parody**

And Then There Were None (1943 play;
  alternative titles: *Ten Little Indians, Ten
  Little N-----s*)

Although she had already adapted *The
Secret of Chimneys* around 1930, *And Then
There Were None* was the first play by Christie based on one of her own novels to be
staged. It opened at St. James's Theatre in the
West End on 17 November 1943. The novel
was already wildly successful at this point,
and Christie's agents were bombarded with
requests for permission to dramatize it.
Christie insisted on doing the job herself.

The story is the same: 10 strangers are
called to a luxury house on an island where,
one by one, they are accused of causing
deaths in the past and, one by one, they
are killed, realizing too late that the murderer is one of them. The most notable
thing about *And Then There Were None* as
a script is that Christie changed the ending.
Although the solution—the whodunit and
whodunit—remains as in the book, not all
the characters die. Instead, two are revealed
to be innocent and escape with their lives.

The play ran for 260 performances before
St. James's Theatre was bombed—World
War II was in full swing—and it transferred
to the Cambridge Theatre, where it ran for
several months more. In 1944, a successful Broadway version was mounted, and
there have been countless revivals around
the world since. These have not always
gone seamlessly. A London revival in the
1960s inspired street protests because of
the title—and ill-timing amid a civil rights
movement—which led to its official change
in the United Kingdom.

The script is very much a product of its
time, and offensive language has been
updated over the years. The new ending
is also a product of its historical context.
Christie was advised or decided—depending on whom one believes—that theater
during the war needed to offer complete
escapism and that audience members would
need someone to root for, hence the romantic resolution (Vera Claythorne and Philip
Lombard, realizing they are innocent and
the sole survivors, decide to marry). "Thank
God women can't shoot straight," says
Lombard, revealing that, despite appearances, Vera has not killed him (*TMT* 78).

Inevitably, directors in peacetime have
sought out the more dramatic ending of the
novel, which also avoids making a chauvinist into a hero. An entirely new script by
Kevin Elyot was staged in 2005 to little success, and numerous amateur and repertory
companies worked with Christie's version,
editing the text slightly (which is technically forbidden by Samuel French). Things
changed in 2015, the year the BBC released
its enormously successful three-part adaptation of the book. That year, a touring production of *And Then There Were None* from
Bill Kenwright Ltd. used a new "official"
ending drawn exclusively from material in
the novel.

This ending, commissioned by Agatha
Christie Ltd., has the murderer confessing
and committing suicide prior to the final
death. His dialogue is drawn from the written confession in the novel—as such, it is
bizarrely stilted and complex compared to
what has come before. Nonetheless, it was
a success, and Samuel French promptly
incorporated it into licensable scripts as an
"alternative ending." *And Then There Were
None* is the most heavily dramatized of
Christie's narratives. In the twentieth century, screen versions, even if claiming to be
based on the novel, have used the play's ending, following public taste. This is reversed
in twenty-first-century adaptations.

Characters: **Armstrong, Dr. Edward**;
Blore, William; **Brent, Emily**; **Claythorne,
Vera**; **Lombard, Captain Philip**; **Mackenzie, General John**; **Marston, Anthony
(Tony)**; Narracott, Fred; **Rogers, Ethel, and
Thomas**; **Wargrave, Sir Lawrence**

See also: *And Then There Were None*
(novel); *And Then There Were None* (2005
play)

And Then There Were None (2005 play)

Playwright and screenwriter Kevin
Elyot had already made a stir scripting episodes of *Agatha Christie's Marple* and the
revamped *Agatha Christie's Poirot* when
he dramatized *And Then There Were None*
for the West End stage. Elyot was still better known for his gay-themed scripts (especially *My Night with Reg*) than for his
Christie work, and the idea behind his
involvement was to break away from the

image of cozy crime often connected to Christie.

Christie had written her own version of *And Then There Were None* for the stage, but Elyot's version was promoted largely on the grounds of keeping the novel's ending—that is to say, every character dies, whereas Christie's script has two surviving and falling in love. Later productions of Christie's script have used a licensed alternative ending and ends with a hanging. Elyot's script, however, goes further, incorporating gore. The script calls for projectile vomiting in the first death, a sex scene, and a detailed hanging that includes twitches and spasms, carefully choreographed. The play opened at the Gielgud Theatre in 2005, directed by Steven Pilmott, with a gaudily elaborate set design by Mark Thompson. It was poorly received and enjoyed only a short run, without a tour or U.S. production.

See also: *And Then There Were None* (1943 play); *And Then There Were None* (novel)

Andersen, Greta

A companion to Ellie Guteman in *Endless Night*, Greta Andersen is a sexy Swiss woman who is secretly collaborating with Mike Rogers to acquire Ellie's money. Mike describes her as "sex personified" and someone who "looked and smelled and tasted of sex" (209)—although Christie did not approve of a sex scene featuring the character in the 1971 film.

Anderson, Esther. See **Walters, Esther**

Angkatell, David, and Edward

In *The Hollow*, David is the young intellectual of the Angkatell family, and an Oxford education has given him left-wing tendencies. However, as the heir to the family estate, he is laughed at by other characters and the implied reader for hypocrisy. A cousin of the Angkatells, Edward is in love with Henrietta Savernake before conveniently realizing that he is *really* in love with his cousin, Midge Hardcastle.

Angkatell, Lady Lucy, and Sir Henry

An extraordinarily vague woman in *The Hollow*, Lady Lucy Angkatell is a matriarch who lives in her own fairylike world and who resumes conversations she has been having in her head out loud, mid-sentence. "Lucy is inhuman," thinks one character—but in fact it was "because Lucy was too human that it shocked one so" (102). Sir Henry is her respectable, henpecked husband who generally stays out of the way.

Anna the Adventuress. See ***The Man in the Brown Suit***

Anne the Adventurous. See ***The Man in the Brown Suit***

Annie

There are Annies without surnames in four novels and one short story; all are servants, as are Annies with surnames elsewhere in the canon. In "The Adventure of the Clapham Cook," Annie is a house-parlormaid, described as "[a] bit forgetful and her head full of young men, but a good servant if you keep her up to her work" (*PEC* 27). This is the model for parlormaids in early Christie. Similar Annies appear in *The Mysterious Affair at Styles, The Secret Adversary, The Murder of Roger Ackroyd* (all house-parlormaids), and *Dumb Witness* (cook). Other Annies in service include Annie Poultny ("The Four Suspects") and Annie Hicks/Bates ("Christmas Adventure"/"The Adventure of the Christmas Pudding"—the surname was presumably changed in expansion because the surname of Christie's daughter was now Hicks).

Anti-Semitism

One of the most contentious topics in Christie scholarship is anti-Semitism. Although academic studies of Christie's work have largely but not entirely ignored the issue, biographers and readers have confronted it more robustly. There are multiple debates around whether or not Christie can be considered anti-Semitic and whether her work espouses, reflects, or comments upon prejudice against Jewish people and communities. In addition, debate rages as to whether Christie's approach to anti-Semitism evolved over the course of her career or merely boiled beneath the surface.

Christie sets the scene for her 1928 novel *The Mystery of the Blue Train* with a paranoid description of a rat-faced "son of a

Polish Jew" who has access to secrets of which even the government is ignorant and who is intent on using them to enhance his personal fortune: "In an Empire where rats ruled," Christie writes in the first paragraph, "he was the king of the rats" (*MBT* 1). The description taps into a widespread British and especially English hostility toward Jewish people on the grounds of their perceived otherness, and in the context of broader European hostilities and conspiracy theories. The pogroms in Imperial Russia, from 1881, saw tens of thousands of Jews immigrate the Great Britain and the United States: by 1919, there were estimated to be 250,000 Jews in Great Britain, up from 46,000 before the pogroms (Board of Deputies of British Jews), and one result was a widespread campaign of anti-Semitism in Britain, from both the left and right wings of politics. Conspiracy theories about Jewish capitalism undermining the British economy were widespread, alongside the characterization of Jews as "dirty, diseased, verminous and criminal" and, above all "foreign," undermining some essential form of Englishness by their very existence ("Editorial"), reinforced in many ways by legislation against immigration—most notably the Aliens Act of 1905.

It is true that Christie drew on stereotypes in writing, and a common defense of Christie's portrayal of Jews is the idea that she is mocking English insularity, as with her stereotype-embracing portrayal of Hercule Poirot. For example, the biographer Charles Osborne has indicated that references to a fictional financier—Herbert Isaacstein in *The Secret of Chimneys* (1925)—as "Mr. Ikey Isaacsteion," "Noseystein," and "Fat Ikey" are supposed to reflect poorly on the English speakers (43). On the other hand, this character, who is "one of the strong, silent yellow men of finance" (*SOC* 225) and "the real power in the room" by virtue of his cobra-like face (131), is characterized outside dialogue as solely focused on oil and profit and, as Bill Peschel has pointed out, even the character's name reflects an anti-Semitic attempt to connote ultra-Jewishness, evoking the racist 1915 music hall hit "Sergeant Solomon Isaacstein" (Peschel 303). There is

something more pernicious than usual in the negative stereotypes associated with Jews in Christie's work, particularly the stereotype of Jews as shrewd, cunning, and money-grabbing. Key plot points in *Peril at End House* and *Lord Edgware Dies* depend entirely on the "fact" that a Jewish person could not be expected to pass over the chance to make a large amount of money, purely because they are Jewish.

The defense that Christie was a product of her time is self-evident—and anti-Semitism was rife in polite English society in the interwar years. Some commentators have claimed that Christie's anti-Semitism is significantly more nuanced than that of many of her peers, including John Buchan and Dorothy L. Sayers; the former claimed in 1930 that "the Jews" had made "Palestine by far the cheapest of our Imperial commitments" (Buchan 12), and the latter's detective novels in the 1920s contain frequent grotesque stereotypes. Christie was not above stereotyping, inevitably, but her pre–World War II Jewish characters, although crudely drawn, were allowed the dignity of emotional nuance: Carlotta Adams in *Lord Edgware Dies* is the most sympathetically-drawn of her victims, whereas Oliver Manders in *Three Act Tragedy* ends up as the romantic hero.

On the other hand, plenty of writers were significantly more alert to the evils of anti-Semitism, and reflected this in their work. Raymond Postgate's *Verdict of Twelve*, written in the run-up to World War II, explores the psychological impacts of Nazism and anti-Semitism specifically. As is clear from Christie's pseudonymous novel *Giant's Bread*, published in 1930, she was not oblivious to the damages and hypocrisies wrought by anti-Semitism and made some effort to think about them. *Giant's Bread* is the text most commonly cited as evidence that Christie was not anti-Semitic; that she felt able, writing under a secret identity, to reveal "depths of sensitivity and compassion" that would not sell in crime fiction (Peschel 306). A central character, Sebastian Levinne, struggles to be accepted by English society despite his best efforts to prove himself "a very Christian brand of Jew" (*GB* 71). He is frequently subjected to abuse ("A dirty foreign Jew. That's all he is!" [5]), which the implied author critiques as "prejudiced" (6), and such perspectives are directly satirized:

> [Neighbors said of the Levinnes:] "Oh, of course—*Jews*! But perhaps it is absurd of one to be prejudiced. Some very good people have been Jews."
>
> It was rumored that the vicar had said: "Including Jesus Christ," in answer. But nobody really believed that. The Vicar ... had odd ideas [but could not] have said anything really sacrilegious [81; emphasis in original].

Nonetheless, the character remains yellow-faced, beady-eyed, lisping, and cunning. Levinne is introduced as a child who delights his friends with exotic stories of "the persecution of the Jews—of Pogroms! ... he had lived for years amongst other Russian Jews and his own father had narrowly escaped with his life.... It was all entrancing" (79). The exclamation point like the word *entrancing* is grotesque in the context of twentieth-century anti-Semitism and how it would escalate, although it is clearly intended to reflect a child's blunt and unemotional interest in learning about new things. This all means that the decision to draw on and actively endorse these stereotypes was deliberate—even if the intention was to speak to readers in a language they understood rather than to sew or cement a dangerous ideology. As noir novelist Dorothy B. Hughes put it, Christie may have considered her own handling of the issue to be "one of forthright liberalism" in its context, but in every objective sense, the novel espouses "familiar English antisemitism" and the Jewish hero is "a beloved friend, a man of fine character, brilliant in all respects, but always, the Jew" (127).

There is also evidence of anti-Semitism persisting in Christie's work even when the issue had become significantly more prominent and critically engaged with in popular culture. In 1948, American representatives of the Council Against Intolerance wrote to Christie and her publishers to object to anti-Semitic language in *The Hollow* (specifically, a wholly unnecessary characterization of a Jewish costumier). Christie decided the best course of action was to ignore these complains, although publishers seem to have gone behind her back in cleaning up some of the references. She seems then to have doubled down, as her next-finished novel was *A Murder Is Announced* in which the comic relief is supplied by Mitzi, a Holocaust survivor who is a compulsive liar. There have been attempts to claim that Mitzi is sympathetically drawn, because she "proves to be genuinely courageous in the final chapter" (York 69)—that is, when Miss Marple uses her as bait in a trap to catch the killer, risking her life. The character's backstory, her narrative role, and this final indignity—being drowned—are inherently problematic. Although there are some Jewish characters in later books (*Mrs. McGinty's Dead* [1952], *After the Funeral* [1953], and *At Bertram's Hotel* [1965]), these are minor players only, and Christie does not engage in or with anti-Semitism in fiction after *A Murder Is Announced*. Whether this speaks to changes in public attitudes or personal convictions is a matter of some debate.

Most of Christie's biographers have defended Christie against accusations of anti-Semitism, with variations on the argument that she was a product of her time and more liberal than most. Usual practice in this case is to refer to Christie's autobiography, in which she describes her horror at having met a Nazi; Janet Morgan argues that Christie's "horizons were limited and her perspective was that of an ordinary, upper-class Edwardian Englishwoman" (265). Laura Thompson concludes that "Agatha might have made cross remarks about Jews ... but it would never have occurred to her that conclusions about her own character might be drawn from this" (145). Gillian Gill, not an officially authorized biographer, recognizes "jingoistic, knee-jerk anti–Semitism" in the books and proscribes to their author prejudice of the "stupidly unthinking" rather than "deliberately vicious" variety (89).

Biographers—whether authorized by an estate or writing out of love for their subject—are almost bound to find a sympathetic explanation for a contentious issue. Christie scholarship has also been unusually infused with personal investment, with early examples taking a confessional tone and several subsequent analyses carrying some degree of unchecked reverence for the author. This means that a wish to explain away troubling aspects of the texts can be present, as can a raw and intense hurt at the presence of these aspects, unconsciously amplifying them. In the end, the most nuanced analysis of Jews in Christie's work is one of the earliest. In 1987, Jane Arnold concluded that "we come full circle. Christie's characters are stereotypes, and her Jews are stereotypes" (279–80); in this, they betray the attitudes of "the typical English antisemite: not violent, not active, simply smugly secure in the knowledge that anyone who isn't English isn't really quite human" (280).

See also: *Giant's Bread*; *A Murder Is Announced* (novel); War

Antoine, Monsieur

Monsieur Antoine is the assumed name of Andrew Leech in *Death in the Clouds* (1935), who employs the protagonist Jane Grey. He reappears in *The Moving Finger* (1943) as Joanna Burton's hairdresser. The character may have inspired the erratic costumier Anton in James Anderson's 1975 Christie tribute, *The Affair of the Blood-stained Egg Cosy*.

Appleby, Colonel

There are two Colonel Applebys in the Christie canon. The first is an American secretary to billionaire Abe Ryland in *The Big Four*. The second is a tiresome old villager who tries to help the police in *The Moving Finger*.

"The Apples of Hesperides" (alternative title: "The Poison Cup"). See *The Labours of Hercules*

Appointment with Death (film). See Cannon Group Film

Appointment with Death (novel; alternative title: *Date with Death*)

The first of two Poirot novels published in 1938, *Appointment with Death* reflects Christie's experiences in Western Asia, with action taking place in Jerusalem and Petra. In a striking opening, Hercule Poirot overhears a young man state that his stepmother has "got to be killed" (*AWD* 3).

Later, in Petra, Poirot and Sarah King, a new doctor who is trying to find her place in the world, observe and sometimes confront the monstrous stepmother, Mrs. Boynton, who is psychologically abusing her extended family on holiday. Soon after, Mrs. Boynton is discovered dead—sitting in the sun like a Buddha, she has been poisoned with digitoxin.

As family secrets and confused emotions are revealed, Poirot identifies the murderer as a fellow traveler, apparently unconnected with the family. Lady Westholme, a Member of Parliament, has a secret in her past about which Mrs. Boynton, a former prison warden, would have known. She killed to preserve her political reputation.

A key theme of this novel is psychological abuse. Merja Makinen writes that this is significant in the context of a World War looming in 1938: "Mrs. Boynton epitomises the monstrous tyrant, the Hitler or Mussolini figure in a personal and familial form, to allow the novel to interrogate on a private scale why the ordinary person may not be able to resist tyranny" ("Contradicting" 87). The victim in Christie's other 1938 novel, *Hercule Poirot's Christmas*, is also a tyrant: this time a patriarch, Simeon Lee. However, Boynton's abuse is even more insidious than Lee's because it is entirely psychological. She takes pleasure in making those around her—meaning, in the insulated world of British tourism, her family—suffer. Most important, for proprietary reasons, they cannot say anything, and there is nothing they can directly challenge. The evil in *Appointment with Death* is on a scale with the evil punished in *And Then There Were None*: killings for which the culprits could not be legally held accountable.

Another theme often cited in relation to *Appointment with Death* is feminism. After all, it features not just a powerful woman as its victim but also a female Member of Parliament and a female doctor—both relatively rare in 1938. In particular, King is notable as a young professional woman with a university education: not a type of person featured by Christie previously. Moreover, she has decidedly feminist views. At one point, she exclaims to a fellow-traveler: "I do hate this differentiation between the sexes…. It's not a bit true! Some girls are business-like and some aren't. Some men are sentimental and muddle-headed, others are clear-headed and logical. There are just different types of brains. Sex only matters where sex is directly concerned" (*AWD* 84–85). The view is shown to be modern and striking—and crucially a pole apart from celebrating the journalists and assistants who had appeared in previous Christie books—in the reaction of the elderly woman to whom King is speaking: "Miss Pierce flushed a little at the word sex and adroitly changed the subject" (85).

However, although this is an extremely early presentation of a female doctor, by the genre's standards as well as the author's, the text never refers to this character as "Dr. King." She is always "Miss King," whereas her male colleague is "Dr. Gerrard." Moreover, the final chapter shows her, five years later, happily married to one of the Boynton sons and reveling in her husband's professional success while clutching him for support during a particularly emotional part of a stage show. The murderer, Lady Westholme, is mocked outright by the characters and the implied author for her insistence on the importance of being a woman in politics.

Moreover, the sentiment about sex differences being "not a bit true" was not even new in the Christieverse. Christie's unpublished first novel, *Snow upon the Desert*, contains the same words, uttered by a powerless woman with more feminist overtones: "It seems to be an accepted idea that every woman will strive to live up to a man's ideal of her—that she will be grateful for his idealisation of her," says the heroine, Rosamund Vaughan. "It's not a bit true! One has, if anything, a contempt for people who can't see you as you are…. One gets sick, tired, *bored* of being admired for impossible, imaginary qualities!" (qtd. in L. Thompson 86; emphasis in original). If anything, King's sentiments are more muted than Rosamund Vaughan's. *Appointment with Death*, then, is forward-thinking in its presentation of women but is not a feminist text.

The novel was first serialized in the United States in *Colliers Weekly* (28 August to 23 November 1937), and later in the United Kingdom in the *Daily Mail* (19 January to 19 February 1938), where it was preceded by the much quoted essay, "Hercule Poirot—Fiction's Greatest Detective." It was published by Collins in the United Kingdom and Dodd, Mead in the United States later that year.

Christie adapted the novel into a play, removing Hercule Poirot, in 1945. In 1988, Peter Ustinov played Poirot on the silver screen for the last time in a movie adaptation released by the Canon Group. A BBC Radio 4 dramatization, starring John Moffatt, aired on 25 August 2001. There are three television adaptations. A British version, part of *Agatha Christie's Poirot*, was broadcast on ITV 1 on Christmas Day 2009, and represents the series failing to keep up with changing times. Adapting the psychologically intense plot, something that audiences of the 2010s would have appreciated, into the series' formulaic parameters, and changing the emotional abuse into physical violence, played poorly with general viewers and Christie fans alike. A French version, part of *Les Petits Meurters d'Agatha Christie*, aired on France 2 on 20 September 2019. A Japanese version, the third Poirot (renamed Suguro Takeru) adaptation for Fuji TV, premiered on 6 March 2021.

Characters: **Abdul**; **Boynton, Carol**; **Boynton**; **Elmer**; **Boynton**; **Genevra (Jinny)**; **Boynton, Lennox, and Nadine**; **Boynton, Mrs.**; **Boynton, Raymond (Ray)**; **Carbury, Colonel**; **Cope, Jefferson**; Gérard, Dr. Théodore; Hunt, Lady Ellen; **King, Dr. Sarah**; Mahmoud; Pierce, Miss; **Poirot, Hercule**; **Race, Colonel Johnny**; Steinbaum, Sir Gabriel; Stone, Sir Manders; **Tatiana, Grand Duchess**; **Westholme, Lady**; Westholme, Lord

See also: *Agatha Christie's Poirot*; *Appointment with Death* (play); Cannon Group Films; Feminism; Fuji TV Adaptations; *Hercule Poirot* (BBC radio series); *Les Petits Meurtres d'Agatha Christie*

Appointment with Death (play)

Christie's own adaptation of her 1938 Hercule Poirot novel *Appointment with Death* was a modest success when it opened on 31 March 1945, but it has been generally neglected by critics, scholars, and performers since then. Now, it is perhaps best remembered because of a letter sent by the author to a minor cast member.

As with *Murder on the Nile*, Christie cut out Poirot, replacing him in proceedings with Colonel Carbery; in the novel, Colonel Carbury assists Poirot but in the background. The plot—Brits gather in Petra, and a dragonlike matriarch dies of digitoxin poisoning—and key theme—psychological abuse—are the same in both versions of the story. However, Christie changed the ending for the stage. In the novel, Lady Westholme, an ambitious Member of Parliament, murdered the revolting Mrs. Boynton to prevent the revelation of her past. In the play, Mrs. Boynton killed herself after learning that she had a terminal illness and made it look like murder. This is explained as part of her sadism: "She specialised in mental cruelty" (*TMT* 166).

The change marks a subtle shift in tonal focus and changing times. By 1945, social mores had changed—partly helped by the increased role of women in public life during World War II—so the thread of women becoming monstrous because they are career-oriented running through the 1938 novel is abandoned. Instead, Mrs. Boynton is a supremely grotesque sadist, and the focus is on her manipulation of those around her. In the context of war, which was still ongoing when the play opened, the idea of a person's accountability persisting beyond death would have been timely.

Lady Westholme morphs in the adaptation from a single-minded professional woman into a conservative comedy figure; these older, class-conscious snobbish women are a constant presence in Christie's stage plays, from Emily Brent in *And Then There Were None* (1943) to Mrs. Bole in *The Mousetrap* (1952). To comic effect, she has a rivalry with a working-class, left-wing man, Alderman Higgs (he pronounces it "'Alderman 'Iggs"), who closes the plot with an announcement that he will run against her for Parliament.

Despite these adjustments, the play was neither escapist enough to engage wartime audiences nor contemporary enough to stimulate them, and it closed after 44 performances. The cast, however, had been strong, and Christie had particular praise for character actor Joan Hickson, who played the twittery Miss Pryce. Hickson had already appeared in a film adaptation of *Love from a Stranger* in a minor role and would go onto appear in several Christie bit-parts. Christie wrote to Hickson, inviting her to lunch, and stating: "I will call you to play my 'Miss Marple' one day, if I can find the time to write another play" (qtd. in Underwood, "Gentle" 45), although this has been widely misquoted as "I hope one day you will play my dear Miss Marple." Christie never did write a Miss Marple play, but several years after her death, Hickson would take the role in a much-feted BBC television series.

Characters: **Boynton, Ginevra**; **Boynton, Lennox, and Nadine**; **Boynton, Mrs.**; **Boynton, Raymond**; **Carbery, Colonel**; **Cope, Jefferson**; **Gerard, Dr.**; Higgs, Alderman; **King, Dr. Sarah**; **Pryce, Miss**; **Westholme, Lady**

See also: *Appointment with Death* (novel)

The Arabian Nights of Parker Pyne. See *Parker Pyne Investigates*

Araby, Mr.

In "The Scoop," Mr. Araby is a tobacconist, "calm, incurious, and unaffected by any emotion" (*SBS* 49). He is from Asia and possesses the "dignified" "silence of the East" (48).

Arbuthnot, Colonel

In *Murder on the Orient Express*, Colonel Arbuthnot is a British military officer involved with Mary Debenham and a "pukka sahib" with a strong sense of honor. He is instrumental in the plot in which 12 individuals connected to a past crime stab the child-killer Cassetti as a form of alternative retribution: "trial by jury," he opines, "is a sound system" (129). He is also racist, with a "natural distaste for being questioned by 'foreigners'" (130).

"The Arcadian Deer" (alternative title: **"Vanishing Lady"**). See *The Labours of Hercules*

Archaeology

Christie's second husband, Max Mallowan (1904–78), was a noted archaeologist, and Christie often accompanied him on digs. The experiences famously informed backdrops for some of her novels, most obviously *Murder in Mesopotamia*, which is set on a dig in Iraq and features characters based on her fellow travelers. However, a casual interest in archaeology preceded Christie's second marriage. "The Adventure of the Egyptian Tomb" (1923) shows that archaeological excavations were part of popular culture, and it has an undetailed description of life in tents, but no real details, because of course the author had no experience. She had traveled widely since girlhood, however, and in 1928–29 attended a dig at the ancient Mesopotamian site of Ur. There, she befriended archaeologist Leonard Woolley and his wife, Katherine, who invited her back. On her second trip, she met Mallowan. They married in 1930 and Christie joined him on digs in Syria and Iraq most years. The early digs at Ur directly inspired *Murder in Mesopotamia*.

On Mallowan's digs, Christie took on a gendered role. Mallowan describes his wife as a "helpmate, an ever-smiling hostess, a brave and happy companion [and] photographer[, who] helped with the cleaning and registration of the small finds" (245). In fact, Christie supervised many of the activities of local workers, and the cleaning was a significant procedure. In her autobiography, she makes herself sound like an amateur, although the attention to detail evidences a scientific, resourceful approach:

> I had my own favourite tools, just as any professional would: an orange stick, possibly a very fine knitting needle—one season a dentist's tool, which he lent, or rather gave me—and a jar of cosmetic face-cream, which I found more useful than anything else for gently coaxing the dirt out of the crevices without harming the friable ivory [*AA* 457].

Like Amy Leatheran, the self-effacing narrator of *Murder in Mesopotamia*, Christie presents herself as an amateur, out of her depth among male intellectuals, but also shows herself quietly getting the job done. (However, this revelation did cause issues in 2021, when researchers tried to ascertain what pigments went into ancient

paints on the artefacts, and were left with knowledge of contamination but not of the brand of face cream used, and therefore its ingredients.) Her archaeological memoir, *Come, Tell Me How You Live*, frames itself as a travel memoir. It opens with a description of picking out outfits and sitting on a suitcase to make the luggage fit, and closes with a picture of marital bliss and offhand remarks about the book being an "inconsequent chronicle" (205). Nonetheless, the main content is very much about dig life. Christie did, however, have a tourist's approach to the excavations: in 1952, when King George VI died, she wrote home her frustration that she would have to wear black and had packed mainly colorful outfits. Although archaeologists do feature prominently in her fiction, the bulk of the "exotic" novels, like *Death on the Nile* and *Appointment with Death*, are about tourists, and some of the most colorful portraits of British insularity in her fiction and memoirs are of travel companions in the Western Asia. This provides gentle satire in *Destination Unknown*, for example, but the Mary Westmacott novel *Absent in the Spring* is entirely about the internal journey of a British tourist stranded in Baghdad, forced by the distance from her ordinary world to evaluate her life choices.

There is general consensus, especially among older scholars, that exotic settings merely form the backdrop to puzzles or dramas of human interest. There is certainly an element of archaeology occurring in the background in some novels: archaeologists who obsess over small details, ignoring real drama before their eyes in *Death in the Clouds*, for example, purely add comic relief and perhaps enable the author to vent frustrations about her husband who, like a husband described in the book, missed her hospital visit because he was wrapped up in his work. In *Death on the Nile*, the description of a little-known dig site serves as a plot point, to indicate a secret assignation. That novel also includes an example of a point made regularly in texts from "The Adventure of the Egyptian Tomb" onward. Poirot states:

> In the course of an excavation, when something comes out of the ground, everything

is cleared away very carefully all around it. You take away the loose earth, and you scrape here and there with a knife until finally the object is there, all alone, ready to be drawn and photographed with no extraneous matter confusing it. That is what I have been seeking to do—clear away the extraneous matter so that we can see the truth—the naked shining truth [*PI* 262].

However, the real interest for Christie seems to have been the human side of archaeology. As the foreword to *Death Comes as the End* illustrates, she believed people remain essentially the same, regardless of temporal or geographic context, and her writing often highlights the continuity of human nature. In *Murder in Mesopotamia*, a skeleton of an ancient murdered woman is found in the middle of the main murder investigation. Still intact with the bones are remnants of a "copper bowl and some pins" and "gold and blue things that had been her necklace of beads"—this long-dead woman is described as "A Mrs. Leidner [the present victim] of two thousand odd years ago" (*MIM* 195), indicating that people and human behavior never change. The same idea is present in the mundane objects, which Christie highlights in *Come, Tell Me How You Live*:

Here, some five thousand years ago, was *the* busy part of the world. Here were the beginnings of civilization, and here, picked up by mid, this broken fragment of a clay pot, hand-made, with a design of dots and cross-hatching in black paint, is the forerunner of the Woolworth cup out of which this very morning I have drunk my tea [55; emphasis in original].

Two substantial Christies are set in ancient Egypt. *Death Comes as the End* is a mystery novel and *Akhnaton* is about that pharaoh. Both plots are focused on human nature—particularly passions between the sexes—and use archaeological research for context about rituals, religious beliefs, and manners. However, the idea is that underneath that, the naked passions that drive human communication are consistent.

Christie famously wrote everywhere she went. However, she did not write about the areas she was in at the time. *Come, Tell Me How You Live* was written in London during World War II, some seven years after the events recounted. By contrast, *Lord Edgware Dies*, a quintessentially London novel, was written in Nineveh. *They Came to Baghdad*, the last of her novels set on a dig, was written in Devon just ahead of a trip to Baghdad.

Christie's archaeological connection has proven fruitful, especially for raising the profile of her husband's research in the decades following their deaths, where her fame has eclipsed his. For this reason, when Mallowan's memoir, titled *Mallowan's Memoir*, was republished in 2001, it was subtitled *Agatha and the Archaeologist*. A 2001–02 British Museum exhibition of Mallowan's findings also incorporated Christie's home videos and was titled *Agatha Christie and Archaeology*. This is also the title of the companion book by Charlotte Trümpler.

See also: *Absent in the Spring*; *Come, Tell Me How You Live*; *Death Comes as the End*; **Mallowan, Sir Max**; *Murder in Mesopotamia*

Arden, Enoch

This name comes from a narrative poem by Alfred, Lord Tennyson, which describes a missing-presumed-dead man returning. It lent its name to a legal principal regarding the reclamation of inheritance. Christie used the name for two characters. In "While the Light Lasts," a soldier, presumed dead in World War I, returns to see his wife, who has remarried. In *Taken at the Flood*, set after World War II, "Enoch Arden" is the assumed name of a visitor to a village, widely thought to be the long-dead first husband of a wealthy widow. While the reference is hardly obscure to readers of English poetry today, it would have been a fairly universal reference for Christie's original readership.

Arden, Linda. See **Hubbard, Caroline**

Are You Happy? If Not, Consult Mr. Parker Pyne. See *Parker Pyne Investigates*

Argyle, Christina ("Tina")

Christina Argyle is an adopted daughter of Rachel and Leo Argyle in *Ordeal by Innocence*, Tina is one of the few mixed-race characters in the Christie canon. She is more calm and collected than her siblings and seems to be the only one who never resented their mother.

Argyle, Jack ("Jacko")

The black sheep of the Argyle family in *Ordeal by Innocence*, Jacko Argyle has died in prison after being sentenced to death for killing his adoptive mother. However, when an alibi emerges, his reputation is reevaluated. He turns out to have been a complex personality, a mixture of magnetism and self-service; in fact, a narcissist who even in death is controlling people.

Argyle, Rachel

Rachel Argyle is the victim in *Ordeal by Innocence,* a well-respected philanthropist who has adopted five children. Rachel appears to have had distinct but highly plausible personas. There is a public one, of a public-spirited woman, "determined to make [her five adopted children] feel wanted, to give them a real home, be a real mother to them" (181). The sentiments, however, have not translated into good parenting, which several characters blame on the lack of a "blood tie" (182). It is not a black-and-white, Jekyll-and-Hyde characterization but an illustration of personalities, ideals, and practicalities in conflict.

Aristides, Mr.

A vastly rich and therefore powerful man in *Destination Unknown*, Mr. Aristides represents the damaging spread of absolute wealth. He is a "shrivelled-up, bent … wrinkled, dried-up, mummified old morsel of humanity" who inspires "awe" by virtue of "his enormous wealth" (190). He is perhaps the only villain in Christie whose culpability is never excused or mitigated but who nonetheless gets away, unpunished. This is again because of his money.

Arlington, General

A friend of Lady Selina Hazy's in *At Bertram's Hotel*. Only mentioned in passing— she mistakes another man for him early on—this character helps Christie set the scene for a novel in which characters can impersonate one another by adopting key mannerisms.

Armstrong, Daisy

In *Murder on the Orient Express*, Daisy Armstrong was an American child, the daughter of Colonel and Mrs. Armstrong, who was kidnapped for ransom some years earlier and killed before the ransom was collected. Her killing is considered the ultimate form of human evil, especially as the man responsible, Cassetti, evaded legal justice. The story of her death was very famously based on the kidnapping and murder of Charles Lindbergh Jr., the son of famed aviator Charles Lindbergh and his wife, writer Anne Morrow Lindbergh.

Armstrong, Dr. Edward

A respected Harley Street doctor with a secret history of drinking, Dr. Edward Armstrong is among the guests on Soldier Island in *And Then There Were None*. Like other guests, he is positioned as someone who has killed in the past, but whom the law cannot touch. He is considered one of the more culpable, because a patient, Louisa Clees, died when he operated on her while he was drunk. The last two survivors on the island believe he is the murderer, U.N. Owen, until his body washes up on the shore.

Arundell, Charles, and Theresa

Charles and Theresa Arundell are the modern, rather grasping nephew and niece respectively of Emily Arundell, children of the late Thomas Arundell, in *Dumb Witness*. They have powered through a previous inheritance, and Theresa, in particular, is an enviable figure of fashion.

Arundell, Emily

Emily Arundell is a wealthy elderly spinster who is killed with phosphorous after writing to Hercule Poirot about an attempt on her life in *Dumb Witness* and the short story on which it is based, "The Incident of the Dog's Ball."

Ascher, Alice, and Franz

Alice Ascher is an elderly shopkeeper and the first victim in *The ABC Murders*. Franz is her drunken husband, whom police suspect of her murder. Alice is killed purely because of her initials—AA—and her location, Andover.

Ashfield

Ashfield was Christie's childhood home in Torquay. She lived at Ashfield until her marriage and on and off thereafter. When she sold it in 1940, it was largely against her will. The property always stayed with her, and she wrote in her autobiography: "I remember the house where I was born. I go back to that always in my mind. Ashfield. How much that means. When I dream I hardly ever dream of Greenway or Winterbrook. It is always Ashfield, the old familiar setting where one's life first functioned" (530).

Ashfield, described extensively with the thinnest of veils in the Mary Westmacott novels *Giant's Bread* and *Unfinished Portrait*, began Christie's love affair with houses. As a child with few social connections and a wild imagination, she built fictional worlds in the property's extensive gardens.

See also: *An Autobiography*; *Giant's Bread*; **Greenway House**; **Styles House**; *Unfinished Portrait*; **Winterbrook House**.

Ashley, Diana

A fun-loving beauty in "The Idol House of Astarte," who is described as possessing "Oriental" charms, and whose decision to host a fancy dress "orgy" in a haunted house, while dressed as the Roman goddess Diana, leads to a man's death.

"A-Sitting on a Tell" (poem)

Structurally resembling Lewis Carroll's "I'll Tell Thee Everything I Can" and presented "with apologies to Lewis Carroll," "A-Sitting on a Tell" opens Christie's 1946 archaeological memoir, *Come, Tell Me How You Live*. It is a comic account of meeting "an erudite young man" (*CTMHYL* 9) who talks earnestly of archaeology, while the narrator is entirely preoccupied with thinking up murder mystery plots. The narrator subsequently realizes that this man is interesting, and she should go digging with him. It is not difficult to put names to these characters. The poem shares one line with is source material, which is also the title of the memoir: "I said, 'Come tell me how you live'" (9). A "tell" is an archaeological term for a mound that holds the remains of a city or village as well as a term for revealing something through a gesture or behavior (as in bluffing during a card game), so the word in the title has multiple meanings.

See also: **Archaeology**; *Come, Tell Me How You Live*; **Mallowan, Max**

"Ask and You Shall Receive." See "The Thumb Mark of St. Peter"

Associés Contre le Crime (alternative title: *Partners in Crime*). See *Bélisaire et Prudence Beresford*

Astor, Anthony. See **Wills, Muriel**

At Bertram's Hotel (novel)

The 10th Miss Marple novel opens conversationally. Christie addresses readers, introducing Bertram's Hotel, a relic from the past, as a location very present in 1965. "If you turn off an unpretentious street," readers are told, having been directed to "the heart of the West End," "and turn left and right once or twice, you will find yourself in a quiet street with Bertram's Hotel" (1). Before the plot has kicked off, then, Christie has introduced the hub of action in her novel as paradoxically belonging to a quiet pocket of the loudest and busiest part of London.

Bertram's "has been there a long time" (1). Other hotels have closed or modernized, but Bertram's has defied both the passage of time and the evolution of values that comes with it. The place has been "patronized over a long stretch of years by the higher *échelons* of the clergy, dowager ladies of the aristocracy up from the country, girls on their way home … from expensive finishing schools" (1), suggesting a vanishing tradition of country houses and expensive education. Bertram's, in short, evokes both a fantasy of the past and a class-based fantasy that seems to revive conservative values and hierarchies.

This is how Christie's books have been read for years—as affectionate, conservative relics of a gilded age that was before even its author's time—but her playful self-awareness cannot be ignored. It is clear from the first page that Bertram's caters chiefly to people who want this fantasy rather than exclusively to "dowager ladies" and prominent clergymen. The hotel has indoor plumbing, a discreet television room (for "the Americans"), and chairs that accommodate people "of any proportion" in comfort; not something for which traditional British furniture is famed (3). The hotel, then, has a certain façade, but to have survived as it has, it has necessarily become all things to all people. Its branding, therefore, is a contradiction.

Miss Marple, who "[l]ooks a hundred" (5), is staying at the hotel courtesy of her well-meaning nephew Raymond West. While having tea with an old friend, she sees the high-living Lady Bess Sedgwick arrive in an "avid state" (17), and a drama unfolds as Lady Bess is reunited with her semi-estranged daughter, Elvira. Meanwhile, the police are investigating a series of robbery and money-laundering operations, and the only eyewitness account implicates a high court judge who is staying at Bertram's. Before long, another robbery takes place, with witnesses identifying a clergyman, Canon Pennyfather, who is also staying at the hotel but goes missing.

The police investigate the fresh link to Bertram's and soon ascertain that the organized crime ring is somehow linked with the hotel. They also suspect the involvement of Lady Bess. When Pennyfather finally appears, he tells the extraordinary story of having been attacked by a man who looked identical to himself, and Miss Marple realizes that the gang is employing doppelgangers of respectable figures who are supposed to be out of town so they can carry out their crimes without fear of discovery. As revelations come to light, a man from Lady Bess's past, Mickey Gorman, arrives and blackmails her. While Miss Marple is discussing the possibility of violence at the hotel with Chief Inspector Davy, there is a gunshot outside. Davy finds Mickey dead and Elvira in a state of panic, claiming the man died protecting her from an unknown assassin's bullet.

Toward the end of the novel, Lady Bess confesses to the murder of Gorman and to masterminding the criminal network. She commits suicide, giving Elvira her much-sought-for blessing. However, Miss Marple refuses to accept this explanation of the facts and reveals that the crime conspiracy extends throughout the whole hotel, to the level of management who source the respectable guests for impersonation and launder stolen money. "Bertram's," says Davy, is "the headquarters of one of the best and biggest crime syndicates that's been known for years" (251). Moreover, Miss Marple reveals that it was Elvira and not her mother who murdered Gorman. He was secretly married to Lady Bess, making the latter's marriage to Elvira's father bigamous, and Elvira believed—mistakenly—that she would inherit nothing as an illegitimate daughter. The young woman is more tied to tradition and blind to the march of progress than any of her older peers.

The mother-daughter bond in this novel is complex and inconsistent. The hedonistic mother, who has no time in life for Elvira, tries to give her daughter the gift of life by taking the fall for the murder. The daughter, desperate for her mother's approval, is caught up in the question of inheritance and personal gain. As with the hotel, which houses "[n]o beatniks, no thugs, no juvenile delinquents [but rather] sober Victorian-Edwardian old ladies" (157), a superficial précis of the relationship is misleading. Elvira is not arrested for her crime. The novel ends with the authorities vowing to catch her, but they have no evidence. It is a bittersweet ending to a novel with an unconventional structure: unusually in a Christie, there is no murder until chapter 23 of 27. Setting aside the frequent references to what would happen "in a thriller" (50, 207), the book interacts with its own generic traditions, showing something contrived and arbitrary in the convention of ending with the villain's apprehension or death.

Leaving the hotel, Miss Marple notes that "it was all too good to be true.... But it was a performance: not real" (252). Bertram's, it is hinted, must close down. Similarly, nostalgia cannot go unchecked (ironically, two real London hotels now claim to have inspired Bertram's and offer tourists "Agatha Christie cream teas"). Nostalgia is the big question tackled in this novel, and Christie reveals it to serve modern agendas by contrasting a calm Edwardian façade with the portrayal of 1960s organized crime. Having a stunted mother-daughter relationship at the heart of the novel shows us that not growing up or moving on can be dangerous.

At Bertram's Hotel has been filmed for television twice: for the BBC as part of *Miss Marple* (starring Joan Hickson and broadcast 25 January 1987) and for ITV as part of *Agatha Christie's Marple* (starring Geraldine McEwan and broadcast 23 September 2007). A serialized radio adaptation starring June Whitfield as Miss Marple was broadcast by the BBC between 25–29 December 1995.

Characters: **Arlington, General; Blake, Hon. Elvira**; Campbell, Inspector; Carpenter, Mrs.; Coniston, Lord; Davy, Chief Inspector; **Gorman, Michael (Mickey); Gorringe, Miss**; Graves, Sir Ronald; Guido; Hazy, Lady Selina; Hoffman, Robert and Wilhelm; Humfries, Mr.; Isaacstein, Abel; **Luscombe, Colonel Derek**; MacRae, Mrs.; **Malinowski, Ladislaus; Marple, Jane**; Martinelli, Contessa; McAllister, Amy; Melford, Mildred and Nancy; **Pennyfather, Canon**; Pomfret, Lord; **Robinson, Mr.; Sedgwick, Lady Bess**; Sheldon, Rose; Simmons, Archdeacon; Swanhilda; Russell, Harry; Wadell, Sergeant; **West, Raymond**.

See also: *Agatha Christie's Marple*; *Agatha Christie's Marple*; *Miss Marple* (radio series); *Miss Marple* (television series); Nostalgia; Theatricality.

"At the Bells and Motley" (alternative titles: "The Disappearance of Captain Harwell," "A Man of Magic")

"At the Bells and Motley" is the third Quin and Satterthwaite story. On a stormy night, Mr. Satterthwaite's car breaks down and he seeks shelter in a pub, the Bells and Motley, where he meets the mysterious Mr. Quin. Together, they learn about a murder and an attendant love triangle that occurred nearby a year previously. With Quin's help, Satterthwaite comes to understand what happened and puts the mind of a love-struck young woman at ease.

"At the 'Bells and Motley'" was published as "A Man of Magic" in the *Grand Magazine* in November 1925 and appears under its present title in *The Mysterious Mr. Quin* (1930). The pub reappears in "The Voice in the Dark."

Characters: Brandburn, Cyrus G.; Foster, Sir George; **Grant, Stephen**; Harwell, Captain Richard; Lecon, Lord; Le Couteau, Eleanor; Masters; Mathias, John; **Quin, Harley; Satterthwaite, Mr.**

See also *The Mysterious Mr. Quin*

"At the Crossroads." See "The Love Detectives"

"At the Gate of Baghdad." See "The Gate of Baghdad"

"At the House in Shiraz." See "The House at Shiraz"

"At the Inquest." See "The Scoop" (novella)

"At the Stroke of Twelve." See "The Adventure of Johnnie Waverly"

"The Augean Stables." See *The Labours of Hercules*

Austin, Celia

Celia Austin is the first victim in *Hickory Dickory Dock*, who pretends to be a kleptomaniac to make herself interesting to psychology student Colin McNabb. In doing so, she accidentally discovers something sinister.

An Autobiography (nonfiction work)

An Autobiography is Christie's own version of her life-story, started in Nimrud, Iraq, in 1950 and concluded in Wallingford, England in 1965. A monumental volume, the original manuscript is significantly longer than the 542 pages that were published in 1977, a year after her death. Her publisher, William Collins, who had published numerous tributes in memoriam, included a foreword, explaining that some repetitions had been elided, and warning readers not to expect any account of her 1926 disappearance, still being talked about at the time.

In fact, the autobiography does deal with the breakdown of Christie's marriage and its aftermath, although it does not dwell on the eleven days in Harrogate. Christie's only published accounts of these days are her 1928 *Daily Mail* interview and her 1934 pseudonymous novel, *Unfinished Portrait*. Indeed, many passages in the autobiography appear almost verbatim in the Westmacott novels, although there are some elements that are expanded upon in fiction but not dwelt upon in here. For instance, a reference to a crush on a schoolmistress, present in *Unfinished Portrait*, does not appear in the equivalent scene in *An Autobiography*. Other moments of honesty—such as a lengthy critique of her own *The Mystery of the Blue Train*—were removed for commercial purposes.

Almost half the book is devoted to Christie's early life, with especial focus on her childhood. There is a definite focus on the characters in her family and professional life, recounted with mild satire. About her own early work, Christie is generally dismissive, although she writes proudly of some of her achievements. She also reflects on her position as a writer, championing innocence and the defeat of evil. Overall, she presents herself a shy woman who happens to be a writer.

In 2011, Christie's estate released Dictaphone recordings she had made during the autobiography's composition. They were complete passages, written in longhand and recited for a stenographer to put into print. These were included in a CD with the book as a kind of audio supplement.

Elements of the autobiography have inspired numerous pieces of fiction and dramatic writing. As the text is under copyright, direct adaptations are rare. The dialogue in the BBC's *Agatha Christie: A Life in Pictures*, a 2004 drama starring Anna Massey and Olivia Williams as older and younger versions of Christie, is taken almost verbatim from the text. In the 2010s, Agatha Christie Ltd. threatened legal action when a novelist writing about Christie included incidents that had no source other than the autobiography.

See also: **Christie, Colonel Archibald ("Archie")**; *Come, Tell Me How You Live*; **"Her Own Story of Her Disappearance"**; **Hicks, Rosalind**; *Unfinished Portrait*; **Westmacott, Mary**

Averil

Averil is one of Joan Scudamore's children in *Absent in the Spring*. She "settled down" with a stockbroker and has little to do with her parents (596).

Babbington, Rev. Stephen

Rev. Stephen Babbington is the first victim in *Three Act Tragedy*. His death is extremely puzzling because no one had a motive to kill him. Babbington is a kindly, elderly clergyman who has never offended anyone except the easily-offended-on-principle Oliver Manders. It is so difficult to find a motive that Hercule Poirot deduces the crime must be motiveless. It transpires that the motive has nothing to do with Babbington personally.

Badcock, Arthur, and Heather

In *The Mirror Crack'd from Side to Side*, Arthur Badcock is quietly unobtrusive and his wife, Heather, is highly involved in village life. Arthur has a secret history as the first of actress Marina Gregg's five husbands, and Heather is a film fanatic who is utterly starstruck at the actress's arrival in St. Mary Mead. She is poisoned after excitedly telling Marina at great length about a time they met in the past.

Badstock, Mrs.

Mrs. Badstock is a working-class woman who meets St. Catherine while scavenging for a discarded pram in "Promotion in the Highest."

"The Baited Trap." See *The Big Four* (novel)

Baker, Cherry, and Jim

Cherry Baker is Miss Marple's young cleaning woman and Jim Baker is Cherry's handyman husband who live on "the development"—new social housing in St. Mary Mead—in *The Mirror Crack'd from Side to Side* and *Nemesis*.

Baker, David

Norma Restarick's boyfriend in *Third Girl*, David Baker is an artist whom Ariadne Oliver calls "the Peacock" because he is so colorful and assertive. There is some ambiguity in his gender presentation, reflecting youthful decadence in the 1960s.

Baker, Mrs. Calvin

A brash American tourist in *Destination Unknown*, Mrs. Calvin Baker turns out to be a secret agent who hates her home country. The stereotypical behavior she exhibits is a kind of clue that her identity is false, although Christie's American tourist characters are almost always drawn along similar lines.

Baldock, Mr.

Mr. Baldock is a gossipy confirmed

bachelor who offers life advice in *The Burden*. Christie's only gay-coded male character in a non-mystery novel, Baldock indicates no authorial homophobia beyond general stereotyping. It is difficult to judge authorial intention from gay-coded characters in the mysteries, because the author exploits cultural prejudices against queer people to mislead the reader about who is and is not guilty.

"The Ballad of the Flint." See *The Road of Dreams* (poetry collection)

"Ballad of the Maytime." See *The Road of Dreams* (poetry collection)

Banks, Gregory, and Susan

Husband to Susan Banks in *After the Funeral*, Gregory Banks possesses an unspecified mental complex, which manifests in extreme guilt. Believing himself morally guilty of murder, he confesses to crimes he never committed. An inconsequential-looking man, of whom his wife's family disapproves, Banks illustrates Christie's negotiation of medicalized psychology throughout the 1950s. Susan is his wife, is an independently-minded aspiring actress and a suspect in the death of her uncle, Richard Abernethie.

Bantry, Colonel Arthur, and Dolly

Colonel Arthur Bantry and his wife, Dolly, are regular characters in the Miss Marple novels. Arthur, a retired colonel, is an unobtrusive magistrate and member of the Conservative Club in St. Mary Mead. Dolly is a close friend of Miss Marple's. With a fecund imagination and an interest in gossip, Dolly provides a good sounding board for Miss Marple's theories. The couple lives in Gossington Hall when introduced in *The Thirteen Problems*. They also appear, centrally, in *The Body in the Library*, where the colonel finds himself the center of gossip after a tacky blonde girl is found dead in his library. They last appear together in *Sleeping Murder* but are mentioned in *A Murder Is Announced*. By 1962, and *The Mirror Crack'd from Side to Side*, Arthur has died, prompting Dolly to sell Gossington Hall to filmmakers.

Barnard, Elizabeth ("Betty")

Elizabeth "Betty" Barnard is a flirtatious 23-year-old waitress engaged to Donald Fraser and the second victim in *The ABC Murders*, She is killed in Bexhill because of her alliterative name.

Barnard, Megan

In *The ABC Murders*, Megan Barnard is Betty Barnard's no-nonsense sister. Megan is described by the traditional Captain Hastings as possessing "a queer modern angularity" (79) She turns out to be the moral center of the investigation, with the most enduring, albeit dysfunctional, romantic relationship.

Barnes, Mrs.

Mrs. Barnes is Joyce Lambert's blustery housekeeper in "Next to a Dog." This is not a sympathetic portrayal of working-class women; she believes tea is a panacea and dares to criticize Terry the dog, with insults that could only have been written by a dog-lover posing as a dog-hater.

Barrow, Miss

Miss Barrow is a secretive woman who travels with Miss Cooke and turns out to be a kind of protection officer hired by Jason Rafiel as a guardian angel for Miss Marple in *Nemesis*. Miss Barrow appears to be the senior partner, as Miss Cooke looks to her for advice.

Barton, Emily

Emily Barton is the voice of conservatism in *The Moving Finger*, a proper and correct spinster who owns the cottage rented by Jerry and Joanna Burton. She opens the novel faintly scandalized by the idea of a young woman smoking and ends it broadening her horizons by going on a cruise with the doctor's manly sister.

Barton, George

The devoted older husband to Rosemary Barton in *Sparkling Cyanide*, George dies while re-creating the night of her death. He is an easily manipulated man who is too unworldly to survive.

Barton, Rosemary

Rosemary Barton is the central character in *Sparkling Cyanide*, dead at the outset. Like Helen in *Sleeping Murder*, Rosemary exists solely in the memories of those who discuss her. She is, essentially, what they need her to be: and they are split on which side of Sigmund Freud's Madonna/whore dichotomy they place her. As several characters point out, her name, according to Ophelia in *Hamlet*, stands for remembrance. Indeed, her existence as a Shakespearean concept models other relationships: Anthony repeatedly thinks of her as Rosaline in *Romeo and Juliet*, casting himself as Romeo and Iris as Juliet, the relative who ultimately eclipses Rosaline/Rosemary in Romeo's affections. It is only at the very end of the novel, once Rosemary and her death have been explained, that Iris is able to conclude the *Hamlet* quotation: "Pray, love, remember" (*SpC* 238).

Bassington-ffrench, Roger

The self-described "bold, bad villain of the piece" in *Why Didn't They Ask Evans?* (288), Roger Bassington-ffrench is a cheeky, charming man who initially assists the young adventurers Frankie Derwent and Bobby Jones before unmasking himself as the murderer. He is Christie's last playful villain, who ends up evading justice for his crimes, and earning the grudging respect of the heroine he tried to kill.

Bates, Annie. See Annie

Bateson, Leonard ("Len")

Leonard Bateson is a medical student, "a friendly soul, with a Cockney accent" and "fiery red hair" (19) who makes a fool of himself by falling in love too hard and not taking anything seriously enough in *Hickory Dickory Dock*. Although the character is in his twenties, he speaks like a 1930s schoolboy, talking about "cut[ting] up a lovely corpse" in class, which was "Smashing" (19), perhaps portraying Christie's discomfort at conveying young adult voices in 1955. She would master this by 1967, with Mike Rogers in *Endless Night*.

Batt, Albert

Starting out as a lift-boy in *The Secret Adversary*, Albert Batt stays with Tommy and Tuppence Beresford as an office boy and later a servant with an unspecified role throughout their careers. He appears in every title, going from a 15-year-old pulp fiction enthusiast in the first title to a keen follower of movies in *Partners in Crime*, a minor character in *N or M?*, a happily married father of three in *By the Pricking of My Thumbs*, and an elderly companion in *Postern of Fate*.

Batt Family

In the Tommy and Tuppence books, Albert Batt acquires a wife, Milly, and three children: Charlie, Elizabeth, and Jean—all are mentioned in *By the Pricking of My Thumbs*.

Battle, Superintendent

Christie was not the first author to create a policeman called Battle; George Ira Brett introduced readers to "the experiences of Inspector Battle of the Criminal Investigation Department" in *The Murder at Jex Farm* (1895).

A physically imposing Scotland Yard man, Battle is impassive and easily underestimated. He works alongside Hercule Poirot in *Cards on the Table* (1936) and takes a more central role in other novels, although never as the protagonist. Battle was created in *The Secret of Chimneys* (1925), returning sporadically throughout the 1920s and 1930s (*The Secret of Chimneys, The Seven Dials Mystery, Cards on the Table,* and *Murder Is Easy*), with a final appearance alongside his troubled daughter in *Towards Zero* (1944). His family life (a wife and five children) is mostly happy, and he largely keeps it separate from his work. He appears to be the father of Colin Lamb, the narrator of *The Clocks* (1966).

Superintendent Battle has enjoyed a surprising lease of life beyond Christie's texts and their adaptations. He appears as a character in Peter Cheyney's "Crime Club Card Game" alongside Poirot and several of Cheyney's own creations and in Carlo Fruttero and Franco Lucentini's comic mystery *The D Case, or the Truth about The Mystery of Edwin Drood* as one of several detectives and the only one who does not take a "Porfirian" (psychological) or "Agathist" (puzzle-centric) approach to the crime. The appeal of the character may lie in the fact that, similarly to Hastings, he could well have been an undisputed hero in any number of books by other writers, but next to a selection of gifted amateurs he is a sidekick.

The BBC Murders

A precursor to *Murder in the Studio*, *The BBC Murders* was an authorized tour of four Christie radio scripts, read live on stage, in a tour of Florida in 2013. Staged in full period costume, the production was presented by Zev Buffman, who had consulted with the Christie estate. The line-up consisted of **Butter in a Lordly Dish, Three Blind Mice, Personal Call,** and **The Yellow Iris.** These plays had previously been performed on American radio in 2009, for *Mystery Series Live—On the Air.* Revivals are occasionally licensed in the United States.

See also: **Murder on Air; Mystery Series Live: On the Air**

BBC Radio Adaptations

Christie's difficult relationship with the British Broadcasting Corporation did not stop her writing several original plays for BBC radio. Separate entries in this volume exist for *The Scoop, Behind the Screen, Miss Marple Tells a Story, Three Blind Mice, The Yellow Iris, Butter in a Lordly Dish*, and *Personal Call.* This entry concerns dramatizations of her work for BBC radio broadcast. This entry does not concern abridged readings of novels, which are a regular feature of BBC Radio.

After a version of Frank Vosper's *Love from a Stranger* in 1936, the BBC broadcast an original adaptation of "The Incredible Theft" in 1938. The other early radio adaptations were of extracts from Christie novels which were, after all, always best-sellers. In 1940, the series *Crime Magazine*, which introduced readers to key detectives such as Sexton Blake, featured an extract from the latest Christie, *Sad Cypress*, with Hercule Poirot played by Lionel Gamlin. Two years later, in December 1942, *Armchair Detective*, a program recommending discussing and recommending new books, hosted by Ernest Dudley, featured dramatized extracts from *The Body in the Library.* The same program featured *Five Little Pigs* two months later, with Billy Milton reading the part of Poirot.

The first full dramatization of a Christie novel came in 1944, when Robert Holmes played Superintendent Battle in a version of *Towards Zero*, part of the long-running *Saturday Night Theatre* (where several Christie titles have appeared in subsequent decades). On 17 June that year, the Home Service broadcast a version of *Alibi*, starring Basil Sydney as Poirot with Arthur Ridley as Dr. Sheppard.

There were two BBC radio adaptations of *Love from a Stranger* in 1945. One on the Home Service, part of *Saturday Night Theatre* on 24 March, starred John Clements as Bruce Lovell. The other, broadcast on the General Forces Programme on 9 May and repeated on 4 July, starred Pamela Brown, John Slater, and Alan Howland. On 27 December 1947, a radio version of the play *And Then There Were None* was broadcast (under its original title) as part of the *Monday Matinee* program. Producer Ayton Whitaker reworked the script and cast veteran radio actors including H. Marion-Crawford (Lombard) and Denys Blakelock (Wargrave) to create something of an event.

On 29 May 1948, the World Service broadcast an adaptation of Arnold Ridley's play version of *Peril at End House.* This starred a familiar figure as Hercule Poirot: Austin Trevor, who had created the role on screen in three films for Twickenham Studios in the 1930s. An adaptation of "The Witness for the Prosecution," which was proving highly popular with U.S. radio audiences, was broadcast on 28 January 1950. This is evidence of British broadcasters paying attention to their transatlantic peers: the story had been in circulation in the United Kingdom since 1925 but had only appeared in an anthology in the United States in 1948 and since then had become a desirable, adaptable property.

In 1953, BBC Radio commenced its first Christie series: *Partners in Crime*, starring husband and wife Richard Attenborough and Sheila Sim, then appearing in *The Mousetrap*—see **Partners in Crime (radio series)**. On 24 April 1954, French actor Jacques Brunius played Poirot for the first of two times in an adaptation of "The Third-Floor Flat." Richard Williams starred as Poirot in a 30-minute adaptation of "Murder in the Mews," airing on 20 March 1955. This is one of the rare pre–1960 BBC

Radio plays that survives, and has been released commercially on CD. Following these and other successes, the BBC Light Programme organized an "Agatha Christie festival" in 1956 (see **Light Programme Festival**).

Although Christie's novels continued to be serialized in abridged on-air readings throughout the 1960s and 1970s, full-cast dramatizations did not return until 1982. The Home Service was replaced with BBC Radio 4 in 1967, and it is on this station that subsequent adaptations have been broadcast, with two exceptions. *The Unexpected Guest*, adapted by Gordon House, aired on the World Service on 30 May 1981. It was rebroadcast on BBC Radio 4 on 12 March 1982 as the *Afternoon Play*. A curiosity from July 1984, a 30-minute adaptation of the ghost story "The Lamp," aired as part of the series *Haunted*. It starred Judy Cornwell and Timothy Bateson.

On 10 September 1983, the *Saturday Night Theatre* slot commenced a "Murder for Pleasure" season with a 90-minute adaptation by Neville Teller of *Ordeal by Innocence*. It starred Alex Jennings as Dr. Calgary. In 1985, the BBC commenced its 21-year series of occasional Hercule Poirot adaptations; a series of Jane Marple adaptations commenced in 1993 (see **Hercule Poirot [BBC radio series]** and **Miss Marple [radio series]**).

In the meantime, standalones were broadcast as well: *The Sittard Mystery*, a five-part serial (aired from 1 February 1990), and *The Pale Horse* was the *Saturday Night Theatre* installment for 3 March 1993; both programs featured John Moffatt, who was playing Poirot elsewhere on Radio 4, among the ensemble casts. Like the Poirot and Marple series, they were dramatized by Michael Bakewell and directed by Enyd Williams.

The Miss Marple series concluded in 2001, and the Poirot series was winding down. In line with Agatha Christie Ltd.'s plans to rebrand—which saw plans (tried out but shelved) for international modernized television adaptations—Above the Title productions made twelve 30-minute plays based on Christie's quirkier stories. The first installment, "Witness for the Prosecution" (7 January 2002), was set in World War II and starred Hywel Bennet who had played the killer in the movie *Endless Night* 30 years earlier.

However, the other seven were set in the modern day. These included: "Philomel Cottage" (14 January 2002), "The Gate of Baghdad" (21 January 2002), "Swan Song" (28 January 2002), "Magnolia Blossom" (4 February 2002), "The Hound of Death" (11 February 2002), "The £199 Adventure" (17 February 2003; based on "The Case of the City Clerk"), "In a Glass Darkly" (24 February 2003), "The Gypsy" (3 March 2003), "The Dressmaker's Doll" (10 March 2003), "The Case of the Perfect Carer" (17 March 2003; based on "The Case of the Perfect Maid"), and "The Last Séance" (24 March 2003).

After the Poirot series wound down in 2006, Radio 4 commissioned fresher—but still period—adaptations, focusing on standalone titles, including two it had already adapted in the 1980s and 1990s. Joy Wilkinson dramatized the following (date of first episode broadcast in brackets): *Crooked House* (four parts, from 15 February 2008), *Endless Night* (one part, 30 August 2008), *Towards Zero* (four parts, from 10 February 2010), *And Then There Were None* (one part, 13 November 2010), *Sparkling Cyanide* (three parts, from 12 January 2012), and *Murder Is Easy* (three parts, from 21 February 2013). These atmospheric dramas, with video game style music, pre-empted the darker turn of the BBC television adaptations from 2015, which have in their turn helped reshape public opinion on Agatha Christie.

Wilkinson dramatized an additional three stories as **Miss Marple's Final Cases** in 2013, which saw June Whitfield return to the role she had played from 1993 to 2001. In 2020, to mark the centenary of Christie's crime debut, BBC Radio 4 broadcast adaptations of three lesser-known titles: a "rediscovered" play, *The Lie* (29 August 2020), and two Mary Westmacott titles, *Absent in the Spring* (31 August 2020) and *The Rose and the Yew Tree* (1 September 2020).

See also: **Hercule Poirot (BBC radio series)**; **Miss Marple (radio series)**; **Miss Marple's Final Cases (radio series)**

BBC Television Adaptations since 2015

The BBC has aimed to produce annual multi-part Christie adaptations for Christmas since 2015. The delivery of these productions has faced multiple challenges, from sexual allegations to the COVID-19 pandemic, but the broadcaster has generally come up with something. These adaptations offer fresh approaches to Christie's texts, highlighting darker, more historically-engaged aspects of the texts than traditional dramatizations.

The first, *And Then There Were None* (airing in three parts from Christmas Day 2015), was a runaway hit and has enjoyed phenomenal success in export. Critically, it was a triumph and, as the first English-language adaptation to maintain the dark ending of the 1939 novel (as opposed to the happy ending of the play and every major movie), it heralded a revival of interest in Christie as a sinister writer, sensitive to the darkness of impending war. The all-star cast featured Charles Dance, Aidan Turner, Miranda Richardson, Toby Stephens, Douglas Booth, Maeve Dermody, and others. It was dramatized by Sarah Phelps, who had made a stir with her adaptations of *Great Expectations* and *The Casual Vacancy* for the BBC, following a stint writing for the gloomy soap *EastEnders*.

Phelps attributed her fresh approach to the fact that she had not seen any other version of the story and had never read Christie at all before reading this novel so she could adapt it; therefore, she claimed, she could access key themes and truths in the text without any preconceptions. Although British tabloid the *Daily Mail* sought to manufacture some outrage at the presence of swearing and partial nudity (which appears in the book), the adaptation was met with adulation by the hard-to-please Christie fandom and brought in millions of new readers. Phelps was quickly commissioned to write the next year's "Christie for Christmas," and the BBC announced that it had optioned six Christie titles (although what constitutes these six has changed several times).

The critical unity was short-lived. Every subsequent adaptation has taken greater steps to challenge traditional ideas of Christie and moved more and more consciously away from the source text itself, injecting increasingly new elements that have divided Christie fans and have come to appear increasingly generic to television audiences. On Christmas Day 2016, the BBC began airing its three-part version of "The Witness for the Prosecution." A three-hour take on a very short story, the plot is not so much inflated as bled dry for long, brooding montages, sex scenes, and even a song. Although Phelps claimed not to have seen the 1957 film, Andrea Riseborough as Romaine singing "Let Me Call You Sweetheart" appears like a throwback to Marlene Dietrich in the equivalent role, singing "I May Never Go Home."

Ordeal by Innocence was supposed to be the 2017 Christmas offering, but after filming concluded, it was one of several productions that was impacted by the #MeToo movement, under which several media professionals broke their silence about sexual abuse from powerful men, and multiple allegations swirled. One of these was a pair of allegations against actor Ed Westwick, who had been filmed in the starring role of the accused murderer (and, in this adaptation, rapist) Jacko Argyll. Although Westwick denied the allegations, which were later dropped, a decision was made to reshoot all his scenes with another actor, Christian Cooke, and the broadcast was delayed until Easter 2018. The production team was faced with several challenges, not least budgeting and the schedules of stars involved—Anna Chancellor, Matthew Goode, Bill Nighy, and others—but also more prosaic things like the weather. Although it had been too hot and sunny during initial filming, reshooting in the winter meant trying to edit out snow. Designers were relieved that the owners of a private property, rented out for filming as the house in the drama, had decided to keep much of the décor installed by the filmmakers. The new version was broadcast in three parts from 1 to 15 April 2018. Christie fans reacted with hostility to the ending: the solution was changed, from Christie's more complex explanation of the crimes to a more simple, binary, abusive father story-line.

It was back to normal for Christmas

2018, with a new offering and new outrage, less manufactured on this occasion, because *The ABC Murders* (26–28 December 2018) involves Hercule Poirot, and the public has very definite ideas about Poirot, mostly stemming from David Suchet's performance. Controversy was deliberately courted, with early images of John Malkovich playing the part without adapted facial hair released. Malkovich gave interviews, insisting that he "didn't see any reason to [read] the book" (qtd. in Lawson 15). The adaptation engages directly with the impending World War II, and the rise of xenophobia—something directly reflecting the situation in Britain at the time, following a referendum on leaving the European Union—presenting Poirot more obviously than any other adaptation as an immigrant, who receives racist abuse.

Phelps also made several flamboyant decisions in the adaptation to illustrate a move away from not only traditional ideas about Christie but also the source texts themselves. Most notably, she made Poirot a former priest—something that has divided fans, although there is a general critical consensus that it is a strong dramatic move, and one grounded in the character's moral conflicts. She also symbolically kills off Inspector Japp in the first episode, illustrating a decisive break from the cozy Poirot-and-friends formula of the ITV series. Hastings does not appear in this version of the story. There is not likely to be a *Poirot* series with Malkovich, but the idea of future standalone Poirots with other takes on the character has been mooted.

The six novels under contract were reannounced in 2018, and it was confirmed that *Death Comes as the End*, one of Christie's few never-filmed novels, would be the Christmas 2019 offering and that Phelps would not be returning to write the script. However, for reasons never revealed but likely concerning budgets, this never materialized and, in 2020, BBC sources confirmed that it was indefinitely on hold. Instead, *The Pale Horse* aired as a two-parter on 9 and 16 February 2020. Starring Rufus Sewell and Sean Pertwee, it is a sexed-up, sensationalized version of the story that removes critiques on capitalism and adds an ambiguous extra twist for shock value. Although the Phelps adaptations established themselves as abrupt departures from nostalgic Little England visions of Christie, to date they are still more concerned with these gestures than with finding their own voice, and critics and viewers alike are beginning to respond negatively.

The COVID-19 pandemic means there was no fresh multipart Christie adaptation in 2021. Actor Hugh Laurie announced in 2021 that he had dramatized *Why Didn't They Ask Evans?* into a three-part miniseries, in which he would also feature. Though made by the same production company, Mammoth Entertainment, this more export-conscious production was picked up by Britbox rather than the BBC.

See also: *The ABC Murders* (novel); *And Then There Were None* (novel); *And Then There Were None*, Screen Adaptations of; *The Pale Horse* (novel); *Partners in Crime* (2015 television series); *Ordeal by Innocence* (novel); *Why Didn't They Ask Evans?* (novel); *Witness for the Prosecution*, Screen Adaptations of; "The Witness for the Prosecution" (story)

Beadon, Badger

A friend of Bobby Jones in *Why Didn't They Ask Evans?*, Badger Beadon is a young twit with a speech impediment who unexpectedly becomes a deus ex machina, breaking through a skylight to rescue the central couple from imprisonment.

Beatrice

Beatrices without surnames appear as maids in *The Sittaford Mystery* and *Sleeping Murder*. Beatrice is also the name of Tommy and Tuppence Beresford's granddaughter in *By the Pricking of My Thumbs* and *Postern of Fate*.

"Beatrice Passes." See *The Road of Dreams* (poetry collection)

"Beauty." See *Poems*

Beddingfeld, Anne

Christie's first female narrator, Anne Beddingfeld becomes a journalist in *The Man in the Brown Suit* for want of a living following her father's death. Thrown into a mystery, she tries to emulate the heroines of popular fiction but finds them too helpless and ends up carving her own path. At one point, she dubs herself "Anna the Adventuress," in a clear parody of *The Perils of Pauline.*

"Before It's Too Late." See **"Triangle at Rhodes"**

"Behind Closed Doors." See **"Miss Marple Tells a Story"**

Behind the Screen (game). See **Games**

"Behind the Screen" (novella)

In 1930, the BBC commissioned six members of the recently-formed Detection Club to produce a collaborative mystery narrative. The contributors—Hugh Walpole, Agatha Christie, Dorothy L. Sayers, Anthony Berkeley, E.C. Bentley, and Ronald Knox—each wrote one chapter and read it on the air over a six-week period. Alongside, the chapters were published weekly in the *Listener.* Christie contributed chapter 2 ("Something Is Missing"), broadcast on 21 June 1930 and published in an issue dated 25 June (although without a title).

Walpole's opener sets a vivid scene of a family on a stormy night, settling down only to discover the body of a blackmailer behind a decorative screen on their premises. From here, Christie introduces the police and a gossipy neighbor, whereas others develop the plot and the puzzle. Unlike "The Scoop," by which point the novelty of the exercise seems to have worn off, "Behind the Screen" exhibits Christie's attempts to outwrite her peers. There is a more than usually detailed description, for instance, of a man's Adam's apple, "jerking up and down, while his long pale fingers twisted and untwisted themselves nervously" (*SBS* 158). She also turns a minor character, the housekeeper Mrs. Hulk, into a fierce and forceful staple of the piece, who is comically offended at the adjective *hulking* and is convinced that the police are out to offend her with "nasty puns" (164–65).

In 1931, an editorial in the *Listener* described the writing process: "the first three authors carried the story along according to their own several fancies; while the last three used their wits, in consultation, to unravel the clues presented to

them by the first three" (*SBS* 228–29). The publication ran a competition adjudicated by Milward Kennedy (another crime writer and Detection Club member), in which readers had to answer four questions correctly about how the murder was committed and by whom. No one seems to have provided correct answers to all the questions, but they all elicited correct responses individually.

Following the broadcast and publication in 1930, "Behind the Screen" was dormant until it was published in book form, alongside "The Scoop," in 1983. It has inspired a game, which uses a board and a video-cassette, called *Agatha Christie: Behind the Screen.* This was published by Spinnaker in 1986. In August 2015, BBC Radio 4 Extra broadcast a series of abridged readings from "Behind the Screen," in which famous actors voiced 15-minute versions of each chapter. Christie's chapter was read by Penelope Keith. *Characters introduced by Agatha Christie*: Larkin, Dr.; **Parsons, Mr.; Rice, Inspector**

Other characters: Benson, Constable; Dudden, Paul; Ellis, Amy; Ellis, Mr.; Ellis, Mrs.; Ellis, Robert; Hall, Sergeant; Hope, Wilfred; Hulk, Mrs.; Grip; Pettigrew, Miss

See also: **The Detection Club;** *The Floating Admiral;* **Games; "The Scoop" (novella)**

"Being So Very Wilful" (story)

The early short story "Being So Very Wilful" does not survive in any archive. The 19-year-old Christie sent it to her mentor, Eden Phillpotts, in 1909. He responded that she was developing her own voice as a writer and had "a natural sense for construction and balance"; predicting that "you might go far" as a writer (qtd. in Morgan 52). He advised her, however, that her 31-year-old heroine was "too old" and told her to drop "poetic quotations" at the beginning of each section (qtd. in Morgan 53), something most mentors to young writers have advised at some point. From Phillpotts' response, it is evident that one of Christie's later trademarks was already in evidence: the comedy of manners, centering on the obnoxiousness of English people abroad. It is also evident that she was not yet writing with an eye to commercial demands, as one of Phillpotts's points was that the text was an awkward length—too long for magazine publication and too short for serialization.

See also: **Phillpotts, Eden**

Belcher, Major Ernest (1871–1949). See **Pedlar, Sir Eustace**

Bélisaire et Prudence Beresford

Bélisaire et Prudence Beresford is a series of films released in France between 2005 and 2012, directed by the notable Pascal Thomas, these featured characters based on Tommy and Tuppence Beresford. The Beresfords, played by the highly respected Catherine Frot and André Dussollier, were reimagined as a middle-aged French couple with connections to the Secret Service. Although the three adaptations are slapstick and veer into the absurd—for instance, in one scene, antagonists deflate like balloons—the characterization is arguably closer in spirit to the characters created by Christie than most of the British renditions.

The first film, *Mon Petit Doigt M'a Dit...* ("My Little Finger Told Me...," 2005) is based on *By the Pricking of My Thumbs*. The second, *Le Crime Est Notre Affaire* (Crime Is Our Business, 2008), takes as its source material the Marple novel *4.50 from Paddington*. The third and final film—although there had been two other French Christie movies, one directed by Thomas in the interim was *Associés Contre Le Crime* (Partners in Crime, 2012), based on the short story "The Case of the Missing Lady" from *Partners in Crime*.

The films' playful, irreverent tone—consciously reimagining the source material—made a strong impression with French audiences, helped by the caliber of people involved and the relatively new "literary classic" status of Christie's work. This directly influenced televisions producers at France 2, creating the loose and playful series *Les Petits Meurtres d'Agatha Christie* in 2009.

See also: **Beresford, Prudence ("Tuppence")**; **Beresford, Thomas ("Tommy")**; *By the Pricking of My Thumbs*; *4.50 from Paddington* (novel); *Partners in Crime* (story collection); *Les Petits Meurtres d'Agatha Christie*

"The Bells of Brittany." See *The Road of Dreams* (poetry collection)

Beltane, Hon./Lord Eustace (6th Lord Cronshaw)

In "The Affair at the Victory Ball," the Hon. Eustace Beltane is a languid, middle-aged poseur, heir to his nephew's title. He collects porcelain figures of the harlequinade and is a suspect in his nephew's murder. He recommends Hercule Poirot to a client in "The Adventure of the 'Western Star.'"

"The Benevolent Butler." See **"The Listerdale Mystery"** (story)

Bentley, James

The misfit James Bentley is awkward and antisocial, which has led to his arrest and trial for murder in *Mrs. McGinty's Dead*. Although Superintendent Spence finds him highly distasteful, he is convinced that Bentley is innocent, meaning there is no choice but for Poirot to investigate the case.

Beresford, Betty. See **Sprot, Betty**

Beresford, Deborah, and Derek

Twins Deborah and Derek Beresford are the children of Tommy and Tuppence Beresford, conceived toward the end of *Partners in Crime* and young adults working for the war effort (codebreaking and fighting, respectively) in *N or M?* Deborah marries a man, also called Derek, but when he dies, she returns to live with her parents, appearing in *By the Pricking of My Thumbs* and *Postern of Fate*.

Beresford, Prudence ("Tuppence")

A clergyman's daughter at a loose end after World War I, Prudence "Tuppence" Cowley encounters her old friend Thomas "Tommy" Beresford and goes into business with him as a detective in *The Secret Adversary*. Over time, the two fall in love, marry, and have children. They appear in the stories constituting *Partners in Crime*, published throughout the 1920s and in subsequent decades in *N or M?*; *By the Pricking of My Thumbs*; and Christie's final novel, *Postern of Fate*. Unlike Poirot and Miss Marple, the Beresfords age with each new appearance. Tuppence, who has a penchant for hats and refuses to stay out of matters, is equally matched with her husband in terms of wits, and the two solve an equal number of cases in *Partners in Crime*—something unusual for a husband-and-wife team in Golden Age crime fiction.

A more developed character than Tommy, Tuppence lacks, as Earl F. Bargainnier points out, "the order and method of Poirot or the enological deductions of Miss Marple" (83). Instead, she has an eager vitality and remains in every text the gleeful amateur, despite the fact that, in most cases, she is one of Christie's professional investigators, even employed by the British government. Tuppence stumbles into cases and *finds* the truth more often than she deduces it—but uses her own skills as a detective, and an often overlooked woman, to get people to talk. Filmmakers tend to make Tuppence younger than Tommy—as in the BBC's *Partners in Crime* (2015) and Pacal Thomas's *Bélisaire et Prudence Beresford*—but in the books, they are roughly the same age, like Agatha and Archie Christie.

Beresford, Thomas ("Tommy")

A simple-hearted, "pleasantly ugly" (*TSA* 4) young man wondering what to do after World War I, Tommy Beresford runs into his old friend Prudence "Tuppence" Cowley and launches a career with her in *The Secret Adversary* (1922). The pair marry, have children, and grow old together over the next 51 years in *Partners in Crime*, *N or M?*, *By the Pricking of My Thumbs*, and *Postern of Fate*. Tommy is a straightforward, eager character who works with his wife in every sense of the word—therefore, he is unusual as a detective hero because not only does he have limits but also knows them and works with them. Moreover, he shares the starring role with his wife, another feature that is not common in crime fiction. Tommy is, crucially, a very ordinary kind of man. In *N or M?*, a government official tries to employ Tommy alone to investigate a spy; of course, Tuppence listens at keyholes and joins him undercover. Tommy is not surprised: "his life with Tuppence had been and would always be—a Joint Venture" (*NOM* 63).

Berroldy, Jeanne. See Daubreuil, Madame

Bessner, Dr. Carl

Carl Bessner is a socially awkward German doctor in *Death on the Nile* and the play adaptation, *Murder on the Nile*, who surprises and distresses the self-entitled Mr. Ferguson by successfully proposing marriage to Cornelia Robson.

"Best of the Year" (magazine feature)

Vol. 21, issue 3 (Jan–Mar 1952) of the British Film Institute's *Sight and Sound* magazine features a "best of the year" segment, in which distinguished figures reflected on their favorite films of 1951. Contributors include Ruby M. Ayres, Cecil Beaton, Benjamin Britten, Agatha Christie, T.E.B. Clarke, Cecil Day-Lewis, John Gielgud, Trevor Howard, Celia Johnson, Michael Powell, Ronald Searle, Peter Ustinov, and Mal Zetterling. All the names remain well-known today, but particularly relevant aside from Christie are Day-Lewis (aka mystery author Nicholas Blake), Gielgud (for whom Christie wrote *Akhnaton*), and Ustinov (Hercule Poirot on screen after Christie's death).

As her favorite films of 1951, Christie selected *The Lavender Hill Mob*, calling it "original … and very amusing," *No Highway* ("Very good and gripping"), and *Seven Days to Noon* (though this she commended chiefly for its "nice shots of London"). In addition, Christie mentions "[a] delightful film about Seals," the title of which she could not recall. This is likely Disney's *Seal Island* (1948), which Christie may have seen rerun.

See also: *Akhnaton*; EMI Films

Betterton, Olive, and Thomas ("Tom")

In *Destination Unknown*, Tom Betterton is a brilliant Canadian scientist who has recently gone missing. Olive, his second wife, is killed in a plane crash and Hilary Craven takes her identity to pursue the case undercover. Tom Betterton turns out to have secrets of his own. He was previously married to Elsa Mannheim.

"Beware the King of Clubs." See "The King of Clubs"

Big Fish Games. See Games

The Big Four (novel; alternative title: *The Man Who Was Number Four: Further Adventures of M. Poirot*)

The Big Four is the one early or vintage Christie novel that most fans feel justified in criticizing or dismissing outright, perhaps because it is not a mystery; it was bound to disappoint as it immediately followed *The Murder of Roger Ackroyd* (1926) and had a very different tone; and it was "a stop-gap" to fulfill a contractual obligation at a difficult time, as Christie acknowledges in her autobiography (*AA* 354). She also admitted that her brother-in-law, Campbell Christie, did most of the work in assembling it from a set of short stories and called it a "rotten book" (qtd. in Morgan 163). To this end, it has been called "pretty dreadful" and "cobbled together" (Barnard 183), as well as a "work of expediency" (Aldridge, *Screen* 278). However, Christie started work on the novelization of the short stories long before the upsetting events of 1926, so the "cobbled together"/not-real-Christie aspect of the book may well be overplayed.

The text began as 12 short stories published in *The Sketch* under the overall title of *The Man Who Was Number Four: Further Adventures of M. Poirot* in 1924. The stories are the following:

1. "The Unexpected Guest" (published 2 January) features Poirot called away to America, just as a man breaks into his home and dies, uttering cryptic last words about a shadowy group called "the Big Four," bent on world domination. "Number One," he says, is Li Chang Yen, a Chinese criminal mastermind who is "the controlling and motive force" (*TBF* 13). Number Two is a rich American. Number Three is a Frenchwoman, and Number Four is terrible: the man states that Number Four is "[t]he *destroyer*" (13, emphasis in original) and dies. Poirot does not head for America but instead vows to hunt the Big Four.

2. "The Adventure of the Dartmoor Bungalow" (9 January) features Poirot and Captain Hastings learning more about Li Chang Yen and investigating a murder in a bungalow, which they attribute to Number Four who is a master of disguise.

3. "The Lady on the Stairs" (16 January) has Poirot and Hastings investigating a scientist's disappearance and crossing paths again with Number Four. They also meet Countess Vera Rossakoff, an old sparring partner of Poirot's, in disguise. This story was expanded more heavily than the others in the novelization.

4. "The Radium Thieves" (23 January) focuses on Poirot identifying Number Three as a French scientist frequently compared to Marie Curie.

5. "In the House of the Enemy" (30 January) features Poirot identifying Number Two as the billionaire Abe Ryland and Hastings working for Ryland in the guise of a secretary.

6. "The Yellow Jasmine Mystery" (6 February) presents Poirot solving an apparently unrelated murder mystery in a country house, but he discovers a hidden message indicating that Number Four, posing as a family friend, committed it. This is the most complete murder mystery of the set.

7. "The Chess Problem" (13 February) features Poirot trying to distract himself from the case by explaining the sudden death of a chess player, only to learn that Number Four was behind it.

8. "The Baited Trap" (20 February) is one that ensnares Hastings, who believes his wife has been kidnapped in Argentina. His captors try to use him to reach Poirot, but Poirot outwits them.

9. "The Adventure of the Peroxide Blonde" (27 February) features Poirot and Hastings meeting an old girlfriend of Claud Darrell, an English actor they suspect of being Number Four. Before she can show them a photograph of him, she is run over and killed.

10. "The Terrible Catastrophe" (5 March) presents Poirot and Hastings taking the case to the Home Secretary and various foreign diplomats. Shortly after, Poirot is taken ill. Hastings is knocked out in a booby trap and, when he regains consciousness, is told that Poirot has died.

11. "The Dying Chinaman" (12 March) presents Hastings, against all advice, vowing vengeance on the Big Four. After receiving a cryptic message from a dying

man, he discovers that Poirot is still alive and laying the ground for a final showdown with the Big Four.

12. "The Crag in the Dolomites" (19 March) features Hastings and Poirot laying a trap for the Big Four. Poirot then reveals that he is not Hercule but his brother, Achille, in disguise. After making a bargain with Countess Vera Rossakoff, he and Hastings escape an explosion that kills Numbers Two and Three. Number One commits suicide, and Number Four vanishes without a trace. Poirot reveals that Achille never existed—that he, Hercule, was in disguise all along, but that he needed the countess to believe he was dead. The story ends with him considering marriage.

The Big Four manages to incorporate virtually every cliché of pulp crime fiction in the 1920s, including a Chinese master criminal, daring escapes in the mountains, explosions, threats to national security, cryptic last words, glamorous and not-so-glamorous blondes, and a dizzying array of murders from arsenical poisoning to electrocution in just a few pages. In light of Christie's subsequent parody of literary clichés in such works as *Partners in Crime* (1929) and *The Body in the Library* (1942), it is tempting to read *The Big Four* as a send-up of the dominant pulpish trends of the day. Indeed, the earliest mounted defense of this book, by H. Douglas Thomson writing in 1931, holds that this is a "sustained burlesque" of "a Sexton Blake atmosphere," which "pillories the novellette cliches" (207). To support this point, Thomson highlights the presence of Achille Poirot, the Mycroft Holmes–esque brother.

However, notwithstanding the frequent comic relief provided by Hastings—who interprets a reference to the Lago di Carezza as one to Handel's *Largo* and a girl called Cara Zia (*TBF* 200, 203), it does appear to have been written as an earnest episodic thriller. Prior to its novelization, it was never marketed as anything but a new set of gripping adventures for Poirot, the popular magazine detective. It should be remembered that in the years preceding

The Murder of Roger Ackroyd (1926), Christie was finding her feet as a writer, experimenting with different styles such as modernism (e.g., "While the Light Lasts"), American action (e.g., *The Clutching Hand*), and Wodehousian satire (e.g., *The Secret of Chimneys*). It is highly likely that this series of stories, certainly written for a paycheck rather than broad exposure, was her way of trying out such pulp tropes as the "yellow peril." The earnestness of the text is evidenced by the fact that Christie herself parodied it later in "The Man Who Was Number Sixteen" (1924), also published in *The Sketch*. As a thriller, Christie recalled, *The Big Four* "was quite popular" (*AA* 354).

Elements of *The Big Four* were dramatized for the radio in the 1940s as part of Harold Huber's radio series *Hercule Poirot*. *The Big Four* was adapted by Alain Paillou as a graphic novel, *Les Quatre*, published in French in 2006. It was translated into English the next year. Inevitably, the book was one of the last to be filmed as part of the almost-exhaustive ITV series *Agatha Christie's Poirot*, starring David Suchet. An adaptation by Mark Gatiss with effectively a new—although equally jingoistic—plot was broadcast on 23 October 2013, as the first episode of the final series. Gatiss defended his approach on social media, describing it as "a loose adaptation of an almost unadaptable mess of a book" (n.p.). This episode reintroduced viewers to the beloved "big four" characters of the series—Poirot, Hastings, Japp, and Lemon (the last does not appear in the book)—three of whom had been absent on-screen since 2002.

The stories themselves—in total, around 2,000 words shorter than the novel—had long been available to internet sleuths and users of the British Library. However, in 2017, they were published for the first time in book form, also as *The Big Four*, by HarperCollins, as part of the revived Collins Crime Club imprint.

Characters: **Aarons, Joseph**; **Ah Ling**; Andrews, Betsy; **Appleby, Colonel**; Bolitho, Dr.; Borgonneau, Professor; Bronson; **Cinderella**; Claude, Mademoiselle; Combeau, Piere; Crowther, Sydney; **Darrell, Claud**; Daviloff, Sonia; Deans; Desjardeux, Monsieur; Foly, Austen; Gospoja,

Madame; Grant, Robert; Halliday, John and Mrs.; Harvey, Captain; **Hastings, Captain Arthur**; Henri, Monsieur; Ingles, John; James; **Japp, Inspector James**; Kent, Captain; Laon, Félix; **Li Chang Yen**; Martin, Miss; Mayerling, Mr.; Meadows, Inspector; **Monro, Flossie**; **Olivier, Madame**; Palmer, Mabel; Paynter, Gerald; Paynter, Mr.; **Pearson, Mrs.**; **Poirot, Achille**; **Poirot, Hercule**; Quentin, Dr.; Ridgeway, Dr.; **Rossakoff, Countess Vera**; **Ryland, Abe**; **Savaronoff, Dmitri**; St. Maur, John; Templeton, Mr. and Mrs.; Treves, Dr.; Whalley, Jonathan; Wilson, Gilmour

See also: *Agatha Christie's Poirot*; *Disappearance of Agatha Christie*; *Hercule Poirot* (Mutual radio series); *Partners in Crime* (story collection)

The Big Four (story collection; alternative title: "The Man Who Was Number Four"). See *The Big Four* (novel)

"The Bird with the Broken Wing" (story)

In the Harley Quin story "The Bird with the Broken Wing," Mr. Satterthwaite is alerted to tragedy via a Ouija board. Watching young people play at table-turning, he hears them read out incomprehensible messages, "Q-U-I-N" and "L-A-I-D-E-L-L" (*MMQ* 240). He promptly rushes to accept an invitation that he had previously declined, to a house called Laidell, where he learns of a forthcoming engagement. He meets the sad and ethereal Mabelle Annesley, whom he likens privately to a bird with a broken wing. She tells him about the elusiveness of happiness and her sighting of a man, whom Satterthwaite recognizes as Mr. Quin, in the woods.

Mabelle is found dead, presumably a suicide, but it soon proves to be murder. Two men who were in love with her are accused of killing her or at least being responsible, but Satterthwaite proves that a quiet man without an obvious motive strangled her with a ukulele string. Satterthwaite meets Quin on the train back and regrets that he had not prevented Mabelle's death. However, Quin points out that Satterthwaite saved the lives of the two young men. He then disappears, leaving a blue stone bird in his wake.

This story is the closest that Christie comes to glamorizing death, as she presents unhappiness as a potentially worse fate for Mabelle. The murderer is, like Satterthwaite, not the kind of man who is easily noticed. The men are different because Satterthwaite protects and celebrates life in others rather than destroying it and trying to be noticed.

No magazine publication of "The Bird with the Broken Wing" prior to 30 September 1951, when it appeared in *Truth*, has been traced. It is possible that Christie did not submit this intensely personal story, with potential suicidal ideation, for magazine publication for private reasons. However, she included it in *The Mysterious Mr. Quin* (1930), and it has subsequently appeared in U.S. magazines and various anthologies.

Characters: Annesley, Gerard; Annesley, Mabel; Graham, Mrs.; Graham, Roger; Keeley, David; Keeley, Madge; **Quin, Harley**; **Satterthwaite, Mr.**; **Winkfield, Inspector**.

See also: *The Mysterious Mr. Quin*; *The Sittaford Mystery*; *13 for Luck!*

Black Coffee (film). See **Twickenham Studios Films**

Black Coffee (play and novel; alternative title: *After Dinner*)

The only full-length play by Christie to feature Hercule Poirot, *Black Coffee* has been described by even ardent Christie apologists as "clichéd and unoriginal" (Curran, "Black Coffee" 41). It is a three-act play in which well-known physicist Sir Claud Amory has developed a formula for an atomic bomb and suspects that a member of his household is planning to steal it. He invites Poirot and Captain Hastings to his home at Abbot's Cleve, but before they arrive, the formula vanishes. He assembles the houseguests and tells them no questions will be asked if the formula is returned immediately. He promptly collapses, and Poirot arrives on the scene to pronounce him dead.

Among the suspects are Richard Amory, Sir Claud's unsatisfactory son; Lucia Amory, Richard's "half–Italian" wife; Sir Claud's "fussy but kind" sister (*BC* 8); their thoroughly modern niece, Barbara; Amory's forgettable secretary, Edward Raynor;

the "suave" and flamboyant Dr. Carelli (17), and the staid butler Tredwell. Poirot solves the case with the help of Hastings and Inspector Japp.

The play was first staged for two weeks at the Embassy Theatre in London. Francis L. Sullivan played Poirot, and critics compared him favorably to Charles Laughton, who had taken the role in *Alibi*, Michael Morton's 1928 adaptation of *The Murder of Roger Ackroyd*. Christie, however, was not impressed that her diminutive detective was being played by a man she described as "broad, thick, and about 6 feet 2 inches tall" (qtd. in Osborne 84). John Boxer played Captain Hastings, and Donald Wolfit was featured as Dr. Carelli. Christie was not around to see the production in London or indeed to approve the change in title from *After Dinner* to *Black Coffee*, which she only learned about by reading the *Sunday Times*. However, she had been involved in rehearsals, and her sister attended the opening night. Christie singled out for especial praise Joyce Bland, who played Lucia, notwithstanding an opening-night catastrophe in which Bland's character pronounced that a door would not open only to have it fly open (Green 89).

After the two-week tryout in December 1930, the script was heavily rewritten for a West End run in April 1931 at St. Martin's Theatre (now famously home to *The Mousetrap*). Efforts to modernize the script included changing the insult "Victorian" to "prewar" and including jokes about contemporary commercial brands, as well as removing a hint of romance for Poirot from the final scene. Sullivan continued as Poirot, but other cast members were changed.

There is some uncertainty around when *Black Coffee* was written and when it is set. Traditional wisdom has been that Christie wrote it, in the words of her grandson, out of "dissatisfaction with *Alibi*" (Prichard i). Christie herself claimed in 1972 that this was her "very first" play, written "in about 1927" (Christie, Introduction, *The Mousetrap Man* 7), although, as Julius Green has shown, she had written several plays before *Black Coffee*. John Curran has made a convincing case for the play

having been written "a few years after the war," "shortly after [*The Mysterious Affair at Styles* (1920)] was published," and probably in 1922 ("Black Coffee" 42). It is well-known that Christie reused ideas from unsuccessful or low-profile efforts and it is notable that *The Secret of Chimneys* (1925) features both a secret formula and a butler called Tredwell. Christie may well have taken up these ideas from the typescript then known as *After Dinner* when writing this light, contract-fulfilling thriller. Certainly, Christie herself described the play as clichéd and admits in her autobiography that she had lengthy trouble in having it staged. She also described it in correspondence at the time as "an aged play of mine" (qtd. in Green 87), so it is likely indeed that the 1930 version was at best a rewrite of a years old manuscript.

When Charles Osborne, an actor and Christie biographer, turned *Black Coffee* into a novel in the 1990s, he took the intriguing step of setting it in May 1934 and referencing *The Big Four* (1924/1927) as the "last case" of Poirot and Hastings (Christie and Osborne 4), although the pair also appear in *Peril at End House* (1932). Since the bulk of Osborne's novelization is a straightforward script-to-prose translation of the play, the temporal shift fails to clear up any of the confusions over timing that appear in the original: namely, there are several references, as Curran highlights, to the immediate aftermath of World War I that would have seemed slightly old-fashioned even in 1930. Osborne's novelization, heavily marketed as "The New Hercule Poirot Novel," was the first of three (followed by *The Unexpected Guest* and *Spider's Web*). It was first published in Finnish translation in 1997 before appearing in English in 1998.

Commonly misrepresented as the only Poirot play, *Black Coffee* is frequently staged around the world by professional and amateur companies. It has been filmed twice. The first time, in 1931, starred matinee idol Austen Trevor, reprising his unlikely role as Poirot following the success of *Alibi* the previous year. The second film, the French *Le Coffret de Lacque* (or *The Lacquered Box*, 1932), adapted the story liberally and made little use of Christie or Poirot in its promotional materials. Neither film exists today. A German television adaptation aired in August 1973. David Suchet, who had been keen to appear in a film production of *Black Coffee* as part of the series *Agatha Christie's Poirot*, eventually played the character in a staged reading as part of the Chichester Festival in July 2012.

Characters: Amory, Barbara; Amory, Caroline; Amory, Edward; Amory, Lucia; Amory, Richard; Amory, Sir Claud; Carelli, Dr.; **Hastings, Captain Arthur**; **Japp, Inspector James**; **Poirot, Hercule**; Raynor, Edward

See also: *Black Coffee* (television adaptation); *Le Coffret de Lacque*; Osborne, Charles; Twickenham Studios Films

Black Coffee (television adaptation)

Black Coffee was the fourth and final adaptation of a Christie stage play for West German television, broadcast on 7 August 1973 and following versions of *And Then There Were None*, *Love from a Stranger*, and *Murder at the Vicarage*. Unlike the other three, it was aired under the English title. Claus Peter Witt, who directed, wrote the screenplay from Peter Goldbaum's translation of the 1930 play. Witt's adaptation makes several changes but does not lose the production's staginess. It also makes the decision to set action, apparently, before World War I—notable given recent suggestions from John Curran ("Black Coffee") that *Black Coffee* was originally written and set at an earlier date than usually presumed. This production starred Horst Bollmann as Hercule Poirot.

See also: *And Then There Were None, Screen Adaptations of*; *Black Coffee* (play and novel); *Love from a Stranger, Screen Adaptations of*; *Mord im Pfarrhaus*

Blacklock, Charlotte ("Lotty"), and Letitia ("Letty")

Charlotte and Letitia Blacklock are sisters in *A Murder Is Announced*. Between the world wars, Letitia ("Letty") was secretary to a millionaire, who died, and Charlotte ("Lotty") developed a problem with her thyroid and became a recluse. After the war, Lotty was said to have died of her goiter, and Letty moved to Chipping Cleghorn.

However, Miss Marple reveals that it was Letty who died (of tuberculosis), and Lotty, who recovered, is living as her sister. This is the motive for the murders: to prevent people from recognizing her so that, in time, she can inherit the money that would have passed to Letty. In this novel, which consciously engages with ideas about rebuilding and reinventing oneself after war, Letty is an unlikely villain or imposter because she is a handsome, late-middle-aged, and likable woman, unlike some of the young, mysterious, and politically opinionated people around her.

Blair, Suzanne

In *The Man in the Brown Suit*, Suzanne Blair becomes a friend and traveling companion of the narrator, Anne Beddingfeld. Mrs. Blair is a brash, sometimes tactless, American tourist; the first of many such characters created by Christie. She indulges in the latest fashions—in this case (in 1924), psychoanalysis.

Blake, Basil

Basil Blake is a young bohemian filmmaker who enjoys outraging the locals with his outré ways in *The Body in the Library*. He is framed for murder at one point but manages to temporarily avert suspicion. His antisocial tendencies are largely performative; he is in fact respectably married to Dinah Lee, and the threat of arrest scares him into conventionality.

Blake, Dinah. See **Lee, Dinah**

Blake, Hon. Elvira

The 19-year-old daughter of Lady Bess Sedgwick and Lord Coniston, Elvira Blake uses cultural ideas about girls being ditzy to camouflage an extraordinarily cold murder plot in *At Bertram's Hotel*. She kills to protect her inheritance, although it actually was not endangered. She understands the letter but not the spirit of estate law, showing that analytical intelligence and worldly intelligence are distinct.

Blake, Meredith, and Phillip

Meredith and Phillip Blake are brothers in *Five Little Pigs* who, in the 16 years since they were young men at the scene of Amyas Crale's murder, have gone in different directions. Phillip is a self-assured stockbroker (as in the rhyme, he "went to market"), whereas Meredith is a sensitive, semi-reclusive herbalist (he "stayed at home"). However, they still live together.

Blanche, Angèle

Angèle Blanche is a French teacher at Meadowbank in *Cat Among the Pigeons*. A malicious and temperamental woman, she also is a blackmailer who is murdered by one of her victims. She turns out not to be Angèle Blanche at all; the real Angèle died shortly before joining the school, and her sister assumed her identity.

Bland, Detective Inspector

Thorough and unprepossessing, Detective Inspector Bland investigates the murders in *Dead Man's Folly* and its source novella, "Hercule Poirot and the Greenshore Folly."

Bland, Josiah, and Valerie

Josiah Bland is a builder who lives with his wife, Valerie, on Wilbraham Crescent in *The Clocks*. Mrs. Bland turns out to be deeply involved in espionage, and the couple is responsible for the murders in this book. Their everyday life as perfectly ordinary citizens—typified by their adopted surname—is effective cover for their criminal activities.

Bleak House (screenplay)

Bleak House (1853), an early mystery novel and a satire on London's emerging criminal justice system, was Christie's favorite work by Charles Dickens. In 1962, MGM, which was producing a series of Miss Marple films starring Margaret Rutherford, asked Christie to write a screenplay based on the book. This was Christie's second screenplay after *Spider's Web* (written in 1956)—neither was filmed. Agatha Christie Ltd. was paid £10,000 for Christie's efforts, and her agent Edmund Cork wanted to ask for an extra £5,000, but this was vetoed by her daughter, Rosalind, for reasons that are not clear (L. Thompson 437).

Christie had strong ambitions for her script, which involved emphasizing "a thriller or detective streak" that she considered underrepresented in adaptations of Dickens's work, and paring down the plot and characters to do without "two thirds of the book [and] those people or incidents which, delightful in themselves, might just as well have figured in any other of Dickens works" (Morgan 331). The draft sent by Christie to MGM, beginning and ending with swirling London fog, was 270 pages and estimated to run four hours. A cutting process described by biographer Janet Morgan as "ruthless" ensued (332), and ultimately the project was abandoned.

See also **MGM Films**

Blenkensop, Mrs.

A false identity assumed by Tuppence Beresford in *N or M?*, Mrs. Blenkensop is an eccentric character, bucking the trend of making a cover as inconspicuous as possible. Mrs. Blenkensop is referred to fondly in *By the Pricking of My Thumbs* and *Postern of Fate*.

Bletchley, Major

Major Bletchley is a tiresome old military man in *N or M?* This character was the cause of a real-life investigation of Christie by MI5, because the name implied some secret knowledge about Bletchley Park. Christie later confirmed that she had chosen the name because she thought the town of Bletchley was boring (Smith 32).

Bligh, Nellie

This character's real name is "something like Gertrude or Geraldine" Bligh, but she is generally referred to as Nellie in *By the Pricking of My Thumbs* (102). Although the reason is not explained, it evokes the home-wrecker Nelly Bly in the American song "Frankie and Johnny." This Miss Bligh, however, is no such thing: involved in community works, she helps at the church.

"Blindman's Buff" (story; alternative title: **"Blind Man's Buff"**). See *Partners in Crime* (story collection)

Blood Will Tell. See *Mrs. McGinty's Dead*

"The Bloodstained Pavement" (story; alternative titles: **"The Blood-Stained Pavement"**; **"Drip! Drip!"**; **"Miss Marple and the Wicked World"**). See *The Thirteen Problems*

Blore, William

The closest source of comic relief in *And Then There Were None*, William Blore is an unsavory private detective based in Plymouth. He tries to join the party on Soldier Island as "Mr. Davies" from South Africa but fools no one. A corrupt former policeman, he is being punished on the island for fabricating evidence against an innocent suspect who died in prison. Blore is lazy and stupid, and as tension escalates and most characters just try to survive, it is Blore who becomes obsessed with getting enough food.

"The Blue Geranium." See *The Thirteen Problems*

Blunt, Gerda. See **Montressor, Helen**

Blunt, Martin Alistair

Martin Alistair Blunt is a worldrenowned banker in *One, Two, Buckle My Shoe*, who is considered a vital force in the development of western capitalism. He also turns out to be the murderer, killing to avoid revelation of the details of his bigamous, careerist marriage. He tries to justify his actions as being for the greater good and suggests that his life is more important than those of his victims—something with which Hercule Poirot disagrees robustly.

"Blunt's Brilliant Detectives" (alternative titles: "A Fairy in the Flat"; "The Affair of the Pink Pearl"; "Publicity"). See *Partners in Crime* (short story collection)

Bob

Bob is a wire-haired terrier in *Dumb Witness* and "The Incident of the Dog's Ball," on which the novel is based. He is a cheerful character who gets on well with Captain Hastings.

Bodlicott, Isaac ("Old Isaac")

Isaac Bodlicott is a gardener and the self-proclaimed oldest man in Market Basing in *Postern of Fate*. Isaac, like Mr. Sampson in *The Mirror Crack'd from Side to Side*, has a higher claimed age than is generally believed. Nonetheless, he is killed for the knowledge he may or may not have acquired over the years.

The Body in the Library (novel)

The idea of a "body in the library" was a cliché long before Christie published a novel by that name in 1942. In 1929, Dorothy L. Sayers had a character, self-constructed as a natural victim, declare, "Me for the corpse in the library" (*Strong Poison* 6), and Christie herself had Ariadne Oliver identified as "the one who wrote *The Body in the Library*" in 1936's *Cards on the Table* (*COT* 12). Christie wrote *The Body in the Library*, her shortest novel, to pillory "clichés belonging to certain types of fiction" (Foreword, *Body in the Library* 5). This is, in short, a comic novel, although it also stands up as a mystery.

Miss Marple appears in her second full-length outing, although she is by now an established character who is "very good at murders" (*BIL* 13), as she has previously appeared in several short stories and *The Murder at the Vicarage*. Her friend, Dolly Bantry, calls on her when the body of a stranger—a tacky young blonde—is discovered in the library of Gossington Hall in St. Mary Mead. Miss Marple travels with Mrs. Bantry to the seaside resort of Danemouth (i.e., Torquay) and meets the Jeffersons, a family connected with the missing dancer Ruby Keene. Ruby's cousin identifies her as the victim. After a missing schoolgirl is found murdered, Miss Marple identifies the killers and clears up a case of mistaken identity. To confuse the time of death, the killers have murdered a schoolgirl and dressed her as Ruby, posing her in the library.

The Body in the Library revels in its artifice. The body is extraordinarily artificial, partly because it is not who it claims to be and partly in its façade constructed by make-up, peroxide, sequins, and show business. There are also more references than usual to crime fiction and things that "only happen … in books" (12), and the book even has Christie name-checking herself for the first and only time. An irritating child who impedes the police boasts that he has "got autographs from Dorothy Sayers, Agatha Christie and [John] Dickson Carr" (53). Then there is the question of forensic science. As P.D. James has pointed out, there is no way the police would confuse dyed hair on a girl's corpse with the natural blondness of a young woman or fail to notice that the victim had bitten her fingernails. Nor, for that matter, would Josie's word be sufficient for an identification, even in 1942. However, James concedes, "we are in Christie Land. We're not dealing with reality. We're dealing with a different form of reality" (qtd. in L. Thompson 385). This "different form of reality" is deliberately celebrated in the novel.

Christie wrote *The Body in the Library* at the same time as *N or M?* Both are set in seaside resorts, but they could not be more different: the former is a parody, and the latter is a wartime thriller. However, her notebooks show that sometimes the distinct works became mixed up: she sketched a sequence for the Miss Marple novel involving Milly Sprott, a rather central character in *N or M?*

The book was published first in February 1942 by Dodd, Mead in the United States, with the U.K. edition from Collins following three months later. It had been serialized in seven parts the previous year in the *Saturday Evening Post*. Television adaptations, both set in the 1950s, have opened both British Miss Marple series: one with Joan Hickson for the BBC aired in 1984, and one with Geraldine McEwan for ITV aired in 2004. BBC Radio 4 aired a 90-minute adaptation, starring June Whitfield, in 1999, and a Russian version appeared as part of *Teatr u mikrofona* in the 1990s. A Paul Lamond jigsaw inspired by the book appeared in 2001. The novel has also spawned an episode of *Les Petits Meurtres d'Agatha Christie,* broadcast in French 2011 and one, in Korean, of *Miseu Ma: Boksooui Yeoshin,* broadcast in 2018.

Characters: Badger, Mr. and Mrs.; **Bantry, Colonel Arthur, and Dolly**; Biggs, Albert; Blake, **Basil**; Blake, Selina; Bond, Tommy; **Briggs**; **Carmody, Michael and Peter;** Chetty, Edie and Mrs.; **Clara**; **Clement, David, and Leonard Jr.**; **Clement, Griselda**; **Clement, Rev. Leonard**; **Clithering, Sir Henry**; **Gaskell, Mark, and Rosamund**; Gregg, Constable; Harper, Superintendent; **Hartnell, Amanda;** Haydock, Dr.; Henniker, **Beatrice**; Janet; **Jefferson, Adelaide, and Frank; Jefferson, Conway**; Jefferson, Margaret; **Keene, Ruby; Lee, Dinah**; Lorrimer; **Marple, Jane**; Martin, Mrs.; McLean, Hugo; **Melchett, Colonel**; Metcalf, Dr.; Muswell; **Palk, Constable**; Prestcott, Mr.; Price, Mary; **Price-Ridley, Martha;** Reeves, Major and Mrs.; **Reeves, Pamela**; Ridgeway, Lilian; **Slack, Inspector**; Small, Florence; **Starr, Raymond;** Turner, Josephine ("Josie"); West, Raymond; Wetherby, Caroline

See also: *Agatha Christie's Marple*; **Forewords to Penguin Books; Games;** *Miss Marple* (radio series); *Miss Marple* (television series); *Ms Ma, Nemesis*; **Russian Radio Adaptations; Theatricality**

"The Book of Queer Women." See *What We Did in the Great War*

The Boomerang Clue. See *Why Didn't They Ask Evans?*

Bosner, Frederick, and William

Frederick and William Bosner are mysterious characters in *Murder in Mesopotamia*. Frederick Bosner was Louise Leidner's first husband, married during World War I and presumed dead after he was revealed to be a spy in the pay of the German government. Louise fears that he has returned from the dead to exact revenge after her marriage to Eric Leidner. Others fear that Frederick's brother, William Bosner, is on the dig in disguise. In fact, Poirot reveals, Frederick Bosner and Eric Leidner are one and the same.

Bourget, Louise

Louise Bourget is the morose and resentful French maid of Linnet Doyle in *Death on the Nile*. In the play *Murder on the Nile*, she is more flirtatious. In both versions, she tries to blackmail the murderer and ends up dead herself.

Bourne, Ursula

Ursula Bourne is a parlor-maid critiqued for her delusions of grandeur in *The Murder of Roger Ackroyd*. She turns out to be secretly married to Roger Ackroyd's stepson, Ralph Paton. Actually a respectable woman of aristocratic stock, she is working in domestic service to secure a living. In this, she represents a stark contrast to Flora Ackroyd, Ackroyd's prim and proper niece, who has resorted to petty theft.

Boyd Carrington, Sir William

Sir William Boyd Carrington is a middle-aged bore in *Curtain*. Formerly the governor of an Indian province, he is well-known as a big game hunter and represents the traditional British *pukka sahib*. Captain Hastings thinks he is marvelous and asks Poirot to let him take Boyd Carrington into his confidence about the investigation, but Poirot refuses vehemently. Poirot thinks Boyd Carrington is tiresome and points out that he repeats anecdotes he has been told as if they had happened to him.

Boyle, Mrs.

Mrs. Boyle is an unwholesome battle-axe in *The Mousetrap* and "Three Blind Mice," whose dialogue reveals a vital clue. When she tells Sergeant Trotter that he is "too young" to be a sergeant (*TMT* 314), she is ignored—the remark is taken as evidence of her fussy, judgmental conservatism. However, she is right: the young man is not who he claims to be. The name, sounding like "boil," is a joke, suggesting that she is an irritant.

Boynton, Carol

Carol Boynton is Mrs. Boynton's stepdaughter who eventually marries lawyer Jefferson Cope in *Appointment with Death*. Nervous and oppressed, she blossoms once Mrs. Boynton has died.

Boynton, Elmer

Elmer Boynton is the deceased husband of Mrs. Boynton, whom she is suspected of having killed, in *Appointment with Death*. "Elmer," a distinctly American Christian name, is one never given by Christie to major characters, but she often used it in references to absent Americans such as Elmer Robson in *And Then There Were None*.

Boynton, Genevra ("Jinny")

The only biological child of Mrs. Boynton in *Appointment with Death*, Jinny Boynton has problems reacting to social situations. She also has a great deal of rage and, for a time, it appears that, because of the abuse she has suffered, she may become one day as monstrous as her mother. However, by the end of the novel, she has been saved—in large part by her mother's death and Sarah King's marriage into the family—and channeled her extreme emotions into acting,

giving an acclaimed turn as Ophelia in *Hamlet*.

Boynton, Lennox, and Nadine

In *Appointment with Death*, the monstrous Mrs. Boynton exerts power over her stepson, Lennox, by pressuring him to marry the weak-willed Nadine and live under Mrs. Boynton's roof. However, Nadine is more spirited than she appears and tries a variety of methods to convince Lennox to move out of the family home.

Boynton, Mrs.

Mrs. Boynton is the grotesque matriarch of the Boynton family in *Appointment with Death* who sits, Buddha-like, beneath the cliffs of Petra, where she is killed. A former prison warden, she is not quite human. Poirot describes her as "[a] human creature born with an immense ambition, with a yearning to dominate and to impress her personality on others" (*AWD* 247). The expression *human creature* is used at three points in connection with her.

Boynton, Raymond ("Ray")

Speaker of the striking opening line in *Appointment with Death*, Raymond Boynton hates his stepmother and wants her dead after living under her coercive control.

Bradbury-Scott, Anthea, and Clotilde

The three Bradbury-Scott sisters (Anthea Bradbury-Scott, Clotilde Bradbury-Scott, and Lavinia Glynne) are compared to Macbeth's witches in *Nemesis*. Anthea, the youngest of the sisters, is thin and vague. Lavinia is described as plain. Clotilde, the older sister, is compared to Clytemnestra for the myth. She is later revealed to have murdered her young ward, Verity Hunt, with whom she was in love. She is in this sense an equivalent character to Dr. James Kennedy in *Sleeping Murder*.

Brent, Edna. See Edna

Brent, Emily

In *And Then There Were None*, Emily Brent is a self-righteous spinster with a fanatical religiosity. Her kind of Christianity—which uses the Bible as a prop with which to assert her own righteousness—detracts from her humanity. She is the fifth of 10 to die on Soldier Island; as the guests are killed in order of culpability, she falls precisely midway. Her conscience is, she insists, completely clear: although she acknowledges that Beatrice Taylor (a servant she dismissed and humiliated) committed suicide as a result, she does not feel guilty, as she believes she acted according to God's will. However, by the time of her death, Brent is writing in her diary that Beatrice is extracting revenge, indicating a level of conscience as the environment forces her to examine her guilt.

And Then There Were None is the most filmed of Christie's novels, and Brent has presented a great challenge to filmmakers, who tend to be allergic to older women—especially those with good lines, as she inevitably has. Therefore, this is the character most commonly changed for the screen. For example, in Harry Alan Towers' three films (1965, 1974, and 1989), the equivalent character (played by Daliah Lavi, Stéphane Audran, and Brenda Vaccaro, respectively) is a social-climbing actress. In the last of these, she is an alcoholic lesbian—as unlike Emily Brent as it is possible to be.

Brent, Gladys. See **Gladys**

Brent, Lady Eileen ("Bundle")

Nicknamed "Bundle" because she is a bundle of energy, Lady Eileen Brent appears in *The Secret of Chimneys* as a Bright Young Thing, part of the Chimneys backdrop. She comes into her own as the star of *The Seven Dials Mystery*, where she is hurled headfirst into a murder mystery. She ends up romantically linked to Bill Eversleigh.

Brent, Sir Clement

The ninth Marquis of Caterham, Sir Clement Brent is the father of Bundle Brent in *The Secret of Chimneys* and *The Seven Dials Mystery*. An old-fashioned, largely disinterested but indulgent figure, he helps set the scene of Bundle's privileged, orthodox, but human background.

Brewis, Amanda

The observant secretary to Sir George Stubbs, Amanda Brewis is in love with her employer in *Dead Man's Folly*. She plays a reduced role in "Hercule Poirot and the Greenshore Folly," the novel's basis.

Brewster, Emily

Emily Brewster is a manly, stentorian woman in *Evil Under the Sun*, who values physical fitness and faintly terrifies the other tourists.

Brewster, Lola

Lola Brewster is a fading Hollywood actress and rival to Marina Gregg in *The Mirror Crack'd from Side to Side*; their rivalry extends to marrying the same man. This character tends to be expanded in adaptations, presumably for the glamour factor, although her role in the story and in showbiz tends to change each time.

Briggs

Briggs is a jobbing gardener in St. Mary Mead, mentioned in *The Body in the Library* and *The Mirror Crack'd from Side to Side*, and also appears as the gardener at Meadowbank School in *Cat Among the Pigeons*. He tires of the younger generation of gardeners that "[d]on't like to get their hands soiled with a bit of honest earth" (CAP 105).

Bright Young Things

The term *Bright Young Things* referred to hedonistic young aristocrats and socialites who dominated England's upper set in the 1920s. Prominent Bright Young Things include the Mitford sisters; Stephen Tennant; Cecil Beaton, whose photographs famously documented the set; and Evelyn Waugh, whose biting satire *Vile Bodies* was filmed in 2003 as *Bright Young Things*. As Alison Maloney points out, citing F. Scott Fitzgerald's *The Great Gatsby* as a portrayal of Bright Young Things in the United States, the hedonism of this class and time was a reaction to the devastation of World War I. The participants, of course, had not been active in the war.

In many ways, the Bright Young Things were heirs to the hedonists of the gay 1890s—although they would have rejected this association. The aim was usually to shock—with short skirts, shorter hair, and smoking in public for women, and ambiguous gender expressions and large quantities of alcohol and drugs for men. The Bright Young Things loudly pursued pleasure, with pranks, fancy dress, and overt sexuality calculated to shock in a period that saw the rise of modernism, expressionism, Art Deco, and the mantra "Make It New."

Although Christie was about 10 years too old to be a part of this set, she wrote about Bright Young Things with indulgence. There is a sense of the aspirational in the presentation of Lady Eileen "Bundle" Brent and her many nicknamed friends in *The Secret of Chimneys* and *The Seven Dials Mystery*, both written in the mid–1920s. Although older characters despair of their antics or try to explain them away, they are generally shown to be resourceful and are rewarded—normally with money and position—for their efforts. Christie takes an uncommonly nuanced approach for a middlebrow writer in the 1920s, showing Bright Young Things as proactive, energetic figures who make good detectives rather than their typical roles of layabouts and dissolutes.

Things were already changing by 1930, when Christie adapted *The Secret of Chimneys* as a play. To this end, Bundle Brent is given less stage time than Virginia Revell, a more timeless anti-heroine, whose evolution from chasing money to settling down is more conventional. By 1932, the publication year of *Peril at End House*, Christie was presenting cocaine addiction as a serious and debilitating phenomenon. There had been references to "dope," drug parties, and wild orgies in *Partners in Crime* and *The Seven Dials Mystery*, but these were tangential, not indulged by the smart set at the heart of the books. Similarly, *Why Didn't They Ask Evans?* gives prominence to morphine addiction, but this is completely divorced from the youthful hijinks of Lady Frances Derwent and Bobby Jones.

Bright Young Things lose their centrality in the 1930s books. They become isolated, dissolute characters, like Ronald Marsh in *Lord Edgware Dies* (1933). In 1939, Christie published *And Then There Were None*, in which Anthony Marston, a charming, irresponsible, and stupid man who belongs to this set, is the first to die. He was Christie's final Bright Young Thing, although Tommy and Tuppence, often imagined in this category, were to age throughout the decades.

See also: **Beresford, Prudence ("Tuppence"); Beresford, Thomas ("Tommy");** Class; *The Secret of Chimneys* (novel); *The Seven Dials Mystery* (novel)

Bristow, Frank

Frank Bristow is an up-and-coming artist from humble stock but possessing genius, who uses his art to convey messages that he is too afraid to explain in "The Dead Harlequin."

British Empire Exhibition. See *The Grand Tour*

Broad, Nancy, and Nora

In *Nemesis*, Nora Broad was a young woman living with her mother, Nancy, 16 years in the past, when she went missing. Because of her low social position and reputation for serial boyfriends, her disappearance was less thoroughly investigated than that of the virginal Verity Hunt, and ultimately her corpse was identified as Verity's. Miss Marple's mission to find justice for Verity and to clear the name of the man accused of killing her is equally a mission to find peace for Nora and her mother.

Brown, Laurence

An ineffectual tutor to Eustace and Josephine Leonides in *Crooked House*, Laurence Brown was employed by Aristide Leonides, the family patriarch, less for his tutorship than to encourage a kind of affair with Aristide's young wife, Brenda. The idea is that this would be "[a] beautiful soulful friendship tinged with melancholy" rather than a full-throttle affair (*CH* 62). Brown was a conscientious objector during World War II and is a nonsmoker, causing many characters to view him as less than a man.

Browne, Anthony ("Tony")

Anthony or Tony is a very common name in Christie's works for attractive young men. A charmer with Spanish ancestry and a mysterious past, Tony Brown becomes one of the heroes of *Sparkling Cyanide*. He has a complicated past, something atypical for Christie heroes, in that he has been in prison. He is initially reluctant to work with Colonel Race, who might recognize him as convict Tony Morelli. However, all is well when he reveals that he is a British agent, who went by the name of Morelli when working undercover.

Brun, Genevieve

Genevieve Brun is a French governess

in *The Secret of Chimneys* who appears to play no major role but turns out to be an imposter. In reality, she is Angèle Mory, or Queen Veraga of Herzoslovakia, on the run from the Comrades of the Red Hand. She has faked her own death and kidnapped the governess to steal her identity. This reflects the novel's context, within a decade of European revolutions and World War I, with aristocrats and nobility forced to go underground and/or assume civilian roles. More than this, however, she is a former gangster with the Red Hand, who murdered Prince Michael of Herzoslovakia to gain the crown.

Buckley, Magdala ("Maggie"), and Magdala ("Nick")

In *Peril at End House*, Magdala is a common name in the Buckley family, and cousins Nick and Maggie share this name. This enables Nick to claim that documents addressed to her cousin were actually addressed to her. When Maggie is shot, it is assumed that Nick was the intended target. However, the idea that someone is trying to kill Nick is a concoction. A bright young thing on the edge of a hard-living crowd, Nick only ever seems able to live vicariously: she copies her style and slang from Freddie Rice and even claims that her cousin's romance and inheritance are hers.

Bulstrode, Honoria

The outgoing headmistress of Meadowbank School in *Cat Among the Pigeons*, Honoria Bulstrode is used to making tough, unpopular decisions, and the best interests of the school are her driving force. Ten years later, in *Hallowe'en Party*, Miss Emlyn, headmistress of The Elms, mentions Miss Bulstrode as an acquaintance.

Bunner, Dora ("Bunny")

In *A Murder Is Announced*, Dora "Bunny" Bunter is Miss Blacklock's oldest friend and "the only link with the past" (174), making her death, as the second victim, particularly striking. It is all the more so when Miss Marple reveals that Miss Blacklock killed her for this reason. Although Bunny has episodes of insight, she is growing old and forgetful, and has been letting slip secrets she has been keeping about her friend's true identity. The act of killing Bunny is a metaphor for painfully cutting ties with the past in the process of reinvention.

The Burden (novel)

The final "straight" novel under Christie's Mary Westmacott pseudonym, *The Burden* deals with sisterly love and the tensions that accompany it. In 1929, when baby Shirley is christened, 10-year-old Laura Franklin overhears her parents lamenting the death of their "high-spirited" son Charles and wishing that Laura had died instead (401). The complicated emotions this engenders translate into a concentrated hatred of Shirley. Shortly later, Laura saves her baby sister from a house fire and becomes extremely protective. In part 2, set in 1946, Laura has become a smothering guardian for her younger sister, especially following their parents' deaths: she is behaving like "[a] heavy Victorian father rather than a sister" (458). This has ultimately led to her failing to achieve any life of her own and her sister hastily marrying the unsuitable Henry Glyn-Edwards in a failed attempt to get away.

Parts 3 and 4 are set 10 years later in 1956. Religious evangelist Llewellyn Knox discovers that Shirley, now remarried, is still unhappy. Trying to become a perfect, caring wife, she has been driven to drink and ultimately suicide. Knox tells Laura about Shirley's death, and Laura confesses to having murdered Henry to protect Shirley 10 years ago. The novel ends with Laura accepting the burden of being loved by, as well as loving, Knox.

The Burden makes several attempts to stay up-to-date with references to psychology—for instance, Knox wonders at one point "if he had an Oedipus complex," for no reason other than he attended a lecture on the subject (534). There is also a persistent strain throughout the novel's 27-year span of societal expectations constraining women. Henry asserts, "What's a wife for, if you can't let loose on her in times of trouble?" (492), and makes sweeping generalizations about "all women" (487). Shirley is so constrained by her life that she invents "fantasies" of "escape" (512) and ultimately kills herself. The gossipy confidant Mr.

Baldock frequently advises Laura to live her own life but on certain terms:

> Why don't you paint your lips pillar-box red and varnish your nails to match? … they're a symbol, a sign that you're in the market and ready to play Nature's game. A kind of mating call, that's what they are. Now look here, Laura, you're not everybody's fancy.… You've got to remember that you're a woman, and play the part of a woman and look about for your man [446–47].

Laura responds that she will always be "plain" and will likely "never marry," an attitude dismissed as "[d]efeatism" (447). Merja Makinen has described the novel's "key focus" as "the idea that we should never choose impose our wishes on other women, since everyone is an unknowable stranger, and that the height of love is to stand back and refuse to interfere" (forthcoming). This is one of the key burdens of sisterly love in the novel; another burden is constructions of gender roles, which spread from outside to within the family.

The *Times Literary Supplement* review critiqued the novel as a "staunchly traditional woman's magazine"-style story, despite "smart modern trimmings," in which "problems are resolved when the mousey heroine puts on some lipstick" (qtd. in Sanders and Lovallo 389). Although this is a fair criticism of some of Christie's work, most notably *The Moving Finger*, it is remarkably irrelevant in a novel that itself critiques these sexist constants over a period of time. However, it fits the concept—entirely a construction of people who have not read them—that the Westmacott novels are light romantic love-stories, written as side projects.

Characters: **Baldock, Mr.**; Ethel; Fairborough, Lady Muriel; **Franklin, Angela, and Arthur; Franklin, Charles; Franklin, Laura; Franklin, Shirley; Glyn-Edwards, Henry**; Graves, Dr.; Henson, Rev. Eustace; Horder, Mr.; **Knox, Llewelyn**; Lonsdale, Susan; Weekes, Miss; Wilding, Sir Richard.

See also **Suicide; Westmacott, Mary**

Burnaby, Major John

Major John Burnaby is an affable retired military man who is the closest friend of Captain Trevelyan and kills him in *The Sittaford Mystery*. Despite the long-lasting friendship, money is more important to Major Burnaby.

Burt, Dr. James, and Milly

The 28-year-old wife of James Burt, Milly is a victim of domestic violence and abuse, which sends her running to John Gabriel, who represents danger but also escape, in *The Rose and the Yew Tree*. Many of Christie's scoundrels are doctors called James.

Burton, Jerry, and Joanna

In *The Moving Finger*, siblings Jerry and Joanna Burton move to the sleepy village of Lymstock so that Jerry can recover from an injury sustained as a pilot. The Burtons are both conventionally good-looking and do not bear a resemblance—she is fair and pretty, whereas he is dark and handsome—leading to speculation that they are not really related. They struggle to fit into the village because of their modern city ways but find resolution through romance: Jerry shows the unworldly Megan Hunter a broader milieu, whereas Joanna settles down with the dependent Dr. Owen Griffith. Their resolution is strictly conservative in an almost parodic way.

Burton-Cox, Desmond, and Mrs.

The young, relatively undercharacterized, prospective fiancé of Celia Ravenscroft, Desmond Burton-Cox is the adopted son of the obnoxious, tactless Mrs. Burton-Cox in *Elephants Can Remember*. Although she is overly concerned with a potential streak of insanity in Celia's family line, Mrs. Burton-Cox does not seem overly worried about establishing Desmond's lineage.

Butler, Judith, and Miranda

In *Hallowe'en Party*, Miranda Butler is a young friend of one victim, Joyce Reynolds. A quiet, nymph-like girl, she is the one who witnessed a murder in the past, which Joyce then recounted as her own story. Miranda is fascinated by her own name and its mythological origins, as well as the first names of her mother, Judith, and Ariadne Oliver. Judith is an extremely conventional friend to Mrs. Oliver.

Butter in a Lordly Dish (radio play)

Written to raise funds for the Detection

Club, *Butter in a Lordly Dish* was aired on 13 January 1948, the first of six 30-minute BBC Radio plays. The other five were by Cyril Hare, Anthony Gilbert, Christianna Brand, E.C.R. Lorac, and Dorothy L. Sayers. Christie's play features well-known prosecutor Sir Luke Enderby, whose silver tongue in the courtroom is said to have sent several men to the gallows. He is particularly credited with the hanging of serial killer Henry Garfield. Sir Luke is seduced by Julia Keene, who serves him a lavish meal including precious butter (hence the title, which Sir Luke quotes) that is scarce in the immediate postwar period.

As they talk about the case, Sir Luke becomes ill and realizes that Julia has poisoned him. She is Garfield's widow. She reminds him that "butter in a lordly dish" is a biblical quotation: "Of course, I've got it," he says before he realizes: "Jael and Sisera. She's the one who brought him butter in a lordly dish and then happened [to drive] a nail through his forehead" (*MITS* 86). In a final twist, she reveals that her husband was never a killer—she killed all the victims. The play ends with her preparing to hammer a nail into Sir Luke's forehead.

Butter in a Lordly Dish is one of the few Christie works in which the perpetrator goes unpunished for the crime and is less a mystery than a twist-based thriller. It opens with an uncommonly satirical reflection on true crime journalism and sensationalism in the reporting of real crime as if it were crime fiction. The central "Blondes on the Beach" case is remembered as "a good murder" by the working-class Florrie because of its sexy details and the "really good-looking" man in the dock, as opposed to the more recent "taxi murder" that is less interesting because the murderer is "an insignificant little chap" (70).

The original broadcast was lost for many years but was recovered by archivist Sean Whyton and released as part of the BBC's *Agatha Christie: The Lost Plays* in 2015. In 2009, National Public Radio in the United States broadcast the first production since 1948, along with three other Christie scripts, in a special series, *Mystery Series Live—On the Air*. The script has been performed a few times on stage, usually as part of *Murder in the Studio*, a Christie play collection that also includes *The Yellow Iris* and *Personal Call*. That set-up started life as *Murder on Air*, performed by Bill Kenwright Ltd.'s Agatha Christie Theatre Company in 2008. A similar staged reading of these radio scripts and *Three Blind Mice* ran in 2012 and 2013 in and around Florida, as *The BBC Murders*. This, too, is occasionally revived. *Butter in a Lordly Dish* was performed in German as *Legale Tricks* on 7 January 2001.

Characters: Enderby, Lady Marion; **Enderby, Sir Luke;** Garfield, Henry; Garfield, Julia; Hayward; **Keene, Julia; Petter, Florrie;** Petter, Mrs.; Warren, Susan

See also: ***The BBC Murders;* German Radio Adaptations;** *Murder in the Studio;* **Personal Call;** *The Yellow Iris* **(radio play)**

By the Pricking of My Thumbs (novel)

The fourth Tommy and Tuppence book, *By the Pricking of My Thumbs* sees the crime-solving couple transition from middle age to old age. It contains several themes and tropes that recur in Christie's later fiction.

The Beresfords are now "an ordinary couple" (3) enjoying a quiet domestic life, their exploits in espionage a distant memory. They visit Tommy's elderly, semi-senile Aunt Ada at her nursing home, Sunny Ridge. She is, they believe a "problem" common to "nearly every family" (5):

> The names are different—Aunt Amelia, Aunt Susan, Aunt Cathy, Aunt Joan. They are varied by grandmothers, aged cousins, and even great-aunts. But they exist and present a problem in life which has to be dealt with…. Arrangements have to be made. Suitable establishments for looking after the elderly have to be inspected…. The days have past when [such women] lived on happily in the homes where they had lived for many years [6].

In this opening, Christie presents social change and the issue of care homes, reflecting her reliance on character types. Aunt Ada is a strong, cantankerous woman. While Tommy visits her, Tuppence is approached by another Sunny Ridge resident who asks her, bafflingly, "was it your poor child behind the fireplace?" (26).

When Ada dies and the other woman, Mrs. Lancaster, disappears, Tommy and Tuppence suspect something is afoot. A mysterious painting among Aunt Ada's effects, which was a gift from Mrs. Lancaster, piques their interest, and they go on a mission to find the house it depicts. The investigation leads them to a tangled family drama and a long-time serial killer in an out-of-the-way village where old traditions like local witches still survive, and older traditions like child sacrifice are practiced in secret.

Mrs. Lancaster turns out to be an infamous serial killer, known sensationally as "Killer Kate." Consumed with guilt over an abortion in her youth, she has taken to killing other children over the years to keep her own baby company and other individuals who learned the truth so she could protect herself. Believing she is cursed, she sees these acts as sacrifices and atonements, professing herself "a Killer of the Lord": "It's the Lord's will that I should murder. So that's all right" (281). Her glib justification of her conduct speaks to mental illness but also to the use and abuse of religion to justify evil acts. Mrs. Lancaster is one of Christie's most terrifying murderers, not because she is irrational but because she speaks "with gentle reasonableness" (282).

The scene with an old lady referencing a "poor child behind the fire" appears, without elaboration and apparently for atmosphere only, in *Sleeping Murder* and *The Pale Horse*. The killer's attempt to poison Tuppence with a milky drink during the dénouement would be mirrored in the final chapters of *Nemesis*, the last Miss Marple novel. Another link to the Miss Marple universe is the presence of Market Basing, Christie's go-to town near St. Mary Mead.

By the Pricking of My Thumbs was, according to its dedication, written to update readers on Tommy and Tuppence's marriage in response to several inquiries. The title comes from act 4, scene 1 of William Shakespeare's *Macbeth*, where it is spoken by witches forecasting wickedness. The book was published in the United Kingdom by Collins and Dodd, Mead in the United States in late 1968. It was selected by author-publisher-critic August Derleth as an outstanding book of 1969 (62).

It has been filmed twice: as a French comedy-thriller, *Mon Petit Doigt M'a Dit...*, in 2005 and as an episode of *Agatha Christie's Marple*, with Miss Marple inserted into the action, in 2006. The Beresfords were played by Catherine Frot and André Dussollier in the former, and Greta Scacchi and Anthony Andrews in the latter.

Characters: Amelia; Anderson, Mr.; **Batt, Albert; Batt Family; Beresford, Deborah, and Derek; Beresford, Prudence ("Tuppence"); Beresford, Thomas ("Tommy"); Bligh, Nellie**; Boscowan, Emma and William; Copleigh, George and Elizabeth ("Liz"); Eccles, James; **Fanshawe, Maria ("Ada"); Lancaster, Mrs.**; Moody, Elizabeth; Murray, Dr.; Packard, Millicent; Penn, Sir Josiah ("Josh"); **Perry, Alice, and Amos**; Smith, Ivor; **Starke, Sir Philip**

See also: *Agatha Christie's Marple*; *Bélisaire et Prudence Beresford*; **Christianity; Market Basing; Shakespeare, William**

Bylo 10 Murzynków. See *And Then There Were None*, Screen Adaptations of

"By Road or Rail." See **"Double Sin"** (story)

Cade, Anthony ("Gentleman Joe")

Anthony Cade is a 32-year-old adventurer who stars in *The Secret of Chimneys*. He is tanned and worldly with a good sense of humor and is presented as quintessentially British, although he turns out to be the heir to the throne of Herzoslovakia. Ascension to the throne cures him of socialist tendencies.

Calgary, Arthur

A geophysicist is an unlikely hero in a detective novel. In *Ordeal by Innocence*, Arthur Calgary returns to England after two years in the Arctic to learn that Jacko Argyll, a man he could have alibied, has died after he was arrested for murder. He infiltrates the dysfunctional Argyle family and is confused by their negative reaction to his efforts.

"The Call of Wings" (story)

Almost certainly written before the mid–1920s, "The Call of Wings" is a semi-supernatural short story about the uncanny. It features extravagantly wealthy hedonist Silas Hamer who, feeling but not expressing that something is missing from his life, becomes haunted by the sound of pipe music, played by a street musician who has no legs—in other words, "a battered derelict of the human race" (*HOD* 190) who has been treated much more poorly by life than him. Despite a stated refusal to "believe ... in anything I can't see, hear and touch" (190), he only finds peace when, throwing himself under a train to protect a homeless man, he lets memory of pipe music engulf him.

The story was included in the U.K. anthology *The Hound of Death and Other Stories* (1933) and in the U.S. anthology *The Golden Ball and Other Stories* (1971). Its first U.S. publication, however, was in the *Magazine of Fantasy and Science Fiction* (June 1952), the cover of which mistitles it "The Sound of Wings." The story has never been adapted for the screen or stage.

Characters: Borrow, Dick; Harmer, Silas; Seldon, Bernard.

See also: *The Hound of Death* (story collection); Music

"Calvary." See *Poems*

Cannon Group Films

Via Golan-Globus Productions and Breton Films Productions Ltd., the Cannon Group released three Christie adaptations to cinemas in the 1980s. Cannon Films was an American company in operation from 1967 to 1994 and rarely garnered strong commercial and financial returns, although among its large output in the 1980s, the Spider Man franchise was a notable success.

The first Cannon Group Christie film was *Ordeal by Innocence* (1985), directed by Desmond Davis. Based on Christie's 1958 novel, it starred Donald Sutherland and Faye Dunaway, with Christopher Plummer and Sarah Miles. The film was not a hit, and an often-cited criticism is Dave Brubeck's jazzy score, incongruous with the bleak cinematography and understated, emotional acting style. In fact, this was a last-minute addition after the film, with a more somber score by Pino Dinaggio, tested poorly with audiences in 1984. Following glossy travel movies like *Death on the Nile* (1978) and *Evil Under the Sun* (1982) from EMI, this smoky noirish thriller, featuring a nude scene, may not have found its target audience. Even a royal premiere in 1985 could not help it.

The Cannon Group tried again in 1988 and 1989, sticking to exotic period color with *Appointment with Death* and *Ten Little Indians*. The former saw Peter Ustinov return to the role of Hercule Poirot for the last time. Directed by Michael Winner, *Appointment with Death* makes a real effort to recapture the glamor of *Death on the Nile* and *Evil Under the Sun*. It was filmed on location in Israel and featured two cast members from *Murder on the Orient Express*—Lauren Bacall and John Gielgud—alongside major stars such as Carrie Fisher, Piper Laurie, Hayley Mills, and David Soul. However, this was not a point in the film's favor, as it invited comparisons with the EMI efforts and was found wanting. Despite remaining relatively faithful to the plot of the novel, the film lacks characterization and innovation, and it makes no effort to compensate for the source text's bloodlessness. Psychological abuse, a key theme of the book, is only lightly explored so in the absence of engaging action, it was a commercial and critical failure. Plans for Winner to direct another Christie movie did not materialize.

By 1989, when Harry Alan Towers' third *Ten Little Indians* film emerged, the production company was in serious financial trouble. No further Christie films were made by Cannon or another company for more than two decades.

See also: *And Then There Were None* **(1943 play);** *Appointment with Death* **(novel); EMI Film Adaptations;** *Ordeal by Innocence* **(novel); Screen Adaptations of** *And Then There Were None*

"The Capture of Cerberus" (1940)

For many years, Christie scholars puzzled over the 12th installment of *The Labours of Hercules*. Although the 1947 volume contains 12 stories, each paralleling one of Hercules's 12 labors, the original *Strand* magazine series (and subsequent American serials) contained only 11. "The Capture of Cerberus" appeared first in book form. In 2009, archivist John Curran published new material in *Agatha Christie's*

Secret Notebooks. Here, he describes archived letters that show that Christie submitted a different "The Capture of Cerberus" in 1939–40, which the magazine refused to publish. Curran's book contains the entire text of this original story, which is very unlike the 1947 version.

Unusually, and problematically, this story deals explicitly with current events, imagining Hercule Poirot's intervention in World War II. Musing on the follies of war at Lake Geneva, Poirot is reunited with his flamboyant old flame, Countess Vera Rossakoff. She tells a friend, Dr. Kaiserbach, that Poirot can "bring the dead back to life" (CC 436)—a reference to Poirot's actions in *The Big Four,* when he recovered her long-lost son.

The doctor seeks a private meeting with Poirot. He is the father of Hans Lutzmann, a young man said to have assassinated a major European fascist dictator, August Hertzlein. Hertzlein's death had been expected to precipitate peace in Europe but in fact mobilized his base, as he became a martyr. Kaiserbach tells Poirot that his son "was a Nazi through and through" and would never have killed Hertzlein (440). The direct reference to Nazis makes clear that Hertzlein is Adolf Hitler, translucently veiled.

Poirot finds Hertzlein living in a mental asylum where he is thought to be a paranoiac with a personality disorder: none of his handlers believe he is who he says he is, since "in every mental institution, there are Napoleons, Hertzleins, Julius Caesars" (449). He deduces that Hertzlein was kidnapped by his own party, and a body double was shot on stage by a stormtrooper so Hertzlein would become a martyr for fascism. This was because Hertzlein had been converted to Christianity by an evangelical monk. Poirot learned this by listening to the kind of gossip that is normally ignored. Hertzlein confirms that he is now antifascist and committed to mobilizing his base "to plan a great campaign, a campaign of peace" (447).

Poirot brings Hertzlein back into the public eye—his equivalent of Hercules conquering death—and the dictator uses his platform to convert young people with "new catchwords": "Peace," "Love," and "Brotherhood" (450). Poirot makes Rossakoff the gift of an ugly dog, Fido, which has been helpful in the investigation, and instructs her to call it "Cerberus" (451).

The publication in *Agatha Christie's Secret Notebooks,* alongside "The Incident of the Dog's Ball," occurred in a blaze of publicity. The story received its true first publication in the *Daily Mail* in the United Kingdom on 28 August 2009, introduced by A.N. Wilson and illustrated by David Young. The two "new" stories were also released as an audiobook, read by David Suchet.

Characters: Fido; **George(s)**; Golstamm; **Hertzlein, August**; **Higgs, Mr.**; Lutzmann, Hans; **Neumann, Dr.**; Poirot, Hercule; **Rossakoff, Countess Vera**; Schultz, Dr. Otto; Schwartz; Von Emmen; Weingarten, Dr.

See also: "**Capture of Cerberus**" (1947); **War**

"**The Capture of Cerberus**" (1947; alternative titles: "Hercule Poirot in Hell"; "Meet Me in Hell!"). See *The Labours of Hercules*

Carbery, Colonel. See **Carbury, Colonel**

Carbury, Colonel

A vague and disoriented British official with responsibility for the Transjordan area, Colonel Carbury calls in Hercule Poirot after the murder of Mrs. Boynton in *Appointment with Death.* Carbury, who enjoys detective fiction, is fascinated by Poirot, treating him as a living relic from a detective novel—creating a small crack in the fourth wall.

Cards on the Table (novel)

In *The ABC Murders,* Hercule Poirot describes to Captain Hastings his idea of the perfect mystery:

> "Supposing," murmured Poirot, "that four people sit down to play bridge and one, the odd man out, sits in a chair by the fire. At the end of the evening the man by the fire is found dead. One of the four, while he is dummy, has gone over and killed him, and, intent on the play of the hand, the other three have not noticed. Ah, there would be a crime for you! *Which of the four did it?*" [23–24; emphasis in original]

In the following year, 1936, Christie published her next Poirot novel, without Hastings but using this premise. In a foreword, she explains to readers that this is a fair play novel rather than one where the "least likely person" is the criminal (*COT* i). She also alludes to the passage in *ABC*, writing that *Cards on the Table* "was one of Hercule Poirot's favourite cases" but that Hastings had "considered it very dull" (i).

The victim is Mr. Shaitana, an elaborately "other," "queer," and "sinister" man who is drawn along orientalist lines (13; see Bernthal, *Queering* 96–98)—Shaitana mocks Poirot for his "*bourgeois* sensibilities" and "the limitations of the policeman mentality" (*COT* 5). He says he has his own kind of Black Museum (a famous collection of artifacts related to criminal cases). However, rather than collecting things, he collects murderers. He proposes a party, where he will invite four murderers who have escaped punishment in the past and four detectives. He does so. At the end of an uncomfortable evening, the eight guests split into two parties and play bridge in two rooms. In the room with the four murderers, Shaitana sits by the fire and, by the end of the evening, he is dead.

Poirot's fellow detective-guests are all characters who have appeared previously but not with him. Ariadne Oliver, who would become a notable Poirot sidekick, had featured in various J. Parker Pyne stories in the mid–1920s. Superintendent Battle had appeared in the two novels set at the country estate Chimneys. Colonel Race, who would go on to star with Poirot in *Death on the Nile* the next year, had been a potential romantic interest in *The Man in the Brown Suit* in 1924.

In this novel, Mrs. Oliver becomes, for the first time, an obvious self-portrait, as she glibly discusses the difficulties of writing to deadlines and formulae, the inconvenience of adherence to accuracy (with a specific story referencing a real fan letter about measurements in *Death in the Clouds*), and the frustrations of creating a larger-than-life European detective character.

The metafictional moments provided by Mrs. Oliver are not the only examples. The whole book takes note of its own artificiality, something emphasized by the running theme of gamesmanship. A card game, bridge, is central to the action and Poirot's main clues are based on the bridge scores: if a cautious man overplays his hand or a confident woman underplays hers, there is a reason.

Another key theme in the novel is colonialism. Three of the four murderers receive some form of comeuppance (two die, and one is arrested—presumably to be hanged—for killing Shaitana). However, one seems to survive the novel without an implied stain on his character. Major Despard, who shot a man on safari, gets both the girl and the last word in the novel, and even reappears with his wife, Rhoda, in *The Pale Horse* (1961).

The novel was published in the United Kingdom by Collins in 1937 and in the United States by Dodd, Mead in 1937. In a review in the *New York Times*, Isaac Anderson stated that the book "is not quite up to Agatha Christie's best work" (23). In contrast, the anonymous reviewer in the *Auckland* [NZ] *Star* considered it "one of the best she has done" (8). It was dramatized for the stage by Leslie Darbon in 1981, and a radio play was broadcast on BBC Radio 4 on 4 May 2002.

A graphic novel, adapted and illustrated by Frank Leclercq, appeared in French and English in 2010. A British television version was broadcast on ITV 1 on 19 March 2006. A French version, part of *Les Petits Meurtres d'Agatha Christie*, aired on France 2 on 3 October 2014. *Chorabali*, a Bengali film adaptation directed by Subhrajit Mitra, was released in 2016.

Characters: Astwell, Mrs.; Batt, Elsie; **Battle, Superintendent**; Benson, Mrs.; Burgess, Miss; **Craddock, Charles, and Mrs.;** Davidson, Dr.; **Dawes, Rhoda; Despard, Major John;** Emery, Dr.; Fred; Graves, Mrs.; Harper, Inspector; Hemmingway, Gerald; Lang, Dr.; L**orrimer, Mr.; Lorrimer, Mrs.; Luxmore, Mrs., and Professor; Meredith, Anne**; Meredith, Major John; O'Connor, Sergeant; **Oliver, Ariadne; Poirot, Hercule; Race, Colonel Johnny; Roberts, Dr.**

Geoffrey; Shaitana, Mr.; Turner, Constable

See also: *ABC Murders* (novel) *The*; *Agatha Christie's Poirot*; Games; *Hercule Poirot* (BBC radio series); Indian-Language Adaptations; *The Pale Horse*; *Les Petits Meurtres d'Agatha Christie*

Cards on the Table (play)

Following the modest success of *A Murder Is Announced* in 1977, Leslie Darbon dramatized the 1936 novel *Cards on the Table* for the stage. Once again, Christie's long-time producer Peter Saunders presented the play at the Vaudeville Theatre, London, where it opened on 9 December 1981.

Darbon's script calls for two sets, and the original production used a revolving set. Following Christie's lead but apparently more for the sake of tradition than for dramatic effect, Darbon removed Hercule Poirot from the story, casting one of his sidekicks, Superintendent Battle, as the main detective. This decision is artistically unfortunate because it loses the novel's symmetry: the four murderers/suspects are matched with four detectives in the book, but here it is four against two (Colonel Race is also absent). There is something twee and dramatic, at the expense of taste, about the script. For example, eccentric novelist Ariadne Oliver asks Mr. Shaitana, the future victim: "Hasn't it struck you, Mr. Shaitana, that murderers have a very nasty habit—murdering people?" (Darbon 5). The play, directed by Peter Dews, received "generally dismissive reviews," according to Charles Osborne (94). It is available for amateur performances but is rarely produced.

See also: *Cards on the Table* (novel); *A Murder Is Announced* (play)

A Caribbean Murder. See **CBS Television Adaptations**

A Caribbean Mystery (novel)

A Caribbean Mystery, the only Miss Marple novel set overseas, is still essentially a domestic mystery. Miss Marple, holidaying on the island of St. Honoré in the West Indies, enters an extended social and family drama in an exotic hotel run like a guest house, and most of the major players are British or American. Miss Marple draws several parallels to her life in St. Mary Mead, once again relying on the maxim that human nature is the same everywhere and on gossip to uncover truths.

The novel was published in 1964 while Miss Marple was reaching a larger audience than ever due to a series of MGM film adaptations that starred Margaret Rutherford. Christie, unhappy with these movies, was shortly to terminate her contract with the studio. The boisterous Miss Marple of the screen was not at all the "old pussy" of the books, and Christie's U.K. publishers Collins took the unusual step of adding to the title page:

> Featuring
> Miss Marple
> The Original Character
> As created by
>
> AGATHA CHRISTIE

Despite the promise of an exotic setting, readers are assured on the first page that they are in an essentially conservative British world. The first words are "'Talk about all this business in Kenya,' said Major Palgrave" (*ACM* 7)—a fairly good indication of the prism through which the wider world will be viewed. Moreover, this is familiar Miss Marple territory. The second paragraph reveals that "Old Miss Marple" is not listening to these "somewhat uninteresting recollections" (7). Instead, her mind is wandering, and mentally she, like the reader, is back in St. Mary Mead. She does not need to listen to Major Palgrave, because his stories follow

> a routine with which she was well acquainted. The locale varied. In the past, it had been predominantly India. Majors, Colonels, Lieutenant-Generals—and a familiar series of words: *Simla. Bearers. Tigers. Chota Hazri—Tiffin. Khitmagars*, and so on. With Major Palgrave the terms were slightly different. *Safari. Kikuyu. Elephants. Swahili*. But the pattern was essentially the same [7; emphasis in original].

The description serves three purposes: (1) presenting narrative comedy, humanizing Miss Marple; (2) presenting the idea that human nature is consistent; and (3) reassuring the reader that this novel will cover familiar ground. It will not be an edgy, new exotic mystery—the kind that a screen Miss Marple would investigate—but, essentially, a village mystery, with Palgrave playing an equivalent narrative role to Colonel Bantry in *The Body in the Library*. Indeed, the novel is so inherently unworldly that the word *Caribbean* was consistently misspelled in the first several drafts (Christie Family Archive).

A hallmark of Christie's 1960s novels is an increased focus on character exploration, often tied to plot development, and extended interior monologues for the central detectives. In *A Caribbean Mystery*, Miss Marple's thoughts are presented more baldly than previously as are those of the people around her. Miss Marple's worldly nephew, novelist Raymond West, has sent her on this holiday to shake her out of her "idyllic rural life" and to focus on "REAL LIFE" (9, emphasis in original). Miss Marple indulges him but inwardly reflects that she has acquired "a comprehensive knowledge" of the kinds of things he means from rural life, even if she does not talk about them: "Plenty of sex, natural and unnatural. Rape, incest, perversions of all kinds. (Some kinds, indeed, that even the clever young men from Oxford who wrote books didn't seem to have heard about)" (9–10).

The parentheses really encapsulate Miss Marple's point. The 1960s would prove to be a decade of protest and liberation as new identity categories and pathologies entered the public lexicon. Miss Marple indicates that she already knows about it; these things have not just been invented, even if "clever young men from Oxford" who put names to them think they have discovered them. West goes on to assure his aunt that her house will be safe while she is away because his friend is looking after it and "[h]e's very house proud. He's a queer," before breaking off, "embarrassed … but surely even dear old Aunt Jane must have heard of queers" (10). She has certainly encountered such men, even if this is the first time in her literary career the idea of "a queer" has been raised.

This moment recalls an account in A.L. Rowse's memoir, *Memories of Men and Women*, published after Christie's death, in which he recalls how he would chide Christie's husband, Max Mallowan, for staying "simply heterosexual" after "the homo side to public school" (Rowse 100). This banter, he notes, would always be out of Christie's earshot, because, as a "dear, good, Christian soul," she never even thought about sex (100). These reminiscences are about the early 1960s—the time that Christie was writing *A Caribbean Mystery*. Although Christie hated being compared to Miss Marple, this may be an example of real life influencing the character.

A Caribbean Mystery has a lightness of touch that was slowly disappearing from Christie's novels in the 1960s. This is evident in the presentation of drugs, compared to how they appear in *Third Girl* (1966). Here, as in *The Mirror Crack'd from Side to Side* (1962), there are mass-produced sleeping tablets and medications, viewed with general suspicion, and poisons that are used to infect medicines. There is also belladonna, slipped into cosmetics, to create mental instability and hallucinations in a victim. Talk of drug addiction is cast as an aside or a red herring. By the time of *Third Girl*, addiction to hard drugs, named and discussed, is simply a backdrop to the degeneracy of the young. It is no longer a secret shame, as cocaine addiction is in *Peril at End House* (1932) and *Death in the Clouds* (1935) but almost a badge of honor, and the lines between addiction and victimhood become consciously blurred as the book progresses. *A Caribbean Mystery* is breezier about the issue.

Two characters introduced in *A Caribbean Mystery* will return: Jason Rafiel, with whom Miss Marple strikes an unlikely alliance, and his secretary, Esther Walters, an understated character who does not achieve a happy ending until *Nemesis* (1971). *Nemesis* begins with Rafiel's death, and he sends Miss Marple on a mission from beyond the grave. This "[f]abulously wealthy" northern supermarket magnate (24) is not an obvious friend—or, some readers have maintained, romantic interest—for the Victorian spinster. He is coarse and pompous, far removed from the likes of Dolly Bantry. However, they function effectively as a duo—perhaps a concession to changing times, as well as notable difference to the MGM Marple, who dominates the screen, boisterously talking over her demure romantic interest, Mr. Springer.

A Caribbean Mystery has been dramatized several times, normally in series and oddly out of sequence—i.e., after *Nemesis*—perhaps because the idea of filming on location is daunting. It was first televised by CBS as *A Caribbean Murder* (22 October 1983), with Helen Hayes in the lead, and was intended to launch a series of modernized Miss Marple stories, although only one would follow. Relocated to Barbados, it was filmed as part of the BBC's *Miss Marple* (25 December 1989), starring Joan Hickson. A BBC Radio 4 dramatization starring June Whitfield aired in November 1997. ITV's *Agatha Christie Marple* featured a dramatization with Julia McKenzie on 16 June 2013. In 2016, it inspired an episode of the French series *Les Petits Meurtres d'Agatha Christie*. Another television legacy is the BBC series *Death in Paradise*, which is set in and around a fictional Caribbean town, "Honoré," a nod to the book's setting, which had also given its name to a Spanish island in Channel 4's *Black Books*.

Characters: Arden, Joe; Daventry, Mr.; de Caspearo, Señora; de Ferrari, Count; Dyson, Gail; **Dyson, Gregory (Greg), and Lucky; Elis, Big Jim**; Enrico; Fernando; **Graham, Dr.**; Hillingdon, Colonel Edward and Evelyn; **Jackson, Arthur; Johnson, Victoria; Kendal, Molly; Kendal, Tim**; Linnett, Mrs.; **Marple, Jane; Palgrave, Major**; Prescott, Canon Jeremy and Miss Joan; **Rafiel, Jason**; Robertson, Dr.; Sanderson, Mr. and Mrs.; **Walters, Esther; West, Raymond**; Western, Harry; Weston, Inspector; Wood, Georgy.

See also: *Agatha Christie's Marple*; **CBS Television Adaptations**; *Miss Marple* **(radio series)**; *Miss Marple* **(television series)**; *Nemesis*; *Les Petits Meurtres d'Agatha Christie*

Carlisle, Elinor

On trial for her aunt's murder in *Sad Cypress*, Elinor Carlisle is—as her Christian name suggests—an embattled figure, struggling against her extreme emotions: her love, hard to classify, for fiancé Roderick Welman; her hatred for Mary Gerrard; and her growing affection for Peter Lord. When Mary dies, she feels guilty for having wished and imagined her dead, but Poirot reassures her that imagining murder is not the same as committing it.

Carmichael, Sir Arthur

In "The Strange Case of Sir Arthur Carmichael," Sir Arthur Carmichael is a 23-year-old man who, despite being "pleasant," "amiable," and "thoroughly normal in every respect," has had a sudden change of personality, becoming "semi-idiotic" (165) and obsessed with the idea of a ghostly cat. It transpires that his soul has been partially decanted into the body of a cat, which has been killed.

Carmody, Michael, and Peter

In *The Body in the Library*, Michael Carmody is the deceased first husband of Adelaide Jefferson, and Peter is their annoying son, who is thrilled to be involved in a real murder and tries to help the investigation. He has autographs from famous writers such as Agatha Christie, contributing to this novel's metafiction.

Carnaby, Amy

In "The Nemean Lion," Amy Carnaby is a sympathetically presented criminal who devises a dog-napping scheme to fund her ill sister's treatment. She returns in "The Flock of Geryon" as Hercule Poirot's client, urging him to save her friend from a cult.

Carter, Mr.

In *The Secret Adversary* and the stories collected as *Partners in Crime*, Mr. Carter is an assumed name for Lord Easthampton, an agent of British Intelligence, who engages Tommy and Tuppence Beresford as unofficial secret agents for the Crown.

Cartwright, Sir Charles

Sir Charles Cartwright is an attractive, middle-aged actor in *Three Act Tragedy* who is always playing a part, both on and off stage. When he sees things he wants such as Hermione Lytton Gore, he plays the part of someone who has them. When the action of the novel begins, he is playing the part of a retired country squire; he later decides to play the part of a detective. Poirot unmasks him as the murderer, whose criminal activities have spread to disguising himself as a butler (John Ellis) so he can be in two places at once. Cartwright is, in every sense, a performer, to the extent that his murder plot includes a "dress rehearsal," killing someone who is not his target so he can test the method. Befitting Cartwright's life as an actor in both work and life, even his name is a fabrication—his real name is Charles Mugg.

Carver, Dr.

An archaeologist in "The Pearl of Price," Dr. Carver is, like many of Christie's archaeologist characters, unhealthily devoted to his field. It is not difficult to read a satirical comment on her husband's work ethic in such characters.

"A Case of Buried Treasure." See **"Strange Jest"**

"The Case of the Caretaker" (story)

This story started life as "The Case of the Caretaker's Wife" but was rewritten for publication in *The Strand* in January 1942. Archivist John Curran places the "composition date" in 1940–41 (*Making* 237). Unlike in the first draft, this version has Miss Marple outside the main action. She is bedridden with influenza when Dr. Haydock arrives with his version of a cure: a manuscript detailing a mysterious death. He asks Miss Marple to provide an explanation. She embraces the challenge and, of course, succeeds. The story contains some elements that would later reappear in *Endless Night* (1967): a "poor little rich girl" (68) who marries a poor man, reveals she has heart problems, and dies after complaining of "the new home [being] tainted and poisoned by the malevolent figure of one crazy old woman" (70)—in this case, a caretaker who curses the couple and their property. As in the novel, the husband turns out to have murdered his wife for money and out of lust for an intensely sexy other woman. The story also contains some character names—Harmon and Murgatroyd—that would reappear in *A Murder Is Announced* (1950).

There are several differences between "The Case of the Caretaker" and *Endless Night*

(detailed under ***Endless Night*** and **Curses**). A key one, however, is the presence of a detective figure, even a tangential one. Miss Marple suspects that Harry Laxton, the husband, married the wealthy Louise for her money, because he also has a romantic history with the dark, sexy Bella Edge—and "gentlemen always seem to admire the same type" (76). The presence of physical clues such as a syringe is immaterial to her deductions.

The story appeared in the U.S. anthology *Three Blind Mice* (Dodd, Mead, 1950) and in the U.K. anthology in *Miss Marple's Final Cases* (Collins, 1979). It has never been dramatized.

Characters: Brent, Miss; Edge, Bella; Edge, Mr.; Harmon, Miss; **Haydock, Dr.;** Laxton, Harry; **Laxton, Louise (Mrs. Harry)**; Laxton, Major; **Marple, Jane**; **Murgatroyd, Mrs.;** Price, Mrs.; Vane, Clarice

See also: **"The Case of the Caretaker's Wife"**; Curses; ***Endless Night*** (novel); *Miss Marple's Final Cases* (story collection); *Three Blind Mice* (story collection)

"The Case of the Caretaker's Wife" (story)

An alternative draft of what became "The Case of the Caretaker," this story was unpublished until it appeared in John Curran's *Agatha Christie's Murder in the Making* (2011), a collection of archived materials with analysis. Curran hints that "The Case of the Caretaker's Wife" was written after the other story, mainly because it has been made to fit better into the Miss Marple universe, the action occurs more obviously in St. Mary Mead, Miss Marple plays an active role in the proceedings, and recurring characters appear (Curran, *Making* 241). In short, this unpublished version has more commercial viability. However, he rightly hesitates to claim certainty. It is equally possible that this version was written first: the sheer number of handwritten corrections to the manuscript suggests a first draft, which is too long for publication in *The Strand*. It is also possible that Christie misplaced the draft and rewrote the story quickly and from memory, which would explain the "bare bones" nature of the manuscript-within-a-manuscript in "The Case of the Caretaker." Both stories contain similar plots.

Characters: Edge, Bella; **Hartnell, Amanda**; Haydock, Dr.; Laxton, Harry; **Laxton, Louise**; **Marple, Jane**; **Murgatroyd, Mrs.**; **Price-Ridley, Martha**; **Wetherby, Caroline**
See also: "The Case of the Caretaker"

"The Case of the City Clerk" (story; alternative title: "The £10 Adventure")

In this short story, a 48-year-old city clerk, Mr. Roberts, calls on Parker Pyne because he is experiencing a midlife crisis. Pyne, after all, advertises his services for "unhappy" people. Roberts wants excitement but has a limited budget: £5. Pyne, who accepts what people can pay and budgets accordingly, arranges an adventure. Soon enough, Roberts finds himself in a dangerous case, traveling around the world and witnessing murder, robbery, and kidnapping. He leaves in his wake a pining grand duchess (played by Pyne's employee, Madeleine de Sara) and returns to his family life, happy with his adventure.

The original version of this story appeared as part of the serial *Are You Happy? If Not, Consult Mr. Parker Pyne* in *Cosmopolitan* in August 1932. The version published in *The Strand Magazine* in November 1932 was slightly different: *The Strand* titled it "The £10 Adventure." However, the sum involved was £5 by the time it appeared in *Parker Pyne Investigates* (1934). It was dramatized for BBC Radio 4 in a modernized version in 2003; by then, the title had to be adjusted again to "The £199 Adventure."

Characters: Bonnington, Lucas; Carslake; **de Sara, Madeleine**; Hooper; Maitland; **Parker Pyne, J.**; Peterfield, Professor; Roberts, Mr.
See also: **BBC Radio Adaptations**; *Parker Pyne Investigates*

"The Case of the Discontented Husband" (story; alternative title: "His Lady's Affair")

Almost a companion piece to "The Case of the Middle-Aged Wife," this Parker Pyne story centers on a young man whose wife is growing tired of him and wants to divorce and remarry. Reginald Wade, "who is 'the inarticulate type'" (PPI 55), consults Pyne because he is unhappy. He explains that he has been married nine years and that he can quite understand his "clever, beautiful" wife "getting fed up with an ass like me" (57). Pyne arranges for Wade to carry out a dalliance with the vampish Madeleine de Sara. Such a plan worked well with Mrs. Packington and Claude Luttrell in "The Case of the Middle-Aged Wife." Sure enough, Iris Wade sees her husband in another woman's arms and has a realization. However, Wade decides that he really is in love with Madeleine and wants to marry her. Pyne chalks this case up as a "FAILURE—owing to natural causes" (71, emphasis in original).

Taken alongside the other story, "The Case of the Discontented Husband" seems to present men as significantly more emotional than women. It is likely that Iris was trying to make her husband jealous all along, and Reggie simply falls into his own trap. It is an ongoing theme in early–1930s Christie that women need to take care of men, who are the weaker sex (see, for instance, *The Sittaford Mystery*). Another notable feature is Pyne's clarification of "[h]uman troubles" "into a few main heads": "ill health," "boredom," "wives who are in trouble over their husbands," and the reverse (58). This is a distinctly middle-class list of "troubles."

The story was published under the title *Are You Happy? If Not, Consult Mr. Parker Pyne* with other Pyne short stories in *Cosmopolitan* in August 1932. It appeared in *Woman's Pictorial* in the United Kingdom two months later as "His Lady's Affair" and, in 1934, appeared in the anthology *Parker Pyne Investigates*.

Characters: **de Sara, Madeleine**; Jordan, Sinclair; **Luttrell, Claude**; Massington, Mrs.; **Parker Pyne, J.**; Wade, Iris; **Wade, Reginald (Reggie)**
See also: *Parker Pyne Investigates*; *The Sittaford Mystery*

"The Case of the Discontented Soldier" (story; alternative title: "Adventure by Request")

A Parker Pyne story, "The Case of the Discontented Soldier" is a light, magazine-ready romp, notable for introducing readers to the sensational novelist Mrs. Ariadne Oliver, who would develop into Christie's fictional alter-ego in later books.

The story concerns the retired Major Charles Wilbraham, who consults Pyne because he is bored: the latter's advertisement recommends consulting him in case of unhappiness. Pyne promises to help Wilbraham and soon sends him a note that indicates a rendezvous. However, when Wilbraham travels to the place, he hears a young woman crying for help and becomes caught up in an extraordinary adventure. After rescuing the woman, Freda Clegg, from near-death, Wilbraham determines to marry her.

The reader learns that both Wilbraham and Clegg were clients of Pyne and that he has brought them together with this outlandish scheme, thought up by the sensational novelist Ariadne Oliver. Mrs. Oliver defends the lack of originality in the story: "The public is conservative, Mr. Pyne; it likes the old well-worn gadgets" (38). Jumping forward in time, Wilbraham and Clegg are happily married. Both remember, but keep to themselves, their previous consultations with Pyne and conclude that, even though Pyne did nothing to help them, he can keep his fee—they have found one another and are happy.

The story was published with other Pyne short stories under the title *Are You Happy? If Not, Consult Mr. Parker Pyne* in *Cosmopolitan* in August 1932. It was published in *Woman's Pictorial* in the United Kingdom two months later, and, in 1934, appeared in the anthology *Parker Pyne Investigates*. It was filmed as part of *The Agatha Christie Hour* in 1982.

Characters: **Clegg, Freda**; **de Sara, Madeleine**; Jerry; Johnny; Lemon, Felicity; Lorrimar; **Oliver, Ariadne**; **Parker Pyne, J.**; Parkins, Mrs.; Percy; Reid, Mr.; **Wilbraham, Major Charles**.

See also: *The Agatha Christie Hour*; *Parker Pyne Investigates*

"The Case of the Distressed Lady" (story; alternative titles: "The Cat and the Chestnut," "Faked!")

In "The Case of the Distressed Lady," J. Parker Pyne is consulted by a guilt-ridden Daphne St. John, who says she has replaced Lady Naomi Dortheimer's diamond ring with a paste replica and wants to return it before anyone notices. Pyne devises a dramatic scheme involving two of his glamorous employees, Claude Luttrell and Madeleine de Silva, performing a dance (as "Michael and Juanita") to disguise a sleight-of-hand routine. In the end, he reveals that he has not switched the rings at all: he knows that Daphne was trying to use him to steal the original and that the one in her possession was paste. Pyne, always a statistician, reminds her that "in eighty-seven per cent of cases dishonesty does not pay" (53).

The story was published with other Pyne short stories under the title *Are You Happy? If Not, Consult Mr. Parker Pyne* in *Cosmopolitan* in August 1932. It was published in *Woman's Pictorial* in the United Kingdom two months later and, in 1934, appeared in the anthology *Parker Pyne Investigates*.

Characters: **de Sara, Madeleine**; Dortheimer, Lady Naomi; Dortheimer, Sir Reuben; **Lemon, Felicity; Luttrell, Claud**; **Parker Pyne, J.**; St John, Daphne, and Gerald

See also: *Parker Pyne Investigates*

"The Case of the Drug Peddler." See **"The Horses of Diomedes"**

"The Case of the Family Taint." See **"The Cretan Bull"**

"The Case of the Forged Notes." See **"The Crackler"**

"The Case of the Gossipers." See **"The Lernean Hydra"**

"The Case of the Kidnapped Pekingese." See **"The Nemean Lion"**

"The Case of the Middle-Aged Wife" (story; alternative title: "The Woman Concerned")

The story that opens the *Parker Pyne Investigates* touches in a lighthearted manner on themes not emphasized by Christie in her mystery fiction. A housewife, Mrs. Packington, is alarmed that her husband has lost interest in her, favoring a young typist, Nancy. She visits J. Parker Pyne, who advertises his services for those who are not "happy." Pyne sets up a scheme, whereby

Mrs. Packington goes dancing with a young gigolo, Claude Luttrell, and is seen by her husband. George Packington soon realizes that he has been blinded by Nancy, "a shrewd little piece" (*PPI* 15), and neglecting his wife. All is resolved satisfactorily, but Pyne starts to notice "vestiges of a conscience" in Claude, the "Lounge Lizard" (17).

Although this story opens the volume, it appears to have been written as the sixth story, because it was not included in the Pyne short stories that appeared in *Cosmopolitan* under the title *Are You Happy? If Not, Consult Parker Pyne* but was published instead in *Woman's Pictorial* in the United Kingdom on 8 October 1932. It nonetheless does a good job introducing Pyne; his philosophy that human beings can be distilled into six "types" and his employee, Claude. It also introduces his secretary, "[a] forbidding-looking young woman with spectacles" called Miss Lemon (5). Miss Lemon would evolve, as Hercule Poirot's secretary, into a modernist human machine.

The story is also notable for featuring a young secretarial mistress called Nancy. Christie's first husband, Archie, had divorced her to marry a secretary, Nancy Neele. It is surprising that the story, written two years into Christie's second marriage and apparently imagining her first in happy continuation, has been ignored by biographers.

In 1934, "The Case of the Middle-Aged Wife" was published as part of *Parker Pyne Investigates*. In 1982, it was one of two Pyne stories filmed, starring Maurice Denham, as part of *The Agatha Christie Hour*.

Characters: **Luttrell, Claude**; **Lemon, Felicity**; **Nancy**; Packington, George; Packington, Maria; **Parker Pyne, J.**

See also: *The Agatha Christie Hour*; *Parker Pyne Investigates*

"The Case of the Missing Lady" (story). See *Partners in Crime* (story collection)

The Case of the Missing Lady (television adaptation). See CBS **Television Adaptations**

"The Case of the Missing Schoolgirl." See **"The Girdle of Hippolyta"**

"The Case of the Missing Will" (story; alternative titles: "Sporting Challenge"; "Where There's a Will")

This early story is very much in the Sherlock Holmes vein, opening with a client—the businesslike Violet Marsh—visiting Poirot and recounting, over several pages, her story. Her story, too, is rather Holmesian, although more modern. She and her uncle rowed bitterly over her graduating from Girton College, Cambridge with a bachelor of science degree; the old-fashioned Andrew Marsh believed that women had inferior brains and should not be educated. He died, leaving her his house and its contents for one year to "prove her wits" (*PI* 284). After this period, his money will pass to various charities. The inference is that a second will, benefiting her, is hidden in the house for her to find. She consults Poirot to help her find it.

Poirot agrees. He and Captain Hastings travel to Devon, and Crabtree Manor, the property. They find a burnt will. However, Poirot realizes that this is a red herring: the real will was written in invisible ink inside an old envelope. He recovers it and makes the ink appear—it inherits Violet Marsh. Although Hastings suggests she lost the bet with her uncle because she could not find the will, Poirot disagrees: she had the wits to "employ the expert" (298).

The story has a similar premise to "Strange Jest" in that an eccentric uncle hides his money and leaves a series of cryptic clues, and his niece and nephew consult Miss Marple for help. Another Miss Marple story, "Motive versus Opportunity," reuses the idea of a will written in invisible ink. In both of those, Miss Marple invokes her trickster relative, Uncle Henry.

The reference to women's education in "The Case of the Missing Will" is distinctive. It is not exactly a feminist story—the educated woman is unable to solve the puzzle—but acknowledges and seems to celebrate advances while satirizing conservative objections. In this sense, the best parallel elsewhere in the Christie canon is *Appointment with Death*. Girton College, the first women's college at the University of Cambridge, was founded in 1869. It was not able to issue degrees, however, until 1948, so the reference to Violet Marsh's bachelor of science degree is inaccurate.

"The Case of the Missing Will" was first published in *The Sketch* in 1923 and appeared in the anthology *Poirot Investigates* in 1924. It is a light, noncrime story, so was heavily expanded by Douglas Watkinson, with two murders thrown in, for an episode of *Agatha Christie's Poirot*, broadcast on ITV in 1993.

Characters: Baker, Mr.; Baker, Mrs.; **Hastings, Captain Arthur**; **Marsh, Andrew, and Violet**; Marsh, Roger; **Poirot, Hercule**; Pike, Albert; Pike, Jessie

See also: *Agatha Christie's Poirot*; **Conan Doyle, Sir Arthur**; *Poirot Investigates*

The Case of the Moving Finger. See *The Moving Finger*

"The Case of the Perfect Maid" (story; alternative titles: "The Perfect Maid"; "The Servant Problem")

One of Christie's more controversial tropes is the idea that nobody looks at the staff. The general extension of this idea is that a character can pass unknown among their peers to commit a crime, if disguised as a servant. "The Case of the Perfect Maid" contains an example of this.

Miss Marple's maid, Edna, asks Miss Marple to help her cousin, Gladys ("Gladdie") Holmes. Gladys has been dismissed from her position in service to sisters Emily and Lavinia Skinner on apparently baseless grounds. The Skinners live in one of four flats at Old Hall, and Emily, the younger sister, is a notorious hypochondriac who spends extended periods in bed. Gossip in the village is that staff are hard to find and that Gladys will be impossible to replace. However, a "domestic treasure," Mary Higgins, appears from apparently nowhere and soon moves in with the Skinners, proving herself "the good, old-fashioned type of servant" (*MMFC* 86).

Miss Marple warns Lavinia that Mary seems "almost too good to be true" (87) and covertly takes the maid's fingerprint using a sucked boiled sweet in her handbag to make a hand mirror sticky. Before long, Mary is missing and so are many valuables from the Old Hall flats. Miss Marple realizes that Mary and Emily are one and the

same, using the fingerprints to prove it. Her main clue was the fact that Emily refused to see a doctor—because she was not in bed but posing as Mary: "Hypochondriacs love doctors—and Emily didn't" (93). Typically, the logic here lies in folk psychology and, in the case of Mary being "too good to be true," realism about changing times over and above nostalgia. However, Gladys is reprimanded by the detective for having ideas above her station and being unable to hold down a job, so there is a sense of discomfort at changing times. Miss Marple's weapons—the contents of her handbag— are equally domestic.

The story was first published as "The Perfect Maid" in *The Strand* in April 1942. It was anthologized in *Miss Marple's Final Cases* (Collins, 1979). The story was first adapted as part of NHK's *Agasa Kurisutī no Meitantei Powaro to Māpuru,* broadcast on 1 August 2004. It has been dramatized for BBC Radio 4 twice: the first, modernized version that did not feature Miss Marple, was broadcast as "The Case of the Perfect Carer" on 17 March 2003, and the second, more direct version was part of *Miss Marple's Final Cases*, aired on 23 September 2015.

Characters: Allerton, Dr.; Carmichael, Mrs.; **Clara**; Clement, Griselda; Devereux, Mr.; Devereux, Mrs.; **Edna**; **Haydock, Dr.**; Higgins, Mary; **Holmes, Gladys**; Janet; Larkin, Mr.; Larkin, Mrs.; **Slack, Inspector**; Marple, Jane; Meeks, Mr.; Melchett, Colonel; Skinner, Emily; Skinner, Lavinia; **Wetherby, Caroline**

See also: *Agasa Kurisutī no Meitantei Powaro to Māpuru*; BBC Radio Adaptations; *Miss Marple's Final Cases* (radio series); *Miss Marple's Final Cases* (story collection)

"The Case of the Retired Jeweler." See **"Tape-Measure Murder"**

"The Case of the Rich Woman" (story; alternative title: "The Rich Woman Who Wanted Only to Be Happy")

First published in *Cosmopolitan* in August 1932 with other J. Parker Pyne short stories under the title *Are You Happy? If Not, Consult Mr. Parker Pyne*, this story has an origin story, revealed in Christie's preface to the 1952 Penguin edition of *Parker Pyne Investigates* (1934). Christie met "a strange woman ten years before when I was looking into a shop window"— the woman cried "with the utmost venom" that she had too much money and knew not what to do with it. The suggestion of charity was met with disdain. Christie reflects that nowadays (25 years later), the tax inspector would take it all (Christie, Foreword, *Parker Pyne Investigates* 7).

That is the premise of this story: Pyne, the statistician-turned-problem-solver, meets a rich woman, the widowed Mrs. Rymer, who does not know what to do with her money and utterly rejects the idea of charity. She is, as the title reminds us, a "woman," not a "lady." She is *nouveau riche* and has all the wrong priorities, puzzled as to why she is unhappy despite her ownership of "three fur coats, a lot of Paris dresses and such like" (*PPI* 91). In an extraordinary act of literary revenge on a woman she met in the 1920s, Christie has Mrs. Rymer thrown into a life of poverty, where she learns to live a happy, simple, servant's life. She ends up giving most of her money to "the hospitals" (108) and decides to live frugally, "[a] grand figure of a peasant woman, outlined against the setting sun" (109).

Characters: Antrobus, Dr.; **de Sara, Madeleine**; Gardner, Mr.; Gardner, Mrs.; **Luttrell, Claud**; **Oliver, Ariadne**; **Parker Pyne, J.**; Roberts, Mrs.; Rymer, Abner; **Rymer, Amelia**; Welsh, Joe

See also: **Class**; **Forewords to Penguin Books**; *Parker Pyne Investigates*.

"The Case of the Sinister Stranger." See **"The Adventure of the Sinister Stranger"**

"The Case of the Veiled Lady." See **"The Veiled Lady"**

"The Case of the Vulture Women." See **"The Stymphalean Birds"**

Caso dos Dez Negrinhos, O. See *And Then There Were None*, **Screen Adaptations of**

Cassetti. See **Ratchett, Samuel**

Castle, Mrs.
Mrs. Castle is the snooty hotel receptionist, with airs above her station, who speaks with tortured vowels in *Evil Under the Sun*.

Miss Gorringe in *At Bertram's Hotel* is drawn along the same lines as Mrs. Castle.

Castletown, Harry. See **Curry, R. H.**

Cat Among the Pigeons **(novel)**
The boarding school mystery was an established subgenre when Christie wrote *Cat Among the Pigeons*. British publishers had already issued such works as Nicholas Blake's *A Question of Proof* (1935), Josephine Tey's *Miss Pym Disposes* (1946), and Nancy Spain's irreverent *Poison for Teacher* (1949), and boarding schools formed the backdrop to countless mysteries for children. Christie's contribution to the field goes slightly against the grain in that, whereas the school provides a closed and introspective community as in the titles mentioned, it also provides a microcosm for certain elements of the wider world, with international students bringing in their guardians' political arguments, class conflict rampant among the staff, and sexual tension boiling into letters to parents.

The setting is Meadowbank, an exclusive girls' school, whereas a parallel narrative details espionage, revolution in Western Asia, and political imposters closing in on the school. *Cat Among the Pigeons* introduces a new country to Christiean geography: the Principality of Ramat, which appears to be based on small principalities in the Yemen, which Christie visited on archaeological digs with her husband. After two deaths, a likably disheveled student— Julia Upjohn—consults Hercule Poirot, whose name she has heard in connection to the case from *Mrs. McGinty's Dead*. Poirot arrives three-quarters into the book and solves the riddle rather quickly. In the process, he identifies an imposter among the students—a woman posing as a young Egyptian princess—and to recover some priceless jewels from a tennis racket. At the end of the novel, Poirot gives Julia one of the stolen jewels.

Although Poirot featured prominently in the blurb and publicity for *Cat Among the Pigeons* in 1959, he only appears in 28 percent of the book. Still, Poirot he is in usual form, complete with George(s) the valet and the elusive Mr. Robinson. It is clear, however, that Christie's heart was not with

Poirot at this point. When the novel was filmed as part of *Agatha Christie's Poirot* (broadcast on ITV1 on 28 September 2008), Poirot was introduced at the outset as an old friend of the headmistress, uncharacteristically giving a talk to the girls. A looser adaptation appeared in the first season of *Les Petits Meurtres d'Agatha Christie* in France on 8 September 2010.

Characters: Arnold, Lydia; Blake, Miss; **Blanche, Angèle**; Bond, Sergeant Percy; **Briggs**; **Bulstrode, Honoria**; Calder, Alice; Carlton-Sandways, Lady Veronica and Major; **Chadwick, Miss**; Edmundson, John; Garnett, Lady; **George(s)**; **Goodman, Adam**; Hope, Henrietta and Mr./Mrs. Gerald; Hurst, Mr. and Mrs.; **Johnson, Elspeth**; **Kelsey, Detective Inspector**; Lorrimer, Vera; O'Connor, Derek; **Pikeaway, Colonel Ephraim**; **Poirot, Hercule**; Rathbone, Denis; Rawlinson, Squadron Leader Robert ("Bob"); **Rich, Eileen**; **Robinson, Mr.**; Rowan, Miss; **Shaista, Princess**; **Shapland, Ann**; **Springer, Grace**; **Summerhayes, Maureen**; Sutcliffe, Joan and Henry; **Sutcliffe, Jennifer**; **Upjohn, Julia, and Mrs.**; **Vansittart, Eleanor**; Yusuf, Prince Ali

See also: *Agatha Christie's Poirot*; *Les Petits Meurtres d'Agatha Christie*

"The Cat and the Chestnut." See **"The Case of the Distressed Lady"**

Caterham, Marquis of. See **Brent, Sir Clement**

Cauldfield, Richard

A "boyish and natural ... charming companion" in the Mary Westmacott novel *A Daughter's a Daughter* (33), Richard Cauldfield is Ann Prentice's new younger beau, whom she has known for three weeks. He is sent away to marry another woman, the unsatisfactory but traditionally age-appropriate Doris.

Cavendish, John, and Mary

Brother to Lawrence Cavendish in *The Mysterious Affair at Styles*, John Cavendish is the next suspect in his stepmother's death after Alfred Inglethorpe. Captain Hastings believes he is in love with John's wife, Mary; she represents untamed passion and open-mindedness, evidenced by her flirtations with the Jewish Dr. Bauerstein. Mary

is also mentioned in "The Adventure of the 'Western Star'" and *Curtain: Poirot's Last Case.*

CBS Radio Adaptations

CBS and NBC are the two American networks that broadcast the most Christie adaptations in the twentieth century. Both networks put Christie adaptations on the small screen and the radio from the 1930s onward.

The first for CBS was part of the Campbell Soup-sponsored *Campbell Playhouse* (1938–40), a vehicle for Orson Welles that followed the *Mercury Theatre on the Air.* Welles had made headlines with his 1938 production of *The War of the Worlds*, which had led to the creation of this series with its lucrative sponsorship deal. The format included one-hour adaptations of famous works of literature, such as Charles Dickens's *A Christmas Carol*, Victor Hugo's *Les Misérables*, and Daphne du Maurier's *Rebecca*, always starring Welles. The offering on 12 November 1939 was *The Murder of Roger Ackroyd*, adapted from Christie's novel by Herman J. Mankewicz, who would go on to co-write the screenplay for *Citizen Kane*. Welles played both Hercule Poirot and the narrator Dr. Sheppard. The supporting cast included Edna May Oliver, Brenda Forbes, and George Couloris.

In the 1940s, Poirot returned to CBS, when the network picked up Harold Huber's Mutual Broadcasting series *Hercule Poirot*, under the title *Mystery of the Week*. On 15 May 1949, a star vehicle for Helen Hayes, *Electric Theater*, broadcast a version of *Love from a Stranger*. Hayes would go on to play Miss Marple on screen, also for CBS, some four decades later.

On 24 February 1949, the last of five episodes of *Suspense!* (1940–62) based on Christie's work was aired. "Where There's a Will," a story anthologized in *The Hound of Death*, was broadcast in a live adaptation starring James Mason and his then-wife, Pamela Mason. A celebrity couple also starred in "The ABC Murders," broadcast on 18 May 1943. Charles Laughton and his wife, Elsa Lanchester, feature in this 30-minute reworking of the 1936 Poirot novel, although Poirot does not feature. Astonishingly, the scriptwriter has attempted to condense the entire complex plot into the short format required for live radio.

Suspense! often broadcast new versions of popular episodes. For instance, it aired eight versions of Lucille Fletcher's *Sorry, Wrong Number*, all starring Agnes Moorehead and using the same script. In addition, it featured three versions of *Love from a Stranger* (all citing Christie's original story, "Philomel Cottage," rather than the playwright Frank Vosper). The first, featuring Alice Frost and Eric Dressler, was broadcast on 29 July 1942. The second, airing on 7 October 1943, featured Welles's return to Christie, alongside Geraldine Fitzgerald. The third, which played on 26 December 1946, starred Lilli Palmer. Anthologist and historian Peter Haining has reported an episode based on the short story "Accident" (*Murder* 61), but this appears not to have occurred.

CBS Television Adaptations

CBS had broadcast several successful radio productions based on Christie's writing when it started airing her work on television. Christie was notoriously hostile to television productions of work, but she was more inclined to accept proposals when they were one-offs, lucrative, and geared for international audiences (thus she would not have to see them).

As well as two early versions of *Witness for the Prosecution* and "Three Blind Mice," CBS gave Tommy and Tuppence Beresford (renamed Blunt here) their screen debut. "The Case of the Missing Lady," airing on 7 December 1950, was a live episode of *Nash Airflyte Theatre* (1950–51), starring Cloris Leachman as Tuppence and future president Ronald Reagan as Tommy. The semi-supernatural story "The Red Signal" was dramatized for the television version of long-running radio series *Suspense* (1942–62). It aired on 22 January 1952 and is widely available today.

Also available, but less widely, is the first—and, so far, only—adaptation of *They Came to Baghdad*. This one-hour installment of *Studio One* (1948–52) was broadcast live on 12 May 1952. It starred a young June

Dayton as Victoria Jones and featured Bea Arthur, Leon Askin, and Jacqueline deWit. This was a remarkably prompt adaptation of a just-published novel.

In the 1980s, CBS produced a string of occasional television specials, including three Poirot cases, two Miss Marple cases, and four standalone. These attracted some big names, including Bette Davis, Olivia de Havilland, Faye Dunaway, Helen Hayes as Miss Marple, and—reprising his role from the EMI movies—Peter Ustinov as Poirot. For budgetary reasons, they were not period pieces but were set in the 1980s, allowing for a certain playfulness: Ustinov's Poirot makes his first appearance in *Thirteen at Dinner* as David Frost's interviewee in a glittery television studio.

First was *Witness for the Prosecution* (4 December 1982), a remake of the 1957 film, starring Diana Rigg, Ralph Richardson, and Deborah Kerr. *Murder Is Easy* followed, airing on Christmas Eve 1983. While *Witness* had been set in England and featured a largely British cast, *Murder Is Easy*, although set in England, was a quintessentially American affair. Subsequent productions would be set in and around California. Helen Hayes, who had appeared in *Murder Is Easy*, starred as Miss Marple in *A Caribbean Murder*, broadcast on 22 October 1983.

Less than a month later, on 5 November, CBS aired its version of *Sparkling Cyanide*, starring Anthony Andrews and Deborah Raffin; one of the screenwriters was mystery author Sue Grafton. In 1985, Hayes returned as Miss Marple, giving the second-to-last performance of her life. *Murder with Mirrors* (20 February 1985), based on Christie's *They Do It with Mirrors*, also starred John Mills and Bette Davis. "We didn't get chummy," stated Davis regarding her work with Hayes (Stine 359). Davis was treated with great reverence by the crew and gave each member a customized mirror when production wrapped. Plans for a series of Miss Marple adaptations faltered, partly because of the success of the BBC's concurrent series in the United Kingdom.

Instead, CBS returned to Poirot, presenting Ustinov with a blaze of marketing in the modern trappings of *Thirteen at Dinner*. In this version of *Lord Edgware Dies*,

Faye Dunaway plays both Jane Wilkinson and Carlotta Adams, who impersonates Wilkinson. The adaptation is notable for featuring David Suchet as Inspector Japp. Jonathan Cecil played Captain Hastings and returned in the two next Poirot adaptations, written into the stories. *Dead Man's Folly,* which also featured Jean Stapleton as a chatty American Ariadne Oliver, aired on 8 January 1986. Ustinov and Cecil returned for one last outing in *Murder in Three Acts* (30 September 1986), featuring Tony Curtis as an actor experiencing a midlife crisis. Ustinov would play Poirot one more time on the silver screen.

By now, Christie was beginning to dominate British television schedules, with the BBC Marple series, various LWT outings, and a new Poirot series in the works. Although there were many discussions about future adaptations, CBS only made one more in the 1980s: *The Man in the Brown Suit,* with Stephanie Zimbalist, Edward Woodward as the murderer, and one-time Poirot Tony Randall, aired on 4 January 1989.

CBS would not televise a Christie work again until 2001. Another modernized production, *Murder on the Orient Express,* starred Alfred Molina as Poirot and is generally considered one of the worst Christie adaptations. It aired on 22 April. The number of suspects is reduced from the symbolic 12 to 9, characters are apparently commuting to work via the Orient Express, and Poirot takes days to solve the crime despite looking up all the relevant details on his laptop within minutes. Following a less-than-enthusiastic reaction, plans for a potential series and even a tie-in edition of the novel were shelved.

See also: *Agatha Christie's Poirot*; **CBS Radio Adaptations**; **EMI Films**; *Miss Marple* **(television series)**; *The Mousetrap,* **Screen Adaptations**; *Witness for the Prosecution,* **Screen Adaptations**

Celia

Protagonist Celia is Christie's self-portrait in the Mary Westmacott novel *Unfinished Portrait,* plagued with self-doubt and a strong moral core. At one point, she thinks: "I'm pretending to be a writer. I think it's almost queerer than pretending to be a wife or a mother" (547).

Chadwick, Miss

A cofounder of Meadowbank School in *Cat Among the Pigeons,* Miss Chadwick loves the school and wants to take over as headmistress from her friend, Honoria Bulstrode, but she is far too sensitive and emotional to be successful in the role. She is so invested in the idea that, in a kind of trance, she murders Eleanor Vansittart, whom she wrongly believes is her greatest competition. Later, she takes a bullet fired by Ann Shapland at Miss Bulstrode and Mrs. Upjohn, and dies, confessing with her last breath.

Challenger, Commander George

Commander George Challenger is a naval commander and friend to Nick Buckley and Freddie Rice in *Peril at End House.* Although Captain Hastings instantly likes Challenger because he has a good, patriotic background and attended Eton, Poirot declares himself free of preconceptions and thus can see the commander for what he is: a cocaine dealer.

Chantry, Valentine

Valentine Chantry is the 39-year-old victim in "Triangle at Rhodes," who has been famous for being beautiful since she was 16. Like so many of Christie's multiply-married celebrity women (such as Marina Gregg in *The Mirror Crack'd from Side to Side* and Arlena Marshall in *Evil Under the Sun*), she is not allowed to survive her own narrative and is killed by her most devoted lover. Christie also shows her to be a character whose personality is interpreted by people rather than reflected by actual behavior.

Chapman, Nigel

Nigel Chapman is a student in *Hickory Dickory Dock* who seems to be a generic, arrogant male with occasional affectations such as using green ink. He turns out to be the secret son of Sir Arthur Stanley, who had changed his name after murdering his mother. He is working with Valerie Hobhouse on an international smuggling operation—diamonds or drugs, it is never clearly specified—and kills three people to cover it up.

Charteris, Isabella

Isabella Charteris is a beautiful young woman who seems to exist mostly for men to fall in love with her, in the Mary Westmacott novel *The Rose and the Yew Tree*. Unlike beautiful women in Christie's crime novels, she is not blamed for this; indeed, her self-sacrifice, out of love, at the end of the novel is its emotional pivot.

"The Chemists and the Pharmacists." See *What We Did in the Great War*

"The Chess Problem" (alternative titles: "A Chess Problem"; "A Game of Chess"). See *The Big Four* (novel)

"The Chocolate Box" (story; "The Clue of the Chocolate Box"; "The Time Hercule Poirot Failed")

Hercule Poirot recounts "The Chocolate Box" to Captain Hastings as "the story of a failure"—an antipode to the "record of my successes" (*PEC* 130). At the end of the story, Poirot urges Hastings to say "Chocolate Box" if he ever gets too conceited. He promptly exhibits egocentrism and fails to understand why Hastings is saying "Chocolate Box" (142–43). The story covers events "in Belgium many years ago" (130) when Poirot was a member of the Sûreté. In the story, Poirot is asked to investigate the death, apparently by heart failure, of Paul Deroulard. Focusing entirely on the method of murder, he misses the more psychological clues and identifies the wrong perpetrator. The solution to this one hinges on color-blindness.

The story was first published in *The Sketch* on 23 May 1923. In February 1925, an altered version appeared in the *Blue Book Magazine* in the United States. This version removes two references to Poirot's sister, Yvonne, among other items, and it is unclear who made the decisions about the changes. It is the revised version that appeared in the 1925 U.S. edition of *Poirot Investigates* and the 1974 U.K. collection *Poirot's Early Cases*. Therefore, the only canonical reference to a Poirot sibling by name (excluding the imaginary Achille) appears in *The Sketch*.

"The Chocolate Box" was filmed as part of *Agatha Christie's Poirot*, broadcast on ITV on 21 February 1993. Notably, the dramatists seemed unable to make Poirot fallible after all; the episode has Poirot (David Suchet) correctly identify the murderer but stay silent out of love for a beautiful woman with whom, in the story, he is certainly not smitten.

Characters: Deroulard, Paul; Deroulard, Madame; de Saint Alard, Monsieur; Felicie; **Hastings, Captain Arthur**; Mesnard, Virginie; **Poirot, Hercule**; **Poirot, Yvonne**; Wilson, John

See also: *Agatha Christie's Poirot*; *Poirot Investigates*; *Poirot's Early Cases*

Chevenix-Gore, Sir Gervaise

Sir Gervaise Chevenix-Gore is a baronet who is murdered in "Dead Man's Mirror." A pompous and extremely wealthy man with many enemies, he is described in terms that would suit the baronets of gothic fiction: "the kind of fellow who made impossible wagers and won 'em" (*MITM* 153). One character says of him: "I always think that he blustered such a lot because he really knew his brains weren't up to it" (234). Like the patriarchs of *Lord Edgware Dies*, *4.50 from Paddington*, and *Crooked House*, he represents a kind of gothic survivalism that is ultimately unsustainable in a sea of permissive modernity. The equivalent character in "The Second Gong" is Hubert Lytcham-Roche.

Chimneys. See *The Secret of Chimneys* (play)

"The Chinese Puzzle Box." See "The Veiled Lady"

"A Choice" (poem). See *Poems*

"The Choice" (story)

Christie wrote "The Choice" when she was about 17, submitted it unsuccessfully to magazines under the name Sydney West, and failed to sell it. The story, currently unpublished and housed in the Christie Family Archive, is described by biographer Janet Morgan as a "prissy parable" that undermines its prissiness with "a tweak" (50). The story resembles "Mrs. Jordan's Ghost" by Christie's mother, Clara Miller, that has a haunted woman and the appearance of a ghost or ghosts whenever a certain piece of music is played. The "tweak" described by Morgan comes in the form of the narrator making a counter-rational decision on the basis that rational decisions have only enhanced feelings of grief and guilt so far. The author was at this time heavily influenced by both her family and the work of May Sinclair, which explains the story's dreamlike tone and gestures toward modernism.

See also: **Miller, Clarissa (Clara)**; **Pseudonyms**

Chorabali. See **Indian-Language Adaptations**

Christianity

A devout member of the Church of England, Christie was raised in an environment of general Protestantism typical to her time and class. As she outlines in her autobiography, her father "was a simple-hearted, orthodox Christian"; her governess, "Nursie," who shaped her formative views, "was a Bible Christian"; and her mother dabbled in a variety of "'high' churches," including "a brief but vivid interest in Zoroastrianism" and experiments in Christian science (*AA* 25).

Every day for most of her life, Christie kept a copy of Thomas à Kempis's *The Imitation of Christ* by her bed. The strength of her faith is evidenced in early anecdotes: as a girl, she worried that her father would go to hell for failing to observe the Sabbath (he played golf on Sundays), and after her divorce in 1928, she no longer took part in Holy Communion. Like Dorothy L. Sayers, Christie occasionally wrote religious fiction and poetry, mostly for children: these works were published in 1965 as *Star Over Bethlehem*.

However, unlike Sayers or G.K. Chesterton, Christie was not a theologian. Faith was important in Christie's life, and religion is reflected in her books—but not religiosity. Although many of her characters attend church and know their Bibles, Christian evangelism is presented as a form of insanity or a shirking of individual responsibility. Emily Brent, a religious fanatic in *And Then There Were None*, sits "[e]nveloped in an aura of righteousness" (*ATTWN* 7) and blithely wreaks havoc on those around her. The murderers in "The House of Lurking Death" and *By the Pricking of My Thumbs* are both elderly women who believe or claim that they are acting for God.

It is often said that, after World War I, as faith in traditional religion declined, detective fiction filled a gap. W.H. Auden discusses such a scenario in his 1948 essay "The Guilty Vicarage," which presents detective fiction as a modern version of the creation story. In this reading, influential in Golden Age scholarship, the murderer represents the serpent in the Garden of Eden. Once they are named, the evil is expunged, allowing world-weary readers the opportunity to indulge a fantasy of restored innocence. As Hannah M. Strømmen points out, however, this fantasy is inherently compromised, as, given the nature of the genre, there is also the promise that a new serpent will come in the next publishing cycle: "the restoration of harmony and the identification of guilt is … a temporary fix" (165).

Nonetheless, the detective in such a reading acts as a kind of secular priest. This is easy to support in Christie specifically. Hercule Poirot frequently acts as a father-confessor, encouraging suspects to unburden to him, and calls himself "Papa Poirot." So clear is the comparison that Sarah Phelps's 2017 television version of *The ABC Murders* gives the detective a backstory as a priest. Miss Marple, too, professes a belief in good and evil, considering herself a champion for the divine principle of retribution in *Nemesis*. Whereas the villains may align themselves with God and the Bible, the sexless amateur detectives act as prophets without denominations or "secular priest[s]" (Hesford 169).

That said, Nick Baldock points out that "overt references to God or theology" are more common in Christie's novels than in those of her peers (Baldock). Religion is, in Christie, part of a national and community tradition. Vicars and priests tend in Christie's works to be elderly, amiable, and muddled. This is true of minor and major characters, regardless of the time of writing. Sometimes, they will be single parents to Bright Young Things who become involved in cases such as the vicar of Marchboldt in *Why Didn't They Ask Evans?* and the father of Prudence "Tuppence" Beresford. One priest breaks the mold: Canon Ambrose Pennefather, a rather worldly and gregarious type, who acts as detective in Christie's play *Murder on the Nile* (not to be confused with Canon Pennyfather of *At Bertram's Hotel*). Notably, this play was based on a novel in which Hercule Poirot had investigated in a role as a kind of secular father-confessor.

Christianity, in its many forms, shaped Christie as a woman and as a writer. However, she coupled its influences with an awareness of a world beyond that of which she wrote, informed by her experiences in Western Asia and elsewhere. Key to Christie's plots and characters is the idea that people do not change, and religion in her writing is an element of this concept.

See also: *Autobiography, An; Star Over Bethlehem* (story collection)

Christie, Colonel Archibald ("Archie"; 1889–1962)

Colonel Archibald Christie was Agatha Christie's first husband, for whom she broke off an engagement to Captain Reggie Lucy to marry on Christmas Eve 1914. It was a war marriage, and Archie was serving with the RAF for much of its early years. Their letters from this period demonstrate the kind of playful affection that is largely performative. The couple had a daughter, Rosalind, in 1919. After the war, Archie joined the Imperial and Foreign Corporation and in 1922 took his wife on the British Empire Tour (chronicled through letters in *The Grand Tour*). Once Agatha was an established, successful writer, the Christies bought a house in Sunningdale, which they named Styles after the house in her first novel, and Agatha became, in her words, "a golf widow" (*AA* 343) as the pastime absorbed her husband.

In 1926, Archie announced that he was having an affair with Nancy Neele, a young secretary, and that he wanted a divorce. After several bitter quarrels and a dramatic disappearance by Agatha, the couple divorced in 1928. A few months later, Archie married Neele. The couple had a son, also called Archibald, in 1930. Archie sold Styles and moved with his new wife to London. He does not seem to have stayed in touch with his first wife, although his brother and sister-in-law, writers Campbell and Dorothy Christie, did. Archie died in 1962.

See also: **Beresford, Thomas ("Tommy"); Disappearance of Agatha Christie; Neele, Nancy; Styles House**

Christie, Rosalind. See Hicks, Rosalind

"Christmas Adventure" (story)

The last of the first series of Poirot stories for *The Sketch*, "Christmas Adventure" was published on 11 December 1923. It is best known now as the inspiration for the novella "The Adventure of the Christmas Pudding" (1960). In the story, Poirot spends Christmas at a country house, where he receives a note warning him not to eat the Christmas pudding. On Christmas Day, some children in the house stage a mock-murder to tease him, and Poirot uses the scene to catch a thief who has hidden the stolen item—a jewel—in the pudding.

The story was subsequently published in two pulp volumes, *Problem at Pollensa Bay and Christmas Adventure* (1943), and *Poirot Knows the Murderer* (1946). It was later included in *While the Light Lasts* (1997) but is not currently available in the United States.

Characters: Cardell, Nancy; Endicott, Emily; Endicott, Mr.; Endicott, Roger; Eric; **Gladys**; Graves; Haworth, Evelyn; **Hicks, Annie**; Jean; Jonnie; Levering, Miss; Levering, Oscar; Pease, Charlie; **Poirot, Hercule**

See also: **"The Adventure of the Christmas Pudding" (story);** *Poirot Knows the Murderer***;** *While the Light Lasts* **(story collection)**

"A Christmas Tragedy" (alternative titles: "The Hat and the Alibi"; "Never Two without Three"). See *The Thirteen Problems*

Christow, Dr. John, and Gerda

In *The Hollow*, John Christow is a Harley Street doctor, working on a cure for "Ridgeway's Disease" (a fictional spinal disease). Like Amyas Crale, Christow is a womanizer and is murdered for it, realizing at the end of his life that he loves his wife after all. Christow has a kind of insistent masculinity: when he is around the ineffectual Edward Angkatell, according to one character, "John ... becomes so much *more* so and Edward becomes so much *less* so" (12; emphasis in original). Gerda, his emotionally neglected wife, realizes, like Miss Marple (and Christie) that it is advantageous for a woman to appear more stupid than she is.

Chupi Chupi Aashey. See **Indian-Language Adaptations**

Cinderella. See **Duveen, Dulcie**

Clancy, Daniel

Detective novelist Daniel Clancy is suspected of murder by the police in *Death in the Clouds*, partly because he wrote a novel with an identical weapon and partly because he is not traditionally masculine.

Clapperton, Adeline, and John

In "Problem at Sea" (and its predecessor, "Poirot and the Crime in Cabin 66"), Adeline is John Clapperton's domineering wife and the murder victim. She speaks loudly and extensively of her many good deeds and her zest for life, and is so interested in being admired and valued that she makes herself hated. Her overshadowed husband eventually snaps and kills her in a kind of midlife crisis. He dies of shock when Hercule Poirot tricks him into a confession.

Clara

In the St. Mary Mead novels, there are two Claras, both maids to local women and both eternally young. In "The Thumb Mark of St Peter" (1928), Clara works for Miss Marple. In *The Murder at the Vicarage* (1930), a similar Clara is in service to Mrs. Price-Ridley. She is still with her in *The Body in the Library* and "The Case of the Perfect Maid" (both 1942). Marple's Clara returns as a former employee in *The Mirror Crack'd from Side to Side* (1962).

Clarke, Franklin

The sporting brother of Sir Carmichael Clarke, Franklin Clarke devises an ingenious plot in *The ABC Murders*. Posing as a mad serial killer, he can camouflage the sane and motivated murder of his wealthy brother. He is in love with Thora Grey.

Clarke, Lady Charlotte

Lady Charlotte Clarke is the elderly, terminally ill wife of Sir Carmichael Clarke in *The ABC Murders*, whose prejudice against beautiful young women hampers the investigation before it provides a valuable clue.

Clarke, Sir Carmichael

Sir Carmichael Clark is a country squire killed in Churston; he is the third victim in *The ABC Murders*.

Class

A perennial issue in the twentieth century, class is one aspect of Christie's novels that is generally glossed. It is taken for granted that her books represent a vision of a long-lost (and never quite real) upper-middle-class Edwardian England, where the only significant characters are well-to-do and servants know their place. There is some truth to this characterization, but it is not the whole story. Christie herself was from an upper middle-class family, and she had a rather conventional upbringing on a large, frequently visited estate where she was privately educated by a series of governesses. In later youth, she lived in France and traveled to Cairo. She always had servants. The family was not overburdened with money, but it was socially privileged.

The novels present, on many levels, conventional middle-class stereotypes. It is true that the plots of several revolve around the idea that nobody looks at servants or staff: without this as a given, the killers in "The Case of the Caretaker," *Death in the Clouds*, *Three Act Tragedy*, and "Yellow Iris" would be unable even to attempt to get away with it. The very fact that servants rarely come under suspicion despite their presence at most crime scenes speaks to their status as not quite human and thus not on a level with the protagonists. Servants slowly disappear from the novels, as they did from wealthy households more generally. Indeed, Christie reflected that she was astonished by just how many servants populated her early works (Wyndham E5). Still, there are usually one or two old retainers even in the late books.

Another typically conservative approach to class is Christie's presentation of the *nouveau riche*. The victim in *The Murder of Roger Ackroyd* is, some may think, bound to die, when the narrator describes him, satirically, as "more impossibly like a country squire than any country squire" (7), and Lord Whitfield, a self-made newspaper magnate in *Murder Is Easy,* is roundly mocked for his pomposity. The impression is given that these are people seeking to emulate something they can never really achieve because they were not born into it. Christie has a similar model for presenting American millionaires. Anyone seeking fundamental social change is presented as naïve. For example, if the angry socialist Mr. Ferguson in *Death on the Nile* would just acknowledge that he is actually Lord Dawlish, he would be happier with his lot and luckier in love.

Lidia Kyzlinkova points out that Christie does not often write about "the working class" except in general terms: "if we do [encounter working-class characters,] there are to be found features that closely correspond to those of the servants. The working class seems quite childish, naive, and honest in the Christie plots" (123). Kyzlinkova's reading gives the lie to criticism that seeks to highlight Christie's empathy for working-class characters by pointing out, for example, that Poirot helps a broken-hearted mechanic in "The Acadian Deer" or that the helpless maid Agnes Woddell is the most heavily-mourned character in *The Moving Finger.* These characters are all, to some extent, infantilized.

However, Christie presented a complex and convincing portrait of a young working-class man in her 1967 novel *Endless Night,* which is written entirely convincingly in the voice of the ruthlessly ambitious Michael Rogers. Nonetheless, that character's crimes stem from a sense of entitlement and a drive toward social mobility: he steals all his life as well as marries and kills a millionaire to acquire a house and a lifestyle to which he is not, by birth, entitled.

Kyzlinkova concludes that it can be "difficult to [know] just when Dame Agatha had her tongue in her cheek and when she was slipping in signs of her own opinions" (126). Ultimately, any reading of class in Christie should take account of the author's aims—"to hold up a mirror to" the world around her (*PTF* 13)—and her own context.

As Danny Nicol writes, "She wanted her novels to be true to life and grounded in the real world. She therefore drew on the reality that was readily apparent from the time in which she lived" (8).

See also: **Bright Young Things**; *Endless Night*; *The Murder of Roger Ackroyd*

Claythorne, Vera

In *And Then There Were None,* Vera Claythorne is the most guilty of the people summoned to Soldier Island for execution. The last to die, she hangs herself after finally accepting responsibility for her past crimes. Now a secretary, she was a nursery governess in the past. Caring for toddler Cyril Hamilton, she allowed him to swim into dangerous waters, where he drowned, so that his inheritance would pass to his uncle, Hugo, whom she wanted to marry.

In most novels, the beautiful young woman, with a history of child care and a status as the last survivor, would have a happy ending, but this novel assigns her a portion of guilt arguably greater than that allotted to the "main" murderer. When Christie adapted the book as a play at the height of World War II, she judged that audiences needed a happy ending and sympathetic characters, so she recast Vera Claythorne and Philip Lombard as two innocent parties who survive the ordeal and agree to marry.

Cleat, Mrs.

Mrs. Cleat is a villager in *The Moving Finger,* considered a prime suspect for sending anonymous letters because she is different. She "[g]oes out to gather herbs and things at the full moon and takes care that everybody in the place knows about it" (*TMF* 122). However, she is a tangential figure. The name may be a reference to Edith Cleeth, who was suspected of sending anonymous letters in the 1930s on the Isle of Wight.

Clegg, Freda

Freda Clegg is a young woman, orphaned in childhood, who has grown bored with life and consults J. Parker Pyne in "The Case of the Discontented Soldier." After paying a fee of three guineas, she becomes embroiled in an extraordinary adventure and ends up marrying a stranger, Major

Wilbraham, who, unbeknownst to her, is another of Pyne's clients.

Clement, David, and Leonard Jr.

David Clement and Leonard Clement Jr. are the children of Griselda and Rev. Leonard Clement; Leonard Jr. is conceived during *The Murder at the Vicarage* and becomes interested in trains, helping Miss Marple with timetables in *4.50 from Paddington*. David is a small child, crawling backward, in *The Body in the Library*.

Clement, Griselda

Although her name is suitable for a vicar's wife, Griselda Clement is unconventionally young and worldly. Nonetheless, her devotion to her husband is genuine. After her introduction in *The Murder at the Vicarage*, in which she is the subject of deep suspicion, she becomes more of a background figure, often exchanging gossip with Miss Marple over the telephone, in *The Body in the Library*, *4.50 from Paddington*, and *The Mirror Crack'd from Side to Side*.

Clement, Rev. Leonard

Vicar of St. Mary Mead, Leonard Clement narrates *The Murder at the Vicarage* as a middle-aged cleric confused by the sexual entanglements he observes. He is also endlessly fearful that his young and free-spirited wife will leave him or prove too good to be true. However, they remain happily married throughout the Miss Marple series. Clement appears briefly in *The Body in the Library*, and, in *The Mirror Crack'd from Side to Side*, it is implied that he has died.

"Cleopatra as the Dark Lady"

In January 1973, historian A.L. Rowse claimed in the *Times* of London that he had identified the "Dark Lady" of William Shakespeare's sonnets as the poet Emilia Lanier (née Bassino). This claim appeared more extensively the same year in Rowse's book, *Shakespeare's Sonnets: The Problem Solved*. Christie, a friend of Rowse, contributed to the discussion with a letter to the *Times*, published on 3 February 1973. In "Cleopatra as the Dark Lady," Christie argues that the female lead of *Antony and Cleopatra* is so convincingly drawn, especially the mix of raw sexuality and emotional frustration, that she may have the same real-life inspiration as the Dark Lady. This argument was critiqued at the time for lacking evidence (Curran, *Making* 371; Rowse 104), although Rowse noted the psychological insight it demonstrated (but apparently failed to notice that nowhere in the letter does Christie agree with his reading [Rowse 103–04]).

The letter also outlines Christie's opinions that Shakespeare's plays should be viewed rather than read in the first instance and that Shakespeare was a frustrated actor who, lacking performance skills, turned to writing. It is not difficult to see Christie reading herself—the frustrated opera singer—into the Bard.

See also: **Shakespeare, William**

"The Clergyman's Daughter" (story; alternative title: "The First Wish"). See *Partners in Crime* (Story Collection)

Clithering, Sir Henry

Former commissioner of Scotland Yard and godfather to Inspector Dermot Craddock, Sir Henry Clithering often vouches for Miss Marple, encouraging his colleagues to listen to her, despite her unconventional approach to detection. He features in each of *The Thirteen Problems* and in *The Body in the Library*, *4.50 from Paddington*, *A Murder Is Announced*, *Nemesis*, and *A Pocket Full of Rye*.

Cloade, Roland ("Rowley")

Cousin and fiancé to Lynn Marchmont in *Taken at the Flood*, Roland Cloade did not see any action during World War II because he worked as a farmer. As a result, he has not changed, although she has, and he appears to be a boring, unrisky presence in her life. However, he reveals hidden depths of passion and aggression toward the end of the novel.

Cloade, Rosaleen

In *Taken at the Flood*, Rosaleen Cloade is David Hunter's sister and the new wife (now widow) of elderly patriarch Gordon Cloade. The woman who presents herself as Rosaleen is shy, petite, and easily manipulated. As an Irish Catholic, she becomes overwhelmed with guilt and treats Hercule Poirot as a kind of father confessor.

It emerges that the real Rosaleen Cloade died in a wartime bombing and that an Irish housemaid, Eileen Corrigan, has been manipulated by David Hunter into taking her place.

"The Clock Stopped" (story)

"The Clock Stopped" is a curious work in the Christie canon. The Yorkshire Copper Works, an industrial manufacturing facility in Leeds, was founded in the 1880s and closed in 1997. Around the time of World War II, it launched the *Yorkshire Magazine* for employees. A regular feature of the magazine was regular creative-writing competitions, open to employees only.

In fall 1949, the magazine ran a competition designed by Christie. Christie contributed a very short opening to a story and asked readers to continue it to a maximum of 800 words. The prizes for the best three entries were listed as £3, £2, and £1, with the winner to be published in that year's Christmas issue. It is unlikely that Christie judged the entries herself.

The story, titled "The Clock Stops," begins with a young typist visiting the home of a blind woman and finding a dead man in the sitting room, surrounded by various clocks, including one labeled "Rosemary." Christie included several notes on how entrants might follow up this opening—so many notes, in fact, that it is difficult to imagine a development not pre-empted in italics.

The author of the present work is unable to locate the Christmas 1949 issue of the *Yorkshire Magazine*, so the outcome of the competition is unclear. However, the story has a strong legacy, as Christie used the exact premise as the basis of *The Clocks* (1963).

Characters: Hollaran, Nancy; Leadbetter, Miss; Spencer, Miss

See also: *The Clocks*

The Clocks (novel)

The Clocks started life in 1949 as a short story competition for employees of the Yorkshire Copper Works. At that time, Christie sketched the beginning of a story, "The Clock Stopped," and asked entrants to complete it in 800 words. Fourteen years later, she took up her own challenge—with a rather higher word-count—and made a novel out of the premise. The opening of *The Clocks* combines the set-up of "The Clock Stopped" with that of Stephen Maddock's 1945 thriller, *I'll Never Like Friday Again*.

Sheila Webb, a stenographer with an agency, is requested to do a job for a blind woman, Millicent Pebmarsh. Sheila lets herself into the house, as per instructions, only to find a dead man, surrounded by various clocks that have been stopped at 4:13, despite the current time of 3 o'clock. When Miss Pebmarsh enters, Sheila runs out, screaming, into the arms of Colin Lamb, an undercover member of British Intelligence, who narrates this book.

The man is a stranger to Miss Pebmarsh and, apparently, everyone else, and Colin works with Inspector Hardcastle to learn the victim's identity, the reasons why he was at 19 Wilbraham Crescent and was murdered, and the name of the perpetrator. He consults Hercule Poirot, who solves the case from his flat, relying on Colin to do his legwork. A complicated picture of spies and espionage emerges, and the surface confusion of the many clocks and why Sheila was called continues to cloud the case. However, Poirot suggests that a lot of this is a smoke screen and that the crime itself is simple. He identifies the victim and names the killer from among the neighbors. He also unmasks a spy in the unlikely form of Miss Pebmarsh and picks up on a guilty secret of Sheila's. She and Colin are romantically linked.

Thematically, *The Clocks* fits in with the chaos and paranoia of the Cold War era. There are (multiple) spies and murderers living in close proximity in a suburban cul-de-sac, and they are unlikely types: not only the blind elderly woman who proves to be an international spy ring's leader but also the murderer living under the significant name "Bland." It is, however, presented with some awareness that this is not quite the real world. Colin is constantly comparing himself to the heroes of spy thrillers, and exchanges at the secretarial bureau are filled with satiric asides about novels and novelists, for whom the typists do freelance work.

Metafiction abounds when Poirot is

introduced—late into the action, as was becoming usual. No sooner has Colin arrived than Poirot has given his opinions on various real murder cases—that of Charles Bravo and the alleged crimes of Adelaide Bartlett, Constance Kent, and Lizzie Borden. However, he explains, those were unsatisfactory to think about because everyone involved is dead, and no new information can be gleaned—instead, "I turned to fiction" (123). Unprompted, he launches into a lengthy account of the strengths and weaknesses of early crime fiction, discussing Anna Katharine Green's *The Leavenworth Case*, Maurice Leblanc's *The Adventures of Arsène Lupin*, and Gaston Leroux's *The Mystery of the Yellow Room*—all documented influences on Christie's writing. Of course, he is scathing about Sherlock Holmes, and then he discusses quite critically the work of Ariadne Oliver (his friend and Christie's fictional alter ego) and two more writers created in *The Clocks*. In his semi-retirement, Poirot is writing a monograph on crime fiction (by the next novel, *Third Girl*, he will have completed it).

The Clocks also explores disability. Miss Pebmarsh has been blind for 14 years before the action of the novel. Disability is rarely a theme in Christie's fiction. In *Crooked House* (1949), the young Eustace is embittered as a result of his disability due to polio, which has thwarted a promising intellect; he is presented as part of the grotesqueness of the Leonides family, like his sister whose obsession with murder mysteries has corrupted her own intelligence to more disastrous effect. In *The Unexpected Guest* (1954), the wheelchair-bound victim has no redeeming qualities; indeed, his disability is a talisman of a sinister past. However, there is a much more nuanced presentation of disability by the time of *The Clocks*.

When her eyesight started to fail, Miss Pebmarsh learned Braille and has become a much-valued member of the community, teaching Braille to children. There is nothing patronizing about how she is presented, although other characters patronize her and are reprimanded. Finally, in her role as a spy, she is afforded the narrative dignity of agency so rarely applied to disabled characters created by able-bodied authors. Parallels could be drawn to Christie's accounts of her increasingly limited mobility and her dislike of being "helped" and patronized into her mid-seventies.

The Clocks was published by Collins in the United Kingdom in December 1963 and by Dodd, Mead in the United States in January the next year. Abridged versions were serialized in *Woman's Own* in the United Kingdom and *Cosmopolitan* in the United States; unusually, these appeared after the book. *The Clocks* has been filmed once, as an episode of *Agatha Christie's Poirot* that was broadcast in 2010.

Characters: Beck, Colonel; **Bland, Josiah, and Valerie**; **Brent, Edna**; Brown, Geraldine; Castletown, Harry; Cray, Sergeant; **Curry, R.H.**; **Curtin, Ernie, and Mrs.**; Duguesclin, Quentin; Elks, Florence; **Gregson, Gary**; **Gretel**; **Hardcastle, Detective Inspector Richard (Dick)**; Hemming, Mrs.; **Lamb, Colin**; **Martindale, Katherine**; McNaughton, Mrs. and Professor Angus; **Oliver, Ariadne**; **O'Malley, Louisa**; **Pebmarsh, Millicent**; **Poirot, Hercule**; **Quain, Cyril**; Ramsay, Bill and Ted; Ramsay, Mrs.; Rigg, Dr.; **Rival, Merlina**; Sunbeam; Waterhouse, Edith and James; **Webb, Sheila**

See also: ***Agatha Christie's Poirot***; **Battle, Superintendent**; **"The Clock Stopped"**; **War**

Clode, Simon

In "Motive vs. Opportunity," Simon Clode is heartbroken when his granddaughter, Chris, dies. In poor health, he consults a highly insalubrious medium, Eurydice Spragg, who seems able to communicate with Chris. This sends Simon "into ecstasies[, proclaiming] she had been sent to him by Heaven" (*TTP* 75). Learning he is shortly to die, he makes a new will, leaving everything to the medium. "Simon Clode" is a soubriquet, applied by Mr. Petherick, who is telling the story.

Close-Up (radio series)

The BBC dedicated an episode of its radio series *Close-Up* to Christie in 1955. Providing an overview of her career to date, especially the record-breaking success of *The Mousetrap*, the program included interviews with many of her theatrical contacts—Peter Saunders (producer), Margaret Lockwood, Richard Attenborough, Francis L. Sullivan (stars of her plays), Allen Lane (publisher), and Christie herself. Lane's prerecorded account details Christie's role in the establishment of Penguin Books. Christie's contribution, also prerecorded, attributes her success to the lack of formal education and emphasizes the importance of giving children time and space to develop their imaginations.

The program was broadcast as the *Light Programme* on 13 February 1955. An archived recording was made available on the BBC website in 2008, until 2018 when it was released as a CD. Transcribed extracts have been widely published over the years.

See also: *Light Programme Festival*

Closed Casket (Hannah). See **Continuation Fiction**

"The Clue of the Chocolate Box." See **"The Chocolate Box"**

Cluedo/Clue. See **Games**

The Clutching Hand **(play)**

It is unclear why Christie adapted Arthur B. Reeve's *The Exploits of Elaine* (1915) as a four-act stage drama. Reeve's novel features his series detective Craig Kennedy, often cited as the American Sherlock Holmes, and was itself based on an episodic film series of the same name. This series had followed the more famous *The Perils of Pauline* and, like its predecessor, starred Pearl White as the heroine. That format would, of course, be parodied extensively in Christie's fourth published novel, *The Man in the Brown Suit* (1924).

Julius Green has suggested that the script may have been a response to the famous bet between Christie and her sister, Madge, in 1916, that she could not write a detective story (62), although the fact that it is not a novel or story suggests otherwise, unless this was a hitherto-unknown exercise employed by Christie to distill the essence of plot. If, as John Curran has suggested, the early play *Black Coffee* (1930) started life as an attempt to adapt *The Mysterious Affair at Styles* (1920) for the stage (see Curran, "Black Coffee"), this script could perhaps be regarded as an early attempt to practice

adapting a detective narrative. It may simply have been a way for Christie and her performance-minded friends to enjoy the action of the films when they were no longer being played at cinemas. It could also have been commissioned, but the loss of much of Christie's professional communications prior to World War II make this difficult to confirm. As Green notes, the American dialogue is not very convincing, and this script has not been published or performed to anyone's knowledge.

See also: **Black Coffee** (play); *The Man in the Brown Suit*

Le Coffret de Lacque **(The Lacquered Box; film)**

French cinema (and television) did not fully embrace Christie until the twenty-first century, but the first French film adaptation was the fifth Christie film, released in 1932. *Le Coffret de Lacque* (The Lacquered Box) starred René Alexandre as M. Preval, a French detective based on Hercule Poirot. The script by Pierre Maudru, H. Fowler Mear, and Brock Williams was based on the 1930 play *Black Coffee*, although Christie's agents were not aware of it until 1936. A minor role was given to a 16-year-old Danielle Darrieux, who would make her second appearance in a Christie adaptation 75 years later in *L'Heure Zéro* (2007).

See also: **Black Coffee** (play); **Poirot, Hercule**; *L'Heure Zéro*

Cole, Elizabeth

Elizabeth Cole is a handsome, middle-aged woman who attracts Captain Hastings's attention in *Curtain*. She is haunted by the death of her sister, Margaret Litchfield, in an asylum. Her real surname is Lichfield.

Coleman, William ("Bill")

William Coleman is a wealthy young man with an amiable but twittish nature who lives on the dig but is not much interested in archaeology in *Murder in Mesopotamia*. Narrator Amy Leatheran describes him as behaving "more like a P.G. Wodehouse book than like a real live young man" (133). The description may be a kind of playful payback for the high volume of references in Wodehouse's work to people reading Christie. Women easily distract Coleman.

Collier/Collins, Beryl

Beryl is John Christow's impassive secretary in *The Hollow*, with more than a touch of Poirot's secretary Miss Lemon about her. In early editions, this character is referred to as Beryl Collier in chapter 3 and Beryl Collins in chapter 16. In more recent editions, she is consistently named Collins.

Collins Crime Club

The idea of crime fiction "clubs" was not new in 1930 when William Collins, Christie's publisher since 1926, launched the Collins Crime Club. Indeed, there was already a Crime Club—a book club—in the United States and a Detection Club—a body of writers—operating out of London. Moreover, Collins had already enjoyed medium success with its "Detective Story Club," later rechristened "The Detective Club" in the 1920s. Like the Crime Club, its predecessor was not really a club but an imprint.

The Detective Club had focused on low-end stock: reprints and magazine-quality novels. The Crime Club would advertise its selectivity with new titles and less lurid dustjackets. It was established, with its signature "hooded gunman" logo, to be "the sign of a good book." Although not in any real sense a club, early promotion encouraged "membership," and there was a club newsletter for some years. It was not without controversy: Dorothy L. Sayers (published by Gollancz) led the charge of disgruntled non–Collins crime writers, protesting advertisements that suggested that Crime Club titles had been independently selected for glory. In fact, all sharing a publisher, it gave the impression that no other publisher was turning out solid crime books.

Undaunted, the imprint launched and enjoyed great success from 1930 to 1992. It was briefly revived in 2015. It published almost all of Christie's novels and several of her short story collections from *The Murder at the Vicarage* (1930) onward. In 1935, crime writer Peter Cheyney produced "The Crime Club Card Game," a complicated game for multiple players with several illustrated cards featuring characters from Crime Club novels—including Christie's Hercule Poirot and Superintendent Battle but mostly Cheyney creations. John Curran's *The Hooded Gunman* (2019) provides a pictorial history of the Crime Club.

See also: **The Detection Club**; **Games**; **Golden Age Crime Fiction**; **Only for Dons**

Collodon, Miss

Miss Collodon is a researcher for Tommy Beresford in *Postern of Fate*. Like Ariadne Oliver (especially in *Elephants Can Remember*), she has an ever-changing hairstyle, reflecting social pressure for older women to continue reinventing themselves.

"Columbine's Song." See *A Masque from Italy*

Come and Be Hanged! See *Towards Zero* **(novel)**

Come, Tell Me How You Live (nonfiction work)

This short nonfiction book was published under the name Agatha Christie Mallowan to distinguish it from her crime writing. In a foreword and epilogue, Christie warns readers that it is an "inconsequent chronicle" (*CTMHYL* 205) and "not a profound book" (17) but simply an account of her time in Syria with her second husband, archaeologist Max Mallowan, in 1930.

The title *Come, Tell Me How You Live* comes from a poem by Lewis Carroll, which Christie parodies in her own piece, "A-Sitting on a Tell," to open the book. Carroll's verse, itself a parody of William Wordsworth's "Resolution and Independence," appears in *Alice through the Looking Glass*.

The observations are generally of people—the people Christie left in England and those she met on her travels. There are several sweeping generalizations: "The prisoners were amiable," she writes, explaining why locals were not paid to help on digs, "in the highest good humour, and seemed to enjoy the work" (45). Later, she discloses that "Turkish men nearly all bear a remarked resemblance to a colored picture of Lord Kitchener that used to hand in my nursery" (89), an observation that says rather more about the writer than her subject. The memoir expresses a fascination with other cultures but not a desire to understand them. Dig work is described—as "[d]etective work" (146)—but only in light terms, and Christie minimizes her involvement when, in fact, she was highly active in it.

The memoir started in the late 1930s but was set aside with the advent of World War II. It was completed later and published, with black-and-white photographs, by Collins in 1946. In 2018, Syrian novelist Haitham Hussein published his own memoir, the title of which translates to *There May Not Be Anyone Left: Agatha Christie.... Come, I'll Tell You How I Live*. In it, he argues against her orientalist generalizations about eastern contentedness.

See also: **Archaeology**; *An Autobiography*; **Mallowan, Sir Max**

"The Coming of Mr. Quin" (story; alternative title: "The Passing of Mr. Quinn")

"The Coming of Mr. Quin" is the first Harley Quin story. At a New Year's Eve party at Royston Hall, the shy Mr. Satterthwaite notices that his hosts and fellow guests are acting strangely. Just after midnight, a mysterious visitor—Harley Quin—arrives at the house, and light shining through a stained-glass window gives the effect of making him look like a harlequin. Quin explains that his car has broken down and by way of small talk discusses an unexplained suicide that took place at Royston Hall 10 years previously.

With prompts from Quin, Satterthwaite uncovers a complex romantic triangle and a deep-rooted murder plot; he explains the suicide that occurred. In a final twist, he realizes that one person affected by those incidents is currently in the house and that his explanation has prevented her suicide. Quin discusses the symbolism of the harlequinade and announces that his car is ready. He disappears into the night.

The story was first published in the *Grand Magazine* in March 1923. It was filmed as *The Passing of Mr. Quinn* (the first British Christie film) in 1928, and a novelization by G. Roy McRae was published the same year. The story, with changes to distinguish it from the film, opens *The Mysterious Mr. Quin*, published by Collins in the United

Kingdom and Dodd, Mead in the United States in 1930.

Characters: Capel, Derek; Conway, Lady Laura; Conway, Sir Richard; **Portal, Alec, and Eleanor**; **Quin, Harley**; **Satterthwaite, Mr.**

See also: **Commedia dell'arte**; *The Mysterious Mr. Quin*; *The Passing of Mr. Quinn* (film)

Commedia dell'arte

Originating in Italy in the sixteenth century, *commedia dell'arte* became popular across Europe and by the late-nineteenth century it was popular among the British upper classes as a Parisian art form. The genre relies on stock characters—archetypes representing the breadth of humanity between them. These include Columbine (the simple, mischievous maid), Harlequin (the ever-present clown servant), Pierrot and Pierrette (the lovers), Pantalone (the wealthy merchant), and Il Capitano (the blackguard), among others. Christie herself is often charged with writing in stereotypes, and the influence of these stock characters on her use of recognizable "types" to convey complex emotions in a few strokes is evident.

A lifelong collector of porcelain figures representing the Harlequinade, Christie was always enticed by *commedia dell'arte*. Her early poems and dramas, such as *A Masque from Italy*, re-create the stories and characters precisely, and they weave in and out of her early fiction. Her first Poirot short story, "The Affair at the Victory Ball," is set during a Harlequin-themed ball, where characters hide and confuse one another behind themed masks. Most obviously, she created the semi-supernatural figure Harley Quin, who assists the perpetual outsider Mr. Satterthwaite in matters of the human heart in *The Mysterious Mr. Quin* and other stories. These stories were her personal favorites, written as and when the need struck her, and they are thematically among her most personal.

This interest in the subject was not unusual among the upper and upper-middle classes in the early-twentieth century. Harlequin-themed costume balls trickle into popular fiction of the period, including

Dorothy L. Sayers's *Strong Poison* (1929) and P.G. Wodehouse's *Right Ho, Jeeves* (1934). In 1944, Christie considered writing a play or ballet based on *commedia dell'arte*, to bring escapism (and a degree of nostalgia) from the horrors of war. She imagined Australian dancer Robert Helpmann, whose ballet of *Hamlet* she admired, in the role of Harlequin. However, this play was never written—although Christie did adapt "The Dead Harlequin" into a play, *Someone at the Window*, which was never staged.

See also: **"The Affair at the Victory Ball"**; *The Mysterious Mr. Quin*; **Quin, Harley**; *Someone at the Window*

"The Companion" (alternative title: "The Resurrection of Amy Durrant"). See *The Thirteen Problems*

Conan Doyle, Sir Arthur (1859–1930)

There is no evidence that Agatha Christie and Arthur Conan Doyle ever met or corresponded, although innumerable writers and filmmakers have imagined meetings. Conan Doyle was a profound influence on Christie, who grew up reading his Sherlock Holmes stories and novels such as "A Scandal in Bohemia" and *The Hound of the Baskervilles*. These hugely influential works were published between 1887 and 1926. The plot and atmosphere of *Baskervilles* directly influenced Christie's "The Lemesurier Inheritance" and *The Sittaford Mystery*.

Like Christie, Conan Doyle became frustrated with his creation, the acerbic consulting detective who became so popular many readers thought he was real, and tried to kill him off in "The Final Problem" (1894), only to revive him, in response to the public outcry and to considerable financial incentives, in 1901. Many of the Holmes stories were published in *The Strand*, which later published Christie. Unlike Christie, however, Conan Doyle preferred not to be remembered for his detective fiction, insisting that his historical fantasies and adventure stories were superior.

An adventurer and propagandist in addition to his work as a writer, Conan Doyle was occasionally consulted by Scotland Yard on difficult cases. The police even consulted him in 1926 when Christie disappeared. However, by now, he was almost entirely consumed by an interest in spiritualism. He asked for an item that had belonged to the missing author and, when presented with a glove, showed it to a medium.

See also: **Disappearance of Agatha Christie; "The Lemesurier Inheritance"; Poirot, Achille; Poirot, Hercule**

Conneau, Georges. See **Renauld, Paul**

Connell, Marjorie

Marjorie Connell is a young secretary in the Mary Westmacott novel *Unfinished Portrait* who has an affair with Dermot. This character is an unflattering portrait of Nancy Neele, the secretary for whom Archie Christie left his wife.

The Conqueror (play)

A one-act play written under the name Sydney West, *The Conqueror: A Fantasy* is an example of Christie's juvenilia. It is currently housed in the Christie Family Archive and has never been published or performed. In it, a sphinx-like figure, which presents itself as Fate incarnate, is exposed by angels to be an imposter.

See also: **Pseudonyms**

Continuation Fiction

The little-studied phenomenon of continuation novels has been a major part of publishing for decades. A continuation novel is one in which an author revives a literary series or character created and made famous by another writer, sometimes deceased, and with the estate's authorization. Most major crime writers and writers in other genres have received the continuation novel treatment, and Christie is no exception. There have been several parodies of Christie's writing and creations, as well as several unofficial resurrections of her characters, but this entry considers those authorized by her family and Agatha Christie Ltd.

In Christie's lifetime, there were numerous requests, always refused, to write new cases for Poirot or Miss Marple for stage or screen and, in one case, for a clergyman to publish a biography of Poirot; Christie's agent apparently lost this manuscript. Years after her death, the estate authorized Canadian professor Anne Hart to write *The*

Life and Times of Miss Jane Marple (1985) and, later, *The Life and Times of Hercule Poirot* (1990), although, unlike William S. Baring-Gould's influential biography of Sherlock Holmes, neither of these adds details that are absent from Christie's published work.

The first example of fiction reviving Christie's characters and authorized by her estate came in 1981, with Julian Symons's *The Great Detectives: Seven Original Investigations*. This glossy book was lavishly illustrated by Tom Adams, the most recognizable of Christie's cover artists, and featured chapters on Poirot and Miss Marple in addition to Sir Arthur Conan Doyle's Sherlock Holmes, Raymond Chandler's Philip Marlowe, Georges Simenon's Jules Maigret, Rex Stout's Nero Wolfe, and Frederic Dannay and Manfred B. Lee's Ellery Queen. Each chapter is a work of fiction, relaying the detective's backstory and imagining episodes from their career. Symons, a crime writer, critic, and author of the nonfiction volume *Bloody Murder* (1972), secured permission from each of these authors or their estates.

The Miss Marple entry shares its narrator, Rev. Leonard Clement, with *The Murder at the Vicarage*. It is, essentially, a potted biography of Miss Marple rather than a story. Similarly, the Poirot entry, purporting to be "based on the notes of Captain Arthur Hastings" (Symons, *Great* 95), is largely based on quotes in published works, with some small exceptions. Given Rosalind Hicks's protectiveness about her mother's legacy, it is likely that there was a restriction on what Symons could do. However, he takes the step of inserting the characters, without naming them, into other chapters, which are more straightforward story narratives. Sherlock Holmes is shown in retirement, helping a Miss Jane "M ... was it perhaps Mantle or Maple...?" (29) with an unfortunate engagement. Similarly, Inspector Maigret meets a cocky Belgian detective and then sees his face on the cover of *The Murder of Roger Ackroyd* (93). Tom Adams's illustrations play along with these ideas.

The first Poirot continuation novel also pairs him with other great detectives of times past, including Holmes and Maigret.

Carlo Fruttero and Franco Lucentini's Italian novel *La verità sul caso D* (1989, English title: *The D. Case, or, the Truth about the Mystery of Edwin Drood*) is a postmodern work of literary criticism masquerading as a novel. It features dozens of fictional detectives such as Sherlock Holmes (and Watson), Hercule Poirot (and Hastings), Dr. Thorndyke (and Astley), Nero Wolfe (and Goodwin), Philip Marlowe and Lew Archer who form an amusing double act, basically doing the same thing at all times—with one being famously considered a rip-off of the other, Father Brown, Superintendent Battle, Sergeant Cuff, Hercule Popeau, Toad-in-the-Hole (the antihero in Thomas de Quincey's "On Murder Considered as One of the Fine Arts"), Porfiry Petrovich, Inspector Bucket, Gideon Fell, Dupin, and Maigret. These characters gather at a conference on Charles Dickens's unfinished novel, *The Mystery of Edwin Drood*, and each proposes an ending. Although the authors were not apparently concerned about copyright infringement, Agatha Christie Ltd. is thanked for permission to use the character of Poirot—although the rights to use Captain Hastings and Superintendent Battle, who also appear, are not mentioned. Intriguingly, Poirot's solution to the mystery—that the novel actually reveals Wilkie Collins's murder of Dickens—is based on ideas about plagiarism, and in this book Poirot confronts his own status as a product of plagiarism, reflecting on Marie Belloc Lowndes's creation, Hercule Popeau.

H.R.F. Keating published a short story in Tim Heald's *A Classic English Crime* (1990) that featured Sven Hjerson, the detective created by Ariadne Oliver in Christie's novels. This story is described in publicity materials as "an affectionate tribute" to Christie, although it is unclear if the estate authorized it. Keating, Christie's successor as president of the Detection Club, had already edited *Agatha Christie: First Lady of Crime* in 1979. "Jack Fell Down" is thoroughly in the Christie mold and is a convincing piece of literary ventriloquism. Hjerson is effectively Poirot, with a "tall, gangling" Finnish veneer (95), and shares many of Poirot's idiosyncrasies.

In 2013, British author Sophie Hannah was approached by Agatha Christie Ltd. to write a Poirot continuation novel. Working with the estate, Hannah published *The Monogram Murders* in 2014. This was followed by *Closed Casket* in 2016, *The Mystery of Three Quarters* in 2018, and *The Killings at Kingfisher Hill* in 2020. It was confirmed in 2020 that a fifth book was under contract. Hannah has stated in various interviews that she models her own plotting after Christie's. Each Poirot novel she writes is planned in detail and approved by Mathew and James Prichard, Christie's grandson and great-grandson respectively. However, Hannah also insists publicly that she does not seek to emulate Christie's writing style, which is why she created a new companion and narrator in her books: Inspector Edward Catchpool, who acts as Poirot's mentee. Catchpool's psychological issues act as a bridge between the original Christie environment and the contemporary context in which the books are written.

The new Poirot novels are set between 1929 and 1931, based on the publishers' research indicating that no canonical Poirot titles were set between those years. In fact, Christie's "The Adventure of the Cheap Flat" is set in early 1930. Miss Marple is seen by publishers as more suited to short stories. In Italy, Nico Orengo published a short apparently unauthorized story following Christie's death, in which Marple mourns the passing of her friends Poirot (in *Curtain*) and Christie (in reality, twelve days prior). "Miss Marple's Worries." Was published in *Tutto Libri* on January 24, 1976. It appears in an official Italian volume of Marple stories, published in 2022.

In English, 2022 sees the publication of a new collection of twelve new Marple stories, each by a different bestseller, employing a range of tones and genres. This publication, featuring Naomi Alderman, Leigh Bardugo, Alyssa Cole, Lucy Foley, Elly Griffiths, Natalie Haynes, Jean Kwok, Val McDermid, Karen M. McManus, Dreda Say Mitchel, Kate Mosse, and Ruth Ware seeks new perspectives, not emulations, with the contributors claiming to have been given free rein, although there is inevitably some regulation on content.

See also: **Adams, Tom; Fictional Portrayals of Agatha Christie; Hjerson, Sven; Marple, Jane; Pastiche and Parody; Poirot, Hercule**

Conway, Bridget

In *Murder Is Easy*, Bridget Conway is an unlikely romantic lead. She is perfectly open about her engagement to Lord Whitfield as motivated purely by his money, but she is not judged for this outlook. She enjoys a bantering relationship with Luke Fitzwilliam, in the style of Beatrice and Benedick in Shakespeare's *Much Ado About Nothing*, and ultimately decides to marry him, not because she loves (or desires) him but because she likes him.

Cooke, Miss

Miss Cooke, also known as Miss Bartlett and Miss Hastings, is a middle-aged woman who travels with Miss Barrow and turns out to be a kind of protection officer hired by Jason Rafiel for Miss Marple in *Nemesis*. Miss Cooke appears to be the subordinate partner, as she looks to Miss Barrow for advice.

Cope, Jefferson

Jefferson Cope is an optimistic American solicitor in *Appointment with Death*, who idolizes Nadine Boynton and tries to convince her to leave her husband for him, but he feels protective about Genevra Boynton and marries her instead.

Cork, Edmund (1894–1988)

Edmund Cork served as Christie's long-suffering and extremely tactful literary agent from 1924 until her death in 1976. Cork earned Christie's professional and personal respect, evidenced by a gradual change in tone in their correspondence: initially, all her letters were addressed to "Mr. Cork" but, by the end, they were to "Edmund." Much of Christie's correspondence to Cork, who worked for Hughes, Massie, is housed in the University of Exeter's special collections.

See also: **Ober, Harold**

Cornish, Detective Sergeant/Inspector Frank

Frank Cornish is a policeman who works under Inspector Craddock in *4.50 from Paddington* and *The Mirror Crack'd from*

Side to Side. By the latter, he has evolved from laughing at old ladies like Miss Marple to listening patiently and has also been promoted from sergeant to inspector.

"The Cornish Mystery" (story)

"The Cornish Mystery" is a short story in which a woman believes she is being poisoned by her husband but dies before Hercule Poirot and Captain Hastings can investigate. Eventually, Poirot determines that she was poisoned with arsenic by a young man who was romancing both her and her niece. Poirot tricks the guilty Jacob Radnor into a confession, playing on the fact that he thinks he can charm detectives in the way he can charm women.

The story was first published in the United Kingdom in *The Sketch* on 28 November 1923 and in the United States in *Blue Book Magazine* in October 1925. It appeared in the U.S. anthology *The Under Dog* (1961) and the U.K. collection *Poirot's Early Cases* (1974). The story was filmed as series 2, episode 4 of *Agatha Christie's Poirot*, broadcast on 28 January 1990.

Characters: Adams, Dr.; **Hastings, Captain Arthur**; Jessie; Pengelly, Edward; Pengelly, Mrs.; **Poirot, Hercule**; **Radnor, Jacob**; Stanton, Freda

See also: *Agatha Christie's Poirot*; *Poirot's Early Cases*; *The Under Dog* (story collection)

Corrigan, Alice, and Edward

Alice Corrigan is an historic murder victim and Edward is the husband who killed her; he now lives as Patrick Redfern in *Evil under the Sun.*

Corrigan, Eileen. See Cloade, Rosaleen

Corrigan, Katherine ("Ginger")

In *The Pale Horse*, Katherine Corrigan is a highly likable, red-headed art-restorer who falls in love with Mark Easterbrook while posing as his wife so that some murderers can be trapped. She is a contrast to the pretentious and entitled Hermia Redcliffe, Mark's wealthy girlfriend who ditches him when his focus threatens to shift toward the murders.

Cosdon, Anthony

The "sleek," "almost plump" Anthony Cosdon is nearly 50 years old with "an impression of immaturity" that makes him appear much younger (*MMQ* 156) in "The Man from the Sea." As he has only six months to live, he plans to commit suicide but is dissuaded. His desire for an easy way out is linked by the implied author to his immaturity.

"Count Ferson to the Queen." See *Poems*

Crabtree, Lily

In "Sing a Song of Sixpence," Mrs. Lily Crabtree is Magdalen Vaughan's late great-aunt who was murdered. Although she is dead before the story starts, she is vividly and entertainingly drawn as an eccentric, conservative figure. Christie later gave the name Mrs. Crabtree to John Christow's favorite patient—a cheerful, working-class woman—in *The Hollow.*

Crackenthorpe, Alfred

Alfred Crackenthorpe is the black sheep of the extensive Crackenthorpe family in *4.50 from Paddington.* Known to the police for his involvement in tinned food smuggling during World War II, he lives extravagantly and charms his way out of most situations. He is murdered with arsenic in the novel.

Crackenthorpe, Emma

Emma Crackenthorpe is a plain, middle-aged woman who runs her father's house, Rutherford Hall, with minimal thanks in *4.50 from Paddington.* In a sense, the novel is Emma's *bildungsroman*, as the arrival of housekeeper Lucy Eylesbarrow from London opens her eyes to a world beyond the family home.

Crackenthorpe, Luther

Luther Crackenthorpe is the cantankerous patriarch of Rutherford Hall in *4.50 from Paddington* who is a hypochondriac. He boasts repeatedly of his forebears' success in making money by inventing biscuits, but has done little himself except hoard the money, alienate his family, and maintain the family home as a kind of fortress against the rest of the world. A miser, but not a villain.

"The Crackler" (story; alternative titles: "The Affair of the Forged Notes"; "The Case of the Forged Notes"). See *Partners in Crime* (story collection).

Craddock, Charles, and Mrs.

A married couple who were under the care of Dr. Roberts in *Cards on the Table*. Mrs. Craddock was flirtatious, and complained, without meaning it, that Charles neglected her. Dr. Roberts seems to have infected Charles Craddock with anthrax, and when it seemed he would not be marrying the widow, poisoned her with a vaccination.

Craddock, Detective Inspector/Superintendent Dermot

Although not technically a nephew of Miss Marple, the handsome Inspector Craddock considers her an honorary great-aunt. He first encounters her in *A Murder Is Announced* and appears in "Sanctuary," *4.50 from Paddington*, and *The Mirror Crack'd from Side to Side*. In addition, he is referenced in *A Caribbean Mystery*. The character is one of the more popular Miss Marple detectives, often appearing in screen productions.

"The Crag in the Dolomites." See *The Big Four* (novel)

Crale, Amyas, and Caroline

Amyas and Caroline Crale are a central, unconventional, and deeply loving couple at the heart of *Five Little Pigs*. Both have been dead for 16 years when action begins: Caroline was hanged for killing Amyas. Consistent with Christie's view of brilliant artists, Amyas is concerned only with his vision. He has dalliances with women but ends them when he has finished the project they inspire, and Caroline is aware of this. However, nobody else understands this dynamic, especially not his latest muse, Elsa Greer, who really believed Amyas would leave his wife for her. Caroline confessed to the crime out of love for her half-sister, whom she believed was the killer.

Cram, Gladys. See **Gladys**

Craven, Hilary

Hilary Craven is the protagonist of *Destination Unknown*: a depressed woman who has recently lost a child and experienced a divorce. She resolves to kill herself, but a secret agent offers her a more patriotic way to die, and she embarks on a spy mission.

Cray, Veronica

Veronica Cray is a glamorous Hollywood actress who has inexplicably rented a cottage in the English countryside in *The Hollow*; she turns out to have a romantic history with John Christow and is something of a fabulist. In the text, she is compared unfavorably to Hedy Lamarr (and found to be too intellectual). Outside the text, Owen Dudley Edwards has compared her to World War II cinema idol Veronica Lake.

Cresswell, Mrs.

Mrs. Cresswell is a housekeeper in "Greenshaw's Folly" who initially appears to be a comic character: she overenunciates and has a ludicrously superior manner. She is revealed to be a conspirator in her mistress's murder and the mother of Nathaniel Fletcher, whom she wants to inherit the estate.

"The Cretan Bull" (story; alternative titles: "The Case of the Family Taint"; "Midnight Madness"). See *The Labours of Hercules*

The Crime Club Card Game. See Games

Le Crime est Notre Affaire **(*Crime Is Our Business*).** See *Bélisaire et Prudence Beresford*

"Crime in Cabin 66" (alternative titles: "Crime in Cabin 66"; "The Quickness of the Hand"). See **"Poirot and the Crime in Cabin 66"**

Crime Is Our Business. See *Le Crime est Notre Affaire*

"The Crime Passionnel"

"The Crime Passionnel" was published in volume 2, issue 2 of *Britannia and Eve* in February 1930. The magazine had previously published Christie's "The Man from the Sea" and would go on to publish "What I Would Do If I Were Starving." The *crime passionnel*, a crime committed in the heat of emotion, has always been more common in life than in highly stylized detective fiction, where the puzzle format tends to require an elaborate pre-planned scheme. In Christie's fiction, when a murder looks like a *crime passionnel*, the chances are that it has been *made* to look like one.

See also: **True Crime**; **"What I Would Do if I Were Starving"**

Crispin, Angus

Angus Crispin is an agent of British Intelligence, who poses as Tommy and Tuppence Beresford's gardener in *Postern of Fate*.

Croft, Bert, and Mildred ("Millie")

Bert and Mildred Croft are a pair of Australian lodgers in *Peril at End House*, who turn out to be con-artists. Mr. and Mrs. Croft are eventually exposed as having forged Nick's will. They are presented with typical Christiean extremeness, as hearty, gossipy Australians. While the performance initially beguiles Hastings, Poirot is suspicious early on: "They were, perhaps just a shade too 'typical' ... That cry of Cooee—that insistence on showing us snapshots—was it not playing the part a little too thoroughly?" (61). As Christie's characters are all stereotypes, the line is an important clue to readers to see the characters as bogus.

Crofton-Lee, Sir Rupert

A well-known explorer and adventurer in *They Came to Baghdad*, he is easily recognized by his distinctive cloak. This makes him easy to impersonate; in fact, Sir Rupert is dead and Edward Goring is passing as him. The character is similar to Sir Stafford Nye, the protagonist of *Passenger to Frankfurt*.

Crome, Inspector

Inspector Crome is the young, overconfident, and out-of-his-depth investigating officer from Scotland Yard in *The ABC Murders*, who tends to think and deduce exactly as the murderer desires.

Crooked House (film)

As described in the entry for *Crooked House*, this novel has proven difficult for filmmakers. Giles Paquet-Brenner directed this film, announced in 2011 but not released until 2017 following several production and cast changes. The film was originally to feature a cast including Julie Andrews and Matthew Goode, but these roles eventually went to Glenn Close and Max Irons. *Downton Abbey* and *Gosford Park* writer Julian Fellowes penned a screenplay that is faithful to the novel, and the film, set in the 1950s so marginally after the action of the book, was shot in London and Bristol.

Although a cinematic release was anticipated, the film ran into several production issues, and it was not considered wise to put it in cinemas alongside that year's much more high-budget and ostentatious *Murder on the Orient Express*. It was released first in Italian cinemas on 31 October 2017 and debuted in the United Kingdom on Channel 5 in December that year.

See also: ***Crooked House* (novel)**

Crooked House (novel)

Christie was never entirely consistent about which of her books she preferred, but *Crooked House* was always mentioned in her lists of favorites. She wrote that she "saved [the idea] up for years, thinking about it, working it out," and that "[p]ractically everybody has liked *Crooked House*" (Foreword, *Crooked House* 5). Because of its solution, in which a child is named as the murderer and is executed after a manner, it has been one of Christie's most controversial books.

Crooked House was published in 1949 but is set in 1945. It is narrated by Charles Hayward, the son of a Scotland Yard assistant commissioner, who returns to England from World War II. He is ready now to marry Sophia Leonides, an Englishwoman from a Greek family, whom he met in Cairo. However, she will not get engaged until the mystery surrounding her great-grandfather's death has been resolved. Originally, the 85-year-old Aristide Leonides was said to have died of heart failure, but the police now know he was poisoned. His young, gold-digging wife Brenda is the prime suspect, but Sophia is worried that this is just what the family wants to believe—because she is an outsider. Charles teams up with Chief Inspector Taverner to investigate.

Aristide was a forceful personality with an extended family living in one large monstrosity of a house. These include his sister-in-law, Edith de Havilland, who is a grand matriarch, and various children, their spouses, and grandchildren. Among these are a self-absorbed actress who instantly tries to turn her family murder into a play and a ghoulish 11-year-old granddaughter, Sophia's sister Josephine, who decides to play Sherlock Holmes and records her investigation in a black notebook. The emotional disconnect in the family is reflected in the home itself: an old solid structure, which has simply been built on over several decades, and the fundamental problems of which have not been architecturally addressed. It is also covered with bindweed, reflecting stifled growth.

During his inquiries, Charles is assisted by Josephine, who calls him "Watson" and who surprisingly pre-empts the second murder, as well as an attempt on her own life. In the end, she goes for a car ride with Edith, which results in a crash and the death of both. Charles recovers her black notebook and realizes the truth. In it, she documents how she killed her grandfather because he would not let her take ballet lessons and explains everything that follows. In a note, Edith explains that she figured out that Josephine was the killer and decided to end her life to avoid retribution but also to stop her. The novel ends with Charles commanding Sophia to marry him and to move out of the crooked house.

Christie was not the first to make the killer a child. Most famously, Margery Allingham did it in *The White Cottage Mystery* (1928), although her five-year-old character shot someone accidentally. Many elements of *Crooked House* mirror *The White Cottage Mystery*, including the make-up of the families and the focus on a stifling family home. However, Allingham's book ends with the child repressing its memory and avoiding punishment: years later, they wake up, recalling the whole thing as a dream. Adults, particularly a governess, are blamed for brewing immorality in an innocent child. Christie's novel does not have this idea of childish innocence: a child's ideas are only insubstantial because they lack the framework and vocabulary to present them, not because they are any less intense or real than those of an adult. This is illustrated with an offhand comment made halfway through, similar versions of which appear in *Curtain*, *Towards Zero*, and *And Then There Were None*:

A child, you know, translates desire into action without compunction. A child is angry with its kitten, says "I'll kill you," and hits it on the head with a hammer—and then breaks its heart because the kitten doesn't come alive again! Lots of kids try to take a baby out of a parma and "drown it" because it usurps attention—or interferes with their pleasures. They get—very early—to a stage where they know that it is "wrong"—that is, it will be punished. Later, they get to feel that it is wrong. But some people, I suspect, remain morally immature [*CH* 89].

Preempting criticism, Christie has Charles express initial disbelief but realize that "Josephine and only Josephine fitted in with all the necessary qualifications" (182). In *Crooked House*, Josephine is absolutely culpable, which is why she is killed at the end.

The solution is shocking enough that Christie was, she claimed, asked by her publishers to change it (see Bernthal, *Queering* 180). There is no evidence of this in her business archives, but there is evidence of early radio and television projects falling through once the producers read up to the end—the idea of a child committing murder on evening television, several years before *The Bad Seed* (1956) was too scandalous. Rosalind Hicks, Christie's daughter, later claimed that there was a "family jinx on the book" (qtd. in Aldridge, *Screen* 213), presumably for this reason. Still, the book was published, to strong reviews, in 1949 following serializations in U.S. and U.K. magazines in 1948–49.

Television historian Mark Aldridge has unearthed two scripts for proposed films, one from 1990 and one from 1993, both ultimately unproduced. In 2011, a film adaptation by *Downton Abbey* writer Julian Fellowes was announced. Following several production issues, this was released with modest fanfare in 2017. There has also been a four-part BBC Radio 4 adaptation by Joy Wilkinson, which aired in 2008, and a Yemeni miniseries, *Locked Doors*, in 2016.

Characters: Agrodopolous, Mr.; **Brown, Laurence**; Ferdinand; Gaitskill, Mr.; Gray, Dr.; Glover; **de Havilland, Edith**; de Havilland, Marcia; **Hayward, Charles, and Sir Arthur**; Johnson; **Jones, Vavasour**; Lamb, Sergeant; **Leonides, Aristide, and Brenda;**

Leonides, Clemency and Roger; Leonides, Electra and Joyce; Leonides, Eustace; **Leonides, Josephine; Leonides**, Philip; Leonides, William; Richard; **Rowe, Janet (Nannie)**; Taverner, Chief Inspector; **West, Magda**; Woolmar, Janet

See also: **BBC Radio Adaptations;** *Crooked House* **(Film);** *Locked Doors***; True Crime**

Crossfield, George

In *After the Funeral*, George Crossfield is the late Richard Abernethie's nephew and heir. A young solicitor, he is the son of the late Laura and Rex Crossfield.

"Ctesiphon." See *Poems*

Cunningham, Dr. Alice

Like Judith Hastings in *Curtain*, this young scientist is presented as missing out on life because she devotes her attention to her work rather than to attracting men. Countess Vera Rossakoff compares Dr. Cunningham unfavorably to herself in the 1947 version of "The Capture of Cerberus."

"The Curious Disappearance of the Opalsen Pearls." See "The Jewel Robbery at the Grand Metropolitan"

Curry, R. H.

According to his identification documents, R.H. Curry in *The Clocks* was a salesman. He is discovered stabbed to death in the first chapter. His real name is Quentin Duguesclin, and he is involved in international espionage, which resulted in his death. A photograph of his dead face is published in newspapers to help identify him.

Curses

Like many middle-class people growing up at the end of the long nineteenth century, Christie was interested in the supernatural. The theme of curses runs throughout her work, sometimes paired with witches, sometimes with gothic tropes, and sometimes as a plot device. Although horror fiction and crime fiction have always enjoyed a degree of crossover, anyone who writes about supernatural elements in crime fiction, regardless of their profiles otherwise, can normally be expected to follow one of two paths: they either ensure that all phenomena like curses are explained rationally (like Sir Arthur Conan Doyle in *The Hound of the Baskervilles*, notwithstanding his contributions to other genres), or they fully embrace it (like Sax Rohmer in *The Dream Detective*). Christie, however, did both. Most often, a detective will find a human explanation for apparent magic (such as *The Sittaford Mystery* and *The Pale Horse*), but sometimes the solution to a riddle is supernatural (such as "In a Glass Darkly" and *Endless Night*).

Curses in detective fiction appear as early as Wilkie Collins's *The Moonstone* (1868). Christie provides a take on this story in "The Lemesurier Inheritance." Similarly, in "The Adventure of the Egyptian Tomb," Hercule Poirot reveals that a murderer is using an apparent curse. In this story, the ever-credulous Captain Hastings, who believes the deaths have a supernatural explanation, represents the general public at a moment fascinated by the apparent curse of Tutankhamen in real life. The presumption that there will be a logical explanation—evident to readers from the very beginning, when Christie shows Hastings and Poirot in conflict—serves to reassure anyone who might be affected by a sensationalized media story.

As Poirot puts it in "Dead Man's Mirror": "it was not a curse that cracked the mirror—it was a bullet!" (*MITM* 186). This remark follows another character's quotation of lines from Alfred Lord Tennyson: "Out flew the web and floated wide. / The mirror crack'd from side to side. / 'The curse is come upon me!' Cried / The Lady of Shallot." The same lines are more famously quoted in *The Mirror Crack'd from Side to Side*, in which they provide a psychological clue. They help pinpoint the moment at which one character becomes overwhelmed by her emotional baggage.

In the longer mysteries, there is less of an impetus to find the rational explanation for a curse because the characters like the reader will (generally) assume human agency for crime, although it still underpins the central mystery. After all, this is a ratiocinative genre. Therefore, mysteries around the odd behavior of teenagers in *Evil under the Sun* and *Spider's Web* are resolved when it turns out they have been dabbling in black magic, trying to curse people who then wound up dead, and believing themselves guilty. Of course, someone else commits each murder in question, but in both cases, it is remarked that older and wiser people have believed in black magic before. Because the puzzle element is resolved in each case, there is never a need to consider the question of one person's curse taking effect through another person's agency. It all appears rational, but there is space for a supernatural interpretation.

However, when the focus is not on cursed people but on cursed land, the corresponding narrative becomes less about human action. In *Endless Night*, the land on which the house is built is said to be cursed. The murderer becomes so incensed by a local woman reminding everyone of this that he kills her and becomes obsessed with the curses. There is perhaps a psychological explanation for this, but it is not explored, and neither are the unnatural deaths of the space's previous tenants. On the surface, at least, the supernatural element stands. Notably, *Endless Night* is an expansion of a short story, "The Case of the Caretaker," in which a caretaker places a curse on the house and fulfills the witch's role; it turns out that she has been paid. In the expansion, the witch character has space to become more real as other elements of the story satisfy the rationality quota. Christie's grandson has explained that this is because the author herself believed in these curses (see Prichard). Obsession with property and its ties to a family or an intangible history can be seen throughout Christie's works, from *Peril at End House* in 1932 to *Endless Night* in 1967. Again, however, the supernatural elements—however pronounced—do not compromise the rationality of the mystery narrative.

Outside of Christie's detective fiction, a curse can be simply a curse. There is no rational explanation for the "dangerous" and "evil" (*MMFC* 129) doll in "The Dressmaker's Doll," which appears without notice and is looking for someone to love it, whereas the curse in "The Gipsy" is demonstrably real.

See also: "The Dressmaker's Doll"; *Endless Night* (novel); *The Mirror Crack'd from Side to Side*

Curtain (novel; alternative title: *Curtain: Poirot's Last Case*)

The last Hercule Poirot novel was written in 1940 at the outset of World War II. In it, Christie documents Poirot's death. Famously, the book was intended for posthumous publication. The most romantic version of how and why Christie came to write *Curtain*, widely reported in her lifetime, states that she feared she would be the victim of a bomb during the war and wanted to ensure that her legacy was complete.

There were also prosaic reasons. As Charles Osborne outlines in *The Life and Crimes of Agatha Christie*, the royalties for this book, bound to be highly lucrative, were assigned to Christie's daughter, Rosalind Hicks, and this was a way of ensuring a legacy in the face of significant tax issues in the 1940s. Mark Aldridge (*Poirot* 315) has also suggested that Christie, horrified by James Bond continuation novels, wanted to ensure that the same fate would not befall her detective—hence killing off Poirot. With minor exceptions, Poirot escaped the continuation-novel phenomenon until Sophie Hannah's *The Monogram Murders* in 2014—unless the novels written by Christie after *Curtain* are counted.

In the end, *Curtain* was published in September 1975, four months before the author's death. She was, by now, no longer capable of producing a novel, and the decision to publish was largely Rosalind's. Predictably, the death of Poirot caused a sensation even before the contents of the book were known. He remains the only fictional character to receive an obituary in the *New York Times*—on the front page, no less.

Captain Hastings returns to narrate *Curtain*, visiting his old friend at Styles Court—the setting of the first novel, *The Mysterious Affair at Styles*—which has now become a guest house. The sadly withered Poirot is very thin and confined to a wheelchair. His body is failing, but his mind remains as sharp as ever. Poirot tells Hastings that he is at Styles to track down his most dangerous adversary, whom he calls "X." X has been present at the scenes of several murders but never directly involved—and Poirot expects X to strike again at Styles.

Poirot will not tell Hastings the identity of X, because Hastings would accidentally give it away. Instead, Hastings's job is to watch the guests, gather information, and report back to Poirot. He does so, inevitably drawing all the wrong conclusions and making the wrong judgments. At the same time, he grows increasingly concerned about his adult daughter, Judith, and her love life. Psychological tensions abound, and, one night, Colonel Luttrell, who runs the guest house with his bullying wife, seems to shoot her accidentally. She survives, tempers continue to fray, and soon a doctor's wife is poisoned. Incredibly, Poirot gives evidence at the inquest to suggest that she committed suicide.

Hastings grows more and more worried about his daughter's relationship with an unsuitable man, Major Allerton. He resolves to poison Allerton, although Poirot foils his plan. There are two more deaths: nervous birdwatcher Stephen Norton, who tends to fade into the background, is shot in the head shortly after visiting Poirot. The next morning, Poirot dies of heart failure. Everything remains mysterious to Hastings until, two months later, he receives an explanatory letter from Poirot (via a law firm). X was Norton, who never killed directly but enjoyed manipulating people into committing murder, and one of his victims was Hastings. Realizing he could not be stopped, Poirot arranged a meeting with Norton and shot him.

Just as *The Mysterious Affair at Styles* is often considered the starting point of the Golden Age, *Curtain*, which shares a setting, can be seen as a postscript to the Golden Age. Just as Christie's breakthrough, *The Murder of Roger Ackroyd*, shattered preconceptions about reliable narrators, *Curtain* shows that even a beloved recurring detective can be a murderer. In this way, it undermines any sense of trust or security in the genre, something highly significant given the wartime context in which it was written.

In a sense, *Curtain* acknowledges that Golden Age crime fiction is too artificial. Poirot's rationale for chasing X in the first place is that he has been tangentially around at least five murders: "Coincidence might account for two cases, or even three, but five is a bit too thick," as Hastings paraphrases it. "There must, unlikely as it seems, be some connection between these different murders" (*C* 23). This comes from a detective who famously cannot take a holiday without a murder taking place. Even Poirot's trademark—the moustache—comes under a subtle attack. It emerges that he has been exaggerating his illness and wearing a wig and false moustache so he can move around the house clean-shaven and unnoticed. Hastings has already noticed that the moustache is starting to look like something "to amuse the children" (14). By the end of the Golden Age, the quirky amateur detective, typified by that moustache, was thought to have had his day.

Although it is as tightly plotted as any other vintage Poirot mystery, *Curtain* is more psychologically astute than, for instance, *The ABC Murders*. Norton's sadism is subtle and depends on the power of words—the ability to influence others—something highly relevant with the rise of orator-dictators in the 1930s. Christie does not dwell on medical explanations for this but configures it in reference to William Shakespeare: throughout, Poirot invites Hastings to compare X to Iago in *Othello*. The emphasis on psychology, especially alongside the "out of date" character stereotypes (crusty colonels, and so on; Symons, "mort" 289) that evoke the interwar genre, disoriented some reviewers: Julian Symons concluded that *Curtain* had "all of 'Roger Ackroyd's' outrageousness but only a fraction of its cunning" (289).

As criticism has evolved and distance has been gained, *Curtain* is considered one of Christie's strongest novels, but it is rarely discussed—partly because it has hardly been filmed. The only adaptation, the final episode of *Agatha Christie's Poirot*, was broadcast on ITV 1 in 2013. There are several fans who will not read (or watch) it because the idea of Poirot dying is too emotionally charged.

Characters: **Allerton, Major; Boyd Carrington, Sir William**; Bradley, Derek and Mrs.; Clay, Freda; **Cole, Elizabeth**; Craig, Ben; Craven, Nurse; **Curtiss**; Etherington, Leonard and Mrs.; **Franklin, Barbara,** and Dr. John; George(s); Hastings, Captain Arthur; Hastings, Judith; Litchfield, Margaret, and Matthew; Luttrell, Colonel Toby, and Daisy; Norton, Stephen; Poirot, Hercule; Riggs, Edward and Mrs.; Sharples, Miss

See also: *Agatha Christie's Poirot*; Continuation Fiction; *The Mysterious Affair at Styles*; Shakespeare, William

Curtin, Ernie, and Mrs.

Mrs. Curtin is a cleaner who works for Millicent Pebmarsh, and Ernie is Mrs. Curtin's spoiled son, in *The Clocks* (1963). Mrs. Curtin is working class and so concerned with looking respectable that she creates the opposite effect. Hostile to change, Mrs. Curtin has strong opinions on the European Economic Community, asserting that "England's good enough for me" (*TC* 48).

Curtiss

Curtiss is Hercule Poirot's last valet, hired just before the action of *Curtain*. Curtiss previously worked at a sanitarium and looks rather like a criminal. Poirot hired him because he is less observant than Poirot's usual valet, George(s).

Cust, Alexander Bonaparte

A door-to-door salesman traumatized by war, Alexander Bonaparte Cust is framed for *The ABC Murders*. In any number of serial killer narratives of the 1930s, the mentally unstable Cust would have been the murderer; Christie's decision to make him a red herring, exploited by the real killer, in turn exploits and exposes her readers' prejudice.

Cyril

Cyril is Celia's brother in *Unfinished Portrait*, modeled after Christie's brother, Louis "Monty" Miller.

Czarnova, Countess

In "The Soul of the Croupier," Countess Czarnova is a regular visitor to the casino at Monte Carlo. A glamorous aristocratic woman, she is in fact losing all her money. Secretly, she is Jeanne Vaucher, who was raised from poverty when she married Pierre Vaucher but later descended into addiction and instability.

The D. Case (Fruttero and Lucentini). See **Continuation Fiction**

Daijoyu Satsujin-jiken (2007). See **NTV Adaptations**

Daijoyu Satsujin-jiken (2018). See **TV Asahi Adaptations**

"Dame Agatha Tells Whodunit." See "The Unsinkable Agatha Christie"

Dane-Calthrop, Maud, and Rev. Caleb

The Rev. Caleb Dane-Calthrop is a vague clergyman, liable to lapse into Latin, in *The Moving Finger* and *The Pale Horse*. His wife, Maud, calls in her friend Miss Marple in the former and persuades Mark Easterbrook to look into matters in the latter. Unlike her husband, she is very direct and to the point, stating that "so many men have obviously married the wrong woman" (*TMF* 73) and telling the world that her husband "has absolutely no taste for fornication" (43). Christie enjoyed creating this character and stated in an introduction that she would "like to meet" her (Christie, Foreword, *Moving Finger*, 6).

Dangerous Women. See *Kiken na Onnatachi*

"Dark Sheila." See *The Road of Dreams* **(poetry collection)**

Darnley, Rosamund

A strong-minded businesswoman, Rosamund Darnley owns her own dress shop in *Evil under the Sun*. Love for Kenneth Marshall undermines her iron will and professional instinct; she feels that she ought to be grateful for having everything, but that something—a family—is missing.

Darrell, Claud

Former actor Claud Darrell has become a criminal mastermind known as Number Four, set on world domination, in *The Big Four*. Darrell is a nondescript Englishman but encounters Hercule Poirot several times in disguise and commits most of the murders in *The Big Four* personally. At the end of the novel, Darrell is declared dead in an explosion, but no body is recovered, so the question of his returning as a Moriarty-style nemesis lingers.

"Dartmoor." See *Poems*

Date with Death. See *Appointment with Death* **(novel)**

Daubreuil, Madame, and Marthe

In *The Murder on the Links*, Madame and Marthe Daubreuil, a mother and daughter, are neighbors of the Renaulds. Madame Daubreuil is suspiciously self-contained, and it transpires that she is really Jeanne Beroldy who, 22 years previously, conspired with Georges Conneau (now Paul Renauld, the victim in the present case) to murder her husband.

When Captain Hastings first sees Marthe Daubreuil, he declares her "a young goddess" (31). Hercule Poirot says he sees "only a girl with anxious eyes" (31). This typifies the difference between their characters and approaches—and is a device that Christie would reuse many times—but it also suggests to readers, misleadingly, that Marthe will be the distressed damsel and chief romantic interest of this novel. In fact, she turns out to be the murderer, with a homicidal streak due to heredity, killing for lust.

A Daughter's a Daughter (novel)

When *A Daughter's a Daughter* was published in 1952, the true identity of its author, Mary Westmacott, was an open secret. The back cover of the first edition accordingly features a three-quarter-page photograph of the author and the words:

MARY WESTMACOTT
known to a large public as
AGATHA CHRISTIE

Based on a then-unperformed play, the book is set during World War II, rather than the 1930s of the original script. The novel follows the play and its dialogue fairly closely, with a few new characters mentioned but not featured. It is of interest to scholars as an example of adaptation from the stage rather than the usual process of a written work adapted to the stage.

The novel centers on the generational conflict between a mother, Ann Prentice, and her daughter, Sarah Prentice, and their mutual jealousies over one another's love affairs. The generational conflict is presented as a clash of prewar and postwar attitudes, whereas the elderly Laura Whitstable provides a voice of reason and experience, speaking as a member of the pre-prewar generation. Laura's common sense reveals itself in breezy anecdotes that culminate in maxims:

> "Have you ever felt really alone, Laura?" Anne asked with curiosity.
> "Oh yes. It came to me when I was twenty-six—actually in the middle of a family gathering of the most affectionate nature. It startled me and frightened me—but I accepted it. Never deny the truth. One must accept the fact that we have only one companion in this world, a companion who accompanies us from the cradle to grave—our own self. Get on good terms with that companion—*learn to live with yourself.* That's the answer. It's not always easy." [9; emphasis in original]

Gillian Gill has noted that the dynamic of open warfare between parent and child is tempered by an intergenerational collegiality between a very old and a very young woman, which also is featured in *The Burden*. Gill also notes that this kind of alliance provides for domestic resolutions in the Westmacott novels, whereas it makes for an effective detective partnership in the mystery novels published under the Christie name (185).

The book has often been used as evidence of a dysfunctional relationship between Christie and her daughter, Rosalind Hicks, although other sources have also been suggested (see *A Daughter's a Daughter,* [play]). In a 1990 piece on Westmacott to mark Christie's centenary, Hicks writes mostly about *Giant's Bread* and *Absent in the Spring*. She mentions "powerful and destructive forms" of love in the other Westmacott novels but barely cites *A Daughter's a Daughter* (Hicks 51). Characters: Cauldfield, Doris; **Cauldfield, Richard**; Edith; Fane, Professor; Grant, Colonel James; **Lloyd, Gerald ("Gerry"); Mowbray, Basil; Prentice, Ann; Prentice, Sarah; Steene, Lawrence; Whitstable, Dame Laura**

See also: *A Daughter's a Daughter* (play); **Hicks, Rosalind; Westmacott, Mary**

A Daughter's a Daughter (play)

This play, written in the late 1930s, deals rawly with tensions between a mother and a daughter. In 1939, Christie explored staging options, but the emergence of World War II stopped this from happening. It was eventually staged in 1956, four years after Christie had adapted it into a novel under the pseudonym Mary Westmacott. By then, Christie had updated the script, setting it between 1945 and 1946.

It is easy—and for most biographers and theatrical critics, irresistible—to draw comparisons between Christie's second marriage, upsetting the daughter from her first marriage, and the same scenario in the play. Certainly, this play and the subsequent novel have been widely examined for evidence of a fraught relationship between Christie and her daughter, Rosalind Hicks. However, biographer Jared Cade suggests that it is grounded in the relationship between her cousin-by-marriage Nan Watts and Nan's daughter, Judith, whose mother feared she was "going off the rails" (184). This would make Christie the wise, hedonistic Dame Laura figure.

The play has also been considered as an entry into the sphere of domestic drama; multiple critics have compared it to the works of J.B. Priestley and Terence Rattigan. The play is notable for containing Christie's first apparently gay character (Basil Mowbray) in a theatrical production—although by the time it was performed, she had created the extremely camp Christopher Wren in *The Mousetrap*.

The first run was a short one at the Theatre Royal, Bath, in 1956, where its authorship was attributed to Westmacott. It received its London debut in 2009 at the smallest West End theater, Trafalgar Studios, with television stars Jenny Seagrove and Honeysuckle Weeks in the major roles and Adam Dalgleish actor Roy Marsden as director. It was because of discomfort about the theme that the play was not performed between Christie's death and that of her daughter, the copyright-holder.

Characters: Cauldfield, Doris; **Cauldfield, Richard**; Edith; **Lloyd, Jerry; Mowbray, Basil; Prentice, Ann; Prentice, Sarah; Steene, Lawrence; Whitstable, Dame Laura**

See also: *A Daughter's a Daughter* (novel); Hicks, Rosalind; Westmacott, Mary

Davies, Mrs.
In *The Floating Admiral*, Mrs. Davies is "a jolly, good-humoured looking woman of fifty" wearing "[a] gold locket and several rings" (*TFA* 55). She talks incessantly, with a high-pitched, insistent voice.

Davis, Giles, and Molly. See **Ralston, Giles, and Mollie**

Dawes, Rhoda. See **Despard, Major John, and Rhoda**

Dawlish, Lord. See **Ferguson, Mr.**

"The Day of His Dreams." See **"The Manhood of Edward Robinson"**

De Bellefort, Jacqueline ("Jackie")
Jacqueline de Bellefort is the hot-tempered ex-fiancée of Simon Doyle and ex-best friend of Linnet Doyle in *Death on the Nile*. Jackie is descended from feudal barons and boasts that honor killing is in her blood. In the play *Murder on the Nile*, she is called Jacqueline de Severac. Jackie and Simon are secretly still in love, and she has masterminded a murder scheme to satisfy his greed, which prompted him to marry Linnet.

De Havilland, Edith
In *Crooked House*, Edith de Havilland is the sister of Aristide Leonides's deceased first wife, Marcia. Aged around 70, Edith is the family matriarch and ultimately takes the law into her own hands.

De la Roche, Comte Armand
Comte Armand de la Roche is the exotic lover of Ruth Kettering in *The Mystery of the Blue Train*. He is a caddish figure, of whom Christie writes: "Men saw through him, women did not." (110).

De Rushbridger, Margaret
Margaret de Rushbridger is an unseen patient at Bartholomew Strange's sanatorium in *Three Act Tragedy*, who is murdered purely because of her memorable name, to mislead investigators as to the motive for other killings.

De Sara, Madeleine
Madeleine de Sara, aka Maggie Sayers, is an exotic vampish character, who works for J. Parker Pyne to help people who are bored or unhappy. Madeleine always plays the part of an exotic, unobtainable woman—usually leading unhappy men into the arms

of more suitable partners. In reality, she is a humble, conventional woman who lives with her parents in Streatham. She appears in "The Case of the Discontented Soldier," "The Case of the Distressed Lady," "The Case of the City Clerk," "The Case of the Discontented Husband," "The Case of the Rich Woman," and "Problem at Pollensa Bay."

De Severac, Jacqueline (Jackie). See **De Bellefort, Jacqueline (Jackie)**

De Sousa, Etienne

Etienne De Sousa is an exotic second cousin of Lady Hattie Stubbs, with a reputation for being a playboy and, in her words, doing "bad things" in *Dead Man's Folly* (71). He is in fact simply a devoted cousin. In "Hercule Poirot and the Greenshore Folly," the novella that is its basis, he is called Paul Lopez.

De Toredo, Angelica. See **Shapland, Ann**

"The Dead Harlequin" (story; alternative title: "The Man in the Empty Chair")

"The Dead Harlequin" is a Quin and Satterthwaite story, first published in the *Grand Magazine* in March 1929 and collected in *The Mysterious Mr. Quin* in 1930. Christie later adapted this story into a play, *Someone at the Window*.

Mr. Satterthwaite purchases *The Dead Harlequin*, a painting by an up-and-coming artist, because he recognizes both the setting—Charnleys, a home he has visited that was the site of a suicide 14 years previously—and the subject, who bears a resemblance to his friend, Harley Quin. Two separate women with connections to the suicide contact Satterthwaite, asking him to resell the painting to them. Satterthwaite gathers these women, the artist, Mr. Quin, and other affected parties at Charnleys. Together, they realize that the painting holds a visual clue to the event, which was not a suicide but a murder.

Characters: **Bristow, Frank**; Charnley, Lady Alix; Charnley, Hugo; Charnley, Lord Reginald (Reggie); **Ford, Monica**; **Glen, Aspasia**; Monckton, Colonel; **Quin, Harley**; **Satterthwaite, Mr.**

See also: *The Mysterious Mr. Quin*; *Someone at the Window*

Dead Man's Folly **(novel)**

The 1956 "Christie for Christmas" was an expansion of an unpublished novella (see "Hercule Poirot and the Greenshore Folly"). The premise is typically playful—the victim at a "murder hunt," part of a charity fete, is murdered in real life—and the execution typically avoids the obvious or gimmicky. The body is not discovered by players of the game, nor does the party idea overtake the action. Unlike the previous year's *Hickory Dickory Dock*, the novel does not overplay its attempt to keep with the time. Although communism, nuclear warfare, and teenage and celebrity culture form subplots, the essential story is more or less timeless.

Hercule Poirot is summoned by his crime writing friend, Ariadne Oliver, to Nasse House, where she is devising a murder game for the local fete, because she has a typically vague sense of foreboding. He meets Sir George and Lady Hattie Stubbs of Nasse House and notices that Lady Stubbs is extraordinarily vacant. He also meets assorted young people, relatives, and international tourists. Lady Stubbs is particularly afraid of an exotic cousin, Etienne de Sousa, who is planning to visit after many years. On the day of the fete, Lady Stubbs disappears, and Marlene Tucker, the 16 year old who was playing the victim in the game, is found strangled.

Poirot is the only person who seems to have been listening to Marlene and to her elderly, drunken grandfather, Merdell, and he has an inkling that they were killed for what they knew. The solution uncovered by Poirot has shades of *Three-Act Tragedy, A Murder Is Announced, Murder in Mesopotamia*, and *Taken at the Flood*. Discussions of heredity surrounding it are reminiscent of those that close *Crooked House*.

Although Nasse House is a fictional setting, the house and its grounds are patently based on Greenway, Christie's holiday home where she wrote the bulk of the book. The novel has an additional intensely personal connection for its author. The elderly Mrs. Folliat, secret mother of Sir George Stubbs, quotes the following lines from Edmund Spenser's *The Faerie Queene*: "Sleep after toyle, port after stormie seas, ease after war, death after life, doth greatly please" (59).

These lines would later appear on Christie's gravestone, at her request.

In the United Kingdom, the novel was serialized in *John Bull Magazine* from 11 August 1956, with a brief interview in which Christie invites readers to compare Mrs. Oliver to herself and a photograph of her baking (although it implies she is cooking lobster thermidor) at Greenway. The U.S. book publication by Dodd, Mead came in October that year, with Collins's U.K. edition following in November. The novel has been filmed twice: in 1986, in a modernized version with Peter Ustinov for CBS, and in 2013, as the last-filmed and penultimate-broadcast episode of *Agatha Christie's Poirot* with David Suchet. It was dramatized for BBC Radio 4 in 2007, with John Moffat in the lead, and in 2009, it was the subject of a hidden object computer game by Big Fish Games.

Characters: Barnes/Brown, Susan; Blake, Jackie; **Bland, Detective Inspector; Brewis, Amanda**; Cottrell, Sergeant Frank; **de Sousa, Etienne**; Hendon; **Hoskins, Police Constable; Folliat, Amy; Folliat, James**; Fox, Betty/Biddy; **George(s)**; Knapper family; **Legge, Alec, and Sally; Masterton, Connie, and Wilfred; Merdell; Oliver, Ariadne; Poirot, Hercule; Stubbs, Lady Harriet ("Hattie"); Stubbs, Sir George; Tucker, Marlene**; Tucker, Marilyn; Tucker, Mrs.; Warburton, Captain James ("Jim"); **Weyman, Michael**

See also: *Agatha Christie's Poirot*; CBS Television Adaptations; Games; Greenway House; *Hercule Poirot* (BBC radio series); "Hercule Poirot and the Greenshore Folly"

Dead Man's Folly (television adaptation). See **CBS Television Adaptations**

"Dead Man's Mirror" (novella; alternative title: "Hercule Poirot and the Broken Mirror")

The longest novella in *Murder in the Mews*, "Dead Man's Mirror" seems from the presence of subplots, multiple and recurring characters, and particularly intricate plotting to be a novel that ran short. It is an expansion of the 1932 short story "The Second Gong" and one of the last Hercule Poirot stories to include a diagram of the crime scene.

Sir Gervase Chevenix-Gore arrogantly summons Poirot to his home to investigate a potential fraud, and Poirot is reluctant to attend—no ego can be allowed to clash with his. However, after attending a party with the gossipy Mr. Satterthwaite, who reminisces about acquaintances from other cases such as *Three Act Tragedy* and "The Man from the Sea," Satterthwaite shares some gossip about Chevenix-Gore and his eccentric relatives that piques Poirot's interest. Arriving at the home, Poirot is surprised to find that nobody was expecting him and that his host will not leave his study. Eventually, Sir Gervase is found dead in his study, an apparent suicide. However, Poirot determines that he was murdered. It is difficult to determine the time of death because of conflicting accounts over when the gong sounded for dinner. The bullet apparently hit the dead man's mirror, but Poirot determines that this is impossible; instead, it passed through a door that should have been closed and hit the gong. This explains the confusion: the gong sounded twice, when struck by the bullet and at dinner time.

There are many suspects for the murder, because Sir Gervase was a rich, unpopular, and stupid man. Of particular interest is his adoptive daughter, Ruth, soon to be disinherited over a secret marriage. Poirot eventually discovers that the murderer is Miss Lingard, a housekeeper who is Ruth's biological mother. He agrees not to tell anyone, including Ruth, about her parentage; thus, to the wider world, Miss Lingard's motive remains a mystery. The novella has been dramatized for television as season 5, episode 7 of *Agatha Christie's Poirot*, broadcast on ITV on 28 February 1993.

Characters: Burrows, Geoffrey; Bury, Colonel; Chevenix-Gore, Vanda, Lady Vanda; Chevenix-Gore, Ruth; **Chevenix-Gore, Sir Gervase**; Coldwell, Susan; Forbes, Ogilvie; Lake, Captain John; **Leith, Duchess of (Maria)**; Lingard, Miss; **Poirot, Hercule**; Riddle, Major; **Satterthwaite, Mr.**; Snell; Trent, Hugo

See also: *Agatha Christie's Poirot*; *Murder in the Mews* (story collection)

Dead Man's Mirror (story collection). See *Murder in the Mews* (story collection)

Death Beat

Death Beat is a proposed stage-musical adaptation of *Hickory Dickory Dock*. Early discussions were held at Greenway among Christie, John Wells—who drafted a script and devised the title—and pianist Alexis Weissenberg, who wrote some songs, around 1963. Peter Sellers was tapped to play Hercule Poirot, Sean Kelly was to be the set designer, and John Dankworth was to orchestrate the score. Christie was, according to biographers, "helpful" and "enormously impressed" by the process (Osborne 278). Impresario Bernard Delfont, who had been involved from an early stage, lost interest in the idea, and nothing came of it. Reportedly, Wells kept a copy of the script in a bottom drawer until his death. In 2019, Weissenberg's estate released one song from the musical, "Atmosphere," via the internet.

See also: ***Hickory Dickory Dock***; **Music**

"Death by Drowning" (alternative title: "Village Tragedy"). See *The Thirteen Problems*

Death Comes as the End (novel)

Christie's only historical mystery novel, *Death Comes as the End* is set "on the West Bank of the Nile at Thebes in Egypt in about 2000 BC" (1). It is one of her few books to include an "author's note," which is needed to explain certain phrases and the timing system. Christie uses and explains the festival of Inundation for timings. The book was famously written at the request of Egyptologist Stephen Glanville, whom Christie thanks in a lengthy dedication for fielding many research questions. It makes strong use of Christie's archaeological knowledge, acquired through her husband Max Mallowan's work in Egypt and elsewhere.

The title comes from a quote by a wise character in chapter 3: "Men are made fools by the gleaming limbs of women, and lo, in a minute they are become discolored carnelians…. A trifle, a little, the likeness of a dream, and death comes as the end" (*DCE* 38). As Adolf Erman explains, the source is *The Instruction of Ptahhotep*, attributed to a vizier of Egypt's King Issi ca. 2675 BC (54); the section with the quote relates to a "Warning Against Women" (60). The

passage thus directly relates to the story, which concerns the disruptive presence of a beautiful woman stepping into a family home.

The protagonist is the widowed Renisenb, a daughter of the Ka-priest Imhotep. She lives in the family property with a large household that includes her brothers and their wives, her grandmother, and two senior servants. When Imhotep returns home with his new concubine, Nofret, nerves are rattled. Nofret is very beautiful and very sophisticated, and no one in the household likes her. Imhotep departs on business, leaving Nofret with the family. Acting through the scribe Hori, she communicates with the priest in his absence, spreading stories about the household, and he sends word that he will disown them all in her favor. Soon, Nofret is killed.

Everyone is a suspect, including Imhotep's three sons: the quiet Yahmose, the aggressive Sobek, and the spoilt and boisterous Ipy. When Yahmose's domineering wife Satipy also dies, Renisenb tries her best to solve the mystery. She works closely with Hori—a cause of concern for another, younger scribe, Kameni, whom her grandmother wants her to marry. Eventually, Hori realizes the identity of the murderer, just as he reveals himself to Renisenb in a dramatic showdown at the scene of the previous killings. It is Yahmose, who believed he was entitled to his father's fortune and was hurt by women who did not see him as a proper man. Following the resolution, Renisenb agrees to spend her life with Hori.

In her foreword, Christie—who always claimed to write foremost about people—argues that "place and time are incidental to the story" (*DCE* 1). That is to say, it could have happened anywhere, because personality types do not change (1). However, the characters, she writes, were "derived from two or three Egyptian letters of the XI Dynasty, found about 20 years ago" (1). This refers to the Hekanakhte papers, discovered in the tomb of Vizier Ipi, which were written by or for a ka-priest and detail agricultural transactions. Their focus explains to decision to focus on "everyday" domestic life in ancient Egypt rather than on luxurious palatial scenes. Original plans for the novel involved a parallel modern-day narrative, which would have incorporated the same themes and character types, but this idea was scrapped at an early stage.

The novelty of the narrative has masked a key theme for many scholars—*Death Comes as the End* is undeniably a feminist work. The household in the novel is nominally patriarchal, but the head of the house is absent, the men are generally useless, and women run the place while wondering: "What does a woman's life come to in the end, after all? It is spent in the back of the house—amongst the other women" (44). Even in the face of murder and family scandal, the women are made to turn on one another, especially on Nofret, who—like Arlena in *Evil under the Sun*—is seen as the personification of evil. She is also frequently described as catlike or animalistic. Men understand Egypt as "[b]roken by war" and "obsessed by death," which is its "lifeblood," but women see "women [as] the life blood of Egypt" (63, 132, 195). Through the course of the novel, dangerous extremism is allowed to fester in the most unlikely of places. Kait, a devoted mother and housewife, is revealed toward the end to have a hidden rage that has boiled over at her own missed opportunities, whereas her incompetent husband found increasing glory. She goes to far as to say that men are good for nothing but breeding. Meanwhile, Yahmose's motive for murder is that he has never been made to feel like a full or adequate man. Renisenb, the protagonist, sees no sex as superior and has an egalitarian, individualist attitude—for example, she thinks women should learn to read—that seems consistent with the view of an early-twentieth-century feminist.

Christie famously changed this novel's ending at Glanville's request. According to her autobiography and that of her husband, this was the only time she had done so and was a cause of regret. Mallowan wrote that Christie's original ending was "more dramatic" (172). Perhaps because the puzzle is unusually easy to solve, some commentators have naturally assumed that the matter changed was the identity of the murderer; indeed, Christie's notebooks show that she considered several options for the perpetrator. However, this was common practice, as Christie would start with a theme or idea and weave a plot—including the mechanics of the mystery—around it. Moreover, although the puzzle is weak, that is not uncommon in 1940s Christie. Finally, interacting as it does with the general theme of gender roles, it is highly unlikely that the book would make much sense with a different murderer and/or motive.

What is unusual is the resolution of Renisenb's love triangle. In most Christie works—indeed, in most books—when a woman must choose between two men, one ends up dead or incriminated, making the other the obvious choice. Here, the man she is meant to marry simply disappears from the action, and she chooses Hori for a love-match at the last minute. This both undermines Renisenb's blossoming independent spirit and denies closure to readers. It is not inconceivable that one or more of her suitors would have sacrificed themselves during the dramatic dénouement. For example, Hori losing his life to save her from Yahmose, causing Renisenb to refuse marriage to Kameni and live independently, would be an artistically satisfying and "more dramatic" ending. However, for obvious reasons, it might not have appealed to Glanville, who was in love with the author and whose involvement in the book concerned her husband.

Death Comes as the End was published in 1945 and has yet to be dramatized in any medium. Adaptations have been proposed over time: a 1984 script by Gerard Scoteman was character focused, and production went so far as to costume designs. However, financial problems ended plans for the film. A second script by Laird Koenig was sent to the Christie estate for approval in the 1990s. Mark Aldridge (*Screen* 201) suggests that this production would also have been too expensive to make. It is likely that the sheer expense of re-creating ancient Egypt has discouraged filmmakers. A BBC mini-series was announced in 2016 and confirmed as the next project in its Christie series, with a screenplay by Gwyneth Hughes, in 2018. However, the production failed to materialize, and in 2020, the BBC indicated that it was no longer on the horizon.

Although much can be done with technology, the COVID-19 pandemic and budgetary restrictions had made location filming challenging.

Characters: **Esa; Henet; Hori; Imhotep; Kait; Kameni; Khay;** Mersu; Montu; **Nofret; Satipy; Sobek;** Teti; **Yahmose**

See also: *Akhnaton;* Archaeology; **Glanville, Stephen; Mallowan, Max**

Death in the Air. See *Death in the Clouds*

Death in the Clouds (novel; alternative title: *Death in the Air*)

A typically Golden Age novel, *Death in the Clouds* features a first-class passenger murdered aboard an airplane, leaving a closed cast of suspects. Hercule Poirot is at his most theatrical; a character who writes crime fiction provides metatextual humor, the murderer is the least likely suspect; and the solution depends on the much-critiqued, typically Christiean idea that nobody looks at the staff.

The plot involves Poirot, who is afraid of flying, aboard the *Prometheus,* an airplane flying from Paris to London. He notices the other passengers, especially two young people—Norman Gale and Jane Grey—who are trying not to notice one another. When Madame Giselle, an elderly French woman in the back of first class, is found dead, it is assumed that she was stung by a wasp, which another passenger—French archaeologist Jean Dupont—killed during the flight. However, Poirot discovers a poisoned dart, which crime writer Daniel Clancy notes belongs to a blowpipe used by South American tribes. A blowpipe is discovered behind Poirot's seat.

At an inquest, the jury tries to accuse Poirot of the murder, but the coroner refuses to accept this. Poirot teams up with Jane, who is a hairdresser's assistant, and Norman, a dentist, to track down the killer. Along with Inspector Japp of Scotland Yard, he learns that Madame Giselle was a moneylender who had upset several people such as the cocaine-addled Countess of Horbury, another passenger on the plane. While Jane, disguised as a secretary, investigates Clancy, Norman, disguised as a blackmailer, investigates the Countess of Horbury.

Madame Giselle's estranged daughter comes forward to claim her inheritance but is soon killed. Through a combination of psychology, an observation of luggage aboard the plane, and an assessment of acting skills, Poirot identifies Norman as the murderer. He was secretly married to Madame Giselle's daughter and killed both women to inherit the money and have a clear path to marry Jane. The key clue is a white jacket among Norman's belongings: although this seems natural for a dentist, it is a strange thing to carry on a plane. Norman disguised himself as a steward so he could insert the dart into his victim's neck without the other passengers taking any notice. Poirot catches the murderer by saying his fingerprints were found on a certain item, to which Norman responds that this is impossible, because he was wearing gloves. By the end, it seems clear that Jane will eventually marry the rather serious Jean.

Jean and his archaeologist father Armand are comic through their dullness, something that can be linked easily to Christie's own experience in the early years of marriage to an archaeologist. Indeed, an episode recalled by Poirot, in which an Englishwoman fell ill in Iraq but her archaeologist husband put his work on the dig before visiting her in the hospital, reflects an experience from the first year of Christie's marriage to Max Mallowan. She wrote to him, disingenuously, that everyone in the hospital thought he was "brutal and human" for neglecting her, but that of course she understood his work must come first (qtd. in L. Thompson 298). As Laura Thompson (314–15) points out, the frequent jokes about archaeologists obsessing over small details about antiquity while ignoring major problems or events in real time find direct parallels, with examples, in her memoir *Come, Tell Me How You Live.*

Elements of the plot closely mirror those of Christie's preceding novel, *Three Act Tragedy:* Poirot is assisted by two burgeoning lovers, both of whom disguise themselves to investigate others from the enclosed crime scene. After proving to himself that the male is an accomplished actor, Poirot reveals that he disguised himself as a servant to commit murder. In both cases, the motive is to be rid of an inconvenient wife and marry the unknowing new lover.

In the United States, the book was first serialized as *Death in the Air* in the *Saturday Evening Post* from 9 February 1935. It was published in book form by Dodd, Mead that March, six days before the final installment of the serial. In the United Kingdom, it appeared in *Woman's Pictorial* from 16 February to 23 March 1935, and was published by Collins that July. It was filmed in 1992 as part of *Agatha Christie's Poirot* in the United Kingdom, where it was also dramatized for BBC Radio 4 in 2003—in both productions, Philip Jackson played Inspector Japp. In 2005, it was animated as a four-part episode of *Agasa Kurisutī no Meitantei Powaro to Māpuru*, and a graphic novel version was released as a tie-in.

Noted cover artist Tom Adams was disgruntled when, in 2007, the BBC aired an episode of *Doctor Who* in which Christie encounters a giant alien wasp, inspired by one of his cover designs for *Death in the Clouds*, which features in the episode (although the published design was slightly different from that used). Adams told the author of this volume that the broadcaster had not only failed to ask permission but also had missed his point. The large wasp in his image only appears big because it is close—in a matter of perspective, its significance is amplified, just as a wasp in the novel is a red herring.

Characters: **Antoine, Monsieur**; Barraclough, Raymond; Bryant, Dr. Roger; **Clancy, Daniel**; Davis; **Dupont, Armand, and Jean**; Fournier, Monsieur; **Gale, Norman**; **Giselle, Madame**; Grandier, Elise; **Grey, Jane**; **Horbury, Lady Cicely, and Lord Stephen**; **Japp, Chief Inspector James**; **Kerr, Hon. Venetia**; **Leech, Andrew**; Mitchell, Henry and Ruth; **Morisot, Anne, and Marie**; Perrot, Jules; **Poirot, Hercule**; **Richards, Anne, and James**; Ross, Miss; Ryder, James; Thibault, Alexandre; Whistler, Dr. James; Winterspoon, Henry; Zeropoulos, Monsieur

See also: **Adams, Tom**; *Agasa Kurisutī no Meitantei Powaro to Māpuru*; *Agatha Christie's Poirot*; **Hercule Poirot** (BBC radio series); *Three Act Tragedy*

Death on the Cards. See **Games**

Death on the Nile (novel)

Death on the Nile was written in two parts, although the first—*Characters in Order of Their Appearance*—is only one chapter long, and the second—*Egypt*—contains the other 30. Most editions after the U.K. editions have omitted the indication of parts. In the first part/chapter, the characters are all introduced through the prism of their relationship with or knowledge of Linnet Ridgeway. She will become Linnet Doyle, the first and main victim of the novel.

The plot begins with a love triangle, but really, it begins with the characters—especially Linnet. A beautiful heiress, nearly 21 with a solid business head and "the world at her feet" (*DOTN* 62), Linnet turns down an aristocratic suitor to marry her best friend's fiancée, Simon Doyle. The penniless Simon's equally poor but European-aristocratic ex-fiancé, Jacqueline (Jackie) de Bellefort, vows revenge on Linnet and is all the more enflamed when the Doyles plan their honeymoon on the River Nile—the location of Simon and Jackie's intended honeymoon.

In fact, most of the Doyles' fellow passengers are present because of Linnet. Her American trustee, Andrew Pennington, is trying wrangle her out of her inheritance. An undercover representative of her English lawyers is there to stop her. Others, including an eccentric novelist currently in a legal dispute with Linnet and a wealthy kleptomaniac obsessed with her pearls, make last-minute decisions to join the cruise. By subterfuge, Jackie, too, is on board. Perhaps the only passenger there by coincidence is Hercule Poirot.

During the voyage, passions come to a head, and Jackie shoots Simon in the leg in front of witnesses. That night, the gun goes missing, and, the next morning, Linnet is found dead. Poirot and his friend, Colonel Race, determine to find the murderer, and there is no shortage of suspects. There is also no shortage of subplots: two jewel robberies, a smuggling operation, fraud, libel, secret alcoholism, and multiple rivalries and resentments simmering beneath the surface. After two more murders, Poirot reveals the dramatic truth: a complex plot whereby Simon and Jackie conspired for him to marry and kill Linnet for her money. The novel ends with Jackie and Simon dead in each another's arms, whereas two troubled young people—a camp man with a mother complex and the beleaguered daughter of an alcoholic—celebrate their new life together as they disembark from the boat.

Linnet and Simon are presented as a modern fairy-tale couple. She is described as a "princess" or "queen" and he as a "Prince Consort" (62, 278). The year it was written, 1937, Walt Disney's *Snow White and the Seven Dwarfs* was in the cinemas, capitalizing on a popular sentiment that two young people could find one another, fall in love, and marry, and everything would be right with the world. Here, the fairy-tale ending is the beginning—or middle—of a destructive plot. Underpinning everything is the pursuit of wealth. Contrasting this couple is a more realistic, less glamorous one that moves from disinterest through hostility toward a genuine relationship (although the action takes place over just a few days, any journey in fiction is a broader journey in microcosm). Tim Allerton, a jewel thief wholly devoted to his mother, and Rosalie Otterbourne, an antisocial young woman under the thumb of her mother, find each other toward the end, and Poirot "thank[s] God" for their happiness (285). In the context of a looming war, where dashing young men would likely be swept off and killed, and marriages would need to be less impulsive than they had been in World War I, this is a deliberate note of realism.

The boat in this novel is a heterotopic space. It is out of place and out of time. On it, the Anglo-American class systems are preserved and played out, but by the end of the journey, things will have changed. It is not just that five passengers will be dead and new cross-class relationships formed, but in the wider world, dramas are developing on the European stage and the class system fetishized in *Death on the Nile* manifestly will not survive World War II. The ship is essentially a reconstruction of British high society in the middle of Egypt, staffed and powered by Egyptian people to a mythical standard of Edwardian luxury, where the only working-class Brits on board either serve the first-class passengers or turn out to be a lord pretending to be poor, and the only turban on board is an accouterment of cultural appropriation donned by a salacious British novelist, trying to shock.

The first of many adaptations was the 1945 "Rendezvous with Death," a 30-minute episode of Harold Huber's Mutual Radio series *Hercule Poirot*. Next was Christie's own stage adaptation, the best-known title of which is *Murder on the Nile*, first staged at the Wimbledon Theatre before a West End debut at the Ambassador's Theatre, London (later to host *The Mousetrap*) on 19 March 1946. A New York run occurred that September. On 12 July 1950, NBC aired a one-hour adaptation of the novel as part of *Kraft Television Theatre*. This episode, titled *Murder on the Nile*, omits Poirot, as does the play of the same name, but it is a unique adaptation.

In 1978, the first major movie based on the novel was released, the second of EMI's Christie series and the first since the author's death. Peter Ustinov played Poirot, heading an all-star cast, and the film was surrounded by a blaze of publicity. In 1997, BBC Radio 4 aired a five-part adaptation starring John Moffatt. In 1999, Paul Lamond Games released a jigsaw based on the novel. Although the packaging details several plot points and characters, the actual story is condensed to a few pages, covering the mechanics of the first murder only, rather like the 1945 radio adaptation.

A television version with David Suchet, part of *Agatha Christie's Poirot*, aired on 12 April 2004, and was filmed on the same boat as the 1978 movie. In 2007, Big Fish Games released an "I-spy" or hidden object game, a low-budget computer application, based on the novel as part of a series of Christie games, and HarperCollins released a graphic novel adapted by François Rivière and Solidor, which had previously been published in French (in 2003). A follow-up to Kenneth Branagh's 2017 movie, *Murder on the Express*, *Death on the Nile* was at last released on 11 February 2022. This follows several delays due to the COVID-19 pandemic, as the film was completed in early 2020.

Characters: **Allerton, Mrs., and Tim; Bessner, Dr. Carl**; Blondin, Gaston; **Bourget, Louise**; Bowers, Miss; Bryce, Toby; Burnaby, Mr.; Carmichael, William; **de Bellefort, Jacqueline; Doyle, Linnet; Doyle, Simon**; Fanthorp, Jim; Fleetwood; **Ferguson, Mr.**; Hartz, Anna and Leopold; Jules; Leech, Mrs.; **Otterbourne, Rosalie, and Salome; Pennington, Andrew; Poirot, Hercule; Race, Colonel Johnny**; Richetti, Guido; Ridgeway, Melhuish; **Robson, Cornelia**; Rockford, Sterndale; Southwood, Hon. Joanna; **Van Schuyler, Marie**; Windlesham, Lord Charles; Wode, Sir George

See also: *Agatha Christie's Poirot*; **EMI Films; Games; Hercule Poirot** (BBC radio series); *Hercule Poirot* (Mutual radio series); *Murder on the Nile*; **NBC Television Adaptations; Twentieth Century Studios Films**

"Death on the Nile" (story)

The Parker Pyne short story "Death on the Nile" bears no relation to the more famous novel of the same name, although both are set aboard Nile steamers. If anything, it is more closely related to the Poirot story "Problem at Sea." Pyne is consulted by Lady Ariadne Grayle, who fears that her husband is trying to poison her. He is unable to stop her death from strychnine poisoning and discovers a fragment of a note, which leads him to suspect—and trap, through purely psychological means—a young man with whom Lady Grayle was infatuated.

The story was first published in the United States with other Pyne short stories in the April 1933 *Cosmopolitan* under the title *Have You Got Everything You Want? If Not, Consult Mr. Parker Pyne*. In the United Kingdom, it appeared with two other stories in *Nash's Pall Mall Magazine* in July 1933 under the overall title *More Arabian Nights of Parker Pyne*. It was appeared in the collection *Parker Pyne Investigates* in 1934. In 1942, a radio adaptation was broadcast by NBC as the last Christie-based episode of *Murder Clinic*.

Characters: Grayle, Lady Ariadne; Grayle, Pamela; Grayle, Sir George; Mac-Naughton, Elsie; **Mohammed; Parker Pyne, J.**; West, Basil

See also: *Murder Clinic; Parker Pyne Investigates*

Death on the Nile (1978 film). See EMI Films

Death on the Nile (2022 film). See Twentieth Century Studios Films

Debenham, Mary

Mary Debenham is a sensible Englishwoman in *Murder on the Orient Express*, secretly in love with Colonel Arbuthnot. Hercule Poirot admires her level-headedness and professionalism. Secretly, she was a secretary and governess in the Armstrong household. Her involvement in a conspiracy to dispatch Daisy Armstrong's killer helps convince Poirot that the scheme was rational, premeditated, and arguably justified.

Delafontaine, Mary

Two women have the name Mary Delafontaine in the Christie canon. The first is a young woman who turns out to have murdered her wealthy aunt in "How Does Your Garden Grow?." The second is an elderly woman, a friend of Ariadne Oliver in *The Pale Horse*, who is murdered by the eponymous criminal organization.

Dermot

Dermot is a portrait of the author's first husband, Archie Christie, in the Mary Westmacott novel *Unfinished Portrait*. He is a dashing military man with a quick temper who deserts his wife for another woman when she is at her weakest.

Derwent, Lady Frances ("Frankie")

In *Why Didn't They Ask Evans?*, Lady Frances Derwent is one of Christie's last Bright Young Thing detectives, possessing a tomboy nickname; unlimited funds; boredom translating into a passion for adventure; and an open-minded interest in amiable, genteel, and poor idiot Bobby Jones.

Despard, Major John, and Rhoda

Major John Despard and Rhoda Dawes meet in *Cards on the Table* as suspects in

Mr. Shaitana's murder. Despard, a cocky adventurer with whom women tend to fall in love, saves Rhoda Dawes from her psychotic housemate, who is trying to drown her. Rhoda, who has always been in her beautiful friend's shadow, has a developed interest in true crime, and Hercule Poirot gives her the knife from *Murder on the Orient Express*. The couple appears as a happy, middle-aged pair in *The Pale Horse*, a standalone novel.

Destination Unknown (novel; alternative title: *So Many Steps to Death*)

Destination Unknown is one of Christie's last spy novels, and its plot is strikingly like that of *They Came to Baghdad*, which had appeared three years earlier. The depressed Hilary Craven contemplates suicide at a Moroccan hotel. An intelligence agent, Mr. Jessop, approaches her, offering her a "more sporting," patriotic way to die (39). Brilliant left-wing scientist Tom Betterton has gone missing, and his wife, Olive, has died in a plane crash. The British government suspects Tom of communist sympathies and defection to the Soviets. Hilary is to take Olive's identity and travel beyond the Iron Curtain to find out what has happened to the scientist.

Embarking on a journey across the globe, Hilary ends up with an international group of intellectuals who have retreated to a secret research facility in the Atlas Mountains. Hidden behind a leper colony, "the Unit" consists of politically extreme intellectuals who live shut off from the outside world so they can focus on their research. They occasionally hear long, stirring speeches about a new world order. Hilary meets Tom, who seems to recognize her as his wife, but learns little from him. She befriends a left-wing American, Andy Peters, who seems, like her, to see the facility not as "an earthly paradise" (129) but as "a prison" where they are "surrounded by a lot of inhuman Robots" (138).

Eventually, Hilary discovers that one of the richest men in the world, Mr. Aristides, runs the whole operation. A well-known financier, Aristides is collecting the world's greatest young minds in one place, so he can have a monopoly on scientific knowledge.

Although people had been drawn to the Unit because of their political philosophies, the whole thing is really "a gigantic financial operation" (179). The whole story is revealed at a press conference. Andy reveals that he is not really a left-wing intellectual: he, too, was in disguise and trying to get to Tom who murdered his first wife, the lover of Andy. He and Hilary declare their love for one another, and—like *The Mystery of the Blue Train* (1928)—the novel ends with the Shakespearean adage that journeys end in the meeting of lovers. The plot is not primarily a mystery, but there is a murderer, and his identity is fairly clued with typical wordplay: Oliver Betterton's dying words are taken to be a warning to Tom about Boris, but they are in fact a warning to Boris about Tom.

The word *unreal* appears several times during the novel. Diplomats are "unreal" in their idiomatic English (26). "[H]eady and intoxicating" orators are likened to stage performers and evangelists (160). The facility or "prison" where Hilary finds herself has an air of "unreality." When she uncovers the truth, Hilary realizes: "why the Unit had seemed unreal to her—because it *was* unreal. It had never been what it pretended to be." Seeing it not as an earnest political operation but as a plain business venture, "everything made sense—hard, practical, everyday sense" (176). There are two potential readings at play here: the mundanity of evil (likely the intended takeaway) and the pervasiveness, the destructiveness to the individual, of capitalism. Hilary is quick to note a range of political ideologies at the Unit. Between them, her companions were "completely Left Wing: 'a fanatical believer in the Superman,'" "a Fascist," and a worshipper of money (180). They believed in their ideologies but only their fervor united them—they had all been lured there for a reason they did not really understand. The rousing political oratory—talk of "the Future," a "new world" free of "[c]orrupt governments and warmongers" (92) appeals to political extremists of all stripes—because it is essentially empty and deflective. Hilary often notes in this novel that populations and people are essentially the same, to the extent that she feels "queer" and "stateless" (83). This is a persistent theme in Christie's works.

Aristides frames his activities as the habits of a collector—someone so rich that he has run out of things to do. He has exhausted fine art and stamp collecting, and turned to "assembling all the brains of the world" (179). However, a further motive is immediately revealed: at some point in the future, Aristides explains, "if [any nations] want a scientist, or a plastic surgeon, or a biologist, they will have to come and buy him from *me!*" (179; emphasis in original). Playing a long game, Aristides has collected the minds of *young* men—as in other Christie thrillers, a cult of youth here is seen to be underpinned by the financial ambitions of an individual. At the end of the book, the intelligence service concedes that Aristides will not be punished for anything he has done—he is too rich to prosecute, and people under his command will take the blame. Although the implied author tells the reader that the solution is apolitical, the fact is that the central venture is an example of venture capitalism, and the villain remains "behind nearly everything" powerful in the western world (190) and therefore untouchable.

Biographer Jared Cade has read elements of the novel as autobiographical. He notes that, like Christie in 1926, Hilary is dealing with a broken marriage and the loss (through death in the book and alienation in the author's case) of a young daughter. As in the autobiographical *Unfinished Portrait*, Cade points out, the protagonist is saved from suicide by a perceptive, attractive man (206). In the Westmacott novel, he shows her love; in this text, he offers her adventure. Authors fictionalizing the Christie disappearance also tend to use the attractive-man-preventing-suicide angle: Kathleen Tynan's *Agatha* features a journalist who falls in love with Christie, whereas Andrew Wilson's *A Talent for Murder* has an intelligence officer who commissions Christie to commit a murder. It is not uncommon to fantasize about a handsome stranger sweeping a suicidal person off his or her feet, and the connection to Christie's life is tenuous. However, it does highlight a keen interest in the suicidal mindset;

and it is known that Christie had suicidal thoughts in 1926.

Published in the United Kingdom in 1954, *Destination Unknown* appeared in the United States in 1955 as *So Many Steps to Death,* a line from the book. Surprisingly, it has never been filmed. Early plans to film updated versions for television (in the 1980s) or cinema (in the 2000s) were abandoned. Beyond a rewritten version for Collins'/Penguin's "English Readers" program in 2012, the novel has yet to be adapted in any form.

Characters: Alverstoke, Lord; **Aristides, Mr.; Baker, Mrs. Calvin**; Barron, Dr. Louis; **Betterton, Olive, and Thomas ("Tom")**; Craven, Brenda; **Craven, Hilary**; Craven, Nigel; **Ericsson, Torquil; Glydr, Major Boris**; Griffiths, Walter; Hetherington, Janet; **Jennson, Miss**; Jessop, Mr.; La Roche, Mademoiselle; Laurier, Henri; LeBlanc, Monsieur; **Mannheim, Dr., and Elsa; Mohammed**; Murchison, Bianca and Dr. Simon; **Neidheim, Helga**; Nielson, **Dr.; Peters, Andrew ("Andy")**; Rubec, Dr.; Speeder, Carol; Van Heidem, Paul

See also: **Suicide;** *They Came to Baghdad;* **War**

Desyat Negrityat. See *And Then There Were None,* **Screen Adaptations of**

The Detection Club

An organization of crime writers founded ca. 1930, the Detection Club continues to the present day. In its early days, the club combined leading British novelists such as Christie, Dorothy L. Sayers, Father Ronald Knox, and Anthony Berkeley (Cox), and consisted mostly of formal meals and informal get-togethers. A stated aim was to promote a certain standard in crime writing, distinct from lowbrow "potboilers" and thrillers.

It was the Detection Club that produced a famous set of "rules," known as the "Ten Commandments" that had been developed by Knox:

(1) The criminal must be someone mentioned in the early part of the story, but must not be anyone whose thoughts the reader has been allowed to follow.
(2) All supernatural or preternatural agencies are ruled out as a matter of course.

(3) Not more than one secret room or passage is allowable.

(4) No hitherto undiscovered poisons may be used, nor any appliance which will need a long scientific explanation at the end.

(5) No Chinaman must figure in the story.

(6) No accident must ever help the detective, nor must he ever have an unaccountable intuition which proves to be right.

(7) The detective must not himself commit the crime.

(8) The detective must not light on any clues which are not instantly produced for the inspection of the reader.

(9) The stupid friend of the detective, the Watson, must not conceal any thoughts which pass through his mind; his intelligence must be slightly, but very slightly, below that of the average reader.

(10) Twin brothers, and doubles generally, must not appear unless we have been duly prepared for them [qtd. in M. Edwards, *Golden Age* 118].

Despite the earnestness of some commentators, these "rules" are clearly tongue-in-cheek and were not actually enforced.

Similarly fanciful is the initiation ceremony for new members that still continues today. The inductee is invited to swear an oath on a skull called Eric. This is a real skull, acquired from a medical student in 1930, although analysis proved it to be female. The oath, written by Sayers, is as follows:

> Do you promise that your detectives shall well and truly detect the crimes presented to them using those wits which it may please you to bestow upon them and not placing reliance on nor making use of Divine Revelation, Feminine Intuition, Mumbo Jumbo, Jiggery-Pokery, Coincidence, or Act of God? [qtd. in M. Edwards, *Golden Age* 119]

The influence of the Detection Club can be seen in several publications of the time, where crime-minded clubs feature prominently. The most notable examples are Anthony Berkeley's *The Poisoned Chocolate Case* (1929), in which members of the fictional "Crimes Circle" are clearly based on the author's colleagues in the Detection Club, and Christie's *The Thirteen Problems* (1929): her stories of the "Tuesday Night Club" started in 1927.

There were collaborative efforts, too, generally to raise funds for the club. The most famous of these is a novel, written by several members, including Christie: *The Floating Admiral*. Christie also contributed to the collaborative novellas "Behind the Screen" and "The Scoop" in 1930–31. Christie was not involved in subsequent round-robin efforts such as "No Flowers by Request" and "Crime on the Coast," but they continued at occasional intervals. The most recent collaborative novel from the Detection Club is *The Sinking Admiral* (2016).

The first club president was G.K. Chesterton, creator of Father Brown. After his death in 1936, his longtime friend E.C. Bentley—author of the highly-influential *Trent's Last Case* and creator of the Clerihew—took over. After his death in 1949, the mantle passed to Dorothy L. Sayers, who embraced the theatricality of a presidential role despite having more or less retired from crime writing. After Sayers died in 1957, Christie became president. However, as she was a shy person, Christie insisted on a co-president to conduct the ceremonies. Liberal politician Lord Gorell took on this role until he died in 1963. After Christie died in 1976, Julian Symons assumed the presidency. The current president is Martin Edwards.

See also: **"Behind the Screen" (novella)**; *The Floating Admiral*; **Golden Age Crime Fiction**; **"The Scoop" (novella)**

Detective Akafuji Takashi. See *Meitantei Akafuji Takashi*

"Detective under a Lacy Hat" (interview)

Published in Croatian, "Detective under a Lacy Hat" is one of the few interviews Christie conducted with her second husband, Max Mallowan (there was an October 1966 interview with Howard Thompson in the *New York Times*). Vinja Ogrizovic interviewed them for a piece that appeared in the Yugoslavian women's magazine *Svijet* on 15 September 1967—Christie's 77th birthday. Later, in the early days of the internet, Ogrizovic translated it into Slovene and English and posted it online.

Ogrizovic describes the mission of obtaining an interview with Christie: she attributes her success to brushing her teeth and bringing flowers. Although chance likely played a role—and the fact that this was not a traditional, belligerent male British journalist—the use of charm probably did have an impact. During the interview, Christie twice ignores a question about whether she thinks like Miss Marple (she would argue against this viewpoint more forcefully in her 1970 letter to *Woman's Day*). She makes her oft-repeated claim that ideas come at banal times such as visiting the opera or going shopping, and is more open than in other interviews about enjoying detective fiction when she was growing up. As in other interviews of the 1960s, she argues against excessive violence in fiction.

The interview concludes the next day, as the parties say goodbye. Ogrizovic discusses learning Arabic languages with Mallowan and talks about a postcard written by Christie to her daughter, Rosalind Hicks. They briefly consider the dangers of living and traveling in the modern world. Ogrizovic concludes that, despite her success, Christie is a very ordinary elderly woman.

See also: **Letter to "Woman's Day"; "'Queen of Crime' Is a Gentlewoman"**

"Detective Writers in England" (article)

The Ministry of Information refused a request from Christie to travel to Cairo in 1945. In one biographer's words, to "make up" for this (Morgan 253), the ministry asked her if she would like to write an article for publication in translation in a Russian magazine "on the four leading detective story writers this century (including yourself, of course)" (qtd. in Morgan 253). Christie agreed that it was "important to 'get together' with Russia in any non-political way" (qtd. in Morgan 253) and agreed to write the piece.

She immediately struggled with the question of the top four figures. The ministry had mentioned Dorothy L. Sayers, but Christie was aware that Sayers had largely abandoned crime fiction by the 1940s. "Rather invidious to single out 4," she wrote to her husband. "To set aside modesty—Myself (!!) Margery Allingham? Dickson Carr? And then who? Bentley? Ngaio Marsh? Anthony Berkeley?" (qtd. in

Morgan 261). In fact, she ended up mentioning all these names and more, strategically forgetting any reference to the number four.

Before turning to the twentieth-century luminaries, the article pays tribute to Sir Arthur Conan Doyle, and Christie asks whether in the Golden Age detective fiction and detectives in fiction have become "too artificial": for this reason, she writes, "my own 'Hercule Poirot' is often somewhat of an embarrassment to me" (DWE 3). The article then details Christie's leading colleagues, starting with Allingham, who is, Christie writes, "foremost" among peers (4; Allingham would return the compliment in her 1950 *New York Times* tribute to Christie). Regarding Sayers, Christie laments her departure from crime writing while implying that Sayers's novels had become too serious and Lord Peter Wimsey had become "a good man spoilt" (4). Next, she discusses H.C. Bailey ("always the same" and better at short stories than novels; 4), John Dickson Carr ("the master magician" 4), Ngaio Marsh ("decidedly popular" and a "genius" 5), Freeman Wills Crofts (the "Master of Alibis" 5), and R. Austin Freeman (damned with faint praise as "interesting" 5).

She then presents honorable mentions to other key names of the age: Michael Innes, John Rhode, Anthony Berkeley, and the "up-to-date" Gladys Mitchell (5). Finally, Christie discusses her own work. She refers to herself as "an industrious craftsman" but also accepts the media-given moniker "Duchess of Death" (5). Finally, she warns any aspiring writers to be careful in their choice of detective, lest they be saddled with him for many years (6).

The article was published in Russian, but it did not appear in an English-language publication until issue 55 of *CADS: Crime and Detective Stories* in December 2008, introduced by archivist Tony Medawar. In 2012, it reached a wider readership when it appeared as a preface to a reissue of the Detection Club's *Ask a Policeman*.

See also: **The Detection Club; Conan Doyle, Sir Arthur; War**

Deyre, Vernon

Vernon Deyre is the central figure in the

Mary Westmacott novel *Giant's Bread*. In this character, Christie gives some of her own traits and history to a completely different type of person: a Jewish male composer. Deyre is brilliant and intense, and loses his identity for many years, in an escalated parable for Christie's own nervous breakdown.

Dhund. See **Indian-Language Adaptations**

Disappearance of Agatha Christie

It is common—but inaccurate—to say that Christie never discussed her 11-day disappearance. Certainly, she preferred to forget it. Nonetheless, it is the most widely discussed aspect of her life. This is partly because Christie, with her global, generation-defying popularity, had a contained, uneventful private life, so the one sensational event in it inevitably attracts attention. The disappearance can be understood easily as an unfortunate but totally explicable event. However, hype around it seems unlikely to die, partly due to the wish of entertainers and readers to find a mystery in the real life of the world's most successful purveyor of mysteries.

Christie's *annus horribilis* was 1926. In April of that year, her mother, to whom she was devoted, died, and in August, her husband Archie asked for a divorce so that he could marry his mistress, Nancy Neele. Christie then experienced what the *Daily Graphic* called "a breakdown," which prompted a trip to the Pyrenees for recuperation—although media speculation attributed this to "overwork," noting that her kind of writing "is not done at top speed without paying a penalty" (Mr. London 6). Christie's autobiography and her semi-autobiographical novels describe emotional scenes as she refused a divorce, and her husband insisted.

On 3 December, following an argument with Archie, Christie wrote to her brother-in-law, Campbell Christie, that she would be taking a break in Harrogate. This letter apparently went unnoticed. She drove off in her car, a Morris Cowley. It was later found at Newland's Corner in a spot known as "Silent Pool," containing an old passport and the author's effects. Christie had disappeared.

The story quickly became a media sensation, with newspapers around the world following it in minute detail. Speculation ran unfettered: theories were freely expressed that Archie had killed his wife, that she had committed suicide, and that the disappearance was a publicity stunt to sell more books. Major search parties—official as well as informal, volunteer-led ones—were organized, and Silent Pool was dredged. One newspaper ran photographic reconstructions of "Mrs. Christie Disguised" to encourage readers to spot her, and writers Edgar Wallace and Paul Trent speculated about a "hysterical breakdown" (Wallace 9) and a "probably nervous breakdown" (Trent 8), deliberately staged to look like suicide, respectively. Among those involved in search efforts was fellow crime writer Dorothy L. Sayers, and the police even consulted Sir Arthur Conan Doyle—although, now fully immersed in spiritualism, he gave one of Christie's gloves to a medium, who told police she could be found near water.

In fact, this was true. Unbeknownst to anybody, Christie had booked into the Swan Hydropathic Hotel (now the Old Swan), a health spa in Harrogate, under the name Teresa Neele. The use of the surname of her husband's mistress was, she later claimed, coincidental. Albert Whiteley, a banjo-player in the Harry Codd Dance Band, spotted her on 14 December. The police and her husband were summoned, and she was ushered to Abney Hall, her sister's residence in Cheadle, on the next day. Both Agatha and Archie maintained that she had no memory of what had happened during the 11 missing days. She saw several doctors and was diagnosed with "an unquestionably genuine loss of memory" (Donald Core and Henry Wilson, qtd. in Cade 141). The Christies quickly separated and divorced in 1928. The story remained a media sensation for some time.

The press speculation was merciless, generally accusing Christie of staging the disappearance either to sell more books or to frame her husband for murder. The furor marked a shift in Christie's approach to the media; she stopped flirting with the press, granting regular interviews and photo sessions, and smiling for journalists. In 1928, in an effort to lay the matter to rest and in response to a libel case, Christie gave a lengthy interview to the *Daily Mail*, which editors published as an article titled "Her Own Story of Her Disappearance." In it, Christie claims total amnesia born of "nervous strain" and suicidal tendencies; she claims that, while in Harrogate, she genuinely believed she was Teresa Neele of South Africa (HOC 11). Things did not quieten down as hoped: the next year, a prank letter signed "Agatha Christie," suggesting that police should not waste public funds searching for a man who had gone missing, was published in the Melbourne *Herald*.

Subsequently, most people meeting Christie socially or professionally were instructed not to mention events. Christie and later her daughter, Rosalind Hicks, reacted angrily when public references were made to the disappearance, especially if there was an implication that it had been staged. Legal action was occasionally considered but always dismissed—mainly to avoid bringing the event back into the public eye, at least in Christie's lifetime.

Under the veil of anonymity, she wrote in more detail about the emotional trauma of Archie's infidelity as well as her mother's death in *Unfinished Portrait* (1934), in which all the key players from this drama appear as fictional characters. Christie's autobiography does not deal explicitly with the disappearance, although it skirts around the event, something that her publishers knew would disappoint readers looking for answers. To this end, publisher William Collins took the unusual step of writing in a foreword that the disappearance would not be covered.

Biographers have, of course, not ignored the disappearance. Indeed, it is the central or exclusive topic of several biographies, including Gillian Gill's *Agatha Christie: The Woman and Her Mysteries* (1990), Jared Cade's *Agatha Christie and the Eleven Missing Days* (1998), and Andrew Norman's *Agatha Christie: The Finished Portrait* (2006). It occupies a sizable chunk of every biography. It has also, inevitably, been the subject of an array of novels, books, plays, and other media forms.

See also: *An Autobiography*; Christie, Colonel Archibald ("Archie"); Fictional Portrayals of Agatha Christie; "Her Own Story of Her Disappearance"; Neele, Nancy; *Unfinished Portrait*

"The Disappearance of Captain Harwell." See **"At the Bells and Motley"**

"The Disappearance of Mr. Davenheim" (story; alternative titles: "Hercule Poirot, Armchair Detective"; "Mr. Davenby Disappears")

The Poirot story "The Disappearance of Mr. Davenheim" is best-known for an offhand comment made by the detective about amnesia. Ever since Christie's disappearance in 1926 and subsequent claims of memory loss, commentators of many stripes have remarked on the grim irony of Poirot's words. Investigating the unexplained disappearance of the famous banker Mr. Davenheim, Poirot suggests that the "'loss of memory' case" is "much abused ... rare, but occasionally genuine" (*PI* 232). His comment is part of the story's—and Christie's—self-referential turn, referring to the "much-abused" device in fiction. However, it has been widely taken to mean that people who disappear might be making up or avoiding their reasons for doing so. In the story, Poirot discovers that Mr. Davenheim has been living a double life as a petty criminal.

Published in *The Sketch* in March 1923, "The Disappearance of Mr. Davenheim" appeared in the anthology *Poirot Investigates* in 1924. In 1962, NBC broadcast a television adaptation, which was the first U.S. appearance of Poirot on the small screen. The 30-minute drama was an episode of *General Electric Theater*, starring Martin Gabel, and was expected to launch a series, although this did not materialize. Another adaptation, part of *Agatha Christie's Poirot*, aired on ITV in 1990. An animated episode of *Agasa Kurisutī no Meitantei Powaro to Māpuru* based on the story was broadcast on NHK in 2005.

Characters: Davenheim, Mr.; Davenheim, Mrs.; **Hastings, Captain Arthur**; **Japp, Inspector James**; Kellett, Billy; Lowen, Mr.; **Miller, Inspector**; **Poirot, Hercule**; Salmon

See also: *Agasa Kurisutī no Meitantei*

Powaro to Māpuru; *Agatha Christie's Poirot*; Disappearance of Agatha Christie; NBC Television Adaptations; *Poirot Investigates*; Psychoanalysis

"The Disappearance of Winnie King." See "The Horses of Diomedes"

Dittisham, Lady. See Greer, Elsa

Dixon, Gladys. See Gladys

"Does Woman's Instinct Make Her a Good Detective?" (article)

The very short essay "Does Woman's Instinct Make Her a Good Detective?" was written to promote the sixth story in what would become *The Thirteen Problems*. This story, "The Thumb Mark of St. Peter," was to appear in the *Royal Magazine* when Christie's piece appeared in the *Star* newspaper on 14 May 1928. In the promotional essay, Christie dismisses any idea of "woman's intuition"—as she does in *Mrs. McGinty's Dead*—and argues instead that women have been trained to notice small things about which men are incurious since prehistoric times. She also argues—less progressively—that women prefer not to do things thoroughly but instead value the concept of the lucky guess, as a "short cut" (DWI... 149).

The essay was reprinted as a postscript to Tony Medawar's *Murder, She Said: The Quotable Miss Marple* (2019).

Dogs

Christie was extremely fond of dogs, and throughout most of her life, she had at least one as a pet. In her life and work, dogs are a constant presence alleviating heavy moments in a domestic setting with uncomplicated companionship. Christie's first dog, which she had at age five, was called

George Washington (Christie's father was American), although Christie called him Tony. Her favorite dog, Peter, was a terrier acquired in the 1920s and was instrumental in Christie's recovery from her traumatic experiences in 1926. As a result, Peter was a co-dedicatee of *The Mystery of the Blue Train*, as was Christie's secretary, Carlo Fisher. They are described in the dedication as "the two distinguished members of the O.F.D.," which stands for "Order of Faithful Dogs"—the distinction is meant as high praise. Peter later inspired a character: Bob the wire-haired terrier in "The Incident

Facsimile edition of *Dumb Witness* (HarperCollins, 2007) with a photograph of Christie's beloved terrier Peter on the cover. Photo by Dean James.

of the Dog's Ball." Bob also appears in *Dumb Witness* and has the voice of a cheeky schoolboy—including actual dialogue—emerging as the most sympathetic character. Poirot solves the case by realizing that a faithful dog would never endanger its mistress. At the end of the novel, Bob takes up residence with Captain Hastings. Peter (in character as Bob) appeared on the front cover of *Dumb Witness*'s first edition.

Christie's last dog was a Manchester terrier, Bingo, described by a friend as "so overbred as to be positively neurotic" (Rowse 108): he would bite indiscriminately. Christie imagined that he believed a devil possessed the telephone, so his barking and biting was an effort to protect his owners from evil spirits (Rowse 108). Hannibal, the Manchester terrier in *Postern of Fate*, is affectionately drawn as arrogant: "he considered himself to be on a much higher level of sophistication and aristocracy than any other dog he met" (33). Bingo (in character as Hannibal) appeared on the back cover. *Postern of Fate* is dedicated to "Hannibal and his master" (Hannibal was most likely a nickname for Bingo as well as a character in the book).

Dogs in other stories play smaller roles. A dog's mouth provides a hiding place for cocaine in "The Capture of Cerberus" (the 1947 version), and it is devotion to an aging, half-blind terrier that motivates the protagonist of "Next to a Dog." In 1974, Christie contemplated writing "a little book about my cats and dogs, possibly in the Christmas Season" (qtd. in Rowse 109) but did not follow through on this idea, citing a (predicted) lack of interest from publishers. In reality, she was no longer writing publishable material at this stage.

See also: ***Dumb Witness; Postern of Fate***

The Donkey

The donkey is the central figure in "The Naughty Donkey." It is disappointed by the gifts being brought to Jesus Christ but comes to realize their true value.

Dorothy and Agatha (Larsen). See **Fictional Portrayals of Agatha Christie**

"The Double Alibi." See **"Triangle at Rhodes"**

"The Double Clue" (story)

In the story "The Double Clue," first published in *The Sketch* in December 1923, Hercule Poirot meets his version of Sherlock Holmes's Irene Adler: Countess Vera Rossakoff. A spate of jewel thefts puts him on the track of this mysterious Russian woman who claims, perhaps without warrant, to be a countess. In the process, he becomes enchanted with her, providing much comic relief. A spiteful, effeminate man is generally suspected because of a cigarette case found at the crime scene that is monogrammed with the initials B.P. Poirot realizes that, in the Cyrillic alphabet, B.P. equates to V.R.—that is, Vera Rossakoff. He reveals the truth but allows the countess to escape and ponders that he may cross paths with her again.

The clue about Cyrillic letters would be recycled in *Murder on the Orient Express*. Poirot and the countess would cross paths in the stories collected in *The Big Four* and *The Labours of Hercules*, although she is mentioned in many of the later novels and stories. "The Double Clue" appeared in the U.S. anthology *Double Sin and Other Stories* (1961) and the U.K. collection *Poirot's Early Cases* (1974). It was dramatized as an episode of *Agatha Christie's Poirot*, broadcast on ITV on 10 February 1991. That adaptation made several changes, partly to soften the countess and create a love story rather than a comic diversion, partly in the context of changed British attitudes to Russia following the then highly topical fall of communism.

Characters: Bird, Katherine; Caroline, Lady; Hardman, Marcus; **Hastings, Captain Arthur**; Johnston, Mr.; Nacora; Parker, Bernard; **Poirot, Hercule**; **Rossakoff, Countess Vera**; Runcorn, Lady

See also: ***Agatha Christie's Poirot***; *The Big Four* (novel); ***Double Sin*** (story collection); **Homosexuality**; *Poirot's Early Cases*

"Double Sin" (story; alternative title: "By Road or Rail")

A short story involving a sleight of hand on a train journey, "Double Sin" sees Hercule Poirot in top priestly form as he uses the vocabulary of "Papa Poirot," referring to his client—who is the criminal—as "my child" several times. This story has Poirot being decidedly un–English ("a strange mix of Flemish thrift and artistic fervour"; *PEC* 176) and Hastings being distracted as usual by pretty, auburn-haired women. It was published in the *Sunday Dispatch* on 23 September 1928, and in *Detective Story Magazine* as "By Road or Rail" the next year. It appeared in the U.S. collection *Double Sin* (1961) and the U.K. collection *Poirot's Early Cases* (1974). An adaptation aired on ITV on 11 February 1990, as part of *Agatha Christie's Poirot*.

Characters: **Aarons, Joseph**; Baker Wood, J.; Durrant, Mary; **Hastings, Captain Arthur**; Kane, Norton; Penn, Elizabeth; **Poirot, Hercule**

See also: *Agatha Christie's Poirot*; *Double Sin* (story collection); *Poirot's Early Cases*

Double Sin (short story collection; alternative title: *Double Sin and Other Stories*)

Double Sin is a 1961 U.S.-only collection of short stories, which is composed of the following: "Double Sin," "Wasp's Nest," "The Theft of the Royal Ruby," "The Dressmaker's Doll," "Greenshaw's Folly," "The Double Clue," "The Last Séance," and "Sanctuary." This unusually diverse stories had either been published in the United Kingdom in *The Hound of Death* or *The Adventure of the Christmas Pudding* or would appear in *Poirot's Early Cases* or *Miss Marple's Final Cases*.

Dove, Mary

Mary Dove is an efficient housekeeper in *A Pocket Full of Rye* who turns out to be an unlikely blackmailer.

"Down in the Wood." See *The Road of Dreams* (poetry collection)

Doyle, Linnet

Not yet 21, Linnet Doyle, the daughter of Melhuish Ridgeway and Anna Hartz, is one of the most admired and envied women in the world because of her wealth and beauty in *Death on the Nile*. She is murdered on her honeymoon after marrying her best friend's fiancé. In the play *Murder on the Nile*, the character is named Kay. A more human spin on the "poor little rich girl" motif, in a similar plot, appears in the figure of Ellie Guteman in *Endless Night*.

Doyle, Simon

Simon Doyle is a boyishly handsome man at the center of the action in *Death on the Nile* and its adaptation, *Murder on the Nile*. Very much a "simple Simon," he is effortlessly attractive to women and inhabits a kind of fairy-tale when he goes from genteel poverty to riches by marrying Linnet Ridgeway. However, it is all part of a plot with his ex-fiancée, Jacqueline de Bellefort, to gain Linnet's money. Simon is judged more harshly than Jacqueline in the text: when she kills him in a murder-suicide after their crimes are revealed, Poirot remarks that he "died an easier death than he deserved" (*DOTN* 285). Unsurprisingly, filmmakers adapting the text tend to position the woman as more culpable than the man.

Dragimiroff, Princess Natalia

Natalia Dragimiroff is a hideous, autocratic, and emotionally sensitive Russian princess in *Murder on the Orient Express*. She is one of the figures first noticed by Hercule Poirot on the train, observing that, despite her appearance, she is a warm, obviously kind person—by contrast, the respectable-looking Samuel Ratchett exudes malice.

Drake, Lucilla, and Victor

Lucilla and Victor Drake are mother and son respectively, related to the Marle and Barton families, in *Sparkling Cyanide*. Blinded by devotion to her insalubrious son, Lucilla bankrolls him and refuses to acknowledge that he is a criminal. Victor is, however, a bad boy, set on money and manipulating women to get it. He and Iris Marle are responsible for the murders.

Drake, Rowena

Rowena Drake is a sensible, handsome, middle-aged woman who hosts the eponymous *Hallowe'en Party*. The shock of her identification as a murderer of children—and lover/disciple to Michael Garfield—lies in the implausibility of respectable, middle-class homeowners engaging in cultish behavior.

Drake, Una, and Vera

Una and Vera Drake are identical twins who take part in a practical joke on Mr.

Montgomery Jones in "The Unbreakable Alibi." With these characters, Christie breaks one of the cardinal rules of Golden Age crime fiction—using identical twins as an explanation for how someone can be in two places at once. It should be noted that the story is a parody of the work of Freeman Wills Crofts.

Draper, Mary. See **Hopkins, Nurse Jessie**

Draper, Ruth (1884–1956). See **Adams, Carlotta**

"The Dream" (story; alternative title: "The Three Strange Points")

In the short story "The Dream," Hercule Poirot investigates the murder of a man who seems to have dreamed about the date and hour of his death in advance. The story explores psychoanalysis but offers a typically dramatic sleight-of-hand explanation for events. Indeed, medical explanations for mysteries are roundly mocked as "preposterous" and contradictory (205), as Poirot represents a purely logical approach to problems. This story also introduces Dr. Stillingfleet, a character who would be mentioned in *Sad Cypress* and appear as a romantic lead in *Third Girl*.

The story was published in the *Saturday Evening Post* on 23 October 1937 and appeared in the U.S. collection *The Regatta Mystery* (1939) and the U.K. anthology *The Adventure of the Christmas Pudding* (1960). It was dramatized as an episode of the television series *Agatha Christie's Poirot* in 1989 and for radio as part of *Krimi-Sommer mit Hercule Poirot* in 2006.

Characters: Adams, Mr.; Barnett, Inspector; Cornworthy, Hugo; **Farley, Benedict**; Farley, Joana; Farley, Louise; Holmes; **Poirot, Hercule**; **Stillingfleet, Dr. John**; Stoddart, Mr.

See also: *The Adventure of the Christmas Pudding* (story collection); *Agatha Christie's Poirot*; *Krimi-Sommer mit Hercule Poirot*; *The Regatta Mystery* (story collection)

"The Dream House of Shiraz." See **"The House at Shiraz"**

"The Dream Spinners." See *The Road of Dreams* (poetry collection)

"The Dressmaker's Doll" (story)

"The Dressmaker's Doll" is a supernatural short story in which a doll appears uninvited at a dressmaker's shop. The dressmaker becomes obsessed with it, believing it to be cursed. She tries to stop a "small ragged girl" (*MMFC* 128) taking it home, only to realize that the doll is longing for love and companionship. This is a story about recognizing the humanity of the Other, something that is explored by Christie more fully in short fiction than in long form and is a theme rarely recognized in her work. It was first published in *Woman's Journal* in 1958 and appeared in the U.S. collection *Double Sin and Other Stories* (Dodd, Mead 1961) and in the U.K. anthology *Miss Marple's Final Cases* (Collins, 1979). A dramatization was broadcast on BBC Radio 4 on 10 March 2003.

Characters: Coombe, Alicia; Elspeth; Fellows-Brown, Mrs.; Fou-Ling; Fox, Sybil; Groves, Mrs.; Margaret; Marlene

See also: **BBC Radio Adaptations**; **Curses**; *Miss Marple's Final Cases* (story collection)

"Drip! Drip!" See **"The Bloodstained Pavement"**

"Drugs and Detective Stories" (article)

"Drugs and Detective Stories" is an article, written and published in 1941, when Christie was volunteering at the University College Hospital, London, in the pharmacy. In it, she reflects on working in the dispensary at the Red Cross Hospital, Torquay, during World War I and the strangeness of performing the same work again after 25 years. Christie outlines the process of writing her first detective novel and the inspiration that came from working in a dispensary. She also admits to a preference for dispatching her characters via poison, which she knew so much about, writing that guns "make me acutely nervous—I know so little about them. When it comes to poison I feel more on my own ground" (DDS xv).

One challenge highlighted by Christie is the need to sanitize death by poison while still informing and sensationalizing. There is, she points out, a pleasure for audiences in reading about a face turning purple, but "vomiting and purgation" would not be well-received (xv). The article concludes rather hastily with disparate throwaway remarks, the most illuminating of which is a comparison of the death of Socrates via hemlock—which Christie calls "dignified"—and the use of castor oil by "Fascist[s]." Castor oil was used by the Nazis in Germany and more openly by the Blackshirts in Italy to torture political enemies and Jews in the most humiliating way possible—forcing laxative effects, dehydration, and death. Christie does not dwell on this, merely remarking that it diabolically undignified.

The article is breezy but evidences commercial calculation and an awareness of broader sociopolitical contexts to her writing. It appeared in volume 26, issue 6 of the *University College Hospital Magazine* in 1941. Although it has been broadly quoted in the intervening years, it was not reproduced entirely until 2016, when it appeared in a special edition of *Curtain*, published in a box set with *The Mysterious Affair at Styles,* to mark the centenary of the writing of that novel. It enjoyed a wider circulation—and translation for international imprints—as an introduction to an anniversary edition of *The Mysterious Affair at Styles* in 2020.

See also: **"How I Became a Writer"**; *The Mysterious Affair at Styles*

Dubois, Martine

Martine Dubois is the mysterious French wife of Edmund Crackenthorpe, whom he married shortly before his death during World War II, in *4.50 from Paddington.* The Crackenthorpes, who never met her, believe that a dead woman found on their property is Martine. However, Lady Stoddart-West, mother of Alexander Eastley's best friend, reveals that she is Martine. She is youthful and elegant, and presents herself as an Englishwoman.

Duguesclin, Quentin. See **Curry, R. H.**

Dumb Witness (novel; alternative title: *Poirot Loses a Client*)

One of the weaker Poirot novels of the 1930s, *Dumb Witness* has a complex structure that flits between different times and flashbacks. In it, Hercule Poirot receives a letter from an old woman who believes that her fall down some stairs was not an accident. However, by the time the letter arrives, its author—Emily Arundell—has died, apparently of liver failure. Poirot and Captain Hastings visit her home, Littlegreen House, in Market Basing under assumed identities so as not to arouse suspicion and determine that she was poisoned. They meet her scheming nieces and nephew—Bella Tanios, Theresa Arundell, and Charles Arundell—and her longtime companion, Wilhemina Lawson, as well as a range of village spinsters and doctors, including Bella's husband, Dr. Jacob Tanios, about whom locals are suspicious because there is "nothing English about him" (16).

As matters escalate, Bella reveals that she is terrified for her life and plans to leave her husband of whom she claims to be afraid. Poirot arranges for her to stay in a nondescript hotel and writes her a note. When Bella commits suicide in the hotel, he explains that she was the murderer, trying to frame her husband, and that her motive was financial independence. Throughout the story, Poirot and Hastings are accompanied by Emily's dog, Bob, who forms a special friendship with Hastings. Hastings ends up adopting him. This is the final Hastings novel before *Curtain: Poirot's Last Case* (1974).

Dumb Witness started life as the short story "The Adventure of the Dog's Ball." It was expanded into a novel in 1936 and published the next year with several marketing innovations to promote Christie as a homely, domestic novelist. Much of this dwelt on the central presence in the story of Bob the wire-haired terrier, who is drawn affectionately and even given a form of dialogue. The book was dedicated to Christie's own wire-haired terrier, Peter—"most faithful of friends and dearest of companions"—and Peter was photographed for the front cover. Peter had already been a co-dedicatee of *The Mystery of the Blue Train* (1928). A note explaining the identity of the model appeared on the inside flap, and a note from "Bob," in Christie's handwriting, dominated the back cover: "If it hadn't been for me, old Monsieur Poirot would not have solved this case. Bob—the *not* so dumb witness!" (emphasis in original). The book was also the first Christie title to appear in a Book Club edition, which featured four photographic plates, including a sketch of Poirot and a similar-looking dog.

The dog is, in many ways, the only likable character encountered by Poirot and Hastings. Their late client was spiteful, changing her will on a whim, and prejudiced against Dr. Tanios on racist grounds, as is acidic local resident Caroline Peabody. Tanios himself is sinister. His wife, Bella, is an extremely manipulative murderer. Charles Arundell is an out-and-out cad, whereas his sister Theresa is irreverent, addressing Poirot as "Hercule." Even the victim's faultlessly loyal and sympathetic companion, Miss Lawson, is guilty of massaging the truth so she can inherit money that should rightly have gone elsewhere. Unpleasant characters are more of a staple in Christie's novels than traditional adaptations and scholarship imply. However, *Dumb Witness* and *And Then There Were None* (1939) are her only novels that feature wholly unsympathetic casts of characters, including the romantic interests.

The prejudice against Dr. Tanios—who turns out to be his wife's enamored patsy—is presented as an eccentricity of old-school Englishness. In the first chapter, it is stated that Bella "had married a Greek. And Emily Arundell's people, who were all what used to be termed 'good service people,' simply did not marry Greeks" (13). Two pages later, Emily reflects that Bella

> was a good woman [but] could not be regarded with complete approval. For Bella had married a foreigner—and not only a foreigner—but a Greek. In Miss Arundell's prejudiced mind a Greek was almost as bad as an Argentine or a Turk. The fact that Dr. Tanios had a charming manner and was said to be extremely able in his progression only prejudiced the old lady slightly more against him [15].

The same sentiment is repeated twice in a short space of time, showing that Emily is set in her ways and that no amount of personal brilliance or contributions to society can change them. The use of an archaic expression ("good service people") and old-fashioned takes on the exotic sinister foreigner ("an Argentine or a Turk") show that this "prejudice" is outmoded. Another character who expresses outright prejudice against Tanios for his Greekness is the equally old-school Miss Peabody, whereas the proudly odious Charles, whose defining characteristic is his dishonest means of acquiring money, argues without reason that Tanios must have "a nose for money all right! Trust a Greek for that" (24).

However, racial prejudice is not trivial in real life or in this novel, as it is a collective prejudice against the exotic and affectionate doctor that enables his beautiful, dull, and crucially English wife to tell conflicting stories that convince most characters and the implied reader of his guilt, despite his lack of motive for murder. The town of Market Basing is shown to be insular when Poirot arrives under the Italian name of Parotti, speaking partially in French, and no one seems to notice anything odd about this. At the same time, Englishness is shown to be judgmental, insular, and never satisfied when Miss Peabody makes a joke at Hastings's expense after dismissing Poirot as "a foreigner":

> "Can you write decent English?" [she asked Hastings.]
> "I hope so."
> "H'm—where did you go to school?"
> "Eton."
> "Then you can't" [104].

The world of Market Basing—self-contained, judgmental, and nostalgic—exists down to the "definitely Victorian" décor of Littlegreen House (70), and the greatest judgment falls on the younger generation that have made choices that challenge the received order: Theresa is assumed to take drugs and drink heavily because of her many "love affairs" (140–41), Charles is considered a bad lot for forging his aunt's signature on a check, and Bella is blamed for having a Greek husband. Poirot's pretext for visiting—to write a biography of Emily's military father—is embraced by locals, but many tell him there is nothing to write about, politely ignoring the father's alcoholism while condemning the same habit without justification in his great-niece. It is a straightforwardly nostalgic community but is not presented in a straightforwardly nostalgic way.

Another link to the Victorian past is spiritualism, including séances, automatic writing, and spiritual possession. Christie had dealt with séances and spiritualism extensively in older work, but she would not return to it until 1961's *The Pale Horse*. The esoteric provides amusing character portraits in the form of the Tripp sisters, but it ultimately provides a clue: the apparent sight of the victim's spirit leaving her body—a vision of phosphorescent green light—proves to be proof that she was poisoned with phosphorus. This is a case of plot and theme serving each other mutually, eliminating the need for a scientific explanation of the poison as the symptoms are revealed via an example, in a nontechnical manner.

The novel was published in the United Kingdom in 1937 and in the United States in 1938 as *Poirot Loses a Client*. This edition included several continuity errors absent from the U.K. version—the name of Bella's son switches from John to Edward several times, and her maiden name is also inconsistent—which remain in some subsequent U.S. editions. As is standard in publishing, the different publishers will have edited proofs independently, and some issues in the original manuscript were evidently missed during corrections.

On 26 March 1996, *Dumb Witness* aired as the 45th episode of the ITV series *Agatha Christie's Poirot*, with publicity again centered on the dog. This was the last episode to air before a four-year hiatus. On 30 November 2006, a BBC Radio 4 adaptation was broadcast. An extremely loose dramatization set in 1950s France aired on the France 2 network in 2013, part of *Les Petits Meurtres d'Agatha Christie*.

Characters: Angus; **Annie**; **Arundell, Charles, and Theresa; Arundell, Emily;** Arundell extended family (Agnes, Arabella, Matilda, Mr. and Mrs.); Biggs, Professor; **Bob**; Carruthers, Miss; Donaldson, Dr. Rex; **Ellen**; Fox, Mary; Gabler, Mr.; **George(s)**; Grainger, Dr.; **Hastings, Captain Arthur; Lawson, Wilhelmina (Minnie)**; Peabody, Caroline; **Poirot, Hercule**; Purvis, William; **Tanios, Arabella (Bella); Tanios, Dr.**

Jacob; Tanios, John/Edward; Tanios, Mary; **Tripp, Isabel, and Julia**; Varley, Mrs.

See also: *Agatha Christie's Poirot*; Dogs; *Hercule Poirot* (BBC radio series); "Incident of the Dog's Ball"; Market Basing; *Mystery of the Week*; *Les Petits Meurtres d'Agatha Christie*

Duó mìn zhèn rén (Death Witness)

Duó mìn zhèn rén (English: *Death Witness*) is a Chinese adaptation of *Witness for the Prosecution* (film), staged in Hong Kong in 2018. This version by Mao Junhui, Pan Shiyun, and Liu Haoxiang was directed by Junhui and staged at the Hong Kong Academy for Performing Arts, starring Carina Lau, Paul Chun Pui, and Tse Kwan Ho. The production mirrored, in some respects, a West End version then playing at the London County Hall, which employed the gimmick of allowing audience members into a jury box. In the Hong Kong version, 12 audience members entered a lottery to become jurors, actively involved in the scene, and give their verdict on whether the accused was innocent or guilty toward the end of the play.

Dupont, Armand, and Jean

Armand and Jean Dupont are obsessive French archaeologists—father and son respectively—in *Death in the Clouds*. At the end of the book, it is implied that Jean may have a future with fellow plane passenger Jane Grey.

Duveen, Dulcie

Dulcie Duveen is a spirited flapper who speaks the first dialogue in *The Murder on the Links*: her cry of "Hell!" upon entering a train carriage scandalizes the "old-fashioned" Captain Hastings (10). He falls in love with her over the course of the book, although she uses him to destroy evidence implicating her twin sister, Bella. Between *The Murder on the Links* and *The Big Four*, Hastings and Dulcie—who introduces herself as "Cinderella," the name by which she becomes known—are married. Cinderella is mentioned heavily in *The Big Four* but does not appear. By *Curtain*, Poirot's last case, she has died in Argentina, leaving her widower and a daughter, Judith.

"The Dying Chinaman." See *The Big Four* (novel)

Dyson, Gregory ("Greg"), and Lucky

An American tourist in *A Caribbean Mystery*, Greg Dyson is fascinated by birds and butterflies. He has married twice: Lucky, with whom he travels, is his second wife. An American botanist with bleached hair, she is killed when mistaken for Molly Kendal. Her real Christian name is not stated; Greg calls her "Lucky" because he considers her his lucky charm.

"Easter, 1918." See *The Road of Dreams* (poetry collection)

Easterbrook, Mark

Historian Mark Easterbrook is the amateur detective in *The Pale Horse*. Although he has a secret in his past—a hasty, youthful marriage to a woman who later died—he is presented as an everyman.

Eastley, Alexander, and Squadron Leader Bryan

In *4.50 from Paddington*, Bryan Eastley is an amiable young widower with a military background who proposes marriage to Lucy Eyelesbarrow. Alexander Eastley is his son and the grandson of Luther Crackenthorpe. He is at the family home during the summer holidays from boarding school. Polite and angelic-looking, he is precocious and gung-ho, becoming a close ally of Lucy. Alexander reflects changing attitudes when he attributes his grandfather's frugality and irritability to "a diet or something" (56). He uses slang like "wizard" (57).

Easy to Kill. See *Murder Is Easy*

Eden, Beryl. See Gilliat, Beryl

"The Edge"

The brief story "The Edge" appeared in *Pearson's Magazine* in February 1927 with publicity stating that it had been "written just before this author's recent illness and mysterious disappearance" (*WLL* 85). It is an intensely personal short story, and Christie repeatedly refused requests to republish it. It is likely that the direct link made in publicity between the story and the personal trauma were too much.

"The Edge" tells the story of Clare Halliwell, a well-put-together English woman, whose lover, Gerald Lee, marries the glamorous hedonist Vivien Lee. Clare visits a cliff-edge and contemplates suicide. When she discovers that Vivien is having an affair, Clare confronts her on the cliff edge, and Vivien commits suicide. Clare becomes overwhelmed with guilt, believing she has killed Vivien, and lives the rest of her life in a mental prison.

Like "Harlequin's Lane" (written and published in 1927), "The Edge" deals with Christie's own confused feelings of betrayal and guilt, hinting at the self-destructive tendencies that came to the fore in her disappearance. The story was not republished in Christie's lifetime, but it appeared in 1997 in the U.K. collection *While the Light Lasts* and the U.S. collection *The Harlequin Tea Set*.

Characters: Cyril; **Halliwell, Clare**; Lauriston, Nurse; Lee, Lady Vivien; Lee, Sir Gerald

See also: *The Harlequin Tea Set* (story collection); *While the Light Lasts* (story collection)

Edgware, Lady. See Wilkinson, Jane

Edgware, Lord

In *Lord Edgware Dies*, the titular victim is George Alfred St. Vincent Marsh, fourth Baron Edgware. He is presented in gothic style as a mad, sadistic aristocrat with likely homosexual tendencies. Hercule Poirot is initially employed to convince Lord Edgware to grant his wife a divorce, although he has already agreed to do so.

Edna

Edna, like Mary and Gladys, is one of those names often given to servants by their mistresses and by their creators in fiction. Christie named Miss Marple's maid in "The Case of the Perfect Maid" and "Tape-Measure Murder" Edna and also gave the name to a shop assistant in *Mrs. McGinty's Dead*. There is also a maid called Edna in *Taken at the Flood*, and a typist, Edna Brent, is murdered in *The Clocks*. These Ednas typically fail to grasp the significance of knowledge they have. The most famous Edna-the-maid was probably created by J.B. Priestley in *An Inspector Calls* (1945), where the well-named character is significant for the aristocratic family's cultivated ignorance of her humanity.

"The Egyptian Tomb." See "The Adventure of the Egyptian Tomb"

Elephants Can Remember (novel)

The premise of *Elephants Can Remember* (1972) is strong. At a social event, novelist Ariadne Oliver is asked by an acquaintance, Mrs. Burton-Cox, to look into a family matter. Her son, Desmond, has a prospective fiancée, Celia Ravenscroft, who is Mrs. Oliver's goddaughter and has lost her parents in mysterious circumstances. Mrs. Burton-Cox wants to know if Celia's father killed her mother, or her mother killed her father. Mrs. Oliver goes to Hercule Poirot for help, and the resulting investigation lies entirely in conversations between middle-aged and elderly characters recalling events of some decades before. Like the premise, the solution is extremely ambitious and evokes vintage Christie, centering on twin sisters, mental illness, and family secrets. The novel could be compared to *Five Little Pigs* for evidence of two distinct approaches from the same author to mysteries where the evidence is all anecdotal and based on emotional memories.

Elephants Can Remember is partly distinguished by extreme interiority and a focus on the private life and private thoughts of Mrs. Oliver. She is Christie's self-portrait and a deliberately constructed one at that: she encouraged readers to see her in the character. In this book, Mrs. Oliver is shown dealing without much success with the need to keep changing her hairstyle—surely a reflection of the need to evolve, fashionably, as a writer and a woman—and introducing a bewildered Poirot to Ribena. As a famous writer too shy to enjoy the considerable attention she receives, she also has several comic opportunities to answer back to fans and hangers-on in her head. The reader gets to experience the answer-back, whereas the fan character who is the reader's stand-in does not.

The stream-of-consciousness form taken by *Elephants Can Remember* is reminiscent of the previous year's *Nemesis*, and both novels could be seen as examples of late-career literary experimentation. However, a more prosaic explanation for this increased interiority also exists. Elderly and infirm, Christie now composed her novels almost exclusively by Dictaphone, aided only by rough notes in her exercise books. As Mark Aldridge points out, *Elephants Can Remember* is full of "similar conversations," and the original typescript, worked over by Collins, was significantly more crowded—for example, with "Mrs. Oliver's musings on elephants" (*Poirot* 289). The publishers also had to change references to India to references to Malaya, since the former "had not been under British rule for twenty-five years" (470).

The last Poirot novel completed by Christie, *Elephants Can Remember* sold well and was received with indulgent criticism. Both these facts have more to do with the author's status than with the content of the book. *Library Journal*'s H.C. Veit called it "endearingly English" and "less a mystery than a lovely gossip," whereas Newgate Callendar (aka Harold C. Schonberg) asserted in the *New York Times Book Review* that the book was critic-proof: "As well criticize the Brooklyn Bridge or the Tower of London"—but nonetheless conceded that "it is, alas, not very good" (qtd. in Sanders and Lovallo 364–65).

Elephants Can Remember was dramatized for BBC Radio 4 in John Moffatt's final outing as Poirot, broadcast on 7 January 2006. A television version aired on ITV1 in the final season of *Agatha Christie's Poirot* on 9 June 2013. The twin ploy and murder-suicide plot at the novel's heart have inspired a Thai horror film *Fad* (alone), which has been remade several times, spawning a franchise, in India.

Characters: Buckle, Mrs.; **Burton-Cox, Desmond, and Mrs.;** Carstairs, Hon. Julia; Fenn, Kathleen; **Garroway, Chief Superintendent; Goby, Mr.; Jarrow, Dorothea ("Dolly"); Lemon, Felicity;** Livingstone, Miss; Matcham, Mrs.; **Meauhourat, Zélie; Oliver, Ariadne; Poirot, Hercule; Ravenscroft, Celia; Ravenscroft, General Sir Alistair and Lady Margaret (Molly);** Rosentelle, Madame; **Rouselle, Mademoiselle;** Sedgwick, Miss; **Spence, Superintendent Bert;** Willoughby, Dr.; Wizell, Fred

See also: ***Agatha Christie's Poirot; Hercule Poirot* (BBC radio series); Indian-Language Adaptations**

"Elizabeth of England." See *The Road of Dreams* (poetry collection)

Ellen

Ellen is a name given to faithful servants, retainers of the days of relics, in *Dumb Witness*, *Peril at End House*, and *The Mystery of the Blue Train*.

Elliott, Lady Noreen

A young, flapper-like adventurer in "The Manhood of Edward Robinson," Lady Noreen Elliott represents the fast-paced unpredictability of the modern (early 1920s) aristocratic set. She steals jewelry and returns it after wearing it.

Ellis, Big Jim

Father to Victoria Johnson's two children in *A Caribbean Mystery*, Big Jim Ellis warns her not to become involved in the murder case. She ignores him and pays with her life.

Ellsworthy, Mr.

The creepy and effeminate Mr. Ellsworthy is twice considered a "[n]asty bit of goods" in *Murder Is Easy* (62, 77). Unlike Mr. Pye in *The Moving Finger*, Mr. Ellsworthy is an example of a character drawn according to typical codes of the day for male homosexuality, who is judged negatively for this. Although he is not the murderer, and his crime is chiefly being different (and hosting "nameless orgies," 108), he is still considered a bad man and the heroic ex-policeman Luke Fitzwilliam is presented as an excellent sport for spitefully embroiling Mr. Ellsworthy in trouble with the law after the main mystery has been resolved.

EMI Films

There are four EMI films of Christie novels, made in the 1970s and 1980s. This series began in Christie's twilight years when she was persuaded, reportedly by Lord Louis Mountbatten, to authorize a film of *Murder on the Orient Express*. Christie had an intense dislike of movies based on her work and consistently refused approaches. Most film efforts before 1974 had not been high quality: as Mark Aldridge (*Screen* 122) points out, the strength of Christie's plots had led a general view among filmmakers and the public that her work was low-brow and disposable. Even critical and commercial successes like *And Then There Were None* (1945) and *Witness for the Prosecution* (1957) had not made efforts for cultural relevance or high artistry. By 1973, however, when Christie agreed to allow the production of *Murder on the Orient Express*, she had written her final published texts, and her books were already being recognized as "classics": enduring, not disposable, products of a vanished age and worldview that held popular appeal and critical merit.

Christie was certainly reassured by the high-caliber names involved in this film, including director Sidney Lumet, producer John Brabourne, and an unprecedented cast of Hollywood heavyweights. There was difficulty casting Princess Dragimiroff in particular: Marlene Dietrich, Katherine Hepburn, and Ingrid Bergman were all considered or approached (Bergman eventually played Greta Ohlsson, for which she won an Academy Award). In the end, that role went to Wendy Hiller. The final line-up also included Lauren Bacall, Jacqueline Bisset, Sean Connery, John Gielgud, Anthony Perkins, Vanessa Redgrave, Richard Widmark, Michael York, and others. Albert Finney played Poirot, with extensive padding and aging make-up, his performance based on finicky mannerisms. The production was filmed in a disused carriage of the Orient Express and captured a sense of nostalgia that pervaded in the 1970s, following the social developments and many civil unrests of the 1960s.

The production received a royal premiere, at which Christie, in her final public appearance, met Queen Elizabeth II for the second time. It received numerous awards, including Bergman's Academy Award for best supporting actress. Christie herself was delighted, and her only criticism of the film was that Finney/Poirot's moustache was not extensive or luxurious enough.

The next film in the series was supposed to begin production in 1976. However, there were some problems. Brabourne wanted to film *Death on the Nile* but, for tax reasons, this was not an option for Christie, who maintained the rights to that novel (most were now with the family trust). She suggested an adaptation of the stage play, *Murder on the Nile*; eventually, it was decided that *Evil under the Sun* would be the next film. However, Christie's death in January 1976 changed things, and *Death on the Nile* became available.

For this, another travel novel, the formula of an all-star cast and an exotic locale—here, an authentic Nile steamer—was recycled. However, Finney, who had been uncomfortable with the transformation required to play Poirot, did not return. He was replaced by Peter Ustinov. Ustinov's performance is bombastic whereas Finney's is idiosyncratic, and it is reflected in the more camp, colorful cinematography and Anthony Shaffer's relatively jaunty script.

Once again, the cast combines big names from two generations: Bond girl Lois Chiles plays the victim, with Jane Birkin, Mia Farrow, Jon Finch, Olivia Hussey, Simon Mac-Corkindale, and others, all fresh from cinematic successes, playing suspects. The cast also includes well-established stars such as Angela Lansbury, David Niven, and Maggie Smith, with Hollywood legend Bette Davis providing waspish one-liners as the battle-axe Mrs. Van Schuyler. The caliber of this cast does not quite match that of *Murder on the Orient Express*, but it is still a roster of A-listers and actors like Harry Andrews who would be (and were) leading names in television films appear in seconds-long supporting roles.

Angela Lansbury, a standout as the flamboyant Salome Otterbourne in *Death on the Nile*, played Miss Marple in *The Mirror Crack'd* (1980), although a fluffy white wig could not mask her age—she was 55, too young for the role. The 1962 novel *The Mirror Crack'd from Side to Side* is really about social change and concerns the modernization of St. Mary Mead. Naturally, filmmakers did not focus on this aspect but on the presence of a movie in production. Action was relocated to 1952, a significant moment nostalgically, as it is the year Queen Elizabeth II ascended the throne, the year rationing began to wind down in Britain, and the year *The Mousetrap* made its debut. Some huge names from the 1950s and 1960s starred as middle-aged actors from a former gilded age: Elizabeth Taylor took the biggest role, Marina Gregg, with Rock Hudson

playing her film director husband and Tony Curtis and Kim Novak playing their rivals. The *Radio Times* summarized this casting as "Hollywood has-beens [playing] Hollywood has-beens" ("Film Guide").

Despite plans to alternate Poirot and Miss Marple movies over the next decade, *The Mirror Crack'd* did not rate as highly at the box office or with critics, as expected, and changes were made. There would be no further Miss Marple movies, with Lansbury committing instead to star in the long-running American Christie-inspired series *Murder, She Wrote*. There would only be one more EMI Poirot film, although Ustinov would return to the role throughout the 1980s.

Evil under the Sun (1982) is high-camp. Once more, the novel is glamorized, with action relocated from an island off the west coast of England to director Guy Hamilton's own beach in the Adriatic. Rather than an original score, the film uses a re-orchestration of Cole Porter numbers, one of which is sung at a piano by Diana Rigg and Maggie Smith in vampish competition. Some of the biggest names in this production are those returning from previous EMI Christie films—Smith, Birkin, and Ustinov—although it also featured Hollywood heavyweights James Mason and Sylvia Miles as a bickering couple and Roddy McDowall as a newly created camp character. Other stars, like Rigg and Nicholas Clay, were then most well known as television stars.

Despite receiving a royal premiere attended by Queen Elizabeth II and the Duke of Edinburgh and a script that followed the formulae of *Death on the Nile*, the film makes no pretense at greatness, and embraces camp and farce. For instance, a lengthy comedy sequence in which Ustinov's Poirot goes "swimming" would have been out of place in any of the previous installments. The film received lukewarm reviews, with critics calling it overlong and fun but tired. No subsequent films were made in this series, although the four that were made remain influential. Ustinov, in particular, became highly associated with the role of Poirot, to the extent that the character dominated his obituaries in

2004, despite a long and varied career, and he went on to play him in four more productions. In the 2010s and 2020s, Kenneth Branagh's Poirot series for Twentieth Century Studios worked clearly in the shadow of the EMI series, with a similar progression from A-list stars to A-minus-list stars between *Murder on the Orient Express* (2017) and *Death on the Nile* (2022).

See also: **CBS Television Adaptations; Cannon Group Films;** *Death on the Nile* **(novel);** *Evil under the Sun* **(novel);** *The Mirror Crack'd from Side to Side;* *Murder on the Orient Express* **(novel); Twentieth Century Studios Films**

"Enchantment." See *Poems*

Endhauzo Paslaptis (The Secret of End House)

A 1981 Soviet miniseries based on Christie's *Peril at End House, Endhauzo Paslaptis* (The Secret at End House) was filmed in Lithuanian in three parts totaling 140 minutes. Vidas Petkevicius played Hercule Poirot, and color filters were ramped up to create as much vibrancy as possible in the depiction of a generic olden-days Cornish coastline.

See also: *Peril at End House* **(novel); Poirot, Hercule**

Enderby, Charles

Charles Enderby is a journalist for the tabloid *Daily Wire* in *The Sittaford Mystery*, who becomes friendly with Emily Trefusis and joins her as an amateur sleuth. Refreshingly, she turns down his marriage proposal. He has exploited her, as his profession exploits so many, for his own ends and returns to her fiancé.

Enderby, Sir Luke

Sir Luke Enderby is a world-renowned prosecuting barrister (a King's Counsel) in *Butter in a Lordly Dish*, who condemns men in the dock on moral grounds but fails to notice that his own womanizing behavior is just as disgraceful. He is made to confront the fact that he has sent an innocent man to his execution.

Endless Night (film)

Sidney Gilliat's film of *Endless Night* was a rare example of Christie licensing her work for theatrical release following her negative experiences with MGM in the 1960s. It is likely that the lack of a detective eased the situation emotionally. Partly financed by the Nottingham Forest Football Club, the film was put together rather quickly for United Artists in 1971 following the decision to shelve a comedy film about divorce that became outdated during production.

Endless Night stars Hayley Mills and Hywel Bennet, with an international supporting cast, including Britt Eckland, Per Oscarsson, and George Sanders in his penultimate role before his suicide. It is a surprisingly literal and even more surprisingly successful translation of the book to the screen. Although marketed as a mystery, with posters carrying the legend "Only 3 people in 100 guess the answer" (apparently a made-up figure), the tagline "Victim … or Killer?" hints at its horror undertones. It is certainly grounded in the context of 1960s–70s British horror.

With critics, the film has fared better in the years since its release than it did at the time. It was not a box office hit and was denied a U.S. release but later did exceptionally well in video sales. Christie herself was reportedly generally pleased with it but furious at the inclusion of a sex scene, which she deemed unnecessary (although the relevant scene in the book describes a woman who "smelt and looked and tasted of sex" [*EN* 211]).

See also: *Endless Night* **(novel)**

Endless Night (novel)

By any estimation, *Endless Night* is an outlier in the Christie canon. Although it has a mystery structure and provides genre-tested twists, it is more intensely and straightforwardly psychological, and deals more explicitly with the psychopathy of a serial killer, than her other work. Of all Christie's novels, it is the only one that would need only minimal revisions to be published as a debut in the twenty-first century and stand a good chance of reaching critical and commercial acclaim. Author-critic-publisher August Derleth selected it as one of the best books of 1968 ("Outstanding 1968 Books" 62).

The novel is narrated by Michael (Mike)

Rogers, a young, working-class, ex-military man who is interested in money and beautiful things. He meets and falls in love with one of the richest women in the world, 20-year-old Eleanor (Ellie) Guteman. The couple becomes enchanted with Gipsy's Acre, an area of land known for being cursed—a local "witch," Esther Lee, warns them to stay away several times. Nonetheless, Ellie buys it and when the pair marry, their friend, Rudolf Santonix, builds them the most beautiful house he has ever designed on the cursed ground. As strange events happen—birds die; Esther Lee harasses the couple, telling them to move out, and eventually dies herself—Ellie is revealed to suffer from a heart condition. Her nurse—originally presented as a friend, the sexy Germanic Greta Andersen—lives with the couple; she and Mike frequently fight over Ellie. Eventually, Ellie dies in a riding accident. Greta stays on with Mike, who comes to depend on her, and they grow close.

When a society friend, Claudia Hardcastle, who has swallowed the same tablets as Ellie, dies of cyanide poisoning, the police start to realize that Ellie may have been murdered. Mike returns from a holiday to discover this news and that Ellie's solicitor, Andrew Lippincott, has been investigating: he knows, for instance, that Mike and Greta have known each other for longer than they have disclosed. It is revealed that Mike and Greta planned Ellie's marriage and murder to acquire her money. Mike is also revealed to have killed several times in the past, starting in childhood when he drowned a classmate to acquire an expensive watch and later in the army when he killed a fellow serviceman for petty cash. However, he is haunted by Ellie and her singing voice, and realizes he could have loved her and lived very happily at Gypsy's Acre. Blaming Greta, he kills her in a passionate erotic episode, and readers learn that this novel has been his confession.

In efforts to situate this novel within the Christie canon, scholarship has traditionally focused on plot aspects that can be traced to other books. The most obvious link—the narrator-murderer—is with *The Murder of Roger Ackroyd*. Pierre Bayard has analyzed the ambiguous language of both novels, where an account of the same scene can be read in two ways, with the presumption of innocence or the knowledge of guilt (43–50). Bayard concludes that *Endless Night* is an attempt to rewrite *The Murder of Roger Ackroyd* while concealing from readers the famous source text, whose solution is surely known to most crime fiction consumers (47–48, 50). The underlying assumption here, of course, is that all Christie novels are essentially the same product, with the same simple aim—bamboozlement—even if they were written 41 years apart.

Others have highlighted similarities with *Death on the Nile*: these include the murder of a 20-year-old American socialite by her new, penniless husband, in collusion with her best friend whom he appears to hate, and the presence of an American solicitor known as "Uncle Andrew" (Osborne 331; Curran, *Secret Notebooks* 413). Charles Osborne and John Curran have also pointed out that the murder itself and some of the supernatural trappings are preempted in 1941's "The Case of the Caretaker" (Osborne 331; Curran, *Secret Notebooks* 414).

Less observed, however, is the novel's thematic relationships within the Christieverse. Christie's novels from the mid–1950s were more experimental than traditionally assumed, frequently exploring new formal models while maintaining a crime and punishment backbone where the puzzle, plotting, and themes are inextricable (Bernthal, "'Dangerous'"). This is most evident in *Endless Night*, where the lie of childhood innocence and its relationship to moral deviance—first raised in *Towards Zero* (1944) and amplified in *Crooked House* (1949), *The Mousetrap* (1952), and *Mrs. McGinty's Dead* (1952)—is given a sustained confessional treatment. The motives for Mike's various crimes all come down to money, but they evolve over time—from a watch and ready cash to a house and a lifestyle. This is also an evolution of human aspiration, from the tangible to the abstract, encouraged under capitalism. However, they have at their root a base and artless motive. There is analysis to be done on *Endless Night* as it pertains to capitalism.

Similar themes are explored in other 1960s texts: *The Pale Horse*, *Hallowe'en Party*, and the "extravaganza" *Passenger to Frankfurt*.

The use of William Blake's *Songs of Innocence and Experience* also reflects Christie's increased reliance on the use of pre–Victorian poetry, plays, and religious writing as structuring texts, for example in *By the Pricking of My Thumbs*, *Hallowe'en Party*, and *Nemesis*. The title comes from "Auguries of Innocence," which Ellie puts to music along with several others, which end up haunting Mike. Notable is "The Fly," which muses on the arrogance of Man to decide that flies can be swiftly killed without consequence, simply because they are small. Christie makes similar observations in *Black Coffee*. The *Innocence and Experience* poems (or songs) are nearly all pairs: optimizing "innocence" anthems, which Ellie sings, and jaded "experience" counterparts showing that these ideals do not work in life. A key theme of the novel, as Christie outlined in an interview, is the central character's awareness that he has missed a chance for a happy, uncomplicated life (Wyndham E5).

Another theme that appears increasingly in 1960s texts is witchcraft. However, although the "witches" in *The Pale Horse* are explained as pawns—willing or otherwise—in the game of murderous conspirators, the apparent foresight of Mrs. Lee, the "witch" or "gipsy," is never rationally explained. Police suspect that Mike paid her to terrify Ellie and then killed her to silence her, but Mike denies this, and appears to have killed her out of fear and superstition. She saw him for what he was. Christie's grandson, Mathew Prichard, has claimed that this is because Christie believed in witchcraft. Whatever the explanation, *Endless Night* integrates folk magic and folk psychology in a way where one works as a plot device to explore the other.

Christie wrote *Endless Night* in six weeks, although her notebooks reveal that she was plotting it from 1961 (Curran, *Secret Notebooks* 414). Reader reports at Collins in 1967 expressed enthusiasm for the novel itself, tempered with concern over its commercial potential as it is an obvious departure from formula, and—viewing the whodunit

as the most important element—the "gimmick" of narrator-as-murderer was by then well-worn (411, 413). Nonetheless, the U.K. (Collins, 1967) and U.S. (Dodd, Mead 1967) editions received critical praise from the outset.

The novel has been filmed four times: twice for the big screen and twice for television. The first film was released in Christie's lifetime, a British production in 1970. A Bollywood version, *Aar Ya Paar*, was screened in 1997. In 2013, the ITV series *Agatha Christie's Marple* aired its final episode, a critically panned adaptation of *Endless Night*, with Miss Marple inserted into the action. A French version aired in 2021 as part of *Les Petits Meurtres d'Agatha Christie*. There has also been a BBC Radio 4 adaptation, by Joy Wilkinson, which aired in 2008.

Characters: **Andersen, Greta**; Constantine, Dimitri; Ed; Hardcastle, Claudia; Keene, Sergeant; **Lee, Esther**; Lippincott, Andrew P.; **Pardoem, Reuben**; Pete; Phillpott, Major (God); Rogers, Mrs.; **Rogers, Eleanor ("Ellie")**; **Rogers, Michael ("Mike")**; **Santonix, Rudolf**; Shaw, Dr.; Van Styvesant, Cora

See also: ***Agatha Christie's Marple***; **BBC Radio Adaptations**; **Curses**; ***Endless Night* (film)**; **Indian-Language Adaptations**; ***Les Petits Meurtres d'Agatha Christie***

"Enter Allen Lane and the Penguins." See **"Sir Allen Lane: A Flair for Success"**

"Entrevista a Agatha Christie." (interview; alternative title: **"Rare Interview with Agatha Christie"**)

"Entrevista a Agatha Christie" is the only television interview with Christie freely available online. It was filmed in Lisbon, Portugal, where Christie spent a week on holiday with her second husband, Max Mallowan. This two-minute, undated interview was filmed in the 1960s and broadcast as part of the magazine program *Fim de Semana* on 6 April 1984. It is now available via the RTP archive.

Christie speaks uncomfortably but politely to the distinguished lawyer Artur Varatojo, who translates her answers into Portuguese, while Sir Max laughs awkwardly and says nothing. Christie, in hat and pearls, answers three questions: (1) Which is the best Poirot book? ("*Murder in* [sic] *the Orient Express*") (2) Does she prefer Poirot or Miss Marple ("Miss Marple"), and (3) Will she send Poirot or Marple to Lisbon one day? (She says she will think about it. She did not.)

See also: "**The Algebra of Agatha Christie**"; *Murder on the Orient Express* (novel)

Entwhistle, Miss, and Mr.

In *After the Funeral*, Mr. Entwhistle is a personal solicitor and close friend to the Abernethie family, specifically Richard Abernethie. He alerts Hercule Poirot to a potential link between Richard's death and the murder of his cousin, Cora Lansquenet. Miss Entwhistle is his niece and assistant.

Ericsson, Torquil

Torquil Ericsson is an intense Norwegian scientist in *Destination Unknown*. He believes scientists are the master race and that the rest of the world should exist in comfortable slavery.

Erskine, Janet, and Major Richard

An old friend of Helen Kennedy/Halliday, suspected to have been her boyfriend in *Sleeping Murder*, Major Erskine is in a tense, unhappy marriage with the jealous Janet.

"The Erymanthian Boar" (story; alternative title: "Murder Mountain"). See *The Labours of Hercules*

Esa

The mother of Imhotep, Esa is an old and wise woman in *Death Comes as the End*. She acts as matriarch, occasionally dropping cryptic pieces of wisdom, and has a steadier hand over the household than her son. The narrative follows her thoughts when she is poisoned, and her overriding concern is to work out how it was done—which she does.

Estravados, Pilar (aka Conchita Lopez)

The exotic granddaughter of Simeon Lee in *Hercule Poirot's Christmas*, Pilar Estravados is considered the most like him. Ironically, she proves to be an outsider, who has assumed her dead friend's identity to gain an inheritance. She ends up marrying another imposter in the extended Lee family. Poirot recognizes that she is not who she claims to be because she has blue eyes, and neither of her parents did. The name Pilar Estravados was used in the 2017 film of *Murder on the Orient Express*, applied to a very different character based on Swedish missionary Greta Ohlsson, so that she could be played by Spanish actor Penélope Cruz.

Eugenia and Eugenics (play)

An unpublished one-act play, *Eugenia and Eugenics* is set in the then-future 1914 and concerns a fictional law about to come into force, preventing those who are not mentally and physically perfect from marrying. The heroine, Eugenia, decides that "an uneugenic husband" is a "more chic" option than a "perfect" one (qtd. in Green 46). The play is housed in the Christie family archive. The title may come from a common joke about the ideal eugenic family being like a circus act in its unnatural physical fitness. A caricature labeled "Eugene, Eugenia and the Little Eugenics" appeared in *Life* magazine in 1913, showing a stern, angry-looking Germanic man and woman with their six stern, angry-looking, muscular children; all are dressed in circus outfits, and they are performing a human pyramid, looking miserable and unattractive.

See also: **War**

Evans, Gladys. See **Gladys**

Eversleigh, William ("Bill")

William Eversleigh starts out as a young twit, constantly asking Virginia Revel to marry him, in *The Secret of Chimneys*. He continues in a similar vein in *The Seven Dials Mystery*, being obviously interested in Bundle Brent, but eventually reveals strong heroism, saving her life and protecting national secrets. He works for George "Codders" Lomax as a civil servant.

Evil Under the Sun (film). See **EMI Films**

Evil Under the Sun (game). See **Games**

Evil Under the Sun (novel)

Evil Under the Sun is one of Christie's more recognizable novels, thanks in part to the glamorous 1982 movie starring Peter Ustinov. The book itself is less about glamour than escapism and the treatment of women in society. Its setting, the fictional

Jolly Roger Island, replete with an Art Deco hotel, is obviously based on Burgh Island, off the coast of Devon, and tourists can (and do) visit it, to follow the action according to the island's geography—and a map in the text.

On holiday, Hercule Poirot notices that sunbathers all look alike: they are not people, he says, but slabs of meat. He soon learns that one guest on the island, Arlena Marshall, is causing a stir: she is there with her husband but carrying on shamelessly with a married man, Patrick Redfern. Arlena, Poirot suspects, is a natural victim. Soon enough, Patrick discovers Arlena's body—she has been strangled. The husband is suspected, as is his daughter—Arlena's step-daughter, Linda—especially when it transpires that Linda's mother was an accused poisoner, and Linda is consumed by guilt over something. However, it turns out that Linda, a troubled teenager, believes she killed her stepmother via black magic. The real murderer was Patrick. He and his wife, Christine, have a killed in the past, and they confused the time of death by Christine posing as Arlena's body. Arlena, Poirot concludes, was not fatally attractive to men but fatally attracted to them—an "eternal and predestined" victim, who could easily be exploited. All along, the motive was money.

The plot twist had previously appeared in "Triangle at Rhodes," and the body-switching device would appear very soon in *The Body in the Library*. However, the novel is about more than plot: Poirot is learning to look at sunbathers and celebrities like Arlena, not as slabs of meat like everyone else views them but as individuals. The book was written in 1939 when World War II was inevitable. It was published once war was a reality: it was first serialized in 1940 and then published in book form in 1941. It is set in the 1930s. The prewar holiday setting will certainly have been a welcome distraction for readers coping with international disaster, and the focus on women's presumed power as nothing of the sort will have been timely. After all, just as women had increased their roles in public life during World War I, they were taking on more jobs now while men were away.

Evil Under the Sun was not considered a remarkable Christie work before the 1982 EMI movie, which transposed the action to a Majorca island and featured an all-star cast and rearranged music by Cole Porter. It then instantly became one of the better-known and most desired Christie properties. In 1999, the BBC broadcast a five-part radio play based on the novel. It was dramatized as an episode of the ITV series *Agatha Christie's Poirot*, notably filmed on Burgh Island, and broadcast in 2001. In 2007, Burgh Island provided the model for Jolly Roger Bay once again, in a computer game by the Adventure Company. A French graphic novel by Didier Quella-Cuyo, illustrated by Thierry Jollet, was published in 2012 and translated into English in 2013. A French adaptation, an episode of *Les Petits Meurtres d'Agatha Christie*, was broadcast in 2019.

Characters: Barry, Major; Blatt, Horace; **Brewster, Emily; Castle, Mrs.;** Colgate, Inspector; **Corrigan, Alice, and Edward; Darnley, Rosamund; Gardner, Carrie, and Odell; Hastings, Captain Arthur; Lane, Rev. Stephen; Marshall, Captain Kenneth and Linda**; Martindale, Jane; **Narracott, Gladys**; Neasdon, Dr.; Phillips, Sergeant; **Poirot, Hercule; Redfern, Christine and Patrick; Stewart, Arlena; Weston, Colonel**

See also: *Agatha Christie's Poirot*; **Curses; EMI films; Games; *Hercule Poirot* (BBC radio series); *Les Petits Meurtres d'Agatha Christie***

"Express to Stamboul." See **"Have You Got Everything You Want?"**

Eyelesbarrow, Lucy
In *4.50 from Paddington*, modernity arrives for the Crackenthorpes in the form of Lucy Eylesbarrow, who has a triple first from Cambridge University but has chosen to work in domestic service, turning a traditionally gendered role into a business endeavor. Lucy is extraordinary as a young, female protagonist in that she has no obvious interest in romance. Nonetheless, as is customary in these narratives, two young men are in love with her. She ends up with two proposals of marriage, and Miss Marple says she knows which one Lucy will accept, although readers never learn Lucy's

choice. The BBC and ITV adaptations opt for one each. Closing the novel without an answer from Lucy grants her narrative authority and personal power normally denied to young heroines and represents an attempt to change the conservative form of the mystery novel with the times.

Eyewitness to Murder. See ***4.50 from Paddington***

"The Face of Helen" (story)

"The Face of Helen" is a Quin and Satterthwaite story about the power of beauty. Satterthwaite bumps into Quin at the opera, where they witness two men fighting over a beautiful woman. Discussing the heights of human passion with Quin, referencing both the operas and the real dramas, Satterthwaite learns of a murder plot and acts to prevent it. The story was first published in *The Story-Teller* in May 1927. It appeared in the anthology *The Mysterious Mr. Quin* in 1930.

Characters: Burns, Charles (Charlie); Eastley, Philip; Master; **Quin, Harley**; **Satterthwaite, Mr.**; West, Gillian; Wilde, Martin

See also: *The Mysterious Mr. Quin*

"A Fairy in the Flat" (story; alternative titles: "Blunt's Brilliant Detectives"; "The Affair of the Pink Pearl"; "Publicity"). See *Partners in Crime* (story collection)

"Faked!" See "The Case of the Distressed Lady"

A Family Murder Party. See ***Petits Meurtres en Famille***

Fane, Walter, and Family

In *Sleeping Murder*, Walter Fane is a colorless solicitor who, long ago, was in love with Helen Kennedy/Halliday. He is married to Eleanor and has two adult sons, Gerald (banker) and Robert (soldier).

Fanshawe, Maria ("Ada")

Maria Fanshawe is Tommy Beresford's Aunt Ada, an elderly and extremely forceful care home resident who takes grim delight in outliving her friends. The name evokes Aunt Ada Doom from Stella Gibbons' *Cold Comfort Farm*.

Farley, Benedict

Eccentric millionaire Benedict Farley is the victim in "The Dream." He seems to exist as the sum of his idiosyncrasies: his distinctive appearance, ancient dressing gown, and aversion to cats. These make him easy to impersonate but are also his mimic's undoing, and the quirks are applied inconsistently.

Farr, Stephen

In *Hercule Poirot's Christmas*, Stephen Farr is the name used by Stephen Grant. The real Farr—son of Simeon Lee's business partner, Ebenezer Farr—has been dead for two years and Grant, Lee's illegitimate son, is using his identity to infiltrate the family home.

Farraday, Stephen

Stephen Farraday is a careerist politician in *Sparkling Cyanide*, who was having an affair with Rosemary Barton. He married his wife, Lady Sandra, purely for money but is shocked, late in the day, to discover that he has fallen in love with her. His narrative arc is one of reformation.

The Fatal Alibi. See ***Alibi*** (play)

Faulkener, Jimmy

The two Jimmy Faulkeners in the Christieverse do not appear to be the same man, although both are young, upper middle-class dimwits who are exploited by villains. Captain Jimmy Faulkener in "The Crackler" is an oblivious mule for counterfeit banknotes. Jimmy Faulkener in "The Third Floor Flat" is an unwitting accomplice in setting up the murderer's alibi.

Feminism

Christie's relationship with feminism has been much studied. Although Christie would not have described herself as a feminist and famously claimed on her passport that her occupation was "housewife," her work has been analyzed for its feminist potential at least since the 1980s.

In 1983, Marty S. Knepper argued that Christie should be considered "a feminist" rather than an "anti-feminist," because her texts show that she "obviously respects women and has feminist sympathies": most notably, Tommy and Tuppence Beresford, the married detectives, are equally matched and truly egalitarian—highly unusual in crime fiction ("Feminist" 383, 399). In 1999, Roberta S. Klein suggested, in the very title of her dissertation, that Christie should be subject to "a feminist reassessment." In her authorized biography, published in 2007, Laura Thompson suggests that Christie was an "unconscious" feminist, not identifying as one but drawing on several of the ideas and principles that feminists were also communicating in her lifetime (26). Merja Makinen agrees that Christie's fiction, although not actively seeking to contribute to feminist analysis, was written with awareness of social change and "in accord with [contemporary] feminist agendas," savvy to "the performativity of femininity, as masquerade" (*Investigating* 22, 57).

Popular culture has been behind the academy, potentially due to the arch-conservatism of traditional screen adaptations. Christie was "discovered" as a feminist writer in the mainstream media around 2015, thanks in large part to a rebranding initiative from Agatha Christie Ltd. that promoted images of Christie surfing in the 1920s and reminded the public that her second husband was 16 years her junior. The populist blog *Eclectic Literature* published an article, "Miss Marple vs. the Mansplainers: Agatha Christie's Feminist Detective Hero," arguing that Christie's use of Miss Marple over Poirot in her later novels speaks to "exhaust[ion] with male know-it-alls" (Bolin n.p.). Meanwhile, both the *Daily Telegraph* and BBC America proclaimed Christie a "feminist icon" (Cohen; Margolis)—the former because she was a single mother who worked and the latter because of strong female characters: Tuppence Beresford, Ariadne Oliver, and Bundle Brent.

Although none of the latter analyses stands up to academic scrutiny, scholarship is increasingly finding fresh applicability in Christie's work. Christie's fiction undoubtedly emphasizes women's experiences and presents women as powerful, resourceful, often intelligent, and often flawed people—in other words, as human beings, often underestimated and undermined by their patriarchal contexts.

See also: *Appointment with Death*

(novel); *An Autobiography*; *Partners in Crime* (story collection)

Ferguson, Mr.

Mr. Ferguson is an angry socialist in *Death on the Nile*, whose sense of entitlement and immense hypocrisy likely stem from his secret aristocratic roots. In reality, he is Lord Dawlish, heir to a fortune; however, this does not impress the object of his affection. The clues to his identity lie in his apparel: he wears the same old school tie as Poirot's friend Captain Hastings (that is, Eton), and despite cheap outer clothing, he dons expensive underwear.

Ffoliot-ffoulkes, Helen. See Van Schuyler, Marie

Fictional Portrayals of Agatha Christie

Christie has appeared as a character in works of fiction across multiple media, most often dealing with her 1926 disappearance. Her extreme shyness and aversion to the limelight has had a paradoxical effect: it has made her highly attractive to audiences who want to find out her mysteries and to creators who can construct a character from a relatively blank canvas. To this end, she has been portrayed variously as intellectual, oblivious, mischievous, prudish, soppy, inquisitive, a committed feminist, an angry imperialist, demure, nymphomaniacal, and even possessed. Generally, she is presented with whatever qualities are most common for female leads at a given moment.

Novels. The first novel about Christie was Kathleen Tynan's *Agatha: The Agatha Christie Mystery*, published in 1978 and filmed the next year with Vanessa Redgrave as Christie and Dustin Hoffmann as a journalist, Wally Stanton, with whom she falls in love. Describing itself as "an imaginary solution to an authentic mystery" (Tynan 5), Tynan's novel looks at Christie's much-publicized 1926 disappearance, which had not been discussed in any detail in her autobiography that had been published the year before. Tynan imagines friendships that Christie might have forged at the hotel in which she stayed after her disappearance and has her confronting her husband's mistress in a dramatic manner.

In 1990, to mark Christie's centenary,

Gaylord Larsen published *Dorothy and Agatha: A Mystery Novel*. It has Christie working with Dorothy L. Sayers to solve a murder. A supremely American effort, its cover shows the two women drinking tea and looking disapproving, and there is little to distinguish the book beyond misapprehensions about British customs. A better-known American, Max Allan Collins, made Christie the detective in *The London Blitz Murders* (2004), which followed his *The Titanic Murders* (starring crime writer Jacques Futrelle, who went down with that ship). The Christie entry is generally considered Collins's weakest entry in a gimmicky series. Christie has also been a girl-detective, alongside a young Alfred Hitchcock, in a series of children's books by Ana Campoy. The Spanish book series, *Agatha & Alfred*, has been optioned for television. In addition, Christie has appeared as a character in two French graphic novels, *Agatha* (Anne Martinetti, Guillaume Lebeau, and Alexandre Franc, 2016) and *Le Detection Club* (Jean Harambat, 2019).

There have been many attempts to weave detective stories out of Christie's disappearance—sometimes she appears as a detective going undercover and sometimes as the subject of the investigation. Examples include Alison Joseph's *Murder Will Out* (2015, spawning a series, *Agatha Christie Investigates*); Roy Dimond's *Silence and Circumstance* (2015); Andrew Wilson's *A Talent for Murder* (2016, spawning a very popular series); and Marie Benedict's *The Mystery of Mrs. Christie* (2020). Lindsay Ashford's *The Woman on the Orient Express* (2016) is the most consciously literary take on the disappearance. It is set in 1928, during Christie's first trip aboard the Orient Express, and imagines her mental state as she reflects on the events of two years prior, as she prevents another woman's suicide.

Stage. On stage, there have been at least four musicals featuring Christie as a character. *Vanishing Point*, a 2014 musical by Rob Hartmann and Liv Cummins, is about three women who famously disappeared: Christie, pilot Amelia Earhart, and evangelist Aimee Semple McPherson. The three women appear on stage, trying to solve one another's disappearances, and the main aim is comedy. The 2014 Korean musical *Agatha* is more serious. The story of an inspiring writer, who is a neighbor of Christie's and is embroiled in a plagiarism scandal, publicity was boosted in 2015 when a pop star, Kim Ryeo-Wook, took on the male lead.

There are less ambitious productions featuring Christie as well. Mary McMahon's *Mystery on the Orient Express* (2000) is a semi-musical aimed at amateur companies and offers anti-intellectual rollicks, with Christie as a kind of compere. *The Mystery at Magpie Manor* by Mary Green and Julia Stanley is a musical for American primary schools, set in the 1920s. Christie appears among several fictional characters in a show that pitches itself as "Downton-meets-Poirot" ("Mystery at Magpie Manor").

Murder, Margaret and Me (2017) by Philip Meeks (originally titled *Murder, Marple, and Me*, 2012) was originally a one-woman show starring Janet Prince and directed by Stella Duffy, although in recent manifestations, there is a cast of three. It imagines a meeting between Christie and Margaret Rutherford, who was to play Miss Marple on screen. Although both women admired one another, both were troubled by the films for different reasons, and Meeks explores their mental conflicts.

Steven Carl McCasland's *Little Wars* (2020) advertises its premise as "the most fantastical what-if dinner party imaginable." Set on the eve of World War II in France, it features six famous writers: Christie, Gertrude Stein, Muriel Gardiner, Alice B. Toklas, Dorothy Parker, and Lillian Hellman. With humor and tension, it comments on hate crimes such as anti-Semitism and homophobia, using the unique and divergent voices of these key women writers.

Film and Television. Christie makes cameo appearances in more film and television productions than it is possible to detail, so only cases where she is a major figure are highlighted here. Although movies about the disappearance are frequently proposed, and treatments are easy to find online, only *Agatha* (1979), the beleaguered adaptation of Tynan's novel by Warner Bros., has been made. This production was troubled for several reasons, including the famous difficulty of leading man Dustin Hoffman, who reportedly demanded rewrites to give his character more screen time and moral authority. There were also issues with Agatha Christie Ltd., which tried to stop the making of the film (see Street).

Christie has appeared in dramatized segments of countless television documentaries, but she has also been a central character in screen dramas. She was played by Peggy Ashcroft in *Murder by the Book* (1987), which also featured Ian Holm as Hercule Poirot, visiting his creator in her twilight years.

In 2004, as ITV began to promote its new series *Agatha Christie's Marple* and its revamped *Poirot*, the BBC sought to cash in with a docudrama, *Agatha Christie: A Life in Pictures*. There are two Christies in this—an old one (Anna Massey) and a young one (Olivia Williams)—and almost all dialogue is taken directly from *An Autobiography*. The result is bizarrely static despite attempts to mine the deliberately serene autobiography for high drama and a focus on her first marriage. The move may have been inspired by *Murder by the Book*, which takes a great deal of its dialogue from essays and archived letters—however, the older drama *adapts* the material rather than *transposing* it into dialogue.

Christie makes appearances in all kinds of historical dramas such as the Spanish hit *Gran Hotel* (2011–13) and is central to a 2020 episode of CBC's *The Frankie Drake Mysteries* (2017–), where she, played by Honeysuckle Weeks, helps the detective locate a missing friend. More famously, the BBC's *Doctor Who* (1962–) features Christie in a 2008 episode. "The Unicorn and the Wasp" stars Fenella Woolgar as Christie and posits a unique explanation for her disappearance: it blames a giant alien wasp that has possessed a local vicar. One gimmick given to this episode was the inclusion, in dialogue, of around two dozen of Christie's book titles: some (e.g., "We are facing a secret adversary") more successfully than others (e.g., "Murder at the vicar's rage").

In 2017, Andrew Wilson's *A Talent for Murder* and subsequent series of novels was optioned for a big-budget television series. British broadcaster Channel 5 promptly commissioned its own series of Christie-as-detective dramas, to air each Christmas. At the time of writing (January 2021), there have been three: *Agatha and the Truth of Murder* (set during the 1926 disappearance), *Agatha and the Curse of Ishtar* (set during her 1929 trip to Iraq), and *Agatha and the Midnight Murders* (set during the Blitz). Following the model of Netflix's *The Crown*, each year's installment has a different actor playing Christie. However, some recurring characters are consistently cast.

No Christie-as-sleuth productions are licensed or endorsed by Agatha Christie Ltd. Mathew Prichard, Christie's grandson, has refused multiple "serious and potentially well-financed offers to do an *Agatha Christie Investigates* type series," considering the idea an act of "trespass on her life" (qtd. in Aldridge, *Screen* 335–36). Inevitably, treatments for various films and miniseries exist. One that has significant traction is a series unauthorized by the estate, *Young Agatha*, by Rebecca Pollock and Kas Graham. Set in Devon in the 1900s, it has a teenaged Agatha Miller solving mysteries unconnected to her future novels.

Radio. Christie appears as a character in several BBC radio productions. *The Mysterious Affair at Harrogate* (Radio 2,11 January 1992) is an episode of *The Pasadenas' Almanac* about the disappearance (a comedy musical). *The Case of the Vanishing author* (Radio 4, 17 June 2002), a drama by Stephen Sheridan, imagines Sir Arthur Conan Doyle, Dorothy L. Sayers, and even Sherlock Holmes joining forces to find Christie during her disappearance. *Psychiatry* (Radio 4,18 October 2007) is an episode of the sitcom *Old Harry's Game* in which a dead woman in hell consults Christie to help solve her own murder—Christie (and Conan Doyle) simply complain that writers are not paid enough and do not help.

Between the Ears: The Impossible Book (Radio 3, 11 June 2016) by Peter Blegvad is an artistic drama about a writer who hears other writers' voices, including Christie's, while traveling on a train—he occupies conflicting realities. Simon Brett's *Eric the Skull* (Radio 4, 22 May 2020) is a comedy drama about the foundation of the Detection Club in the late 1920s. This time, Fenella Woolgar plays Dorothy L. Sayers to Janie Dee's Agatha Christie.

The sheer range of texts and media in which Christie has appeared as a character demonstrate that the Christie phenomenon is entirely pervasive and that there is no consensus as to her character or the tone in which she is to be presented and enjoyed.

See also: **Agatha Christie Ltd.**; *An Autobiography*; *Come, Tell Me How You Live*; **Disappearance of Agatha Christie**

Fiddlers Five (alternative titles: *Fiddle de Dee*; *Fiddlers All*; *Sixpence Off*; *This Mortal Coil*)

The original version of *Fiddlers Three* (1972), Christie's final play. *Fiddlers Five*, originally titled *This Mortal Coil*, was also given alternative titles *Fiddle de Dee*, *Sixpence Off*, and *Fiddlers All*. The play opened in Bristol in 1971 and toured briefly. Critics were polite but not kind about this farce, which centers on a man who needs his father to live to a certain date if he is to claim a grand inheritance. Christie acknowledged the poor reviews but was highly committed to its staging—potentially for the West End—much against the wishes of her daughter.

Rosalind Hicks wrote to her mother in no uncertain terms about the damage the play could do to her reputation: not just because it is poorly written (which it undeniably is) but also because of a scene that celebrates the cunning of high earners cheating the Inland Revenue. Christie responded furiously, and it was left to her producer friend Peter Saunders to soothe damaged egos. The play was rewritten and retried as *Fiddlers Three* in 1972.

See also: *Fiddlers Three*; **Hicks, Rosalind**

Fiddlers Three

Christie's final play, *Fiddlers Three*, is a revised version of *Fiddlers Five,* which had gone on tour to mediocre reviews in 1971. In a new production, directed by Allan Davis, who had supervised several changes to the plot, structure, and characters, the play starred Doris Hare in a role for which Irene Handl had been approached. It opened at the Yvonne Arnaud Theatre, Guildford, on 1 August 1972 and although Christie hoped for a West End run, this did not happen. The play, a farce about hiding a body to avoid death duties, has rarely been staged since.

Characters: Blunt, Sally; Bogusian, Felix; Fletcher, Sam; Jones, Gina; Moss, Mr.; Nolan, Dr.; Panhacker, Henry; Panhacker, Jonathan; Trustcott, Mr.

See also: *Fiddlers Five*

Finch, Sally

Sally Finch is an American student on a Fulbright scholarship in *Hickory Dickory Dock*. A practical and efficient woman, she is also one of the more humane students in the hostel on Hickory Road and is more friendly than others to Mr. Akibombo, although in an infantilizing way. She and Len Bateson end up engaged to be married.

"Find the Cook." See **"The Adventure of the Clapham Cook"**

"Finessing the King." See ***Partners in Crime*** (story collection)

Finn, Jane

Christie started writing *The Secret Adversary* after overhearing a conversation about someone called Jane Fish. The name struck her as highly amusing, so she placed the scene into a novel, altering "Fish" to "Finn." Tommy Beresford overhears the name, which he remembers because it intrigues him, and this leads him and Tuppence Cowley into a hunt for the woman discussed.

A First Class Murder. See **Games**

"The First Wish." See **"The Clergyman's Daughter"** and **"The Red House"**

Fisher, Charlotte ("Carlo," 1901–76)

Charlotte "Carlo" Fisher was Christie's secretary, scribe, and close personal friend for many years, to whom Christie dedicated *The Mystery of the Blue Train* (in a joint dedication with her dog) and *And Then There Were None*. She inducted Fisher into an "Order of Faithful Dogs," giving her the jovial post nominals, "O.F.D." Fisher also served as governess to Rosalind Christie (later Prichard, then Hicks). Fisher was particularly invaluable in the years following Christie's *annus horribilus*, 1926. Her role in this has been fictionalized (and sensationalized) in Roy Diamond's novel, *Silence and Circumstance*.

After parting ways professionally, the two women remained friends. In 2016, Fisher's personal library, including a complete set of first editions signed and dedicated by Christie, went to auction. To this date, her editions of Christie's books circulate the market and fetch large sums.

See also: **And Then There Were None** (novel); **Hicks, Rosalind**; *The Mystery of the Blue Train*

Fitzwilliam, Luke ("Fitz")

The main protagonist in *Murder Is Easy*, a youngish former policeman who acts here as a private citizen. His oldest friend is Jimmy Lorrimer, who introduces him to his cousin Bridget Conway as a means of getting to Wychford-under-Ashe to investigate the murders.

Five Little Pigs (novel; alternative title: **Murder in Retrospect**)

Five Little Pigs is Christie's epistolary novel. The bulk of it takes the extraordinary form of five written testimonies from the key witnesses/suspects in a murder case, recounting the same events. Framing these reports is a narrative in which Carla Lemarchant asks Hercule Poirot to prove that her mother, Caroline Crale, did not kill her husband, Amyas, 16 years previously, when Carla was a child. After going through the narratives and reading them psychologically, Poirot identifies the murderer. Arguably, the novel is more successful in concept/synopsis than in execution, but it nonetheless frequently tops the "favorite" lists of Christie fans and scholars who have read beyond the best-known titles.

The title comes from the nursery rhyme, "This Little Piggy," that structures it. The counting rhyme is traditionally said by parents counting their children's toes, and Christie's novel applies each line to a potential suspect in Amyas's murder:

This little piggy went to market. (Phillip Blake became a stockbroker.)
This little piggy stayed home. (Meredith Blake became a reclusive herbalist.)
This little piggy had roast beef. (Elsa Greer has enjoyed social elevation through various marriages.)
This little piggy had none. (Cecelia Williams, the governess, has spent her life in service to others.)
And this little piggy cried "wee wee wee" all the way home. (Angela Warren has been living with disfigurement.)

The novel is about love. Caroline and Amyas have an unorthodox marriage, but they love one another, and their young daughter. Poirot reveals at the end that Amyas was murdered by his young model-cum-mistress Elsa Greer, who found out that he loved his wife and not her and would lose interest once he had painted her portrait. He discovers that Caroline went willingly to the gallows because she believed that her half-sister, Angela, had murdered him and felt guilty for having assaulted her some years earlier. Love is a destructive force in *Five Little Pigs*.

At the end of the novel, Poirot confronts Elsa, who has since married several times and become Lady Dittisham. He tells her that Caroline will receive a posthumous pardon from the state but that police are unlikely to want to charge a woman of Lady Dittisham's position. In perhaps Christie's starkest ending, Elsa tells him that Caroline and Amyas never died—they "escaped" and, when she killed the man she loved, "I died" (233). She leaves in a chauffeur-driven car, a fur rug around her knees. Love may be destructive, but a life without it is an empty kind of death. By contrast, Caroline survives through her daughter, the similarly-named Carla.

There are elements of the personal in *Five Little Pigs*. The gardens of Christie's favorite holiday home, Greenway, inspired a scene in the novel: the battery on Greenway's grounds is relocated precisely as the location where Amyas paints Elsa and is the scene of his death. Furthermore, it has not gone unnoticed—for instance, by Laura Thompson, Jared Cade, and A.L. Rowse—that the charming, womanizing Amyas Crale shares his initials with the unfaithful Archie Christie.

The novel was first serialized in the United States in *Collier's Weekly* from September to November 1941, under the title *Murder in Retrospect*. It appeared in the United States (Dodd, Mead) in book form in 1942 under the same title and in the United Kingdom (Collins) as *Five Little Pigs* in 1943. Christie adapted it for the stage as *Go Back for Murder* in 1960, cutting out Poirot, as had become her habit.

It was first dramatized for BBC Radio 4 in 1994, and a Russian radio play was broadcast in 2000. A version appeared on British television as part of *Agatha Christie's Poirot* in 2003. In 2011, it was adapted into an episode of *Les Petits Meurtres d'Agatha Christie*.

Characters: **Blake, Meredith, and Phillip;** Caleb, Jonathan; **Crale, Amyas, and Caroline;** Depleach, Sir Montague **Dittisham, Lady;** Dittisham, Lord; Edmunds; Fogg, Quentin; **Greer, Elsa;** Hale, Inspector/Superintendent; **Lamarchant, Carla;** Mayhew, George; **Mayhew, Mr.;** Poirot, Hercule; Rattery, John; **Warren, Angela;** Williams, Cecilia

See also: *Agatha Christie's Poirot; Go Back for Murder; Greenway House; Hercule Poirot* (BBC radio series); *Les Petits Meurtres d'Agatha Christie;* **Russian Radio Adaptations**

Fletcher, Harry

In "Greenshaw's Folly," Harry Fletcher is a "handsome fellow … but a rogue" (*ACP* 235), whose son, Nat Fletcher, is thought unsuitable to inherit the family property because of his parentage.

***The Floating Admiral* (round-robin novel)**

In 1931, the Detection Club published its first collaborative novel, *The Floating Admiral*, to raise funds. This ambitious experiment featured 13 authors. Agatha Christie, Dorothy L. Sayers, Victor L. Whitechurch, G.D.H. and Margaret Cole, Henry Wade, Milward Kennedy, Ronald Knox, Freeman Wills Crofts, Clemence Dane, Edgar Jepson, and Anthony Berkeley (Cox) contributed a chapter each, and club president G.K. Chesterton added a prologue to tie it together. Unlike novellas produced by the club for radio serials in 1930 and 1931, *The Floating Admiral* was not planned. Instead, each writer would receive the manuscript so far and add to it. With their submission, each attached, in a sealed envelope, their solution to the mystery. The 12th chapter by Berkeley proposes the main solution, based

on what has come before, but the other solutions appear in an appendix.

The story concerns a body found floating in the River When. Predictably, contributors variously ignore leads created by their colleagues and develop avenues of their own. For instance, John Rhode's chapter, "Inspector Rudge Begins to Form a Theory," is followed by Milward Kennedy's "Inspector Rudge Thinks Better of It." Christie's contribution, the fourth chapter, is titled "Mainly Conversation." As with her chapter in "The Scoop," it does a strong job introducing characters with comic absurdity. Particularly striking is Christie's portrait of the voluble Mrs. Davies, with her talk of "Eyetalians" (*TFA* 55).

The solutions proposed and the manners of their delivery are typical of their authors. Dorothy L. Sayers's is the lengthiest. Christie's is the most elaborate. Christie proposes that at the heart of the murder plot is a man who has been living for years as his dead sister. Christie also seems to have forced one character, the Rev. Peter Mount, to become the Rev Philip Mount, by creating for him two children, called Alec and Peter.

The book was published in 1932 and reprinted in 1983 and 2010.

Characters *introduced by Agatha Christie*: **Davies, Mrs.;** Mount, Alec; Mount, Peter.

Other characters: Arkwright, Mrs.; Ayres, Harry; Dakers, Edwin; Denny, Sir Wilfred; Emery; Emery, Mrs.; Fitzgerald, Elma; Fitzgerald, Walter; Grice, Dr.; Hawkesworth, Superintendent; Hawkins, Bob; Hempstead, Police Constable Richard; Holland, Arthur; Holland, Mrs.; Mount, Mrs.; Mount, Rev. Peter (later Philip); Pennistone, Admiral; Skipworth, Mr.; Twyffit, Major; Ware, Neddy.

See also: **"Behind the Screen"** (novella); **Detection Club, the;** "The Scoop" (novella)

"The Flock of Geryon" (alternative title: **"Weird Monster").** See *The Labours of Hercules*

Fogg, Justin

In *Go Back for Murder*, young solicitor Justin Fogg investigates a 16-year-old murder and falls in love with Carla La Marchant. He is the son of Quentin Fogg, who does not appear in the play but does appear in *Five Little Pigs*, the novel on which it is based. Christie created Justin for the play, to replace Hercule Poirot.

Folliat, Amy

Amy Folliat is an elderly lodger whose family built and traditionally owned Greenshore House in "Hercule Poirot and the Greenshore Folly" and Nasse House in its expansion, *Dead Man's Folly*. Although she keeps family secrets—including insanity and murder—to herself, they weigh on her heavily.

Folliat, James. See **Stubbs, Sir George**

Folliat, Jimmy

In "The Manhood of Edward Robinson," Jimmy Folliat is the absent fiancé of Lady Noreen Elliott. It is unclear if this is the same character as James Folliat, who is presumed dead in *Dead Man's Folly* but emerges as a man in early middle age. The ages and backgrounds would line up.

Ford, Monica. See **Glen, Aspasia**

Foreword to the *Crime Collection*

Between 1969 and 1972, Paul Hamlyn published 24 hardback omnibus editions of Christie's books, each volume containing three titles under the banner *Crime Collection*. The books were attractively presented in black covers with gilt lettering and red page-edges. The books were wrapped in dust-jackets that are extremely of their time. For the first edition—an omnibus of *The Murder of Roger Ackroyd*, *They Do It with Mirrors*, and *Mrs. McGinty's Dead*—Christie contributed a brief foreword, writing: "I am very glad indeed there is to be this distinguished edition of my books, and I hope my many loyal readers will appreciate it, and enjoy re-reading those of my books which are their favourites" (Foreword, *Crime Collection* n.p.). Under this is printed her autograph.

Forewords to Penguin Editions

In 1953, Penguin published its second set of Christie books, with Christie providing forewords for each. The set was composed of *The Body in the Library*, *Crooked House*, *Death Comes as the End*, *Death on the Nile*, *The Labours of Hercules*, *Miss Marple and the Thirteen Problems*, *The Moving Finger*, *The Murder of Roger Ackroyd*, *The Mysterious Mr. Quin*, and *Parker Pyne Investigates*. The forewords provide light introductions in which Christie discusses how these books came to be written and what she is most pleased with about them.

Introducing *The Labours of Hercules*, Christie suggests that the premise of playing with "Poirot's Christian name" was "irresistible." Some stories, she writes, "wrote themselves" but others were extremely difficult. In particular, she cites "The Capture of Cerberus" (the final story), which archival research by John Curran has shown was completely rewritten to avoid political tensions. This is the origin of a famous sentiment often slightly misquoted: "The really safe and satisfactory place to work out a story in your mind is when you are washing up. The purely mechanical labour helps the flow of ideas.... I strongly recommend domestic routine for all those engaged in creative thinking" (Christie, Foreword, *Labours* 3).

In *Miss Marple and the Thirteen Problems*, Christie suggests that her grandmother may have inspired Miss Marple and states that Miss Marple is more suited to short stories, while Poirot better suits novels. In *The Mysterious Mr. Quin*, she identifies Harley Quin's origins in the *commedia dell'arte* Dresden figurines on her mother's mantelpiece and discusses her first publication, "Harlequin's Song," in *Poetry Review*, for which she was paid a guinea. *Parker Pyne Investigates*, another short story collection, is introduced with an account of how Christie devised the character—as with Poirot, she saw a man and built a narrative around him—and of the origins for "The Case of the Rich Woman."

The foreword to *Crooked House* identifies it as one of Christie's proudest achievements. Introducing *The Body in the Library*, Christie outlines "cliches belonging to certain types of fiction," including "'the body in the library' for the detective story," confirming that the novel is a parody she had long wanted to write (Christie, Foreword, *Body* 6). Similarly, she calls *The Moving Finger* her attempt to tackle "a classic theme"—that is, the poisoned pen letter. She professes a fondness for Megan Hunter, a character in the novel, and says she "would also like to meet the vicar's wife, but am afraid I never shall" (Christie, Foreword, *Moving* 6).

The foreword to *Death on the Nile* partially contradicts that of *The Moving Finger*: introducing *Nile*, Christie writes that exotic settings can be fun, providing much-needed escapism. However, regarding *The Moving Finger,* she writes that village settings are preferable because "[e]xotic settings [can] detract from the interest of the crime itself" (Foreword, *Moving Finger* 6). The origins of *Death Comes as the End* are given: Christie cites "a well-known Egyptologist" who asked her over dinner to write a mystery set in Ancient Egypt: the reference is to Stephen Glanville (Foreword, *Death Comes as the End* 5). Christie reveals that she considered a tomb-robbing plot before settling on a domestic one.

See also **Penguin Books**

Fortescue, Lancelot ("Lance")

The attractive black sheep of the Fortescue family in *A Pocket Full of Rye*, Lance Fortescue is a kind of prodigal son who returns from Kenya with a new wife and gains his father's affection. His callous use of women is noticed but not challenged, because of male privilege. This becomes more sinister when he is unmasked as the murderer who has charmed women in the execution of his crimes, and Miss Marple reflects that he is a particularly evil killer who needs to be brought to justice.

Fortescue, Patricia ("Pat")

The daughter of an Irish peer and recently-married wife to Lance Fortescue in *A Pocket Full of Rye*, Pat Fortescue is considered suspicious because she has been married three times. However, after Lance is outed as the murderer, she is proved to be blameless, even a victim. Miss Marple advises her to return to her childhood home when she needs to reclaim innocence and stability in life.

Fortescue, Percival ("Percy/Val"), and Jennifer

In *A Pocket Full of Rye*, Percival is the sensible oldest son of Rex Fortescue, and Jennifer is his bored wife with a secret family connection.

Fortescue, Rex, and Adele

Rex and Adele Fortescue are the first and second victims in *A Pocket Full of Rye*, who are killed in ways that parody the queen and king of the nursery rhyme. Rex is an industrialist, owner of the Blackbird Mines, and an unfriendly patriarch. Adele, his second and significantly younger wife, is glamorous but classless, and is not considered a good fit for the socially aspirational family, faintly embarrassed about its own humble origins. She was having an affair with tennis player Vivian Dubois.

"Four and Twenty Blackbirds" (story; alternative title: "Poirot and the Regular Customer")

"Four and Twenty Blackbirds" is a Hercule Poirot story in which an old man's deviation from his usual eating habits precedes his death. Poirot uncovers a dramatic plot involving twin brothers and a young man dressed as an old man. The story was first published as "Poirot and the Regular Customer" in *Collier's* in 1940 and *The Strand* in 1941. Contrary to some claims, it did not appear in *Mystery Magazine* in April 1926. It was anthologized in *Three Blind Mice* (1950) in the United States and in *The Adventure of the Christmas Pudding* (1960) in the United Kingdom. It is one of three Christie titles derived from the nursery rhyme "Sing a Song of Sixpence" (the others are "Sing a Song of Sixpence" and *A Pocket Full of Rye*).

The story was filmed as part of *Agatha Christie's Poirot*, broadcast on ITV on 29 January 1989. It was also dramatized as part of *Agasa Kurisutī no Meitantei Powaro to Māpuru*, broadcast on NHK on 10 April 2005. A German radio play, part of *Krimi-Sommer mit Hercule Poirot*, aired on SWR on 9 July 2006.

Characters: Bonnington, Henry; Gascoigne, Anthony; Gascoigne, Henry; **George(s)**; Hill, Amelia; Lorrimer, George; MacAndrew, Dr.; Molly; **Poirot, Hercule**

See also: *The Adventure of the Christmas Pudding* (story collection); *Agasa Kurisutī no Meitantei Powaro to Māpuru*; *Agatha Christie's Poirot*; *Krimi-Sommer mit*

Hercule Poirot; Nursery Rhymes; *Three Blind Mice* (story collection)

4.50 from Paddington (novel; alternative titles: *Eyewitness to Murder; Murder She Said; What Mrs. McGillicuddy Saw!*)

Inspector Craddock, Miss Marple's most famous honorary nephew, makes his third of four appearances in this book. Craddock is one of the few detective inspectors who has time for Miss Marple and creates a cozy, familiar tone in a novel in which much of the action occurs without her being present. He is used to similar effect in *The Mirror Crack'd from Side to Side*, the only other novel in which Miss Marple appears but is largely absent.

On a train from London, middle-aged spinster Elspeth McGillicuddy is half-asleep when she sees, through the window, a train on a parallel track. As they round a corner, the blinds in the other window fly up, and Elspeth sees a woman being strangled. The conductor does not believe her, and the police find no body on the other train or by the tracks, so she visits her friend Miss Marple, the only person likely to believe her.

Miss Marple does not disappoint. Upon determining the only plausible hiding place for a corpse—the grounds of a sprawling country estate, Rutherford Hall—she enlists a young woman, Lucy Eylesbarrow, as her spy. Lucy, an intelligent woman who has taken up housekeeping because she enjoys it, easily secures employment. She meets Emma Crackenthorpe, a stressed spinster in her forties whose life is consumed with keeping up the house and caring for her perfectly healthy but highly irritable father, Luther Crackenthorpe. She also meets Emma's surviving brothers, the worldly artist Cedric and the serious Harold; Bryan Eastley, widower of their sister Edith; and Bryan's young, precocious son, Alexander, and his good friend James Stoddart-West. She notes that Emma is particularly fond of Dr. Quimper, Luther's meek, unassuming physician.

While playing with the boys, Lucy discovers the body in an old sarcophagus in a disused barn. It is the body of a beautiful, clearly foreign woman. Speculation mounts that it is the corpse of Martine, the mysterious wife of Emma's, Harold's, and Cedric's deceased brother Edmund, who died shortly after marrying her in World War II. However, the real Martine makes herself known, and the police struggle to identify the body. After the whole family is poisoned, resulting in one death, Miss Marple arrives at Rutherford Hall for the first time, claiming to be Lucy's aunt. She also arrives at the solution and sets a trap so that Elspeth McGillicuddy will see the murderer leaning over her and identify him. The murderer is Dr. Quimper, the mystery woman was his estranged wife, and he killed her so that he would be free to marry Emma.

Miss Marple reflects that she is "really very, very, sorry that they have abolished capital punishment because ... if any man ought to hang, it's Dr. Quimper" (254–55). The death penalty in Britain had not been formally abolished when this book was published, but it had just come out of an 18-month moratorium following public and political pressure, and it would be formally abolished in 1969.

4.50 from Paddington is a country house novel but not a nostalgic one. The house in the book, like the family that inhabits it, is unsustainable, occupying a small amount of a large space, cut off from the rest of the world, and unaware of a corpse on the grounds until Lucy discusses it. While it is initially introduced as a charming escape from the world—"a real country place all surrounded by town," where one "[c]an't see another house" in any direction (42)—it becomes clear that Emma Crackenthorpe, who runs and will inherit it, is isolated and alone. Under the thumb of Luther Crackenthorpe, the family lives frugally, without visitors, lavish meals, or even a "sense of family" (42). So alone is Emma that she clings to the dream of marrying Dr. Quimper, virtually the only male stranger who enters the house, other than Inspector Craddock, despite his being unsuitable—and, in the end, she remains alone.

While the family has spread out, around the world—except Emma and her father—it has not given up the unsustainable property or lifestyle. If this is presented as destructive, so too, is Quimper's attempt to buy into it. Initially, the realization that the dead woman is not Martine is a relief to the family: "she can't have had anything to do with us!" cries Emma (224). However, when she is identified as Quimper's wife, she comes to represent the wider world; a person sacrificed so that her husband can join the liminal family unit.

There have been numerous adaptations since the book was published in 1957. The first film, *Murder She Said*, opened MGM's Miss Marple series with Margaret Rutherford in 1961—this was also Miss Marple's first appearance on the silver screen. A British television adaptation aired in 1987 as part of the BBC's *Miss Marple*, and ITV released its own version, part of *Agatha Christie's Marple*, in 2004. There has also been a British radio play, broadcast on BBC Radio 4 in 1997, a hidden object computer game released by Big Fish Games in 2010, and a 2008 French movie, *Le Crime Est Notre Affaire*, replacing Miss Marple with characters based on Tommy and Tuppence Beresford.

In addition, there have been three Japanese screen adaptations: a four-part episode of the anime series *Agasa Kurisutī no Meitantei Powaro to Māpuru* airing in 2005 (with an accompanying manga version) and standalone television movies for NTV and TV Asahi in 2006 and 2018, respectively.

Characters: Bacon, Inspector; Baker, William; **Clithering, Sir Henry; Cornish, Detective Sergeant Frank; Crackenthorpe, Alfred; Crackenthorpe, Emma; Crackenthorpe, Luther;** Crackenthorpe, other relatives (Cedric, Edmund, Harold, Henry, Lady Alice, Josiah); **Craddock, Detective Inspector Dermot; Clement, Griselda; Clement, David, and Leonard Jr.;** Darwin; **Dubois, Martine**; Eade, Mr. and Thomas; **Eastley, Alexander, and Squadron Leader Bryan;** Eastley, Edith ("Edie"); Edwards; Ellis, Miss; **Eyelesbarrow, Lucy;** Hart, Mrs.; **Haydock, Dr.; Hill, Florence;** Hillman; Johnstone, Dr.; Joilet, Madame; Kidder, Mrs.; **McGillicuddy, Elspeth**; Morris, Dr.; **Quimper, Dr.;** Rogers, Dickie; Stoddart-West, James; Stoddart-West, Sir Robert; **Stravinska, Anna**; Webb, Geraldine; Wells, Mr. and Ronnie; West, David; **West, Raymond;** Wetherall, Detective Sergeant Bob

See also: ***Agatha Christie's Marple; Bélisaire et Prudence Beresford;*** Games; Houses; MGM Films; *Miss Marple* (radio series); *Miss Marple* (television series); NTV Television Adaptations; TV Asahi Adaptations

"The Four Suspects" (story; alternative title: "Some Day They Will Get Me"). See *The Thirteen Problems*

"The Fourth Man"

"The Fourth Man" is a short story first published in the *Grand Magazine* in 1925 and collected in *The Hound of Death* (1933) and *The Witness for the Prosecution* (1948). It was filmed in 1982 as part of *The Agatha Christie Hour*.

On a train, three elderly friends discuss, idly, the existence of the human soul. They are surprised when the fourth man in the carriage, a stranger who seemed to be sleeping, tells a story. He, Raoul Letardeau, talks about Filicie Bault, whom they have been discussing as a case of someone with multiple personalities. Raoul knew Felicie in childhood. In an orphanage, she was hypnotized by an egotistic singer, Annette Ravel, with whom Raoul was once in love. Annette exerted extraordinary power over Felicie. When Annette died, she possessed Felicitie. Raoul leaves the carriage.

Characters: Bault, Felicie; Clark, Dr. Campbell; Durand, Sir George; Letardeau, Raoul; Parfitt, Canon; Ravel, Annette ("Ravelli"); Slater, Miss

See also: ***The Agatha Christie Hour; The Hound of Death*** (story collection); ***The Witness for the Prosecution*** (story collection)

"Foxglove in the Sage." See **"The Herb of Death"**

Franklin, Angela, and Arthur

In the Mary Westmacott novel *The Burden*, Angela and Arthur Franklin are emotionally distant parents who die in a plane crash. They conceived their daughter, Shirley, after their beloved son Charles's death and are resented by their other daughter, Laura, who craves their love and attention, even after their death.

Franklin, Barbara, and Dr. John

Barbara is a histrionic hypochondriac

who tries to poison her husband, John, but accidentally kills herself in *Curtain*. Dr. John Franklin is a research chemist so absorbed in his work that he fails to notice most things going on around him. Toward the end of the novel, he reveals that he is in love with his research assistant, Judith Hastings, who is the daughter of Captain Hastings.

Franklin, Charles

Charles Franklin is the younger brother of Laura Franklin in *The Burden*, who died in infancy and has been elevated in death to almost saintly proportions.

Franklin, Laura

Laura Franklin is the protagonist in the Mary Westmacott novel *The Burden,* who feels unwanted as a child after hearing her parents wish that she had died instead of her younger brother. The novel follows her resentments and reconciliation with her sister, Shirley.

Franklin, Shirley

A tragic figure in the Mary Westmacott novel *The Burden*, Shirley Franklin is never truly loved. She is conceived by her parents in the aftermath of their son Charles's death, and is always viewed as a kind of replacement for him She is resented by her older sister Laura, who believes that she has absorbed all their parents' love and attention. She marries twice and never finds real happiness; she kills herself.

Fraser, Donald ("Don")

A quiet on-and-off fiancé to Betty Barnard in *The ABC Murders*, Donald Fraser struggles to reconcile his grief over Betty's death with the fact that he is in love with her sister, Megan. Readers are subtly encouraged to suspect him of the murders, but he ends up as the romantic lead.

Freemantle Freddie

Freemantle Freddie is an escaped convict in *The Sittaford Mystery*; he is the narrative equivalent of Seldon the convict in Sir Arthur Conan Doyle's *The Hound of the Baskervilles*.

Fremder Kam ins Haus, Ein. See *Love from a Stranger,* **Screen Adaptations of**

Fremder Klopft An, Ein. See *Love from a Stranger,* **Screen Adaptations of**

"From a Grown-up to a Child." See *Poems*

"A Fruitful Sunday" (story)

This story was first published in the *Daily Mail* on 11 August 1928. It appeared in the U.K. collection *The Listerdale Mystery* (1934) and the U.S. collection *The Golden Ball* (1971). A young working-class couple finds a ruby necklace during a Sunday picnic, just after reading about the theft of such a necklace that is worth £50,000. They struggle over what to do before learning that the necklace they have is an imitation given away as a publicity stunt. All is well, and the couple plans to go to the cinema.

Characters: McKenzie Jones, Mrs.; Palgrave, Edward ("Ted"); **Pratt, Dorothy ("Jane")**

See also: **Class**; *The Golden Ball* **(story collection)**; *The Listerdale Mystery* **(story collection)**.

Fuji-sanroku Renzoku Satsujin-jiken

Fuji-sanroku Renzoku Satsujin-jiken is the second Japanese television adaptation of *The Unexpected Guest* following *Kirifuri-sanso Satsujin-jiken* (1981), this aired on 18 February 2001. Directed by Itoh Hisharu, it stars Asano Yuko, Nogiwa Yoko, and Mitramura Kunihiko.

See also: *Kirifuri-sanso Satsujin-jiken*; *The Unexpected Guest* **(play and novel)**

Fuji TV Adaptations

As part of an effort to expand Christie's international reach during a rebrand in the 2010s, Agatha Christie Limited struck deals with two Japanese television production companies, Fuji TV and TV Asahi. The first installment was highly publicized, including on buses.

A two-part Japanese adaptation of *Murder on the Orient Express*, *Oriento kyuukou satsujin jiken* was broadcast on Fuji TV from 11 January 2015. It features Nomura Mansa, a highly-regarded classically trained actor, as Suguro Takeru, a version of Hercule Poirot, and features a cast of well-known Japanese actors. Visually and stylistically, the first part is almost a direct replica of Sidney Lumet's 1974 adaptation, with costumes, make-up, and accents directly modeled after it. The second part, however, tells the backstory in detail. The two episodes, totaling almost five hours in length, were directed by Keita Kôno and the teleplay was written by Kôki Mitani.

It was followed by *Kuroido Goroshi*, based on *The Murder of Roger Ackroyd*, in April 2018. Mitani also wrote this one, and Mansai Nomura returned as Poirot. The third installment of the series, reprising the dramatist and star, aired on 6 March 2021. *Shitonoyakusoku* (Promise of Death) is based on *Appointment with Death*.

See also: **Appointment with Death** (novel); *The Murder of Roger Ackroyd*; **Murder on the Orient Express** (novel).

Fullerton, Lavinia. See **Pinkerton, Lavinia**

Funerals Are Fatal. See *After the Funeral*

Gabriel, Major John Merryweather

In *The Rose and the Yew Tree*, he is "a VC in the war, an opportunist, a man of sensual passions and of great personal charm" (11). After Isabella's death, he becomes Father Clement, an "incredible" man whose "heroism, endurance, compassion, and courage" are praised by all (11). At the beginning of the novel, Hugh considers these two men as different people. Selfless love is what transforms one man into the other.

Gale, Norman

Also known as James Richards, Norman Gale is a young dentist, with whom Hercule Poirot seems to collaborate, only to expose him as a murderer, in *Death in the Clouds*. Gale murders a blackmailer and his secret wife, Anne Richards, to make his move on the attractive Jane Grey. Although he seems like a romantic hero, the first clue that he is not a good man is that he is a dentist—a profession inspiring fear in Poirot.

"A Game of Chess." See "The Chess Problem"

Games

As long as crime novels have existed, they have been likened to games, set by the author and played by the reader. Sherlock Holmes's oft-repeated expression "The game's afoot" refers to game that is hunted, but with the domestication of popular fiction in the early-twentieth century, concurrent with the rise of detective fiction, it came to stand for the perceived self-contained, homely diversion of murder mysteries.

Christie began her career appealing to sportsmanship, claiming that she wrote her first novel after her sister wagered that she could not write a fair, baffling mystery. Throughout her career, critics compared her to a card-sharp or crossword-setter. The ideas of games and playing are reflected in her work, and often a game turns deadly. Sometimes, it is self-consciously a murder game (*A Murder Is Announced*, *Dead Man's Folly*), and other times, the games are more general, still maintaining that concept of fair or foul play. Rules for card games provide clues in *Cards on the Table* and "The King of Clubs," whereas the idea of playing meaning safety is violated in *Hallowe'en Party*, when a girl is drowned while apple-bobbing.

The 1930s—the height of the Golden Age—saw British and American writers embracing the game-playing angle, sometimes thematically (see above) and sometimes more dramatically. Ellery Queen's *The Roman Hat Mystery* (1929) had introduced a "Challenge to the Reader," a point at which readers were informed that they had seen all the same clues as the detective and should be able to solve the mystery—Christie would later take this up insisting that a 1965 screen adaptation of *And Then There Were None* should include a "mystery minute" along similar lines. Dennis Wheatley produced a series of "crime dossiers"—publications in which the clues to a mystery were physically reproduced so that the reader could sort through them—throughout the 1930s. Perhaps the culmination of this transatlantic game-playing is *Cluedo* (or *Clue*), a murder mystery board game for three to six players, devised by Anthony Pratt in 1943 and sold from 1949.

Given the global visibility of the Agatha Christie brand, it is unsurprising that Christie's works have inspired real games throughout history. The first semi-official Christie game was a card game in 1935. Crime writer Peter Cheyney produced *The Crime Club Card Game*, which features some 50 colorful cards containing detectives, villains, weapons, and locations, alongside complicated rules for play. The cards feature various characters created by members of the Collins Crime Club (mostly by Cheyney himself). Hercule Poirot and Superintendent Battle are among them.

In 1994, to promote an episode of *Agatha Christie's Poirot*, a card game based on *Hercule Poirot's Christmas* was released as a promotional item with chocolate mints. The game includes 52 text-filled cards containing clues and story elements, and a sealed solution. A third card game came in 2019, the Agatha Christie Ltd.-authorized *Death on the Cards*, with extremely simple gameplay designed to appeal to casual and dedicated fans alike. It does not deal with any book or plot but uses stock character types with "detective" cards representing Poirot, Miss Marple, and the Beresfords.

There has been one board game based specifically on a Christie novel: *And Then There Were None*, part of Ideal Games' *Mystery Classic* series. It is a four-player game, aesthetically similar to *Cluedo*. However, the gameplay is closer to the later *Death on the Cards*, in that it is possible to play as the murderer. It was released in 1968. It was followed by a game called *Murder on the Orient Express*, which has nothing to do with the novel and is a Sherlock Holmes game. There has also been an officially branded Agatha Christie board game, a trivia game, released in 2010.

More successful have been jigsaw puzzles, where a condensed version of the story is provided in a booklet and a jigsaw contains a visual clue before the puzzle assembler checks the solution in sealed envelope or mirror writing. Official Christie jigsaws produced by Paul Lamond Games in the 1990s and 2000s include *The Body in the Library*; *Death on the Nile*; *[Hercule] Poirot's Christmas*; *How Does Your Garden Grow?*; *The King of Clubs*; *Remember, Remember* ("Murder in the Mews"); and *The Veiled Lady*. The 750-piece jigsaws were expanded to 1,000 pieces in 2002 rebranding. Paul Lamond Game produces numerous branded entertainments, including murder mysteries. Other Agatha Christie-branded offerings include two dinner party games, complete with videotapes (later DVDs, then links), instructions, and recipe suggestions. *A First Class Murder* (2002) is based on "The Plymouth Express," whereas *The Pyramids of Giza* (2002) is based on "The Adventure of the Egyptian Tomb."

The first Christie computer game was *The Scoop*, based on the Detection Club novella. This was made in 1986 by Telarium, part of Spinnaker, for Apple II software, and was released for MS-DOS in 1989. It is now widely circulated online as freeware. The player assumes the role of a journalist investigating the crimes. Following this, Spinnaker remade *The Scoop* (alongside *Behind the Screen*) as interactive VHS games (see below).

The 2000s provided a new era of Christie computer games. The Adventure Company launched a series of point-and-click games, initially for Windows but later expanded to Apple, Nintendo, and other software, in 2005 with *And Then There Were None*. Given that everyone on the island dies in the novel, a new playable character based on the boatman was created. This extremely popular game allows players to choose their own ending, so the last two survivors—apart from the player—either live or die depending on how it is played. It also changes the solution to the novel, making the murderer Emily Brent and giving her a backstory rooted in offhand comments in the original text. The book's solution is included as a playable postscript.

It was followed in 2006 by *Murder on the Orient Express*, with David Suchet voicing Hercule Poirot. This time, graphics were improved, and again the ending was slightly altered—the child whose murder is at the heart of the plot survives—whereas the player assumes another newly created character, a young woman who helps a bedridden Poirot solve the case. Likely, Suchet did not have the time to record extensive lines for his character, which would explain why Poirot is not playable. He is a playable character, in a way, in *Evil under the Sun* (2007). The premise here is that Poirot is recounting the case to Captain Hastings during World War II, and Hastings (the player) retraces his steps. Essentially, then, one is playing as Poirot, no longer voiced by Suchet but by Kevin Delaney.

Throughout the 2000s, Big Fish Games released four cheaply produced "i-spy" hidden-object games, then a popular diversion, based on *Death on the Nile*, *Peril at End House*, *Dead Man's Folly*, and *4.50 from Paddington*, in that order. There have been two video games based on *The ABC Murders*. The first was an ignominiously received Nintendo DS game in 2009, designed by DreamCather Interactive and in the vein of the *Professor Layton* series. Another version, a return to the point-and-click adventure format, was published by Anuman for various software in 2016. In 2021, Microids released *Young Poirot*, another point-and-click adventure game carrying the Christie brand.

There have been three Christie games combining video footage and real-world game-play. "Agatha Christie: Behind the Screen," based on the collaborative novel of the same name, included a 30-minute VHS and eight cards along with a solution booklet. It was produced in the United States by Spinnaker in 1986 and followed by "Agatha Christie: The Scoop" (based on the collaborative novella), along similar lines in 1987. The releases crowned half a decade of failed attempts on Spinnaker's part to secure rights for Agatha Christie video games. An international release, "After the Funeral" (2007), was an "interactive DVD" to coincide with the relevant episode of *Agatha Christie's Poirot*. It featured clips from the episode and Suchet, in character as Poirot, setting questions to the players. Agatha Christie Limited has had some notable misses seeking to broaden its reach, with initiatives like a live-tweeted *The Body in the Library* (2012) and an app based on *The Mysterious Mr. Quin* (2015) quickly forgotten.

Efforts to translate Christie into playable media remain constant, and future oddities will doubtless emerge.

See also: ***Cards on the Table*** (novel); **Collins Crime Club; Golden Age Crime Fiction**

Gapp, Flossie. See Rival, Merlina

Gardner, Carrie, and Odell
Carrie and Odell Gardner are American tourists in *Evil Under the Sun*, who believe they are running out of sites to see in Europe. Carrie is highly loquacious and bores her fellow guests. Her husband says little but "Yes, darling."

Garfield, Michael
Michael Garfield is a beautiful gardener who admires and pursues beauty in *Hallowe'en Party*. He attracts women and girls to religious levels of devotion and "sacrifices" them in the service of creating beauty on Earth. Toward the end of the novel, he is revealed to be Miranda Butler's father, which makes his grooming and attempted murder of her doubly sinister.

Garroway, Chief Superintendent
In *Elephants Can Remember*, Chief Superintendent Garroway investigated the murder-suicide of Sir Alistair and Lady Ravenscroft several years ago and is now retired. He was never fully satisfied with the official verdict on the case.

Gaskell, Mark, and Rosamund
Rosamund Gaskell (née Jefferson) was the daughter of Conway Jefferson and first wife of Mark Gaskell but died before the events of *The Body in the Library*. Her widower has secretly married Josie Turner. Mark appears a minor character but is revealed to be Josie's accomplice in a highly choreographed and ruthless murder-for-inheritance plot.

"The Gate of Baghdad" (story; alternative titles: "At the Gate of Baghdad"; "The Gate of Death")
A story that appears in *Parker Pyne Investigates* (1934), "The Gate of Baghdad" opens with a quotation from James Elroy Flecker's *The Gates of Damascus* that would provide the title for Christie's last-written novel in 1974: "*Postern of Fate, the Desert Gate, Disaster's Cavern, Fort of Fear...*" (128). The story is J. Parker Pyne's first murder case. On a bus from Damascus to Baghdad, he encounters an array of international characters, one of whom is murdered. Once Pyne has solved the crime, the killer commits suicide by smoking a cigarette that contains prussic acid.

Prior to its collection in *Parker Pyne Investigates*, the story was included with other Pyne stories under the title *Have*

You Got Everything You Want? If Not, Consult Mr. Parker Pyne in the United States in the April 1933 *Cosmopolitan*. In the United Kingdom, it appeared as "At the Gate of Baghdad" in a three-story special, *The Arabian Nights of Parker Pyne,* in *Nash's Pall Mall Magazine* in June 1933. On 21 January 2002, the BBC aired a 30-minute radio dramatization starring Richard Griffiths and Patricia Routledge.

Characters: Hensley; Loftus, Squadron Leader; Long, Samuel; O'Rourke, Lieutenant; **Parker Pyne, J.**; Pentemian, Madame; Pentemian, Monsieur; Poli, General; **Pryce, Miss**; Pryce, Netta; Smethurst, Captain; Williamson, Lieutenant

See also: *Parker Pyne Investigates*; *Postern of Fate*

"The Gate of Death." See "The Gate of Baghdad"

"Genteel Queen of Crime"

One of Christie's most famous interviews was with Nigel Dennis for *Life* magazine, where it was published on 14 May 1956. A long piece spanning as many pages as a story, it is presenting with a three-quarter page illustration by Ronald Searle of Hercule Poirot and Miss Marple watching a "roomful of other Christie characters, either killing or being killed" in full Edwardian evening wear (Dennis 87). It also includes photographs of Christie in Paris, on set of *Witness for the Prosecution* in London, with her second husband on the grounds of Greenway, and in the 1920s, as well as an image of the search for her in 1926. It closes with an illustration of a bathtub surrounded by apple cores.

As in similar interviews, Dennis takes pains to present Christie as an eccentric part of a vanished world. He opens with a description of her eating apple after apple in her bathtub, noting that both she and it were "born in the reign of Queen Victoria" (87). (When this description of her was repeated in *Woman's Day* in 1970, Christie was embarrassed enough to deny it.)

Christie presents herself in a deliberately unthreatening, conservative way. She is quoted here saying, "I specialise in murders of quiet, domestic interest.... Give me a nice deadly phial to play with and I am

happy," which licenses the gendered (mis) categorization Dennis goes on to make: that her work exhibits a "feminine dislike" of manual violence (88). The interview goes through Christie's early ambitions to become an opera singer—thwarted by shyness—and her apparent bafflement at her own fame: "I don't know why people should want to write about me," she says (91). It details the well-rehearsed story of a bet between sisters spawning *The Mysterious Affair at Styles.* She even describes herself as an "amateur typist" (102).

However, Dennis digs a little deeper, pointing out a "rebel's hostility to all" in her prose, highlighting satirical character portraits (91), and citing a piece of misdirection that has also been cited by Michael Gilbert and Tim Heald at different times: Poirot asking a butler to check a date on a calendar, only to reveal that he was not interested in the date but in the butler's eyesight (97). Dennis compares the openings of Christie's *The Body in the Library* and Mickey Spillane's *Vengeance Is Mine,* finding the latter too earnest and seeing comedic potential in the "restrained," "classical" model Christie represents (98). He describes Christie's disappearance in 1926 in some detail, but there are no indications that he asked Christie about it in the interview. She was famously silent on this topic throughout her life.

The interview proceeds in this manner: the subject presents herself as utterly uninteresting and the interviewer presents the opposite. It culminates in him drawing out some examples of personality: Christie discusses her frustrations with Poirot ("I can't kill him.... However, I can put him in a wheelchair" [102]), and makes quips about having to diet and not enjoying alcohol. She also says something that has become a famous quote, often attributed to her: "An archaeologist is the best husband a woman can have: the older she gets, the more interested he is in her" (102). Here, this is attributed to a "witty wife" from her excavation days, and Christie later vehemently denied having said it herself. However, as early as 1952, the quotation had been attributed in society pages to Christie ("Archeologist Husband" 8).

See also: **Mayhem Parva**; **"Queen of**

Crime' is a Gentlewoman"; *Witness for the Prosecution* (play)

"The Gentleman Dressed in Newspaper."
See *Partners in Crime* (story collection)

George
Aside from Poirot's valet, George(s), there are two unsurnamed Georges. One is a chatty gardener in "Philomel Cottage." The other is a St. Mary Mead ticket-collector in "Sanctuary."

George(s)
George is Hercule Poirot's valet, referred to in text as "George" and by his employer as "Georges." George is an "extremely English-looking person" (Christie, "Under Dog" 23), and the gallicization of his name is an act of irony. Like Poirot's secretary, Miss Lemon, George is completely lacking in imagination. Poirot considers him the perfect manservant, and his impeccable knowledge is strictly limited to social protocols, although his speech patterns occasionally betray working-class roots. He is far removed from the more traditional servant-outwitting-his-master of early-twentieth-century popular literature. George is also Poirot's longest-serving ally, first appearing in "The Under Dog" (1926) and last written about in *Elephants Can Remember* (1972), also surviving Poirot in *Curtain* (written around 1940, published in 1975).

George also appears or is mentioned in *After the Funeral*; "The Capture of Cerberus" (1940); *Cat Among the Pigeons*; *The Clocks*; *Dumb Witness*; "Four and Twenty Blackbirds"; *Halloween Party*; *Hickory Dickory Dock*; various stories in *The Labours of Hercules*; *Mrs. McGinty's Dead*; *Murder in the Mews*; *The Mystery of the Blue Train*; "The Mystery of the Spanish Chest"; *One, Two, Buckle My Shoe*; *Peril at End House*; *Taken at the Flood*; *Third Girl*; and *Three-Act Tragedy*.

Gérard, Dr. Théodore
Théodore Gérard is a French psychologist in *Appointment with Death*, who mentors the newly-qualified Dr. Sarah King and whom she hero-worships. He is briefly suspected of Mrs. Boynton's murder.

German Radio Adaptations
As well as the 2006 SWR series *Krimi-Sommer mit Hercule Poirot* (Summer of Crime with Hercule Poirot), German radio has produced several Agatha Christie dramatizations, including *Der Mord an Roger Ackroyd, oder, Alibi* (*The Murder of Roger Ackroyd*), broadcast on North German Radio (NDR) on 14 January 1956, directed by Friedrich Pütsch; *Zeugin der Anklage* ("The Witness for the Prosecution"), broadcast on ORF on 25 June 1995, directed by Maria Meiner; *Legale Tricks* (*Butter in a Lordly Dish*), broadcast on WDR. on 7 January 2001, directed by Wilfried Müller; and *Das Krumme Haus* (*Crooked House*), broadcast on Deutschlandfunk Kultur on Friday, 28 June 2019, directed by Irene Schuck.

See also: *Krimi-Sommer mit Hercule Poirot*

Gerrard, Mary
Mary Gerrard is a young woman for whom Laura Welman develops a strong affection in *Sad Cypress* (Mary is later revealed to be her daughter). She is beautiful and attracts the attentions of Roderick Welman. The combination of these two relationships causes Eleanor, Laura's niece and Roddy's fiancée, to resent her bitterly. Mary is poisoned with morphine for a reason she could never understand.

Giant's Bread (novel)
The first novel Christie published pseudonymously, *Giant's Bread* is a tangible attempt to break out of the genre format and to write a novel of ideas. The narrative sprawls over five "books," spanning in time from the Boer War to the aftermath of World War I and the novel grapples with themes of artistic obsession, finding one's purpose, and relationship between private life, high art, and commercialism.

After a prologue, it begins as a *bildungsroman*, following the "touchy sensitive" (56) Vernon Deyre through his childhood—which bears striking similarities to the upbringing Christie would describe in her autobiography. Vernon lives an isolated life with a neurotic mother, a wise nurse, and hundreds of imaginary friends in his extensive family grounds. He makes two friends:

a tomboy cousin known as Joe and a neighbor, Sebastian Levinne, who is the son of a Jewish refugee. Although the child Vernon hates music with a visceral passion, he grows obsessed with the medium and eventually writes an opera, which Sebastian and a worldly actress, Jane, help make a commercial success. World War I interrupts this career, and Vernon makes a hasty wartime marriage with a besotted friend, Nell. Vernon is declared dead and Nell remarries and sells his childhood home, but he reappears under a different name, having escaped a prisoner of war camp and suffered amnesia. Recovering his memories and his identity, he rebuffs Nell's fresh advantages and focuses on writing his masterpiece—an opera explored in the prologue.

There is an exchange half-way through that would reward critical scrutiny. It is 1914 and Joe is telling Sebastian of Vernon's marriage to Nell. Joe opines that it would not have happened without the war, and reflects: "isn't war wonderful? What it's doing for people, I mean…. There's going to be a new world after it…. All the cruelty and the wickedness and the waste of war. And they'll stand together so that such a thing shall never happen again." Sebastian reflects that "the war had, as he phrased it, 'got' Joe…. It made him sick to read the things that were printed and said about the war. 'A world fit for heroes,' 'The war to end war,' 'The fight for democracy.' And really all the time, it was the same old bloody business it always had been" (215). The passage does not reflect but actively critiques the conservative jingoism of which Christie has been widely accused, and which in later conflicts has weaponized Christie in its nostalgia.

Another theme dealt with by Westmacott, in contrast to the common view of Christie, is anti-Semitism. Even as a child, Vernon feels Sebastian is "a member of an enemy race" who is "queer[ly] un–English" (80) and even declares "war" on him repeatedly (78–79). Sebastian's Jewishness later makes him exotic and "fashionable" (181), but he is always limited and surrounded by abuse because of "[h]is yellow Mongolian face" (87), despite his mother's attempt to assimilate, wearing "tweedier tweeds than her neighbour's" (82).

The distinctive theme of *Giant's Bread* is music, which William Weaver suggests appears here as "a kind of possession, or rather obsession, which seizes its foreordained victim and forces him to follow it" (190). It is frequently compared to religion: "I tried to escape from music—but it got me … in the same way that religion got those people at the Salvation Army meeting" (*GB* 310). Music here is superhuman and destructive in its pursuit of otherwise unphrasable truths: Vernon considers "the way he was using his sorrow, his desire—transmuting it into terms of sound" to be "base, cruel" (327). Christie herself originally wanted to be an opera singer but was told that her voice was too weak. The character of Jane, who has a medical assessment similar to the one described by Christie in her autobiography, also has too weak a voice but pursues her dream career for a brief spurt until she loses her voice and does not regret it.

There is more indirect autobiography. When the amnesiac Vernon is asked for his name, he picks the first name in his head: George. This is the name of his wife's new husband, about whom he has just read in *The Sketch*. In 1929 when she wrote *Giant's Bread*, Christie was still recovering from her divorce with Archie, whose affair with a secretary, Nancy Neele, had prompted Agatha to disappear for 11 days. During this time, suffering from memory loss, she checked into a hotel under the name Teresa Neele. In a 1929 interview, her last official word on the matter, Christie explained that claimed to have read about the missing novelist and assuming she must be dead. She would later revisit events in more detail as Westmacott in *Unfinished Portrait* (1934).

Initial discussions of high and low art are typically middlebrow: "They say it's simply the—*the*—latest!! Everything out of time on purpose…. And you have to read Einstein in order to understand it …" says one character of Vernon's opera. "Yes, dear," replies another. "I shall tell everyone it's too marvellous. But, privately, it does make one's head ache!" (*GB* 5; emphasis in original). However, the novel digs beyond the playful discussions of hypocrisy that also pervade Christie's crime fiction. Engaging with Ezra

Pound's modernist mantra "make it new," Sebastian points out that Vernon, as a true artist, "isn't creating something new. He's discovering something that's already there. Rather like a scientist" (113). Although Vernon himself dismisses discussions of quantum theory as "clearly mad" (158), he goes on to reflect intensely, in terms he can only understand through music, on the relationship between space, time, and humanity. Although he thinks of himself as lowbrow, when Sebastian and Jane market the opera as a "highbrow" "musical spectacular" (184)—and its author as an anonymous Russian—it is a critical success. The novel, written with the knowledge that it would sell more poorly than it would under its author's real name, mounts a sustained attack on artistic classification.

Characters: Chetwynd, George; Deyre, Myra; **Deyre, Vernon;** Fleming, Mr.; Frances, Nurse; Green, Mr.; Harding, Jane; Katie; Levinne, Mr. and Mrs.; **Levinne, Sebastien;** Nina, Aunt; Pascal, Mrs.; Robbins, Miss; Susan; Sydney, Uncle; **Vereeker, Nell; Waite, Josephine ("Joe");** Winnie

See also: **Disappearance of Agatha Christie; Music;** *Unfinished Portrait*; **Westmacott, Mary**

Gilby, Miss

Miss Gilby is a stern schoolmistress in the Mary Westmacott novel *Absent in the Spring*, remembered by her now-middle-aged pupil in the midst of a Damascus moment in the desert. Her bullying tactics are partially blamed for the repressed, damaging direction taken by Joan Scudamore's life.

Gilchrist, Miss

One of Christie's most psychologically sophisticated portrayals of a killer, Miss Gilchrist is a paid companion to Cora Lansquenet, whom she kills for a painting in *After the Funeral*. She is described as demure, old-fashioned, and "a *lady-like* murderer" (*ATF* 192; emphasis in original). Her motive is to open her own tea-shop, reflecting the damage in a nostalgic vision of English life in this highly theatrical novel.

Gilliat, Beryl

Beryl Gilliat is the second wife of Simon Gilliat and mother of Roland Gilliat in "The Harlequin Tea Set." She tries to murder her stepson, Timothy Gilliat, so that her biological son will inherit more money. A frantically busy middle-aged woman, her initial dialogue is nearly always introduced with the startled word "Oh."

"The Gipsy" (alternative title: "The Gypsy")

In the semi-supernatural short story "The Gipsy," sailor Dickie Carpenter is afraid of "gypsies." His fear comes from a recurring childhood nightmare, in which a woman discomforts him by appearing, and looking sad, at family functions. In adulthood, he is occasionally confronted by Mrs. Haworth, a "gypsy" who warns him not to do a certain thing. Each time, he ignores her, and something bad happens. The final incident involves a warning to avoid a surgical operation. He ignores the warning and dies in the operating theater.

Macfarlane, a friend in whom he has confided, visits Mrs. Haworth, who tells him that he, too, possesses second sight. He starts to see bloody visions. Mrs. Haworth tells Macfarlane she will not see him again. Determined to prove her wrong, he travels to her cottage the next day, but she has died. The death fulfills both her last prophesy and one from long ago that her marriage would end in tragedy.

The story appears in the anthology *The Hound of Death* (1933) in the United Kingdom. In the United States, it appears in the collection *The Golden Ball* (1971). It was adapted for television as part of *The Agatha Christie Hour* (1982).

Characters: Carpenter, Dickie; Haworth, Maurice; **Haworth, Mrs. Alistair;** Lawes, Esther; Lawe, Rachel; Macfarlane; Rowse, Mrs.

See also: *The Agatha Christie Hour*; **Curses;** *The Golden Ball* **(story collection);** **The Gun Man;** *The Hound of Death* **(story collection).**

Giraud, Monsieur

Monsieur Giraud is a character who appears in *The Murder on the Links* and is mentioned in *The Big Four* and *Death in the Clouds*. A detective of the Paris Sûreté, he has an approach to detection that is comically opposed to Hercule Poirot's, and the two become rivals. Whereas Giraud happily discards a length of lead piping he considers unimportant, Poirot insists that no clue is too small to be relevant. Meanwhile, Giraud's focus on footprints and fingerprints is greatly mocked by Poirot, who insists on the significance of "psychology" on several occasions. Ultimately, Poirot dismisses Giraud as an inferior being: "Ah, he is smart, Giraud, he can do his tricks. So can a good retriever dog" (*MOL* 149–50). In *The Murder on the Links*, Giraud initiates a wager with Poirot concerning who will arrest the murderer first. He loses and gives Poirot 500 francs, with which the Belgian detective buys a dog-shaped decoration, naming it Giraud.

"The Girdle of Hippolyta" (story; alternative titles: **"The Case of the Missing Schoolgirl"; "The Disappearance of Winnie King"**). See *The Labours of Hercules*

"The Girl in Electric Blue." See **"The Plymouth Express"**

"The Girl in the Train" (story)

"The Girl in the Train" is a breezy short story in which the dull, middle-class George Rowland grows frustrated after his uncle fires him and boards a train without any interest in his destination. On board, he meets a beautiful but desperate young woman, who begs him to hide her from her dangerous uncle. He does so and later learns that this woman, who calls herself Elizabeth, is the Grand Duchess Anastasia of the Baltic kingdom of Catonia, running away from an arranged marriage. Sometime later, George learns that Elizabeth was in fact a doppelgänger for the grand duchess, whose uncle she was to divert while the real Anastasia married in secret (not to the agreed fiancé). George and Elizabeth agree to marry.

The story is very much a magazine story, and shares some elements with "Jane in Search of a Job" and "The Golden Ball." Calling the grand duchess Anastasia is an intriguing choice, given that in 1924 rumors were rife that the real Grand Duchess Anastasia of Russia, who had been executed in 1918, had survived and was living anonymously. Anna Anderson, the most famous of many young women claiming to be Anastasia, had garnered significant attention in 1922.

"The Girl in the Train" was published in the *Grand Magazine* in February 1924 and collected in *The Listerdale Mystery* (1934) in the United Kingdom and *The Golden Ball* (1971) in the United States. It was filmed as part of *The Agatha Christie Hour*, broadcast on ITV on 21 September 1982.

Characters: Anastasia of Catonia, Grand Duchess; Betty Bright Eyes; Elizabeth; Gaigh, Lord Roland; Jarrold, Inspector; Karl, Price; Mardenberg; Osric, Prince; Peter; Rogers; Rowland, George; Rowland, William; Stürm

See also: *The Agatha Christie Hour*; *The Golden Ball* (story collection); "Jane in Search of a Job"; *The Listerdale Mystery* (story collection)

The Girl with Anxious Eyes. See *The Murder on the Links*

Giselle, Madame

Madame Giselle is a notorious French moneylender/blackmailer, also known as Marie Morisot, who is murdered on a plane in *Death in the Clouds*. She has a mysterious daughter, Anne Morisot. She is not murdered because of her blackmailing directly, but for the fortune she has accrued.

Gladys

The quintessential Christie maid is called Gladys. As Curtis Evans has written, "The classic adenoidal maid in Christie probably is poor Gladys Martin, found murdered with a clothes peg clipped to her nose in *A Pocket Full of Rye*" (n.p.). Evans's point is a strong one, about how Christie's writing connects adenoids with a lack of intelligence and—although he does not explore this directly—a certain social class. However, Gladys Martin is not the only adenoidal Gladys in Christie's work. Names like Edna, Edith, and Gladys frequently recur in her work for just such characters. There are at least 24 Gladyses in Christie's published fiction, 10 of whom have no given surname and all but four of whom are maids.

The name itself has mysterious origins. It could come from the Latin *gladiolus*, meaning "small sword," or from the Welsh *gwladus*, referring to a princess or flower;

alternatively, it could come from *claudelle*, meaning "lame." It was common practice before the twentieth century for ladies to rechristen their personal maids, usually to avoid having to remember new names, and the girls were often assigned the name "Gladys" so, like "Abigail," it became a generally working-class name by the twentieth century. The Gladyses trail off after the 1940s, because servants more generally trail off in Christie's fiction after World War II, as they did from her social circle.

Gladyses without surnames appear in "Christmas Adventure" (1923), "The Under-Dog" (1926), *The Murder at the Vicarage* (1930), *Death in the Clouds* (1935), *Unfinished Portrait* (1934), "The Lernean Hydra" (1939), *Taken at the Flood* (1948), *Crooked House* (1949), "Sanctuary" (1954—depending on when this is set, Gladys may or may not be Gladys Martin in *A Pocket Full of Rye*), and *Sleeping Murder* (1976—this Gladys is not a maid but a carer for her father).

The following texts contain Gladyses with surnames (in brackets after the date): "The Affair of the Pink Pearl" (1924, Holmes), *The Murder of Roger Ackroyd* (1926, Jones), "The Tuesday Night Club" (1927, Linch), *The Murder at the Vicarage* (1930, Cram—this is the only novel to contain two Gladyses; both are maids), "A Christmas Tragedy" (1930, Sanders—not a maid, but a doomed wife on holiday), "The Scoop" (1930, Sharp—a gleefully gloomy waitress, who pronounces the "u" in "morning glory"), *Three-Act Tragedy* (1934, Lyndon), *Why Didn't They Ask Evans?* (1934, Evans/Roberts—apparently two characters, who prove to be one, before and after her marriage; she is instrumental to the novel's "trick" and comedy—the investigators never realize that their maid was also a maid they have been hunting down), *One, Two, Buckle My Shoe* (1940, Nevill—not a maid but a good-looking secretary, whose boyfriend appears to bring trouble. Unsuitable boyfriends are a theme with Christie maids in the 1940s), "Tape-Measure Murder" (1941, Brent), *Evil Under the Sun* (1941, Narracott), *A Pocket Full of Rye* (1953, Martin—the supreme Gladys, she is a former maid of Miss Marple's and the third murder

victim; it is empathy for her senseless murder that drives the detective forward. Although the character is seen as worthy of empathy, she is nonetheless presented as unthinking; indeed, the crime is so horrible because she could not possibly have been a threat to anyone by virtue of her insignificance), and *The Mirror Crack'd from Side to Side* (1962, Dixon).

Glanville, Stephen (1900–56)

Professor Stephen Glanville was a friend of Christie's through her second husband, Max Mallowan. An Egyptologist, Glanville studied at Oxford University and was made assistant in the Department of Egyptian and Assyrian Antiquities at the British Museum before taking up positions at University College, London and Kings College, Cambridge. He published several Egyptological works, including *Daily Life in Ancient Egypt* (1930), *The Legacy of Egypt* (1942), and *The Growth and Nature of Egyptology* (1947).

Although his friendship with Mallowan was professional, his closeness to Christie was intense. The two frequently exchanged letters—on Glanville's part, these were long and emotional (opening "Agatha darling"), and she is said to have kept them in a drawer with those of her first husband. He shared his deepest confidences with Christie, and confessed to a friend that he was in love with her. The two became close friends in the 1940s when Christie's husband was on various digs in Western Asia, and Glanville's wife and children were in Canada. Christie's 1943 novel, *Five Little Pigs*, is dedicated to him, and that year he famously convinced her to set a novel in ancient Egypt. This became *Death Comes as the End* (1944) and, unusually, he was allowed to read drafts at most stages of the writing process and even make editorial suggestions.

Mallowan was not at all happy about this collaboration. Glanville summarized Mallowan's concerns as a view that "archaeology should not demean itself by masquerading as a novel" (qtd. in L. Thompson 331), although it is possible that he resented the closeness of the collaboration, something he did not experience.

Glanville had also been instrumental in the writing of *Akhnaton* in 1937. However, the book was published, and gushing letters were sent back and forth. Glanville accompanied Christie and her daughter that year to the West End production of *And Then There Were None*, and he helped her with certain aspects of *Murder on the Nile* in 1944. The friendship became more formal and conventional that year, when Glanville left his wife and intensified his relationship with a mistress. He became, foremost, Mallowan's friend once more.

See also: **Archaeology**; *Death Comes as the End*; **Mallowan, Sir Max**

Glen, Aspasia

Aspasia Glen is an accomplished actress in "The Dead Harlequin," known as "the woman with the scarf" who has a secret past, as she had previously played the part of a gormless nursery governess, Monica Ford, to help Hugo Charnley commit murder. Like Carlotta Adams in *Lord Edgware Dies*, this character was inspired by American actress Ruth Draper.

Glydr, Major Boris. See **Peters, Andrew ("Andy")**

Glyn-Edwards, Henry

Henry Glyn-Edwards is the charming, narcissistic first husband of Shirley Franklin in *The Burden*. He conducts multiple affairs, driving his wife to drink, and ultimately dies of polio.

Glynne, Lavinia

The three Bradbury-Scott sisters (Anthea Bradbury-Scott, Clotilde Bradbury-Scott, and Lavinia Glynne) are compared to Macbeth's witches in *Nemesis*. Lavinia is the most worldly and therefore most human of the three sisters. She reacts to the name "Verity" while her sisters do not, and she does the housework. Unlike her sisters, she tries to help Miss Marple.

Go Back for Murder (play)

As Julius Green points out, the stage adaptation of *Five Little Pigs* is "the only play Christie ever wrote with the word 'murder' in the title" (484; *Murder on the Nile* was originally *Hidden Horizon*). This was also her last dramatization of one of her novels, being completed and staged in 1960.

As usual, she cut Hercule Poirot out of the adaptation and the title shows a dramatic focus on time.

In place of Poirot is Justin Fogg, a young solicitor, who takes up Carla Le Marchant's case in part because his father worked for her mother. The mystery plot mirrors that of the novel: Caroline Crale, Carla's mother, was hanged many years ago for murdering her husband, Amyas. Seeking to prove or disprove her innocence, Justin investigates five alternative suspects from the case and identifies one of them as the killer.

The play calls for time-switches, as events of the past are acted out on stage—and this means that the lead actress generally plays both Carla and Caroline. Other cast members play the same characters in the present and 16 years in the past. The play opened at the Duchess Theatre in the West End on 23 March 1960 to generally good reviews. *The Unexpected Guest* had closed at the same venue that January.

Characters: **Blake, Meredith, and Philip; Crale, Amyas, and Caroline; Fogg, Justin; Melksham, Lady;** Rogers, Jeff; Turnball; **Warren, Angela; Williams, Cecilia**

See also: *Five Little Pigs*

Goby, Mr.

Mr. Goby is a mysterious, nondescript private investigator with no social skills, first introduced in the 1928 novel *The Mystery of the Blue Train* and revived in several late titles: *After the Funeral* (1953), *Third Girl* (1966), and *Elephants Can Remember* (1972).

The Goddess of Revenge. See **Ms Ma, Nemesis**

"Gold, Frankincense and Myrrh." See *Star Over Bethlehem* (story/poetry collection)

Golden Age Crime Fiction

There are differing views on the period of the Golden Age of crime fiction, but it is generally situated between the world wars (thus 1918–39). Some argue that it begins with E.C. Bentley's *Trent's Last Case* (1913), and many critics cite Dorothy L. Sayers's *Busman's Honeymoon* (1937), Agatha Christie's *And Then There Were None* (1939), or even Christie's *The Mousetrap* (1952) as its endpoint.

More agreed upon is the nature of Golden Age crime fiction: it centralizes the puzzle element of a whodunit plot, tends to involve an amateur detective, and is either British or Anglocentric. Christie is the dominant name in Golden Age crime fiction; other key figures include Dorothy L. Sayers, Margery Allingham, Nicholas Blake, Gladys Mitchell, John Dickson Carr, Freeman Wills Crofts, John Rhode, Anthony Berkeley (Cox), Ngaio Marsh, and Michael Innes.

Throughout the 1930s and more so in the 1940s, partly in response to the political situation, criticism arose of the apparently socially disengaged, highly stylized genre. Two famously excoriating essays include Edmund Wilson's "Who Cares Who Killed Roger Ackroyd?" (1945) and Raymond Chandler's "The Simple Art of Murder" (1944). Chandler was representative of the U.S. hard-boiled school of crime writing, seeking to reflect the complexity and brutality of crime; to take bodies out of the library and put them on the "mean streets."

Traditional crime fiction scholarship—such as Julian Symons's *Bloody Murder* and John Scaggs' *Crime Fiction*—has held up British Golden Age fiction and American hard-boiled fiction as two competing schools in the evolution of crime fiction scholarship. It is harder to uphold this distinction in the age of domestic noir, which combines elements often thought to distinguish the two. Golden Age crime fiction enjoyed a resurgence of interest in the late 2010s/early 2020s, with the British Library publishing its highly nostalgic "crime classics" series of "forgotten" Golden Age novels, some of which became surprise bestsellers.

See also: **Collins Crime Club**; The **Detection Club**

"The Golden Ball." (story; alternative title: "Playing the Innocent")

Almost like a J. Parker Pyne story but from the perspective of the client, "The Golden Ball" is a brief comic adventure. George Dundas, fired by his uncle for laziness, is urged to "seize the golden ball of opportunity" (*TLM* 349; this line only appears in the anthologized version). He ends up meeting and distractedly agreeing to marry the eccentric socialite Mary Montresor. On a drive, the couple stumbles upon a house and enters to investigate, where they are apparently attacked by a man and a woman. After George fights back and is ready to call the police, Mary reveals that the assailants are actor friends of hers, testing out his suitability for marriage. He has passed the test so she will marry him. George returns to his uncle to let him know that he now is marrying a wealthy woman and has thus seized the golden ball.

The story was first published in the *Daily Mail* on 5 August 1929 under the title "Playing the Innocent." It was anthologized with slight alterations in *The Listerdale Mystery* (1934) in the United Kingdom and *The Golden Ball and Other Stories* (1971) in the United States. A 15-minute adaptation for NBC was screened live on 17 January 1950 as season 2, episode 18 of *Fireside Theatre*, with George Nader as George and Eve Miller as Mary.

Characters: Dundas, George; Leadbetter, Ephraim; Montresor, Mary; Pardonstenger, Mrs.; Wallace, Bella; Wallace, Rube

See also: *The Golden Ball* (story collection); *The Listerdale Mystery* (story collection); NBC Television Adaptations

The Golden Ball (story collection; alternative title: *The Golden Ball and Other Stories*)

In 1971, Dodd, Mead published a collection of short stories that had not previously been collected in the United States. Most had been published in the United Kingdom in either *The Listerdale Mystery* or *The Hound of Death*. The remaining two would appear in the United Kingdom sometime after Christie's death in *Problem at Pollensa Bay*. The *Golden Ball and Other Stories* is composed of **"The Listerdale Mystery," "The Girl in The Train," "The Manhood of Edward Robinson," "Jane in Search of a Job," "A Fruitful Sunday," "The Golden Ball," "The Rajah's Emerald," "Swan Song," "The Hound of Death," "The Gypsy," "The Lamp," "The Strange Case of Sir Arthur Carmichael," "The Call of Wings," "Magnolia Blossom,"** and **"Next to a Dog."**

The Golden Ball (television adaptation).

See **NBC Television Adaptations**

"Good Night for a Murder." See **"Murder in the Mews" (novella)**

Goodman, Adam

Adam Goodman is the strong and handsome new gardener at Meadowbank, a girls' school, in *Cat Among the Pigeons*. As virtually the only male presence, he attracts a lot of attention—unfortunate, because he is really an undercover spy for the Special Branch. His real name is Ronnie.

Goring, Edward

A strikingly handsome assistant to Dr. Rathbone in *They Came to Baghdad*, Edward Goring attracts but vaguely intimidates the protagonist Victoria Jones by appearing such a perfect gentleman. With a background in the Royal Air Force, he is in fact a criminal mastermind, who knows better than anyone else when to switch between charm and intimidation.

Gorman, Michael ("Mickey")

Michael Gorman Irish doorman in *At Bertram's Hotel*, who dies, apparently taking a bullet for Elvira Blake. In fact, Elvira shot him, after discovering that he had married her mother, Lady Bess Sedgwick, making Lady Bess's subsequent marriages bigamous and Elvira illegitimate.

Gorringe, Miss

The snobbish and superior chief receptionist in *At Bertram's Hotel,* much in the mold of Mrs. Castle in *Evil under the Sun*.

Graham, Dr.

There are two Dr. Grahams in the Christie universe, and both are reluctant coroners. The first appears to deal with Maggie Buckley's death in St Loo in *Peril at End House*. The second is the resident doctor on the island of St Honoré in *A Caribbean Mystery*; he is inching toward retirement.

***Le Grand Alibi* (The Grand Alibi; film)**

A poorly-received 2008 French film based on *The Hollow* and directed by Pascal Bonitzer, who also coordinated the screenplay. *Le Grand Alibi* (The Grand Alibi) dispenses with the character of Hercule Poirot, replacing him with a French policeman, Lieutenant Grange. The film dispenses with the psychological tension at the heart of the novel, focusing more on the mystery element, as subplots are expanded and alibis become the focus. A cameo from iconic French actress Emmanuelle Riva could not recover the film in the eyes of critics and audiences.

See also: ***Bélisaire et Prudence Beresford***; **The Hollow (novel)**

The Grand Tour

In 1922, Archie and Agatha Christie left their young daughter Rosalind with her grandmother and set out on a 10-month tour of the British Empire to promote the British Empire exhibition. This was a notable event in which the Christies became among the first Brits to take up surfing and where Christie began work on her 1924 novel, *The Man in the Brown Suit*, largely at the insistence of Major Ernest Belcher, the inspiration for Sir Eustace Pedlar.

This book was published 90 years later, edited by Christie's grandson, Mathew Prichard. It contains her letters home to her mother, Clara Miller, from South Africa, Australia, New Zealand, Hawaii, and Canada. This is the most candid Christie has ever been in print; since the letters were not intended for publication, they are more personal and often more humorous than her other published work. She complains of a "strange family" (*TGT* 68), "unEnglish" houses (69), the "stupid … people" who dug up, and damaged, an ancient skull (70), and the "sanitary arrangements [which are] embarrassing to one of Victorian upbringing" (135).

She also writes at some length about family matters and her collection of wooden animals acquired on the travels (which would be photographed for a feature in *The Sketch* in 1923), references Wilfrid Pirie, a man to whom she was nearly engaged, and admits jealousy at her sister Madge's success with a play in the West End. The book includes numerous holiday snaps of Christie, her travel companions, and the locations they visited.

See also: **Christie, Colonel Archibald ("Archie")**; *The Man in the Brown Suit*; **Miller, Clarissa ("Clara")**; **Pedlar, Sir Eustace**; **Prichard, Mathew**

Grandmaster. See **Indian-Language Adaptations**

Grant, Jim

Jim Grant is a suitor to whom Celia is briefly engaged in the Mary Westmacott novel *Unfinished Portrait*; he is a fictional portrait of Captain Reggie Lucy to whom the author was briefly engaged. "Jim was not a lover," Celia concludes. "He was too self-conscious" (464). Reggie proposed marriage to Agatha Miller on the Torquay golf course after flirtations over roller-skating along the Princess Pier. The couple was keen to take their time, and in the interim Agatha met Archibald Christie.

Grant, Stephen

There are two Stephen Grants: a discharged horse handler in "At the Bells and Motley" and a man living as Stephen Farr in *Hercule Poirot's Christmas*.

Graves, Mr.

Count Foscatini's unassuming "valet-butler" (268) in, who tries to mislead the police with an elaborate story in "The Adventure of the Italian Nobleman." In the relevant episode of *Agatha Christie's Poirot*, he was given the name Edwin.

"Great Unsolved Mysteries." See **"A Letter from Agatha Christie"**

The Great War. See **War**

"The Green Gate" (story)

An unpublished early supernatural short story, "The Green Gate" is housed in the Christie Family Archive.

See also: **"The House of Beauty"**

"Greenshaw's Folly" (story)

In 1954, Christie was commissioned to write a story that would raise funds for a new stained-glass window in her home church, at Churston Ferrars, Totnes. She produced the novella "The Greenshore Folly," but this proved difficult to place because of its awkward length. Frustrated and vowing to expand it into a novel (it became *Dead Man's Folly*), she wrote another story quickly. For legal reasons, it had to share a title with its predecessor. Nonetheless, the final product was called "Greenshaw's Folly."

Miss Marple is called in by her nephew, Raymond West, when the mistress of Greenshaw's Folly is murdered after drawing up a new will. Confronted with a locked-room mystery, Miss Marple soon unravels a complex scheme involving one character masquerading as another and the use of a bow and arrow. Like other late Miss Marple short stories such as "Sanctuary," "Greenshaw's Folly" is more ponderous and philosophical than the early stories. It is not just about the puzzle but also contains reflections on changing times—Miss Marple deplores her nephew's "modern tendency" to process death by making light of it (247)—and a subplot.

"Greenshaw's Folly" was published in the United Kingdom in the *Daily Mail* in December 1956, and the next year had its American debut in *Ellery Queen's Mystery Magazine*. It appeared in the U.K. anthology *The Adventure of the Christmas Pudding* (1960) and in U.S. collection *Double Sin* (1961). A screen adaptation, including elements of "The Thumb Mark of St. Peter," was broadcast as part of *Agatha Christie's Marple* on ITV 1 in 2013.

Characters: Bindler, Horace; Cayley, Sergeant; **Cresswell, Mrs.;** Easterly, General; **Fletcher, Harry**; Fletcher, Nathaniel ("Nat"); Greenshaw; Laura; Greenshaw, Miss; Greenshaw, Nathaniel; Greenshaw, Nettie; **Marple, Jane**; Naysmith, Mr.; Oxley, Louisa ("Lou"); Pollock, Alfred; Pollock, Thomas; **West, Joan, and Raymond**

See also: *The Adventure of the Christmas Pudding* (story collection); *Agatha Christie's Marple*; *Double Sin* (story collection); **"Hercule Poirot and the Greenshore Folly"**

"The Greenshore Folly." See **"Hercule Poirot and the Greenshore Folly"**

Greenway House

The best-known of Christie's houses, Greenway was her holiday home starting in 1938. Located on the River Dart in England's West Country, Greenway House and its surrounding estate were built in the eighteenth century but have roots as far back as the 1490s. The young Agatha Miller had seen and admired Greenway with her mother. Christie and Max Mallowan bought the house in 1938: she described it in her autobiography as "the most perfect of the various properties on the Dart" (479) and in a letter to Mallowan as "the loveliest place in the world" (qtd. in Morgan 237).

During World War II, the U.S. Coast Guard requisitioned Greenway for 51 military personnel who were stationed there from January 1944 until just before D-Day in June 1944. During this time, the library served as the officers' mess room. While there, Lt. Marshall Lincoln Lee painted a striking frieze of 12 murals, showing the men's arrival and experiences at Greenway (and, inexplicably, featuring a female nude). The frieze survives and is now a prominent tourist attraction.

In later life, Christie relied increasingly on her daughter and son-in-law, Rosalind and Anthony Hicks, to maintain Greenway, one of her favorite properties, while she was away. A series of passive-aggressive letters to Rosalind accusing her of not taking good enough care of the property survives. In 1968, the Hickses started living in Greenway, where they stayed until Anthony's death in 2005. Christie spent her last Christmas there in 1973.

The house became a Grade II-listed building in 1985. The property was given to the National Trust in 2000, and the gardens were opened to the public that year. After the Hickses' deaths, the property was extensively rejuvenated and every item inside it catalogued. The house opened gradually to visitors from 2007. It is now extremely popular with tourists, who take a ferry to Greenway from Paignton.

Greenway inspired several of Christie's novels, some of which she wrote there. The grounds particularly have been identified in her fiction: the battery overlooking the river is re-created precisely in *Five Little Pigs*, as the scene of the crime, and appear in *Towards Zero*. Meanwhile, the boathouse appears as the scene of the crime in *Dead Man's Folly* and *Hercule Poirot and the Greenshore Folly*, of which that novel is an expansion. So strong is the connection that the commissioned cover art for *The Greenshore Folly* includes an extensive illustration of Greenway, and the television adaptation of *Dead Man's Folly*, the last-made episode of *Agatha Christie's Poirot*, was filmed on its grounds. Although there is a Greenway House in the Harley Quin story "The Shadow on the Glass," it does not appear to be based on this one.

See also: *Dead Man's Folly* (novel); *Five Little Pigs*; Hicks, Rosalind; *Ordeal by Innocence* (novel); War.

Greer, Elsa

In *Five Little Pigs*, Elsa Greer is the "little piggy [who] had roast beef." As a young woman, she was a muse to the bohemian artist Amyas Crale, who was in the process of painting her portrait when he died. Since then, she has married several rich men but never found fulfillment. A woman who never grows up and never leaves her gilded cage, she is one of the few Christie characters to get away, in the legal sense, with murder—her life is punishment enough.

"A Greeting." See *Star Over Bethlehem* (story/poetry collection)

Gregg, Hubert (1914–2004)

Hubert Gregg is probably best known for writing the song "Maybe It's Because I'm a Londoner," but he was also one of Christie's most frequent theatrical directors. He worked with her first on *The Hollow* (1951) and subsequently on several of her plays. Although he originally turned down the chance to direct *The Mousetrap*, because he wanted to make it as an actor in America, he later demanded that he be allowed to direct it, and got his wish.

Gregg authored a vituperative memoir, *Agatha Christie and All That Mousetrap,* in 1980. That volume claims credit for almost every one of her theatrical innovations, including the title *The Mousetrap* and the dramatically satisfying ending of *Witness for the Prosecution*, and reveals Christie's rarely-discussed business side. The dislike does not appear to have been mutual: since he did not read Christie's novels, Gregg likely never found out that he is one of the few real people mentioned in *After the Funeral*.

See also: *The Hollow* (play); *The Mousetrap* (play); Saunders, Sir Peter.

Gregg, Marina

Marina Gregg is a Hollywood film star coming out of retirement in *The Mirror Crack'd from Side to Side*. Gregg has been married five times and is enjoying her new role as an English landowner. A magnetic, sheltered woman, she treats life almost as if it were a film, and the murder plot she concocts is highly melodramatic, involving threatening letters and attempts on her life. Gregg is consistently searching for fulfillment and has adopted several children, although her only biological child was born with severe special needs because she contracted rubella during pregnancy.

Christie rebuffed suggestions that this character was based on Gene Tierney. In the year *The Mirror Crack'd from Side to Side* was published, Tierney made a highly publicized return to acting after recovering from her premature child's death.

Gregson, Gary

In *The Clocks,* he is a prolific popular novelist who uses the Cavendish Secretarial Bureau. One of his plots inspires a crime. Detection Club expert Martin Edwards has suggested that Gary Gregson is based on John Creasey, on the grounds of a "prolific, sometimes careless quality of writing" ("The Clocks" n.p.).

The Grey Cells of M. Poirot. See *Poirot Investigates*

Grey, Jane

In *Death in the Clouds*, Jane Grey is the romantic lead. A young, pretty woman down on her luck and lacking an aim in life, she feels overlooked when she travels on the *Prometheus*. Getting involved in the murder investigation gives her a new lease on life. The name not only evokes the same overlooked quality suggested by Christie with Katherine Grey in *The Mystery of the Blue Train* but also England's shortest-reigning queen, Jane Grey, who was executed after nine days; this character fears that, like the queen, she will fail to make an impact.

Grey, Katherine

In *The Mystery of the Blue Train*, she is an often overlooked young woman who has just come into a large inheritance and is overwhelmed by distant relatives coming out of the woodwork for her money. She gets on well with Hercule Poirot and acts as his sounding-board during the investigation. As with Jane Grey in *Death in the*

Clouds, her surname indicates that she is not considered a colorful presence in the wider world, although she is a hero of this narrative.

Grey, Thora

The beautiful, ruthlessly efficient secretary to Sir Carmichael Clarke in *The ABC Murder*, she inspires envy in Lady Clarke, who wants her to be the killer.

Grey, Thyrza

One of the three self-proclaimed witches in *The Pale Horse*, Thyrza Grey is tall and masculine. Her rejection of traditional femininity is part of the women's projection of otherness.

Grierson, Alan

Janet and Rodney Grierson's 13-year-old son, who has learning difficulties, in "In the Cool of the Evening." He has made friends with a strange creature in his parents' garden; this turns out to be God.

Gudgeon

The imposing, extremely loyal butler in *The Hollow*, who has been compared to P.G. Wodehouse's creation Jeeves. He was memorably played on screen by Edward Fox, as part of *Agatha Christie's Poirot*.

Gumnaam. See **Indian-Language Adaptations**

The Gunman

"The Gunman" is a figure about whom Christie dreamed as a girl. The recurring dream has been widely discussed by biographers and Christie covered it in detail in her autobiography, and in her semi-autobiographical Mary Westmacott novel, *Unfinished Portrait*.

In both texts, he is described as wearing a French "powder-blue uniform" and having intensely blue eyes (*UP* 355; *AA* 37). In both texts, it is emphasized that there is no danger of him hurting anyone, but the fear he engenders is "symbolic" (*UP*, 255):

> It was his mere presence that was frightening. The dream would be quite ordinary—a tea-party, or a walk with various people, usually a mild festivity of some kind. Then suddenly a feeling of uneasiness would come. There was someone—someone who *ought not to be there*—a horrid feeling of fear: and then I would see him—sitting

at the tea-table, walking along the beach, joining the game. His pale blue eyes would meet mine, and I would wake up shriek-ing: "The Gunman, the Gunman!" [*AA* 37; emphasis in original]

The short story "The Gipsy" includes a similar scenario. Dickie Carpenter has a recurring dream which involves a strange presence.

> She—the gipsy, you know—would just come into any old dream…. I'd be enjoying myself no end, and then I'd feel, I'd know, that if I looked up, she'd be there, standing as she always stood, watching me…. With sad eyes, you know, as though she under-stood something I didn't…. Can't explain why it rattled me so—but it did! Every time! I used to wake up howling with ter-ror [*HOD* 75; ellipses in original].

All three accounts go on to discuss dream-ing about old friends and then their faces or voices turning into those of the Gunman (or Gun Man, or gypsy).

The autobiography does not analyze the dream beyond the sensation described above of fearing "someone who ought not to be there." In *Unfinished Portrait*, the stranger with whom Celia is sharing her story takes over the narrative at the end, revealing that he himself is the Gun Man: "It was the Gun Man again, you see [… he] had pursued her all these years [and] she had met him face to face [… H]e was just an ordinary human being" (591). Now Celia has faced her "symbol for fear," she is free "to grow up" and live a rich and happy life: the Gun Man concludes: "I shall never see her again" (591).

In "The Gipsy," the terrifying figure is actually a supernatural protector, warning Dickie in dangerous situations. The more he ignores her, when she seems to materi-alize in real life, the closer he gets to death. Eventually, having ignored the gypsy, he dies. This alternative resolution to the Gun-man story shows the damage of fearing out-siders *because* they are outsiders, while the version in the novel shows the destructive power of an enemy *within* an inner circle.

In his Freudian account of Christie's 1926 disappearance, Andrew Norman has argued that the Gunman story reveals sep-aration anxiety, the fear "that her parents

might abandon her" (27), and knowledge that her self-contained childhood was lim-ited—something also evidenced in her cre-ation of detailed fantasy worlds, as she played by herself. Norman concludes that a "fear of change, of losing her home, but more importantly of being separated from her loved ones, was a cardinal feature of Agatha's make-up" (35).

See also: *An Autobiography*; "The Gipsy"; *Unfinished Portrait*

Guteman, Ellie. See **Rogers, Ellie**

Guthrie, Alexander

Alexander Guthrie is a bright-spirited, elderly art critic in *After the Funeral* and is a friend to Cora Lansquenet.

"The Gypsy." See **"The Gipsy"**

Haggard, Blanche

In the Mary Westmacott novel *Absent in the Spring*, Blanche Haggard is one of Joan Scudamore's oldest friends, who has been married five times. Her hedonism contrasts Joan's obsession with keeping up appear-ances, causing the latter to reevaluate her life choices.

Halliday, Helen. See **Kennedy, Helen Spen-love**

Halliday, Major Kelvin

Gwenda Reed's late father in *Sleeping Murder*, who was committed to a mental hospital after insisting he had murdered his second wife, Helen Kennedy. Most people believed Helen had run away with another man, but Miss Marple proves that she was killed.

Halliwell, Clare

Clare Halliwell is a "fresh and pleasant and very English" (*WLL* 57) parish worker in "The Edge," who struggles with many of the complex emotions experienced by Christie in the late 1920s.

Hallowe'en Party (novel)

In 1969, the Christie for Christmas was a new Hercule Poirot mystery. It was serial-ized in *Woman's Own* in the United King-dom and *Cosmopolitan* in the United States, in both cases after book publication by Col-lins and Dodd, Mead respectively.

Unusually for a book this late in his—and

his creator's—career, Poirot appears at the very beginning, summoned by Ariadne Oliver, as in early 1950s cases like *Mrs. McGinty's Dead* and *Dead Man's Folly*. At a children's Hallowe'en party, which Mrs. Oliver attended, a 13-year-old girl announced that she once witnessed a murder. Nobody listens, because this girl, Joyce Reynolds, is a known fabulist, but, by the end of the night, she has drowned in an apple-bobbing bucket. The apple-loving Mrs. Oliver is traumatized and calls Poirot for help.

Poirot learns that Joyce tended to repeat stories other people have told, as if they happened to her. He comes to realize that Joyce's friend, Miranda Butler, is the one who witnessed the murder. In a race against the clock, he saves Miranda from the murderers who—by now—have killed three children including the teenaged au pair whose death Miranda witnessed in the past. Now is the respectable hostess of the Hallowe'en party, and another is a beautiful man, Michael Gardner, who can enchant women, and whose sole motive is money to build a beautiful garden. He has a messianic draw over Miranda who, it transpires, is his secret daughter, and nearly convinces her to offer herself as a human sacrifice in the pursuit of a New World, defined by beauty.

The book reflects a growing preoccupation in late Christie with youth, beauty, and cultish allegiance. It is the last time Poirot is drawn to male beauty and, for the first time, he views it critically. Contrasting the magnetic beauty Michael Garfield to that of an artificial garden and that of nature itself, he wonders about its effects and impacts, no longer viewing beauty as an end in itself—which the murderer does—but as a form of power.

Joyce is also Christie's youngest murder victim. However, she had made children victims before, most notably in *Dead Man's Folly*, and made a younger girl the murderer in *Crooked House*. In the previous year's *By the Pricking of My Thumbs*, a very elderly woman had been named as a murderer—and a cultish victim, like Miranda—showing that, in Christie, age is not a barrier to victimhood or culpability.

Hallowe'en Party is notable also for being

the only Christie novel to include the word *lesbian*. It is said by one of the young people in a "man of the world way," trying and failing to shock Poirot (*HP* 177). When the novel was filmed, as part of *Agatha Christie's Poirot*, in 2010, this was expanded into a full lesbian subplot. The novel has also been dramatized as a radio play, which aired on BBC Radio 4 in 1993, and a French television drama, part of *Les Petits Meurtres d'Agatha Christie*. A graphic novel version by Chandre was released in French in 2007 and English in 2008.

Characters: Ambrose, Nora; Benfield, Charlotte; **Bulstrode, Honoria; Butler, Judith, and Miranda;** Drake, extended family (Edmund, Frances, and Hugo); **Drake, Rowena;** Emlyn, Miss; Ferguson, Dr.; Ferrier, Leslie; Fullerton, Jeremy; **Garfield, Michael; George(s);** Goodbod, Mrs.; Holland, Desmond; Leaman, Harriet; Llewellyn-Smythe, Mrs.; McKay, Elspeth; **Oliver, Ariadne; Poirot, Hercule;** Raglan, Timothy; Ransom, Nicholas; Reynolds, Ann; **Reynolds, Joyce, and Leopold;** Reynolds, Mrs.; Richmond, Alfred; Seminoff, Olga; **Spence, Superintendent Bert;** White, Janet; Whittaker, Elizabeth

See also: ***Agatha Christie's Poirot; Hercule Poirot*** (BBC radio series); ***Les Petits Meurtres d'Agatha Christie;* Religion**

Hamilton, Cyril Ogilvie, and Hugo

In *And Then There Were None*, Cyril Ogilvie Hamilton was a toddler in Vera Claythorne's care; she allowed him to drown so that his inheritance would pass to his uncle, Hugo. However, Hugo became suspicious of Vera and broke off his engagement to marry her, later discussing his concerns in a bar, which led to Vera's invitation to Soldier Island, where she would be punished. Toward the end of the novel, Vera starts to hear voices from both Cyril and Hugo, igniting her conscience. Also mentioned is Mrs. Hamilton, Cyril's mother.

Hannah

In "The House of Lurking Death," she is Lady Lucy Radclyffe's long-serving maid, who turns out to be a religious maniac, using biblical quotations, out of context, to justify extreme violence. This is a theme Christie would revisit some four decades later in her musings on idealists and lunatics in works such as *By the Pricking of My Thumbs* and *Hallowe'en Party*.

Hannah, Sophie (1971–). See **Continuation Fiction**

Hannibal. See **Dogs**

Hardcastle, Detective Inspector Richard ("Dick")

A tall police official investigating the murders in *The Clocks*, Detective Inspector Richard Hardcastle has highly expressive eyebrows, of which he makes full use, and is an old friend of Colin Lamb's.

Hardcastle, Midge

A cheerful relation to the Angkatells, Midge Hardcastle is in love with Edward Angkatell in *The Hollow*. Midge represents Christie's attempt to show the upper classes living in reduced circumstances, although the images of Midge working part time in a dress shop and lunching in a café rather than at home may not inspire the sympathy in modern readers that they do in her cousin.

Hargreaves, Lois

Tommy and Tuppence Beresford's client in "The House of Lurking Death," Lois Hargreaves is a smartly presented but internally chaotic young woman. She has a habit of doodling three intertwined fish on any surface or document to hand, something done by Christie herself, which inspired the cover art for the Greenway Editions of her novels in the 1960s and 1970s.

Hargreaves, Mrs.

Mrs. Hargreaves is an unpleasant woman in "The Water Bus," who "didn't like people" (*SOB* 31). Rather like Ebenezer Scrooge, she experiences a life-changing vision that makes her like and nearly love humanity. Her transformation is less straightforward than that in *A Christmas Carol*. She is already considered a friendly, conscientious community pilar; the cynicism is purely internal—and although she gets swept away in visions of joyful human contact and diversity, she acknowledges that a change of personality is impossible.

"The Harlequin Tea Set" (story)

It is hard to know when the last Harley Quin story was written, especially since Christie wrote them as and when the fancy took her. It was first published in a multi authored anthology, *Winter's Crimes*, in 1971. This advertised it on the cover as "new" and references to young people smoking pot put it at least in the mid–1960s. Most likely, the story was written around 1970 when Christie was asked to provide something for the anthology. Certainly, it bears the hallmarks of her late fiction: filled with nostalgia, reminiscence, and highly uneven pacing. There is a sizable diversion about the irritations of wearing dentures. It is also an evocative, emotional, final outing for Quin and Mr. Satterthwaite, the reticent protagonist of the Quin stories, "now of an advanced age" (*PPB* 85), who has not seen him for many years, since the stories collected in *The Mysterious Mr. Quin* in 1930.

When his car breaks down en route to an old friend's house, Satterthwaite waits in a café/ shop, the Harlequin Café. He is not really surprised when Harley Quin appears, for the first time in decades, now accompanied by a dog called Hermes. They reminisce, and Satterthwaite tells Quin about his elderly friend, Tom Addison, and Addison's complicated family history. A woman enters the shop—she proves to be Beryl Gilliat, Tom's daughter-in-law, buying a new multicolored set of tea cups. Satterthwaite asks if Quin will join him at Addison's, but Quin declines, and leaves Satterthwaite with one word: "Daltonism."

At the house, Satterthwaite meets or re-meets the various children and grandchildren of Tom Addison. When he sees Beryl drop a red tea-cup and replace it with a blue one, he stops one of the grandsons drinking out of it. He recalls that Tom is color-blind (a condition once called Daltonism) and suggests that his grandson has inherited this trait; that Beryl was, for reasons of greed, trying to poison him via a switched tea-cup ruse, and that he would not have noticed the red and blue cups had been switched. Once he makes it clear that he has guessed what is going on, Beryl disappears on a motorbike. Sometime later, Satterthwaite sees an apparition of the would-be-victim's long-dead mother, and tells her that her son is safe. She disappears.

Hermes the dog delivers a note of congratulations from Quin, and disappears into the sea.

On an emotional level, the story is an artistic triumph. It breathes longing, loss, and nostalgia. On a technical level, it is perhaps the opposite, although all the elements of Christie the crime writer at her peak are there. Following its publication by Macmillan, it remained uncollected until *Problem at Pollensa Bay* (1991) in the United Kingdom and *The Harlequin Tea Set* (1997) in the United States.

Characters: Addison, Pilar; **Addison, Tom;** Ali; **Gilliat, Beryl;** Gilliat, Lily Addison; Gilliat, Roland; Gilliat, Simon; Gilliat, Timothy; Hermes; Horton, Dr.; **Inez; Leith, Duchess of ("Maria");** Maria; **Quin, Harley;** Satterthwaite, Mr.

See also: **Dogs;** *The Harlequin Tea Set* **(story collection);** *Problem at Pollensa Bay* **(story collection)**

The Harlequin Tea Set (story collection; alternative title: *The Harlequin Tea Set and Other Stories*)

In 1997, when *While the Light Lasts* was published in the United Kingdom, Putnam published a similar collection, *The Harlequin Tea Set*, in the United States. Both volumes contain nine short stories, previously published in magazines or newspapers but not placed in anthologies in the author's lifetime. However, "Christmas Adventure" and "The Mystery of the Baghdad Chest," which appear in *While the Light Lasts*, are absent. Instead, "The Mystery of the Spanish Chest," the expanded version of the "Baghdad Chest" story, appears, as the other had already been collected in *The Regatta Mystery and Other Stories* (1939) in the United States. Additionally, "The Harlequin Tea Set," a story that had been published in *Problem at Pollensa Bay and Other Stories* (1991) in the United Kingdom, closes the volume. Although early editions of *While the Light Lasts* include background notes by Tony Medawar for each story, *The Harlequin Tea Set* only includes notes on the highly unusual "Manx Gold" as a foreword and afterword. Bizarrely, these explanatory notes have been omitted from subsequent editions.

The book is composed of **"The Edge," "The Actress," "While the Light Lasts," "The House of Dreams," "The Lonely God," "Manx Gold," "Within a Wall," "The Mystery of the Spanish Chest,"** and "The Harlequin Tea Set."

"Harlequin's Lane" (story)

There is a myth that Christie stopped writing in the immediate aftermath of her December 1926 disappearance, as she negotiated the breakdown of her first marriage. This has, inevitably, proven a good way for Christie apologists to explain away the shortcomings of *The Big Four* (1927) and *The Mystery of the Blue Train* (1928), overplaying the input of others in those books. However, Christie's magazine publication trail shows that she continued to write.

"Harlequin's Lane" was published in *The Story-Teller* magazine in May 1927 and later collected in *The Mysterious Mr. Quin* (1930). Of the stories collected in that volume, it hints perhaps most strongly at the supernatural nature of Harley Quin, who appears at opportune moments to help the effeminate Mr. Satterthwaite get to the bottom of problems of human nature. The "Love Detectives" meet on a road variously known as "Harlequin's Lane" and "Lovers' Lane," which terminates a disused quarry, which has become a rubbish tip. They get involved in a family drama: Satterthwaite meets a dancer who has given up her passion for marriage. He warns her that Harlequin—the figure of love, escape, and romance—"is only a myth" (*MMQ* 391). Later Satterthwaite sees the dancer strolling with a harlequin down Harlequin's Lane. The Harlequin is Harley Quin, but his face is that of her lover from long ago. She is found dead in the quarry. Quin denies having been on the road at all, and Satterthwaite realizes: "I see things other people do not" (396). It is a story about empathy, but also about the destructive power of sexual passion, something very much on Christie's mind in 1927 as her marriage was ending in divorce.

Characters: Denman, John; Ivanovich, Sergius; Kharasanova, Anna; Korsakoff, Rimsky; Oranoff, Prince; **Quin, Harley;** Roscheimers, Lady; Roscheimers, Lord; **Satterthwaite, Mr.**

See also: **Commedia dell'arte**; *The Mysterious Mr. Quin*

"Harlequin's Song." See *A Masque from Italy*

Harmon, Diana (Bunch), and Rev. Julian

In *A Murder Is Announced* and "Sanctuary," Diana "Bunch" Harmon is an honorary niece of Miss Marple's. Nicknamed because of her plumpness, she is playful and optimistic. Her husband is younger than he acts: Christie writes that he was born destined for late-middle-age. His idea of an amusing anecdote concerns muddling the nomenclature of ancient monarchs. The couple has children, Edward and Susan, and a cat named Tiglath Pilesar.

Hartnell, Amanda

Miss Marple's next-door neighbor, she is confidently involved in village life and is "much dreaded by the poor" (*MAV* 5). Appears in *The Body in the Library*, "The Case of the Perfect Maid," *The Murder at the Vicarage*, *The Mirror Crack'd from Side to. Side*, and "Tape-Measure Murder."

Hastings, Captain Arthur

Even in Christie's heyday, Captain Arthur Hastings was considered "easily the stupidest of all modern Watsons" (Haycraft 132) and "the most splendidly obtuse Watson in crime fiction" (Symons, "mort" 289). The narrator of the early Poirot short stories and several novels, he fulfills the role of Dr. Watson in the Sherlock Holmes stories by Sir Arthur Conan Doyle. However, whereas Watson famously sees but does not observe, Hastings often fails to see.

He is not, as convention has it of narrators, slightly stupider than the average reader, but significantly more so—enabling the reader to laugh at him and side with Poirot. As Poirot puts it in *Lord Edgware Dies*, Hastings is "intensely ordinary" and will always think what the murderer wants him to think (62), something that he considers intensely valuable, as does the reader. Poirot frequently chides Hastings for being too invested in the British class system and for his refusal to look through keyholes or, in one case, a lady's underwear. Hastings, he claims, "is an admirable man but, alas, intensely English" (LP 2).

When Poirot mocks Hastings's Englishness, Christie is mocking traditional crime-fiction conventions. "*Mon ami*," Poirot says mockingly in *The ABC Murders*. "You fix upon me a look of doglike devotion and demand of me a pronouncement à la Sherlock Holmes!" (56). She is also mocking traditionalism itself from the moment this character—named after a battle lost by the English—proclaims himself Sherlock Holmes in *The Mysterious Affair at Styles* and mocks his petite Belgian friend's delusions of grandeur, only to be sportingly outwitted. Although Dorothy L. Sayers critiqued Christie in 1928 for "still cling[ing] to the Watson formula" (Sayers, Introduction 33), Christie was in some ways undermining it through parody with Captain Hastings.

Either way, she tired of him almost as soon as she had created him, sending him away to South America at the end of *The Murder on the Links* in 1923, although he would return on and off until *Curtain*, written around 1940. Even in this, though, Christie was parodic, affronting Hastings' propriety by having him fall in love with a flapper who drinks and swears and his intelligence by having him unable to distinguish his future wife from her twin sister. The love plot, something Christie and many of her peers saw as a "fettering convention" of the genre (Sayers, Introduction 39), is also given a twist. As Dolores Gordon-Smith points out:

> Hastings was not the only detective to mix up love and murder, but the usual procedure was to be convinced of the beloved's innocence and clear her name (as Philip Trent and Lord Peter Wimsey do in *Trent's Last Case* and *Strong Poison*), then propose. Hastings is, as far as I know, the only one to be convinced of his girl's guilt whilst offering marriage [Gordon-Smith 22].

Like Countess Vera Rossakoff, Hastings is mentioned by Poirot in several of the late novels and short stories, long after he has ceased to appear. Often, Poirot compares his unimaginative staff, George and Miss Lemon, unfavorably to Hastings, missing the latter's imagination. These remarks become particularly pronounced in "The Mystery of the Spanish Chest," a

1960 rewriting of "The Mystery of the Spanish Chest." Rewriting that story, Christie replaced Hastings with Lemon, making Poirot's observation that he wishes she was more like him particularly notable.

Hastings, Judith

There is more than a dash of Rosalind Hicks, Christie's daughter, in Judith Hastings, the adult daughter of Captain Hastings in *Curtain*. Specifically, Christie worried that her daughter took life too seriously, as Hastings does of Judith. She also bears some similarities to Dr. Alice Cunningham, Countess Rossakoff's daughter-in-law in the 1947 version of *The Capture of Cerberus*. An intellectual scientific researcher, she has definite views on things but tends to absorb those views from people she respects, so she does not yet know her own mind. In low-level conflict with her father, she provokes him by flirting with an unsuitable man, before revealing that she is in love with her supervisor, Dr. Franklin.

"The Hat and the Alibi." See "A Christmas Tragedy"

"Have Ye Walked in the Wood Today?" (poem)

The unpublished poem "Have Ye Walked in the Wood Today?" by Christie, written ca. age 13, shows the influence of Agatha Miller's mother on her early work, as the young author tried to find her voice. It is filled with archaic language and imagery—for example, autumnal leaves become a "carpet of gold" (qtd. in L. Thompson 42).

See also: *The Road of Dreams*

"Have You Got Everything You Want?" (story; alternative titles: "Express to Stamboul"; "On the Orient Express")

The Orient Express features in this Parker Pyne story, which was written and published in 1933, at the time Christie was writing *Murder on the Orient Express* and had fresh memories of traveling on that train. In it, an American newlywed abroad the train is worried about something. She notices that J. Parker Pyne, who advertises his services for unhappy people in the *Times*, is a fellow passenger and asks him for help. The woman is Elsie Jeffries, and she is concerned about her "straitlaced," "puritan" husband Edward, whom she is traveling to meet in Constantinople (*PPI* 115). After finding a mysterious message in Edward's study, Elsie is concerned that he is planning an unpleasant surprise, potentially life-threatening, for her during the journey.

The next day, a smoke bomb goes off, and Elsie's jewels are missing. At Stamboul, Pyne contacts Edward, who appears and hands the jewels over to his wife. It emerges that he replaced the jewels with paste before leaving for Constantinople and that an accomplice was to remove the replicas on the train so that Edward could replace them in Baghdad. He made the switch because he was being blackmailed in a scam (resembling that in "The Stymphalian Birds"). Pyne advises him to confess all to Elsie, except the part about the scam, because "[i]f a woman has to choose between a mug and a Don Juan, she will choose Don Juan every time" (126).

The story was published with other Pyne short stories under the title *Have You Got Everything You Want? If Not, Consult Mr. Parker Pyne* in the United States in the April 1933 *Cosmopolitan*. In the United Kingdom, it appeared as "On the Orient Express," as the first installment of *The Arabian Nights of Parker Pyne* in *Nash's Pall Mall Magazine* in June 1933. It appears as the seventh installment of *Parker Pyne Investigates* in 1934.

Characters: Jeffries, Edward; Jeffries, Elsie; **Parker Pyne, J.**; Subayska, Madame

See also: *The Labours of Hercules*; *Murder on the Orient Express* (novel); *Parker Pyne Investigates*

Have You Got Everything You Want? If Not, Consult Mr. Parker Pyne. See *Parker Pyne Investigates*

Havering, Zoe

Zoe Crabb Havering is the wife of Roger Havering in "The Mystery of Hunter's Lodge" who disguises herself as housekeeper Mrs. Middleton to fake an alibi in an elaborate murder plot. The clue that she played the part of the housekeeper is that she used to be an actress, performing as Zoe Carrisbrook—always a suspicious backstory in Christie. She initially gets away with it but is later killed in an airplane crash.

Haworth, Mrs. Alistair

Mrs. Alistair Haworth is the eponymous character in "The Gipsy," for whom the gift of supernatural vision is a curse. "Alistair" appears to be a maiden name rather than a first name, as she is remembered at one point as "Miss Alistair, the pretty lamb" (*HOD* 84). Nonetheless, it may evoke the occult figure Aleister Crowley (1875–1947).

"Hawthorn Trees." See *Poems*

Haydock, Dr., and Penelope

Dr. Haydock is the village doctor in *The Murder at the Vicarage*, perhaps most notable for emphatically opposing the death penalty, only to insist upon it when confronted with an actual murderer. A far mellower Haydock narrates "The Case of the Caretaker" and appears in *The Moving Finger, The Mirror Crack'd from Side to Side* (1962), *Sleeping Murder*, and "The Case of the Caretaker's Wife." He is mentioned in "Death by Drowning," "The Case of the Perfect Maid," and *4.50 from Paddington*. Penelope, his wife, is discussed in *The Mirror Crack'd from Side to Side*.

Haymes, Philippa ("Pip")

In *A Murder Is Announced*, Philippa Haymes says she is a widow because she is ashamed that her husband was an army deserter during World War II. However, he ultimately dies a heroic death. Several clues in *A Murder Is Announced* are linguistic, including that surrounding mysterious twins called "Pip and Emma." For various reasons, the reader is invited to assume that Pip is a boy—when in fact it is short for Philippa, and the clue has been there in her name all along.

Hayward, Charles, and Sir Arthur

The 35-year-old son of Sir Arthur Hayward, Charles Hayward narrates *Crooked House*. This character represents the return of British masculinity, as he comes back to England after war service and becomes involved in his fiancée's domestic life, investigating her grandfather's murder. Usually referred to as "the Old Man," Sir Arthur is an assistant commissioner of Scotland Yard.

Hazy, Lady Selina

An elderly friend of Miss Marple's in *At Bertram's Hotel*, Lady Selina Hazy has enjoyed life, but her abilities and faculties are starting to fade. She is more enthusiastic than helpful as Miss Marple investigates.

Heilger, Romaine. See Vole, Romaine

Helier, Jane

Jane Helier is an actress who is part of the Tuesday Night Club in *The Thirteen Problems*. She is indulged by other members of the group as ditzy and oblivious, something she plays up. When it becomes her turn to recount a mystery in "The Affair at the Bungalow," she describes a scheme she is secretly plotting, to see if anyone will figure it out. She later appears in "Strange Jest."

Henderson, Ellie

In "Problem at Sea," she is "a woman of forty-five who was content to look her age" (*PEC* 222); a contrast to the histrionic victim, Adeline Clapperton, who clings to her fading youth. She is a similar character to Rosamund Darnley in *Evil Under the Sun*; both are level-headed, admirable middle-aged women who take some pity on, and romantic interest in, the overshadowed husband of a glamorous, difficult woman who dies.

Henet

The family servant, Henet is a snide and unpleasant woman in *Death Comes as the End*, who nonetheless retains the trust of those in authority, because of her well-practiced sycophancy. Women tend to see through her while men do not. She is characterized by a nasal, whining voice.

Henry, Uncle

Miss Marple mentions her mischievous Uncle Henry in several village parallels. He is particularly significant in "Strange Jest," where his sense of humor helps her get to the bottom of another playful uncle's psychology, but is also cited in "Tape-Measure Murder."

"Her Own Story of Her Disappearance" (interview)

Christie's 11-day disappearance in 1926 was

a turning point in her relationship with the press. Reporting on the case was relentless and inhumane, and Christie maintained a lifelong hostility toward journalists as a result. She only spoke publicly about her disappearance once, in an interview granted to the *Daily Mail* in February 1928. In this, she was encouraged by her sister-in-law, Nan Watts, after the event had been referenced in a high-profile libel case, as an example of a "hoax on the police" (qtd. in "HOS" 11). To lay the matter to rest, Christie gave a lengthy account of events. In the end, it made no difference to rampant speculation and, perhaps because it detracts from the mystery of things, it is rarely quoted now.

In the interview, published as an essay with occasional interruptions on 16 February 1928, Christie describes her "state of high nervous strain" and initial intention to commit suicide. She states that she "drove aimlessly about" without thinking and eventually crashed her car (11). This is the moment, Christie maintains, that she was no longer "Mrs. Christie"; "I lost my memory. For 24 hours after the accident my mind was an almost complete blank" (11). "I had become," she explains, "a new woman"—a happy South African, Teresa Neele, the name under which she checked into the Harrogate Hydro Hotel (11). Christie insists that she did not realize while staying there that she was "Mrs. Christie": "I read every day about Mrs. Christie's disappearance and came to the conclusion that she was dead" (11).

See also **Disappearance of Agatha Christie**

"The Herb of Death" (story; alternative title: "Foxglove in the Sage"). See *The Thirteen Problems*

Hercule Poirot (BBC radio series)

The collective name *Hercule Poirot* has been retrospectively granted to 27 BBC Radio 4 dramatizations of Hercule Poirot novels and a novella between 1985 and 2007. These in fact appeared in several different long-running series or slots, such as the *Afternoon Play, Saturday Night Theatre, The Saturday Play,* and *Murder for Christmas.* All adaptations were dramatized by Michael Bakewell. All but one were produced and directed by Enyd Williams. All but two starred John Moffatt as Poirot.

Casting Poirot proved problematic. Veteran actor Maurice Denham was initially cast in a six-part special, *The Mystery of the Blue Train* (at the tail-end the Christie/train fever brought about by the 1974 movie *Murder on the Orient Express*). This was directed by David Johnston and aired for the 1985–86 new year, with the first episode broadcast on 29 December 1985.

In 1986, *Hercule Poirot's Christmas* aired in five parts, from Christmas Eve, meaning the episodes were broadcast roughly on the same days (but 48 years later) that they were set. Both Denham and Johnston were replaced; Peter Sallis, not quite able to mask his Yorkshire accent, took the role of Poirot, whereas Enyd Williams stepped in as producer/director. Williams would retain this position for nearly two decades, but Sallis was not considered a success.

For *The Murder of Roger Ackroyd*, a 90-minute special airing exactly one year later, John Moffatt was approached to play Poirot. Moffatt, a Shakespearean actor, brought gravitas to the role and was an instant hit. He reprised the role in *The Murder on the Links*, broadcast on Christie's 100th birthday (15 September 1990), and in all subsequent installments.

These include: *Lord Edgware Dies* (five parts, from 18 March 1992—released in the United States as *Thirteen at Dinner*), *Sad Cypress* (five parts, from 14 May 1992), *Murder on the Orient Express* (five parts, from 18 December 1992), *Hallowe'en Party* (one part, 30 October 1993), *Five Little Pigs* (one part, 18 June 1994), *Murder in Mesopotamia* (five parts, from 26 December 1994), *Death on the Nile* (five parts, from 2 January 1997), *Evil Under the Sun* (five parts, from 6 April 1998), *After the Funeral* (one part, 28 April 1999), *The ABC Murders* (one part, 22 April 2000), *Peril at End House* (five parts, from 20 November 2000), *Appointment with Death* (one part, 25 August 2001), *Cards on the Table* (one part, 4 May 2002), *Three Act Tragedy* (five parts, from 8 July 2002), *Death in the Clouds* (one part, 3 May 2003), *Taken at the Flood* (five parts, from 13 October 2003), *One, Two, Buckle My Shoe* (five parts, from 30 August 2004), "The Adventure of the Christmas Pudding" (a 45-minute special on 24 December 2004), *The Mysterious Affair at Styles* (five parts, from 5 September 2005), *Elephants Can Remember* (one part, 7 January 2006), *Mrs. McGinty's Dead* (five parts, from 3 March 2006), *Dumb Witness* (two parts, from 7 December 2006), and *Dead Man's Folly* (four parts, from 6 August 2007).

There was some attempt to keep recurring characters consistently cast, although Captain Hastings, Inspector Japp, and Ariadne Oliver each had at least two people play them. Notably, Philip Jackson, who played Japp in the television series *Agatha Christie's Poirot*, reprised the role in four radio plays. Julia McKenzie, who would take over the screen role of Miss Marple from Geraldine McEwan in *Agatha Christie's Marple*, took over the role of Mrs. Oliver from Stephanie Cole in three radio plays.

The BBC does not have an endless pool of radio players and some actors turn up again and again in these productions, playing similar roles and lending credence to a notion that Christie wrote in stereotypes: certainly the dramatizations depend on undeveloped character "types." For the 1992 production of *Murder on the Orient Express*, a special effort was made to bring together an all-star cast (Sylvia Syms, Francesca Annis, Peter Polycarpou, and Joss Ackland, among others) and original music by Michael Haslam was commissioned. Most of the dramatizations use rearranged stock music, often in the Cole Porter/Noel Coward/Irving Berlin vein.

John Moffatt seems to have retired after *Dead Man's Folly*, at age 85. He died in 2012, just before his 90th birthday. Already by then, BBC Radio 4 had moved away from the Bakewell/Williams/Moffatt formula, and its Christie offerings had started veering toward the macabre and standalone.

See also: **BBC Radio Adaptations**; **Poirot, Hercule**

Hercule Poirot (Mutual radio series)

Also known as *The Adventures of M. Hercule Poirot* and *Hercule Poirot: Detective Extraordinary*, the Mutual Broadcasting radio series was played across networks in the United States with sponsorship from Mutual Insurance. It ran from 22 February 1945 to 17 February 1946, broadcast in 30-minute slots on Wednesday nights, before legal disputes over scriptwriting halted it. Conceived by its star, Harold Huber, the series relocated much of the action to New York and gave Poirot a glamorous assistant, Miss Fletcher. Huber's radio background was from the long-running CBS program *Suspense*, which also featured Christie adaptations. The Mutual Broadcasting System had also produced several Christies, including three straightforward Poirot adaptations, under its *Murder Clinic* banner, although the new program was designed to be like any number of American detective series at the time: Sherlock Holmes, Nero Wolfe, Philo Vance, Perry Mason, and Ellery Queen all had pulpy audio adventures so it was not surprising to put Poirot in the limelight.

As well as containing original stories with typically lurid titles—such as "The Case of the Roving Corpse" and "The Trail Led to Death"—the series also drew on Christie's own plots and themes. One episode, "Rendezvous with Death," seeks to present *Death on the Nile* in under 30 minutes, whereas "The Deadest Man in the World" includes a villainous Dr. James Sheppard but otherwise seems unrelated to *The Murder of Roger Ackroyd*.

Each episode begins with a clock ticking and Huber, as Poirot, saying: "Time and the little grey cells—they will always solve the mystery," a slight misquote of *The Big Four*. The host then introduces, "complete with bowler hat and magnificent [or 'brave'] moustache, London's [or 'your'] favorite detective, Hercule Poirot." The first episode was introduced by Christie herself. Due to a faulty telephone line, a pre-recorded message was played. Christie was paid £65 a week for the series, and paid no attention to it. In 1949, Huber sought Christie's permission to produce a Poirot television series. Christie declined and Poirot would not reappear on the screen for another 13 years.

After the series ended, Huber reprised the role of Poirot in a similar program, *Mystery of the Week*, for CBS. The radio series was partially remade in Australia in the 1950s, with Alan White as Poirot.

See also: *Mystery of the Week*

Hercule Poirot (television pilot). See **NBC Television Adaptations**

"Hercule Poirot and the Broken Mirror." See **"Dead Man's Mirror"** (novella)

"Hercule Poirot and the Greenshore Folly." (story; alternative title: **"The Greenshore Folly"**)

The novella that became *Dead Man's Folly* in 1956 was written in 1954 to raise funds for a new stained-glass window at St. Mary the Virgin Church in Churston Ferrars, Totnes. However, her agent had trouble finding anywhere to publish "The Greenshore Folly," because it was too long for a magazine and too short for a book. Although Christie was urged to reduce it, she refused, deciding instead to put it aside and later expand it into a novel. Instead, she wrote a completely different Miss Marple story, "Greenshaw's Folly," the royalties for which went to the church window appeal.

Although this background was well-known, the manuscript itself was illusive for many years, before it turned up on an online auction website. It was quietly purchased and, in 2014, Agatha Christie Ltd. arranged for it to be published in book form, with a jacket design by the iconic cover artist Tom Adams, which was transposed onto various local benches by artist Mandi Pope. At the center of the publicity was Christie's holiday home, Greenway, in Devon. This is well-known as the basis for the fictional Nasse House in *Dead Man's Folly* (and for "The Greenshore Folly," which tells the same story), and is painted into the cover design. The book was launched at Greenway, which had also been used the previous year in the last-filmed episode of *Agatha Christie's Poirot*, as Nasse House.

The novella is useful to researchers who wish to explore how Christie expanded her work, because it is identical in plot and structure to *Dead Man's Folly*, and it is easy to compare the two texts, to see which passages have been added or lengthened.

Characters: **Bland, Detective Inspector; Brewis, Amanda; Folliat, Amy; George(s);** **Hoskins, Constable; Legge, Alec, and Peggy; Lemon, Felicity;** Lopez, Paul; Merdle; **Oliver, Ariadne; Poirot, Hercule; Stubbs, Sir Lady Harriet (Hattie); Stubbs, Sir George; Tucker, Marlene;** Warborough, Captain James (Jim); **Weyman, Michael.**

See also: **Adams, Tom;** *Dead Man's Folly;* Greenway House

"Hercule Poirot and the Sixth Chair." See **"Yellow Iris"** (story)

"Hercule Poirot, Armchair Detective." See **"The Disappearance of Mr. Davenheim"**

"Hercule Poirot: Fiction's Greatest Detective" (article; alternative title: **"How I Created Hercule Poirot"**)

Probably Christie's most famous essay, "Hercule Poirot: Fiction's Greatest Detective" was published as an introduction to a serialization of *Appointment with Death* (abridged and retitled *Date with Death*) in the *Daily Mail* on 15 January 1938. In it, Christie describes how she created Poirot and how she developed him as a figure distinct from Sherlock Holmes and his imitators. Then, in the most widely-quoted passages, she confesses to "a coolness" between Poirot and his creator ("FGD" 8). She describes a certain resentment at receiving letters saying how much she must love the character with whom she has been saddled and confesses to sometimes wondering:

> "Why—why—why did I ever invent this detestable, bombastic tiresome little creature? ... Eternally straightening things, eternally boasting, eternally twirling his moustache and tilting his egg-shaped head. Anyway, what is an egg-shaped head?" (8).

This quote is remarkably reminiscent of comments made by Ariadne Oliver, Christie's alter ego, about her own invention, the quirky Finnish Sven Hjerson, in *Cards on the Table*, published two years earlier. Mrs. Oliver concludes that, if she ever met Hjerson in real life, she would commit her greatest murder yet (*COT* 68).

See also: *Cards on the Table* (novel); **"A Letter to My Publisher"**

"Hercule Poirot in Hell." See **"The Capture of Cerberus"** (1947)

"Hercule Poirot, Insurance Investigator." See **"The Tragedy at Marsdon Manor"**

Hercule Poirot Klärt den Mord im Orient-Express Auf

Hercule Poirot made his German television debut in an episode of *Die Galerie der Großen Detektive*, broadcast on 24 August 1955. Peter A. Horn dramatized this 50-minute episode of the anthology series, which showcased one adventure for each "great detective" from literature (starting with Sherlock Holmes). Heini Göbel played Poirot, cigar in hand. This was the first screen adaptation of the novel, and it is not clear whether Christie or her team was aware of it.

See also: *Murder on the Orient Express* (novel); NBC Television Adaptations

Hercule Poirot's Casebook. See *Agatha Christie's Poirot*

Hercule Poirot's Christmas (novel; alternative titles: *A Holiday for Murder; Murder at Christmas; Murder for Christmas*)

The publishing phenomenon of a "Christie for Christmas" was in full swing when the second Hercule Poirot novel of 1938 was published. Certainly written with an eye to festive sales, *Hercule Poirot's Christmas* is a distinctly Christean spin on the seasonal mystery. It is, of course, set in a country house—like "Christmas Adventure," it has Poirot taking part, against his better judgment, in "the old traditional festivities" of a British family Christmas (78), although this time he joins the party after the murder. By the end, he has vowed never to enjoy another crackling open fire, preferring modern central heating.

The mystery is, rarely but not uniquely for Christie, a locked room one. Although Mark Aldridge has critiqued it as "[a] regression of style for Agatha Christie," because it features a country house (*Poirot* 139), it is, like *Appointment with Death*, published in the same year, an early exploration of the theme of family—a preoccupation of Christie in the 1940s and 1950s. Indeed, the country house setting is shown to be grotesque, as will country house settings in *Crooked House* (1949) and *They Do It with Mirrors* (1952): Gorston Hall is "furnished in the more flamboyant of old fashioned styles" (*HPC* 36). There is a caustic line that sums up the arch-traditional setting and the psychological focus: "Grand old tradition. Christmas. Promotes solidarity of family feeling" (78).

The tyrannical Simeon Lee gathers his family together for a "sentimental family Christmas" at Gorston Hall (26). However, on Christmas Eve he makes it clear that he is changing his will. A crash of furniture and a piercing scream draws everyone's attention to his locked study, and soon he is discovered in a pool of blood, his throat cut. Uncut diamonds from his illicit adventures in South America have also gone missing from his safe. As family tensions surface, Poirot is called in to assist Superintendent Sugden of the police, and it emerges that two of the guests are not the family members they claim to be but have less savory connections to Simeon Lee. It also becomes clear that he has illegitimate children.

One of these, it turns out, is Superintendent Sugden himself, who killed Lee in an act of revenge for his mother, whom Lee treated poorly. In an unusual variation on the idea that detective fiction is a game, Poirot reveals that the locked room crime was committed with various items obtained from a joke shop—such as a pig's bladder to produce a scream and obscure the time of death. He also proves that Sugden is Lee's son by holding a moustache from a joke shop over a Lee family portrait and noting the resemblance. This is very similar to the revelation of the murderer's heritage in Sir Arthur Conan Doyle's *The Hound of the Baskervilles*, a text that had previously inspired *The Sittaford Mystery*.

The victim is as grotesquely evil and commanding over his family as Mrs. Boynton in *Appointment with Death*. The language used of him, particularly before he has appeared, is notable: he is "tyrannical," "he dictates our lives to us," and his children "are his slave[s]" (20). Politics form a backdrop to the novel—wars, pacifism, and colonialism are all discussed extensively by characters that have experienced them—and it should be remembered that *Hercule Poirot's Christmas* was written in the context of the rise of fascist dictators across Europe. The family itself is monstrous and particularly troubling is the free and easy talk of incest. The festive traditions allow the reader to explore traditional family structures as "family dirty linen" is aired in daylight (106)—neither is positive or sustainable in the twentieth century.

The other key feature of this novel is blood. An oft-quoted but seldom analyzed dedication to the author's brother-in-law James Watts runs in part:

> You complained that my murders were getting too refined—anaemic, in fact. You yearned for a "good murder with lots of blood." A murder where there is no doubt about its being murder!
>
> So this is your special story—written for you [6].

There is a lot of blood in the story, but it is not a matter of gore or violence—it is a matter of plot. There is in fact too much blood at the crime scene, something one character notes by repeatedly quoting *Macbeth*: "*Who would have thought the old man to have had so much blood in him?*" (74; emphasis in original)—a quote that lent the book two working titles. It transpires that the murderer sprinkled fresh ox's blood over the corpse to obscure the time of death—so it would look like he had only just been killed. This is the world of Christie where forensic science, even in 1938, is significantly behind reality.

The presence of blood, however, does not actually address Watts's criticism, which was also a famous criticism of Raymond Chandler. The narratives *are* essentially bloodless in that they do not dwell on violence, and that is something Christie insisted upon (see "Genteel Queen of Crime"). However, as Gill Plain has pointed out in *Twentieth Century Crime Fiction*, that does not mean that they are not *about* bloody violence and the extremes of passion. A novel ostensibly written in response to the charge that Christie's work needs "lots of blood" deliberately reworks that charge's premise.

The book was published in the United Kingdom in 1938 but, oddly, appeared on American bookshelves in February 1939 under the more generic title *Murder for Christmas* (the paperback would be rechristened again as *Holiday for Murder*). The first of many dramatizations was for BBC Radio 4, with Maurice Denham playing Poirot, in 1986. Next was an episode of *Agatha Christie's Poirot* for ITV in 1994. There have been two French television adaptations: the four-part *Petits Meurtres en Famille*, directed by Edwin Baily in 2006, was so successful it spawned a campy series, *Les Petits Meurtres d'Agatha Christie*. In 2018, this series featured another adaptation of *Hercule Poirot's Christmas*. There has also been a card game based on the book, released promotionally in 1994 to promote the ITV adaptation, and a mystery jigsaw, *Poirot's Christmas*, from Paul Lamond Games in 2000.

Characters: Best, Grace; Champion, Charlton, Mr.; Walter; Estravados, Juan and Jennifer; **Estravados, Pilar;** Farr, Ebenezer; **Farr, Stephen; Grant, Stephen; Horbury, Sydney; Johnson, Colonel;** Kench, Joan; Lee, Adelaide; Lee, Alfred and Lydia; **Lee, David, and Hilda;** Lee, George and Magdalene; Lee, Harry; **Lee, Simeon; Lopez, Conchita;** Poirot, Hercule; Reeves, Emily; **Sugden, Superintendent;** Tressilian

See also: *Agatha Christie's Poirot;* **Games;** *Hercule Poirot* (BBC radio series); *The Mousetrap; Les Petits Meurtres d'Agatha Christie; Petits Meurtres en Famille;* **Shakespeare, William**

"Heritage." See *The Road of Dreams* (poetry collection)

Herjoslovakia. See **Herzoslovakia**

Hersheimmer, Julius P.

One of the richest men in the world, he is an American multi-millionaire in *The Secret Adversary*. He appears as a potential love interest for Tuppence Beresford (then Cowley), and readers are invited to suspect him of being too good to be true. In the end, he is simply a brash American who marries his delicate cousin, Jane Finn. Tuppence rejects his proposal of marriage and chooses instead to marry Tommy, who is poor but with whom she is in love. The character also offers Christie's first attempt to write "in American"; an over-zealous use of sometimes nonsensical superlatives that has been gently mocked by some U.S. readers.

Hertzlein, August

August Hertzlein is a fascist dictator,

transparently modeled on Adolf Hitler, in the original (rejected) version of "The Capture of Cerberus."

Herzoslovakia

The small Balkan kingdom of Herzoslovakia first appears in *The Secret of Chimneys* in 1925, where battles over its throne and its oil are central to the plot. As a holiday destination, it is the setting for the 1940 Poirot story "The Stymphalean Birds." The kingdom is also referenced, with a different spelling, in *One, Two, Buckle My Shoe* (1940). A "Herzoslovakian Minister" is mentioned briefly in the 1954 play *Spider's Web* (9).

The only sustained study of Herzoslovakia is "The Balkan Theme in *The Secret of Chimneys*" (2016) by Graham St. John Stott and Aysar Yaseen. They conclude that Christie's stereotyped presentation of the kingdom, with obvious parallels to Romania and other countries, is strategic: "Christie uses the all too familiar Balkan stereotypes of backwardness and brigandage, but not—as was usually the case at the time—as an Other to illustrate British virtue, but as a mirror to British vice" (1).

See also: *The Labours of Hercules*; *One, Two, Buckle My Shoe*; *The Secret of Chimneys* (novel)

Hickory Dickory Death (See *Hickory Dickory Dock*)

Hickory Dickory Dock (novel; alternative title: *Hickory Dickory Death*)

By the mid–1950s, Christie's publishers were urging her to engage with youth culture and to add more diversity to her books. *Hickory Dickory Dock* represents her attempt to fulfill this edict; whether or not she succeeded is a matter of opinion, although the mystery element of the novel is almost universally regarded as strong. Once again, Christie evokes a nursery rhyme to structure the action, although the relevance here is loose. Indeed, the strongest link to "Hickory Dickory Dock" is the setting, Hickory Road.

Hercule Poirot is shocked, first by his efficient secretary Miss Lemon making two mistakes and then by the reason: she has a sister who is troubled.

Poirot struggles to understand that his "completely machine-made," "precision instrument" (6) of a secretary could have anything as human as a family or family problems. He learns that Lemon's sister, Mrs. Hubbard, is a warden at a student hostel on Hickory Road, London, where "things are going on" (8). Here is the first clue that we are entering unfamiliar Christie territory: this is going to be a novel about young, diverse people. Miss Lemon says with concern that "some of [the students] are actually *black*, I believe" (7; emphasis in original), to which Poirot responds, "Naturally" (7). Thus, Christie addresses and dismisses the concerns of some of her readers who might prefer a whitewashed, insular world in her fiction.

Poirot goes to the hostel to investigate, and learns that small things have been going missing. There appears to be a kleptomaniac at work. He addresses the students, who are postgraduates so in their early twenties, ostensibly giving an unrelated lecture about crime and criminality. This prompts one, Celia Austin, to confess privately that she is behind most—but not all—of the thefts. The shy Celia has been trying to impress a psychology student, Colin McNabb, to whom she is attracted, and believed she would be more interesting to him with a neurosis or complex. Poirot is inclined to let matters rest—"a girl is entitled to attempt desperate measures to get her man" (45)—but before long Celia is dead.

Investigating the death, Poirot and the police learn about various rivalries and suspicious behavior among the hostel's residents. They also observe strange behavior from its proprietor, the eccentric Mrs. Nicoletis, who is clearly an alcoholic and, it becomes obvious, is involved in smuggling either drugs or diamonds. Mrs. Nicoletis is murdered as well, and then another murder is committed. Poirot comes to connect the murders with a diamond smuggling operation, which also links to some of the original thefts—those not accounted for by Celia but hidden among her crimes.

He uncovers a large criminal operation involving some of the most competent students and a murder plot centered around the homicidal figure of Nigel Chapman, whose contrarian, left-of-center ideas have been indulged henceforth. He emerges as a fatally attractive figure, who corrupts intelligent women, and it is revealed that his identity is assumed: he is, in reality, the wayward son of a great chemist, and in his youth, he murdered his mother. By the end of the novel, Miss Lemon's sister is contemplating a relaxing cruise, and Miss Lemon is back to her old machine-like efficiency.

This novel provides evidence of a creeping—but, at this stage, still affectionate—distrust of the young. Postgraduate students (so, clever young adults) appear more influential than they are worldly. Miss Marple's aphorisms aside, that is the reverse of how young people had appeared even earlier in the 1950s, for example in *They Do It with Mirrors*. The presentation of Mr. Akibombo, as a childishly naive but very clever man who needs to be coached not only in English but also basic socializing, is outright offensive, and shows Christie's limitations as a novelist rather than broadening her reach, as she and her publishers had intended.

Hickory Dickory Dock was published in 1955 by Collins in the United Kingdom and by Dodd, Mead in the United States, following abridged serializations in *John Bull* and *Collier's*. It has been dramatized for television twice: as part of *Agatha Christie's Poirot* in 1995 and as part of *Les Petits Meurtres d'Agatha Christie* in 2015. Around 1963, a script and score were completed for a stage musical, *Death Beat*, which was to star Peter Sellers as Poirot. However, no production was ever mounted.

Characters: **Akibombo, Mr.**; Ali, Achmed; **Austin, Celia**; **Bateson, Leonard ("Len")**; Bultrout, Miss; Chandra Lal, Mr.; **Chapman, Nigel**; Cobb, Sergeant; Combe, Alice; Endicott, Mr.; **Finch, Sally**; **George(s)**; Geronimo; Halle, Rene; **Hobhouse, Valerie**; Hubbard, Mrs.; **Johnston, Elizabeth**; Jones, Montagu; **Lane, Patricia ("Pat")**; **Lemon, Felicity**; Lucas, Mrs.; **Nicoletis, Christina**; Maria; McNabb, Colin; McRae, Detective Constable; **Poirot, Hercule**; Ram, Gopal; Reinjeer, Miss; Robinson, William; Sharpe, Inspector; Stanley, Nigel; Stanley, Sir Arthur; Tomlinson, Jean

See also: **Agatha Christie's Poirot; Death Beat; Nursery Rhymes; Les Petits Meurtres d'Agatha Christie**

Hicks, Annie. See Annie

Hicks, Rosalind (1919–2004)

The only daughter of Christie, Rosalind was born on 5 August 1919. She enjoyed a close but often fraught relationship with her mother, and their disagreements are sometimes borne out in Christie's accounts of quarrels between parents and daughters in, for instance, "The Capture of Cerberus" (1947), *Curtain*, and *A Daughter's a Daughter*. Rosalind married Major Hubert Prichard in 1940, and they had one son, Mathew, in 1943, a year before Major Prichard died in action during World War II. In 1949, she married solicitor Anthony Hicks, with whom she lived until her death in 2004.

Extremely protective of her mother's reputation and legacy, Rosalind was well-known for her strongly worded opinions both before and after her mother's death. Sometimes, the two clashed professionally, most notably over the question of staging *Fiddlers Five*. Throughout the 1980s and 1990s, she vetoed most media proposals for Christie's work and often clashed with producers to whom permission had been granted over how they should proceed. She held a 36 percent stake in Agatha Christie Ltd. that controlled the rights to most of Christie's work. Her mother personally gifted her the copyright to *Curtain* and the playscript *A Daughter's A Daughter,* the latter of which she refused to release or license, partly because of its presentation of a troubled mother-daughter relationship.

See also: **Agatha Christie Ltd.; Christie, Colonel Archibald; *A Daughter's a Daughter* (novel); *A Daughter's a Daughter* (play); Prichard, Mathew**

Hickson, Joan (1906–98)

In many eyes the definitive screen Miss Marple, Joan Hickson played the role on television in the BBC's *Miss Marple* series (1982–92). She also narrated several audiobooks. Hickson, a character actor, is often said to have been Christie's own pick for the role, a story that stems from a letter Christie wrote her in the 1940s, suggesting she would float Hickson for the role if she ever wrote a Miss Marple play. When she took the role, Hickson had already appeared in cameo roles in three Christie films: *Love from a Stranger* (1937), *Murder She Said* (1962), and *Why Didn't They Ask Evans?* (1980). She had also had a stage role in *Appointment with Death* (1945) and a varied non–Christie career, including in the *Carry On* films. Hickson was made an Officer of the Order of the British Empire (OBE) in 1987, upon which occasion Queen Elizabeth II is thought to have said it was especially for her portrayal of Miss Marple.

See also: *Miss Marple* (television series)

Hidden Horizon. See *Murder on the Nile*

Higgs, Mr.

In both versions of "The Capture of Cerberus," Mr. Higgs is an "odoriferous" dog-keeper (CC 444). In the 1940 version, he is a dog-stealer, and in the 1947 version, he is a dog-handler.

Hill, Florence

Faithful Florence Hill is a favored maid of Miss Marple's in *4.50 from Paddington* and *The Mirror Crack'd from Side to Side*.

Hill, Gladys. See **Gladys**

Hindai Tokkyū Satsujin-jiken. See **TV Asahi Adaptations**

Hinchcliffe, Miss ("Hinch"), and Murgatroyd, Amy

In *A Murder Is Announced*, Miss Hinchcliffe and Amy Murgatroyd cohabit a cottage in Chipping Cleghorn. Their relationship plays out along traditional gendered lines, with Hinch in slacks, her hair in a "manlike crop" (15), striking many "a manly stance" (60) and the "fat and amiable" Murgatroyd (16) being twittery and dependent. The couple has the strongest romantic bond in the novel and, when Murgatroyd is murdered, Hinch's heartbreak is described vividly.

The presentation of a lesbian couple in this explicitly postwar novel is significant. Christie toyed with featuring a male-male couple in one of her next books, *Mrs. McGinty's Dead*, but never did so. Although Hinch and Murgatroyd are only ever called "friends," the nature of their relationship is beyond question and has been played up

in some screen adaptations, while other dramatizations have cut the characters out altogether. In the 1940s and 1950s, British magazine culture was full of stories about women loving (or even marrying) women. With frequent stories of couples—one manly, one feminine—living in villages, as Alison Oram points out in *Her Husband Was a Woman!*, a "postwar shift" was in play (Oram 139). Accounts of female-female couples following World War I had emphasized novelty and sometimes patriotism, as trans men or women dressed as men were presented as people trying to pass for male to serve their country. By contrast, there were no such stories in and after World War II (133), and these couples tended to be pathologized, with lesbianism represented in the media and literature as "a psychiatric problem" (143). Christie's presentation of the pair as a real, flawed, loving, and ultimately human couple, is therefore remarkable.

"His Lady's Affair." See **"The Case of the Discontented Husband"**

Hjerson, Sven

In Christie's fictional universe, Ariadne Oliver is the creator of Sven Hjerson, a gangling vegetarian Finnish private detective. Hjerson, a source of embarrassment to Mrs. Oliver, is immensely popular with her readers, but she feels immensely frustrated with him (see: **Oliver, Ariadne**). It takes no imaginative leap to see the character as a device for Christie to share frustrations about her own relationship with Hercule Poirot. The (nonexistent) books in which Hjerson appears include *The Dying Goldfish*, *The Affair of the Second Goldfish*, and *The Cat It Was Who Died*. Hjerson is mentioned by Mrs. Oliver in *Cards on the Table*, *Mrs. McGinty's Dead*, *Dead Man's Folly*, *The Pale Horse*, *Third Girl*, and *Hallowe'en Party*. He is mentioned by other characters in *The Clocks*.

In 1990, H.R.F. Keating published a Hjerson story, "Jack Fell Down," in the style of Poirot stories, as part of a Christie centenary celebration. In 2021, a new Anglo-German-Swedish television series, *Agatha Christie's Sven Hjerson*, set in the modern day, was announced.

Hobhouse, Valerie

Valerie Hobhouse is a young businesswoman lodging with the postgraduate students on Hickory Road in *Hickory Dickory Dock*. A coldly professional type, she is secretly highly involved in smuggling and has many aliases, including Mrs. da Silver, Irene French, Olga Kohn, Nina Le Mesurier, Gladys Thomas, Moira O'Neele, Madame Mahmoudi, and Sheila Donovan.

The idea of a businessperson using international work trips as cover for illegal activities is as old as international work trips, but Christie's decision to make the active player in this smuggling ring a woman shows an effort to change with the times. Unlike Dr. Sarah King in *Appointment with Death* or even Angela Warren in *Five Little Pigs*, Valerie never attracts any comment by posing as a high-flying professional woman. Indeed, the idea is presented as so normal that she is able to use her job as a cover, something career-minded women in Christie's earlier texts would not have been able to do.

A Holiday for Murder. See *Hercule Poirot's Christmas*

Holland, Elsie

In *The Moving Finger*, she is a beautiful governess to the Symmingtons' children, and has absolutely no personality. As protagonists Jerry and Joanna Burton point out, she lacks sex appeal, an undefinable attractive quality that the plain Megan Hunter possesses. Nonetheless, Richard Symington is sufficiently attracted to her to murder his wife, showing that lust is a symptom, not a cause, of his mid-life crisis.

The Hollow (novel; alternative titles: *Murder after Hours*; *The Outraged Heart*)

An unusual novel, *The Hollow* was published in 1946, advertised in the blurb as "a human story about human people." It is unlike other Christie novels because it is like the first half of one novel and the second half of another, combined. Indeed, the first 10 chapters could easily belong to a Mary Westmacott narrative, and Poirot only arrives in chapter 11.

The book is dedicated to actor Francis L. Sullivan, who had played Hercule Poirot on stage and screen, and his wife Frances

Perkins ("Danae"), "with apologies for using their swimming pool as the scene of a murder." Christie was great friends with the Sullivans, and often escaped London during World War II to spend time with them, being particularly struck by their outdoor swimming pool. Appropriately, the crime scene that occurs at such a pool in this novel is extremely theatrical.

The eccentric, absent-minded Lady Lucy Angkatell and her husband, Sir Henry, are hosting a weekend get-together at their country house, the Hollow. Among the guests are the womanizing Dr. John Christow; his downtrodden wife, Gerda; and his mistress, the modernist sculptor Henrietta Savernake. Also present are numerous Angkatells and extended relatives. Hercule Poirot is to arrive soon. At the property, the party is surprised by the arrival of glamorous actress Veronica Cray, who is staying at a nearby property and who turns out to be an old flame of John Christow's. Passions ignite.

Arriving at the Hollow, Poirot sees something so "highly artificial" he assumes it is a "cheap" joke (93–94): Dr. Christow lies aside an outdoor swimming pool, his blood trickling into it. Over his body stands his wife, holding a gun, and the rest of the household is standing around. It looks too theatrical to be true but, Poirot realizes, it is real. Before he dies, Christow says one word—"Henrietta" (95)—and Henrietta seizes the gun from Gerda, flinging it into the pool. Although it looks like Gerda shot her husband, she insists she just found the gun and picked it up. The gun she was holding turns out not to have been the one that killed her husband, but a second weapon, the correct one, is found in a basket of eggs.

As Poirot investigates, all kinds of contrived and theatrical clues appear, seeming to implicate most members of the family and even the stately butler, Gudgeon, in turn. It turns out that the family members are implicating themselves deliberately, to throw suspicion off the real killer: Gerda. Christow's last word was a plea to Henrietta to look after his wife. Guilty over how she has been treated, and for the sake of her children, the household has conspired to cover for her. Poirot confronts Gerda, who quietly commits suicide, and it is agreed that the truth will not come out. However, the previously creatively blocked Henrietta is now able to produce a masterpiece of modernist sculpture, underscored by real human emotion.

Writing about *The Hollow*, Owen Dudley Edwards has suggested that the title has its roots in Alfred Tennyson's "Maud—A Monodrama":

I hate the dreadful hollow behind the little wood,
Its lips in the field above are dabbled with blood-
    red heath,
The red-ribbed ledges drip with a silent horror of
    blood,
And Echo there whatever is asked her, answers
    "Death." [Tennyson 281]

According to Edwards, the novel uses this poem as a reference point for Christie to "work ... through the disappointment, heartbreak and suffering of her personal life via the cute and beguiling morals of the whodunnit" (n.p.). He adds that the surname "Christow" belonging to the victim and killer, provides an "obvious" clue to emotional source material. "Agatha Christie's detective stories," he writes, "are often ... inspired by the triangular relationship destroying her marriage to Colonel Archie Christie who deserted their home in 1926 for Nancy Neele" (n.p.). When Gerda confesses in *The Hollow*, it is difficult not to link the emotional content with accounts of Christie's divorce in her autobiography, the pseudonymous *Unfinished Portrait*, and indeed *Five Little Pigs* (published in 1943, where the victim is the significantly-initialed Amyas Crale):

> It was all a lie—everything! All the things I thought he was. I saw his face when he followed that woman out that evening.... I'd trusted John. I'd believed in him—as though he were God. I thought he was the noblest man in the world. I thought he was everything that was fine and noble. And it was all a *lie*! I was left with nothing at all. I—I'd *worshipped* John! [*TH* 234; emphasis in original].

Last-minute penance from the adulterer and a collective effort to help the wife may well be considered a kind of fantasy. Christie did not explore the impact of adultery in much detail after *The Hollow*, except

(briefly but to great effect) in the play version of *Witness for the Prosecution* and the late novel *Endless Night*. This reading also affirms the reading by Nicholas Birns and Margaret Boe Birns of a "'hollow' quality of the characters reverberates back on to the estate" (160) and the latter's suggestion that the novel can be read as an emotional self-portrait (M. B. Birns 33).

Besides its emotional core, the novel has several subplots more typical to Christie's pre-war crime fiction. These include a young man being cured of socialist tendencies by falling in love with a good woman. With Henrietta Savernake, Christie celebrates modernism, describing the creative process in detail and showing raw, emotional content in abstract structures. This is also a feature of her early Westmacott novels and 1920s short fiction. Like the socialism subplot, it could be seen as an effort to evoke a time and setting before World War II, the effects of which were red raw in 1946. However, references to 1940s movie stars suggest a contemporary setting.

The Hollow also features an ill-judged anti-Semitic character portrait. It is difficult to disagree with the Council Against Intolerance in America, which wrote to Christie in 1948 and 1949 to object to the presentation of costumier Madame Alfred, a minor character who is described as a "vitriolic little Jewess" and "a Whitechapel Jewess with dyed hair and a voice like a corncrake" (126, 127). Calls to change these sentences to, for example, "vitriolic little woman" were ignored for no obvious reason, and although modern editions merely reference a "vitriolic voice," the "Whitechapel Jewess" comment remains. With the horrors of the Holocaust fresh public knowledge in the late 1940s, it is remarkable tone-deafness, and even more horrifying that on the heels of this criticism Christie wrote the character of Mitzi, a Holocaust survivor whose function is comic relief in *A Murder Is Announced*.

The Hollow was first published as a serial in the May 1946 *Collier's* in the United States, where it was titled *The Outraged Heart*. Later that year, it was published in book form (as *The Hollow*) by Collins in the United Kingdom and Dodd, Mead in the

United States. Some U.S. paperbacks have used the title *Murder after Hours*. Christie dramatized *The Hollow* as a stage play of the same name, omitting Poirot as had become her custom, in 1951. There have been two loose, big-screen adaptations, neither featuring Poirot: *Kiken na Onnatachi* (1985) in Japan and *Le Grand Alibi* (2008) in France. A British television version, part of *Agatha Christie's Poirot*, aired in 2004 and a French television version, part of *Les Petits Meurtres d'Agatha Christie*, aired in 2021.

Characters: **Alfrege, Madame**; **Angkatell, David, and Edward**; Angkatell, Geoffrey; **Angkatell, Lady Lucy, and Sir Henry**; **Christow, Dr. John, and Gerda**; Christow, Terence ("Terry"); Christow, Zena; Clark, Sergeant; **Collier/Collins, Beryl**; Crabtree, Mrs.; **Cray, Veronica**; Forrester, Mrs.; Grange, Inspector; **Gudgeon**; **Hardcastle, Midge**; Lewis, Miss; Mears, Mr.; Mears, Mrs.; Medway, Mrs.; Patterson, Elsie; Pearstock, Mrs.; **Poirot, Hercule**; Radley, Dr.; Tremlet; Saunders, Doris; **Savernake, Henrietta**; Simmons, Miss

See also: *Agatha Christie's Poirot*; Anti-Semitism;*Le Grand Alibi*; *Kiken na Onnatachi*; *Les Petits Meurtres d'Agatha Christie*; Theatricality

The Hollow (play; alternative title: *The Suspects*)

Christie adapted *The Hollow* (1946) for the stage ca. 1948, largely fueled by dissatisfaction with other people's dramatizations of her work. She adapted it at her daughter Rosalind's home in Wales and offered it to producer Bertie Meyer, who declined it and gave it to Peter Saunders. Saunders brought on board Hubert Gregg, most famous for having written "Maybe it's Because I'm a Londoner," to direct it. Christie, Gregg, and Saunders would become inextricably linked over the next decade or so, to the extent that her name and that of *The Mousetrap* dominate the titles of both men's autobiographies. Gregg would later claim, with little evidence, that he had effectively to rewrite *The Hollow* to make it performable.

The plot follows that of the novel fairly closely, preserving the central drama and underlying relationships. As would become usual, Christie removed Poirot from the story—not a difficult matter on this occasion, as he makes a late appearance in the novel. Christie was keen that comedy should not dominate too much and flatly refused to include Poirot, although Saunders urged her that a "personality" would be useful. To address this, character actress Jeanne de Casalis was (mis)cast in the role of the eccentric Lady Angkatell. The play opened on 7 June 1951 at the Fortune Theatre, London.

Characters: **Angkatell, Edward**; Angkatell, Henrietta; **Angkatell, Lady Lucy, and Sir Henry**; **Christow, Dr. John, and Gerda**; Colquhoun, Inspector; **Cray, Veronica**; Doris; **Gudgeon**; **Hardcastle, Midge**; Penny, Detective Sergeant

See also: *The Hollow* (novel)

Holmes, Gladys. See **Gladys**

Homosexuality

For decades, a myth surrounded Christie to the effect that she did not write about homosexuality or sexual deviancy of any kind. Twenty-first-century scholarship and a revisionist approach in screen adaptations have given the lie to this approach. However, there is no critical consensus on Christie's approach to the topic of homosexuality.

The "type" of Christie character most readily associated with homosexuality is the artistic, effeminate male. Such men appear steadily throughout the canon, with the first appearance in "The Double Clue" (1924) and the last being a "pansy type" in *The Rats* (1963). With the exception of the character in *The Rats*, none of these men is guilty of whatever crime is under investigation. They are, instead, the obvious suspects because they are presented as undesirable company for the more strait-laced protagonists.

Some LGBTQ⁺ scholars have argued that Christie's presentations of gay stereotypes are casually homophobic (Altman). However, others maintain that Christie uses the expectation of prejudice on the part of her readers to narrative advantage: if a man in particular is read as gay or queer, readers who suspect him of guilt on that score alone will have their presumptions checked when his effeminacy proves a red herring (Bernthal, *Ageless*). In *Murder on the Orient*

Express, the real murderers invent an imaginary suspect—a small man "with a womanish voice"—to distract investigators, and in *The Moving Finger*, the hero's sister is so keen to suspect the "born gossip" Mr. Pye, despite the fact that the murderer is believed to be an unmarried woman, justifying her suspicions on the grounds that "Mr. Pye *is* a middle-aged spinster" (47, 195, emphasis in original). One of Christie's recurring detective-sidekicks, the "effeminate" art collector Mr. Satterthwaite, also falls into this camp. Satterthwaite's position outside of conventional masculinity and other characters' prejudice enable him, like Poirot, to see investigations from a unique angle.

Some "womanish" men are, apparently, punished by heroes for their abnormalities. In "The Double Clue," Poirot frames the lisping Bernard Parker for theft, because he—Poirot—has developed romantic feelings for the real thief, Vera Rossakoff. In *Murder Is Easy*, the hero, after trying and failing to prove the unwholesome antiques dealer Mr. Elsworthy guilty of murder, informs the police that Elsworthy is hosting satanic orgies, and gloats over the upsetting possibilities in store for that young man. However, Christie's later uses of the same stereotype are more nuanced. In *The Mousetrap*, a neurotic and fashionable youth who makes the protagonist's husband uncomfortable is revealed to be a victim of both prejudice and trauma. He is also revealed to be a war hero.

Male homosexual activity is directly alluded to once. The eponymous baron in *Lord Edgware Dies* treats his wife with indifference and sadism. Hastings catches him at the beginning of an assignation with his butler, Alton, who resembles a Greek god, and he is presented as something of a gothic monster, with "lips … drawn back from the teeth in a snarl, the eyes … alive with … insane rage" (33). Hastings wonders at the man's depraved double-life, and this character, who is murdered, is judged more harshly by the narrative than men who simply do not go through with marriage and courtship.

Many of Christie's women are manly, but this does not denote homosexuality. The one indisputable instance of a same-sex relationship in Christie concerns two women in *A Murder Is Announced*. A Miss Marple mystery, the novel concerns a post-war village in which nobody knows who their neighbors really are. Practically the only villagers who are not living under false names are Miss Hinchcliffe and Miss Murgatroyd, who cohabit on a farm. Hinchcliffe is described as "man-like" and "her friend" is "fat and amiable" (13). The latter treats the former as a lord-and-master. The couple appears like a middle-aged heterosexual couple, except that they are both women. At the time Christie wrote, several newspapers were running stories about women who had married each other during World War II, most presenting the couples along similar lines (Oram). When Murgatroyd is murdered, Hinchcliffe vows vengeance in the novel's most emotionally powerful scene. Christie's presentation of a lesbian couple is not ostensibly polemical, but the fact that she presents a same-sex couple whose shared sex has nothing to do with their narrative function is notable.

In the final Marple novel, *Nemesis*, the teenaged Verity Hunt is killed by her adoptive mother, Clotilde Bradbury-Scott, who is incensed that Verity has fallen in love with a young man and not with Clotilde herself. Miss Marple explains that Verity "wanted a normal life" but that Clotilde "loved her too much" and so became "depraved" and killed her (328, 329). The emphasis on the "normality" of heterosexual romance has been criticized. However, the novel is a reworking of the then-unpublished *Sleeping Murder*, the incestuous desire at the heart of which is a man's for his younger half-sister. It is the familial power dynamic between the two women, and not the matter of their shared gender, that the narrative condemns as an abnormal foundation for sexual passion.

Between 2004 and 2013, the British television network ITV released several episodes of *Agatha Christie's Poirot* and *Agatha Christie's Marple* featuring explicitly homosexual characters, rewriting the solutions to some mysteries to make the villains gay men or lesbians. To assist screenwriters, the Christie estate employed a researcher to discover characters who might be identified as gay or lesbian in the books. The producers—and the Christie estate—defended the move of bringing characters out of the closet and explicitly identifying them as homosexual; Christie's grandson, Mathew Prichard, claimed: "If you read the books carefully, it's all there. This is just more overt" (qtd. in Bernthal, *Queering* 238).

However, Christie herself had little desire to engage with homosexuality beyond its usefulness as a tool for misdirecting readers. In the permissive 1960s, her self-consciously conservative narratives poke fun at younger people thinking they have discovered sexual diversity. A trendy novelist in *A Caribbean Mystery* seeks and fails to shock his aunt by stating that "a queer" is looking after his house (4), and in *Hallowe'en Party*, a young boy tries to show his worldliness by speculating that a schoolmistress might be a "lesbian" (177). Using the vocabulary of sexual diversity and mocking its use, Christie challenges the idea that her own work is out of touch. She does not present, as some commentators have suggested, a world in which homosexuality does not exist, but rather a world blinded by taxonomies and snap judgments. See also: *Agatha Christie's Marple*; *Agatha Christie's Poirot*; "The Double Clue"; Ellsworthy, Mr.; *Hallowe'en Party*; Hinchcliffe, Miss, and Murgatroyd, Amy; *The Mousetrap*; *The Moving Finger*; *Murder Is Announced* (novel); *The Rats*; Satterthwaite, Mr.

Hope, Evelyn. See **Upward, Robin**

Hopkins, Nurse Jessie

Jessie Hopkins is a calm and competent district nurse in *Sad Cypress*, whose sensible demeanor contrasts the earthy frivolity of Nurse O'Brien. She is revealed to be Mary Draper, an Australian aunt of Mary Gerrard's, in disguise and plotting a series of murders for inheritance. In this war-conscious novel, her role as the murderer symbolizes a growing distrust of the security and authority represented by nurses.

Horbury, Lady Cicely, and Lord Stephen

Lady Cicely Horbury is a cocaine-addled countess and Lord Stephen her cuckolded husband, presumably the Earl of Horbury, in *Death in the Clouds*.

Horbury, Sidney

Sidney Horbury is the unsavory valet to Simeon Lee in *Hercule Poirot's Christmas*, he appears to help the police but is self-evidently afraid of them. He is likely involved in blackmail.

Hori

A family scribe, Hori is caught between both sides of family quarrels, as he must write the letters between family members in *Death Comes as the End*. He works closely with Renisenb to identify the murderer and is in love with her. Christie initially considered making him a lawyer and/or the narrator.

"The Horses of Diomedes" (alternative title: "The Case of the Drug Peddler"). See *The Labours of Hercules*

"The Hound of Death" (story)

The title story in *The Hound of Death* (1933) appears in the U.S. anthology *The Golden Ball* (1971). If it was published in magazine form, likely in the 1920s, this has not been traced. Either way, it was probably written earlier, when Christie was experimenting with form and genre. It is set just after World War I. A supernatural story, it concerns a Belgian nun who possesses supernatural powers and may have knowledge of the end of the world.

The narrator, Anstruther, learns of Sister Mary Angelique from an American journalist. He hears about her powers, which brought down a lightning bolt in Belgium, killing German soldiers and leaving a mark that resembled a hound. He also hears that Sister Marie Angelique is in Cornwall, where Anstruther is visiting his sister. In Cornwall, he meets Dr. Rose, currently tending to the nun, who speaks of her strange visions, of a hound and the end of the world. After both Rose and the nun, along with Rose's wealthy uncle, die in a surprise natural disaster, Anstruther wonders if mysterious forces are at work. He learns that Rose had been trying to harness the nun's powers to kill his uncle and hold power over death. However, he consciously decides that it is all a coincidence, to avoid thinking about the alternative.

The story has obvious echoes of what would come in Europe—Nazi attempts to harness esoteric powers and assure world dominance. It also looks back to stories from World War I such as the story of the Angel of Mons, appearing over Belgian battlefields to assist British soldiers in 1914. "The Hound of Death" was dramatized for BBC Radio 4 in 2002.

Characters: Anstruther, Mis; Anstruther, Mr.; Ryan, William P.; **Marie Angelique, Sister**; Rose, Dr.

See also: **BBC Radio Adaptations; Christianity; Curses; *The Hound of Death* (story collection); War**

The Hound of Death (story collection; alternative title: *The Hound of Death and Other Stories*)

This unusual collection of (mostly) supernatural stories was first published by Odhams Press as part of a promotional series. Readers of the magazine *The Passing Show* collected coupons and sent them off with seven shillings to receive one of six books. As well as *The Hound of Death*, they could receive titles by Edgar Rice Burroughs, May Edington, Marjorie Bowen, John Rhode, or George Goodchild. As a promotional book and one not under a Collins contract, *The Hound of Death*, with a cover illustration by Dermonay, was not published in the United States.

The Hound of Death collects many of Christie's earlier works that were not considered commercially viable. Although several had appeared in magazines, they tended to be reworkings of her juvenilia, and most are not conventional crime stories. The exception is "The Witness for the Prosecution," which would go on to have a life of its own through successful adaptations in a variety of media. In 1936, William Collins acquired the rights to publish its own commercial edition of *The Hound of Death*, identical to the Odhams one, via a deal allowing Odhams to reproduce the latest Christie collection, *Murder in the Mews*.

The collection contains the following stories (U.S. book publications in parentheses): "**The Hound of Death**" (*The Golden Ball*, 1971), "**The Red Signal**" (*The Witness for the Prosecution*, 1948), "**The Fourth Man**" (*The Witness for the Prosecution*), "**The Gipsy**" (*The Golden Ball*), "**The Lamp**" (*The Golden Ball*), "**Wireless**" (*The Witness for the Prosecution*), "**The Witness for the Prosecution**" (*The Witness for the Prosecution*), "**The Mystery of the Blue Jar**" (*The Witness for the Prosecution*), "**The Strange Case of Sir Arthur Carmichael**" (*The Golden Ball*), "**The Call of Wings**" (*The Golden Ball*), "**The Last Séance**" (*Double Sin*, 1961), and "S.O.S." (*The Witness for the Prosecution*).

"The House at Shiraz" (story; alternative titles: "At the House in Shiraz"; "The Dream House of Shiraz")

The third of Parker Pyne's "Arabian" adventures, "The House at Shiraz" is regarded by Christie scholar Charles Osborne as the most "psychologically penetrating" (119). In the story, Pyne is in Shiraz (now Tehran) investigating the mystery of an English aristocrat who has become a local recluse. He learns that she fell in love with a German pilot many years ago, but after her maid died, she secluded herself. Later, he realizes that it was the opposite: Lady Esther Carr became insane and died; her maid, Muriel King, has been living as her in seclusion. A clue here is that the lady's "dark flashing eyes" (*PPI* 165) betray her: Lady Carr's parents were both blue-eyed so could not have had a dark-eyed daughter.

The story was published with other Pyne short stories under the title *Have You Got Everything You Want? If Not, Consult Mr. Parker Pyne* in the United States in the April 1933 *Cosmopolitan*. In the United Kingdom, it appeared as "At the House in Shiraz," as the third section of *The Arabian Nights of Parker Pyne* in the June 1933 *Nash's Pall Mall Magazine*. It appeared in the anthology *Parker Pyne Investigates* in 1934.

Characters: Carr, Lady Esther; King, Muriel; **Parker Pyne, J.**; Schlagal, Herr

See also: *Parker Pyne Investigates*

"The House of Beauty" (story)

"The House of Beauty" is an unpublished short story written by a teenaged Christie under the name Mac Miller, "The House of Beauty" was later rewritten as "The House of Dreams." Christie identified it in her autobiography as her first promising work. On another occasion, she referred to the actual writing of the story as far more boring and mechanical than thinking up the plot. This original version has more heightened esoteric elements than the published one. It was typed up in purple ink on her sister Madge's Empire typewriter.

See also: **"The House of Dreams"**; Houses; Watts, Margaret ("Madge")

"The House of Dreams"

An expansion of "The House of Beauty," part of Christie's juvenilia, "The House of Dreams" was published in the *Sovereign Magazine* in January 1926. It tells the story of John Segrave, a city clerk who dreams repeatedly about a beautiful country house. When he falls in love with the unconventional Allegra Kerr, whom he tells of his dreams. She tells him she has nightmares, not dreams, and that she can never marry. John travels to West Africa and now his dreams of the house are interrupted by an unspecified, evil "Thing." Later, he learns that Allegra has madness in her family, and, ten years later, she dies in an asylum. By now, John has become obsessed with his dreams about the house. Obsessed with a desire to move into it, he dies.

The story has been compared to Edwardian ghost fiction, specifically that of E.F. Benson (39). It is certainly an example of Christie experimenting with imagery and metaphor, as complex feelings of guilt and responsibility John feels about Allegra manifest as introspection, obsession, and idealism. The story appeared in the U.K. anthology *While the Light Lasts* and the U.S. anthology *The Harlequin Tea Set* in 1997.

Characters: **Kerr, Allegra**; Segrave, John; Segrave, Sir Edward; Wetterman, Maisie; Wetterman, Rudolf

See also: *The Harlequin Tea Set* (story collection); "The House of Beauty"; *While the Light Lasts* (story collection).

"The House of Lurking Death." See *Partners in Crime* (story collection)

Houses

In Christie's writing, houses reflect their inhabitants, something that becomes more pronounced over time. Houses and their grounds formed self-contained worlds in Christie's childhood. As a girl who let her imagination run wild in the gardens of Ashgate in Torquay, she would visit friends in similarly grand homes, which were her introductions to their own equally extensive worlds. She was not formally educated in a boarding school, so her introduction to the world was through the lens of the family home.

Christie formed deep attachments to many of her residences and reflected this kind of feeling in her early work. Houses become obsessions—dangerously so—in "The House of Beauty" and *Peril at End House*. In the latter, End House, a crumbling, unsustainable old mansion, is a motive for murder. Its owner kills to obtain enough money to support the house. At the same time, Christie wrote about country houses—the type of house most readily identified with her work—but less often than is typically thought. Indeed, the country house was already a cliché of the genre when Christie wrote *The Mysterious Affair at Styles*: the setting helps establish the novel and Hercule Poirot *within* a canon. It is, fundamentally, a useful setting: it allows for a range of characters mostly from the same social class, in a closed setting, often meeting for a weekend. This enables a limited number of suspects, a neat time-frame, and a mappable location for puzzle plots, especially locked-room mysteries.

Nonetheless, Christie defended writing about country houses, betraying a certain class insularity by seeming unable to differentiate "a country house" from "a house": "You *have* to be concerned with a house: with where people *live* … it must be a background that readers will recognize, because explanations are so boring … a country house is obviously best" (qtd. in Wyndham E5; emphasis in original). There is, in this explanation, a definite closedness in the choice of setting, beyond the number of suspects: it is a closed-minded worldview that assumes readers belong to the author's social class—although, one could argue, as long as they are participating in the narrative by reading it, they do.

Even so, a Christie country house is not, as many commentators have hinted, an old-fashioned country house, closed off from the real world in a haze of aspirational nostalgia. Charlotte Charteris points out (91): "Critics have come, particularly within the context of the country house setting ... to associate Christie almost exclusively with the 'closed' and 'closely related society' proscribed by W.H. Auden," but this misses the fact that Christie's country houses are always presented as relics, struggling to survive in the modern world. Styles Court, for instance, has adapted into a "war household" (22). The grandest and most lavishly-upkept country estate in Christieland is Chimneys, in *The Secret of Chimneys* and *The Seven Dials Mystery* (both comic novels betraying the influence of P.G. Wodehouse). Even these relics of older times, however, are presented as overrun by Bright Young Things, using the secret passages and endless grounds to hedonistic ends.

In the post–World War II novels, the grand houses that have survived have been forced to adapt. Thus *Crooked House* (1949) and *They Do It with Mirrors* (1952) both feature once-grand buildings that have been added to rather than maintained: architecturally, they are inconsistent, and both the Gables in *Crooked House* and Stoneygates in *They Do It with Mirrors* are overcome with bindweed. This symbolizes the stifled nature of the ever-diversifying families living within them, unprepared to face the real world. Gossington Hall, at the heart of Miss Marple's village St. Mary Mead, is so traditional and old-fashioned that it is a scene of the parodic, deliberately clichéd *The Body in the Library* in 1942, but 20 years later, it is shown to have been bought and gaudily refurbished by Hollywood actors trying to make a show of being English homemakers—on modern, American terms, of course—in *The Mirror Crack'd from Side to Side*.

By 1957, in *4.50 from Paddington*, the country estate is a noted anachronism. The family home in that novel is located in an apparently timeless and spaceless vacuum, cut off from the nearest village and the nearest town, and almost a world unto itself. It is ruled by an idiosyncratic elderly hypochondriac, sustained by his

family's former glory in the world of biscuit manufacturing. Its grounds consist of "a lot of unused old buildings; broken down pig sties, harness rooms, workshops that nobody ever goes near" (*450FP* 52). There is no sense of nostalgic opulence about the country house.

Instead, there is a focus on building and rebuilding. In *Endless Night*, published in 1967, a house once again provides a motive for murder. However, Mike Rogers does not kill, as Nick Buckley does, to maintain a family property, but to establish one. He wants to build his dream house on cursed land, and it is this ambition that spurs him to marriage, and affair, and murder. The sleek, modern house on compromised foundations once again reflects its owner.

See also: **Ashfield;** *Endless Night* **(novel); Greenway House; "The House of Beauty";** *Peril at End House* **(novel); Styles House; Winterbrook House**

"How Does Your Garden Grow?" (story)

This 1935 Hercule Poirot story features Miss Lemon in her first appearance as the detective's secretary, although she had already featured as Parker Pyne's secretary. Here, she is described in extensive detail, as an angular modernist accessory: a very modern woman whose aim seems to be to become an unthinking machine. Nonetheless, missing Hastings' "romantic mind" very much (*PEC* 249), Poirot appeals to her imagination to help him solve the case. The case concerns a woman poisoned with strychnine: the problem is that everybody ate and drank the same thing that evening. Because he spots an uneven display of oyster shells in the garden, Poirot determines that she was given poisoned oysters in private, and the shells were hidden in plain sight. He identifies the murderers and acts as a much-needed "friend" to the victim's rough-mannered maid, who is the police's main suspect.

Although Miss Lemon's two-dimensional presentation is shown to be an affectation—she is, Poirot knows, "capable of human emotion" but does her best to repress it (239), the story is a good example of Christie using stereotypes. The benevolent but suspicious old spinster is as straightforward a character as the surly maid who finds herself torn between "distrust of a foreigner" and "the pleasurable enjoyment of her class in" gossiping to Poirot (241). However, the implied reader's natural prejudice will be against the servant and will not view middle-class young lovers with suspicion. When Poirot reveals that these are the murderers and that the maid is not only innocent but also entitled to her inheritance, the narrative twist is enforced by the unspoken prejudices that form the basis of Christie's characterization.

The story was published in 1935 in *Ladies' Home Journal* in the United States and *The Strand* in the United Kingdom. It appeared in the U.S. anthology *The Regatta Mystery* (1939) and the U.K. anthology *Poirot's Early Cases* (1974). A television adaptation aired on ITV on 6 January 1991 as part of *Agatha Christie's Poirot*. A jigsaw puzzle based on the story was released by Paul Lamond Games in 2001. On 23 July 2006, SWR in Germany broadcast a radio adaptation as part of *Krimi-Sommer mit Hercule Poirot*.

Characters: Barrowby, Amelia; Delafontaine, Henry; **Delafontaine, Mary**; **Lemon, Felicity**; **Poirot, Hercule**; Rieger, Katrina; Rudge; **Sims, Inspector**

See also: *Agatha Christie's Poirot*; *Games*; *Krimi-Sommer mit Hercule Poirot*; **Nursery Rhymes**; *Poirot's Early Cases*; *The Regatta Mystery* (story collection)

"How I Became a Writer"

"How I Became a Writer" was a Christie essay published in *The Listener* in August 1938, likely to promote the movie *Love from a Stranger* (1938), for which the magazine printed production stills. The content is similar to the commonly-reproduced introduction to *Appointment with Death*. It was part of a series of articles by popular authors, under the banner *I Became a Writer*.

See also: "Hercule Poirot: Fiction's Greatest Detective"; *Love from a Stranger*, Screen Adaptations of

"How I Created Hercule Poirot." See "Hercule Poirot—Fiction's Greatest Detective"

Howard, Evelyn ("Evie")

Evelyn Howard is Emily Inglethorpe's manly, stentorian friend with a telegraphic style of speech in *The Mysterious Affair at Styles*. She is presented as extremely masculine so that the reader will not suspect she is having an affair with anyone, let alone with Emily's husband. However, Poirot later reveals that the extent of Evelyn's and Alfred's animosity was such that it *had* to be performative.

Hubbard, Caroline

When she has been unmasked as veteran stage actress Linda Arden in *Murder on the Orient Express*, Hercule Poirot claims that "Mrs. Hubbard" has been this woman's greatest role. An obnoxious American tourist who talks incessantly, she seems annoying but not sinister—a cover for a ringleader in a revenge plot to kill Samuel Ratchett. Unlike her Caroline Hubbard persona, Linda Arden is a tragic, heartbroken figure, who has not been able to recover from the murder of Daisy Armstrong and its traumatic aftermath. She has been played on stage by some highly distinguished performers, including Lauren Bacall in 1974 and Michelle Pfeiffer in 2017.

Hudd, Georgina ("Gina")

The granddaughter of Carrie Louise Serrocold in *They Do It with Mirrors*: her mother, Pippa San Severiano, was adopted, which causes her aunt, Mildred Strete, to resent Gina as an intruder into the family. She is half–Italian and is married to all-American Walter Hudd but flirts with the Restarick brothers. Only Carrie Louise sees that, despite Gina's behavior, she is clearly in love with her husband. Gina represents the young, modern woman who is not overly attached to her roots—she drives fast cars, kisses men to whom she is not married, and treats unfolding family drama as a joke. It is discovered that her biological family tree includes a notorious poisoner, but Gina turns out to be the product of her upbringing, not her heredity.

Hunt, Verity

Verity Hunt is the central victim in *Nemesis,* who died 16 years before the events of the novel. Like several of Christie's female victims, this character exists chiefly in the recollections of others, nearly all of whom construct her as the perfect victim: a kind, beautiful, pure young woman. Marple determines that she was killed by her possessive guardian, Clotilde Bradbury-Scott, because she wanted to get married. Her name, a combination of words for "truth" and "search," typifies her role in the novel as a symbol for imagined lost innocence. Tellingly, the body buried as hers belonged to somebody else; throughout *Nemesis*, she is denied her own story.

Hunter, David

A charming Irishman in *Taken at the Flood*, he represents the allure of danger, especially to Lynn Marchmont, who has grown frustrated with her fiancée, Rowley Cloade. When David suddenly—and unconvincingly—confesses to murder, he says "he had a good run for his money.... I'm a gambler—but I know when I've lost my last throw" (190).

Hunter, Megan

One of Christie's favorites of her own creations, Megan Hunter has not received critical attention, perhaps because her narrative arc in *The Moving Finger* appears problematic. Megan is 20 years old but acts and appears much younger. Her mother, Myrna Symmington, is "apologetic" about her, coddling her as being "at that awkward age [when she has] just left school but [not] properly grown up" (31). The narrator, Jerry Burton, notices at this point that Megan has not "just left school" but is already a woman. Megan's stepfather tends to forget that she exists. When she talks to Jerry, who supplies her with her first martini, Megan exhibits extreme naïveté but also an inquiring mind as she makes intelligent observations on Shakespeare, which Christie shared. Her social awkwardness, then, is a problem of her neglectful upbringing.

Toward the end of the novel, Miss Marple uses Megan as bait in a trap to catch the murderer—her stepfather—and she risks her life in the process. Jerry is so impressed that he takes her to London for a makeover and is struck by her beauty and dancing skills. The two marry and adopt a dog. The villagers are delighted that Megan has found her feet.

It is unsettling to read in the twenty-first century that a young woman can only have value and happiness when she is beautiful and married. However, the city of London represents independence from the world of an insular village, and it is clear that, despite her rather generic narrative arc, Megan has come into confidence and tapped into an existing spirit of independence, rather than dependence. After all, she acquires the dog without asking her husband's permission, and the novel closes with a wedding gift from Jerry's sister Joanna—a dog's lead and collar.

Portrayals on screen have more straightforwardly sided with the villagers, who see Megan transforming from an awkward girl into a sexy woman under the wing of an older boyfriend.

"The Hydra of Lernea." See **"The Lernean Hydra"**

"Hymn to Ra." See *The Road of Dreams* **(poetry collection)**

"I Wore My New Canary Suit." See *Poems*

"The Idol House of Astarte" (story; alternative titles: **"The Solving Six and the Evil Hour"**; **"The 'Supernatural' Murder"**). See *The Thirteen Problems*

Ils Étaient Dix. See *And Then There Were None*, **Screen Adaptations of**

Imhotep

A mortuary priest in *Death Comes as the End*, Imhotep is nominally the head of the house but is easily influenced by those around him. Christie initially sketched out the character as "old fusser—kindly—a nuisance" (Curran, *Secret Notebooks* 231) and stuck close to this.

"The Importance of a Leg of Mutton." See **"The Adventure of the Dartmoor Bungalow"**

"In a Dispensary." See *The Road of Dreams* **(poetry collection)**

"In a Glass Darkly" (story)

Written for radio broadcast but rejected by the BBC as too supernatural, "In a Glass Darkly" is an extremely strong example of the short story form. During World War I, the unnamed narrator is staying with friends. While he is dressing for dinner, he has a psychic vision, seeing in the mirror a man with a scar on the left side of his face strangling a beautiful woman. At dinner, he meets the other house guests, including his friend's sister, Sylvia Carslake, whom he recognizes from the vision. Her fiancé, Charles Crawley, is introduced—and he has a scar on the left side of his face.

Years pass, and, when the narrator delivers news to Sylvia that her brother was killed in action, he learns that she has broken off her engagement to Crawley. Determined to protect her from the fate he witnessed, the narrator, who has been wounded on the right side of his face, marries her. Eventually, they fall out of love, and when Sylvia meets an attractive man, Derek Wainwright, the narrator becomes jealous and violent. When he sees his reflection—and realizes the scar on the right of his face is reversed to the left in a mirror—he knows that the premonition was in fact a warning. He determines to treat Sylvia well.

This story was published in *Collier's* on 28 July 1934 and appeared in the U.S. collection *The Regatta Mystery* (1939) and the U.K. collection *Miss Marple's Final Cases* (1979). It has been dramatized twice: for television as part of *The Agatha Christie Hour* (broadcast on ITV on 14 September 1982) and in a modernized version for BBC Radio 4, broadcast on 24 February 2003.

Characters: Carslake, Alan; Carslake, Neil; Carslake, Sylvia; Crawley, Charles; Oldham, Major; Oldham, Mrs.; Wainwright, Derek

See also: *The Agatha Christie Hour*; BBC Radio Adaptations; *Miss Marple's Final Cases* (story collection); *The Regatta Mystery* (story collection)

"In Baghdad." See *Poems*

"In the Cool of the Evening." See *Star Over Bethlehem* (story/poetry collection)

"In the House of the Enemy." See *The Big Four* (novel)

"In the Market Place" (story)

A short story written under the name Sydney West when Christie was about 17, "In the Market Place" is a straightforward morality tale. A greedy man finds a magical marketplace that can give him anything he desires. He takes on many gifts and trinkets, returning twice but is still unhappy. Many years later, he returns, says he wants nothing, and is rewarded with real treasure. The manuscript is held in the Christie Family Archive. The author typed in purple ink and sent it to at least one magazine, which rejected it.

See also: **Pseudonyms**

"In the Third Floor Flat." See "The Third-Floor Flat"

"The Incident of the Dog's Ball" (story)

A short story later expanded into *Dumb Witness*, "The Incident of the Dog's Ball" was not published in Christie's lifetime. It is possible that, as with "Hercule Poirot and the Greenshore Folly," she saw potential to expand it and put it aside. Archivist John Curran, who published the story in 2009, suggests that it was written in 1932, although by this point stories featuring both Poirot and Captain Hastings were relatively uncommon: as Curran points out, most of these were written in 1923 or 1924 (*Secret Notebooks* 453–54).

The basic idea is the same in both story and novel: an old woman writes to Poirot for help, citing an incident with a dog's ball; he and Hastings arrive to find that she is dead; he investigates references to a picture being "ajar" and identifies a downtrodden niece as the murderer. Some characters and names are similar, too, in both manuscripts.

The story was discovered among the effects of Rosalind Hicks, Christie's daughter, after her death in 2004. To promote Curran's book, *Agatha Christie's Secret Notebooks*, in which the story appeared, "The Incident of the Dog's Ball" was published in *The Strand Magazine* in December 2009.

Characters: **Bob**; Davidson, Mollie; **Ellen**; Graham, James; **Hastings, Captain Arthur**; Lawrence, Dr.; **Lawson, Miss**; **Poirot, Hercule**; Pym sisters; Wheeler, Matilda

See also: **Dogs**; *Dumb Witness*

"The Incredible Theft" (novella)

"The Incredible Theft" is a novella expanded from "The Submarine Plans," in which Hercule Poirot is called to investigate the theft of government secrets and an apparent sighting of a ghost at the home of Lord Mayfield, an ambitious politician. There is anger at this: "Why drag in a foreigner we know nothing about?" (*MITM* 100). Relying more on his knowledge of human psychology than on physical evidence, Poirot unravels both mysteries: the ghost was the invention of a maid who had been sexually assaulted and wanted to explain her scream, whereas the documents were not stolen but hidden by Lord Mayfield, who was being blackmailed and pressured into handing them over to a foreign power. This novella casts a critical eye at patriotism.

The novella was first published in six parts in the *Daily Express*, from 6 April 1937. It was collected in *Murder in the Mews* that June. A BBC radio play of "The Incredible Theft" was broadcast on 10 May 1938 as part of *Detectives in Fiction*. Poirot was played by E.M. Stephan. In the United States, Harold Huber played Poirot in an adaptation for *Mystery of the Week* (1947–48). David Suchet played him in the relevant episode of *Agatha Christie's Poirot*, broadcast on ITV on 26 February 1989.

Characters: Carlile; Carrington, Air Marshall Sir George; Carrington, Lady Julia; Carrington, Reggie; Leonie; **Macatta, Mrs.**, McLaughlin, Sir Charles ("Lord Mayfield"); **Poirot, Hercule;** Vanderlyn, Mrs.

See also: *Agatha Christie's Poirot*; **BBC Radio Adaptations;** *Murder in the Mews* **(story collection);** *Mystery of the Week*; **"The Submarine Plans"**

Indian-Language Adaptations

In 1960, Premendra Mitra directed the first Bengali Christie film, *Chupi Chupi Aashey* (Silently He Comes), based on *The Mousetrap*. It starred Chhabi Biswas and Jahar Ganguly as the young couple based on Giles and Molly Ralston, and Tarun Kumar as Inspector Ghoshal, based on Sergeant Trotter. Popular singer Sandhya Mukhopadhyay sang an original song for the title sequence. This is the only known Indian-language Christie movie shot in black and white.

1965 saw the spectacular Bollywood effort, *Gumnaam* (Nameless), based on *And Then There Were None*. With a threadbare plot, lavish, colorful choreography,

and extensive dream sequences enabling extensive chorus singers to burst into the deserted mansion only to disappear, it remains highly popular with British and American audiences. The film was directed by Raja Nawathe and starred Manoj Kumar, Nanda, Pran, Helen, and Mehmood. Although it does not credit its source material—indeed, few films in this entry do—it is so popular and significant that it is frequently included in "official" lists of Christie adaptations, including those produced or endorsed by Agatha Christie Ltd.

A loose retelling of the story in Tamil appeared in 1970. Veena-player S. Balachander produced, directed, and composed the music for *Nadu Iravil* (In the Middle of the Night). This film was completed in quickly in 1965 to capitalize on the success of Balachander's 1964 thriller *Bonmai* but failed to find a distributor for five years. When it did, it was a modest success. It relocates the action to a domestic house and posits a link between all the suspects, which rather undermines the novel's main premises.

Almost as popular as *Gumnaam* in the United Kingdom is *Dhund* (The Fog), a 1973 Hindi film based on *The Unexpected Guest*. This has been remade in other Indian languages: *Tarka* (Logic, 1989) is a Kannada version with a less lavish set and more straightforward story-plot. *Puriyaadha Pudhir* (Mystifying Puzzle, 1990), a Tamil version, was a box-office flop. This film bears no relation to the 2017 hit of the same name. *Aar Ya Paar* (Now or Never), a 1997 Hindi film directed by Ketan Mehta, is sometimes cited as an unofficial adaptation of *Endless Night*, but it is more properly a version of James Hadley Chase's *The Sucker Punch*.

The 2003 Bengali film *Shubho Mahurat* (title roughly equivalent to "Break a Leg") is generally considered a hidden gem. Directed by Rituparno Ghosh and based on *The Mirror Crack'd from Side to Side*, it starred vert actress Raakhee as Ranga Pishima, the equivalent character to Miss Marple, with Nandita Das as her journalist niece. The film has received several accolades, and although it was screened in the United Kingdom on Channel 4 almost immediately, it has not been released commercially in the United Kingdom or the United States.

Christie adaptations gathered momentum in the 2010s. In 2011, Thakkali Srinivasan directed *Aduthathu* (Next), a Tamil film based on *And Then There Were None*, with the plot involving a survivor-themed reality television program, with the ten characters lured to the island for a competition. Controversially, the same premise was used for K.M. Chaitanya's 2015 Kannada version, *Aatagara* (Player). Although both directors have claimed that their versions of *And Then There Were None* are unique, there are several similarities in the two plots, both of which involved work by Kannan Parameshwaran.

A 2012 Malayalam take on *The ABC Murders*, B. Unnikrishnan's *Grandmaster* is only loosely connected to Christie, drawing equal influence from Henning Mankell's Kurt Wallander. This relatively successful thriller was the first Malayalam film to receive an international release on Netflix, and garnered two national awards. Subhurajit Mitra's 2016 Bengali film *Chorabali* (Quicksand) is an easily accessible adaptation of *Cards on the Table*. It stars Tarun Chanda, Sayani Datta, and Shataf Figar, turning the novel's Orientalist slant on its head by looking awry at the British Raj.

In 2020, director Vishal Bhardwaj read many Christie works and watched Alfred Hitchcock films during lockdowns imposed because of the COVID-19 pandemic. He approached Agatha Christie Ltd. for the rights to make a socially distanced film, one of the first officially licenses Indian adaptations, to shoot in 2021. This turned into a high-profile major deal for a multi-movie franchise featuring new characters in films inspired by various books. The inspiration for this model comes from the success of the French series *Bélisaire et Prudence Beresford* and *Les Petits Meurtres d'Agatha Christie*, although viewers can expect a very different tone.

See also: *The ABC Murders* (novel); *And Then There Were None* (novel); *Cards on the Table* (novel); *The Mirror Crack'd from Side to Side*; *The Unexpected Guest* (play)

Inez

Maria's beautiful daughter in "The Harlequin Tea Set," Inez is a young woman of the "dark Spanish type" (*PPB* 99). Mr. Satterthwaite seems to assume that because she is spending some time in a house with two attractive men—who happen to be her cousins—she will fall in love with one of them. He wonders which, but this idea goes nowhere.

Inglethorpe, Alfred

Alfred Inglethorpe is Emily's much younger husband who murders her in *The Mysterious Affair at Styles*. Christie spun Inglethorpe's character from the premise that she wanted her murderer to have a thick black beard. He does his best to incriminate himself, so that he will be charged and then acquitted when new evidence is released, exploiting the law against double jeopardy. Christie invented this character after deciding that the murderer in her first book should boast a big black beard.

Inglethorpe, Emily

Emily Inglethorpe is the matriarch of Styles Court and the murder victim in *The Mysterious Affair at Styles*. "Emily" appears to have been a suitably Victorian name for many of Christie's elderly female victims.

"Ingots of Gold" (story; alternative titles: "Miss Marple and the Golden Galleon"; "The Solving Six and the Golden Grave"). See *The Thirteen Problems*

The Innocent. See *Ordeal by Innocence* (novel)

"An Interview with Agatha Christie" (1966 interview)

An interview granted to Paul Carson to promote the 1965 movie *Ten Little Indians*, then opening in American cinemas, this was published in the *Gastonia Gazette* in North Carolina on 1 May 1966. In it, Christie reflects on the inadequacy of "low life brawls, naked passion," and "sensational" stories: "She won't read them, won't write them," Carson explains (42). "For her the mystery is the thing"—and the mystery belongs "in a polite leisured class setting." Christie reflects on her early, unpublished work, describing her efforts as "stories of unrelieved gloom" and praises Eden Phillpotts for mentoring her (42).

Asked if she would "stop writing if she could," Christie reiterates a common theme in early interviews: the idea that she writes purely for money: "Yes, of course, I would if I won the pools and could pay off all my back income tax. No one ever enjoyed writing. Far too much of an effort of concentration. In the evening you feel dead" (42). The interview was published with a now-famous photograph of Christie by Angus McBean, strangely altered to give the impression that she is smiling.

See also: *And Then There Were None, Screen Adaptations of*; **Phillpotts, Eden**

"An Interview with Agatha Christie" (1970 interview)

Christie's final years were spent at Winterbrook House, her home with Max Mallowan in Cholsey, Wallingford, Oxfordshire. Although she famously resisted interviews, she granted one in 1970 to a local schoolboy who knocked on her door and asked to interview her for his school magazine. Questions covered her influences (Sherlock Holmes), the difference between Miss Marple and Hercule Poirot (the difference between "common-sense" and police training), and the routine of writing ("I prefer writing during the morning"). In September 2015, the interview was displayed at the Wallingford Museum as part of that town's first annual Christie celebration.

See also: "'Queen of Crime' Is a Gentlewoman"; **Winterbrook House**

Introduction to *Hercule Poirot* (radio series introduction)

Introduction to *Hercule Poirot* was a prerecorded introduction by Christie to the 1945 Mutual radio series *Hercule Poirot* in the United States. Efforts were made to switch to Christie live, but these failed, so the recording was played. In the brief introduction, Christie implies that Poirot is a real person and suggests that a career on the radio would appeal to his vanity.

See also: *Hercule Poirot* (**Mutual radio series**)

Introduction to *The Mousetrap Man* (book introduction)

However theatrical impresario Peter Saunders wished to be remembered, it became clear in his lifetime that he would always be best-known as the first producer of Christie's runaway stage success *The Mousetrap*. For this reason, the title of Saunders's wide-ranging 1972 memoir is, with both wry humor and an eye to sales, *The Mousetrap Man*, and Christie wrote the introduction. Saunders's memoir is much kinder to Christie than director Hubert Gregg's also-cynically-titled *Agatha Christie and All That Mousetrap* (1980), written after her death.

Christie's contribution is brief and mostly concerns a condensed history of her own theatrical writing. Contradicting her autobiography and the findings of archivists, which contradict both, she states that her first play "must have been *Black Coffee* in about 1927" (Christie, Introduction, *Mousetrap Man* 7). She goes on to relate a story that also appears in her autobiography, about turning up to an evening in her honor at the Savoy, only to be turned away by staff and being too shy to contradict them (8). Finally, she commends Saunders for his "kindness to me over my shy fits," his "consoling" manner, his belief in the *Mousetrap* (it is well known that Saunders spearheaded several publicity initiatives to keep the production going), and his luck (9).

See also: *Black Coffee*; *The Mousetrap*; **Saunders, Sir Peter**

"Investigation by Telegram." See **"The Mystery of Hunter's Lodge"**

"The Invisible Enemy." See **"The Lernean Hydra"**

"An Island" (poem). See *Poems*

"The Island" (story). See *Star Over Bethlehem* (story/poetry collection)

"Islot of Brittany." See *Poems*

Itoshino Cendrillon. See *Meitantei Akafuji Takashi*

"I've Forgotten You" (song; see **"Yellow Iris"** [story])

"Jack Fell Down" (Keating). See **Continuation Fiction**

Jackson, Arthur

Arthur Jackson is Jason Rafiel's attendant

and effective guard dog in *A Caribbean Mystery*. He is "a man of extreme muscular development heightened by his training. His not to reason why, his but to do" (242).

Jackson, Fred

Fred Jackson is a fishmonger in St. Mary Mead, known for chatting up the maids, in *The Murder at the Vicarage* and *A Pocket Full of Rye*.

Jameson, Inspector

Inspector Jameson is an eager-to-please but fundamentally unintelligent policeman who appears in "Murder in the Mews" and *The ABC Murders*.

"Jane in Search of a Job" (story)

A perky short story, "Jane in Search of a Job" was published in the *Grand Magazine* in August 1924. It may have its origins in rumors widely spread at the time about Grand Duchess Anastasia of Russia, believed to have survived the assassination of her family in 1918 and to be living as an ordinary woman.

The 26-year-old Jane Cleveland, who is running short on money, answers an advertisement in a newspaper looking for a young woman who matches her description for unspecified work. Applying for the job, she learns that she is to stand in as a double for the Grand Duchess Pauline, the sole survivor of the imperial family of Ostrava, which was killed in a communist revolution. The grand duchess tells Jane, who looks strikingly like her, that an attempt may be made on her life, so she needs a lookalike to divert them. Traveling with a stern elderly princess, Jane is held up at gunpoint, imprisoned, and drugged.

Later, she learns that a jewel robbery has occurred nearby, perpetrated by a woman matching her description and wearing her regular clothes. She realizes that there was no Grand Duchess Pauline but that she was tricked by a gang of thieves. Jane is cleared of suspicion by Detective-Inspector Farrell and falls in love with a young man she met on the journey. "Jane in Search of a Job" appears in the U.K. collection *The Listerdale Mystery* (1934) and the U.S. collection *The Golden Ball* (1971). It was filmed as part of *The Agatha Christie Hour*, broadcast on ITV on 9 November 1982.

Characters: Anchester, Countess of; Cleveland, Jane; Farrell, Detective Inspector; Kranin, Colonel; Pauline of Ostrava, Grand Duchess; Poporensky, Princess Anna Michaelovna; Streptitch, Count Feodor Alexandrovitch

See also: *The Agatha Christie Hour*; "The Girl in the Train"; *The Golden Ball* (story collection); *The Listerdale Mystery* (story collection)

Janet

Janet is an elderly maid in *After the Funeral* who forms a friendship with Marjorie, the young cook. She may have been trained by Miss Marple, who mentions a former maid, Janet, in *The Body in the Library* and *Nemesis*. Another Janet without a surname is an imperfect maid to Mrs. Carmichael in "The Case of the Perfect Maid." There is another Janet, Tommy and Tuppence Beresford's granddaughter, who is mentioned in *Postern of Fate*.

Japp, (Chief) Inspector James

Inspector Japp is to Hercule Poirot what Inspector Lestrade is to Sherlock Holmes. A Scotland Yard man who inevitably requires Poirot's help and takes the credit for himself, this character is nonetheless more sympathetic to the detective than Sir Arthur Conan Doyle's creation and is more like a friend than a grudging colleague. Introduced in the first novel, Japp makes clear that his relationship with Poirot goes back to 1904 and the Abercrombie forgery case.

Japp appears in the following Poirot texts: *The ABC Murders*; "The Adventure of the Cheap Flat"; "The Adventure of the Italian Nobleman"; "The Affair at the Victory Ball"; *The Big Four*; *Black Coffee*; "The Capture of Cerberus" (1947); *Death in the Clouds*; "The Disappearance of Mr. Davenheim"; "The Flock of Geryon"; "The Girdle of Hippolyta"; "The Kidnapped Prime Minister"; *Lord Edgware Dies*; "The Market Basing Mystery"; "Murder in the Mews"; *The Mysterious Affair at Styles*; "The Mystery of Hunter's Lodge"; "The Mystery of the Baghdad Chest"; *One, Two, Buckle My Shoe*; *Peril at End House*; "The Plymouth Express"; *The Secret Adversary*; and "The Veiled Lady."

He is one of the few characters to appear in both the Poirot universe and that of

Tommy and Tuppence Beresford, as he makes an additional cameo in *The Secret Adversary*. His last appearance is in the 1947 version of "The Capture of Cerberus," and this postdates his previous last appearance by some seven years. Christie dispensed with him, then, around the same time she dispensed with Captain Hastings, indicating a desire to move away from the Holmes context completely around the time of World War II, and the end of crime fiction's Golden Age.

Jarimat fi Aldhdhakira (A Crime in Memory)

Jarimat fi Aldhdhakira (A Crime in Memory) is a 1992 Syrian miniseries based on *Sleeping Murder*, which was broadcast in Dubai in 1993. The adaptation is composed of 20 episodes and replaces Miss Marple with a doctor.

See also: *Sleeping Murder*

Jarrow, Dorothea ("Dolly")

Dorothea Jarrow is the twin sister to Margaret Ravenscroft, whom she impersonates after killing Margaret in *Elephants Can Remember*. All she needs for the deception is a series of wigs, but living as her sister proves more difficult.

"Jealousy Is the Devil." See "The Shadow on the Glass"

Jefferson, Adelaide, and Frank

In *The Body in the Library*, Adelaide is the widow of Frank Jefferson, and, via another marriage, mother to Peter Carmody. By the end of the novel, she has agreed to marry again, this time to Hugo McLean. Frank is a deceased son of Conway Jefferson.

Jefferson, Conway, and Margaret

Rich, elderly, and wheelchair-bound, Conway Jefferson is an old friend of Colonel and Dolly Bantry in *The Body in the Library*. Bereaved after the loss of his wife Margaret and two children in a plane crash, which also left him without legs, he had taken an interest in the young, gold-digging Ruby Keene, causing family tensions.

Jennson, Miss

Miss Jennson is an angular, bespectacled woman in *Destination Unknown*; Andy Peters suspects that, because she is easily overlooked, she may well hold a great deal of secret knowledge and fascist ideals may fester in her unchecked.

"Jenny by the Sky." See *Star Over Bethlehem* (story/poetry collection)

"The Jewel Robbery at the Grand Metropolitan" (story; alternative titles: "The Curious Disappearance of the Opalsen Pearls"; "The Jewel Robbery at the 'Grand Metropolitan'"; "The Theft of the Opalsen Pearls")

Although charges that Christie failed to play fair with her readers rarely stand up, she sometimes set up deliberately simple, self-contained fair-play puzzles. "The Jewel Robbery at the Grand Metropolitan," first published in *The Sketch* in 1923, is an example. In this case of a robbery at a high-end hotel, there are two possible suspects—a ladies' maid and a chambermaid—and one of them did it. The story was collected in *Poirot Investigates* in 1924. It was the basis for the play *Road to Memory* (1932) by W.E. Fuller. It has been dramatized for television twice: as episodes of *Agatha Christie's Poirot* (1993) and *Agasa Kurisutī no Meitantei Powaro to Māpuru* (2004).

Characters: Celestine; **Hastings, Captain Arthur**; Opalsen, Ed; Opalsen, Mrs.; **Poirot, Hercule**

See also: *Agasa Kurisutī no Meitantei Powaro to Māpuru*; *Agatha Christie's Poirot*; *Poirot Investigates*; *Road to Memory* (play)

John

St. John is the highly debated author of Revelation, the final book of the Christian Bible. In "The Island," he is shown to be living on an island with the Virgin Mary. When Jesus takes Mary away to make her Queen of Heaven, John begins to write.

Johnson, Anne

Anne Johnson is Dr. Eric Leidner's devoted assistant in *Murder in Mesopotamia*. A traditional woman whom Amy Leatheran compares to a matron, she strongly resents Mrs. Leidner's presence on the dig and is secretly in love with Eric. It is unclear whether this character, who dies one of the cruelest deaths in the canon, is based on a real person as each Leidner is.

Johnson, Colonel

Colonel Johnson is a chief constable who works with Hercule Poirot in *Three Act Tragedy* and *Hercule Poirot's Christmas*. He hails from either Yorkshire (in *3AT*) or "Middleshire," a fictional county vaguely representing the midlands (*HPC*).

Johnson, Elspeth

Elspeth Johnson is matron at Meadowbank School, who cares more about the school than about people, in *Cat Among the Pigeons*.

Johnson, Victoria

The second victim in *A Caribbean Mystery*, Victoria Johnson is an innocent local woman with a common-law marriage and children who works at the hotel. She is killed for what she saw or did not see. The character represents Christie's efforts at awareness of other cultures, living peacefully and disrupted by British tourism. She also represents an inversion of narratives about the dangers for Britons traveling abroad.

Johnston, Elizabeth

A law student in *Hickory Hickory Dock*, Elizabeth Johnston is from Jamaica and is "particularly well balanced and competent" (23). Other students call her "Black Bess."

Jones, Gladys. See Gladys

Jones, Robert ("Bobby")

The joke about this character in *Why Didn't They Ask Evans?* is that he shares a name with a world-famous golfer but is terrible at golf. With Lady Frances "Frankie" Derwent, he is one of Christie's last Bright Young Thing adventurers. The son of a vicar, Bobby is thrown into an upper-middle class world at the same time as he is thrown into a murder mystery.

Jones, Vavasour

In *Crooked House*, Vavasour Jones is the author of a melodrama for the stage, "The Woman Disposes," which is generally "cribbed from *Arsenic and Old Lace*" (180). The character's name is a joke, combining the exotic/elaborate and the prosaic, and the idea of the play is a satire on reductive entertainment masquerading as shocking and new.

Jones, Victoria

Victoria Jones is the highly down-to-earth protagonist of *They Came to Baghdad*. She is unrepentantly greedy and a happy fantasist who lies unblushingly and convincingly. After being fired as a typist for impersonating her boss, she stumbles into an adventure traveling around the world to pursue a shadowy political organization. She also sees romantic potential in the young Edward Goring before unmasking him as a criminal.

Judy

Judy is a fictional portrait of Rosalind Hicks as a girl, with the same nickname ("Teddy"), in the Mary Westmacott novel *Unfinished Portrait*.

Kait

The wife of Sobek in *Death Comes as the End*, Kait appears utterly devoted to her children and is a quiet, even-tempered wife. However, toward the end of the novel, she reveals a hidden rage at the limited opportunities available for women, which could be turning her into a monster.

Kameni

Renisenb is supposed to marry Kameni in *Death Comes as the End*, Kameni is a scribe, younger and more handsome than Hori. His is not a distinctive personality.

Keene, Julia

Julia Keene's real name is Julia Garfield in *Butter in a Lordly Dish*. She is the widow of a man hanged for murder, and her obsession with the late Henry Garfield has led her to commit multiple homicides with increasing violence.

Keene, Ruby

A victim in *The Body in the Library*, Ruby Keene is a 17-year-old dancer, with bleach-blonde hair and a tacky dress. She is known as a gold digger, whom the rich, bereaved Conway Jefferson wished to adopt. In this highly artificial and self-aware novel, Keene is not only misidentified (the body identified as hers belongs to another girl, Pamela Reeves, and Ruby's corpse is identified as Pamela's) but also goes by two names: Keene is a stage name, and her real name is Rosey Legge. The name is significant, however: in real life, a teenager called

Ruby Keen was strangled in a tawdry, sensational case that made headlines in 1939. Therefore, the character is supremely, metafictionally, artificial.

Kelsey, Detective Inspector

Detective Inspector Kelsey is the investigating officer from Scotland Yard in *Cat Among the Pigeons*. He has worked with Poirot before as a sergeant in an unspecified case. There had already been an Inspector Kelsey, working with Poirot in *The ABC Murders*, but that character was xenophobic, and this one is extremely friendly.

Kendal, Molly

The young, friendly wife of Tim Kendal and co-owner of the Golden Palm Hotel in *A Caribbean Mystery*, Molly Kendal believes she is going mad. She is experiencing anxiety, blackouts, and memory loss, and at one point finds blood on her hands. However, her husband, apparently a reformed rogue, is deliberately drugging her so he can have her declared insane and gain control of her money. At the end of the novel, Molly decides to continue running the hotel, with help from the wealthy Jason Rafiel's extensive network.

Kendal, Tim

Married to Molly Kendal, Tim Kendal co-owns the Golden Palm Hotel with her in *A Caribbean Mystery*. An extremely likable and accommodating man in his thirties, he has a secret history as a blackguard, disapproved by Molly's family; he married her under a different name to gain their consent. In fact, his past is darker than even Molly knew: he killed his first wife. The second marriage was likely for money alone, as Tim is behind a dual plot to kill Major Palgrave (who recognized him from a photograph of the old murder case) and several others, as well as to have Molly declared insane.

Kennedy, Dr. James

Half-brother to Helen Spenlove Kennedy in *Sleeping Murder*, James Kennedy is an amiable, middle-aged doctor who turns out to be insane, possessive, and perverted. His control over his half-sister has extended to murdering her and framing her husband for the crime because he did not want to lose her. Unmasking him as a kind of gothic monster, Miss Marple compares him to the incestuous Barrett (Elizabeth Barrett Browning's father) in *The Barretts of Wimpole Street*.

Kennedy, Helen Spenlove

Helen Spenlove Kennedy is the long-dead first victim in *Sleeping Murder*. Miss Marple's investigation, on behalf of Helen's stepdaughter, Gwenda Reed, is in one sense a mission to let Helen's spirit rest easily and peacefully. Like Arlena Stewart in *Evil Under the Sun* and Verity Hunt in *Nemesis*, Helen exists chiefly in how she is constructed by people who remember her. That her abusive half-brother can have her labeled a nymphomaniac simply because she wanted to escape him speaks to widespread cultural misogyny and the silencing of women's voices. Writing in the 1950s, Christie pre-empted some twenty-first century discussions with this narrative arc.

Kerr, Allegra

Allegra Kerr is an unconventional, confident, and slightly esoteric woman in "The House of Dreams," with whom John Segrave falls in love. Her mother died in an asylum, and John accepts that she will likely share that fate, which she does.

Kerr, Hon. Venetia

A high-living friend to Lady Horbury, Venetia Kerr has a cocaine habit and is in love with Lord Horbury in *Death in the Clouds*.

Kettering, Derek

The roguish husband of Ruth Kettering in *The Mystery of the Blue Train*, and the prime suspect for her murder. Although his father-in-law puts a mistress, Mirelle, in his path, he proves to be devoted to his wife. Since this book was written in the aftermath of marital unfaithfulness and divorce, it is not difficult to see some wishful thinking in the character. Christie's other roguish young men tend to remain true to form. See, for instance, her revisions to the character of Leonard Vole in the stage version of *Witness for the Prosecution*.

Kettering, Hon. Ruth

The daughter of Rufus Van Aldin in *The Mystery of the Blue Train*, Ruth Kettering is an American socialite who is murdered for the "Heart of Fire," a jewel with which she is traveling. She is presented as unworldly, with money doing all the talking for her—even her extramarital affair with the Comte de la Roche is more about money than anything else.

Khara Sangayach Tar. See ***Witness for the Prosecution*, Screen Adaptations of**

Khay

Khay was Renisenb's first husband, who is dead before the action begins, in *Death Comes as the End.*

"The Kidnapped Prime Minister" (story)

Written for *The Sketch* in 1923, the short story "The Kidnapped Prime Minister" has Hercule Poirot, like Sherlock Holmes before him, involved in top-secret wartime government operations. It begins optimistically with Captain Hastings asserting that "the problems of war are things of the past," so he can now tell this story (*PI* 195). Poirot is called on to investigate the disappearance of British Prime Minister David MacAdam, who experienced two kidnapping attempts as he traveled to France to sign a military declaration at a conference of Allies. The setting is certainly World War I: Hastings has just been "invalided out" (195). While the police are investigating in France, Poirot returns to England, convinced that he has been misled by the prime minister's secretary, Captain Daniels. He recovers MacAdam in time for the prime minister to travel to France and make a lasting impression at the conference.

It is a jingoistic story, where the culprit's motive is to embarrass the British (always "English") government, and the prime minister, known as "Fighting Mac," is "more than England's Prime Minister—he *was* England" (196; emphasis in original). However, it is tempered with the gentle satire of the Poirot stories. Poirot suspects that Daniels is a spy because "he speaks too many languages for a good Englishman" (213). The story was first published in *The Sketch* on 25 February 1923 and appears in the collection *Poirot Investigates* (1924).

A television adaptation, part of *Agatha Christie's Poirot*, was broadcast on ITV on 25 February 1990. A two-part animation, part of *Agasa Kurisutī no Meitantei Powaro to Māpuru*, was broadcast on NHK in September 2004.

Characters: Barnes, Inspector; Ebenthal, Bertha; Daniels, Captain; Dodge, Bernard; **Edith**; Estair, Lord; Everard, Mrs.; **Hastings, Captain Arthur**; **Japp, Chief Inspector James**; Lyall, Captain; MacAdam, David; Norman, Major; O'Murphy; **Poirot, Hercule**

See also: ***Agasa Kurisutī no Meitantei Powaro to Māpuru; Agatha Christie's Poirot; Poirot Investigates***

"The Kidnapping of Johnnie Waverly." See **"The Adventure of Johnnie Waverly"**

***Kiken na Onnatachi* (Dangerous Women)**

Kiken na Onnatachi (Dangerous Women) is a Japanese film based on Christie's *The Hollow*. Directed by Yoshitarô Nomura, it features Mariko Fuji, Romoe Hiiro, and Kimiko Ikegami, with a screenplay by Motomu Furuta. The film uses the basic premise of *The Hollow* but switches the action to 1980s Japan and does not feature the same characters as the book. It was released in Japanese cinemas on 25 May 1985.

See also: ***The Hollow* (novel)**

***The Killings at Kingfisher Hall* (Hannah).** See **Continuation Fiction**

King, Dr. Sarah

A young and newly qualified English doctor traveling in Western Asia in *Appointment with Death*, Sarah King is one of Hercule Poirot's key allies, who observes the dysfunctional Boynton family with increasing anger. Often cited in feminist scholarship, King is a rare example of a female physician in Golden Age detective fiction, and she is notable for insisting on equity between the sexes. She eventually marries Raymond Boynton and supports his career development without significant reference to her own.

King, Victor

Victor King is an international jewel thief with many aliases in *The Secret of Chimneys*. He also is known as Monsieur Chelles, Inspector Lemoine (the investigating officer in this novel), Captain O'Neill, and Prince

Nicholas of Herzoslovakia, whose identity he adopts in America.

"The King of Clubs" (story; alternative titles: "The Adventure of the King of Clubs"; "Beware the King of Clubs")

Elements of the 1923 story "The King of Clubs" were expanded into elements of *The Hollow*, *Taken at the Flood*, and *Spider's Web*. However, in short story form, they serve as straightforward plot devices, rather than centering the emotional drama as they do in the subsequent works. This is a story in which Hercule Poirot is still being introduced to Christie's readers: how he deports "his egg-shaped head," his approach to "an imaginary fleck of dust," and his reification of "Order and Method [as] his gods" (*PEC* 77) are all lengthily described.

The plot has Poirot and Captain Hastings investigating a "solid middle-class English family, the Oglanders" (77). While they played bridge, famous dancer Valerie Saintclair staggered into their room in blood-stained clothes and cried "Murder!" At a neighboring villa, they found theatrical impresario Henry Reedburn dead. A Mauranian prince who, scandalously, wishes to marry the dancer consults Poirot. Investigating the scenes of the crime and the bridge party, Poirot notices one card, the king of clubs, is still in the pack. Therefore, he deduces that the game was never played and actually was staged. He learns that the victim was blackmailing Valerie because of her humble origins—she is, in fact, the Oglanders' estranged daughter—and another character accidentally killed him during fisticuffs. Poirot decides to lie to the prince so that the wedding can proceed.

First published in *The Sketch* on 21 March 1923, "The King of Clubs" later appeared in the U.S. collection *The Under Dog* (1951) and the U.K. collection *Poirot's Early Cases* (1974). It was dramatized as part of *Agatha Christie's Poirot*, broadcast on ITV on 12 March 1989. In 1999, Paul Lamond Games produced a jigsaw puzzle based on the story.

Characters: Feodor, Count; **Hastings, Captain Arthur**; **Oglander family**; Paul, Prince of Maurania; **Poirot, Hercule**; Reedburn, Henry; Ryan, Dr.; **Saintclair, Valerie**; **Zara**

See also: ***Agatha Christie's Poirot***; ***Double Sin*** (story collection); **Games**; ***The Hollow*** (novel); ***Poirot's Early Cases***; ***Spider's Web*** (play); ***Taken at the Flood***

Kirifuri-sanso Satsujin-jiken

Kirifuri-sanso Satsujin-jiken is a Japanese television adaptation of *The Unexpected Guest*, directed by Ogini Yoshito and broadcast on 15 May 1980. The cast featured Kurihara Komaki and Hayashi Ryuzo. The second Japanese version of the play aired 21 years later.

See also: ***Fuji-sanroku Renzoku Satsujin-jiken***; ***The Unexpected Guest*** (play and novel)

Knight, Miss

Miss Knight is the stern, matronly housekeeper for Miss Marple in *The Mirror Crack'd from Side to Side* and also is mentioned in *Nemesis*. Miss Marple finds herself severely limited by Miss Knight's insistent caring.

Knighton, Major Richard

A charming secretary to Rufus Van Aldin in *The Mystery of the Blue Train*, Major Knighton turns out to be a con artist and murderer known as "The Marquis," who works in cahoots with Ada Mason (really an actress, Kitty Kidd). He disarms people with his personal charm and his apparent insignificance.

Knox, Llewelyn

Llewelyn Knox is an evangelical religious missionary who suffers a breakdown and retreats from life in the Mary Westmacott novel *The Burden* before learning to love and be loved as his story coincides with Laura Franklin's.

Krimi-Sommer mit Hercule Poirot (radio series; Summer of Crime with Hercule Poirot)

A German radio series produced by Südwestrundfunk (Southwest Broadcasting; SWR), *Krimi-Sommer mit Hercule Poirot* (Summer of Crime with Hercule Poirot) was broadcast in 2006. It consisted of eight weekly 40-minute adaptations of Hercule Poirot short stories, starring Felix von Manteuffel as Poirot and directed by Stefan Hilsbecher.

Episodes include (with broadcast date in

parentheses): "Eine Tür fällt ins Schloss" (A Door Slams, 2 July; adaptation of "Problem at Sea"), "24 Schwarzdrosseln" (Twenty-Four Black Thrushes, 9 July; adaptation of "Four and Twenty Blackbirds"), "Der Traum" (16 July; "The Dream"), "Der verräterische Garten" (The Treacherous Garden, 23 July; adaptation of "How Does Your Garden Grow?"), "Urlaub auf Rhodos" (Vacation on Rhodes, 12 August; adaptation of "Triangle at Rhodes"), "Last Blumen Sprechen" (19 August; adaptation of "Yellow Iris"), "Tod I'm Dritten Stock" (Death on the Third Floor, 26 August; adaptation of "The Third Floor Flat"), and "Poirot und Der Kidnapper" (Poirot and the Kidnapper, 3 September; adaptation of "The Adventure of Johnnie Waverly").

See also: **German Radio Adaptations**

Kuroido Goroshi. See **Fuji TV Adaptations**

The Labours of Hercules (story collection; alternative title: *The Labors of Hercules*)

In a foreword to the 1953 Penguin edition, Christie wrote that "Poirot's Christian name made the writing of this series of short stories quite irresistible. I started on it in a fine frenzy of enthusiasm—damped down in as short while by the unforeseen difficulties" (3). The book consists of 12 stories, each reflecting one of the 12 mythical labors of Hercules or Heracles. Although the stories were originally published in magazines and are self-contained, Christie objected strongly to them being published individually—for instance, in the anthology *13 for Luck!*—and preferred to consider them as a collective. Therefore, this entry discusses *The Labours of Hercules* as a whole, like *The Big Four*.

The gimmick here is that Poirot, once again on the verge of retirement, decides to look into his classical namesake. From learning about Hercules, who had to perform 12 feats for the King of Mycenae as penance for killing his family, Poirot decides to take on 12 final cases before retiring. Each case will resemble one of Hercules's labors. According to Christie, some of the stories "wrote themselves," but others were extremely difficult (3). In particular, she cites "The Capture of Cerberus" (the final story), which archival research by John

Curran has shown was completely rewritten to avoid political tensions.

The stories are as follows:

(1) "The Nemean Lion," in which Poirot investigates the kidnapping of a Pekingese dog and in the process prevents a murder.

(2) "The Lernean Hydra," where the hydra, a beast that grows new heads when it is decapitated, is a metaphor for gossip, which ends up in murder.

(3) "The Arcadian Deer," in which Poirot plays a Mr. Satterthwaite-like role, investigating the reasons behind a beautiful mechanic's lovesickness.

(4) "The Erymathian Boar," set in Switzerland, in which Poirot works with the Swiss Police to prevent a murder at his mountainside hotel.

(5) "The Augean Stables," in which Poirot uses the tabloids' interest in sex scandals to cover up a political scandal for the prime minister.

(6) "The Stymphalean Birds," set in the Christiean kingdom of Herzoalovakia, centers on an ambitious young man being blackmailed. Poirot uncovers a complex plot that implicates respectable English guests instead of the ugly foreign women suspected by the young man.

(7) "The Cretan Bull," in which Poirot investigates an old aristocratic family and a line of insanity running through it, for the benefit of a young woman marrying into it.

(8) "The Horses of Diomedes," which concerns Poirot's efforts to stop a young woman becoming a drug addict.

(9) "The Girdle of Hippolyta," about a kidnapped schoolgirl and a stolen Reubens painting.

(10) "The Flock of Geryon," which sees the return of the criminal in the first story, now as a client. Poirot investigates a religious cult, and finds prosaic explanations for apparently supernatural occurrences.

(11) "The Apples of Hesperides," in which Poirot crosses the globe on a quest to recover a priceless renaissance goblet.

(12) "The Capture of Cerberus" [see below].

The stories work as standalone mysteries but also fit together to create a linear narrative. There are recurring themes throughout, many of which have mythic origins. A particular theme is beauty—male and female—which draws Poirot into cases just as it is a spur in many archetypal narratives.

Here, Poirot is also extremely domestic. The opening story sets this out clearly: what is a lion for Hercules is a Pekingese for Hercule. The most socially "important" case is "The Augean Stables," because it involves the highest echelons of politics, but Poirot initially refuses the case before he hears a comparison to the relevant labor. The fact that most of the stories turn out to be murder cases speaks more to generic expectations than to the premise—there is an idea that Poirot is taking cases he normally would not touch, simply because they fit the Herculean theme.

The stories were serialized in *The Strand Magazine*, monthly from November 1939, and these publications were preceded by publications in the United States in *This Week*, a newspaper supplement, in weekly installments from September 1939 to May 1940. *The Strand* rejected the 12th labor, so only 11 were published in the original 1939–40 run. "The Capture of Cerberus" in its original form moved away from the idea of domesticating the labors and dealt in unsubtle parallels with the rise of Adolf Hitler. The editors judged it inappropriate for light escapist fiction, although it is only the series' least subtle example of engaging with the political moment. "The Erymanthian Boar" deals with Jewish refugees from Germany. "The Augean Stables" is about propaganda and misinformation for the greater good. "The Stympahlean Birds" hinges on xenophobia. "The Cretan Bull" would not have been written without the context of eugenics. "The Apples of Hesperides" concerns lost colonial treasures and, tangentially, the loss of empire. "The Flock of Geryon" is about the dangerous magnetism of individual public speakers (a theme dealt with more overtly in the original draft of "Cerberus").

Christie was unable to write a new version in time for magazine publication. However, she wrote a completely new story under the same title for the book publication—it was also printed in the United States in *This Week* under the title "Meet Me in Hell!" in 1947. The published version of "Cerberus" has Countess Vera Rossakoff meeting Poirot on the London Underground and telling him she will see him in Hell. Hell, it transpires, is a night club. Poirot's visa to this confusing modern den leads him to investigate a jewel robbery and a drug racket with the help of an aggressive but obedient guard dog. Like *The Big Four*, *The Labours of Hercules* ends with a hint that, in his retirement, Poirot might marry the flamboyant Russian woman. This is, of course, an in-joke about the fashion, perceived by Christie and her peers as unfortunate, for marrying off one's hero.

The Labours of Hercules was published in 1947, and the U.S. version preceded the U.K. version by several months. It was one of the final books adapted for the television series *Agatha Christie's Poirot*, in an episode broadcast on ITV 1 on 6 November 2013. This dramatization takes considerable liberties with the plot, combining some characters and elements from various stories, and dispensing with the mythological framing. It also features a character named Lemesurier—a nod to "The Lemesurier Inheritance," often considered the one Poirot story that was never filmed.

Characters: **Abdul**; Andersen, Dr.; Anderson, Thelma; Burshaw, Miss; **Carnaby, Amy**; Carmichael, Lady; Carnaby, Emily; Casey, Patrick; Chandler, Admiral Sir Charles; Chandler, Hugh; Clayton, Elsie; Clegg, Emmeline; Cole, Mr.; **Cunningham, Dr. Alice**; Drouet, Inspector; Dublay; Ferrier, Dagmar; Ferrier, Edward; Frobisher, Colonel George; **George(s)**; **Gladys**; Grace, Patience; Grandier, Madame; Grant, General; Grant, Pamela ("Pam"); Grant, Sheila; Gustave, Inspector; Hammett, John; Harrison, Nurse; Harte, Mrs.; Hawker, Anthony; Hearn, Detective Inspector; **Higgs, Mr.**; Hoggin, Lady Millicent ("Milly"); Hoggin, Sir Joseph; **Japp, Chief Inspector James**; Keble, Ellen; King, Beatrice; King, Winnifred ("Winnie"); Larkin, Beryl; Leatheran, Miss; Lementeuil, Inspector; **Lemon, Felicity**; Lutz, Dr. Karl; Maberly, Diana; Marrascaud; Moncrieff, Jean; Nita; Oldfield, Dr. Charles; Perry, Percy; **Poirot, Achille**; **Poirot, Hercule**; Pope, Lavinia; Power, Emery; Rice, Mrs.; Ricovetti; **Rossakoff, Countess Vera**; Samoushenka, Katrina; Samuelson, Mrs.; San Veratrino, Marchese di; Schwartz, Mr.; Simpson, Alexander; Stevens, Detective Inspector Charles;

Stoddart, Dr. Michael; Varesco, Paul; Wagstaffe, Inspector; Waring, Harold; **Williamson, Ted**

See also: *Agatha Christie's Poirot*; "The Capture of Cerberus" (1940); War

"Lady of Mystery in Pakistan"

An interview with the editor of *Illustrated Weekly*, given at a party in Karachi and published on March 6, 1960. There are some editorial inaccuracies (not least in identifying Christie's favorite of her own books as "*Seven Little N-----s*"). Christie describes her writing process, her friends in Scotland Yard, and whether she would set a mystery in Pakistan. As in her interview in Lisbon, Christie politely indicates that this is unlikely. Journalist Sanam Maher unearthed this interview in September 2019.

See also: "**Entrevista a Agatha Christie.**"

"The Lady on the Stairs." See *The Big Four* (novel)

Lamarchant, Carla

Carla Lamarchant is the daughter of Caroline Crale in *Five Little Pigs* and consults Hercule Poirot 16 years after her father's murder, for which her mother was hanged, to determine the truth. The names "Carla" and "Caroline" are deliberately similar; in the stage version, *Go Back for Murder*, Christie stipulates that the same actor should play both roles.

Lamb, Colin

Colin Lamb is a secret service agent who narrates *The Clocks*. Lamb is not his real name, and it is implied that he may be Superintendent Battle's son. He poses as a marine biologist and ends the novel with the promise of marrying Sheila Webb.

"Lament of the Tortured Lover." See *Poems*

"The Lamp" (story)

The title of "The Lamp" comes from the *Rubáiyát of Omar Khayyám*, in which the "Lamp [with] Destiny to guide / Her little Children stumbling in the Dark" is said to be "A Blind Understanding" (qtd. in "The Lamp" 94). It is a ghost story, in which a widow, Mrs. Lancaster, learns that her new house is haunted by a child. When Mrs. Lancaster's young son, Geoffrey, dies, she realizes that the ghost now has a companion and is at peace.

The first traced publication for "The Lamp" is in the 1933 volume *The Hound of Death*. It appeared in the U.S. collection *The Golden Ball* (1971). It was dramatized in 1984 as part of the BBC radio series *Haunted*.

Characters: Lancaster, Geoffrey; Lancaster, Mrs.; Raddish, Mr.; Williams, Master; Williams, Mr.; Winburn, Mr.

See also: **BBC Radio Adaptations**; *The Golden Ball* **(story collection)**; *The Hound of Death* **(story collection)**

Lancaster, Mrs.

Mrs. Lancaster is the most relevant of several pseudonyms used by Lady Julia Starke in *By the Pricking of My Thumbs*. Also known as "Killer Kate" and living under various names including Mrs. Warrander and Mrs. Yorke, she is an elderly woman who has been murdering children for several years and has come to believe that she is acting in the name of God.

Lane, Patricia ("Pat")

A highly intelligent student of archaeology in *Hickory Dickory Dock*, Patricia Lane has one weakness: her love for Nigel Chapman, which clouds her judgment sufficiently that she enables him to murder Celia Austin, Mrs. Nicoletis, and later herself. Poirot does not approve of her because she makes little effort with her appearance; he compares her unfavorably to Countess Vera Rossakoff.

Lane, Rev. Stephen

The Rev. Stephen Lane is a fanatical, misogynistic vicar in *Evil under the Sun*. He sees the sexually confident Arlena Stewart and believes she epitomizes evil.

Lansquenet, Cora

Richard Abernethie's larger-than-life sister in *After the Funeral*, Cora Lansquenet is murdered, apparently after announcing at his funeral that he had been killed. Cora's eccentricities make her easy to impersonate, however, confusing the time of and motive for her demise. She is the widow of artist Pierre Lansquenet but does not discriminate between good and bad art.

Lansquenet, Pierre

The deceased husband of Cora Lansquenet in *After the Funeral*, Pierre Lansquenet was a French artist.

"The Last Days of Nimrud"

One of the "Nimrud Odes" Christie wrote, mainly for her husband's enjoyment, during excavations in the 1950s, "The Last Days of Nimrud" is a jaunty piece of doggerel, the tone of which masks a serious observation. It was written around 1958, so not quite in the last days of the expeditions (they would come in 1960). Instead, it reflects the 1958 Iraqi revolution and the opening of ancient spaces for tourists. Christie reflects on the commodification of ancient sites and includes herself in a vision of a grotesque tourist attraction—"A famous Novelist's on view / For forty fils a peep" (qtd. in Morgan 280). The poem has not been collected or published, although Janet Morgan quotes extracts in *Agatha Christie: A Biography*.

See also **Archaeology**; "**Nursery Rhyme of Nimrud**"

The Last Séance (play)

In her autobiography, Christie writes that one of her early efforts was "a grisly story about a séance," which she later rewrote for publication (*AA* 193). This became "The Last Séance" in 1926. In the 2010s, producer and researcher Julius Green unearthed a one-act play script—dated 1922, also titled "The Last Séance," and telling the same story—and concluded that this was the original draft referred to by Christie in her memoir. However, as the autobiography refers to it among other stories written around 1909, it is likely that the script is one of several reworkings.

Christie sent it to Hughes, Massie on 9 November 1922, and its composition can be dated to earlier that year: she wrote home from the Grand Tour on 9 May that she had "written a Grand Guignol sketch"—partly, it seems, out of jealousy of her sister, Madge, who had just had a play licensed for the West End (*TGT* 171). In the same letter to her mother, Christie writes: "I shall be furious is [Madge] arrives 'on the film' before I do!" (171).

Green has done much to unearth the influence of Grand Guignol—the French-inspired vogue for "horror theater"—on Christie's early theatrical efforts. *The Last Séance* is certainly in this tradition and it is, as she says, more a sketch than a play. A four-hander about a medium who is performing one last séance, it culminates in an exceptionally bloody and dramatic death. The script has never been published and apparently has never been performed.

See also: *An Autobiography*; "The Last Séance" (short story)

"The Last Séance" (story; alternative titles: "The Stolen Ghost"; "The Woman Who Stole a Ghost")

An early play that Christie later reworked for publication, "The Last Séance" is heavily inspired by the French theatrical tradition of Grand Guignol. The presence of a client called Madame Exe is further evidence of a French influence, as it follows a tradition in French literature to name characters like this for verisimilitude, or perhaps of popular accounts of psychiatric case studies.

It is the story of Simone, a medium who has been exhausted by her years of mediumship. A client, Madame Exe, makes particularly challenging demands for Simone to contact her dead child. Madame Exe is full of grief over her loss and longs to touch her daughter, who materializes during the séances, but she cannot. Simone announces that she will perform one final séance, which will involve manifesting the child, Amelie. Madame Exe claims suspicion that it is a scam and insists on typing up Raoul Dubereuil, Simone's lover, to avoid any trickery. When Simone produces the clearest manifestation yet, Madame Exe runs out to grab Amelie, and Simone dies, painfully.

This story was first published in the United States as "The Woman Who Stole a Ghost" in *Ghost Stories* (November 1926) and in the United Kingdom as "The Stolen Ghost" in *Sovereign Magazine* (March 1927). It was collected under its present name in the U.K. collection *The Hound of Death* (1933) and in the U.S. collection *Double Sin and Other Stories* (1961).

Four years before revising it for magazine publication, Christie wrote a one-act play with the same plot, also titled *The Last*

Séance, but it was never published or performed. The story has been adapted for television as an episode of *Shades of Darkness* (27 September 1986) and for BBC Radio 4 in a modernized version, broadcast on 24 March 2003.

Characters: Amelie; Daubreuil, Raoul; Elise; Exe, Madame; Genir, Dr.; **Letellier, Simone**; Roche, Professor

See also: *Double Sin* (story collection); *The Hound of Death* (story collection); *The Last Séance* (play); *The Last Séance* (television adaptation)

The Last Séance (story collection; alternative title: *The Last Séance: Tales of the Supernatural*)

The Last Séance is an edited volume of previously published short stories with supernatural themes, published internationally without annotation by Harper-Collins in 2019. The publishers pitched this volume as "shin[ing] a light on the darker side of Agatha Christie, one that she herself relished" (blurb), in line with general drives to position Christie as the architect of all aspects of modern genre literature in the mid- to late 2010s. In some cases (especially those stories featuring series detectives who offer rational solutions to seemingly impossible scenarios), the "supernatural" criterion is stretched. The majority of entries with true extra-logical themes were published in *The Hound of Death*. However, just as that volume contained the incongruously non-supernatural "The Witness for the Prosecution," so have other volumes contained surprisingly extra-logical stories such as "The Dressmaker's Doll" and "In a Glass Darkly," whose original book publication took the form of appendages to *Miss Marple's Final Cases*.

Anthologies of previously collected stories are nothing remarkable in themselves, and this was followed by similar themed volumes, *Murder under the Sun* and *Midwinter Murder* in 2020. However, it warrants mention here as the first Christie volume to contain "The Wife of the Kenite" (previously published in the multi-author *Bodies from the Library*).

The book contains "**The Last Séance**," "**In a Glass Darkly**," "**S.O.S.**," "**The Adventure**

of the Egyptian Tomb," "The Fourth Man," "The Idol House of Astarte," "The Gipsy," "Philomel Cottage," "The Lamp," "The Dream," "Wireless," "The Wife of the Kenite," "The Mystery of the Blue Jar," "The Strange Case of Sir Arthur Carmichael," "The Blue Geranium," "The Call of the Wings," "The Flock of Geryon," "The Red Signal," "The Dressmaker's Doll," and "The Hound of Death."

The Last Séance (television adaptation)

The 1926 short story "The Last Séance" was dramatized for television in 1986 and broadcast as a one-hour episode of the British ITV series *Shades of Darkness*. Directed by June Wyndham-Davies, this episode featured Jeanne Moreau, Norma West, Anthony Higgins, Annie Leon, Amanda Walker, and Annette Wilkie-Miller. It aired on 27 September 1986 as the second episode of the second season. The cinematography is of surprisingly high quality for a 1980s ITV production, and it is generally considered a superior episode. Although a copy of the tape exists in archive, it is the only episode of *Shades of Darkness* that has never been released on video or DVD.

See also: "The Last Séance" (story)

"The Last Song of Columbine." See *A Masque from Italy*

Latimer, Ted

An extremely attractive gigolo in *Towards Zero*, Ted Latimer is described in *Towards Zero* as having a "[t]ouch of the Dago" about him (45), although this reference has been edited out of recent English editions.

Lawson, Edgar

Edgar Lawson is a young, troubled man who is a delinquent at the Stoneygates facility in *They Do It with Mirrors*. He has wild tantrums, claiming to be the son of various distinguished men such as Winston Churchill and, eventually, Lewis Serrocold. The latter is true, and he conspires with his secret father to kill so that the facility can remain in operation. Miss Marple deduces that he is overplaying the role of an insane man: he is a sane person pretending to be mad.

Lawson, Wilhelmina ("Minnie")

In *Dumb Witness*, Wilhelmina Lawson is Emily Arundell's companion and sole heir to her fortune. A muddled woman, she sees the murderer but misinterprets what she sees. Although she likes children and animals, she is incapable of managing them.

Laxton, Louise

Louise Laxton (also known as Mrs. Harry Laxton) is a "poor little rich girl" (*MMFC* 68) in "The Case of the Caretaker" and "The Case of the Caretaker's Wife" in the vein of Linnet Doyle in *Death on the Nile* and Ellie Rogers in *Endless Night*. Dr. Haydock says, "Louise's ideas were vague and somewhat melodramatic. Riches prevented you [sic] from coming into contact with reality" (69), summarizing something that is implicit in the novel characters.

Leadbetter, Mrs.

Mrs. Leadbetter is an elderly racist in *Taken at the Flood*, who tries to turn Hercule Poirot away from a venue over which she holds no jurisdiction. As soon as she sees him, she snorts, "Foreigners!," and tells Poirot to go back "where you came from" (141). When he says that "would be difficult," she responds: "That's what we fought the war for, isn't it so that people could go back to their proper places and stay there" (141). Poirot knows not to "enter into a controversy" and changes the subject (141).

Leatheran, Nurse Amy ("Amy Seymour")

Nurse Amy Leatheran is the narrator of *Murder in Mesopotamia*, who reappears some 32 years later in *Passenger to Frankfurt*. She is a friendly, no-nonsense type, who claims at the beginning of her account to know nothing "anything about writing" (*MIM* 13). In the magazine version of *Murder in Mesopotamia*, she is called Amy Seymour.

Lee, David, and Hilda

In *Hercule Poirot's Christmas*, David is Simeon Lee's most artistic son, who has physically taken after his mother. He hates his father and plays a funeral march on the piano during a family Christmas gathering. His wife, Hilda, is magnetically kind, partly because she is physically unattractive and therefore unthreatening.

Lee, Dinah

Dinah Lee is a tacky blonde woman, who turns out to have a great deal of sensitivity and substance, and is secretly married to Basil Blake in *The Body in the Library*.

Lee, Esther

Considered a witch in *Endless Night*, she is a local gypsy who warns of a curse of Gypsy's Acre, where Mike and Ellie Rogers build a home. She turns out to have been hired—and killed—by Mike to scare Ellie, but not all her comments can be she easily explained.

Lee, George, and Magdalene

The second (and dullest) son of Simeon Lee in *Hercule Poirot's Christmas*, George Lee is a Member of Parliament for Westringham and has little conversation beyond feigned civility. Magdalene Lee is his wife.

Lee, Simeon

The victim in *Hercule Poirot's Christmas*, Simeon Lee ties with Mrs. Boynton in *Appointment with Death* for the position of Christie's most detestable murder victim. Lee is a tyrannical patriarch with a history of abusing people, property, and businesses, and his extensive family believes that he treats them like slaves. He is conscious of and proud of his wickedness, and does not think twice before telling the world that he would like to sleep with his granddaughter. His wife, Adelaide, is dead when the action begins. It is said that his wickedness was too much for her, and she died of a broken heart.

Leech, Andrew. See Antoine, Monsieur

Legge, Alec, and Sally

Alec Legge is an atomic physicist and Sally is his wife in *Dead Man's Folly*, where they are at an unhappy point in their marriage due to a clash of egos: Alec is obsessed with his work, and Sally misses her career as an artist. They are less developed in "Hercule Poirot and the Greenshore Folly," the earlier version of this novel. There, Peggy Legge (equivalent to Sally; no pun apparently intended) is blonde, not red-headed, and she plays a fortune-teller called Esmeralda (Madame Zuleika in the novel) during the fete.

Legge, Rosy. See Keene, Ruby

Leidner, Dr. Eric

Dr. Eric Leidner is the Swedish-American lead archaeologist in *Murder in Mesopotamia*, who is actually Frederick Bosner, an American spy for the German government, in disguise. Based at the University of Pittstown, Dr. Leidner is described several times as nervous and unremarkable, thus making him an unlikely spy. The other barrier to identifying him before Poirot reveals the solution is that Leidner is well-known in his own right. In a novel conscious of the disruptive power of war, this is significant: Bosner/Leidner reflects the ease with which respectable figures in the twentieth century could rebuild their personas or even start again and still achieve success after high-level scandals—something that would become even more topical with the advent, then aftermath, of World War II.

Leidner, Louise

The "Lovely Louise" has married twice in *Murder in Mesopotamia*, first to Frederick Bosner, an American soldier turned German spy during World War I, and second to Eric Leidner, a Swedish-American archaeologist, who turns out to be Bosner in disguise. When Hercule Poirot investigates her murder, he determines that Louise's personality is the key to the mystery. In reconstructing her, he determines that she must have possessed more than "mere material beauty" to have affected men in the ways she did (247). She stood, he claims, outside of traditional feminine sexuality because, although she liked men, she preferred her own company; he compares her to "*La Belle Dame sans Merci* of the legend" (247). In the magazine version, *No Other Love*, she is named Louise Trevor.

The character is famously based on a real person, Katharine Woolley (1888–1945), whom Christie had met shortly before meeting her second husband on a dig at Ur. Katharine, the wife of Leonard Woolley, was a remarkable personality—mercurial, snobbish, egotistical, ruthless with friends who had outlived their usefulness, and extraordinarily magnetic. Both Christie and Max Mallowan, her husband, described Katharine in their memoirs as equally "entrancing" (*AA* 377; Mallowan 37) and "impossible" (*AA* 377) or "poisonous" (Mallowan 38). She authored a novel, *Adventure Calls*, about a woman called Colin who impersonates her twin brother, in 1929—the same year Radclyffe Hall's *The Well of Loneliness* was published.

Leith, Duchess of ("Maria")

A central character in "The World's End," a minor character in "Dead Man's Mirror," and a character that is mentioned in "The Harlequin Tea Set," the Duchess of Leith flaunts her wealth, which creates a lasting friendship with the class-conscious Mr. Satterthwaite.

"The Lemesurier Inheritance" (story)

A short story first published in 1923, "The Lemesurier Inheritance" is set over several years but opens in wartime, when Hercule Poirot and Captain Hastings—fresh from solving *The Mysterious Affair at Styles* (1920)—hear about an ancient family curse. Over the next few years, the heirs to the Lemesurier estate die in a series of apparent accidents until Poirot intervenes. The plot has several echoes of Sir Arthur Conan Doyle's *The Hound of the Baskervilles* (1901), not least of which is the shared name of the ancestor, Sir Hugo, whose licentiousness and paranoia first fueled the curse.

The story was published in *The Magpie*'s Christmas 1923 edition. It was anthologized in the United States in *The Underdog* (Dodd, Mead 1951) and in the United Kingdom in *Poirot's Early Cases* (Collins, 1974). It has never been dramatized in any medium, and is one of only three then-widely-published Poirot short stories that was not filmed as part of the ITV series *Agatha Christie's Poirot* (1989–2013): the other two ("The Submarine Plans" and "The Market Basing Mystery") inspired novellas, which were filmed in the series.

Characters: Claygate, Lady; Gardiner, John; **Hastings, Captain Arthur**; Higginson; Lemesurier, Captain Vincent; Lemesurier, Gerald; Lemesurier, Gerald; Lemesurier, Hugo; Lemesurier, John; Lemesurier, Major Roger; Lemesurier, Ronald; Lemesurier, Sadie; **Poirot, Hercule**; Saunders, Miss

See also: **Curses; Conan Doyle, Sir Arthur;** *Poirot's Early Cases, The Under Dog* **(story collection); War**

Lemoine, Inspector. See **Victor, King**

Lemon, Felicity

Miss Felicity Lemon's evolution from ornament and archetype to rounded character has been gradual, taking place throughout and beyond the literary canon. She is first introduced as a grim-faced, efficient secretary to J. Parker Pyne in "The Case of the Middle-Aged Wife" and "The Case of the Distressed Lady." She later appears as Hercule Poirot's secretary in "How Does Your Garden Grow?," where her "unprepossessing appearance" and "passion for order" (*PEC* 238) are introduced in detail, and the reader is told that, "though capable of thinking, she never thought unless told to do so" (238). In "The Nemean Lion" and "The Capture of Cerberus," she proves an inadequate substitute for Captain Hastings, as her displeasure at having to use imagination is made clear.

Poirot is shocked in *Hickory Dickory Dock* to learn that Miss Lemon has a sister, Mrs. Hubbard: he has always thought of her as "a precision machine" (6), not a human being with emotions and relatives: "she was a machine—the perfect secretary" (5). Miss Lemon also appears in *Dead Man's Folly* (and the original novella, "Hercule Poirot and the Greenshore Folly"), "The Mystery of the Spanish Chest," *Third Girl*, and *Elephants Can Remember*.

Less a human being than a collection of angular bones, "flung together at random" (*PEC* 238), Miss Lemon is Poirot's ultimate modernist secretary and reflects a modernist interest in machines, which several contemporary novelists such as Elizabeth Bowen used in physical descriptions of women.

Since the television series *Agatha Christie's Poirot*, Miss Lemon has become a well-known part of the Christieverse. The decision was made to give Miss Lemon an expanded role in the series, partly to avoid using Poirot's butler, George—the same production team was making *Jeeves and Wooster,* which features a valet, and wanted no perceived overlap. In adapting the character, dramatists expanded the role partly to suit audience tastes—she was made a sympathetic, motherly character—and partly to suit actor Pauline Moran's interests in the esoteric.

Lemprière, Joyce. See **West, Joan/Joyce**

Leonides, Aristide, and Brenda

In *Crooked House*, Aristide Leonides is the victim—an 85-year-old patriarch with a storied history in business and trade. He has built Three Gables, the stifling family home where his extended family lives, dependent on his extraordinary wealth. As in the nursery rhyme, he is the "crooked man who built a crooked house" (3). His much younger (now 35) second wife, Brenda is the prime suspect for his murder, mainly because she is not considered an authentic part of the family.

Leonides, Clemency, and Roger

In *Crooked House*, the Leonides family has a hereditary "ruthlessness" that translates strangely to Roger—he is "kind" and "lovable" but has "a terrific temper" (22–23) in contrast to his coldly logical wife, Clemency. She is a dispassionately logical scientist who daunts some of the men with her academic credentials. Roger's lack of success in business causes others in the family to see him as a failure.

Leonides, Electra, and Joyce

Electra and Joyce Leonides are the daughters of Aristide Leonides, who died in war, in *Crooked House.*

Leonides, Josephine

Josephine Leonides is the 11-year-old sister of Sophia and Eustace Leonides, and the daughter of Magda and Philip Leonides, in *Crooked House.* An ugly elfin girl, she treats the crimes like events in a murder mystery, inserting herself into narratives as a detective. Ultimately, she is revealed to be Christie's youngest murderer, lacking both impulse control and a moral framework. This character challenges notions of childish innocence and her actions are a result of both nature and nurture.

"The Lernean Hydra" (alternative titles: "The Hydra of Lernea, or the Case of the Gossipers"; "Invisible Enemy"). See *The Labours of Hercules*

Lessing, Ruth

As her name suggests, Ruth Lessing is

ruthless. A secretary to George Barton in *Sparkling Cyanide*, she is in love with him and therefore heartbroken when she accidentally kills him. She is also in a romantic relationship with Victor Drake, with whom she conspires to commit murder. Her efficient work ethic and even her ruthlessness are praised throughout as professionalism, something that becomes sinister when she is unmasked.

Lestrange, Estelle

In *The Murder at the Vicarage*, Estelle Lestrange is a newcomer to St. Mary Mead who keeps herself to herself and is compared by long-standing villagers to a sphinx. A woman around whom rumors and mythologies spring, she in fact has her own secrets: namely, a troubled first marriage to the late Colonel Protheroe, making her the mother of Lettice Protheroe, and a terminal illness. The surname may be a tribute to Gladys Mitchell's edgy detective, Adela Lestrange Bradley, introduced in 1929 in *Speedy Death*. Mitchell would go on to parody *The Murder at the Vicarage* in *The Saltmarsh Murders* (1931).

Letellier, Simone

This character has no surname in the short story "The Last Séance" but is named Letellier in the play on which it is based. She is a French medium who has grown tired and exhausted, and commits, reluctantly, to one last séance, which kills her. Her most exerting client is the grieving Madame Exe.

"A Letter from Agatha Christie" (article)

On 20 October 1968, the magazine supplement to the *Sunday Times* ran a special feature of "Great Unsolved Mysteries" with an especial focus on the case of Charles Bravo. A letter from Christie covered three quarters of a page and outlined her opinion on the case. Christie had long been fascinated by the Bravo case, and it had spawned several ideas for fiction, including an undeveloped idea about a "widow having an affair with a doctor" that was not developed (L. Thompson 380) and, most obviously, *Ordeal by Innocence*, where it is held up as an analogy (88).

Bravo, a barrister, was poisoned in 1876, and the case was never solved. Much of the aftermath focused on his wife, Florence, who had been conducting an affair with an older man, Dr. James Manby Gully, and on the housekeeper, Mrs. Cox, who lied to the police and had been threatened by the victim with losing her job. In her letter, Christie argues that Dr. Gully was likely the murderer as the only person with both motive and mental aptitude. She dismisses Florence as too financially secure to have a motive for the murder and Mrs. Cox as too timid to commit the murder.

See also: **True Crime**

"A Letter to My Publisher" (omnibus contribution)

This letter, signed "Hercule Poirot," was written for publication in the 1936 Dodd, Mead omnibus *Hercule Poirot: Master Detective*. It is dated 15 April 1936. In the letter, Poirot writes about his early work in Brussels, on the Abercrombie Forgery Case in 1904 (thus shaving some early years from his life and career as they are recounted in *The Mysterious Affair at Styles*). As that novel makes clear, Poirot met Inspector Japp on the Abercrombie case. He details his relationship with Captain Hastings, whom he explains is now married in the Argentine, and not working with Poirot any more. In fact, Hastings would return for *Dumb Witness* (1937).

There are several jokes to the effect that every case Poirot investigates is meant to be his last. The letter also covers Poirot's taste in literature, his smoking habits, and the value he sets by order and method. It concludes with a statement—not entirely true—that all the details in the letter are also available in the novels and that "[I]f you Americans, with your magnificent buildings and your furious speed and excitement, wish to know about Hercule Poirot, let them read his cases with precision" (LP 6).

The first U.K. publication of this letter was by HarperCollins in 2016, as a supplement to a special edition of *The Mysterious Affair at Styles* and *Curtain*, titled *Styles: Hercule Poirot's First and Last Cases*.

Letter to *Woman's Day* (unpublished letter to magazine)

In this unpublished letter to a women's

magazine, written in 1971, Christie objects to being described in an editorial as a Miss Marple–like figure, stating that she prefers to be compared to Ariadne Oliver. She also rejects the notion that she has been critically neglected, citing as evidence the newspaper critics attending her 80th birthday celebrations. The letter is housed in the University of Exeter's Special Collections.

See also: **Marple, Jane**; **Oliver, Ariadne**

Levinne, Sebastien

Confronting anti-Semitism throughout his life in the Mary Westmacott novel *Giant's Bread*, Sebastien Levinne starts as Vernon Deyre's boyhood friend, and once they are adults, he produces Vernon's work for visionary stage productions.

L'Heure Zero (Zero Hour; film; released in the United States as *Towards Zero*)

Pascal Thomas directed this 2007 French film based on *Towards Zero*. He had already directed one Christie film and would make two more: all comic installments of *Bélisaire et Prudence Beresford*. However, *L'Heure Zéro* is a more serious mystery than Thomas' Christie series. The film features some luminaries of French cinema including François Morel as Commissaire Martin Bataille (based on Superintendent Battle in the book) and Danielle Darrieux as the matriarch who is murdered. Darrieux had appeared as a very young woman in *Le Coffret de Lacque*, the first French Christie film, in 1932. Although it stays relatively close to the book's plot, the film is set in modern-day France rather than 1940s Cornwall. Another screen adaptation of *Towards Zero*, an episode of *Agatha Christie's Marple*, was also released in 2007.

See also: ***Bélisaire et Prudence Beresford***; ***Towards Zero*** (novel)

Li Chang Yen

In *The Big Four*, Li Chang Yen is "Number One" in a group of four international agents out for world domination. The most intelligent of the four, he has a cruel and devious intellect. This character draws on numerous contemporary clichés surrounding the "yellow peril"—Chinese criminal geniuses such as Sax Rohmer's Dr. Fu Manchu.

The Lie (play; alternative title: The Sister-in-Law)

A long-puzzled-over remark in Christie's autobiography refers to her having written "a rather gloomy play about incest" in the 1920s (*AA* 335). Although some commentators have linked this with her best-known unpublished work, the novel *Snow Upon the Desert*, Julius Green provides a convincing case for this being *The Lie*. A full-length undated play housed in the Christie Family Archive, *The Lie* concerns in part the idea of a marriage considered incestuous under British law at the time, between a divorced man and his ex-wife's sister.

The Lie is not a mystery play but a domestic drama revolving around a lower middle-class matriarchal household. Hannah Reeves, a woman in her forties, lives with her elderly mother and wants desperately to see both her adult daughters happy. Nan, the oldest, is married to the wealthy and generally decent John Gregg, whereas her 17-year-old sister Nell (nearly always "Little Nell") spends a great deal of time with the couple. Both daughters are hedonists to a degree. Feeling ignored by John, Nan has embarked on a brief affair with an acquaintance. When Hannah finds out, she begs Nan to tell John the truth, but instead Nan tries to enlist the sweet and wholesome Nell to lie on her behalf and say they spent the night together. Nell tries and fails to tell John this lie, and, with passions raised, John and Nell discover that they are in love with one another and consider elopement. In the end, it is agreed that, for social and economic reasons, the best thing would be for Nan and John to stay married, whereas Nell marries a man she does not love and moves to Canada. After all, she reflects, "love may come."

The play was unknown for many years but, since his account of the unpublished scripts in *Curtain Up*, Julius Green has championed this one in particular. He arranged the first stage performance—a costumed reading—at the Palace Theatre, Paignton, on 15 September 2018, and a BBC Radio 4 dramatization by Green and Martin Lewton was broadcast on 29 August 2020.

Inevitably, Green has framed the limited discussion of this text, emphasizing an autobiographical reading that highlights Christie's own divorce in 1928 and suggesting that this play was a way of working through her emotions in the build-up. The matriarchal household is certainly reminiscent of Christie's own upbringing. There is also an interesting reference to golf—Christie described herself as a "golf widow" (*AA* 336) and the "other woman" in her first marriage garnered favor with her husband by attending golf games that she would not; the same thing happens in *The Lie*. Christie also broke off an early engagement-for-convenience to marry for love, which resulted in an unhappy marriage that only lasted as long as it did for the sake of her daughter, something described by Hannah in the play. However, other themes and exchanges, which do have a kind of grim authenticity about them, are clearly taken from elsewhere. The radio broadcast in 2020 drew out a broader array of critical perspectives, with one listener comparing the piece to Henrik Ibsen's *A Doll's House* (Poulter n.p.).

Christie's revised version of the text changed the title to *The Sister-in-Law*, but Green, who has become a champion for its broader exposure, has chosen to stage and broadcast it under its working title (Green 69). The radio production received positive critical responses but broadly negative reactions on social media. It is possible that the crime-fiction-esque title may have misled listeners about what to expect, in an echo of the immediate reception for her psychological stage thriller *Verdict* in 1958.

See also: **BBC Radio Adaptations**; **Christie, Colonel Archibald ("Archie")**

Light Programme Festival (radio series)

The *Light Programme Festival* was a series of radio broadcasts run by the BBC in 1956, following various successful productions in 1954–55. Following the February 1955 broadcast of a special episode of *Close-Up* devoted to Christie, for which she took the almost unprecedented step of recording an interview, producers met with Christie and her agents to discuss the idea of a series of programs, dubbed a "festival," that would dominate the airwaves in February and March 1956.

The "festival" kicked off with an adaptation of "Death by Drowning" (19 February), with Betty Hardy starring as Miss Marple. There followed several Poirot adaptations, each starring a different actor—a move that will have pleased Christie, who wanted actors to remember that the role was bigger than them.

On 22 February, Austin Trevor, who had played Poirot on screen in the 1930s, reprised the role one last time in a 90-minute version of *The Mysterious Affair at Styles*. On 26 February, Kenneth Kent played Poirot in "The Adventure of the Clapham Cook." A version of *The ABC Murders* on 29 February starred John Gabriel. Richard Williams, who had played Poirot in "Murder in the Mews" the previous year, played Captain Hastings.

The offering on 4 March was "The Case of the Kidnapped Dog," starring Cyril Shaps as the detective; this was based on "The Nemean Lion," one of the *Labours of Hercules*. Jacques Brunius took the lead—a role he, like Trevor, had previously played on the BBC, in *Murder in Mesopotamia* (7 March). The festival concluded with a rebroadcast of *Butter in a Lordly Dish*, Christie's 1948 radio play.

See also: **BBC Radio Adaptations**; *Butter in a Lordly Dish*

Linch, Gladys. See **Gladys**

Lindstrom, Kirsten

In *Ordeal by Innocence*, a Swedish housekeeper, initially a nurse and masseuse, who has been with the Argyles since World War II. She has cared for the children from their infancy, but has been successfully manipulated by Jacko Argyle into murdering Rachel Argyle. She is a sad, plain, middle-aged woman, and her particular arc reminds readers that this demographic is not as sexless or immune to sex appeal as is traditionally presented in literature.

"The Listerdale Mystery" (story; alternative title: "The Benevolent Butler")

In the short story "The Listerdale Mystery," an upper-middle-class family living with reduced means moves into a surprisingly cheap luxury property. Once there, they resolve to find out what happened to its missing owner, Lord Listerdale. They find out that he faked his own disappearance, regretting his corrupt lifestyle, and has devoted his time to helping families like theirs live well despite relative poverty.

"The Listerdale Mystery" was first published in the *Grand Magazine* in 1925. It appeared in the United Kingdom in the 1934 volume to which it lends its title. In 1971, it appeared in the U.S. anthology *The Golden Ball*.

Characters: Anderson; Carfax, Colonel Maurice; Listerdale, Lord; Lowe, Samuel; Masterson, James ("Jim"); Quentin, Mr.; St. Vincent, Barbara; St. Vincent, Mrs.; St. Vincent, Rupert

See also: *The Golden Ball* (story collection); *Listerdale Mystery The* (story collection)

The Listerdale Mystery (story collection)

The Listerdale Mystery is the second of four Christie books published in 1934 (or the third of six counting *Mr. Parker Pyne, Detective*, published in the United States before its 1935 U.K. edition, and the pseudonymous *Unfinished Portrait*), *The Listerdale Mystery* collects 12 short stories published throughout the 1920s. These are nonseries stories and generally not mysteries. Several of the stories have been dramatized for stage, screen, and/or radio, and they tend to reference more diverse cultural influences than Christie's typical detective stories. The collection was published in the United Kingdom by Collins in June 1934, and it did not appear under the Collins Crime Club imprint. Between them, the stories appeared in two later U.S. editions: *The Witness for the Prosecution and Other Stories* and *The Golden Ball and Other Stories*.

The book is composed of the following: "The Listerdale Mystery," "Philomel Cottage," "The Girl in the Train," "Sing a Song of Sixpence," "The Manhood of Edward Robinson," "Accident," "Jane in Search of a Job," "A Fruitful Sunday," "Mr. Eastwood's Adventure," "The Golden Ball," "The Rajah's Emerald," and "Swan Song."

Litchfield, Margaret, and Matthew

In *Curtain*, Margaret Litchfield died in Broadmoor after confessing to having killed her tyrannical father, Matthew. She was manipulated into killing him by Stephen Norton. Elizabeth, Matthew's daughter and Margaret's sister, changed her name to escape her past and now lives as Elizabeth Cole.

"A Little Cowslip" (poem)

One of Christie's first literary efforts was a poem, written at age 10 or 11 in an exercise book, beginning:

> There was once a little cowslip
> And a pretty flower too
> But yet she cried and petted,
> All for a robe of blue [qtd. in L. Thompson 41].

The cowslip becomes a bluebell in her coveted blue robe but learns that her unhappiness is innate, and that achieving the perfect outer appearance has not changed it. Many years later, Christie recalled the verse in her autobiography, but differently:

> I know a little cowslip and a pretty flower too,
> Who wished she was a bluebell and had a robe of blue [*AA* 190].

Despite making it a much stronger piece of poetry in her recollection, Christie nonetheless critiqued her early work ruthlessly as she presented it: "*Could* anything be more suggestive of a complete lack of literary talent?" (190; emphasis in original). This would have been written in 1901, the year her first poem, "The Trams," was published.

Little, Dorothy ("Dotty")

In *Postern of Fate*, Dorothy Little is a local representative of the Women's Institute known as the "Parish Pump" because she absorbs and disseminates all conceivable local gossip.

Little Murders in the Family. See *Petits Meurtres En Famille*

Little Wars (McCassland). See **Fictional Portrayals of Agatha Christie**

Lloyd, Gerald ("Gerry/Jerry")

Gerald Lloyd is a weak-willed failure of a man who reverses his fortune and becomes successful, buoyed by his love for the unfortunate Sarah Prentice in the Mary Westmacott novel *A Daughter's a Daughter*. He tries to get her to leave her husband and marry him. He is referred to as "Gerry" in the novel and "Jerry" in the play.

Locked Doors (television series)

Locked Doors is a Yemeni miniseries based on Crooked House, with action relocated to the Yemen. The first episode aired on 6 June 2016.

See also: **Crooked House** (novel)

Lomax, Hon. George ("Codders")

An ancient civil servant in The Secret of Chimneys and The Seven Dials Mystery, he is a comic character who is generally oblivious. Nonetheless, his ineptitude spurs on narrative action. His ridiculous proposal of marriage to Bundle Brent in The Seven Dials Mystery, for example, spurs the action that ultimately leads to her marrying Bill Eversleigh.

Lombard, Captain Philip

According to the conventions of popular fiction, Philip Lombard, a young and attractive man with a military background and a strong libido, should be the hero of And Then There Were None. However, he is eventually revealed to be one of the most culpable characters in the novel. Even before this revelation, he is described in animalistic terms: as wolf-like, with a cruel smile.

He is one of 10 guests on Soldier Island who have been invited by "U.N. Owen," forced to confront their past crimes and are killed one by one. Lombard, supremely confident and assured that he will survive the massacre on Soldier Island, acknowledges that he has killed in war and was responsible for the deaths of 21 African tribesmen. He does not see a problem with this, believing it was a case of his life or theirs.

Lombard is the last character to be murdered but the third-last to die, as Vera Claythorne shoots him, believing him to be the murderer, and then hangs herself before the real killer writes a confession and commits suicide. When Christie adapted the book into a play at the height of World War II, she judged that audiences needed a happy ending and sympathetic characters, so she made Claythorne and Lombard two innocent parties who survive the ordeal and agree to marry.

The London Blitz Murders (Collins). See Fictional Portrayals of Agatha Christie

"The Lonely God"

The short story "The Lonely God" was written by Christie in her early adulthood before her first novel. "The Lonely God," dismissed by its author as "regrettably sentimental" (AA 193), was inspired by reading Ernest Temple Thurston's notoriously sentimental and highly Edwardian-religious The City of Beautiful Nonsense (1909). It was expanded in 1926 for publication in The Royal Magazine but did not appear in anthologies until 1997, in While the Light Lasts (U.K.) and The Harlequin Tea Set (U.S.).

The god of the title is the most overlooked of several religious figurines on display in the British Museum. It watches the visitors, including two lonely people who keep running into one another and who eventually fall in love. The lonely god, which had served as their point of reference when meeting, and which they had spoken of as their guardian spirit, watches them depart. They no longer need him.

Characters: Greta; Hurley, Tom; Lonely Lady, the; Oliver, Frank

See also: **While the Light Lasts** (story collection)

Lopez, Conchita. See Estravados, Pilar

Lord, Dr. Peter

Peter Lord is the young, colorless doctor of Laura Welman in Sad Cypress. He enlists Hercule Poirot to prove Elinor Carlisle's innocence when she is on trial for murder. At first, he denies being in love with her, but later he embraces it, and Elinor accepts him as a much-needed voice of stability. He represents the outside world and a release from the ties of family after she breaks off an existing engagement to her cousin, Roddy Welman. The character's name unsubtly parodies Dorothy L. Sayers's aspirational detective, Lord Peter Wimsey, whom he does not in any way resemble.

Lord Edgware Dies (film). See Twickenham Studios Films

Lord Edgware Dies (novel; alternative title: Thirteen at Dinner)

Published in 1933, Lord Edgware Dies puts Hercule Poirot and Captain Hastings at the heart of London high society. Sexy American actress Jane Wilkinson asks Poirot to convince her husband Lord

Edgware to agree to a divorce so she can remarry. Poirot does so, but Lord Edgware says he has already agreed. Shortly later, Lord Edgware is stabbed to death, and a witness places Jane at the scene. However, 12 other witnesses swear she was at dinner on the other side of London. Besides, as Lord Edgware agreed to the divorce, she has no obvious motive. When Carlotta Adams, an impressionist who has impersonated Jane in the past, appears to commit suicide, it is clear that Carlotta went to Lord Edgware disguised as Jane; however, it also becomes clear that she was hired by someone to carry out the impersonation. Poirot investigates Lord Edgware's dysfunctional family and staff, as well as the world of show business.

After another murder and a chance remark at the theater, he realizes that Carlotta's impersonation was not at the crime scene but at the dinner: the 12 witnesses only knew Lady Edgware casually and would not have known an imposter from the actual person. Jane herself murdered her husband, because her new romantic interest, an Anglo-Catholic duke, would have been unable to marry a divorced woman for religious and social reasons. Jane confesses by letter and hopes that her actions have granted her sufficient fame to warrant a waxwork in Madame Tussauds.

The novel's starting point was the second victim, Carlotta, famously based on impressionist Ruth Draper. Christie had seen Draper perform and had become captivated by how minimal props, movements, and vocal inflections could invoke well-known personalities. Her notebooks corroborate an account in her autobiography that the idea of a celebrity impersonator gave Christie the idea that became Lord Edgware Dies. The idea extends, however, beyond the idea of a woman appearing to be in two places at once. Although Carlotta is one of the more rounded murder victims—one contemporary reviewer described it as unfair that Christie created a victim for whom readers could feel sympathy—all the society people around her, including the murderer, are remarkably superficial. There is one point at which Ronald Marsh, the profligate heir to the Edgware barony, almost acknowledges

his own fictional status. Describing himself as "[t]he well-known Wicked Ne'er-do-Weel [sic] Nephew," he admits that he asked his uncle for money, adding: "And that same evening—that very evening—Lord Edgware dies. Good title that, by the way. Lord Edgware Dies. Look well on a bookstall" (115).

Christie wrote Lord Edgware Dies on a dig in Syria, which is one reason that the picture of London society it paints is so satirical; it is written with the biting observation of someone who has stepped away from it. The author wrote home that it was progressing easily and that the final novel would feel "cheap" and insubstantial. Nonetheless, it contains extensive detail on social masquerade. The depiction of aristocrats is a well-worn one, with Lord Edgware appearing as a snarling degenerate who is fixated on his Greek-godlike butler, whereas Lady Edgware's new fiancé is presented with similarly gothic strokes as an apparently homosexual Anglo-Catholic apparently fixated on his mother. However, in presenting these tropes, Christie also invites commentary by weaving them into the crime narrative. The murder weapon is overlooked because it is both feminine and working class: it is a knife for removing corns that belongs to a lady's maid. The pince-nez used in Jane's disguise belongs to the same maid. Because nobody seriously investigates the servants, the truth about these clues remains elusive, and working-class paraphernalia introduces destructive forces into Lord Edgware's aristocratic world.

The novel was published in the United States as Thirteen at Dinner, reflecting a superstition about the number of people at a dinner table, which is mentioned briefly in the novel, and in the next year's Cards on the Table. The book is not one of Christie's best-known, but it has enjoyed success with readers and television audiences. Part of this is its versatility. For instance, Jane's ability for disguise can support at least four readings of the novel: for some, this is a strong example of the basic logic at the heart of the genre—if clues are data, they add up to this unlikely scenario (e.g., Curran, Secret Notebooks). For others, it reflects the culture of celebrity, where people assume that they know a famous figure even without a personal meeting, and those who have had the meeting never really know the individual (e.g., Schwartz). Similar readings focus on gender (e.g., Bernthal, *Ageless*). Then again, it could be taken as a commentary on class—all social roles are performative, and any entrant into aristocratic circles is suspect (e.g., York).

Lady Edgware is not the only character who is "doubled" in this novel. Lord Edgware himself has similarities with the Duke of Merton, his wife's next husband—not least, both are coded as sexually deviant. His butler, Alton, who looks like a Greek god, is mistaken more than once for the movie-star Bryan Martin, another suspect. Finally, there are two Lord Edgwares: the fourth baron, who dies, and the fifth baron (Ronald Marsh), who inherits the title.

Appropriately, given its theatrical setting, the first edition advertised "The Return of Hercule Poirot," with a large photograph of Charles Laughton as Poirot in a production of the play *Alibi*. The book itself was quickly dramatized, in a film with Austin Trevor in 1934. In 1985, CBS aired *Thirteen at Dinner*, a modernized television adaptation starring Peter Ustinov as Poirot. This is notable for being Ustinov's first television turn as Poirot and for featuring David Suchet as Inspector Japp. Suchet played Poirot in the relevant episode of his own series, *Agatha Christie's Poirot*, in 2001. The novel inspired an episode of *Les Petits Meurtres d'Agatha Christie* in 2012.

The same year, a French graphic novel, adapted and illustrated by Marek, was published. Although a translation by David Brawn was prepared and a cover designed for a U.K. edition, it has not been released in English. There has also been a BBC Radio 4 serial, broadcast in five parts from March 1992.

Characters: **Adams, Carlotta**; Adams, Lucie; Alton; Bennet, Alice; Carroll, Miss; Corner, Lady and Sir Montague; Driver, Genevieve (Jenny); Edgware, Lady; Edgware, Lord; Ellis; **Hastings, Captain Arthur**; Heath, Dr.; **Japp, Chief Inspector James**; **Marsh, Captain Ronald, and Hon. Geraldine**; **Marsh, Lord George**; Martin, Bryan; Merton, Dowager Duchess of; Merton, Duke of; **Poirot, Hercule**; Ross, Donald; **Van Dusen, Mrs.**; Wilburn, Mrs.; **Wilkinson, Jane**

See also: *Agatha Christie's Poirot*; **CBS Television Adaptations**; *Hercule Poirot* (**BBC radio series**); **Homosexuality**; *Les Petits Meurtres d'Agatha Christie,*; **Theatricality**; **Twickenham Studios Films**

Lorrimer, Mrs.

In *Cards on the Table*, Mrs. Lorrimer—an expert bridge-player, aged 63—is present at Mr. Shaitana's party because, 20 years earlier, she poisoned her husband. A combination of guilt over the past deed, knowledge that she has a terminal illness, and sympathy for Anne Meredith, whom she thinks killed Shaitana, prompts her to confess to Shaitana's murder. Poirot does not accept her confession, because she lacks the psychology to commit a crime on impulse: she would leave nothing to chance. Mrs. Lorrimer is later killed by Dr. Roberts, the real murderer, and her death is staged to look like suicide. Both the Lorrimers, then, die by poison.

***L'ospite Inatteso* (The Unexpected Guest; television movie)**

The first European screen adaptation of *The Unexpected Guest*, this Italian version aired on Rai 1 on 6 May 1980. It was directed by Daniele D'Anza and starred Paolo Bonacelli as Michael Starkwedder. A surprising soundtrack was provided by the French electro-rock band the Rockets: an instrumental version of "Anastasis" from the band's third album, *Plasteroïd*. The adaptation was followed one week later by *Verso L'ora Zero* (*Towards Zero*).

See also *The Unexpected Guest* (**play**); *Verso L'ora Zero*

"The Lost Mine" (story)

"The Lost Mine" is an early story, in which Poirot recounts his experiences recovering a lost mine in Burma, which had belonged to a Chinese family for centuries. Wu Ling, the owner of papers revealing its location, had been murdered and the papers stolen. Poirot discovered that an English banker, Pearson, was behind the whole business. In gratitude, the directors of Burma Mines Ltd. granted him 14,000 shares in the business. With an air of narrating a "Just So" story, Poirot tells Hastings that this is why he holds shares in a Burmese mine and that there is no other way he would invest in anything so uncertain. The story was first published in *The Sketch* on 21 November 1923 and collected in the U.S. version of *Poirot Investigates* (1925), then in *Poirot's Early Cases* (1974). A radio version featured in Harold Huber's series *Hercule Poirot* (Mutual Broadcasting, 1945). The story was televised as part of *Agatha Christie's Poirot*, airing on ITV on 21 January 1990.

Characters: Dyer; **Hastings, Captain Arthur**; Lester, Charles; **Miller, Inspector**; Pearson, Mr.; **Poirot, Hercule**; Wu Ling

See also: *Agatha Christie's Poirot*; *Hercule Poirot* (**Mutual radio series**); *Poirot Investigates*; *Poirot's Early Cases*

Louise

There are two Louises who are not given surnames by Christie. Both are maids in short stories: "Yellow Iris" and "The Manhood of Edward Robinson." Louise the maid in *Murder on the Nile* also has no surname, although her equivalent character in *Death on the Nile* is Louise Bourget.

"The Love Detectives" (story; alternative title: "At the Crossroads")

The eponymous detectives are Harley Quin and Mr. Satterthwaite, neither of whom is technically a detective. This story was first published in 1926 but it missed collection in *The Mysterious Mr. Quin* (1930) and first appeared in book form in the United States in *Three Blind Mice* (1950) and in the United Kingdom in *Problem at Pollensa Bay and Other Stories* (1991).

One of the well-connected Mr. Satterthwaite's good friends is a chief constable, Colonel Melrose, whom he is visiting when news comes that the unwholesome Sir James Dwighton has been murdered. Both his wife and her younger lover confess to the crime, but the police suspect his valet. Harley Quin arrives, apparently from nowhere, and helps Satterthwaite realize the emotional truth and therefore the truth of the case. The wife and her lover killed Sir James, then planted evidence and faked confessions that could easily be

undermined, so they could clear themselves of suspicion. This bears a striking resemblance to the solution of *The Murder at the Vicarage*, published in 1930—so, too, does the nature of the false evidence: a smashed clock, designed to mislead about the time of death. It is therefore unsurprising that the story was not published in the Quin collection released that year.

Characters: Curtis, Inspector; Delangua, Paul; Dwighton, Lady Laura; Dwighton, Sir James; **Janet**; Jennings; **Melrose, Colonel**; Miles; **Quin, Harley**; **Satterthwaite, Mr.**

See also: *The Murder at the Vicarage* (**novel**); *The Mysterious Mr. Quin*; *Problem at Pollensa Bay* (**story collection**); *Three Blind Mice* (**story collection**)

Love from a Stranger (play)

There has been some debate over the authorship of *Love from a Stranger*, a wildly successful melodrama in what would now be called the domestic noir genre, which opened in the West End on 31 March 1936. Although some have claimed that Christie adapted her 1924 short story "Philomel Cottage" with help from playwright Frank Vosper, and others have argued that Vosper did the work alone, Julius Green has arrived at the most plausible and thoroughly evidenced solution. Vosper wrote the script, basing it on both the short story and a little-known three-act play, *The Stranger*, that Christie had written in 1932 (Green 112–13).

When he started work on the play in 1935, Vosper was already a successful young playwright, author of *Murder on the Second Floor* (1929), which became a novel, and *People Like Us* (1929). The play mines Christie's for sensation, drama, and suspense, removing some of the character sketches and creating something firmly marketed at filmmakers. The story, however, remains the same: a young woman meets a charming man, marries him, and slowly realizes that he is a murderer. Ultimately, she must kill him before he kills her. Emlyn Williams, author of *Night Must Fall*, which competed somewhat with his friend Vosper's play, claimed that Vosper had originally intended to make *Love from a Stranger* reminiscent of "the Patrick Mahon case," referring to the Crumbles case, in which Mahon "cut [a] woman up and no one believed it, he was such a charmer" (Williams 384). He presumably did not follow this strand because Williams's *Night Must Fall* was based on the same case. In fact, Christie had written obliquely about the Crumbles case in *The Scoop* (1930–31).

Vosper wrote a lead role, roguish Bruce Lovell, for himself, although he dropped out of the theatrical run after one week and was replaced by Basil Sydney. Edna Best took the star part, Cecily Harrington. The West End production was a runaway success, and on 21 September 1936, a Broadway production opened, with Vosper playing Bruce once more, to Jessie Royce Landis's Cecily. Vosper would not live long to enjoy the success of *Love from a Stranger*. He died in 1937, falling from an ocean liner into the sea. Despite a great deal of speculation about murder—centered on his sexuality and stoked to publicize his plays and posthumously published novel, *Murder on the Second Floor*—his death was ruled an accident.

The play has enjoyed a significant media life in English and German. There have been three movies (1937, 1947, and 1957) and four television adaptations (1938, 1947, 1958, and 1967). The BBC aired a radio version with the West End cast in 1936 and two more in 1945. In the United States, *NBC Mystery Theater* adapted it in 1944, CBS aired an adaptation starring Helen Hayes (who would go on to play Miss Marple) in 1949 as part of its *Electric Theater* program, and WKNA's *The Theatre Guild on the Air* broadcast a production in 1952. The short story "Philomel Cottage" has also been broadcast on U.K. and U.S. radio several times.

Publicity still from *Love from a Stranger* with John Hodiak as Manuel Cortez and Sylvia Sidney as Cecily Harrington. Eagle-Lion Films, 1947.

See also: **BBC Radio Adaptations; CBS Radio Adaptations;** *Love from a Stranger,* **Screen Adaptations of; NBC Radio Adaptations;** "Philomel Cottage"; *The Stranger*

Love from a Stranger, Screen Adaptations of

The volume of screen adaptations of *Love from a Stranger* in Christie's lifetime shows three things. First, it reveals the dramatic appeal of the play. Second, it betrays an appetite among screen producers for Christie's work. Third, it indicates the difficulty in acquiring the rights from her: *Love from a Stranger* was, after all, the property of dramatist Frank Vosper. He and his estate were much more willing than Christie to sell rights. For three decades, audiences could be assured of one film and one television adaptation around the same time, as well as numerous radio versions (four British, six American, and various others).

Trafalgar Films produced the first and most famous cinematic version in 1937, one year after the play's debut and within months of Vosper's death. Ann Harding, one of the first "talkie" stars, played Carol (Cecily in the play, Alix in the story) and the then-less famous Basil Rathbone, two years from playing Sherlock Holmes, co-starred as Gerald Lovell. In the United Kingdom, this film was known as *A Night of Terror*. It was a huge success, and the BBC broadcast a live television adaptation of the play on 23 November 1938, from Alexandra Palace.

Ten years later, a pattern emerged. Sylvia Sidney and John Hodiak appeared in a U.S. remake directed by Richard Whorf in 1947. In the United Kingdom, this was known as *A Stranger Walked In*. The BBC broadcast another live version on 25 May 1947.

It was another decade until the next film and television versions. *Ein Fremder kam ins Haus* (A Stranger Came into the House) is a 1957 German movie starring Fritz Tillmann and Elfriede Kuzmany. It is dramatized and directed by Wilm ten Haaf. On 26 December 1958, the BBC broadcast yet another television adaptation. The last television version was a West German adaptation, *Ein Fremder Klopft An* (A Stranger Knocks), aired on 5 December 1967. There have been no screen adaptations since, although revivals of the play since 2010 have done very well, given the popularity of "domestic noir" as a crime fiction subgenre.

See also: *Love from a Stranger* (play); "Philomel Cottage"

"Love Passes." See *The Road of Dreams* (poetry collection)

Lucas, Harry. See **Rayburn, Harry**

Lucy, Captain Reginald (Reggie) (1880–1969). See **Grant, Jim**

Luscombe, Colonel Derek

Colonel Derek Luscombe is the fiscally-minded and highly paternal guardian of Elvira Blake in *At Bertram's Hotel*.

Luttrell, Claude

Appearing in three J. Parker Pyne stories, Claude Luttrell is "one of the handsomest specimens of lounge lizard to be found in England" (*PPI* 47–48), whom Pyne occasionally employs to help out those clients seeking adventure. He acts as a gigolo in "The Case of the Middle-Aged Wife" and an exhibition dancer in "The Case of the Distressed Lady." In "The Case of the Rich Woman," he suggests that his "Schedule A" performance (that is, romancing the client, as in the first story) will not be sufficient and bows out of the case.

Luttrell, Colonel Toby, and Daisy

The Luttrells are owners of Styles Court in *Curtain*, which has been converted into a guest house since its earlier incarnation in *The Mysterious Affair at Styles*. Daisy Luttrell is a nagging wife, and her husband, Toby, is briefly manipulated by Stephen Norton into trying to kill her. However, he comes to regret his decision, and they are reconciled. When Hastings first sees her, he is reminded of Evelyn Howard, who stayed at Styles Court in *The Mysterious Affair at Styles*.

Luxmore, Mrs., and Professor

In *Cards on the Table*, Major Despard confesses to shooting Professor Luxmore on safari. Luxmore was delirious and dangerous, and Despard deemed the action necessary. However, Mrs. Luxmore believed he had murdered her husband out of love for her and has been spreading this story around polite society.

LWT Adaptations

LWT, a production company for ITV in the United Kingdom, was particularly keen to make an Agatha Christie series in the 1970s and 1980s but had to approach the estate carefully. Christie had been famously hostile to television, and her daughter was a proud guardian of her legacy. The plan was to propose a Poirot or Miss Marple series, but eventually Miss Marple went to the BBC. Obtaining the rights to Poirot proved a long-term endeavor.

The producers started with lengthy, multi-part adaptations of some lesser-known Christie works, "Bright Young Thing" mysteries of the 1920s and 1930s, dramatized by Pat Sandys. *Why Didn't They Ask Evans?* came first, offering a fairly literal translation of the 1934 novel with Francesca Annis and James Warwick playing the amateur sleuths. John Gielgud made a striking cameo as the clerical father of Warwick's character, Bobby Jones. This aired on 30 March 1980, not in the three parts intended but as a three-hour feature, and reactions were closely monitored: it was very much a water-testing moment for television producers and the Christie estate, to see if successful adaptations could be made. To this end, the budget was extensive by television standards: more than £1 million. In a further publicity drive, Peter Ustinov, then playing Poirot on the big screen, introduced the program when it aired on U.S. television in 1981.

The next offering, *The Seven Dials Mystery*, from the 1929 novel, followed on 8 March 1981. A similarly lengthy drama, this one starred Cheryl Campbell with John Gielgud cameoing again, this time as her befuddled and aristocratic father. James Warwick also returned in a similar role to that he had previously played, but now his character was a murderer. Other cast members included Harry Andrews as Superintendent Battle, Leslie Sands, Terence Alexander, and Rula Lenka. Like its predecessor, *The Seven Dials Mystery* was well-received.

The aim had always been for a series, and *The Agatha Christie Hour* (1982) tested these waters. The next year, *The Secret Adversary* was aired as the pilot for *Partners in Crime*, a 10-part collection of one-hour dramas based on Tommy and Tuppence short stories. For this program, particularly the pilot, the formula of *Why Didn't They Ask Evans?* and *The Seven Dials Mystery* was repeated, even casting Annis and Warwick as the central couple. If the rights to these characters had not been acquired, LWT would likely have attempted a version of *The Secret of Chimneys*, which shares characters and settings with *The Seven Dials Mystery*. The series was stagey and short-lived but did lead to LWT obtaining permission to produce what became *Agatha Christie's Poirot* in the late 1980s.

See also: ***The Agatha Christie Hour***; ***Partners in Crime*** **(1983 television series);** ***The Seven Dials Mystery*** **(novel);** ***Why Didn't They Ask Evans?*** **(novel)**

Lyndon, Gladys. See **Gladys**

Lytton Gore, Hermione ("Egg")

The last of Christie's Bright Young Things with unusual nicknames (like "Socks," "Bundle," and "Tuppence" in various 1920s texts), "Egg" is an energetic, enthusiastic young woman who idolizes Sir Charles Cartwright in *Three Act Tragedy* before growing up and choosing the less glamorous Oliver Manders.

MacArthur, General John

A retired military hero in *And Then There Were None*, General MacArthur accepts an invitation to Soldier Island because polite society seems to be ignoring him for some reason. That reason is the same as why he is on the island: during World War I, he abused his position by sending Arthur Richmond, the lover of his wife Leslie, to the front line, where he died. Leslie, too, died, and the general is haunted by her memory. He is the only character on the island to quietly accept his fate. When Christie adapted the novel for the stage at the height of World War II, she changed the character's name to General Mackenzie, presumably to avoid any confusion with General Douglas MacArthur (1880–1964), a U.S. military hero.

Macatta, Mrs.

Mrs. Macatta is a Member of Parliament who is expected to be "the great force in government in ten years' time" (*MITM* 128) in *The Seven Dials Mystery* and "The Incredible Theft." She is not presented positively but is a caricature of a barking woman who has given over her life to "worthy causes," judging others of her sex harshly and assuming manly traits—rather like Lady Westholme in *Appointment with Death*.

Mackenzie, General John. See **MacArthur, General John**

MacWhirter, Angus

Angus MacWhirter is a suicidal man in *Towards Zero*, who is encouraged not only to live but also to find his role in bringing harmony and justice to the people around him.

"Magnolia Blossom" (story)

A melodramatic story, "Magnolia Blossom" was likely written long before its publication in the *Royal Magazine* in 1926. It bears the trademarks of Christie's juvenilia: heightened romantic prose, an interest in the dissonance between what people say and what they think, and two-dimensional characters whose moral compasses come into tension with the force of lust. However, it also deals with adultery and leaving a marriage, something very much on the horizon for Christie in 1926.

Theodora "Theo" Darrell is embarking on an affair with Vincent Easton when she hears that her husband, Richard, has been involved in a career-ending scandal at his "big city firm" (*ACH* 96). She rushes back to Richard and promises to stay by his side whatever happens, even when he admits to financial crimes. Theo believes "she must stick by him" out of duty, because "she owed him loyalty" despite not loving him (103). Richard says that Vincent Easton must be selling his confidential documents, fueling the scandal, and asks Theo to flirt with him so they can be recovered. Theo recovers and burns some papers from Vincent. She returns to Richard who is ungrateful and believes she slept with Vincent for the papers. Enraged, she tells him about the affair and leaves for "freedom," because she cannot stay with a man who had "sold me, your own wife, to purchase safety" (107).

The protagonist is referred to as "Theo" when with a man but "Theodora" when alone with her thoughts. She has not yet discovered her own personality or adjusted to her persona in life. This small touch shows an experimental streak gently nurtured by Christie throughout the 1920s. The title refers to the protagonist's resemblance, especially when dressed up in white to woo Vincent, to "a magnolia flower" (100): in time, the flower can blossom.

"Magnolia Blossom" appeared in the U.S. collection in *The Golden Ball* (1971). An adaptation of the story appeared in the U.K. collection *The Agatha Christie Hour* (1982), a tie-in for the 1982 television series of the same name. It was later appeared in *Problem at Pollensa Bay* (1992). On 4 February 2004, BBC Radio 4 broadcast a 30-minute modernized version.

Characters: Darrell, Richard; Darrell, Theodora ("Theo"); Easton, Vincent

See also: *The Agatha Christie Hour*; **BBC Radio Adaptations**; *The Golden Ball* (story collection); *Problem at Pollensa Bay* (story collection)

"Mainly Conversation." See *The Floating Admiral*

Les Maîtres du Mystère (The Masters of Mystery; radio series)

French radio station RTF broadcast two Christie adaptations in the 1950s as part of the series *Les Maîtres du Mystère* (The Masters of Mystery, 1952–74). *Le Meurtre de Roger Ackroyd* (The Murder of Roger Ackroyd) starred Henri Crémieux as Hercule Poirot. It was dramatized by Jean Cosmos and aired on 22 October 1957. On 25 November 1958, it aired a Miss Marple adaptation, *La Plume Empoisonnée* (The Moving Finger), dramatized by Hélène Misserly and starring Denise Gence.

Les Maîtres du Mystère was produced by Pierre Véry and was a long-running, popular program that is still occasionally repeated on French radio stations. It featured adaptations of a range of British novelists including E.C. Bentley, Dorothy L. Sayers, John Creasey, and Georgette Heyer, as well as European and American writers such as Friedrich Dürrenmatt, Oscar Wilde, Raymond Chandler, Léo Malet, and Charlotte Armstrong.

See also: **Golden Age Crime Fiction**; *The Moving Finger*; *The Murder of Roger Ackroyd*

Malinowski, Ladislaus

Ladislaus Malinowski is a free-living racing car driver in *At Bertram's Hotel* with an expensive, exotic lifestyle. Elvira Blake is in love with him and jealous of his close relationship with her mother, Lady Bess Sedgwick, who better fits his world than she does.

Mallowan, Sir Max (1904–78)

The second husband of Agatha Christie, Max Mallowan was an archaeologist, 16 years her junior. The couple met on a dig with Leonard and Katharine Woolley at Ur and married in Edinburgh on 11 September 1930. Both lied about their ages on their wedding certificate: his is given as 31 (he was 26) and hers as 37 (she was 39). At the time of their marriage, Mallowan was an apprentice to Leonard Woolley. By 1932, he had become a field director working with the British Museum. Christie regularly accompanied him on excavations and was actively involved in the proceedings. Among their most notable discoveries were the Nimrud Ivories, dating from the seventh century BCE, many of which are on display in the British Museum.

Mallowan served in World War II in the Volunteer Reserve with the Royal Air Force and, after the war, was appointed professor of Western Asiatic archaeology at the University of London before he was elected to a fellowship at All Souls College, Oxford. Mallowan authored several works on archaeology, including *Nimrud and Its Remains* in 1966. He was appointed a Commander of the British Empire (CBE) in 1960 and knighted in 1968. After Christie's death, her widower, who had felt somewhat in her shadow, enjoyed some short flirtations with other women before marrying his longtime secretary, Barbara Parker. He died in 1978 and was buried next to his first wife.

See also: **Archaeology**; *Come, Tell Me How You Live*; *Murder in Mesopotamia*

"The Mallowans"

Appearing in the "Talk of the Town" section of *The New Yorker* in October 1966, "The Mallowans" was a rare joint interview of Christie and her husband, Max Mallowan. Unusually, it focuses mostly on Sir Max's achievements, covering his archaeological findings in Nimrud and her role in cleaning the ivories. The interview was conducted by Geoffrey Hellman.

See also: **Mallowan, Sir Max**

"The Man from the Sea" (story)

"The Man from the Sea" is a remarkably accomplished example of the short story as an art form. In this sixth entry of *The Mysterious Mr. Quin* (1930), the recurring characters are Harley Quin and Mr. Satterthwaite. It was written on holiday in the Canary Islands, and Christie's husband Max Mallowan considered it one of her finest, "most profound" stories (Mallowan 205).

The story opens with Satterthwaite feeling ennui (explained to himself as "feeling old" [*MMQ* 255]) and finding that even his "valuable Art collection ... seemed at that moment strangely unsatisfying"; he wants a human connection (255–56). On holiday on a Spanish island, he watches a dog die of exhaustion and feels depressed. He encounters Anthony Cosdon who conversely feels unable to find "solitude" (263) and reveals that the mysterious Harley Quin is also on the island. As Cosdon asks, "what's it all for?," Satterthwaite recognizes in him the "dumb bewildered questioning" of the dead dog (266). Cosdon reveals that he only has six months to live and strongly implies that he is thinking of jumping off a cliff, before leaving Satterthwaite to his thoughts.

Satterthwaite is invited into a villa, La Paz, by its owner of 22 years, an unnamed Englishwoman, who tells him how she witnessed her abusive husband jump from the cliff and drown decades ago. She then had a brief affair with an Englishman visiting the island, which produced a son, John, after he had left. John is now a grown man who "wants to know all about his father—he wants details" (287), which his mother is too ashamed to share. She is contemplating suicide so that John can marry without the revelation of the stain of illegitimacy. Satterthwaite makes her promise to do nothing for 24 hours. As Cosdon is on his way to jump, Satterthwaite manages to engineer a meeting between him and the woman, who recognizes him as John's father. The couple is happily reunited and looking forward to life. At the clifftop, Satterthwaite finds Quin, who reflects cryptically on the relationship between love and death, then disappears in the direction of the cliff-edge.

"The Man from the Sea" was first published in *Britannia and Eve* (vol. 1, issue 6) in October 1929, then collected in *The Mysterious Mr. Quin* (1930). It has not been dramatized in any medium.

Characters: **Cosdon, Anthony**; John; **Leith, Duchess of (Maria)**; **Quin, Harley**; **Satterthwaite, Mr.**

See also: *The Mysterious Mr. Quin*; **Suicide**

The Man in the Brown Suit (novel; alternative titles: *Anna the Adventuress*; *Anne the Adventurous*)

The first novel Christie published with agency representation was also the first with a female narrator. Anne Beddingfeld, a young woman whose elderly father has died, is left with some money and no direction as she dreams of being swept off her feet by "a stern and silent Rhodesian" like the men she has seen in films (*MBS* 19). She travels to London without much of a plan, only to see a man die in the Underground and becomes convinced that it was murder. She sees a man in a brown suit fleeing the scene. Recovering a cryptic note dropped by the man, she deciphers the name of a luxury cruiser and decides to set sail and investigate.

On board, the man she observed in London stumbles into her cabin after he has been shot, and she helps him evade his captors. He introduces himself as Harry Rayburn. Anne and Harry become involved in an international scheme involving stolen, smuggled diamonds and a shadowy arch-criminal known as the Colonel. There are numerous near-death experiences, with Anne imagining herself as a heroine of the silent cinema. In the end, with help from Colonel Race of British intelligence and a chatty American tourist, she recovers the diamonds, identifies a fellow passenger as the Colonel, and agrees to marry Harry (the man in the brown suit, who turns out to be a titled millionaire).

Anne is an early example of a professional heroine in Christie. To facilitate her investigation, she becomes a journalist. Throughout the novel, she encounters problems because of her sex, although the tone is always light. In her pursuits, Anne imagines herself as "Anna the Adventuress," her own spin on the star of *The Perils of Pamela*, her favorite film series. This is a not-so-subtle allusion to *The Perils of Pauline*, an oft-repeated and occasionally remade genre-defining 1914 series of short movies starring Pearl White as the helpless Pauline, consistently tied to train tracks and awaiting a savior. This series was followed by *The Exploits of Elaine*, also starring White, the book of which Christie adapted for the stage as *The Clutching Hand*. However, this man-made model of heroic womanhood fails to hold good: Pamela (like Pauline) is generally helpless, and her problems are fixed by handsome men coming to her aide. Anne, however, comes to the aid of helpless handsome men.

Early reviews noted another generic innovation. Writing in the *New Statesman*, J. Franklin called the book "remarkable especially for a brand new device for concealing the villain's identity" (qtd. in Sanders and Lovallo 27). The device referred to is the use of a narrator-murderer. Some passages, interspersed with Anne's narrative, are extracts from the diary of Sir Eustace Pedlar, who transpires to be the Colonel. Christie would use this device to more extreme, and notable, effect two years later, in *The Murder of Roger Ackroyd*.

However, the narrator-murderer device on this occasion may not be deliberate innovation but a coincidence of late plot changes. Pedlar is the only character that Christie publicly admitted was based on (rather than inspired by) a real person. A pompous, bullying, but magnetic type, he was based on Major Ernest Belcher, an extraordinary man with whom the Christies traveled during their 1922 world tour. Belcher encouraged Christie to write this book and even suggested a title (*The Mill House Mystery*, quickly dropped), as well as insisting she base a character on him. However, when Christie told him that she had killed off the character on whom he was based, Belcher wanted to be cast as the murderer. Christie dedicated the novel to Belcher.

Another relic of the Grand Tour in *The Man in the Brown Suit* is the presence of wooden animals. During her travels, Christie acquired several wooden animals, with which she was photographed in 1923 for a spread in *The Sketch*. Tourists in this novel acquire the same souvenirs, one of which serves as a hiding place for the diamonds.

The novel's first publication was in the *London Evening News*, as a serial titled *Anne the Adventurous*, from November 1923 to January 1924. Christie remembered this in her autobiography as *Anna the Adventuress* (a name Anne gives herself in the book and the title of a book by

E. Phillips Oppenheim), which she considered "as silly a title as I had ever heard … though I kept my mouth shut, because … they were willing to pay me £500" (*AA* 319). It was published by The Bodley Head in the United Kingdom and Dodd, Mead in the United States in 1924.

The first television adaptation was a much-anticipated final installment of CBS's modernized Christie telemovies, broadcast in January 1989. In 2005, a French graphic novel was produced, translated into English in 2007. In 2017, an adaptation aired on French television as part of *Les Petits Meurtres d'Agatha Christie*. Surprisingly, the novel's potential for a computer game adaptation remains unexploited.

Characters: Batani; **Beddingfeld, Anne**; **Blair, Suzanne**; Carton, L.B.; Chichester, Rev. Eardsley, Sir Laurence; Mr.; Flemming, Mr. and Mrs.; Grunberg, Anita; James, Caroline; Jeannie; **Lucas, Harry**; Meadows, Detective Inspector; Minks, Arthur; Nasby, Lord; Pagett, Guy; Pagett, Mrs. and children; Parker, Harry; Paulovitch, Count Sergius; **Pedlar, Sir Eustace**; Pettigrew, Miss; **Race, Colonel Johnny**; **Rayburn, Harry**

See also: **CBS Television Adaptations**; *The Clutching Hand*; Feminism; *The Grand Tour*; *The Murder of Roger Ackroyd*; *Les Petits Meurtres d'Agatha Christie*

The Man in the Brown Suit (television adaptation). See **CBS Television Adaptations**

"The Man in the Empty Chair." See "The Dead Harlequin"

"The Man in the Mist." See *Partners in Crime* (story collection)

"A Man of Magic." See "At the Bells and Motley"

"The Man on the Chancel Steps." See "Sanctuary"

"The Man Who Knew" (story)

The brief early short story "The Man Who Knew" was written between 1918 and 1923, so after *The Mysterious Affair at Styles* and before Christie's second Poirot novel, *The Murder on the Links*. It was not published in Christie's lifetime and first appeared in print with some of her archival notes in John Curran's *Agatha Christie's Murder in the Making* (2011). At fewer than 2,000 words, the story was later expanded into "The Red Signal" (1924) and serves of interest chiefly as a point of comparison: as Curran notes, Christie's evolving technique is evidenced in her decision to change the villain who appears only at the end into a trusted character who appears early on in "The Red Signal" (*Making* 135).

Characters: Dalton, Cyril; Freshnam; Haverfield, Agnes; Lawson, Derek; Sir James; Western, Noel; Western, Stella

See also: **"The Red Signal"**

The Man Who Was Number Four. See *The Big Four* (novel)

"The Man Who Was Number Sixteen" (story; alternative title: "The Man Who Was No. 16"). See *Partners in Crime* (story collection)

Manders, Oliver

Oliver Manders is an angry communist who is reformed by the love of a good woman in *Three Act Tragedy*.

"The Manhood of Edward Robinson" (story; alternative titles: "The Day of His Dreams"; "Romance and a Red Runabout")

The short story "The Manhood of Edward Robinson" takes place over Christmas. It concerns a mild-mannered man, Edward Robinson, who harbors fantasies about having wild adventures, escaping the dull tedium of his life with his fiancée, Maud. One day, he is suddenly thrown into a dramatic escapade involving a beautiful woman and ends up grateful for his mundane life with Maud. This kind of frothy cautionary tale is typical of Christie's early magazine stories, and the general message is consistent with her juvenilia (e.g., "In the Marketplace" and "A Pretty Cowslip").

The story was published in the *Grand Magazine* in November 1924 and appeared in the U.K. collection *The Listerdale Mystery* (1934) and the U.S. collection *The Golden Ball* (1971). It was adapted for television as the final installment of *The Agatha Christie Hour* in 1982.

Characters: Champneys, Gerald; **Elliott, Lady Noreen**; **Folliat, Jimmy**; Larella, Agnes; **Louise**; **Maud**; Robinson, Edward

See also: *The Agatha Christie Hour*; *The Golden Ball* (story collection); *The Listerdale Mystery* (story collection)

Mannheim, Dr., and Elsa

In *Destination Unknown*, Dr. Mannheim was an eminent Polish scientist who briefly escaped turmoil with his daughter during World War II. Elsa, the daughter, married, and was murdered by, Tom Betterton.

"Manx Gold" (story)

In 1929, Alderman Arthur B. Crookall offered Christie £60 to promote the Isle of Man for tourism. Working with the "June Effort," Christie devised a treasure-hunt inspired by the geographies and mythologies of the island. The hunt involved four "treasures" in the form of antique coins hidden in snuff boxes around the island, accompanied by instructions about where to redeem them for £100 cash. Clues to the locations of these snuff boxes were provided in the form of "Manx Gold," a Christie story, published in the *Daily Dispatch* in May 1930 and then again as a booklet. Although the story was boisterously publicized and the island saw some increased tourism, it did not have quite the desired effect.

The story features first cousins and "from time to time" fiancés Juan and Fenella (*WLL* 142), very much at home among Christie's Bright Young Thing detectives. Like the couple in the Miss Marple story "Strange Jest," they hear that an eccentric uncle has died and has written to his relatives stating that they must solve some cryptic clues to recover his hidden treasure. He has hidden a fortune in an unexpected form in four snuff boxes around the Isle of Man. There are five clues that must be solved by Juan and Fenella, as they pit themselves against a murderous cousin. The reader also has access to these clues, one by one. At the end of the story, Juan and Fenella hand their evil cousin over to the police and, having found all four boxes, agree to marry.

The public did not respond as planned. The first snuff box was found before the relevant clue had been published, as the winner had worked it out from other details in the text. The second clue was solved in the proper manner, with the finder claiming it

had been too easy. The third box was recovered by someone who had not even read the story but simply guessed. The final clue remained unsolved, even when the competition was extended, meaning Christie had to write a postscript explaining it in the narrative voice of Juan. Moreover, since the competition excluded Isle of Man residents, there was a certain amount of resentment, and fake snuff-boxes were planted by locals.

In 1997, the story appeared, with detailed notes by Tony Medawar, in *While the Light Lasts*.

Characters: Corjeag, Ewan; Fayll, Dr. Richard; **Mylecharane, Fenella, and Juan;** Mylecharane, Myles; Skillicorn, Mrs.

See also: **Bright Young Things**; *The Harlequin Tea Set* (story collection); **"Strange Jest"**; *While the Light Lasts* (story collection)

Marchmont, Adela

Mother to Lynn Marchmont in *Taken at the Flood*, Adela Marchmont has been devastated by the war and a lack of direction in its aftermath: "During the war she had taken in evacuees from London, had cooked and cleaned for them, had worked with the W.V.S., made jam, helped with school meals. She had worked fourteen hours a day in contrast to a pleasant easy life before the war. She was now, as Lynn saw, very near a breakdown. Tired out and frightened of the future" (23).

Marchmont, Lynn

A demobbed WREN, returning to her family home and long-term fiancé in *Taken at the Flood*, Lynn Marchmont grows frustrated that, although she has changed, nothing else around her has.

"Margery Allingham—A Tribute" (article)

A peer of Christie's and perhaps the most straightforwardly conservative of the Golden Age "Queens of Crime," Margery Allingham (1904–66) created the gentleman sleuth Albert Campion. Two years after her death, the *Penguin Book News* published a "Margery Allingham—A Tribute" with contributions from a selection of distinguished voices, most notably Christie. Christie's substantial tribute has been used as a foreword in two posthumous collections of Allingham stories: *The Return* of *Mr. Campion* (1991) and a reissue of *The Allingham Minibus* in 2019. This followed Christie's reference to Allingham in 1945 as "foremost" among peers ("Detective Writers in England" 4).

Christie's tribute includes the oft-quoted line "Margery Allingham stands out like a shining light" ("MA-T"), which she goes on to qualify, praising the author for making each character and setting distinctive and memorable. She highlights the "intermingled" sense of "the fantastic and the real," inviting comparisons between Allingham and some of Christie's own favorite writers, Virginia Woolf and Elizabeth Bowen. Christie also makes the intriguing point that she "barely knew" Allingham and that "I am rather glad that I know her only by the words that came with such art from her pen." Like Christie's shy demeanor, Allingham biographer Julia Jones notes that Allingham struggled with a stutter for years and felt uncomfortable in social gatherings (41, 97). Although some accounts portray Allingham as considerably less generous about Christie's work than Christie was about her work, Allingham's tribute to Christie appeared in the 4 June 1950 *New York Times* timed with the publication of *A Murder Is Announced*, Christie's 50th whodunit, in which Allingham said about Christie, among other laudatory comments, "In her own sphere, there is no one to touch her" (BR2).

Christie's tribute describes Allingham's strengths and weaknesses as a writer, and Christie confesses that she "did wonder whence whether Margery Allingham might not be a pseudonym of Dorothy Sayers," since Campion is extremely similar to Sayers's Lord Peter Wimsey—perhaps another veiled critique. The tribute nonetheless concludes with a genial "Bravo!" (Christie, "MA-T").

See also: **The Detection Club**; **Golden Age Crime Fiction**

Marie Angelique, Sister

Sister Marie Angelique is a Belgian nun who has become a refugee in "The Hound of Death" and is plagued by destructive visions which seem to bring about their own fulfillment. The most famous real sister Marie Angelique was an abbess of Port-Royal in the seventeenth century, who was influential in the spread of Jansenism, a movement in Catholicism that emphasizes predestination.

Market Basing

Market Basing is Christie's go-to fictional town, located just outside of various centers of action. It first appears in "The Market Basing Mystery," a 1923 Poirot short story, and is near enough to the Chimneys estate in *The Secret of Chimneys* and *The Seven Dials Mystery* that characters go there for shopping, and its police department deals with emergency calls. The 1937 Poirot novel *Dumb Witness* is also set in Market Basing. Although Christie toyed with taking Poirot back there, briefly, in *Five Little Pigs*, she never did. Instead, it mostly appears in Miss Marple cases—*4.50 from Paddington*, *The Mirror Crack'd from Side to Side*, and *Nemesis*, with a brief mention in *A Caribbean Mystery*—and it is given a county, Melfordshire, in the Tommy and Tuppence novel *By the Pricking of My Thumbs*. Elsewhere, it is said to be in Berkshire or Greater London. Archivist John Curran has suggested that later incarnations of Market Basing were based on Wallingford, where Christie bought a house, Winterbrook, in 1934 (*Secret Notebooks* 219).

See also: **St. Mary Mead**

"The Market Basing Mystery" (story)

A Poirot story, "The Market Basing Mystery" was first published in *The Sketch* in 1923. It appeared in the U.S. anthology *The Under Dog* (1951) and the U.K. anthology *Poirot's Early Cases* (1974). Market Basing is one of Christie's often-cited fictional towns and appears here for the first time. The story was the basis of the novella "Murder in the Mews," although the setting and characters are different—the plot, however, is similar enough that this story is one of the few that was never filmed as part of the ITV series *Agatha Christie's Poirot*.

Poirot, Captain Hastings, and Inspector Japp, investigate a locked-room mystery: the death by gunshot of Walter Protheroe. Although it looks like suicide, Protheroe is holding the gun in the wrong hand, and could not, apparently, have inflicted the wound upon himself. Poirot learns that a third party staged his suicide to look like murder, so a blackmailer could be implicated and hanged.

Characters: Clegg, Miss; Giles, Dr.; **Hastings, Captain Arthur**; **Japp, Chief Inspector James**; Parker, Mr.; Parker, Mrs.; **Poirot, Hercule**; Pollard, Constable; Protheroe, Walter

See also: **"Murder in the Mews" (novella)**; *Poirot's Early Cases*; *The Under Dog* **(story collection)**.

Marle, Iris. See **Barton, Rosemary**

Marle, Iris

Sister to Rosemary Barton in *Sparkling Cyanide*, Iris Marle receives less attention from men but is a far more put-together and interesting person. She is the intended victim when George Barton dies.

Marmalade Moon (play)

A revised version of *New Moon*, *Marmalade Moon* is a one-act play script that has never been produced or published and is currently housed in the Christie Family Archive. It is a four-hander, in which two couples are celebrating, in turn, a honeymoon and the anniversary of a divorce. By the end of the play, both couples have split up and reconciled. It has echoes of George Bernard Shaw's *Getting Married* (1905).

See also: *New Moon*

Marple, Jane

As a character, Miss Jane Marple is enduring and beloved in part because she is generally misunderstood. She is not, simply, a sweet old lady who happens to solve crimes, although this is how she presents herself to suspects and policemen, and this is also how she is generally discussed, including by fans and critics. A key point of Miss Marple as a sleuth is that cultural stereotypes about older women being harmless and irrelevant give her access to spaces denied to more traditionally threatening figures—and this is also true in popular culture. Despite an inherently ruthless nature, she is many people's favorite fictional character, regarded warmly as a universal great-aunt.

Christie's recorded inspirations for Miss Marple are Caroline Shepherd, the gossipy heart of *The Murder of Roger Ackroyd*, and her own "Auntie-Grannie" (Margaret Miller, her father's stepmother and her mother's adoptive mother). In common with Miss Marple, Christie wrote, Auntie-Grannie was "a cheerful person [who] always expected the worst of everyone and everything, and was, with almost frightening accuracy, usually proved right" (*AA* 435). This is part of Miss Marple's appeal as a sleuth: she has no illusions about human nature. Indeed, she states in "Strange Jest" that "human nature" is a thing of "unbelievable" "depravity" (*MMFC* 33). From a life spent in her own insular village, St. Mary Mead, she has observed the spectrum of human behavior play out in microcosm, and in her investigations, she draws on "village parallels"—stories she remembers from St. Mary Mead—to explain why someone acts the way they do, and what it means.

A quiet, unassuming, often overlooked elderly spinster, Miss Marple was created in 1927, within a decade of World War I. The context for the tendency to overlook her and the surprise value in her contributing significantly to social progress by capturing so many murderers lie in her status as a "superfluous woman." The idea of "superfluous women" gained traction in the United Kingdom in the mid-nineteenth century, when women began noticeably to outnumber men in the population; with the extreme loss of male life during World War I, the disparity continued. Significant numbers of women had assumed traditionally male jobs during the war, but most of these were given back to men when it was over, and with the rise of suffrage and (limited) social reforms, as well as the population discrepancy, millions of women were destined simply not to marry.

This concept is illuminatingly discussed by Marion Shaw and Sabine Vanacker in their seminal monograph, *Reflecting on Miss Marple*. Shaw and Vanacker link the phenomenon of "superfluous women" with public expressions of "guilt and resentment," focused on "women leading apparently useless, or at least sterile, lives," adding up to a legacy of "[f]ear of the unmarried woman, and an accompanying misogyny" (38). This, they point out, make Miss Marple a marginalized figure, presented as someone thought to be "useless"—and they link this to Christie herself, going through a divorce when she created Miss Marple, "tacitly join[ing] the ranks of 'surplus women'" (37).

Miss Marple is "a figure whom society in its ageism condemns as, at best, charmingly quaint and, at worst, as a tire-some nuisance, prove more inexorably logical than the most skillful policemen" (Shaw and Vanacker 64). Like Hercule Poirot, Miss Marple gathers information by listening to gossip, inviting confidences via an unthreatening demeanor, and understanding human nature. She notices things missed by male investigators, and, more than in Poirot's case, these things are often domestic: in *The Body in the Library*, for example, she sees significance no one else sees in discarded nail clippings, the nature of quarrels between two lovers, and a working-class girl wearing what looks like her best dress to an event for which she would naturally "dress down." It all adds up to make Miss Marple not just underestimated but, in a gentle way, an anti-establishment figure.

In the early 1950s, Christie bolstered Miss Marple from the rank of her secondary detective to that of a potential rival for Poirot. She still wrote more Poirot books but greatly increased the volume of Miss Marple novels issued, sometimes one a year. Moreover, although Poirot was beginning to retreat, entering his narratives at progressively later stages, Miss Marple's page-time increased. The last-written Miss Marple novel, *Nemesis*, from 1971, is in large part the sleuth's internal monologue. Miss Marple ages in a way: she is always old and always "Victorian," but in the early texts, she presents herself in a specifically Victorian way, complete with black lace. In the 1950s novels, she is essentially Edwardian, and in the last books, she is tweed-clad and not a million miles away from Christie herself. She is consistent in her outdated views, often referring to "gentlemen" "in the tone of one speaking of some alien and dangerous species," a manner described as "Victorian" (*450FP* 166–67) but later reveals more of her "Victorian" attitudes such as her "view of foreigners" (not positive) and her highly problematic attitude to rape (*N* 76).

Robert Barnard has described Miss Marple's development as a process of "fluffification," writing that, "over the years the binoculars are put away, the gardening becomes genuine rather than just a convenient passion, the gentle, appealing manner becomes a real guide to her human qualities rather than a smokescreen" (108). In short, Barnard claims that Miss Marple develops from a character who uses stereotypes about old women as a cover under which to operate to genuinely embodying those qualities. However, it is difficult to reconcile this view of the character with the texts themselves: it is perhaps more the case that Miss Marple on screen and in popular analysis fulfills those qualities she exploits in the books. Indeed, the more the reader enters her head in the later books, the more the reader learns that her twittery manner is strategic and that her drive for justice and retribution is ruthless. Only the first novel, *The Murder at the Vicarage*, directly points out that she is not as nice and gentle as she seems—but the rest consistently demonstrate it.

Miss Marple appears "merely a gentle, fussy-looking elderly spinster" (*MMFC* 31) but is hard-nosed, driven, and ruthless. A particular aspect of her style of detection is the use of traps to catch the killers, with live human bait. Nearly every Miss Marple novel includes a sequence in which Miss Marple has identified the murderer but has no evidence, so she sets someone up—normally a troubled young person and more often than not a woman—to pretend they know something. When the villain tries to kill the person, the police step in, and order is restored. In both versions of Miss Marple's last case (*Sleeping Murder*, written for posthumous publication, and *Nemesis*), Miss Marple herself acts as bait—a form of closure, just as Hercule Poirot's death is the culmination of his playing God in *Curtain*.

Christie's friend A.L. Rowse certainly believed she had "put something of herself" into Miss Marple (110), although Christie repeatedly denied this claim, preferring to be compared to the much less threatening

Ariadne Oliver. Miss Marple is a popular character because she does not challenge the status quo. That same status quo is why she is so fundamentally misunderstood, on and off the page.

Miss Marple appears in the following novels and U.K. short story collections: *The Murder at the Vicarage*, *The Thirteen Problems*, *The Body in the Library*, *The Moving Finger*, *A Murder Is Announced*, *They Do It with Mirrors*, *A Pocket Full of Rye*, *4.50 from Paddington*, *The Adventure of the Christmas Pudding*, *The Mirror Crack'd from Side to Side*, *A Caribbean Mystery*, *At Bertram's Hotel*, *Nemesis*, *Sleeping Murder*, and *Miss Marple's Final Cases*. She also appears in the uncollected story "The Case of the Caretaker's Wife."

Marriot, Inspector

Inspector Marriot is a good-natured Scotland Yard inspector who works with Tommy and Tuppence Beresford in "The Affair of the Pink Pearl," "The Adventure of the Sinister Stranger," "Finessing the King," "The Gentleman Dressed in Newspaper," "The Crackler," and "The Sunningdale Mystery."

Marsdon, Anthony ("Tony")

Anthony Marsdon is an attractive colleague of Deborah Beresford in decoding during World War II in *N or M?* He turns out to be a Nazi spy. The character appears similar to but is distinct from Anthony Marston in *And Then There Were None*.

"The Marsdon Manor Tragedy." See **"The Tragedy at Marsdon Manor"**

Marsh, Andrew, and Violet

In "The Case of the Missing Will," Andrew Marsh is Violet Marsh's late uncle; an old-fashioned but playful type, he disapproves of women's education but leaves his niece all his money, on the condition that she solves a puzzle he set her. A handsome, businesslike woman, Violet is Hercule Poirot's client. From her personality to her name, she exudes the influence of Sir Arthur Conan Doyle on Christie's early short stories, as she could easily have been a client of Sherlock Holmes. She holds a bachelor's degree and has been involved in heated exchanges with her uncle over her decision to study at the University of Cambridge.

Marsh, Captain Ronald, and Hon. Geraldine

Captain Ronald Marsh is the nephew, and the Honorable Geraldine Marsh is the daughter, of the fourth Baron Edgware; they are in a relationship in *Lord Edgware Dies*. Ronald becomes Lord Edgware upon his uncle's death, whereas Geraldine celebrates the loss of an abusive parent. They experience financial and mental health problems, respectively, which make them prime suspects in the murder investigation.

Marsh, Lord George. See **Edgware, Lord**

Marshall, Arlena. See **Stewart, Arlena**

Marshall, Captain Kenneth, and Linda

In *Evil under the Sun*, Kenneth Marshall is Arlena Stewart's current husband, who is framed for her murder. He has a history of trying to save women by marrying them, having previously married a woman acquitted for her first husband's murder. Linda is his teenaged daughter from that marriage. She is young for her age and sheltered. She tries to kill her stepmother using voodoo and, when Arlena dies, believes she has succeeded.

Marston, Anthony ("Tony")

Anthony Marston is a self-absorbed playboy and the first of the "ten little soldier boys" to die in *And Then There Were None*. He is on the island to be punished because, in the past, he killed John and Lucy Combes in a hit and run. At the beginning of the novel, he is described as the most alive of the characters—perhaps because he genuinely feels no guilt for his actions, which is why the murderer gives him the first, easiest death.

Martin, Alix, and Gerald

Alix and Gerald Martin are newlyweds in "Philomel Cottage" who both come to realize they know very little about one another. When Alix realizes that Gerald is an infamous wife-murderer, she tricks him into listening to a story while she slowly poisons him. The equivalent characters in Christie's play version, *The Stranger*, are Enid Bradshaw and Gerald Strange. In Frank Vosper's

Love from a Stranger, they are Cecily and Bruce Lovell.

Martin, Bryan

A film actor "of the Greek god type" in *Lord Edgware Dies* (9), Bryan Martin is just as artificial a person as Jane Wilkinson, whom he tries to implicate in her husband's murder in a most theatrical manner. That he cannot be distinguished, at a distance, from Lord Edgware's butler shows that he is more an archetype than a character, befitting the world of celebrity to which he belongs.

Martin, Gladys. See **Gladys**

Martindale, Hilda. See **Bland, Josiah, and Valerie**

Martindale, Jane. See **Redfern, Christine**

Martindale, Katherine

In *The Clocks*, Miss Katherine Martindale owns the Cavendish Secretarial Bureau and is nicknamed "Sandy Cat" by her employees. Apparently a comic figure, she turns out to be involved in a murder conspiracy with a secret relationship to Josiah and Valerie Bland, and is the murderer of Edna Brent. This character started out as Miss Spencer in "The Clock Stopped."

Mary

Mary is the mother of Jesus Christ, shown in the "Star Over Bethlehem" to be tempted by an angel with foreknowledge of her son's death. She also appears in "The Naughty Donkey." In "The Island," she lives on an island—presumably Patmos—with St. John and is taken over the water, by Jesus, to become the Queen of Heaven.

Mary, Aunt

In "Next to a Dog," the no-nonsense, elderly Aunt Mary rejects modern fads and is convinced that Joyce is looking "peaky" because she has become a vegetarian (*PPB* 183).

Mason, Ada

In *The Mystery of the Blue Train*, Ada Mason is the equivalent of Jane Mason in "The Plymouth Express," and her real name is Kitty Kidd. She is an actress posing as a maid to Ruth Kettering, so she can help execute a murder and robbery.

A Masque from Italy (lyric drama)

Christie was Agatha Miller when she wrote *A Masque from Italy*. A lyric drama subtitled "The Comedy of the Arts," it forms the first half of her 1925 poetry collection *The Road of Dreams* and may well have been performed by the author and her friends at some point, as they frequently mounted small productions. However, no record of a performance survives. It takes the form of a series of "songs," sung by characters from the *Commedia dell'arte*, a key influence on the author's formative work. According to Julius Green, the authority on Christie's stage writing, she put these songs to music in the early 1920s (37). Green also speculates that "it may have been written as a puppet-show" (38). However, references in the text to players removing their masks suggests conventional performance.

At the heart of the story is the love between Harlequin and Columbine. Whereas Pulcinella and Pierrette are content to dance around merrily, Harlequin and Columbine engage in a doomed romance characterized by playfulness and trickery. Expanding the typescript for publication in 1925, Christie inserted a 10th song or poem, "Pierrot Grown Old," which reflects on the power of love enduring after death and separation. The Harlequin-Columbine story and characters would remain influential in Christie's work, most notable in the character of Harley Quin.

Christie later recalled that "Harlequin's Song" from this set was her first published poem and that she was paid one guinea for it.

Characters: Columbine, Harlequin, Pierrette, Pierrot, Puchinello, Pulcinella

See also: **Commedia dell'arte**; *Poems*; *The Road of Dreams*; **Quin, Harley**

Masterton, Connie, and Wilfred

In *Dead Man's Folly* and "Hercule Poirot and the Greenshore Folly," on which it is based, Wilfred Masterton is a West Country Member of Parliament, and Connie is his wife who is "good at organising things" (TGF 15) and who persuaded Sir George Stubbs to host a fete on his grounds.

"The Matter of the Ambassador's Boots." See **"The Ambassador's Boots"**

Maud

The fiancée of Edward Robinson in "The Manhood of Edward Robinson," Maud represents the safe tedium of a normal life. He starts the story tired of her and ends the story glad of her.

Mayhem Parva

The British writer Colin Watson coined the term *Mayhem Parva* in *Snobbery with Violence: English Crime Stories and Their Audience* (1971), which examines social attitudes in and surrounding Anglocentric detective fiction. Watson devotes a chapter to "the little world of Mayhem Parva" (*Snobbery* 165), which H.R.F. Keating defines in an introduction as an element of "mystery fiction of the type generally linked to the name of Agatha Christie" (*Snobbery* 11). Watson defines Mayhem Parva as a setting for gentle English crime stories,

> a cross between a village and a commuters' dormitory in the South of England, self-contained and largely self-sufficient. It would have a well-attended church, an inn with reasonable accommodation for itinerant detective-inspectors, a village institute, library and shops—including a chemist's where weed killer and hair due might conveniently be bought [169–70].

To elaborate, Watson uses examples from Christie, identifying stock characters drawn along conservative lines. The setting, he holds, is "a museum of nostalgia." He holds that "a corpse in the tea-tent" is not disconcerting in these circumstances, but comforting, because the writers of such fiction are not "concerned with reality" (171). Later, in a piece for the BBC, Watson contrasted Mayhem Parva to "Wicked Belgravia," the terrain of hard-boiled, typically American fiction. The distinction, Watson holds, lies in Golden Age crime fiction's "establishment of convention" ("Mayhem Parva" 48), something flouted by the latter. In this piece, Watson extends the analysis to include other "female writers of mystery" such as Dorothy L. Sayers and Ngaio Marsh (63), indicating that he may have shifted his definition of Mayhem Parva from lines of geography—Marsh was a New Zealander—to lines of sex.

The term has become influential and has been embraced and used disparagingly by a number of commentators to describe "cozy" crime fiction, with Christie's name never far behind. Although some scholars such as Keating, John Scaggs, and Robert Barnard would endorse its application, others such as Alison Light, Nicola Humble, and J.C. Bernthal would take issue fundamentally.

See also: **Nostalgia**; **St. Mary Mead**

Mayhew, Mr.

Mr. Mayhew is a defense attorney in *Five Little Pigs* and "The Under Dog." The surname is also given in the stage version of *Witness for the Prosecution* to another defense attorney, who appeared in the 1925 story as John Mayherne.

McGillicuddy, Elspeth

In *4.50 from Paddington*, Elspeth McGillicuddy witnesses a murder while returning on the train from her London shopping and is roundly disbelieved except by her friend Miss Marple. Detectives suggest her imagination has run away with her because she was reading detective fiction on the train, but Miss Marple knows that she is unimaginative. Like Dolly Bantry in *The Body in the Library* but with this key difference, she is in some ways a stand-in for the reader, eccentrically drawn.

McNaughton, Mrs., and Professor Angus

Residents of Wilbraham Crescent, this couple typifies provincial domestic boredom in *The Clocks*. Professor McNaughton's greatest concern seems to be that his wife will think he is swearing when he refers to a local dam. Mrs. McNaughton claims to recognize the dead man from a photograph, but Inspector Hardcastle believes she just wants to be involved in the case.

McNeil, Inspector

Inspector McNeil is an officer from Scotland Yard who appears in both "The Adventure of Johnnie Waverly" and "The Million Dollar Bond Robbery."

Meauhourat, Zélie

After Mademoiselle Rouselle, she was a governess or au pair to Celia Ravenscroft in *Elephants Can Remember*. The nicknames of the two au pairs, Maddie and Zellie, evoke "Mademoiselle," because they are French.

Meitantei Akafuji Takashi (Detective Aka-fuji Takashi)

Meitantei Akafuji Takashi is a two-part Japanese television series broadcast on NHK in December 2005 and set in prewar Tokyo. It was expected to branch out into a larger series with original stories, but this did not happen. The two episodes filmed and broadcast feature Shiro Ito as the eponymous detective. These are based on the Hercule Poirot novels *The ABC Murders* and *Murder on the Links*, and the character involves more than a nod to Poirot. The episodes aired back-to-back on 30 December 2005. Following the anime series *Agasa Kurisutī no Meitantei Powaro to Māpuru* on the same network, this experiment proved a strong interest in Christie for Japanese television and prompted Agatha Christie Ltd. to strike deals with two production companies, Fuji TV and Asahi TV.

See also: *The ABC Murders* (novel); Asahi TV Adaptations; *The Murder on the Links*; NTV Adaptations

Melchett, Colonel

Colonel Melchett is the avuncular chief constable for Radfordshire who heads the police force at St. Mary Mead; he is one of the authority figures who frequently vouches for Miss Marple. He appears in *The Murder at the Vicarage*, *The Body in the Library*, "Death by Drowning," and "Tape-Measure Murder."

Melksham, Lady. See Greer, Elsa

Melrose, Colonel

Colonel Melrose is a chief constable who appears in *The Secret of Chimneys*, *Murder of Roger Ackroyd*, *The Seven Dials Mystery*, "The Love Detectives," and *Sleeping Murder*. He seems to have a wide network of personal friends, among whom he counts Hercule Poirot, Mr. Satterthwaite, and Miss Marple. His jurisdiction is in and around Market Basing.

Merdell

Merdell is a drunk, 92-year-old boatman in *Dead Man's Folly* and "Hercule Poirot and the Greenshore Folly," *Dead Man's Folly* pre-expanded form. His ramblings go unnoticed until his granddaughter, Marlene Tucker, listens and makes a mental connection. This costs both parties their lives, as Merdell has remembered secrets about the Folliat family.

Meredith, Anne

In *Cards on the Table*, Anne Meredith is a charming, manipulative young woman who gains sympathy from most people she meets despite her roles as thief and murderer. A paid companion originally from the British Raj, she murdered her employer, Mrs. Benson, by substituting hat paint for syrup of figs. She tries to kill Rhoda Dawes, the best friend with whom she lives, when the handsome Major Despard shows an interest in Rhoda rather than Anne, but drowns in the process.

In a likely coincidence, "Anne Meredith" was one of three pen names used by crime writer Lucy Malleson, best known as Anthony Gilbert. Malleson first wrote as Meredith in *Portrait of a Murderer* (1933) and *The Coward* (1934), two years before *Cards on the Table* was published, and would revive the pseudonym many times between 1937 and 1962. There is no evidence that Christie was aware of these titles, although she would certainly have been familiar with Malleson and her work as Gilbert.

MGM Films

In Christie's professional life, few topics were as contentious as the MGM film adaptations of her work. She had sold the rights to several of her books to them, expecting a short-lived television series to be made, and was generally embarrassed by the low-budget camp black-and-white films that resulted in the 1960s. She particularly disliked members of the public assuming that she had written the scripts. The four Marple films made by MGM were directed by George Pollock, who also directed the 1965 version of *Ten Little Indians*.

Murder She Said (1961) was the first in the set. With the working title *Meet Miss Marple*, making intentions for a series clear, it starred Margaret Rutherford as Miss Marple. This character was not so much that of the books as a vehicle for Rutherford's colorful, attention-grabbing performances. Rutherford, a distinguished character actor, is now best known either as Miss Marple or as the similarly eccentric Madame Arcati in

David Lean's 1945 version of Noel Coward's *Blithe Spirit*. She had needed some cajoling to take the role, as she generally avoided murder plots due to a complicated family history—but the promise of childish innocence and life affirmation convinced her to take the role.

Christie admired Rutherford and was not as horrified at this film as some have suggested, writing to her agent that it was not as bad as she thought it would be and that she would be happy to let it fly under the radar. She even dedicated her next novel, *The Mirror Crack'd from Side to Side* (which features filmmakers causing havoc in St. Mary Mead), to Rutherford, "in admiration" (*TMC* front end paper). However, she was angered by the next offerings, which took greater liberties.

Rutherford played Miss Marple again with a sidekick, Mr. Stringer, played by her real-life husband Stringer Davis, in *Murder at the Gallop* (1963) and *Murder Most Foul* (1964), based on two Poirot novels (*After the Funeral* and *Mrs. McGinty's Dead*, respectively). With jaunty music, slapstick refrains, and occasional innuendo, the films' threadbare plots relate only slightly to their source material.

More offensive still were the next (and last) two MGM Christie films. Christie was furious at *Murder Ahoy!* (1964), a fourth Miss Marple film set aboard a ship that was not based on any book. The saucily tedious *The Alphabet Murders* (1965) was based on *The ABC Murders*, retitled because it would be distributed in ABC cinemas. Tony Randall, famous for *The Odd Couple*, starred as Poirot, and Robert Morley played a bumbling Captain Hastings. The film opens with Poirot and Hastings in a sauna and does not improve. Rutherford and Davis even make appearances as Miss Marple and Mr. Stringer. Christie insisted on a note appearing on the title page of *A Caribbean Mystery*, her 1964 novel, stating that this book contained "The Original Character" (*ACM*, title page).

In theory, the last straw was a proposal to adapt *Murder on the Orient Express*, a personal favorite of Christie's novels, which she was horrified to imagine might be made to include Miss Marple—even, she half-joked to her agent, driving the train. Moreover, the studio had caused her considerable grief over her own screenplay for a film of Charles Dickens's *Bleak House*. The contract with MGM was terminated prematurely. The experience bolstered Christie's long-running hostility to filmmakers, and, despite frequent requests, she would not approve another production until the 1970s.

See also: **Fictional Portrayals of Agatha Christie; Marple, Jane; Poirot, Hercule; Rutherford, Margaret**

Michael Parkinson's Confession Album (nonfiction contribution, 1973)

Christie's contribution to *Michael Parkinson's Confession Album—1973* has become popular with fans and amateur scholars, partly because it is presented in a visually appealing one-page layout including an unusually legible sample of her handwriting. Another reason for its popularity is that the elderly Christie was here looking back at her long life, and it presents her in a very human life.

Parkinson's *Confession Album* is a series of questionnaires, filled in by various celebrities. Christie wrote her contribution under the name Agatha Christie Mallowan. In a cover letter, she wrote to Parkinson: "Filling up your confessional brought back to me very strong memories of my early Victorian youth. I well remember all our family and friends filling up various confessional albums belonging to my grandmother, great aunt and so on" (Parkinson 23). This may explain why she agreed to such a personal media intrusion.

In this "confession," Christie describes various "favourites": her favorite animal (dogs), flower (lily of the valley), authors (Elizabeth Bowen and Graham Greene), poets (T. S. Eliot, W.B. Yeats, and Alfred Lord Tennyson), color (green), charity (Little Sisters of the Poor), and even names (Charles, Isabella, and Rodney). She lists her "idea of misery" as "noise and long vehicles" and "crowds" (23). She also lists her favorite quotations and describes her state of mind as "peaceful" (23).

See also: **Nostalgia**

Michel, Pierre
Pierre Michel is a conductor for the Blue

Train in *The Mystery of the Blue Train* who returns as a major character, a conductor for the Orient Express in *Murder on the Orient Express*. In that novel, he reveals his traumatic past, as his daughter killed herself after being suspected of a murder masterminded by Samuel Ratchett. Recycling a minor character from a previous novel in this manner is a masterstroke of misdirection; readers who remember him cannot expect him to suddenly develop high narrative significance. In part, this can be attributed to the oft-critiqued truism underlying several of Christie's plots: the idea that nobody looks at the servants.

"Midnight Madness." See **"The Cretan Bull"**

Miller, Clarissa ("Clara," 1854–1926)

Clarissa "Clara" Miller, née Boehmer, was Christie's mother. Born in Dublin, Ireland, she was greatly affected by the death of her father in 1863. This led to her 28-year-old mother giving up her and her siblings. They were raised by an aunt, and the experience of feeling unwanted would haunt Clara for the rest of her life. It also transferred into several Christie novels, most notably *They Do It with Mirrors*, *Mrs. McGinty's Dead*, *Ordeal by Innocence*, and *The Mirror Crack'd from Side to Side*. As Christie wrote in her autobiography, being adopted "made [Clara] distrustful of herself and suspicious of people's affection" (*AA* 17). In 1878, Clara married Frederick Miller, whose stepmother, Margaret Miller, was the aunt who raised her.

The young Agatha Miller was devoted to her father and less close to her mother, whom she saw as "an enigmatic and arresting personality—more forceful than my father" (16). She diagnosed Clara as possessing "a natural melancholy" (16) and "deeply miserable" (18) but nonetheless loved her fiercely, especially after her father's early death in 1901. Clara, Christie decided, had "ideas [that] were always slightly at variance with reality" (21)—of course, the highly creative Christie, who inhabited a world of imaginary friends, inherited these traits—but, like the much-indulged Carrie-Louise in *They Do It with Mirrors*, what most people dismissed as dreamlike thinking often

turned out to be true. Rumors grew in the Miller family that Clara was in fact psychic. She encouraged these to an extent with an ever-evolving interest in mystical religions and a fashionable penchant for séances, as well as a belief in the supernatural, which all informed her daughter's very early and very late writing.

Although it is well-known that Christie's sister Madge was a writer before she was, it is less well-known that their mother wrote and published work as well. Like Madge and—initially—Christie, she used male pseudonyms, and her work is difficult to trace. She wrote and self-published several love poems for her fiancé in the 1870s, including one titled "The Modern Hymen." Under the pseudonym Callis Miller, she wrote a supernatural story, "Mrs. Jordan's Ghost," which survives in the Christie Family Archive and is steeped in Victorian melodrama; Christie later built on this story in her unpublished "The Choice." Clara was not a natural writer, but she was an inventive storyteller and would improvise bedtime stories for her children. She would forget what had happened the next night, however, and simply invent a new one. This led the young Christie to conclude plots in her own head, as she went to sleep.

Clara's death in 1926 precipitated a mental health crisis for Christie, who suffered a well-publicized breakdown when her marriage collapsed in the same year. Indeed, on the rare occasions she referred to that year, she would describe her mother's death and her husband's infidelity in the same sentence. The pain of losing her mother who had warned against the marriage, only to have the marriage break down, is illustrated in the pseudonymous *Unfinished Portrait*, in which Clara appears as "Miriam"; she had similarly been called "Marian" in her husband's fictionalized account of their courtship, "Henry's Engagement."

See also: *An Autobiography*; **Miller, Frederick**; *Unfinished Portrait*.

Miller, Frederick (1846–1901)

Christie's father, Frederick Miller, was an American stockbroker. His daughter was devoted to him and, after his death in

1901, reportedly listened outside her mother's door every night to make sure she was still breathing. Miller was instrumental in developing his daughter's story-telling skills. He used to create (and write out) stories about his courtship with her mother and share them during family time.

See also: **Miller, Clarissa (Clara)**

Miller, Inspector

Inspector Miller is a "conceited, ill-mannered and quite insufferable" (*PEC* 107) investigating officer in "The Lost Mine," "The Disappearance of Mr. Davenheim," "The Under Dog," and "The Mystery of the Spanish Chest," who is compared negatively to Inspector Japp. He is not as accommodating of Hercule Poirot's eccentricities as Japp is.

Miller, Louis Montant ("Monty," 1881–1929)

Christie's brother Monty Miller was something of an embarrassment to the family. Expelled from Harrow, he became a drug addict and eventually lived reclusively in a small Dartmoor bungalow with a string of caregivers paid for by his brother-in-law, James Watts, before dying of a cerebral hemorrhage. Monty was a magnetic personality—described by Jared Cade as a "charming but feckless ... ne'er-do-well" (19), who was known during military service as "Puffing Billy" (171). His erratic behavior included firing gunshots at visitors to the family home, Ashfield (38). Although Christie rarely spoke publicly about Monty and never about his addictions, he has been read by biographers and critics as direct inspiration for several attractive cads in her work, including Cyril in *Unfinished Portrait* (Sova 82), Richard Warwick in *The Unexpected Guest* (Cade 171), Victor Drake in *Sparkling Cyanide*, and Philip Lombard in *And Then There Were None* (Brodbeck and Donovan n.p.).

See also: **Ashfield**; **Miller, Clarissa ("Clara")**; **Miller, Frederick**; **Watts, Margaret ("Madge")**.

Miller, Margaret ("Auntie-Grannie," 1827–1919)

Margaret Miller (née West) was an influential figure in Christie's childhood. She was her father's stepmother, her mother's aunt, and her mother's adoptive mother, so she was known by Agatha and her siblings as "Auntie-Grannie." She lived in Ealing, and Christie cited her gossipy cynicism as a key influence on the development of Miss Marple.

See also: **Marple, Jane**; **Miller, Clarissa ("Clara")**; **Miller, Frederick**; **"The Trams"**

Miller, Margaret ("Madge"). See **Watts, Margaret ("Madge")**

"The Million Dollar Bond Robbery" (story)

In this short story, a young woman approaches Hercule Poirot to clear her fiancé of suspicion in the robbery of $1million in U.S. bonds. Poirot traces the route taken by the bonds on an ocean liner and uncovers their whereabouts. The story was published in *The Sketch* in May 1923 and collected in *Poirot Investigates* (1924). In January 1991, ITV broadcast the relevant episode of *Agatha Christie's Poirot*.

Characters: Farquhar, Esmée; **Hastings, Captain Arthur**; **McNeil, Inspector**; **Poirot, Hercule**; Ridgeway, Philip; Shaw, Mr.; Vavasour, Mr.

See also: *Agatha Christie's Poirot*; *Poirot Investigates*

Mirelle

Mirelle is a temperamental European dancer in *The Mystery of the Blue Train*, not dissimilar in character and function to Nadina in *The Man in the Brown Suit*. She has flickering eyelids and a catlike stare.

Miriam

Miriam is a fictional portrait of Christie's mother, Clarissa ("Clara") Miller, in the Mary Westmacott novel *Unfinished Portrait*.

***The Mirror Crack'd* (film).** See **EMI Films**

***The Mirror Crack'd* (novel).** See *The Mirror Crack'd from Side to Side*

The Mirror Crack'd (play)

Rachel Wagstaff adapted *The Mirror Crack'd from Side to Side* (1962) into a play, *The Mirror Crack'd*, in 2010, and revised the script in 2018. The production opened at the Salisbury Playhouse on 15 February 2019, followed by a very limited U.K. tour to Cardiff, Exeter, Cambridge, and other locations. This is the first authorized Miss Marple stage adaptation since Leslie Darbon's *A Murder Is Announced* (1977) and the third overall. It has a cast of 11 and, unlike screen adaptations of the novel, does not shy away from the book's 1960s context. Wagstaff's other theatrical credits include *Birdsong* (2010) from Sebastian Faulks' novel, *Flowers for Mrs. Harris* (2016) from Paul Gallico's *Mrs. 'Arris Goes to Paris*, *The Girl on the Train* (2018) from Paula Hawkins's novel, and *The Da Vinci Code* (2021), from Dan Brown's novel.

The play was mounted in the context of BBC screen adaptations emphasizing multigenerational darkness, to a mixed response of awe and condemnation from critics and Christie fans. Therefore, Wagstaff's play opens with Miss Marple asleep in an armchair, while dancers in mini-skirts and dressed as Teddy Boys dance. Miss Marple is presented as a figure of the past, unsure about and unfamiliar with 1960s youth culture (which is not really present in the novel, although changing times most certainly are). The play received generally good reviews. Susie Blake starred Miss Marple, and Simon Shepherd played Inspector Craddock, reconfigured here as a gruff and pompous policeman, whose methods and manners contrast those of the heroine.

See also: *The Mirror Crack'd* (film); *The Mirror Crack'd from Side to Side*

The Mirror Crack'd from Side to Side (novel: alternative title: The Mirror Crack'd)

Although the glamor of Hollywood film stars in a picturesque village has dominated adaptations—and discussions—of *The Mirror Crack'd from Side to Side*, Christie wrote it with the theme of changing times. The working title was "Development Murder," a reference to a block of council flats erected in Miss Marple's village, St. Mary Mead, which is referred to throughout the novel. This is the last of Christie's village mysteries and is in many way a retrospective of Miss Marple's St. Mary Mead cases. Indeed, the novel looks back in extended asides on the events of *The Murder at the Vicarage* (1930), *The Thirteen Problems* (1932), and *The Body in the Library* (1942), with updates on which of the characters have died, which servants

have moved on and built lives out of service, and so on.

The scene of the crime, Gossington Hall, was also the setting for *The Body in the Library*. It has now been sold to movie star Marina Gregg who is making a film nearby with her husband, director Jason Rudd. At a charity party on the grounds, Marina is accosted by a fan who tells a story about having met her years ago; she freezes and stares at a painting of a Madonna and child. Shortly afterward, the fan, Heather Badcock, drinks from Marina's glass and dies. As tension and the body-count mount, it becomes clear that Marina is the intended victim. While Inspector Craddock investigates the movie world, Marina's embittered adoptive child, and her ex-lovers, Miss Marple solves the crime largely from her armchair, listening to gossip and perusing film fan magazines. She considers a movie-star's life akin to that of a hospital nurse: "highly specialised" work, a background of gossip and innuendo, and a certain glamour attaching to powerful men (124). This analogy provides an extreme example of the Christiean maxim that people are essentially the same regardless of circumstance.

Miss Marple reveals that Marina poisoned Heather, whose story had concerned going to meet her during the war, despite suffering from rubella. Marina had caught rubella from the encounter and given birth to "[a]n imbecile child, [now] in a sanatorium in America" (129). This had caused her untold grief, and the murder was committed on the spur of the moment. Subsequent killings were to cover her tracks. At the end of the novel, Marina is—it is heavily suggested—killed with sleeping tablets by her husband who wants to protect her from the consequences of her actions. She has always lived, he says, an insulated life enabled by Hollywood and is unable to function in the real world.

The year the novel was published, Hollywood star Gene Tierney returned to the screen, and the press discussed her past freely. This involved years of institutionalization following the death of her premature first child in 1943; Tierney had contracted rubella, likely from meeting a fan. The similarity to events in Christie's forthcoming novel did not escape her publishers, who asked her to make some alterations. Reluctantly, Christie did so, although the similarities to Marina's backstory remain striking in the published novel. Indeed, many commentators, including the Christie estate, have stated outright that Tierney inspired the character, although there are no archived materials to indicate this.

The world of showbiz is presented as one not of glamour but of modernity. Marina's multiple marriages despite only being in her forties are considered par for the course, even by villagers who know her chiefly as a character in magazines and onscreen. These publications, such as *Movie News* and *Amongst the Stars*, are mentioned alongside "Hoovers," "dishwashers," and other annoyances of modern life (124). Miss Marple is self-aware enough to know that her prejudices are just that; that times and trappings change: "In a sense, of course, nothing was what it had been. You could blame the war (both the wars) or the younger generation, or women going out to work, or the atom bomb, or just the Government—but what one really meant was the simple fact that one was getting old" (8).

It is a sentiment that runs throughout the early 1960s novels, but by *Third Girl* (1966), there is a definite despair at "the younger generation" and the changing of the times. Here, however, St. Mary Mead—and Miss Marple—survive, even if forced to adapt. The council building itself looks uniform and characterless, and Miss Marple ventures into it feeling like "Columbus setting out to discover the new world" (18), but the people who live in it are individuals. Sarah Martin and Sally West have discussed this as a deliberate tension as a "manifestation of community"; an illustration of identity being imposed but individually negotiated by a new generation who represent the future of the village (23–24).

Regarding the plot, the idea of the intended victim being the killer is an old Christie trick. It had previously been used several times, most notably in *Peril at End House* (1932) and *A Murder Is Announced* (1950). Perhaps fittingly, as the final novel where St. Mary Mead dominates the action,

The Mirror Crack'd from Side to Side includes complicated relationships, subplots, and coincidences. In her autobiography, Christie laments that there were too many of these in *The Murder at the Vicarage*, so it is surprising that, for instance, she made the insignificant Arthur Badcock—husband of the first victim—Marina's long-forgotten first husband. This move, which adds nothing to the plot, has never been reflected in screen adaptations and is a convoluted coincidence of the kind common to Miss Marple novels such as *The Murder at the Vicarage; One, Two, Buckle My Shoe* (1940); and *4.50 from Paddington* (1957).

When the novel was published in 1962, filming had wrapped on the MGM movie *Murder She Said*, starring Margaret Rutherford. Not impressed with the production, Christie was not as heartbroken as some commentators have assumed—not yet—and remained a firm admirer of Rutherford's. She dedicated this book to her. The book was not filmed with Rutherford, but it did become the next British Miss Marple movie, *The Mirror Crack'd*, with a too-young Angela Lansbury heading an all-star cast in 1980.

A television dramatization, the last episode of the BBC's *Miss Marple*, was broadcast on 27 December 1992, and the BBC aired a radio version on 19 August 1998. On 2 January 2012, ITV aired its own version as part of *Agatha Christie's Marple*. The novel has also been filmed in Bengali (*Shubho Mahurat* [Good Luck], 2004), twice in Japanese (*Daijoyu Satsujin-jiken*, 2006 and 2018), in French (as part of *Les Petits Meurtres d'Agatha Christie*, 2017), and in Korean (as part of *Ms Ma, Nemesis*). In 2019, Rachel Wagstaff's stage adaptation, *The Mirror Crack'd*, opened its first tour.

Characters: Allcock, Councillor and Mrs.; **Badcock, Arthur, and Heather; Baker, Cherry, and Jim;** Bantry, Colo **nel Arthur, and Dolly;** Bardwell; Bence, Margot; **Brewster, Lola; Clara; Clement, Griselda; Clithering, Sir Henry;** Clithering, Colonel and Mrs.; **Cornish, Detective Inspector Frank; Craddock, Detective Inspector Dermot; Dixon, Gladys;** Fenn, Ardwyck; Gilchrist, Dr. Maurice;

Gregg, Marina; Grice, Joshua and Mrs.; Groves, Eddie; Guiseppe; Harry; **Hartnell, Amanda**; Hartwell, Mrs.; **Haydock, Dr., and Penelope**; Hill, Florence; **Knight, Miss**; Laycock; **Marple, Jane**; McNeil, Donald; Meavy, Mrs.; **Preston, Hailey**; Quilp, Andrew; **Price, Lily**; **Rudd, Jason**; **Rudd, Jason**; **Sampson, Mr.**; Sandford, Dr. and Mrs.; Sims, Dr.; Tiddler, Detective Sergeant William; Truscott, Robert; **West, Raymond**; **Wetherby, Caroline**; Wilde, Alison; **Zielinsky, Ella**

See also: *Agatha Christie's Marple*; **EMI Films**; **Indian-Language Adaptations**; *The Mirror Crack'd* (play); *Miss Marple* (radio series); *Miss Marple* (television series); *Ms Ma, Nemesis*; **NTV Adaptations**; **St. Mary Mead**; **TV Asahi Adaptations**

Miseu Ma: Boksooui Yeoshin. See *Ms Ma, Nemesis*

Miss Marple (radio series)

The collective name *Miss Marple* has been applied retrospectively to 12 BBC Radio 4 dramatizations of Miss Marple novels between 1993 and 2001. These were produced and directed by Enyd Williams, dramatized by Michael Bakewell, and starred June Whitfield as Miss Marple. Some were five-part serials, and some were 90-minute *Saturday Plays*. Whereas the BBC's Poirot series used new or customized music for each episode, the Miss Marple adaptations all opened with the same music: Mozart's clarinet concerto in A major, K.622. This decision was made to create a sense of continuity and familiarity, which the dramatists felt runs throughout the Miss Marple novels.

Dramatizations include, in order: *The Murder at the Vicarage* (26–30 December 1993), *A Pocket Full of Rye* (11 February 1995), *At Bertram's Hotel* (5–29 December 1995), *4.50 from Paddington* (29 March 1997), *A Caribbean Mystery* (30 October–27 November 1997), *The Mirror Crack'd from Side to Side* (29 August 1998), *Nemesis* (9 November–7 December 1998), *The Body in the Library* (22 May 1999), *A Murder Is Announced* (9 August–6 September 1999), *The Moving Finger* (5 May 2001), *They Do It with Mirrors* (23 July–20 August 2001), and *Sleeping Murder* (8 December 2001).

See also: **BBC Radio Adaptations**; **Marple, Jane**; *Miss Marple's Final Cases* (radio series)

Miss Marple (television series; alternative title: *Agatha Christie's Miss Marple*)

A highly-acclaimed BBC television series based on the 12 Miss Marple novels, *Miss Marple* was broadcast on BBC 1 between 1983 and 1992, and remains a perennial favorite with fans and general consumers around the world. The BBC gained the rights to the novels incrementally, from a cautious estate, throughout the 1980s. Initially, rights were not available for *A Caribbean Mystery*, *They Do It with Mirrors*, or *The Mirror Crack'd from Side to Side*, because these had all been filmed or were being filmed at the time elsewhere, so they were the last installments of the series.

Christie had a troubled relationship with the BBC and was not an admirer of television adaptations, so, in the decade or so after her death, the estate was highly selective about the projects it allowed. In the 1980s, most Christie television productions were from LWT, a production company of rival broadcaster ITV, although the BBC was jostling for permission to produce a series.

Casting the lead was a vitally important element, and Joan Hickson (1906–98) was an early choice. Hickson, a noted character actor with a varied career, had famously been spotted by Christie, who said she would make a good Miss Marple when she appeared in the stage version of *Appointment with Death* in 1945.

The first episode of *Miss Marple* was a lengthy, three-part take on *The Body in the Library*, recreating the novel's plot faithfully, albeit with a slightly updated 1950s setting. The decision was made early on to set all episodes in that decade, capitalizing on the nostalgia being pedaled from government in 1980s Britain. Inspector Slack, the policeman from that novel and *The Murder at the Vicarage*, became a recurring sidekick for Miss Marple in five episodes, played by David Horovitch. *The Body in the Library* aired on 26, 27, and 28 December 1984 to positive reviews.

The next seven episodes (*The Moving*

Finger; 21 and 22 February 1985) had two parts each, not quite as leisurely as the pilot but maintaining the traditional television format of a drama being as long as it needs to be. The third, *A Murder Is Announced* (28 February, 1 and 2 March 1985), was in three parts, and the fourth *A Pocket Full of Rye* (7 and 8 March 1985) was in two parts. A one-part episode, *The Murder at the Vicarage*, was broadcast on Christmas Day 1986. The inconsistent lengths have led to various edits in repeat and export broadcasts.

The next three installments were all two-parters: *Sleeping Murder* (11 and 18 January 1987), *At Bertram's Hotel* (25 January and 1 February 1987), and *Nemesis* (8 and 15 February 1987). The series slowed down after 1987, in part because producers were running out of source material, and it took time for some rights to become available. The final four episodes were broadcast as one-off one-parters over subsequent Christmas periods: *4.50 from Paddington* (25 December 1987), *A Caribbean Mystery* (25 December 1989), *They Do It with Mirrors* (29 December 1991), and *The Mirror Crack'd from Side to Side* (27 December 1992).

As source material began to run out, conversations were held about adapting the short stories—an idea of creating original plots was vetoed almost before it was raised. Serious consideration was given to filming "Greenshaw's Folly," presumably because of its novella length, but Hickson disapproved of the prospect, because, at her advanced age and with slowly declining health, she did not feel able to commit to filming all the short stories and did not want to leave the project unfinished. Instead, it ended once all 12 novels had been adapted.

The series is influential and was clearly an uncredited model against which the ITV series *Agatha Christie's Marple* positioned itself. When the latter series opened with a controversial take on *The Body in the Library* in 2013, the BBC started promoting DVDs of its own series as "Proper Marple." Although the adaptations are often held up as highly faithful to the novels—even as visual versions of them—some scholarship challenges this view. Alison Light discussed *Miss Marple* as an example of how Christie's fiction is deliberately manipulated in popular culture, writing that, "[w]atching any of the recent dramatisations featuring 'Miss Marple' on television, one could be forgiven for believing Agatha Christie to be the high priestess of nostalgia rather than the 'Queen of Crime'" (62).

See also: **Agatha Christie's Marple**; **Hickson, Joan**; **Marple, Jane**; *Miss Marple* **(BBC radio series)**

"Miss Marple and the Golden Galleon." See "Ingots of Gold"

Miss Marple and the Thirteen Problems. See *The Thirteen Problems*

"Miss Marple and the Wicked World." See **"The Bloodstained Pavement"**

"Miss Marple Tells a Story" (story; alternative title: "Behind Closed Doors")
This short story was written as a 20-minute radio broadcast for the BBC. It was read by Christie herself on 11 May 1934 as part of the *National Programme*. For the fee of 30 guineas, Christie had originally produced a supernatural story, "In a Glass Darkly," but this was rejected by the BBC producer, and "Miss Marple Tells a Story" was written quickly in its place.

It is the only story narrated by Miss Marple, and the conceit is that she is relating her experiences to her nephew and niece. The beginning and end are mostly devoted to the "old lady" flourishes—"I'll tell you my little story" (95); "I've been running on too long …" (105)—but at the heart is a relatively dispassionate narrative. The story concerns Mr. Rhodes, an old friend of the solicitor Mr. Petherick, asking Miss Marple to save him from the death penalty: he is accused of murdering his wife. Miss Marple astounds the two men by declaring the case "remarkably simple" (102). This is one of several Christie mysteries in which the solution depends on nobody looking at the servants.

After the radio broadcast, the story was published as "Behind Closed Doors" in the *Home Journal* (vol. 3, issue 66) on 25 May 1935. It was collected in *The Regatta Mystery* (Dodd, Mead, 1939) in the United States and *Miss Marple's Final Cases* (Collins, 1978) in the United Kingdom.

Characters: Carruthers, Mrs.; Granby,

Mrs.; Gwen; Hill, Mary; **Marple, Jane;** Olde, Sir Malcom; **Petherick, Mr., and Mr.;** Rhodes, Mr.; Rhodes, Mrs.; **West, Joan, and Raymond**

See also: "**In a Glass Darkly**"; *Miss Marple's Final Cases* (story collection); *The Regatta Mystery* (story collection)

Miss Marple's Final Cases (radio series)

June Whitfield returned to the role of Miss Marple for a special set of three 30-minute dramas based on short stories in 2015. Broadcast to mark celebrations for Christie's 125th birthday, the series features "Tape-Measure Murder" (16 September 2015), "The Case of the Caretaker" (23 September 2015), and "Sanctuary" (30 September 2015). Unlike previous BBC Radio 4 Miss Marple adaptations, these episodes were dramatized by Joy Wilkinson, who took over from Michael Bakewell to script the Christie adaptations after John Moffatt's last outing as Hercule Poirot in 2007. These short dramatizations are darker than the feature-length ones, and confront the detective's—and broader human—mortality, albeit lightly.

Wilkinson explained in a blog post for the BBC that she intended to kill Miss Marple off in this series—to "give her three last chances to regain her wits and verve," starting with Miss Marple's "depressed" nature in "The Case of the Caretaker" (a story in which she is recovering from illness) but changed this idea to reflect an "arc" as the character moves during the series "from depression to a renewal" rather than something "elegiac" (Wilkinson).

See also: **BBC Radio Adaptations;** *Miss Marple* (radio series)

Miss Marple's Final Cases (story collection; alternative titles: Miss Marple's Final Cases and Two Other Stories; Miss Marple's 6 Final Cases and 2 Other Stories)

Miss Marple's Final Cases is a posthumous collection published in 1979 in the United Kingdom, containing eight short stories that had not previously been collected in Britain. In the United States, these stories had appeared in *The Regatta Mystery* (1939: "**Miss Marple Tells a Story**" and "**In a Glass Darkly**"), *Three Blind Mice* (1950: "**Strange Jest**," "**Tape-Measure Murder**,"

"**The Case of the Caretaker**," and "**The Case of the Perfect Maid**"), and *Double Sin* (1961: "**The Dressmaker's Doll**" and "**Sanctuary**"). Like most of the posthumous anthologies, excluding themed collections of previously collected stories, *Miss Marple's Final Cases* has a sense of the piecemeal about it. There were clearly not sufficient uncollected Miss Marple stories to sustain a full volume, so two supernatural stories were included.

Miss Perry (play)

In 1962, Christie met with her friend, actress Margaret Lockwood, for whom she had written *Spider's Web* some years earlier. The two women seem to have agreed that Christie would write a play for Lockwood and her daughter. This, like *Spider's Web*, would be a comedy. There is some confusion about when *Miss Perry* was written, with estimates ranging from 1962 to after 1970, and this is likely due to Christie repeatedly altering the typescript and pursuing performances—with or without the Lockwoods—well into the 1970s. Although it appears to have made it to a table-read, the play has never been performed or published. In 2012, collector Ralf M. Sultiens acquired a carbon copy annotated by Christie and sold individual pages from it to other collectors and enthusiasts. J.C. Bernthal has dated this from textual references to 1964. The other known copy, undated but probably slightly later, is held in the Christie Family Archive.

The play is much lighter than *Spider's Web* and more a farce than a comedy thriller. A beautiful woman turns up at a town inn and announces that she is a fairy—fully trained, she has the relevant A-levels. The locals try and fail to make sense of her apparent powers. In the end, it transpires that Miss Perry is an actress, who has been sent to prevent a criminal plot.

See also: *Spider's Web* (play)

"**Mr. Davenby Disappears.**" See "**The Disappearance of Mr. Davenheim**"

"**Mr. Eastwood's Adventure**" (story; alternative titles: "The Mystery of the Second Cucumber"; "The Mystery of the Spanish Shawl")

In the short story "Mr. Eastwood's Adventure," a crime writer suffers from writer's block. He is caught up in an extraordinary adventure, which cures him of the predicament. Anthony Eastwood's first attempt at a mystery, abandoned because the story is too stupid, is "The Adventure of the Second Cucumber," likely a humorous play on the Sherlock Holmes title "The Adventure of the Second Stain." He ends up writing the much more commercial-sounding "The Mystery of the Spanish Shawl." Both these have been used as alternative titles for "Mr. Eastwood's Adventure." It was first published in August 1924 in *The Novel Magazine* and appeared in the U.K. collection *The Listerdale Mystery* (1934) and the U.S. collection *The Witness for the Prosecution and Other Stories* (1948). In 1994, a Russian radio version was broadcast.

Characters: Boris; Carter, Detective Sergeant; Driver, Inspector; Eastwood, Anthony; Ferrarez, Carmen; Ferrarez, Don Fernando; Fleckman, Conrad; Gibson, Mother; Rogers; Seamark; Rosenberg, Anna; Verrall, Detective Inspector

See also: *The Listerdale Mystery* (story collection); Russian Radio Adaptations; *The Witness for the Prosecution* (story collection)

Mr. Parker Pyne, Detective. See *Parker Pyne Investigates*

Mitzi

A domestic helper at Little Paddocks in *A Murder Is Announced*, Mitzi is a refugee from Eastern Europe and apparently a Holocaust survivor. She is also a brazen, fantastical liar, which seems to be her mechanism for coping with trauma she cannot process. Although readers are sometimes encouraged to feel sorry for Mitzi and to recognize that she is being exploited, she is ultimately a figure of fun, and her presentation in a post–World War II novel is problematic.

Mohammed

There are two Mohammeds: a dragoman aboard the SS *Fayoum* in "Death on the Nile" and a beautiful Moroccan servant in *Destination Unknown* who arouses "strange desires" in the hero (167).

Mon Petit Doigt M'a Dit.... See *Bélisaire et Prudence Beresford*

The Monogram Murders (Hannah). See Continuation Fiction

Monro, Flossie

Flossie Monroe is a cheap and unsophisticated actress with bleach-blonde hair, known as "the Peroxide Blonde" in *The Big Four*. She gives Poirot valuable information that helps him remain alert to his nemesis, "Number Four" (aka Claud Darrell), and is killed for her trouble.

Montressor, Helen

Alistair Blunt's distant cousin in *One, Two, Buckle My Shoe*, she has cultivated a plain, unthreatening persona that allows her to blend into the background. In fact, she is the disguised Gerda Blunt, Alistair's actress first wife, whose existence has been hidden. Still very much in love, the couple is working together to cover up their history; Alistair has bigamously married a wealthy woman to advance his career. During the novel, she also poses as Mrs. Albert Chapman.

Moon on the Nile. See *Murder on the Nile* (play)

Mord im Pfarrhaus (Murder in the Rectory; television adaptation)

A West German adaptation of Moie Charles and Barbara Toy's play, *Murder at the Vicarage*, the television production *Mord im Pfarrhaus* (Murder in the Rectory) was the third of four based on Christie plays. It followed versions of *Love from a Stranger* and *And Then There Were None*, and preceded a production of *Black Coffee*. Broadcast on 21 November 1970, *Mord im Pfarrhaus* was the first of the set to be transmitted in color. A far-too-young Inge Langham (then aged 46) played Miss Marple as a "strong and forthright" "busybody" (Aldridge, *Screen* 290).

See also: *And Then There Were None*, Screen Adaptations of; *Black Coffee* (television adaptation); *Love from a Stranger*, Screen Adaptations of; *Murder at the Vicarage* (play)

More Arabian Nights of Parker Pyne. See *Parker Pyne Investigates*

Morelli, Tony. See **Browne, Anthony ("Tony")**

Morisot, Anne, and Marie. See **Richards, Anne, and James** and **Giselle, Madame**

Morley, Henry

Gossipy dentist Henry Morley is killed in *One, Two, Buckle My Shoe*. His death is not personally motivated but strictly pragmatic, so that the killer can access his "true" victim and alter some dental records. Christie emphasizes Morley's personal life, driving home the loss of innocent life during political maneuvers that tend to be, like the murders here, motivated by ego.

Morris, Eileen (1887–1945). See *What We Did in the Great War*

Mory, Angèle. See **Brun, Genevieve**

Mostyn, Kay. See **Doyle, Linnet**

Mostyn, Simon. See **Doyle, Simon**

"Motive v. Opportunity" (story; alternative title: "Where's the Catch?"). See *The Thirteen Problems*

The Mousetrap (play)

Breaking almost every theatrical record, *The Mousetrap* began its legendary West End run in November 1952, closed due to COVID-19 in 2020, and reopened in 2021. The play, based on a 1947 radio play and 1948 novella (both called "Three Blind Mice"), was not expected to enjoy a substantial run, partly because it was staged in one of the smallest West End theaters, the Ambassadors. For this reason, producer Peter Saunders mounted a concerted publicity effort such as "specially designed" posters, "which [were] very unusual in those days" (121) and, crucially, star casting.

Married actors Richard Attenborough and Sheila Sim starred as Detective Sergeant Trotter and Mollie Ralston, and Christie anticipated a healthy six-month run. The title had to be changed to avoid confusion with another, recently-closed play called *Three Blind Mice*. It is unclear who suggested *The Mousetrap*, which is the title of a play-within-a-play in William Shakespeare's *Hamlet*. Inevitably, director and self-promoter Hubert Gregg, who was not involved in the production until well into its run, claimed in his memoir to have come up with the title (95).

The play follows the plot of the "Three Blind Mice": at a snowbound guesthouse, a policeman arrives with news that a serial killer is on the loose. The killer, whistling "Three Blind Mice," strikes, and, slowly, various characters reveal their secret identities that have roots in an old murder case. Finally, the policeman himself is revealed to be the murderer, not a policeman at all but a man who was abused as a child. His development arrested by the trauma, he is taking revenge on the adults who wronged him in childhood.

The Mousetrap's longevity is, by now, self-fulfilling. However, although its early success might be due to good writing and good publicity, it must have stayed running for a reason. Christie attributed this to a good balance of humor and suspense, alongside believable characters. Federica Crescentini, discussing the play, has noted that *The Mousetrap* "presents a disrupted postwar England" (109):

> As the characters try to hide their secrets, the play reveals details about the period when the action takes place. The recurring comic moments balance the dramatic situation: an isolated house in a desolate, unsafe postwar England, during winter at its peak. At Monkswell Manor, people of dubious identity are threatened by the tune and words of a nursery rhyme, which becomes a symbol of both menace and childhood [116].

Further, Crescentini notes, the play is almost unique among crime drama in the 1950s for reflecting the immediate "conditions of postwar England" (116). Like *A Murder Is Announced*, it is set in a world of rationing, using identity cards, and taking one's companions at their word about who they are and their background. As in *A Murder Is Announced*, nearly everyone present is living under a false name, and presumptions can never be made about a person's history. The seemingly unimpeachable police officer is nothing of the sort, and the spectacularly camp Christopher Wren who skips, flirts, and makes the men uncomfortable turns out to be a war hero.

The play marked its 1,000th performance on 22 April 1955 and became the longest-running West End show of any kind on 12 April 1958. On 23 March 1974, it transferred theaters from the Ambassadors to St. Martin's without missing a performance. Indeed, it managed not to close until the COVID-19 pandemic forced all West End productions to cease or be placed on hold in 2020.

The Mousetrap has not been filmed in English, although it has been filmed in several other languages (see **The Mousetrap, Screen Adaptations of**). There were early plans in the play's first year or so for John Boulton to make a movie starring Richard Attenborough, and the rights were sold on the proviso that it would not be released until at least six months after the West End run had closed. A later sale with the same stipulations to was made to representatives of Romulus Films. All parties involved in both transactions are long dead.

Characters: Boyle, Mrs.; Casewell, Miss; Metcalf, Major; Paravicini, Mr.; **Ralston, Giles, and Mollie; Trotter, Detective Sergeant**; Wren, Christopher ("Chris")

See also: *The Mousetrap*, Screen Adaptations of; "Three Blind Mice" (novella); *Three Blind Mice* (radio play); War

The Mousetrap, Screen Adaptations of

This entry concerns the many screen adaptations of "Three Blind Mice" and *The Mousetrap*. The novella's dramatic potential was visible early on, partly because of its origins as a radio play, making it easy to adapt for television screens around 1950. Subsequently, the wild success of the play in London made it an attractive property for overseas broadcasters, and this has remained the case due to the play's longevity.

There have been no English-language screen productions since the play opened in 1952, because Christie, her agents, and her estate have forbidden any screen adaptation of *The Mousetrap* from airing until 18 months after its West End run. Although there was a year's closure due to COVID-19, the two film producers who bought the rights in the 1950s are long-dead.

The first two television versions of "Three Blind Mice" were both in English. The first, a BBC television production, was based on the radio play and broadcast live on 21 October 1947. It starred John Witty and Jessica Spencer. On 31 October 1950, CBS broadcast a version of the novella as part of its anthology series *Sure as Fate*. These are the only two English-language adaptations, and the rest are based on the play (although some credit the novella).

There were three adaptations in consecutive years in the mid–1950s. *Die Fuchsjagd* (The Fox Hunt), directed by Werner Simon, aired on German television on 13 April 1954. *Musefælden* (The Mousetrap), a Danish adaptation by Mogens Brandt, aired on 27 August 1955. *Três Ratinhos Cegos* (Three Blind Mice), an episode of the Brazilian anthology program *Teledrama*, was broadcast on 21 January 1956. In 1960, the first Bengali Christie film, *Chupi Chupi Aashey* (Silently He Comes)—also the first cinematic version of *The Mousetrap*—was released.

In 1976, the year Christie died, when the lights outside St. Martin's Theatre were dimmed, a Greek version of *The Mousetrap* was broadcast. Spiros Milionis directed *Pontikopagida* (Mousetrap), part of *To Theatro dis Desteras*, which played on 28 June 1976. A two-part Russian television version starring Vaiva Mainelyte aired in 1986. The Soviet Union produced a Russian movie based on the play, the well-received *Myshelovka* (Mousetrap), in 1990.

See also: *The Mousetrap*; "**Three Blind Mice**" (novella); *Three Blind Mice* (radio play)

The Moving Finger (novel; alternative title: *The Case of the Moving Finger*)

The title of *The Moving Finger* comes from Edward FitzGerald's translation of Omar Khayyám's *Rubáiyát* and refers to the writing on the all in the Book of Daniel. It is a fairly straightforward novel in which a wounded pilot, Jerry Burton, and his sister, Joanna, move to a quiet English village, determined to distract themselves from their problems by getting involved in local gossip. They receive an anonymous letter implying that they are not brother and sister.

It soon emerges that several letters have been sent to women around the village, including Mona Symmington, the wife of a local solicitor and mother, by her first husband, of the intelligent but awkward 20-year-old Megan Hunter. The letters are full of outlandish and patently untrue, often sexual, allegations. Jerry takes an avuncular interest in Megan. When Mrs. Symmington apparently commits suicide after writing "I can't go on" on a scrap of paper, a coroner concludes that the letter-writer is "morally guilty of murder," but the villagers persist in murmuring that there is "no smoke without fire" (56). Jerry allows Megan, who is struggling, to live with him and Joanna, since her stepfather seems to have forgotten her existence and is entirely focused on looking after his two young sons with their governess, a young woman who is the only one who has not received an anonymous letter.

After a second death, which is very definitely a murder, the plain-speaking Mrs. Dane-Calthrop calls in her friend from a neighboring village, Miss Marple, who "knows a great deal about wickedness" (120). This is determined to be a good thing because Scotland Yard officials and psychiatrists have manifestly failed to get to the root of this clearly local and personal mystery. Miss Marple arrives, learns the facts, hears the gossip, and listens to Jerry's largely symbolic dream (which is in fact an abstract presentation of the major clues). Following some more plot developments, she identifies the murderer as Richard Symmington, who sent the letters so that, when he killed his wife, it would look like suicide. He killed her so he could marry the governess and later killed the maid when she realized that no anonymous letter had arrived in the mail. The suicide note is also explained along psychological lines: such a message would not be written on scrap of paper; it was taken from notes made during a telephone call.

Miss Marple, however, has no evidence. As in other cases, she uses an innocent character to set a trap, persuading Megan to blackmail her stepfather, so the police can walk in on him attempting to murder her. Impressed with Megan's pluck, Jerry treats her to a day out in London, where, seeing her look glamorous, he falls in love with her. Jerry and his sister end up married to locals and serve as the fuel for village gossip.

Christie called this novel her attempt to tackle "a classic theme"—the poison-pen letter (Foreword, *The Moving Finger* 6). The power or strategic use of sensational gossip also featured in two of the short stories in *The Labours of Hercules* (1947). There had been a real case with some similarities: from 1930 to 1933, anonymous letters with sexual allegations and threats had followed a village schoolmistress (Whittaker) and its postmistress (Creeth) on the Isle of Wight, even after the former moved away. Creeth, the only one who could have known Whittaker's new address, was eventually charged with sending the letters but was found not guilty ("Unsolved Mystery":). However, the letters stopped.

Christie's twist on the well-worn theme appears to be that the letters are not based in reality nor are they false rumors disguising one true one but are completely made up by the sender. However, this had already been an element of Richard Llewelyn's 1937 play, *Poison Pen*, in which a vicar's sister invents local scandals because she is bored, and the letters she sends drive various affected parties to murder. Christie's real twist here is the use of gender stereotypes: everyone assumes the letter-writer is a woman, but it is a (respectable, married, professional) man, and the clues to this are that he never sends a letter to the only beautiful and therefore hated-by-most-women young woman in the village and has no access to real gossip on which to base his stories. The gender stereotypes in this novel are not innovative, but they are being used (see **Hunter, Megan**).

Although it is one of the shortest Miss Marple novels—and shorter still in the British Penguin and all U.S. editions, which take text from the magazine abridgement—*The Moving Finger* contains some of Christie's most striking village characters. Christie herself was particularly fond of Megan Hunter and Maud Dane-Calthrop, with the latter revived in *The Pale Horse* (1961). There is also Mr. Pye, the most widely cited example of a gay character in her work; the beautiful but utterly vapid governess Elsie Holland who is so lacking in "SA" (sex appeal) that only a man in a midlife crisis can find her attractive; and Jerry Burton, the RAF veteran wounded in a domestic plane crash, whose attempts to present himself to the reader as an everyman are undermined by his satirical name: a mix of British slang for the German enemy (Jerry) and a death wish (Burton).

The novel was serialized in *Collier's Magazine* from March 1942; this abridged text was used in the U.S. edition (Dodd, Mead, 1942). It was published in the United Kingdom by Collins the next year. The book has been filmed three times: as part of the BBC's *Miss Marple* with Joan Hickson (broadcast 22 February 1985), as part of ITV's *Agatha Christie's Marple* with Geraldine McEwan (broadcast 12 February 2006), and as part of *Les Petits Meutres d'Agatha Christie* (broadcast 11 September 2009). A French radio version was broadcast on RTF on 25 November 1958 and a British version on BBC Radio 4 on 5 May 2001.

Characters: **Appleby, Colonel**; Baker, Beatrice; **Barton, Emily**; **Burton, Jerry, and Joanna**; **Cleat, Mrs.**; **Dane-Calthrop, Maud, and Rev. Caleb**; Elford, Florence; Ginch, Miss; Griffith, Aimée; Griffith, Dr. Owen; **Holland, Elsie**; **Hunter, Megan**; Kent, Dr. Marcus; **Marple, Jane**; Nash, Superintendent; Partridge; **Pye, Mr.**; Rose; Symmington, Brian and Colin; **Symmington, Mona, and Richard ("Dick")**; Woddell, Agnes

See also: *Agatha Christie's Marple*; Homosexuality; *Les Maîtres du Mystère*; Mayhem Parva; *Miss Marple* (radio series); *Miss Marple* (television series); *Les Petits Meurtres d'Agatha Christie*

Mowbray, Basil

Basil Mowbray is a gossipy, effeminate friend of the Prentice family, who describes Dame Laura Whitstable as "a wonderful Period Piece … so divinely grim" in the Mary Westmacott novel *A Daughter's a Daughter* (118). This is an example of a character who has been read as queer-coded, and his flamboyance is played for straightforward comic effect.

Mrs. McGinty's Dead (novel; alternative title: *Blood Will Tell*)

Hercule Poirot's 1952 outing sees the return of Ariadne Oliver, who has now fully evolved into Christie's fictional alter ego and shows plenty of professional causticity. In the novel, Poirot investigates the death of charwoman Mrs. McGinty, whose lodger, James Bentley, has been arrested for her murder, supposedly for the sum of £30. Poirot travels to the village of Broadhinny and has the unique experience of staying in a rundown bed-and-breakfast, where he teaches his landlady how to make omelets. He comes to believe that Bentley is innocent and uncovers a plot involving the child of a famous murderer. In the process, he meets an up-and-coming playwright who frustrates Mrs. Oliver during their work to adapt one of her novels for the stage.

Like many Christie works, the title comes from a children's rhyme, although this is a little-discussed aspect, partly because the rhyme is fairly tangential to the plot (it does not influence structure, unlike in *And Then There Were None*, *Five Little Pigs*, and *A Pocket Full of Rye*, for instance). Another is that the rhyme is now little known. In the United States, it was sufficiently obscure for the book to be published as *Blood Will Tell*, reflecting a theme of heredity touched on by the text. Not a nursery rhyme or containing song, "Mrs. McGinty's Dead" is a game, where children chant, "Mrs. McGinty's dead," followed by "How did she die?," and then a series of actions to be repeated, "just like I."

One theme in *Mrs. McGinty's Dead* is magazine culture. As a working-class woman, Mrs. McGinty had a passionate interest in Sunday newspapers and gossip magazines, which proves to have been relevant to her death. As in *The Mirror Crack'd from Side to Side*, sensational journalistic gossip holds clues for the detective—in this case, the sordid world of true crime journalism, which Christie generally avoided. Unlike many of her peers, she did not write fiction-style accounts of real murders, although she certainly incorporated elements of actual crimes into her novels and did contribute an account of two, "The Tragic Family of Croyden" and "A Letter from Agatha Christie," to newspapers. In fact, James Bentley in this novel bears something of a resemblance to 19-year-old Derek Bentley, who became a *cause célèbre* in British tabloids in 1952 when he was sentenced to execution for a murder committed by a 16-year-old friend of his: Bentley was hanged in 1953, despite 200 Members of Parliament requesting a stay of execution. The outrage this provoked was instrumental in the repeal of the death penalty.

A key and often discussed element of the novel is the subplot in which Robin Upwood is trying to write a play featuring Mrs. Oliver's detective character Sven Hjerson. Christie has manifest fun writing Mrs. Oliver, who views her own green-and-white Penguin books with disapproval (Penguin was famously founded with Christie's writing in mind) and calls her books "frightful tripe," a statement heartily ignored by fans (133). Upwood considers the Hjerson of fiction a "nasty old man" and wants to make him 35, with political ideals and several girlfriends (131). Mrs. Oliver protests that Hjerson hates women, but Upwood insists, he "can't be a pansy" (131)—after all, he reasons, "a play has got to have glamour" (132).

Modern readers cannot miss the real-life parallels here, especially if they have read the following in Christie's autobiography, describing Michael Morton's wishes, in 1928, to adapt *The Murder of Roger Ackroyd* as a play: "I much disliked his first suggestion, which was to take about twenty years off Poirot's age, call him Beau Poirot and have lots of girls in love with him" (*Autobiography* 434). Without this knowledge, however, readers are likely familiar with speculation over Poirot's sexuality, which seems to be based purely on his eccentricities and the fact that he has no canonical girlfriend (discussions of Countess Vera Rossakoff being, at this juncture, inappropriate). The exchange therefore allows Christie to address publicly something she did not usually discuss in print.

It is oddly fitting that the first adaptation of the novel as a film took extreme liberties, including the replacement of Poirot with Miss Marple (played by Margaret Rutherford). In fact, Christie had inadvertently pre-empted this title four decades earlier,

in "The Manhood of Edward Robinson," when an author complains of a publisher: "Ten to one he'll change the title and call it something rotten like 'Murder Most Foul' without so much as asking me" (*TLM* 183). MGM's *Murder Most Foul,* a title on which Christie was not consulted, was released to cinemas in 1963. A BBC Radio 4 adaptation, this time featuring Poirot, was broadcast in 2006. The novel has also been filmed as an episode of *Agatha Christie's Poirot,* which aired in 2008. It was adapted into an episode of *Les Petits Meurtres d'Agatha Christie* in 2015.

Characters: **Amy**; Benson, Mr.; **Bentley, James**; Blake, Vera; Burch, Bessie; Burch, Joe; Carpenter, Eve; Carpenter, Guy; **Edna**; Elliott, Mrs.; Frieda; Gamboll, Lily; **George(s)**; Groom, Janet; Henderson, Deirdre; **Hjerson, Sven**; **Hope, Evelyn**; Horsfall, Pamela; Kane, Eva; Leech, Cecil; McGinty, Mrs.; **Oliver, Ariadne**; **Poirot, Hercule**; Rendell, Dr.; Rendell, Sheelagh; Scuttle, Mr.; Selkirk, Eve; **Spence, Superintendent Bert**; Stanisdale, Judge; Summerhayes, Major Johnnie; **Summerhayes, Maureen**; Sweetiman, Mrs.; Upward, Laura; **Upward, Robin**; Vasseur, Robert; West, Michael; Wetherby, Edith; Wetherby, Roger; **Williams, Maude**

See also: *Agatha Christie's Poirot; Alibi* **(play);** *Hercule Poirot* **(BBC radio series); MGM Films; Nursery Rhymes; Penguin Books,** *Les Petits Meurtres d'Agatha Christie;* **True Crime**

Ms Ma, Nemesis *(The Goddess of Revenge; Miseu Ma: Boksooui Yeoshin)*

This South Korean television series aired on SBS TV in October and November 2018. The 32 episodes were aired in groups of four, back-to-back on Saturdays—a ploy to allow commercial breaks in what were essentially two-hour episodes. South Korean law prohibits commercial breaks within programs. A long narrative overarches the series, with mysteries within, based on various Miss Marple novels.

It is set in the late 2010s and uses muted colors to give the impression of sinister luxury. The Miss Marple character is replaced with Ms. Ma, played by Yunjin Kim—a woman falsely imprisoned when she is accused of killing her daughter. She breaks out of prison to find the murderer. Other cast members include Jung Woon-in and K-pop star CNU (Shin Dong-woo). As well as adapting *Nemesis*, as the title suggests, the series is based on *The Body in the Library*, *The Moving Finger*, *A Murder Is Announced*, and *The Mirror Crack'd from Side to Side*.

See also: **Marple, Jane**; *Nemesis*

Mugg, Charles. See **Cartwright, Sir Charles**

Mullins, Iris ("Dodo")

The villain in *Postern of Fate*, Iris Mullins poses as a friendly neighbor to the Beresfords but is later revealed to be a psychopathic fascist. She is described as rather manly: "a tall masculine-looking woman in tweed trousers and a Fair Isle pullover," with a "deep and slightly hoarse" voice (223). She is known to British Intelligence as "Dodo," because she represents the revival of extinct ideologies.

Murder after Hours. See *The Hollow* (novel)

Murder Ahoy! See **MGM Films**

"Murder and Our Sporting Instinct"

An article published in *Tit-Bits* on 22 September 1930, in which Christie considers the consumption of murder mysteries as a diversion or hobby.

See also: **Games**.

Murder at Christmas. See **Hercule Poirot's Christmas**

The Murder at Hazelmoor. See *The Sittaford Mystery*

Murder at the Gallop (film). See **MGM Films**

Murder at the Gallop (novel). See *After the Funeral*

Murder at the Vicarage (play)

Moie Charles and Barbara Toy dramatized Christie's 1930 novel *The Murder at the Vicarage* as the first Miss Marple stage play in 1948. In 1949, Christie was consulted on the script, considering it generally "very good" but "rather too cosy novelish" (qtd. in Green 241). It opened at the Playhouse Theatre, London, on 16 December 1949, to good reviews. A far-too-young Barbara

Mullen played Miss Marple, and although Christie was publicly kind about the casting, she later wrote to her daughter that she had "hated Murder at the Vicarage and a Miss Marple of twenty-odd" (qtd. in Green 546). Mullen would later revive the role in the same play more than 20 years later.

Other cast members, directed by Reginald Tate, included Jack Lambert as Rev. Leonard Clement, Betty Sinclair as Mary, and Francis Roberts as Inspector Slack. The action takes place entirely in the vicarage study and follows the main murder plot of the novel, cutting subplots and their attendant characters such as Dr. Stone and Mrs. Lestrange. The result is more of a family drama backdrop to the puzzle. A rather sensational ending has Miss Marple held at gunpoint.

See also: **Marple, Jane**; *The Murder at the Vicarage* (novel)

"Murder at the Vicarage" (story). See **"Sanctuary"**

The Murder at the Vicarage (novel)

The first Miss Marple novel is not the character's debut: she appeared in a series of short stories in 1928 but was not yet known to a wide audience when Collins and Dodd, Mead published *The Murder at the Vicarage* in 1930. It was a big year for Collins, which used the novel as one of the inaugural titles in its Crime Club imprint. It was also a big year for Christie: she married Max Mallowan, had her first West End play staged, and published three books. It is hardly surprising that, in her autobiography, she claimed to have no memory of how, why, or when she wrote *The Murder at the Vicarage*. Upon rereading, her main comment was that it had "too many characters, and too many sub-plots" (*AA* 434–35).

The narrator is the Rev. Leonard Clement, a middle-aged Anglican vicar in the village of St. Mary Mead, who has married a much younger woman, Griselda. At the family dinner table and later in his wife's "[t]ea and scandal" with village busybodies (*MAV* 5), several local scandals emerge: Colonel Protheroe, a magistrate, is widely disliked; his daughter, Lettice, is causing a scandal by posing in her bathing suit for local artist Laurence Redding; and those two are suspected of having an affair. In fact, the vicar learns, Redding is having an affair with Anne Protheroe, the colonel's wife and Lettice's stepmother. Later, after being called away on a bogus mission, Clement returns to discover Protheroe shot dead in his study. Soon, Redding and Anne independently confess to the murder, but their confessions cancel one another out, and the investigation proceeds under the assumption that each thought one another guilty and elected to take the blame.

This device evokes one deployed in *The Mysterious Affair at Styles*, but the twist here is that the couple *did* commit the murder, conspiring to appear innocent by making palpably false confessions. There are several subplots to unwind before this can be revealed: the colonel's dying ex-wife living in the village under an assumed name, an escaped criminal hiding in the village, an archaeologist who turns out to be a fraud, a curate who has been stealing from the church, and the mysterious behavior of Griselda who seems to be having an affair (it is later revealed that she is pregnant with her husband's child). The detective is Jane Marple, who is present throughout action. This book also provides the first example of Miss Marple offering up an innocent character for sacrifice, something she does in nearly every one of her novels to trap the murderer(s). In this case, she sets a "little trap" (289), which involves the local doctor putting his life in danger by suggesting to the murderers that they have been witnessed attempting to poison the curate. This tricks them into confessing as they convene to plan their next move.

Although the stories that became *The Thirteen Problems* introduced Miss Marple as the sole elderly woman in a room full of men and bright young things, *The Murder at the Vicarage* introduces her in the context of a circle of aged village gossips. At the outset, Clement compares her to her neighbor, Miss Wetherby: "Miss Marple is a white-haired old lady with a gentle, appealing manner—Miss Wetherby is a mixture of vinegar and gush. Of the two Miss Marple is the more dangerous" (13). She goes on to chide the vicar for being "unworldly" and to speak cryptically on village matters by way

of anecdotes about similar people (18). Over the course of the novel, Clement comes to respect her—first by seeing the patronizing treatment of her by police officials and her nephew, and later by witnessing her deductive powers. He concludes that "Miss Marple is rather a dear" (298).

As Christie acknowledges in her autobiography, Caroline Shepherd in *The Murder of Roger Ackroyd* was one of Miss Marple's inspirations. The character's development—particularly her use of gossip and reliance on a network of wives and servants—is in strong evidence here. The ways people talk about one another, the things they notice, and their own predictable unofficial surveillance activities inform not just the plot of the novel but also the plot that the murderers hatch. With a map and clear descriptions of village locations and activities, this novel also provides the most complete design of St. Mary Mead, giving body to places and characters that would reappear over the next several decades. The village itself, however, had been mentioned as early as 1928's *The Mystery of the Blue Train*.

Although Miss Marple was preceded in print by Anna Katharine Green's Miss Amelia Butterworth, Patricia Wentworth's Miss Silver, and Dorothy L. Sayers's Miss Climpson, Christie's name was already the preeminent one in detective fiction when Miss Marple hit the bookshelves. Her arrival led contemporary critics to herald "an entirely new kind of detective, and a lady detective into the bargain" (Thomson 210). Writing of this strange new "Cranfordian … spinster and … gossip," H. Douglas Thomson insisted that Miss Marple was a character with promise but, would she reappear, she was "exasperat[ingly] limit[ed]" by being confined to "her native heath" (210–11). In so writing, he perhaps embodied the critical male presumptions gently undermined by Miss Marple in this and subsequent outings.

A highly adapted novel, *The Murder at the Vicarage* generally appears in media without the first "The." Thus was it staged in 1949 in a dramatization by Moie Charles and Barbara Toy. A German version of this play was filmed in 1970 as *Mord im Pfarrhaus* (Murder in the Rectory). The first television adaptation of the novel was broadcast as part of the BBC's *Miss Marple* in 1986, and the BBC aired a radio version in 1993. *The Murder at the Vicarage* was filmed as the second episode of ITV's *Agatha Christie's Marple* in 2004. The next year, a French graphic novel, *L'Affaire Protheroe* (The Protheroe Affair), adapted by an artist who goes by the single name Norma, was published. A French screen adaptation, part of *Les Petits Meurtres d'Agatha Christie*, aired in 2016.

Characters: Abbott, Henry; Abbott, Mrs.; Adams, Mary; Archer, Bill; Archer, Mrs.; Bailey; Baker, Mrs.; Bucknall, Joe; Carter, Mollie; **Clara**; Clement, Dennis; **Clement, Griselda**; **Clement, Rev. Leonard**; **Cram, Gladys**; Elwell; Emily; Fanny; **Gladys**; Hargreaves, Major; Hartley-Napier, Susan; **Hartnell, Amanda**; Hawes, Rev. Christopher; **Haydock, Dr.**; His, Mary; Hurst, Constable; **Jackson, Fred**; Lestrange, Estelle; Manning; **Marple, Jane**; Melchett, Colonel; Pratt, Mrs.; **Price-Ridley, Martha**; **Protheroe, Anne**; **Protheroe, Colonel Lucius**; **Protheroe, Lettice**; Quinton; **Redding, Lawrence**; Reeves; Roberts, Dr.; Rose, Lily; Sadler, Mrs.; Simmons, Mrs.; **Slack, Detective Inspector**; Stone, Dr.; **West, Raymond**; **Wetherby, Caroline**

See also: *Agatha Christie's Marple*; **Collins Crime Club**; **Mayhem Parva**; *Miss Marple* (radio series); *Miss Marple* (television series); *Mood im Pfarrhaus*; *Les Petits Meurtres d'Agatha Christie*; **St. Mary Mead**

Murder by the Book. See **Fictional Portrayals of Agatha Christie**

Murder Clinic (radio series)

Murder Clinic was an influential radio anthology series, airing from 1942 to 1943 on WOR, the main station of the Mutual Broadcasting Service, which would go on to make Harold Huber's *Hercule Poirot* series. Airing in the mornings, it featured 30-minute adaptations of short stories and novels by leading contemporary crime writers. There were five episodes based on Christie stories. Three featured Hercule Poirot, played by a different actor each time; one featured Miss Marple; and one featured J. Parker Pyne.

The first Christie adaptation was "The Blue Geranium," starring Vivian Ogden as Miss Marple, on 12 January 1942. On 6 October that year, Maurice Tarplin starred as Poirot in "The Tragedy at Marsdon Manor" (spelled "Marsden Manor" in listings); this is one of the only six recordings from the series that currently survive. Another actor took the role in "Triangle at Rhodes" on 9 February 1943 and yet another, Ted de Corsia, in "Yellow Iris" on 25 July. The last Christie offering of 1943 and of the series was "Death on the Nile," the Parker Pyne story, on 5 September. At the time of publication, this is the only adaptation in any medium of that story.

See also: **Marple, Jane**; **Parker Pyne, J. ("Christopher")**; **Poirot, Hercule**

Murder for Christmas. See *Hercule Poirot's Christmas*

Murder in Mesopotamia (novel; alternative title: *No Other Love*)

Christie's second and final novel with a female narrator, *Murder in Mesopotamia* draws on her experiences with her husband, Max Mallowan, on archaeological digs in Western Asia. Some of the characters and settings are very clearly based on real people and places she encountered.

Nurse Amy Leatheran is called to an archaeological dig in Iraq to look after Louise Leidner, the American wife of lead archaeologist Eric Leidner. She seems to be imagining that her deceased first husband, Frederick Bosner, is haunting her, threatening to kill her because she has moved on from him. Louise married Bosner hastily during World War I before he was outed as a German spy and proclaimed dead. The general consensus is that, hungry for drama, she has invented the ghost. However, Louise is killed in her bedroom, and medic Dr. Reilly calls in Hercule Poirot, who is in the area. Poirot questions the suspects and finds most significant the dead woman's character. In this, his activities mirror those of an archaeologist, as he works to reconstruct a personality he has never met based on often conflicting accounts and physical evidence.

Once he has solved the mystery of her "haunting beauty" (247) and attractiveness for men, he is able to solve the case. Her second husband, Dr. Leidner, was in fact her first, Frederick Bosner, in disguise. He killed her because she was falling for another man on the dig. This novel also includes one of the most violent murders in the Christie canon. The second victim, Anne Johnson, is a devoted assistant to Dr. Leidner. She is in love with him, but he kills her to stop her revealing what she realizes. He replaces her drinking water with hydrochloric acid, and the physical effect is vividly described. Poirot says his case against Leidner is "[p]sychologically perfect.... But there is no proof" (281). However, Leidner/Bosner instantly confesses, declaring himself "tired" (282), and the narrative reaches a satisfactory conclusion.

The setting of the archaeological dig obviously draws on Christie's experiences as an archaeologist's wife, and certain details about life on the dig—not least conversations around unearthed bones and artefacts—have the ring of truth. Equally clearly drawn from life are musings on the dangers of a hasty wartime marriage: Agatha and Archie Christie married on Christmas Day 1914 in something of a whirlwind, and the marriage famously did not work out. There is also the figure of Father Lavigny, a Roman Catholic priest and specialist in dead languages, who examines the artifacts onsite. Few novelists would have thought to include such a figure, but he seems to be based on a real person, Father Leon Legrain, who, according to Max Mallowan, seems to have been a much more earthly, amusing, and talented person than his fictional counterpart (Mallowan 38).

The real-life inspirations for some characters may never be known. Dr. Reilly is described as "a black-haired, long-faced man who said all sorts of funny things in a low, sad voice" (*MIM* 15), which reads authentically, but there is no record of an equivalent character on Mallowan's digs. Mallowan noted that he himself appears in the novel "as [David] Emmott, a minor but decent character" (Mallowan 208). Emmott is a quiet young American who ends up married to the outspoken Sheila Reilly.

More famously based on a real person is "Lovely Louise," the central victim. Katherine Woolley, wife of dig leader Leonard Woolley, was an extraordinary woman who made a lasting impression on Christie. The portrait of her as Louise Leidner is more honest than flattering (see **Leidner, Louise**), but, Mallowan noted in his memoir, when she read the book, "Katherine did not recognise certain traits which might have been taken as applicable to herself, and took no umbrage" (208).

One aspect of *Murder in Mesopotamia* often critiqued by fans and in traditional scholarship is the solution. It is, many point out, quite implausible that a woman would not recognize that her second husband is the same person as her first, even if he has grown a beard, adopted an accent, and allowed 15 years to pass. However, some have argued that this misses the point. In an article subtitled "Feeding the Orientalist Machine," Esther Pujolràs-Noguer argues that, in this novel, the victim "goes through a process of orientalisation," assuming all the narrative blame, including for her own death, by virtue of her otherness. The fact that Bosner/Leidner is able to marry the same woman twice, writes Pujolràs-Noguer, positions him as "a master in deception" and a dangerous national traitor, with his wife/victim dehumanized to the extent that her perception is not actually relevant (Pujolràs-Noguer, forthcoming). The focus is on the murderer's skill, for all Poirot's comments on the victim's personality. Another reading of the novel sees an artistic significance in the double-husband motif, which reflects the presentation of Western characters setting up camp in Iraq: "*Murder in Mesopotamia* depicts the allure of the Other, yet suggests that human nature is often the same the world over, no matter how exotic the surroundings" (Laing and Frost 118).

Murder in Mesopotamia was serialized, abridged in the *Saturday Evening Post* in the United States between 9 November and 14 December 1935. It was published in book form by Collins in the United Kingdom and Dodd, Mead in the United States the next year. Also in 1936, an abridgement was serialized in the British weekly magazine *Woman's Pictorial* under the title *No Other Love*.

Several names are different in this version, indicating that names were changed in the final book manuscript late in the process.

There have been two BBC radio adaptations of this novel. The first, broadcast live on 7 March 1956, starred French after Jacques Henri as Poirot. The second, which aired in five installments in December 1994, starred John Moffat. A television version, part of *Agatha Christie's Poirot*, aired on ITV on 2 June 2002. The same year, a French graphic novel adapted by François Rivière was published. It was translated into English in 2008.

Characters: **Abdullah**; Byrd, Dr.; **Bosner, Frederick, and William;** Carey, Richard; **Coleman, William ("Bill")**; Curshaw, Sister; Emmott, David; Ibrahim; Jervis, Lieutenant; **Johnson, Anne**; Kelsey, Major; Kelsey, Mary; Lavingny, Father; **Leatheran, Nurse Amy; Leidner, Dr. Eric; Leidner, Louise;** Maitland, Captain; Mansur; Mercado, Joseph; Mercado, Marie; Pennyman, Major; **Poirot, Hercule; Reilly, Dr. Giles, and Sheila;** Verrier; **Yusuf, Ali**

See also: *Agatha Christie's Poirot;* **Archaeology; BBC Radio Adaptations;** *Hercule Poirot* (BBC radio series); **Mallowan, Sir Max**

Murder in Retrospect. See *Five Little Pigs*

Murder in the Calais Coach. See *Murder on the Orient Express* (novel)

"Murder in the Mews" (novella; alternative title: "Good Night for a Murder")

A novella based on the 1923 story "The Market Basing Mystery," "Murder in the Mews" relocates the action to Guy Fawkes Night, a British commemoration of a foiled attempt to destroy Parliament that takes place on 5 November annually. In it, Hercule Poirot and Inspector Japp are musing on the festival—"an interesting survival," Poirot remarks, wondering if people who observe it know whether they are celebrating the death or the ambition of Guy Fawkes (*MITM* 11–12). Japp observes that fireworks would mask a gunshot (12), and the men are promptly called to a death-by-gunshot. Although the death of Barbara Allen appears to be a case of suicide, it is noticed that the door is locked, but the key is missing, and the gun is held in the wrong hand. The police start to suspect murder. However, Poirot uncovers a plot whereby a third party made a suicide look like murder. The victim's name evokes the Scottish ballad, "The Death of Barbara Allen," which is not referenced in the text but provides a clue about the romantic passions (and blackmail) that led to the death.

The novella first appeared in *Redbook* in September 1936 and in *Woman's Journal* in December 1936. It was collected in *Murder in the Mews: 4 Poirot Stories* (Collins, 1937) in the United Kingdom and *Dead Man's Mirror* (Dodd, Mead, 1937) in the United States. The neatness of the plot, a small element of which was recycled in *Peril at End House* (1931), and the Britishness of the set-up have made it a favorite among the shorter works. It was first dramatized for the radio as part of the BBC *Light Programme*, broadcast on 20 March 1955 starring Richard Williams as Poirot. It was later filmed as part of the ITV series *Agatha Christie's Poirot*, starring David Suchet, and broadcast on 15 January 1989. A 750-piece jigsaw puzzle based on the story, titled *Remember, Remember,* was produced by Paul Lamond Games in 2001.

Characters: **Allen, Barbara**; Eustace, Major; **Japp, Chief Inspector James**; Laverton-West, Charles; Plenderleith, Jane; **Poirot, Hercule**

See also: *Agatha Christie's Poirot;* **BBC Radio Adaptations; Games;** "The Market Basing Mystery"; *Peril at End House* (novel)

Murder in the Mews **(story collection; alternative titles:** *Dead Man's Mirror; Murder in the Mews: 4 Poirot Stories***)**

Murder in the Mews is a collection of four novellas, first published in the United Kingdom by Collins in 1937 with an identical edition from Odhams Press shortly after. Permission for this was granted to Odhams in exchange for the rights for Collins to reprint *The Hound of Death and Other Stories.* The U.S. edition, retitled *Dead Man's Mirror,* did not initially include the novella *The Incredible Theft,* presumably because it concerned British politics and featured no murder, although this was inserted into editions from 1987 onward. The volume is dedicated to Sybil Heeley, a children's author and daughter of actor Wilfred Lucas Heeley. She likely bonded with Christie over shared American heritage in their mutual childhood home, Torquay; both women were also acquainted with Rudyard Kipling. The original blurb compares Christie to crossword-setter Torquemada (aka Edward Powys Mathers), who later described the contents as "awkwardly shaped" (Torquemada 7) in a lukewarm review.

The book is composed of "**Murder in the Mews,**" "**The Incredible Theft**" (see above), "**Dead Man's Mirror,**" and "**Triangle at Rhodes.**"

Murder in the Studio (radio script collection; alternative title: *Murder on Air*)

Originally titled *Murder on Air, Murder in the Studio* is a 2019 collection of three Christie radio scripts—***The Yellow Iris,*** ***Butter in a Lordly Dish,*** and ***Personal Call.*** They are available for license from Concord Theatricals (Samuel French), which permits their performance either as stage dramas or as staged readings. In professional productions since 2009, they have been played as staged "radio productions" by seated actors in period dress.

Murder in Three Acts (novel). See *Three Act Tragedy*

Murder in Three Acts (television adaptation). See CBS Television Adaptations

A Murder Is Announced (novel)

A Murder Is Announced was published in 1950, with an initial run of 50,000 and a blaze of publicity, describing itself—erroneously—as Christie's 50th novel. It is one of the better-known Jane Marple mysteries and the most self-consciously postwar of Christie's village novels.

The tone of the novel is set from the beginning, which sees the village paper boy Johnnie Butt make his deliveries around the village of Chipping Cleghorn. In the first paragraph, the reader learns, for instance, that Colonel and Mrs. Easterbrook read the *Times* and the *Daily Graphic*; that Mrs. Swettenham and her son take the *Times* and the *Daily Worker*; and that Miss Blacklock's household takes the *Telegraph*, the *Times*, and the *Daily Mail*. The choice of newspaper is a shorthand for the character: readers know that Colonel Easterbrook will be conservative and formal, that Mrs. Easterbrook will be a gossip, that Edmund Swettenham will be an angry idealist, and that Miss Blacklock's household is more egalitarian. Every villager, the reader is told, reads the local newspaper, the *Chipping Cleghorn Gazette*—this evokes prewar village community, although in the context of the accompanying papers, the unity may start to look unsustainable. This impression is amplified as an astonishing number of false identities emerge, proving that in a postwar world it is no longer possible to know one's neighbors.

In the *Gazette*, an announcement appears: "*A murder is announced and will take place on Friday, October 29th, at Little Paddocks at 6.30 p.m. Friends please accept this, the only intimation*" (12; emphasis in original). As original drafts—and the original title, *A Murder Has Been Arranged*—indicate, the similarity to traditional marriage announcements is deliberate. It causes a stir among the locals, and no one is more baffled than the residents of Little Paddocks, which is owned by the very sensible Letitia Blacklock. By 6:30 p.m., several villagers have gathered at Little Paddocks, hardly any of them admitting that the notice in the paper has drawn them there. As the clock strikes, the lights go out, a stranger barges in, and two shots ring out.

The intruder, a Swiss youth called Rudi Scherz, has died, and Miss Blacklock has been shot at. Miss Marple, who is in the area, helps the young Inspector Craddock with the investigation. They learn that Scherz had been told to arrive at this time as part of a joke and also learn that Miss Blacklock is about to inherit a great deal of money—as long as she outlives Sonia Goedler, the dying wife of her former employer. Goedler's extended family comes under suspicion, and it emerges that most of the people living at Little Paddocks are not who they claim to be—the people who would inherit if Miss Blacklock predeceases Goedler are among them.

There are two more murders—one apparently aimed at Miss Blacklock, and one because of an eyewitness statement. As Craddock continues to struggle, Miss Marple gathers clues from gossip, a family photograph, and observations of people's jewelry and furniture. She reveals that Miss Blacklock committed the murders because Scherz recognized her—not as Letitia, who was to inherit the money, but as Charlotte, her sister. The second victim, her oldest friend, was killed because she kept mixing up "Letty" and "Lotty," unable to keep secret the false identity of which she was aware. To catch Miss Blacklock, Miss Marple sets up a scene involving Mitzi, the household help who is a compulsive liar. She convinces Mitzi to announce to the police, in front of Miss Blacklock and others, that she saw the murder. The police make a show of disbelieving Mitzi, and she is left alone with her employer. Miss Blacklock is caught trying to drown Mitzi in the kitchen.

The novel closes with two young people who are misfits in the village—a single mother and a socialist intellectual—settling down to respectable married life. They do, however, cancel their order for the *Chipping Cleghorn Gazette*. The newsagent and his wife agree that this must be a mistake: everyone in Chipping Cleghorn reads the *Gazette*.

As a mystery, the novel rewards close reading, with many clues planted in dialogue and apparent typographical errors ("Letty"/"Lotty" is one example, but so, too, is the fact that two letters apparently by the same person spell "enquire"/"inquire" differently). This caused several editorial issues in the preparation of the manuscript, as Christie had to manually correct and chastise helpful typists and editors at almost every stage of the process. Moments of comedy can serve a triple purpose. Julia Simmons complains that the houseguests "all said the same things in turn" upon arriving at the house: "'I see you've got your central heating on' and 'What *lovely* chrysanthemums!'" (59; emphasis in original). This is comedy, social commentary, and a clue: the central heating is on so a fire does not have to be lit, which would provide a source of light, and the flowers are visible because the water in the vase is needed to fuse the lights—suggesting that the blackout has been planned in advance.

A Murder Is Announced straightforwardly gives the lie to the charge that Christie did not engage in social commentary. The impacts of war are everywhere—from discussions of coal rationing (especially in relation to the central heating) to the black-market trade in meat (which creates an underground network that is a good source of gossip), the presence of a refugee persecuted by the Nazis, and the creation of a gluttonous and ration-defying cake christened "Delicious Death" by those who consume it. "Delicious Death" appears to be based on a real cake, as Christie dedicated the novel "to Ralph and Anne Newman, at whose house I first tasted DELICIOUS DEATH!." There have been frequent attempts over the years to create a recipe, including more than one "official recipe" for sickly chocolate cakes issued by Agatha Christie Ltd.

The novel is politically right-of-center, in a manner more explicit than elsewhere. There is the slow reformation of Edmund, whose socialism softens toward the end as he embraces the idea of marriage. Moreover, there is the narrative treatment of Mitzi. She is presented as a hysterical figure of fun who tells outlandish lies and has a kind of persecution complex (some might say justifiably, since she was imprisoned in a concentration camp). Her exact origins are uncertain, and although at least one character urges Craddock not to "be too prejudiced against the poor thing because she's a liar," adding that there may be "a sub stream of truth behind her lies," the reader is nonetheless invited to laugh at "her atrocity stories" that grow more and more elaborate (57, 58). R.A. York notes that Mitzi is "treated with regrettable levity" (134) but adds that her usefulness to the police goes toward redressing the balance. It may also be taken, however, as narrative condescension. Shane Brown has summarized the uncomfortable reaction of modern readers:

> Certainly, sensitivities regarding these issues were not what they are today, but how can one excuse the ridicule of a refugee character who has witnessed Nazi atrocities in a book written just a few years

after the end of the war? And how could that book be penned by the same author who, two years earlier, had included the devastating anti-refugee assault on Poirot in *Taken at the Flood*, clearly meant as a damning indictment of negative attitudes toward refugees at the time? For whatever reason, Christie seemed to be critical of xenophobia (even if she sometimes unintentionally presented her opposition in a naive, clumsy, or patronizing way) and yet complicit regarding antisemitism [78].

An intolerant ethos undeniably underpins *A Murder Is Announced*, although the book is also gently critical of conservatism for its own sake. By the end, the reformed Edmund and Phillippa may have acquired respectability, but they are still misunderstood. Edmund's novel, *Elephants Do Forget*, is frequently "corrected" by helpful locals who miss the rather obvious point of the title, pointing out that it should be *Elephants Don't Forget* (255). The partners still buy the *Daily Worker* and assert themselves by refusing to place an order for the local *Gazette*. However, Christie shows the newsagent unable to believe that anyone could possibly get by without it and insisting that they misspoke (256). By far, the most sympathetic characters in the novel are a same-sex couple, who have been positively identified as lesbians by fans, scholars, dramatists, and Christie's own grandson (see Bernthal, *Ageless* 239). When one of these characters dies, Christie encourages sympathy because it is the most senseless of the murders, with no blame at all on the victim's part, and her partner is presented, movingly, as heartbroken. Although Hinchcliffe and Murgatroyd are only ever called "friends" who love each other, the homosexual relationship is evident as they are presented in language consistent with then-extremely-fashionable newspaper reports of lesbian couples living together in villages and suburbs.

As Charles Osborne (242) has pointed out, some of the plot points—including the house name Little Paddocks—are pre-empted in the 1930 story "The Companion," whereas the novel *Elephants Do Forget* is not dissimilar in title to Christie's 1972 novel, *Elephants Can Remember*. The village of Chipping Cleghorn and some

of its inhabitants reappear in "Sanctuary" (1954).

Miss Marple's television debut was in 1956, when NBC aired a one-hour adaptation of *A Murder Is Announced*, starring Gracie Fields, complete with Yorkshire accent. Later television versions of the novel include a three-part episode of the BBC's *Miss Marple* in 1985; an episode of ITV's *Agatha Christie's Marple* in 2005; two Japanese versions (NTV, 2007 and TV Asahi, 2019); an episode of *Les Petits Meurtres d'Agatha Christie* in France (2015); and an arc in the 2018 South Korean series *Ms Ma, Nemesis*. Shortly before her death, Christie granted Leslie Darbon the rights to adapt *A Murder Is Announced* for the stage. The play was produced in 1977 and reaped mixed reviews. A radio dramatization by Michael Bakewell was broadcast in five parts on BBC Radio 4 from 9 August 1999.

Characters: Ashe, Mr.; **Bantry, Colonel Arthur, and Dolly;** Barker, Ned; Bedingfield, Mr.; Bellamy, Florence; **Blacklock, Charlotte (Lotty), and Letitia (Letty);** Blacklock, Dr.; **Bunner, Dora ("Bunny");** Butt, Johnnie; Butt, Mr. and Mrs.; **Clithering, Sir Henry; Craddock, Detective Inspector Dermot;** Cutie; Easterbrook, Colonel Archie and Laura; Edwards, Constable; Finch, Miss; Goedler, Belle and Randall; **Harmon, Diana (Bunch), and Rev. Julian**; Harmon, Edward; Harmon, Susan; Harris, Myrna; **Hartnell, Amanda;** Haymes, Captain Ronald; Haymes, Harry; **Haymes, Philippa (Pip); Hinchcliffe, Miss ("Hinch");** Huggins, Jim; Huggins, Mrs.; Julia; Legg, Constable; **Marple, Jane; Mitzi; Murgatroyd, Amy; Price-Ridley, Martha;** Rowlandson, Mr.; Rysedale, Sir George; **Scherz, Rudi;** Simmons, Elinor; **Simmons, Julia, and Patrick**; Spragg, Jessie; Stamfordis, Dmitri; Stamfordis, Sonia; Stamfordis, Emma and Pip; Swettenham, Edmund; Swettenham, Mrs.; Tiglath Pilesar; Tyler, Fred; **West, Raymond; Wetherby, Caroline**

See also *Agatha Christie's Marple*; Anti-Semitism; Games; Mayhem Parva; *Miss Marple* (radio series); *Miss Marple* (television series); *A Murder Is Announced* (play); *Ms Ma, Nemesis*; NBC Television Adaptations; NTV Adaptations; *Les Petits*

Meurtres d'Agatha Christie; TV Asahi Adaptations; War

A Murder Is Announced (play)

In 1975, shortly before her death, Agatha Christie granted Leslie Darbon the rights to adapt *A Murder Is Announced* (1950) for the stage, in a production to be presented by Peter Saunders, producer of—among others—*The Mousetrap* (1952). The play was eventually produced in 1977 to mixed reviews. Despite its shortcomings as a piece of drama, overtly simplifying the plot in some areas while overloading dialogue with complicated subplots in others, it is occasionally revived and frequently performed by amateur theater companies. This likely has much to do with the character list: there are five men and seven women, the majority of whom are middle-aged—amateur theater frequently struggles fill young and male roles in particular.

Darbon's script reduces the novel considerably, cutting out the third murder and several characters including Colonel and Mrs. Easterbrook, Julian and Bunch Harmon, and Miss Hinchcliffe and Miss Murgatroyd. It maintains the essential mystery plot but frames it not in a postwar context but in "Christie time," thus focusing on the puzzle and cozy humor as opposed to considering social issues raised by the novel. This move also means switching the character of Mitzi from one persecuted by the Nazis to a more generic Eastern European fabulist, something all dramatists of *A Murder Is Announced* have done.

Following a run at the Theatre Royal, Brighton, the play opened on 21 September 1977 at the Vaudeville Theatre in the West End. The cast, directed by Robert Chetwyn, included Dulcie Gray as Miss Marple and James Grout as Inspector Craddock. Darbon went on to adapt one more Christie novel for presentation by Saunders: a much less successful version of *Cards on the Table* (1936) in 1981.

See also: **Cards on the Table** (play); *A Murder Is Announced* (novel)

A Murder Is Announced (television adaptation). See NBC Television Adaptations

Murder Is Easy (novel; alternative title: Easy to Kill)

Christie's first publication in 1939 was *Murder Is Easy*, which would quickly be overshadowed by *And Then There Were None* in the same year. Former policeman Luke Fitzwilliam meets the elderly Miss Pinkerton on a train, and she tells him she is on her way to Scotland Yard to report at least four murders. Initially, he dismisses her as a harmless eccentric, but then he finds that she, too, has died. He travels to "the little country town of Wychwood-under-Ashe" (24), which is, essentially, a Christie village. There he meets a colorful array of suspects, including a male witch—Mr. Ellsworthy, often cited as Christie's most explicitly and negatively drawn gay character—and an attractive gold-digger, Bridget, who is open about planning to marry the nouveau-riche Lord Whitfield for his money. Although many in the village had motives for at least one of the five recent deaths, nothing seems to connect them. Luke arrives at the truth almost by chance when he catches a church warden in a lie about a pet budgerigar.

A key point of the novel is psychopathy. The murders are not unmotivated, but, almost uniquely within the genre at this point, the killer's motives are flimsy enough that the reader must accept that she is insane. There is an element of the sensational when Honoria Waynflete is unmasked: she tries to strangle Bridget with "the strength of the insane" (243). There is also an element of Dorothy L. Sayers's maxim that one should never look for a motive because anything might drive someone to murder. However, Christie explores Waynflete's psychological make-up, and the clues are not so much connected with the mechanics of the actual murders as with the killer's state of mind, making the motivation the key clue. The key point is that conflicting accounts of the same incident make it clear that in her youth, Waynflete once strangled a budgerigar because her then-fiancé Lord Whitfield showed it, instead of her, affection.

This was not the first time that Christie had connected killing animals as a child with killing humans as an adult as have several developmental psychologists before and since. She would go on to make the same point in *And Then There Were None*, which closes with the murderer's confession, including an account of torturing insects in childhood. *Curtain,* written around the same time, has an account of a child killing a cat that crosses a kind of empathy barrier and results ultimately in a career of psychopathy—the same story would later appear in *Towards Zero*. In the context of the late 1930s, where war was becoming an inevitability and demographic tensions were being deliberately stirred, the point about the development of destructive personality traits would have been timely.

There is continuity with other Christie novels. For example, Superintendent Battle, an occasional Christie investigator, appears here, although, as usual, not in a major role. Like the Salisbury Plain in the world of Mr. Quin, Wychwood has a pub called the Bells and Motley. There are also witches, which would become fixtures in the late village novels, although for the only time here the main witch is a man. Mr. Ellsworthy, a spiteful, lisping effeminate antiques dealer, is drawn according to contemporary gay stereotypes—one of these, most common used by middlebrow writers of the period, is the presence of "long, artistic fingers" (60). He is presented as an antisocial force in the village, bringing decadent "orgies" (108, not necessarily meaning sex parties) and corrupting (again, not sexually) the local young women who are no longer marriageable. This presentation has been read as outright homophobia and as a strategic exploitation of stereotypes to mislead the reader: Ellsworthy will be the obvious suspect in a prejudiced readership, and therefore the surprise when a church warden is unmasked will be all the more striking. However, it must be noted that, at the end of the novel, despite the fact that Ellsworthy is completely innocent, his deviancy is punished when Luke uses his old police contacts to scare the young witch with "a nasty surprise" (259).

In the United States, the book was published as *Easy to Kill*, using the condensed magazine serial text and the title under which it was serialized in the *Saturday Evening Post* in 1938. Reasons for this are unclear but are likely connected with Christie's notorious lateness in returning corrected manuscripts. Interestingly, like *The Moving Finger*, which also uses a magazine abridgement for its U.S. edition, the gay-coded character has a much reduced presence. Another difference between the U.K. and U.S. editions is that Lavinia Pinkerton becomes Lavinia Fullerton. Although some have speculated that the name Pinkerton, evoking the U.S. detective agency, may have been changed to avoid confusing American audiences, this is unlikely. Surely the point of the name is that it provides an early clue that the character is not as disconnected from reality as she appears. In a similar manner, Waynflete's Christian name hints at her own pride. It is more likely that the name Fullerton came first and that it was changed in the final manuscript after the serial was submitted to U.S. magazines.

The novel, with its rural setting and wise older women, has a Miss Marple feel to it, and it has been incorrectly categorized as one on numerous occasions, first by Jacques Barzun and Wendell Hertig Taylor in *A Catalogue of Crime* in 1971. It is understandable: as Charles Osborne wrote, "Miss Marple would easily have fitted" (168). More recent errors of this type can be linked to one or both English-language screen adaptations. The first, aired on CBS in 1982, featured Helen Hayes who would go on to play Miss Marple in two adaptations in the same loose series. The second, aired on ITV in the United Kingdom in 2009, was part of *Agatha Christie's Marple*, and inserted the character into the story. There has also been a BBC Radio 4 version in three parts, broadcast in 2013, and an episode of *Les Petits Meurtres d'Agatha Christie*, aired on France 1 in 2015. A stage play by Clive Exton was mounted in London in 1993.

Characters: Abbot, Mr.; Anstruther, Mrs.; **Battle, Superintendent**; Carter, Harry; **Conway, Bridget**; **Ellsworthy, Mr.**; Fitzwilliam, Luke ("Fitz"); Gibbs, Amy; Horton, Major; Humbleby, Dr. John Edward; Humbleby, Mrs.; Jones, Mr.; Lorrimer, James ("Jimmy"); Mildred, Aunt; **Pierce, Mrs.**; Pierce, Tommy; **Pinkerton, Lavinia**; **Ragg, Gordon**; Reed, John; Rose, Mrs.; Thomas, Dr.; Wake, Alfred;

Waynflete, Honoria; Whitfield, Lord; Wonky Pooh

See also: *Agatha Christie's Marple*; BBC Radio Adaptations; Mayhem Parva; *Murder Is Easy* (play); *Les Petits Meurtres d'Agatha Christie*

Murder Is Easy (play)

Clive Exton's dramatization of Christie's 1939 novel *Murder Is Easy* opened at the Duke of York, London, on 23 February 1993. It ran for six weeks to mediocre reviews. This may have surprised producers, as Christie was doing extremely well for domestic television audiences. Exton was a much-feted lead dramatist for *Agatha Christie's Poirot*, a runaway success on ITV, and the high-profile cast included Irene Sutcliffe, Peter Capaldi, Nigel Davenport, Charlotte Attenborough, and Ian Thompson.

Murder Is Easy (television adaptation). See **CBS Television Adaptations**

Murder, Margaret and Me (Meeks). See **Fictional Portrayals of Agatha Christie**

Murder Most Foul. See **MGM Films**

"Murder Mountain." See "The Erymanthian Boar"

The Murder of Roger Ackroyd (novel; alternative title: Who Killed Ackroyd?)

Conventional scholarship finds *The Murder of Roger Ackroyd* difficult to discuss because, according to traditional wisdom, its entire value lies in its twist solution, and such studies tend to avoid spoilers. However, although the revelation that the narrator is the murderer is undoubtedly responsible for the novel's infamy, its contribution to the development of detective fiction extends beyond this. Notably, the title names the victim and not the narrator, detective, or distinctive theme (unlike, say, *The Memoirs of Sherlock Holmes* or *The Secret of Chimneys*). This means that the solving of the crime is, apparently, the key feature; as is increasingly well-known, Christie and the Golden Age of detective fiction have done much to shift public perceptions of the genre, to the extent that a puzzle-centric gloss is often applied to her predecessors.

"Mrs. Ferrars," the narrator Dr. Sheppard relates, "died on the night of 16–17 September" (1). She committed suicide and apparently left no note, although village gossip quickly fixes upon her husband's death some time before: rumors are rife that she murdered him, perhaps so she could marry local landowner Roger Ackroyd. Much of this is gleaned through Sheppard's sister, Caroline, who lives with him and has an overriding interest in gossip. Ackroyd is *nouveau riche* after making his money selling wagon wheels and now presents himself as "more impossibly like a country squire than any country squire could really be" (7). He lives with his ghastly sister ("all chains and teeth and bones" [36]); his niece, Flora; his secretary; his butler; and his housekeeper. His mysterious adoptive son, Ralph Paton, may or may not be in the area and is engaged to marry Flora. Shepherd meets his new neighbor, Hercule Poirot, whom he initially believes to be a retired hairdresser.

Sheppard visits Ackroyd, who tells him that Mrs. Ferrars confessed to him that she did indeed kill her husband, that she was being blackmailed, and that would not tell him the blackmailer's name. Ackroyd then receives a letter and, after 10 minutes, Sheppard leaves him. That evening, Sheppard is summoned to Fernley Park, Ackroyd's home, by a mysterious telephone call stating that Ackroyd has been murdered. When he arrives, the butler, Parker, is surprised to see him. However, for peace of mind, they check on Ackroyd and find him dead in his study. Poirot, an old friend of Ackroyd's, takes it upon himself to solve the case, and Sheppard fancies himself to be playing Watson to Poirot's Holmes, although the detective confides more in the doctor's gossipy sister, Caroline.

The key investigative tool is gossip, which Poirot accesses via Caroline's network of wives and servants. One chapter, "A Game of Mah Jong," both summarizes the case and opens new avenues of investigation in the form of dialogue around a table during a game. Multiple secrets, including relationships, theft, and a marriage, are uncovered, before Poirot reveals, in private, that he knows Dr. Sheppard is the murderer. He faked the telephone call and misled witnesses about the time of Ackroyd's death using a rigged Dictaphone. Sheppard ends his narrative with an address to the reader, in which he boasts of his cleverness, never lying but carefully omitting the crime in his account of the relevant evening. Finally, he announces an intention to commit suicide, poetically reflecting the novel's opening, with the death of Mrs. Ferrars.

Prior to its dénouement, *The Murder of Roger Ackroyd* is, as Dennis Sanders and Len Lovallo note, "a conventional mystery" and "classic Christie" (32). In fact, it is so extremely conventional that it almost reads as parody. Almost every cliché now applied to Christie—and at the time applied to even older crime fiction that Christie and her peers were innovating—is present in the first 24 chapters. The village setting, the country-house crime scene, and the *nouveau riche* victim are all tropes. Similarly clichéd are the surly butler, the suspicious drug-addled American who flits in and out of the narrative, the theft of money, a beautiful young woman in a love triangle, a secret marriage, and a cross-class love affair. Poirot may not be a conventional detective, but here he directly emulates Sherlock Holmes, retiring to grow vegetable marrows just as Holmes retired to keep bees, and he apparently enlists Dr. Sheppard as a sidekick, comparing him early on to Captain Hastings (21–22). Sheppard's medical title makes him even more like Watson than Hastings was, and that it is a domestic and not military practice makes him appear completely unthreatening as a literary presence.

However, the solution brings the novel into the world of 1926, where the only clue to modernity henceforth has been the news that Poirot might own "one of those new vacuum cleaners" (20). Not only does the revelation that Sheppard is the murderer introduce the concept of the unreliable narrator to the genre but also introduces a direct engagement in self-conscious literary criticism that would be seized upon by other writers such as John Dickson Carr in *The Hollow Man*. Moreover, the solution is bound up in the use of modern technology: Sheppard uses a Dictaphone to confuse the time of Ackroyd's death, by making the dead man appear to speak after his murder. While this may have its roots in Sir Arthur Conan Doyle's "The Mazarin Stone," where a gramophone record is used to simulate a live instrument, it is a decidedly contemporary touch. In fact, it is so very of the time that the same trick was used in two other popular crime novels published around the same time: J.J. Connington's *Death at Swaythling Court* (1926) and S.S. Van Dyne's *The Canary Murder Case* (1927), which was quickly filmed. This modernity is driven home by the fact that only Poirot notices that the words witnesses heard Ackroyd speak through the door—"The calls on my purse have been so frequent of late..."—are oddly formal. He was dictating a letter. Even the police, however, used to living in the world of stylized fiction, have not seen anything strange in these words. The book is in many senses a self-conscious innovation.

The impact of *The Murder of Roger Ackroyd* has been sensationalized, but it was great: the title itself became a trope. William Newbold's 1928 attempt to write a sensational explanation for the long-mysterious Voynich manuscript was published as *The Cipher of Roger Bacon*. When Edmund Wilson mounted a searing critique on British crime fiction in 1945, he titled it "Who Cares Who Killed Roger Ackroyd?" (although the article does not mention the book), and Gilbert Adair's first foray into crime fiction parody in 2006 was titled *The Act of Roger Murgatroyd*. Christie herself revisited the title's eccentric formula with *Lord Edgware Dies* (1933), although this latter title lacks the original's double meaning. *The Murder of Roger Ackroyd* is both a story about a murder investigation and an account of the murder itself, something confirmed by Dr. Sheppard in his confession when he indicates that he started writing it possibly even before the murder, intending it to be "an account of one of Poirot's great failures" (*MRA* 309). One wonders if it would have had quite the same impact under its working title, *The Man Who Grew Vegetable Marrows*.

As one of the most recognizable titles, this novel has a higher profile than most of Christie's and is frequently targeted in scholarship looking to engage with detective fiction or 1920s literature more broadly. An extreme example is Pierre Bayard's *Que a tué Roger Ackroyd?* (1998; English translation *Who Killed Roger Ackroyd?*, 1999), in which he argues that Poirot—and Christie—are mistaken in identifying Sheppard as the murderer. Bayard focuses on the act of interpreting the clues and reads Sheppard's confession, which does not directly include a confession, as a culmination of being accused by the detective, the ultimate arbiter of Truth. In Bayard's reading, Caroline Sheppard (and, by extension, her successor, Miss Marple) is the murderer. This discussion of the dynamics of interpretation among character, writer, and reader, would later find its extension in Bayard's *La vérité sur "Dix Petits nègres"* (2019).

This was Christie's first novel published by William Collins after her unsatisfactory dealings with The Bodley Head. The new working relationship has continued beyond Christie's death. Although, as a self-consciously *written* text, it does not naturally lend itself to adaptation, *Roger Ackroyd* was dramatized by Michael Morton as *Alibi* in 1928, and this was filmed as the first Poirot movie in 1930. In 1935, the Royal National Institute for the Blind issued the world's first audiobooks, and this novel was among them. By 1955, a *Times Literary Supplement* editorial had already elevated to the level of "a classic" in an editorial otherwise dismissing female-authored and Golden Age crime writing ("In the Best Tradition" 124). The book has also been adapted as a graphic novel, published in French in 2004 and English in 2007.

The novel has been adapted for radio widely. A famous 1939 adaptation starred Orson Welles as both Poirot and Dr. Sheppard on the tail of Welles's controversial *The War of the Worlds*. In 1956, a German version aired on NDR, directed by Friedrich Pütsch. A French radio adaptation starring Henri Crémeux as Poirot aired in 1957, as part of *Les Maîtres du Mystère*. In 1987, the BBC aired *The Murder of Roger Ackroyd* as the first of 25 adaptations starring John Moffatt.

The difficulty of making the novel visual is apparent in the relevant episode of *Agatha Christie's Poirot*, which aired on British television in 2001. In contrast to this condensed, compromised adaptation, a Russian version, *Neudacha Poirot* (also broadcast in 2001), takes five hours to tell the story, replete with a narrator and an effort to make the production a visual novel. *Kuroido Goroshi*, a Fuji TV production in Japan, was broadcast in 2018, following an ambitious take on *Murder on the Orient Express*.

Characters: Ackroyd, Flora; Ackroyd, Mrs. Cecil; **Ackroyd, Roger**; **Annie**; Blunt, Major Hector; **Bourne, Ursula**; Davis, Inspector; Ellerby, Major Ferrars, Ashley; Ferrars, Mrs.; Folliott, Mrs.; Folliott, Richard; Gannett, Miss; Hammond, Mr.; Hayes, Superintendent; Jones, Constable; Jones, Sally; Kent, Charles; **Melrose, Colonel**; Parker, John; **Paton, Captain Ralph**; **Poirot, Hercule**; Raglan, Inspector; Raymond, Geoffrey; Russell, Elizabeth; **Sheppard, Caroline**; **Sheppard, Dr. James**

See also: *Agatha Christie's Poirot*; *Alibi* (play); CBS Radio Adaptations; Class; Fuji TV Adaptations; German Radio Adaptations; *Hercule Poirot* (BBC radio series); *Les Maîtres du Mystère*; Marple, Jane; Mayhem Parva; *Neudacha Puaro*; *Les Petits Meurtres d'Agatha Christie*

Murder on Air. See *Murder in the Studio*

The Murder on the Links (novel; alternative title: The Girl with Anxious Eyes)

Golf would quickly become a sore topic for Christie, but it was a key part of her married life when she wrote the second Hercule Poirot novel. *The Murder on the Links*, her third book with The Bodley Head, has as its crime scene a golf course on private grounds in France.

Poirot and Hastings receive a letter from Paul Renauld, a millionaire in France, stating that he fears for his life. They arrive at his property only learn that Renauld was murdered the previous night. His wife, who seems oddly calm, has been gagged and tied up by masked robbers. However, when she is called to identify the body, she goes completely to pieces. Crossing swords with a pompous French detective who disdain's Poirot's focus on psychology, the detectives uncover a blackmail plot with links to an old case.

Poirot eventually reveals that Renauld and his wife had, in the past, killed her abusive husband, disguising it as a robbery, and fled to France under their current names. Being blackmailed by neighbors, they decided to run away, faking Renauld's death. They would re-create the robbery idea, using the body of a vagrant who died on the grounds. However, on the night, Renauld was stabbed by one of the blackmailers. The then-necessary romantic subplot concerns Captain Hastings, who meets a highly suspicious young woman and, once she has been cleared, kisses her.

There are some obvious influences on *The Murder on the Links*. Christie herself cited Gaston Leroux's 1908 novel, *The Mystery of the Yellow Room*, more on the grounds of a "high-flown, fanciful type of writing" than of plot specifics (*Autobiography* 282). In a part of her autobiography that was withdrawn from publication, Christie suggested that the setting in France was a product of her having "read a lot of French detective stories" at the time (qtd. in Aldridge, *Poirot* 12). At the same time, she argued that this was where the influence of Sir Arthur Conan Doyle started to wane in her work.

However, there are some plot similarities between the puzzle-solution in *The Murder on the Links* and that in Conan Doyle's "The Adventure of the Abbey Grange." Both involve staged break-ins and robberies-gone-wrong attributed to international gangs in the collaborative murder of an abusive husband. In her autobiography, however, Christie gave the plot-influence as a real case that had been "a *cause célèbre* … in France," involving "some tale of masked men who had broken into a house, killed the owner, tied up and gagged the wife," only for the wife's version of events to be disproved (*Autobiography* 281). From this scant information, biographers and scholars have drawn some elaborate conclusions about the nature of the case and its influence. Laura Thompson's biography insists that *The Murder on the Links* suffers because it is "based … too closely upon a real French murder case" (130), but the only case it might be is quite dissimilar.

In 1908, Marguerite Steinheil, a French socialite with several well-connected lovers, was found bound and gagged at her home in Paris, where her husband and stepmother had been killed. She claimed that a gang of robbers had committed the crime, but this was disproved, and Steinheil was caught trying to frame a servant. She was acquitted at trial in 1909 and lived in England until her death in 1954. There is a clear link between this and the murder plot in Christie's novels, but "The Abbey Grange" has an equally obvious influence, and the idea of a successful criminal trying to repeat their efforts is new.

The most obvious indication that Christie was moving away from the Doylean influence here lies in her treatment of Captain Hastings. Already, Christie "was getting a little tired of him," so she decided to "marry [him] off" (282). It is done in a mildly parodic way. Hastings, essentially a conservative character, falls in love with the most unsuitable woman for him—a foul-mouthed, deceitful flapper who will not even share her name for most of the book so becomes known as Cinderella. Formally, the move is clearly sign-posted in both the prologue: the novel opens with Hastings's remark that cheap modern novelists who want to shock to sell books are advised to begin with "'Hell!' said the Duchess" (9), only to announce Cinderella's appearance with the dialogue "Hell!" (10).

At the same time, Poirot's comical rivalry with an ultra-modern detective, Giraud (who is made to look ridiculous), reassures readers that there are not too many modernizations in store. "Methods are very different now," Giraud pontificates at an early stage, to which Poirot responds: "Crimes, though, are very much the same" (75). Another element of Poirot's traditionalism, highly pronounced throughout this novel and in short stories of the period, but strategically dropped later in the decade, is a passionate belief in heredity—the idea that character tendencies pass down family lines.

Hastings's marriage leads him to move to Argentina, returning to narrate novels and stories only occasionally. This means dispensing with the Holmes/Watson formula and thus the need for a narrator. The next step toward this kind of formal innovation would be the next Poirot novel, *The Murder of Roger Ackroyd*, in 1926, where the narrator is revealed to be the murderer. In fact, as soon as 1924, Christie would experiment with a version of this in *The Man in the Brown Suit*.

The first radio adaptation of *The Murder on the Links* was as a serialized part of Harold Huber's *Mystery of the Week* in 1947. It was later adapted for BBC Radio 4 for a broadcast on the centenary of Christie's birth (15 September 1990). A television adaptation, part of *Agatha Christie's Poirot*, was broadcast on ITV on 11 February 1996. A French graphic novel, adapted by François Rivière, was published in 2004 and translated into English in 2007. On 30 December 2005, a Japanese television version appeared as the second installment of *Meitantei Akafuji Takashi*, and a French version, part of *Les Petits Meurtres d'Agatha Christie*, aired on 10 October 2014.

Characters: **Aarons, Joseph**; Arrichet, François; Auguste; **Berroldy, Jeanne**; Bex, Lucien; **Cinderella**; **Conneau, Georges**; **Daubreuil, Madame, and Marthe**; Durand, Dr.; Duveen, Bella; **Duveen, Dulcie**; **Hastings, Captain Arthur**; **Giraud, Monsieur**; Grosier, Maitre; Hautet, Monsieur; **Japp, Inspector James**; Marchand, Monsieur; Oulard, Denise; Oulard, Leonie; **Poirot, Hercule**; **Renauld, Eloise, and Paul**; **Renauld, Jack**; Stoner, Gabriel

Murder on the Nile (play; alternative titles: *Hidden Horizon; Moon on the Nile*)

Christie dramatized *Death on the Nile* (1937) as a play, originally titled *Moon on the Nile*, in 1942. By 1943, she had changed the title again to *Hidden Horizon*, a line from the Egyptian Book of the Dead. It was written as a vehicle for Francis L. Sullivan, who had played Hercule Poirot in *Black Coffee* (1930) and *Peril at End House* (1940), but Christie removed Poirot from the story, replacing him with the avuncular Canon Ambrose Pennefather. The official explanation for this was that Poirot tends to dominate the action as a bombastic character, although there may also have been an element of tempering Sullivan's feelings of ownership over the character.

The play, which is somewhat convoluted, struggled to find a backer and eventually opened regionally in January 1944 with Sullivan in the lead. It would take two more years to open in the West End, retitled *Murder on the Nile*. The production at the Ambassadors Theatre featured David Horne in the lead, with a cast that also included Helen Hayes, who would later play Miss Marple on screen, as Helen ffoliot-ffolkes. It opened on Broadway in September that year with Halliwell Hobbes in the lead. The run at the Plymouth Theatre was only 12 performances.

The essence of *Death on the Nile*'s "trick" survives the translation to stage, but characters are largely reduced or combined to make a cast of 13, whereas all action takes place in the saloon bar of the S.S. *Lotus*. An example of character reduction is the loss of the eccentric novelist Salome Otterbourne. Her characteristics are merged with those of Marie Van Schuyler into the new character, Miss ffolliot-ffolkes, an extremely English snob. Her death is merged with that of Louise the maid, who is, in the play, shot when about to reveal something rather than stabbed because of attempted blackmail.

The play's ending is different as well. In the novel, the two murderers die in a murder-suicide when they realize there is no way out (it is a typically convenient Christie death because Poirot has no evidence). In the play, Pennefather confronts one murderer who has a gun. He gives her a choice: "take your own life" or face justice, with the chance of spiritual healing (*MOTN* 64). She chooses to face justice. The 2012 touring production has the curtain fall before she makes the choice. It is little known that Christie provided an alternative ending, in which it is revealed that most of the action was a fantasy sequence and that Canon Pennefather has talked her out of her actions. The play ends back in the "present" as she steps away from the boat.

The play was poorly received by critics and audiences. Nonetheless, it was televised in 1950 as an episode of the U.S. series *Kraft Television Theatre*, starring Lex Richards, Guy Spaull, and Patricia Wheel.

Characters: **Bessner, Dr.; de Severac, Jacqueline ("Jackie"); ffoliot-ffoulkes, Helen**; Grant, Christina; **Mostyn, Ka;**

Mostyn, Simon; **Louise**; McNaught, Mr.; **Pennefather, Canon Ambrose**; Smith, William

See also: *Death on the Nile* (novel)

Murder on the Nile (television adaptation). See **NBC Television Adaptations**

Murder on the Orient Express (game). See **Games**

Murder on the Orient Express (novel; alternative title: *Murder in the Calais Coach*)

The solution to *Murder on the Orient Express* is so well-known that it has almost become a joke. When Richard Rodney Bennett's suite from the 1974 film adaptation was played at the BBC Proms in 2003, host Timothy West was able to follow it with the words, "They all did it!," eliciting laughter. So well-known is the basic twist that the novel has become an international favorite, frequently adapted and selling consistently well, despite not being as widely read as other Christie works. The twist ending, the presence of series detective Hercule Poirot, and the world of colonial opulence summoned by the title have combined to make it an attractive property for filmmakers that has in turn made it a classic of the genre.

The novel sees Poirot aboard the Orient Express, surprisingly well-populated for the time of year with an international, cross-class array of passengers. Poirot is approached by the very unpleasant Samuel Ratchett, who wants him for a bodyguard; Poirot refuses. That night, a snowdrift traps the train, and Ratchett is stabbed to death several times. During his investigation, Poirot learns that Ratchett was in fact the gangster Cassetti, who was responsible for the abduction and murder of an American girl, Daisy Armstrong. He slowly draws connections between the Armstrong case and 13 other individuals on the train—12 passengers and a conductor had their lives smashed by Cassetti's crimes. At the end of the novel, Poirot proposes two solutions to the crime: the first, inadequate, one is that Cassetti was killed by an intruder who disappeared into the snow. The second is the theory that 11 passengers and the conductor conspired to execute Cassetti, whom the law had failed to punish. When the conspirators admit to the truth of this and testify to the heartbreak they have endured, Poirot decides to present the intruder story to the police.

Murder on the Orient Express is transparently inspired by two real events. The most famous is a case that was front-page news when Christie wrote the book in 1933. The previous year, Charles Lindbergh Jr.— the son of famous aviator Charles Lindbergh and his wife, writer Anne Morrow Lindbergh—was kidnapped. After ransom had been paid, the toddler's corpse was found not far from the Lindbergh home in May 1932, and the coroner determined that Charles Jr. had been dead for two months. The crime caused an international media sensation and triggered calls for the perpetrator to be executed. Eventually—after Christie's book was published—a single man, Bruno Hauptmann, was executed, although few people suspected that he was the mastermind or even directly involved in events. The case caused great upheaval and sorrow in the Lindbergh family; for example, a staff member under suspicion in the household of the toddler's grandmother, Elisabeth Cutter Morrow, committed suicide and was later proved innocent (see FBI). These events are reflected in Christie's book, and their emotional legacies are explored. For example, Pierre the conductor is the father of a maid who killed herself when she came to be regarded as a suspect. Ratchett represents a real figure of evil, and the crowd justice administered to him allowed contemporary readers a fantasy of resolving an emotionally-charged current event that was unlikely to ever reach an "entirely satisfactory" (*MOE* 243) conclusion in real life.

The other main inspiration was Christie's second journey aboard the Orient Express, in 1931. On this occasion, rain washed away sections of the track, causing a 24-hour delay. Christie used the time to observe her fellow passengers and the placement of light-switches and candle-holders, also learning about a 1929 incident when a blizzard stranded a different Orient Express for several days. Following the journey, Christie wrote her husband, to whom the novel would be dedicated, a long letter detailing the events and especially the reactions of her fellow passengers. She was struck by an "amusing wife of 70 with a hideous but very attractive face" (qtd. in Morgan 202) who would become the Princess Dragomiroff; "lady missionaries who never seemed to be there because they had scant food" (202)— who were turned into Greta Ohlsson; and especially "an elderly American lady" (201), Mrs. Hilton, who was "full of USA bewilderment" and kept saying things would be done differently "in the States" (202). She and "a very talkative Bulgarian lady" who vowed "never to travel again" and would not stop talking about her daughter (203–04) became the entertaining Caroline Hubbard. On her first Orient Express journey, also taken alone, Christie had noted with interest the mix of nationalities and personalities that only came together on such a journey. This focus would become central to the plot: where would such diverse people work together? Only on a train, says Poirot, or in America. From there, he unravels the Armstrong kidnapping story.

The novel was published in 1934 following a six-part 1933 serialization in the *Saturday Evening Post*. In the United States, it was retitled *Murder in the Calais Coach* to avoid confusion with Graham Greene's *Stamboul Train* (1932), which was known in that country as *Orient Express*. It has been widely reprinted and always sold well. In 2001, a magazine, *The Agatha Christie Collection*, launched, with each issue accompanied by a Christie book. The first was *Murder on the Orient Express* and, if magazines and partworks had been included in bestseller lists, it would have topped that month's charts. A graphic novel version by François Rivière was released in 2007.

In the 1940s, playwright Ben Hecht inquired about adapting the book for the stage, but Christie's agents communicated that Christie was thinking of dramatizing it herself. This version would "not [have been] a conventional 'whodunnit'" but would have opened with the death of Daisy Armstrong (Morgan 269). This project never came to fruition, but a stage version in 2017 by Ken Ludwig does indeed open with the Armstrong kidnapping.

The first dramatization was for West German television, as an episode of *Die Galerie der Großen Detektive* (The Great Detectives Gallery), broadcast on 24 August 1955 and starring Heini Göbel as Poirot. MGM's plans to film the book as a Miss Marple story with Margaret Rutherford caused Christie to end her contract with the studio and to speculate that MGM would end up having Miss Marple driving the train.

A modernized television version aired on CBS on 22 April 2001 with Alfred Molina as Poirot. In the United Kingdom, it was filmed as part of *Agatha Christie's Poirot* with David Suchet, broadcast on ITV 1 on Christmas Day 2010 (this very dark version emphasized religious convictions and ethical doubts, marking a one-episode tonal shift for the program). A two-part Japanese telemovie, *Oriento kyuukou satsujin jiken*, was broadcast from 11 January 2015.

The Japanese dramatization owes much of its aesthetic to the 1974 British film, directed by Sidney Lumet, which became a *cause célèbre* at the time. Albert Finney headed an all-star cast in this version, which was the last film authorized by Christie. As R.J. Cardullo points out, the 1975 film *Breakheart Pass* starring Charles Bronson and based on Alistair MacLean's novel of the same name modified Christie's *Murder on the Orient Express* for the Western genre (5). A 2017 remake, directed by and starring Kenneth Branagh, similarly featured a starry cast and spearheaded a series of movies that would proceed with *Death on the Nile*.

A two-part Soviet radio play starring Vsevolod Yakut as Poirot was broadcast in 1966, with sound effects eschewed for a dramatic orchestral score. A BBC Radio version in five parts aired on Radio 4 from 1992 to 1993, with John Moffatt, who had been an extra in the 1974 movie, in the lead. A third voice dramatization was produced by Audible in 2017 and starred Tom Conti. This proved extremely popular, and Audible is exploring further Christie dramas.

Murder on the Orient Express has been made into two video games. The Adventure Company produced the first, point-and-click game in 2006, with David Suchet providing the voice of Poirot and a new, playable character inserted. The second, a version of Snap using Mah Jong tiles and slowly revealing the story, was released for mobile devices in 2017.

Characters: Andrenyi, Count Rudolph and Countess Helena; **Arbuthnot, Colonel**; **Arden, Linda**; Armstrong, Colonel John; **Armstrong, Daisy**; Armstrong, Sonia; Bouc, Marcel; **Cassetti**; Constantine, Dr.; **Debenham, Mary**; **Dragomiroff, Princess Natalia**; Dubosc, Lieutenant; Foscarelli, Antonio; Goldenberg, Helena; Hardman, Cyrus; **Hubbard, Caroline**; MacQueen, Hector; Marceau, Antoinette; Masterman, Edward; **Michel, Pierre**; Michel, Susanne; **Ohlsson, Greta**; **Ratchett, Samuel ("Cassetti")**; Schmidt, Hildegarde

See also: *Agatha Christie's Poirot*; CBS Television Adaptations; EMI Films; Fuji TV Adaptations; Games; *Hercule Poirot* (BBC radio series); Russian Radio Adaptations; True Crime; Twentieth Century Studio Films

Murder on the Orient Express (play)

Agatha Christie Ltd. commissioned the Tony Award-winning Broadway playwright Ken Ludwig to adapt *Murder on the Orient Express* for the stage in 2015. The play opened at the McCarter Theatre Center in Princeton, NJ, on 14 March 2017, and a revised full production was co-produced by Hartford Stage Company in Hartford, CT, on 15 February 2018. The play has since had several productions across the United States and internationally, and U.S. amateur rights were released in 2019.

Ludwig's script features Hercule Poirot, making it the first Christie stage play to do so since Arnold Ridley's *Peril at End House* (1949). There are several changes to the plot, presumably to make it more dramatic, including the addition of a shooting. The cast of 12 suspects/killers is reduced to eight, which sacrifices the novel's focus on formal and informal criminal justice— the killers in the book form their own jury of 12—while keeping the cast manageable and maintaining the famous twist to the extent that one can still say "they all did it." The original production of the play made use of period music by Cole Porter, Samuel Barber, and Sergei Prokofiev, although the published script replaces these with music out of copyright in the United States by Irving Berlin, Gustav Mahler, and Gioachino Rossini.

Like several contemporary theater pieces, the script is heavily influenced by film and television. This is evidenced in the music instructions, short snappy scenes, a dramatic one-minute prologue, and the use of onstage flashbacks: at dramatic moments, characters not speaking act out the action described. The shadow of Sidney Lumet's 1974 movie looms large: for one thing, Colonel Arbuthnot is described in the script as Scottish, testament to Sean Connery's memorable performance. For another, the "flashback" enactment of the crime directly mirrors that in Lumet's film.

Hildegarde Schmidt is cut from the play. Instead, Greta Ohlsson (a missionary in the book) takes the role of Princess Dragimiroff's companion—although her "usual" companion, "Miss Schmidt," is mentioned (Ludwig 20). Countess Andrenyi, who travels in the book with her husband, here travels alone and is also a trained doctor, thus eliminating the need for Dr. Constantine. However, M. Bouc is given the Christian name Constantine. The valet Masterman, the private eye Hardman, and the salesman Foscarelli also are dropped. The criminal Cassetti—who lives and dies as Samuel Ratchett—is given the Christian name Bruno. This is presumably a reference to Bruno Hauptmann, who was executed for the murder of Charles Lindbergh Jr. in the case that inspired the Daisy Armstrong case in *Murder on the Orient Express*.

Despite a great deal of publicity and a striking set, the play received mixed reviews upon opening and was largely overshadowed by Kenneth Branagh's movie of the same year.

See also: EMI Films; *Murder on the Orient Express* (novel); Twentieth Century Studios Films

Murder on the Orient Express (television adaptation). See CBS Television Adaptations

Murder on the Orient Express (1974 film). See EMI Films

Murder on the Orient Express (2017 film). See **Twentieth Century Studios Films**

Murder She Said (film). See **MGM Films**

Murder She Said (novel). See *4.50 from Paddington*

Murder with Mirrors (novel). See *They Do It with Mirrors*

Murder with Mirrors (television adaptation). See **CBS Television Adaptations**

"Murderers Are Wicked" (article)

"Murderers Are Wicked" is an extract from Christie's autobiography, published as an article in the *Ottawa Journal* on 29 October 1977 to promote the book's publication. In it, Christie reflects that, in an age fascinated by criminal minds and motivations, there is a danger of pulling focus from innocence, which the criminal justice system and popular culture should protect and defend.

Murdoch, Cynthia

Captain Hastings believes he is in love with Cynthia Murdoch in *The Mysterious Affair at Styles*. She is, like Christie, a volunteer nurse, and her medical knowledge helps readers understand the poisons involved.

Murgatroyd, Amy. See Hinchcliffe, Miss ("Hinch") and Murgatroyd, Amy

Murgatroyd, Mrs.

Mrs. Murgatroyd is a "half-witted malevolent old crone" (CCW 225) who is the widow of a caretaker in "The Case of the Caretaker's Wife" and "The Case of the Caretaker." She places a curse on a young couple and sees that it is fulfilled. She is the equivalent to Esther Lee in *Endless Night*, although that character seems to be a real witch and is an innocent victim.

Musefælden. See *The Mousetrap*, Adaptations of

Music

In her autobiography, Christie describes music as one of her "principal pleasures" in childhood (AA 121). She particularly enjoyed the opera and, as a girl, singing in amateur operettas, describing the experience as freeing: "I felt no stage fright. Strangely enough for a terribly shy person, who very often can hardly bring herself to enter a shop and who has to grit her teeth before arriving at a large party, there was one activity in which I never felt nervous at all, and that was singing" (123). Christie later studied piano and singing in Paris, and considered turning professional but was bluntly told that she lacked the vocal gravitas. This exchange is mirrored in the pseudonymous *Giant's Bread*.

Christie continued, however, to write music and lyrics. The earliest surviving examples are a piano waltz, "One Hour with Thee," and a set of lyrical ballads inspired by the harlequinade, published in *The Road of Dreams*. She later wrote songs and potentially the accompanying music for the radio play *The Yellow Iris* and was involved in discussions for the abandoned musical *Death Beat*. An early short story, "The Call of Wings," uses pipe music as a metaphor for the inexplicable something that is missing in the life of a wealthy hedonist: it represents something more than itself.

In early Mary Westmacott novels, especially *Giant's Bread*, opera music appears in terms of obsession. It is a form of art that expresses the highs and lows of the human condition with an intensity that transcends language barriers. Despite social fashions making it elite or dictating its form, it is, in Christie's formulation, essentially universal. The nuances of this, and some of the explicit history of Richard Wagner's connection to the Nazi movement, are explored in-depth in *Passenger to Frankfurt*. When characters lack the vocabulary to describe their feelings, they occasionally turn to opera: for example, Major Blunt in *The Murder of Roger Ackroyd*, twice compares himself to Faust and says, "There's an opera about it" (MRA 111, 114). Opera enables Christie to explore extreme passions in the short stories "Swan Song" and "The Face of Helen."

More commonly, music appears as part of upper middle-class life and its props and accessories are woven into murder plots. A piano stool conceals the weapon in *They Do It with Mirrors*. A gramophone record apparently holding after-dinner music contains a voice recording accusing houseguests of past crimes in *And Then There Were None*. As William Weaver points out, humming and singing often hides a clue to a suspect's mental state or unlocks a hidden truth for the hummer (187–89). P.L. Scowcroft (n.p.) points out that Christie's music connection was not unique: peers such as Dorothy L. Sayers and Edmund Crispin (aka the composer Robert Bruce Montgomery) were also practicing musicians, whereas "other crime authors, among them Ellis Peters, Cyril Hare, V.C. Clinton-Baddeley, Robert Barnard, Mary Kelly and A.E.W. Mason, reflected their own love of music in their writings" to, in Scowcroft's opinion, a greater extent that Christie ever did. This reading may have to do with the careful artifice of Christie's writing: music appears to be a middle-class prop, but it is shown at the same time *to be* such a prop, one that is actively used, while also hiding shared emotions and deeper truths.

See also: *An Autobiography*; *Giant's Bread*; *A Masque from Italy*; "Swan Song"

Mutton Chop

Mutton Chop is a friend of Tommy Beresford from the Secret Service in *Postern of Fate*.

"My Flower Garden." See *Poems*

Mylecharane, Fenella, and Juan

Fenella and Juan Mylecharane are first cousins and occasional fiancés in "Manx Gold." Fenella exhibits Tuppence-esque enthusiasm and a penchant for old shanties. Juan is a typical Bright Young Thing.

Myshelovka. See *The Mousetrap*, Adaptations of

The Mysterious Affair at Styles (novel; alternative title: *Mystery at Styles*)

Christie's debut novel is set in 1916, when the bulk of it was written. It concerns the murder of Emily Inglethorpe at her country home, Styles Court, and the efforts of retired Belgian policeman Hercule Poirot to solve it. The most popular of various stories about how Christie came to write it while serving with the Voluntary Aid Detachment (VAD) during World War I appeared on publicity for the book and even on its dust jacket. It influenced reviews and how the book was read and marketed, and is still widely repeated:

> This novel was originally written as the result of a bet, that the author, who had previously never written a book could not compose a detective novel in which the reader would not be able to "spot" the murderer, though having access to the same clues as the detective. The author has certainly won her bet [blurb].

The "bet" was reportedly with Christie's sister, Madge. Another story goes that Christie ran out of detective stories to read while ill so resolved to write her own. Both anecdotes, although doubtless true in part, consciously present the novel as an entertainment, evoking gamesmanship and home comforts, rather than as a novel of commentary or ideas.

The country house setting and amateur detective were already staples of the genre when Christie decided to employ them, something evidenced by novels E.C. Bentley's *Trent's Last Case*, published in 1916 when Christie started work on *Styles*, and parodying these conventions. The decision to make Poirot Belgian, however, was a conscious attempt to establish difference with Sherlock Holmes and his successors:

> Who could I have as a detective? … There was Sherlock Holmes, the one and only—I should never be able to emulate *him*.… Then I remembered our Belgian refugees.… Why not make my detective a Belgian? I thought.… Anyway, I settled on a Belgian detective.… A tidy little man. I could see him as a tidy little man.… He would have rather a grand name—one of those names that Sherlock Holmes and his family had.… How about calling my little man Hercules? [*AA* 256–57; emphasis in original]

Nonetheless, the Holmes formula is strong in *Styles* and is used to comic effect when, before the murder, Hastings announces that he has always fancied himself as a Sherlock Holmes. Of course, he is quickly relegated to the Watson position.

Styles is very much a war novel. Cynthia Cavendish is, like her creator, a VAD, and the household and social events are almost exclusively run by women—because men are, of course, away. Hastings opens the narrative describing being "invalided home from the Front" (*MAS* 9). Although he initially considers Styles Court to be "another world," conversation inevitably turns to the "great war ... running its appointed course" (13) and it is acknowledged from the outset that war has affected how the household and life in general are run. Styles is "a war household" (22).

Christie failed at first to find a publisher but persisted despite numerous rejections. The manuscript was finally accepted by John Lane, founder of The Bodley Head—not a natural choice as it published the notorious *Yellow Book* and other provocative titles. Christie's fee—which she later considered scandalously low—was £25, and the book was serialized in the London *Times* before its publication in book form in the United States in 1920 and the United Kingdom in 1921. The intention had been for an October publication in both countries in time for sales in the Christmas season. In Christie's contract with Lane, from which she extricated herself as soon as she could, she agreed to publish a minimum of six books. *Styles* was a great success, quickly selling 20,000 copies.

Before publication, Christie had to make two major changes. One was to the spelling of "cocoa." An editorial assistant insisted that it should be spelt "coco" and, despite Christie producing dictionaries as evidence that her spelling was correct, could not be shaken. Therefore, early editions of the novel include this misspelling. The other change was to the final chapter. Originally, Christie had written a dramatic courtroom dénouement, but Lane advised her that this was unbelievable and betrayed her lack of knowledge about courtrooms. She returned a short time later with a new final chapter, relocated to a drawing room. The idea of Poirot gathering the suspects in a drawing room for the final reveal would become one of her trademarks. In 2011, John Curran printed the original ending in *Agatha Christie's Murder in the Making: More Stories and Secrets from Her Archive*, and it has since appeared in some editions of the novel.

Styles has been adapted for radio and television. The first BBC radio adaptation, in 1956, starred Austin Trevor, playing Poirot for the first time since he had appeared in three Twickenham Studios films in the early 1930s. The second BBC radio version, starring John Moffatt, was broadcast in 2005. The first screen adaptation was a 1990 episode of *Agatha Christie's Poirot* and the second aired in 2016, part of *Les Petits Meurtres d'Agatha Christie*. In the United States, where the book is out of copyright, there have been numerous attempts to mount stage, radio, and screen productions; a few examples are the 2013 production by the Chautauqua [CA] Playhouse, the 2016 production by the St. Clair [MI] Shores Players, and the May–June 2021 Austin [TX] Playhouse virtual production.

Characters: **Annie**; Bauerstein, Dr.; **Cavendish, John, and Mary**; Cavendish, Lawrence; Dorcas; Earl, William; **Hastings, Captain Arthur**; Heavyweather, Sir Ernest; Hill, Amy; **Howard, Evelyn ("Evie")**; **Inglethorpe, Alfred**; **Inglethorpe, Emily**; **Japp, Inspector James**; Mace, Albert; Manning; **Murdoch, Cynthia**; **Poirot, Hercule**; Raikes, Farmer; Raikes, Mrs.; Summerhaye, Superintendent; Wells, Elizabeth; Wells Mr.; Wilkins, Dr.

See also: **Abercrombie Forgery Case**; *Agatha Christie's Poirot*; **BBC Radio Adaptations**; *Curtain*; **"Drugs and Detective Stories"**; **Hercule Poirot** (BBC radio series); **Penguin Books**; *Les Petits Meurtres d'Agatha Christie*; **Styles House**; **War**

The Mysterious Mr. Quin (story collection)

Christie's most unique and neglected contribution to conventional crime fiction, *The Mysterious Mr. Quin* (1930) collects 12 stories she had written as and when the feeling struck her, about the reserved, womanish Mr. Satterthwaite and his semi-supernatural companion, Harley Quin. These stories, all mysteries which flirt with the greater mysteries of psychology and emotional connectedness, had not appeared as a series in any magazine, although in the book, Christie designated each story a "chapter." She dedicated the book "To Harlequin the Invisible"—an implication of the intensity of attachment she felt to the figure of Harlequin, and indeed to Harley Quin, who represents that figure.

Magazine publications for 11 of the stories have been traced, but a source for *The Bird with the Broken Wing*—an unusually emotional story which, like many of the ones collected here, involves suicide—could not be found. Christie may have written this to replace "The Love Detectives," which had appeared in a magazine but would not be collected until *Three Blind Mice* in 1950. The most notable change to magazine versions occurs with the first story, "The Coming of Mr. Quin," which was originally published 1925 as "The Passing of Mr. Quinn." The title and the spelling of Harley Quin's name were likely changed to distance this text from the 1928 Twickenham Studios movie, *The Passing of Mr. Quinn*, which Christie hated.

The Mysterious Mr. Quin is composed of "**The Coming of Mr. Quin,**" "**The Shadow on the Glass,**" "**At the 'Bells and Motley,'**" "**The Sign in the Sky,**" "**The Soul of the Croupier,**" "**The Man from the Sea,**" "**The Voice in the Dark,**" "**The Face of Helen,**" "**The Dead Harlequin,**" "**The Bird with the Broken Wing,**" "**The World's End,**" and "**Harlequin's Lane.**" Some recent editions have added the two other Quin and Satterthwaite stories, "The Love Detectives" and "The Harlequin Tea Set."

"The Mystery at Marsdon Manor." See **"The Tragedy at Marsdon Manor"**

The Mystery at Styles. See *The Mysterious Affair at Styles*

"The Mystery of Hunter's Lodge" (story; alternative title: "Investigation by Telegram")
The short story "The Mystery of Hunter's Lodge" offers an entertaining image of Hercule Poirot the hypochondriac. He is in bed with "*la grippe*" or influenza (*PI* 96), speculating that he might not die on this occasion, when a new case comes his way. He sends Captain Hastings to Hunter's Lodge to investigate the murder of the American millionaire Harrington Pace. Hastings reports back, and Poirot solves the crime from bed. He is unable to provide evidence, so the killers are not arrested—but they promptly die in a plane crash. The story was first published in *The Sketch* in 1923

and collected in *Poirot Investigates* in 1924. It was dramatized for television as part of ITV's *Agatha Christie's Poirot* in 1991.

Characters: Crabb, William; **Hastings, Captain Arthur**; Havering, Hon. Roger; **Havering, Zoe**; **Japp, Inspector James**; Middleton, Mrs.; Pace, Harrington; Pace, Mrs.; **Poirot, Hercule**; Windsor, Lord

*See also: **Agatha Christie's Poirot**; **Poirot Investigates***

"The Mystery of the Baghdad Chest" (story)
This story was expanded into "The Mystery of the Spanish Chest" for inclusion in *The Adventure of the Christmas Pudding* (1960). The plot of this shorter story is similar, although it features more recurring characters such as Captain Hastings—whom Christie would replace with Miss Lemon—and Inspector Japp—who would become Inspector Miller.

An attractive woman, Marguerita Clayton, asks Hercule Poirot to help prove that her lover, Major Rich, did not kill her husband and hid his body in a chest. Poirot reconstructs the crime, which took place during a dance, and determines that a partygoer who was in love with Mrs. Clayton did it. Unlike in "The Mystery of the Spanish Chest," Poirot concludes that Marguerita is at fault: attractive, naïve women, he says "a very dangerous" (*WLL* 232). Much of Christie's 1920s fiction blames the women with whom men fall in love, an attitude that shifted as her work matured.

"The Mystery of the Baghdad Chest" was published in *The Strand Magazine* in the United Kingdom and the *Ladies' Home Journal* in the United States in 1932. It appeared in the anthologies *The Regatta Mystery and Other Stories* (1939) in the United States and *While the Light Lasts* (1997) in the United Kingdom. Although the story has not been dramatized officially, it seems to have been the primary source material for "The Mystery of the Spanish Chest," an episode of *Agatha Christie's Poirot* broadcast on ITV on 17 February 1991.

Characters: Burgoyn; Clayton, Edward; Clayton, Marguerita; Curtiss, Major; Chatterton, Lady Alice; **Hastings, Captain Arthur**; **Japp, Inspector James**; Poirot,

Hercule; Rich, Major Jack; Spence, Mr.; Spence, Mrs.

See also: *Agatha Christie's Poirot*; "The Mystery of the Spanish Chest"; *The Regatta Mystery* (story collection); *While the Light Lasts* (story collection)

Mystery of the Blue Geranium (story collection)

The second Christie U.S. paperback, first published in 1940 by Bantam, *Mystery of the Blue Geranium and Other Tuesday Club Murders* contains five stories from *The Thirteen Problems* (known in the United States as *The Tuesday Club Murders*). It was reprinted twice; each edition has a new and equally lurid cover. The first paperback in the United States had been a 1939 Arrow edition of *Thirteen at Dinner*. This volume contains "The Blue Geranium," "The Companion," "The Four Suspects," "A Christmas Tragedy," and "Death by Drowning."

See also: *The Thirteen Problems*

"The Mystery of the Blue Jar" (story)

In the early short story "The Mystery of the Blue Jar," a young man, Jack Hartington, believes he can hear the cry of a ghost, and—convinced by a beautiful woman and a psychic doctor—seeks to communicate with the spirit via a blue jar that apparently holds significance. The whole set-up is revealed to be a ruse, by which the doctor and the woman can obtain the jar. The villains leave Jack a note, sneering that "the day of the supernatural" (that is, the day of the charlatan) is not "over," "especially when tricked out in new scientific language" (163)—a fairly typical middlebrow repudiation of psychoanalysis. The story shows Christie experimenting with ways to reconcile the supernatural and mystery genres. The story was published in the *Grand Magazine* in July 1924 and appeared in the U.K. collection *The Hound of Death* (1933) and the U.S. collection *The Witness for the Prosecution* (1948). It was dramatized as an episode of *The Agatha Christie Hour* in 1982.

Characters: Hartington, Jack; Hoggenheimer; Lavington, Dr.; Marchaud, Felise

See also: *The Agatha Christie Hour*; *The Hound of Death* (story collection); Psychoanalysis; *The Witness for the Prosecution* (story collection)

The Mystery of the Blue Train (novel)

Two years before *The Mystery of the Blue Train* was published, Hercule Poirot became a household name with the publication of *The Murder of Roger Ackroyd*, and his creator became one with her much-publicized 11-day disappearance. Whereas the next year's offering, *The Big Four*, was quickly forgotten, the 1928 novel was introduced in a blaze of publicity, as "Poirot's Greatest Case!" with advertisements bearing a praise quote not from any of Christie's peers but from Poirot himself. *The Mystery of the Blue Train* sold extremely well and has become a popular entry to the canon, although Christie herself was no fan of the book.

In an interview with Francis Wyndham, she called it "the worst book I ever wrote," adding, "I hate it" (E5). Her autobiography expands upon this, recounting her difficulty writing it: "I had no joy in writing, no *elan*" (AA 347), and it was written purely for money. "I have always hated it," Christie concludes, because it is implausible, "commonplace, full of clichés, with an uninteresting plot," while acknowledging that some readers prefer it to her other work (358). In a passage removed by the publishers, she added that such readers always went down in her estimation.

It is certainly a lazily written book and gives the lie to the idea that Christie bounced back from the traumas of 1926 after a year cobbling together *The Big Four*. Evidently, writing this novel was hard work. It is an expansion of the short story "The Plymouth Express" and is extraordinarily generic in execution. The bulk of the novel was dictated to her secretary, Carlo Fisher—a method she would subsequently use for short stories and only employ for novels again in her twilight years, when her health failed her. It is to Fisher and Peter, Christie's pet terrier, that the book is dedicated—both as "Distinguished Members of the O.F.D." (which means "Order of Faithful Dogs"). Not meant to be a snub or insult, the dedication indicates the value of unconditional friendship during the difficult task of composition. The majority of commentators disagree outright with the author's summary of the book, and Jared Cade perhaps hits the mark, noting that Christie's dismissals of it represent an "attempt to distance herself and others from the painful aspects of her past" (148).

Like "The Plymouth Express," *The Mystery of the Blue Train* concerns a wealthy woman, murdered on a train while carrying a priceless jewel, which is stolen. The setting, however, is a much more luxurious train. Ruth Kettering, daughter of an American millionaire, is making a much-publicized journey on *Le Train Bleu*, in possession of a ruby called the Heart of Fire, over which much blood has been spilt. She is killed and the jewel stolen in an astonishing act of violence. Hercule Poirot—working with a plain young woman, Katherine Grey, who is trying to find her place in the world—uncovers a conspiracy.

Le Train Bleu was one of several "Blue Trains" in the twentieth century, so named because of its dark-blue sleeping carriages and known for its promise of luxury. It ran between Calais and the French Riviera between 1886 and 2003, originally created as a second Wagon-List train, after the success of the Orient Express. Before the Christie novel, it had inspired a ballet, also called *Le Train Bleu*, by Serge Diaghilev. The idea of a priceless gem was also not new to crime fiction. Indeed, Christie had used it herself, not just in "The Plymouth Express" but also in "The Adventure of the 'Western Star,'" and the idea goes back to Wilkie Collins's *The Moonstone* (1868). The name "The Heart of Fire" evokes imperialism and violence.

The novel is also notable as the first full-length Poirot case that has the detective traveling alone (without Captain Hastings), instead forming a friendship with a traveling companion. Christie had tried out this idea in several short stories and would repeat it many times. The companion being a young, likable woman named Grey who is not accustomed to money but has come into it would be repeated in *Death in the Clouds*. In addition, it introduces the village of St. Mary Mead, Grey's home village, which would become the iconic setting of the Miss Marple mysteries from 1928 (this book's publication year) onward. Christie scholar Marty S. Knepper has suggested that in this—and in the presentation of an overlooked woman as "a detective in embryo"—Christie "lay[s] the groundwork" for a writing career beyond Poirot ("*Blue Train*" 38). Another link with future canon is the introduction of Mr. Goby, a mysterious private investigator. It is likely that the train's attendant, Pierre Michel, reappears as a conductor on the Orient Express in *Murder on the Orient Express* five years later.

Finally, it is difficult to disagree with Christie's verdict that the novel lacks *joie de vivre*. The narrative is not lifeless but competent: the author was incapable at this point of turning out dull prose. Indeed, it is typically aware of its own clichés, with Poirot describing the investigation as a 'roman policier'" (*MBT* 205) and the implausibility of Katherine's presence as a working-class woman on the train, explained away: "Cheese-paring old women are always dying in villages and leaving fortunes of millions to their humble companions" (57). However, Mark Aldridge has pointed out a "notable coldness—and even viciousness—towards many of its characters" (*Poirot* 39). This is something that would become more sophisticated in most subsequent titles: Christie's coldness toward her characters is something of an unsung trademark, and *The Mystery of the Blue Train* is arguably the first and most striking example of it.

The book was published by Collins in the United Kingdom and Dodd, Mead in the United States in 1928. Columbia Pictures wanted to film it in the 1970s, following the success of EMI's *Murder on the Orient Express*, but were not successful in acquiring the rights. In 1986, BBC Radio 4 broadcast a multi-part adaptation with Maurice Denham as Poirot, the first of its late-twentieth-century Poirot series. In 2005, a French graphic novel by Marc Piskic was released. It was translated into English two years later. A screen adaptation aired on ITV in 2006 as part of *Agatha Christie's Poirot*.

Characters: **Aarons, Joseph**; **Alice**; Carrege, Monsieur; Caux, Monsieur; **de la Roche, Comte Armand**; Demiroff, Olga; **Ellen**; Evans, Charles ("Chubby"); Frampton, Lord Edward; **Goby, Mr.**; **Grey,**

Katherine; Harfield, Mrs. Samuel; Ivano-vitch, Boris; **Kettering, Derek**; **Kettering, Hon. Ruth;** Kidd, Kitty; **Knighton, Major Richard**; **Mason, Ada**; **Michel, Pierre**; **Mirelle**; **Papopolous, Dmitri**; Papopolous, Zia; **Poirot, Hercule**; Tamplin, Hon. Lenox; Tamplin, Viscountess Rosalie; **Van Aldin, Rufus**; Viner, Amelia

See also: *Agatha Christie's Poirot*; Anti-Semitism; Disappearance of Agatha Christie; *Hercule Poirot* (BBC radio series); *Murder on the Orient Express* (novel); St. Mary Mead

"The Mystery of the Plymouth Express." See **"The Plymouth Express"**

"The Mystery of the Second Cucumber." See **"Mr. Eastwood's Adventure"**

"The Mystery of the Spanish Chest" (story)
This expansion of "The Mystery of the Baghdad Chest" appears to have been completed for the 1960 volume *The Adventure of the Christmas Pudding*, in which it was published. Christie removed the narrator, Captain Hastings, who had not featured in Poirot's cases for many years, and added references to him ("*Ce Cher Hastings*—how he would have enjoyed himself" [64]). She also expanded the role—specifically, the comedy role—of Miss Lemon, Poirot's secretary. The action seems to have been updated as well, and an early reference to Countess Vera Rossakoff—Poirot's potential romantic interest—classes her as "[a] folly of earlier days" (61). The essential plot of the two stories is the same, but the ending of the revised version shifts the blame somewhat from the beautiful woman, who was the motive for the crime to the man who committed it.

"The Mystery of the Spanish Chest" was serialized in three parts in *Women's Illustrated*, prior to its publication in *The Adventure of the Christmas Pudding*. It was later collected in the U.S. volume *The Harlequin Tea Set* (1997). The story was adapted, although "The Mystery of the Baghdad Chest" seems to have formed primary source material, into an episode of *Agatha Christie's Poirot* in 1991.

Characters: Burgess, William; Chatterton, Lady Abbie; Clayton, Arnold; Clayton Margherita; **George(s)**; Johnston; **Lemon, Felicity**; McLaren, Commander Jock; **Miller, Inspector**; **Poirot, Hercule**; Rich, Major Charles; Spence, Jeremy; Spence, Linda

See also: *Agatha Christie's Poirot*; "The Mystery of the Baghdad Chest"; "The Mystery of the Spanish Chest"; *The Regatta Mystery* (story collection); *While the Light Lasts* (story collection).

"Mystery of the Spanish Shawl." See **"Mr. Eastwood's Adventure"**

Mystery of the Week (radio series)
Harold Huber's *Hercule Poirot* series for Mutual Broadcasting was a hit with listeners but ultimately failed following legal disputes with unacknowledged and unpaid writers. Huber went to rival broadcaster CBS with a new Poirot series. The new series similarly transported Poirot to a New York setting and was extremely successful. It ran in two seasons from 1 April 1946 to 21 November 1947.

Like its forerunner, it included a mix of new stories and adaptations of Christie's published work, with more emphasis than before on the latter. The advertised script writer was Alfred Bester. Short stories directly adapted include "The Lost Mine," "The Million Dollar Bond Robbery," "The Incredible Theft," "Problem at Sea," and "The Adventure of the 'Western Star.'" There were 77 thirteen-minute standalone mysteries. Some novels, including *The Murder on the Links*, *The Big Four*, and *Dumb Witness*, were among the 55 five-part serials, broadcast on consecutive week nights. Other five-part episodes had such titles as "The Case of the Long Burial," "The Case of the Missing Mind," and "The Case of the Lively Corpse."

See also: *Hercule Poirot* (**Mutual Radio Series**)

The Mystery of Three Quarters (Hannah). See **Continuation Fiction**

Mystery Series Live: On the Air (radio plays)
Hosted by Angela Lansbury for National Public Radio in the United States, this set of four Christie radio plays was recorded at meetings of the International Mystery Writers' Festival in Kentucky. The plays broadcast in their U.S. debuts include *Three*

Blind Mice, Personal Call, Butter in a Lordly Dish, and *The Yellow Iris*. They were aired in August and September 2009. Three years later, the same four plays were performed in staged readings in Florida under the banner *Agatha Christie's The BBC Murders.*

See also: **The BBC Murders**

N or M? (novel)

Christie discusses this novel with deceptive breeziness in her autobiography:

> I had decided to write two books at once.... I had no other things to do. I had no wish to sit and brood.... One was *The Body in the Library*, which I had been thinking of writing for some time, and the other one was *N or M?*, a spy story, which was in a way a continuation of the second book of mine, *The Secret Adversary*, featuring Tommy and Tuppence. Now with a grown-up son and daughter, Tommy and Tuppence were bored by finding that nobody wanted them in wartime. However, they made a splendid come-back as a middle-aged pair, and tracked down spies with all their old enthusiasm [489].

Importantly, the year described is 1940 when Britain was at war. This description makes the writing of *N or M?* sound like escapism, whereas the uncharacteristically immodest use of "splendid" suggests that the characters exist as separate entities to be praised as old, comfortable friends rather than the author's creations. The focus on diversion, as opposed to "sit[ting] and brood[ing]," is almost a defense mechanism against some critiques of the novel, because it is, for the first time in Christie, set explicitly during World War II, and the spies confronted are Nazis. Writing two books in parallel resulted in a fresh and humorous tone for each, that never drags, although it means that the same hotel guest plays a minor role in both novels.

A jaunty thriller, *N or M?* brought significant grief to its author. She delivered it to her agent, Edmund Cork, in 1940 but soon received word that no U.S. magazine would accept it for serialization. With the United States not yet in World War II, it was thought that a thriller with an anti–Nazi message would alienate a large number of her readers. Christie wrote back furiously, with block capitals explaining that the book

had been a chore to write. It would not be published until late 1941. Even then, Collins, the British publishers, asked Christie to revise and extend it, prompting her to consider terminating her contract in favor of Victor Gollancz. Earlier, she had proposed (in vain) a new ending in which the Beresfords deal with the bombing of their home. Her own property in Sheffield Terrace had suffered this fate—something that would serve to inform a considerable strand of *Taken at the Flood* (1948).

Working titles for *N or M?* include, in order, "Mr. and Mrs. Beresford," "T and T," and "Second Innings," so it is not surprising that the plot sprang from these characters, making a return after their appearances in short stories throughout the 1920s. The story begins with the Beresfords wondering what to do: "It's bad enough having a war," says Tuppence, "but not being allowed to do anything in it just puts the lid on" (6). The tone, then, is one of familiar lightness, despite the current events. Soon enough, Tommy is asked to travel to the island resort of Sans Souci and to be on the lookout for a Nazi spy, codenamed N or M. Tuppence, disguising herself as a Mrs. Blenkensop, maneuvers her own way onto the island.

Although it is not a straightforward murder mystery, *N or M?* contains murders and clues, and the spies, N and M, are eventually unmasked from among the least likely guests on the island—in this case, a charming young man and a British widow who uses her small child like a prop to avoid suspicion. Meanwhile, a nervous young German, perhaps the obvious suspect, turns out to be a British intelligence agent. The novel ends with the Beresfords' adult children, who know nothing of their parents' war work, patronizing them for having done so little to help.

Shortly after the initial publication, MI5, the British intelligence service, investigated Christie over the presence of a minor character, Major Bletchley. In real life, Bletchley Park was the location of a top-secret code-breaking exercise—which would decode the German Enigma ciphers—and there were concerns that Christie had some specialist knowledge. According to Christie, this was all a misunderstanding—she had simply been "stuck at Bletchley [railway] station" one day and "found the place so boring that she thought it the ideal name for a tiresome old major" (Smith 32).

Another coincidental name is that of the spy who turns out to be M: Antony "Tony" Marsdon. A not dissimilar character named Anthony "Tony" Marston had appeared in 1939's *And Then There Were None*. The similar names may have inspired video-game developers in 2005 when adapting the latter as a point-and-click computer game for the Adventure Company. In *Agatha Christie: And Then There Were None*, the character Anthony Marston turns out to be a Nazi.

Despite publishers' misgiving, the book sold well—well enough, in fact, that Christie was later asked to write propaganda for Britain and for Russia; she refused both requests. Before it had even been published in the United Kingdom, Milestone, a U.S. film company, made an offer for worldwide film rights. However, nothing came of this. The book was not filmed for seven decades. In August 2015, BBC 1 aired a three-part adaptation as the second half of *Partners in Crime*, a series that was ignominiously received.

Characters: **Batt, Albert; Beresford, Deborah, and Derek; Beresford, Prudence ("Tuppence"); Beresford, Thomas ("Tommy"); Blenkensop, Mrs.; Bletchley, Major;** Cayley, Alfred; Cayley, Elizabeth; Grant, Mr.; Haydock, Commander; Maguire, Patrick; **Marsdon, Anthony ("Tony");** Meadowes, Mr.; Minton, Sophia; O'Rourke, Mrs.; Perenna, Eileen; Perenna, Sheila; Polonska, Vanda; **Sprot, Betty, and Millicent; von Deinim, Carl**

See also: *The Body in the Library*; *Partners in Crime* (BBC television series); War

Nadu Iravil. See **Indian-Language Adaptations**

Nancy

In "The Case of the Middle-Aged Wife," Nancy is a young secretary who catches the eye of George Packington. He makes a fool of himself, bestowing gifts on her without realizing that she is a gold-digger, before realizing his error and returning to his wife. Notably, the character shares a name with the young second wife of Christie's first husband.

Narracott, Gladys. See **Gladys**

Narracott, Inspector

Inspector Narracott is a West Country police inspector in *The Sittaford Mystery* and *Personal Call*. "Narracott" is one of Christie's go-to West Country surnames. It is also given to a boatman (Fred) in *And Then There Were None,* a maid (Gladys) in *Evil under the Sun,* and a drunkard who experiences a divine revelation (Jacob) in "Promotion in the Highest."

"The Naughty Donkey." See *Star Over Bethlehem* **(story/poetry collection)**

Nazorkoff, Paula

Paula Nazorkoff is a world-class soprano in "Swan Song" who ends up killing a man on stage in what she knows will be her final performance as Tosca. Nazorkoff's birth name is Bianca Capelli, and she is "a prima donna," with the "laugh of a child, the digestion of an ostrich, and the temper of a fiend" (*TLM* 244).

NBC Radio Adaptations

NBC established its Christie credentials in the long-running series *Mollé Mystery Theatre* (also known as *NBC Mystery Theater*), which ran from 1943 to 1948 before transferring to CBS. This anthology program featuring 30-minute episodes included an adaptation of *Love from a Stranger* on 25 April 1944. "The Mystery of the Blue Jar," a mystery story that flirts with the supernatural, was adapted for broadcast on 20 February 1945, and the script was reused on 9 May 1956. A version of *Witness for the Prosecution,* featuring a new ending not included in either the short story or the stage play, aired on 31 May 1946. In 1949, a fresh adaptation of *Witness for the Prosecution,* by Agnes Eckhardt, was broadcast as part of NBC's *Radio City Playhouse.*

See also **CBS Radio Adaptations**; **NBC Television Adaptations**

NBC Television Adaptations

American broadcaster NBC had broadcast several successful radio productions based on Christie's writing when it started putting her on television. Christie was notoriously hostile to television productions of work, but she was more inclined to accept proposals when they were one-offs, lucrative, and for international audiences (that is, she would not have to see them). NBC aired the first Christie television adaptation in the United States in 1949, with an episode of *The Chevrolet Tele-Theatre* based on "The Witness for the Prosecution" (see *Witness for the Prosecution*, **Screen Adaptations of**).

On 17 January 1950, NBC's *Fireside Theatre* (1949–58), an anthology program, aired a 15-minute adaptation of "The Golden Ball" alongside a version of John Reinhardt's "Just Three Words." This was not a well-known Christie story, nor a typical (that is, mystery) one, and cheap rights were likely a reason for its inclusion in this low-budget series. Typically, *Fireside Theatre* (sometimes called *Jane Wyman Presents*) dealt with public domain stories or thrillers acquired cheaply from freelancers.

The same year, *Kraft Television Theatre* broadcast *Murder on the Nile*, a one-hour adaptation of *Death on the Nile* that, like the play (also called *Murder on the Nile*) omitted the character of Hercule Poirot. This 50-minute production starred Guy Spall and Patricia Wheel and aired on 12 July. A print still exists in the Library of Congress.

Rare prints—mostly bootleg—also exist of NBC's best-known Christie television production. An episode of *Goodyear Television Playhouse* based on *A Murder Is Announced* was broadcast live on 30 December 1956. The first screen outing for Miss Marple, it saw a miscast Gracie Fields tackle the role, complete with Yorkshire accent. The cast also included stage veteran Jessica Tandy and a young Roger Moore in his screen debut. Condensing a complex novel to one hour (including commercials), William Templeton's adaptation cuts many characters, but changes are not as widespread as in Leslie Darbon's stage version, and the action ends with the identification of the killer.

Just as the 1949 production of "The Witness for the Prosecution" followed a U.K. television version the same year, NBC's *Ten Little Indians* was broadcast on 18 January 1959, five days after ITV's production in the United Kingdom. This adaptation starring Nina Foch and Barry Jones, also exists and is commercially available (see *And Then There Were None*, **Screen Adaptations of**).

NBC gave Hercule Poirot his U.S. screen debut in an adaptation of "The Disappearance of Mr. Davenheim," broadcast as an episode of *General Electric Theater* (1953–62) on 1 April 1962. This program was introduced by future president Ronald Reagan, who had previously played Tommy Beresford on screen for CBS. By 1962, radio Poirot Harold Huber had given up trying to obtain permission to play the detective on screen. Allowing this production with Martin Gabel was a big deal, and publicity was, for a 30-minute television episode, immense. There was a general impression that "Hercule Poirot," as the episode was titled, could become a series and this was treated as a pilot. Gabel gave several interviews about his approach to the character and even his wife, actor Arlene Francis, got involved, insisting to journalists that Gabel *was* Poirot. Nina Foch, who had played Vera Claythorne in *Ten Little Indians*, returned as Mrs. Davenheim. Although the series never materialized, Gabel was sufficiently attached to the character that he expressed an interest in the 1960s in mounting the later-shelved Poirot musical *Death Beat*, and upon his death in 1986, several obituaries referenced the role.

See also: *And Then There Were None* **(play)**; **CBS Television Adaptations**; *Death on the Nile* **(novel)**; **"The Disappearance of Mr. Davenheim"**; **"The Golden Ball" (story)**; *A Murder Is Announced* **(novel)**

Neele, (Chief) Inspector

The open-minded investigating officer in *A Pocket Full of Rye*, who has heard of Miss Marple's prowess on the grapevine, may or may not be Chief Inspector Neele, drawn along similar lines, from *Third Girl*.

Neele, Nancy (1899–1958)

Nancy Neele was the second wife of Archibald "Archie" Christie, Agatha Christie's first husband. When she and Archie met and began their affair, Neele was a secretary in her twenties and a friend of Major Ernest Belcher. She and Archie married in 1928. She gave birth to their son, named after his father, in 1930. When Agatha disappeared in 1926, she checked into a hotel under the telling pseudonym "Teresa Neele." The character Marjorie Connell in the Mary Westmacott novel *Unfinished Portrait* is transparently based on Neele.

See also: **Christie, Colonel Archibald ("Archie"); Disappearance of Agatha Christie;** *Unfinished Portrait*

Neidheim, Helga

Helga Neidheim is a fascistic German endocrinologist in *Destination Unknown*. Despite despising organized religion, she disguises herself as a nun.

"The Nemean Lion" (alternate title: "The Case of the Kidnapped Pekingese"). See *The Labours of Hercules*

Nemesis

Collins's design for *Nemesis* in 1971 features a large pink question mark, which appears knitted, and the point of which is a ball of pink wool. The contrast to the rather edgy one-word title is deliberate: it promises readers an unlikely Nemesis figure: a safe and comforting, homely type of detective. It promises Miss Marple. *Nemesis* is generally considered Christie's last fully coherent novel, although it has been used in research to show signs of a failing vocabulary and, by extension, a potential dementia diagnosis for its author.

Nemesis is told largely from Miss Marple's perspective. It is in many ways an extended interior monologue. It opens with her reading death notices in the *Times* and finding out that her friend Jason Rafiel, encountered in *A Caribbean Mystery* (1964), has died. She is soon summoned by his solicitors, who tell her he has asked her to investigate a mystery for him. There is little else to go on but that. However, she soon finds that she has been booked onto a tour of England's stately homes and invited to stay with three elderly sisters. From this, she discovers that she is to clear Rafiel's wayward son of a murder charge from many years ago—that of his young girlfriend, Verity Hunt. After a thorough investigation with several asides about sexual propriety for the young, Miss Marple learns that Verity was not killed by Michael but by her guardian, Clotilde Bradbury-Scott, who was in love with her and did not want her to marry. Miss Marple has proven herself

Nemesis, the goddess of retributive justice.

This is the final Miss Marple novel, and there is evidence that it was written as a conclusion to that character's career. For one thing, whereas Miss Marple traditionally uses another character to trap the murderer into a confession, on this occasion she uses herself. This is the first time that Miss Marple's life is directly in danger, as she is given a poisoned glass of milk by her host who killed Verity. It is a culmination of her methodology over several decades. Another point is that *Nemesis* has a similar crime plot to *Sleeping Murder*, the novel Christie wrote as "Miss Marple's Last Case" in the 1940s or 1950s and put aside for publication after her death (it would be published in 1976). In both books, an attractive young woman is murdered over a decade before action begins by a guardian who is inappropriately in love with her and who frames the husband or fiancé for the crime. As Christie continued to refer in interviews to *Curtain*, the final Poirot book, which had also been written in advance but not to *Sleeping Murder*, she may have forgotten it and written the novel as an imperative.

The key difference between the two murder plots is that, unlike the love felt by James Kennedy for his half-sister in *Sleeping Murder*, the feelings of Clotilde Bradbury-Scott are homosexual. Christie is generally more charitable to lesbians than to gay men, and the perversity here is more about the abuse of power in such a relationship than Bradbury-Scott's sexuality. Like Helen, the victim in *Sleeping Murder*, Verity Hunt was killed because "she wanted a normal woman's life" (230)—in both books, configured as heterosexual marriage and children: "She wanted marriage and the happiness of normality" (230), which is "[a] different kind of love" to that her guardian felt for her. She may have had a crush on Clotilde, Miss Marple concedes, but this is a normal part of female adolescence and is only dangerous when it spills into adulthood. Like Helen, Verity has been painted after death as a nymphomaniac despite her pursuit of the nuclear ideal. Like Helen, her name is significant: the clue to the mystery is to realize that one is still trying to find the true nature of "Verity Hunt."

This is a conservative novel. Miss Marple, despite proclaiming herself Nemesis while wearing a fluffy pink shawl like a headdress, is a conservative figure. There is a long and—to contemporary readers—uncomfortable exchange between Miss Marple and an archdeacon about the lax morals of modern girls. Girls, says the archdeacon, are too interested in sex instead of love, and, he appears to say, they are to blame for being raped. The conclusion somewhat negates these attitudes, but they are here, given considerable space, and not challenged as they are presented. Similarly, Miss Marple's conservatism manifests itself as outright racism: a "Victorian view of foreigners. One never *knew* with foreigners." (76; emphasis in original) This is, she acknowledges to herself, "[q]uite absurd," and "she had many friends from various foreign countries. All the same ..." (76). The ellipsis makes it clear that even though she and her creator have changed with the times, there is a fundamental feeling of difference they cannot shake.

As well as Jason Rafiel, who is a looming presence in the novel, his secretary returns from *A Caribbean Mystery*. Esther Walters, whose narrative arc was not resolved in the previous novel, now has a happy, quiet domestic life as a Mrs. Anderson. In *A Caribbean Mystery*, she had been a prim and proper widowed secretary suddenly transformed into weeping distress when it was revealed that the man with whom she was having an affair was a murderer. She is now a much more friendly, remarried woman. Her husband is younger than she is ("much better, my dear," says Miss Marple. "In these days men age so much better than women" [43]). Christie herself, of course, was married to a younger man. Esther's happy married life pre-empts a theme that will be at the heart of the novel. She only appears in an early chapter to give some details of the Rafiel backstory, but her presence shows the kind of resolution for a previously troubled character that Verity was pursuing.

Nemesis has been adapted for BBC television (part of *Miss Marple*, broadcast 8 and 15 February 1987) and radio (broadcast November 1998), and for ITV (part of *Agatha Christie's Marple*, broadcast 1 January 2009). In all three cases, it was dramatized before *A Caribbean Mystery*, meaning different actors played Jason Rafiel each time and sometimes as different characters. It gave its title to a Japanese television series, *Miseu Ma, Boksooui Yeoshin* (*Miss Ma, Nemesis*), loosely based on the character and various Miss Marple plots. It has also inspired, with other Miss Marple novels, the 2018 South Korean series *Ms Ma, Nemesis*.

Characters: **Anderson, Esther; Baker, Cherry, and Jim;** Barker, Sister; **Barrow, Miss;** Bentham, Mildrid; Birkin, Jonathan; Blackett, Miss, Brabazon, Archdeacon; **Bradbury-Scott, Anthea, and Clotilde; Broad, Nancy, and Nora;** Broadribb, Mr.; Butler, Henry; Butler, Mrs.; **Cooke, Miss;** Crawford, Joanna; Douglas, Inspector; **Glynne, Lavinia;** Hopkins, Gary; **Hunt, Verity; Jackson, Arthur;** Jameson, Richard; **Janet; Knight, Miss;** Lucas, Mary; Lumley, Miss; Marple, Jane; Merrypit, Mrs.; Prescott, Canon Jeremy and Joan; Price, Emlyn; **Rafiel, Jason; Rafiel, Michael;** Risely-Porter, Geraldine; Schuster, Mr.; **Temple, Dr. Elizabeth;** Walker, Colonel and Mrs.; Wanstead, Professor; **West, Raymond, and Joan**

See also: *Agatha Christie's Marple*; *A Caribbean Mystery*; Homosexuality; Market Basing; *Miss Marple* (radio series); *Miss Marple* (television series); *Ms Ma, Nemesis*; *Sleeping Murder*

Neudacha Puaro (Poirot's Failure; television adaptation)

Neudacha Puaro (Poirot's Failure), the five-part Russian television adaptation of *The Murder of Roger Ackroyd*, takes the unusual step of transplanting the novel almost word-for-word to the screen. The title translation of "Poirot's Failure" is what the narrator in the book intended the story to be. Directed by Sergey Ursulyak, it is, like the novel, narrated by Dr. Sheppard—here played by Sergei Makovetsky. However, it is more than an illustrated audiobook, as it includes some small plot changes and omits some characters. One device used repeatedly is the creation of newsreels, formed from stock footage and at one point sampling Orson Welles's 1939 radio broadcast of *The Murder of Roger Ackroyd*. Konstantin Raykin plays Poirot. This is the most atmospheric and ambitious of the Russian Christie screen adaptations.

See also: *The Murder of Roger Ackroyd*

Neumann, Dr.

Dr. Neumann is a psychoanalyst in the 1940 version of "The Capture of Cerberus." He specializes in patients who believe they are famous military figures and has "cured three Hertzleins [the story's version of Hitler], four Bondolinis, five President Roosevelts and seven Supreme Deities" (CC 443). There was a real psychologist—a disciple of Carl Jung, Erich Neumann—whose work on delusions and archetypes came to prominence around a decade after this story was written. Christie likely saw the literary appeal in a name implying "New Man" in the context of attempts to upheave world order. She used the same surname in her 1970 Nazi-themed "extravaganza," *Passenger to Frankfurt*.

"Never Two without Three." See **"A Christmas Tragedy"**

Nevill, Gladys. See **Gladys**

New Moon **(unpublished play)**

New Moon is a one-act play that was later expanded into *Marmalade Moon*. Both scripts are unpublished and are housed in the Christie Family Archive.

See also: *Marmalade Moon*

"Next to a Dog" (story)

The brief story "Next to a Dog" reflects Christie's love of dogs. In it, young widow Joyce Lambert cannot find work because she refuses to travel abroad, leaving her pet dog, Terry. She meets Arthur Halliday, whom "[m]any people called ... handsome" (190) but does not think of him or anyone in those terms. She agrees to marry him mainly, it seems, to give Terry a stable home. When Terry dies, she breaks off the engagement and takes a job abroad. There, she meets Mr. Allaby, who "looked a little like a dog" (200) and who had tried to save Terry's life. She marries him. The story is both a tribute to Christie's favorite animal and an early exploration of obsessive love. References to a young man who died

in France suggest that it was written after World War I but perhaps sooner than 1929 when it was published in the *Grand Magazine*. It was anthologized in *The Golden Ball* (1971) in the United States and *Problem at Pollensa Bay* (1991) in the United Kingdom.

Characters: Barnes, Mr.; **Barnes, Mrs.;** Halliday, Arthur; Lambert, Joyce; Lambert, Michael; **Mary, Aunt**; Terry

See also: **Dogs;** *The Golden Ball* **(story collection);** *Problem at Pollensa Bay* **(story collection)**

"The Next Victim." See **"The Adventure of the Egyptian Tomb"**

Nicholson, Dr., and Moira

These characters enable a subversion of pulp fiction norms in *Why Didn't They Ask Evans?* Dr. Nicholson is a sinister-looking Canadian psychologist with no social skills, "exactly like a scientific super-criminal on the films" (252). Moira is his delicate, shrinking wife who seems constantly traumatized. In the end, the doctor is revealed to be a useful idiot, completely unaware of any criminal activities, and his wife is a high-ranking member of a global criminal network.

Nicoletis, Christina

Christina Nicoletis is the mercurial Greek owner of the hostel on Hickory Road in *Hickory Dickory Dock*. Unpredictable and equally a comic and sinister figure, she is in over her head in a smuggling ring and is a secret drinker. She is later revealed to be Valerie Hobhouse's mother. After the novel was published, a Mr. Nicoletis wrote to say that Christie had defamed his mother, who asserted that Christie had stayed in her lodging at one time. In a letter to her agent, Edmund Cork, Christie stated that she had fabricated the name (Morgan 302).

A Night of Terror. See *Love from a Stranger, Screen Adaptations of*

"The Nile." See *Poems*

Nimrud Book of Dreams **(nonfiction work)**

Over breakfast, Christie would tell her husband, Max Mallowan, about her dreams of the previous night. Mallowan's mind tended to wander on these occasions. On a dig in Nimrud in the 1950s, with the kind of humor that is born of frustration, Christie recorded her dreams on paper, bound them, and presented them to her husband. This was the *Nimrud Book of Dreams*.

In a cover-letter, self-deprecatingly signed "A. Snooze," Christie describes this project with mock-grandeur as her answer to "Napoleon's famous Dream Book" and suggests that it will "shed a valuable light on the psychology of the dreamers" (Morgan 276)—not a school of thought to which she subscribed. Max Mallowan is addressed as "Professor Mallowan," the arch-formality being a joke along the lines that professional matters and not his marriage were his preoccupation, and Christie refers humorously to his "unsympathetic attitude towards dreams" (276).

Nimrud Odes. See **Odes to Friends**

No Other Love. See *Murder in Mesopotamia*

Nofret

In *Death Comes as the End*, Imhotep's new concubine, Nofret, is young and beautiful, and highly resented in the house. She boasts of her knowledge of foreign cities and represents the outsider in the family home. She seems powerful and is frequently condemned as "wicked" before and after her murder.

Norreys, Hugh

Hugh Norreys is the narrator of the Mary Westmacott novel *The Rose and the Yew Tree*, presented as an everyman, albeit a rather judgmentally masculine one, who has been seriously injured in a bus accident and who, for the most part, observes the passions of those around him.

Norreys, Teresa

Teresa Norreys is the wife of Robert Norreys and the sister-in-law of Hugh Norreys in the Mary Westmacott novel *The Rose and the Yew Tree*. Teresa pushes Hugh in his wheelchair and interprets situations for him. She lets him know "the female perspective" on things, such as Gabriel's attractiveness (129). Teresa vigorously defends the status quo out of loyalty to her deceased relatives who would have been "horrified" at having a Labour voter in the family; this is presented as an admirable thing.

Norton, Stephen

A shy, stammering bird-watcher who winces at the sight of blood, Stephen Norton appears on the margins of most scenes in *Curtain*. However, he turns out to be its Iago-like villain, one that can only be stopped by a bullet that Hercule Poirot fires himself. Norton—compared to Iago in Shakespeare's *Othello* before and after his revelation as "X"—preys on human weakness. He manipulates people into killing one another via subtle undermining remarks that appear innocuous. He is responsible for at least seven deaths, including his own.

Nostalgia

In 1991, Alison Light published a groundbreaking analysis of Christie's social relevance, disputing the view of Christie as "a 'natural' Tory … jolly and bucolic[,] inherently backward-looking," whose fiction offers a vision of "tranquil and hidebound English life [in] a village sealed in aspic, intent on keeping modernity at bay" (Light 62). To illustrate this point, Light cites a scene from the BBC's *Miss Marple* and argues that the nostalgic conservatism of it "owed as much to a Toryism of the 1980s as it did to any conservatism on Christie's part" (63).

Light's work opened avenues for scholarship in the subsequent three decades but did not affect public attitudes: Christie would remain, in the popular imagination, a museum of nostalgia for many years thanks in large part to television adaptations and tourist initiatives. Nonetheless, it must be noted that criticisms of outdated nostalgia in the canon were rife before even the highly nostalgic 1974 film of *Murder on the Orient* Express. As early as 1961, crime writers Julian Symons and Edmund Crispin were arguing that Christie's brand of fiction had not really recovered from World War II and subsequent conflicts: it "was inspired by a dream of reason, by an idea that things could be solved in a purely rational way, which simply looked silly in the age of Hitler, the atomic bomb, the age we live in at present" (Symons and Crispin 392). It was only Agatha Christie Ltd.'s considered rebrand in 2015, which heralded a new series of dark BBC adaptations and insistences that Christie was the grandparent of the modern thriller, that public attitudes began to shift dramatically.

However, as long as there has been Christie scholarship, those scholars have noticed social change, especially in the Miss Marple novels. For instance, St. Mary Mead changes with the times: it may be two steps behind the rest of the modern world, but it changes (see *The Mirror Crack'd from Side to Side*). More commonly cited, however, is the 1965 novel *At Bertram's Hotel*, in which an old-fashioned Edwardian hotel that appears to perfect to be believed turns out to be a front for a decidedly modern criminal enterprise. R.A. York identifies as supremely theatrical: "Theatrical falsity here, very significantly, lies in the preservation of the past; Bertram's Hotel has become a stage set because the way of life it implies, that of a genteel upper class, is no longer secure" (44–45). However, as Marty S. Knepper notes, the plot twist itself "shows that living in the past, wallowing in nostalgia, is unnatural" ("Thirteen Problems" 49).

See also: *At Bertram's Hotel*; **Mayhem Parva**; *Miss Marple* **(television series)**

NTV Adaptations

Japanese television network NTV broadcast three live-action adaptations of Miss Marple novels following the success of *Agasa Kurisutī no Meitantei Powaro to Māpuru* and *Meitantei Akafuji Takashi* on rival station NHK. *Uso o Tsuku Shitai* (I Want to Lie) is based on *4.50 from Paddington*. The feature-length debut of director Ryûchi Inomata, it was broadcast on NTV on 11 April 2006. *Daijoyu Satsujin-jiken* (Murder of a Great Actress), directed by Yasunobu Kusuda, aired on 9 January 2007. It is based on *The Mirror Crack'd from Side to Side*. The final offering on 6 March 2007 was *Yokoku Satsujin* (Notice of Murder), based on *A Murder Is Announced*, and sometimes translated as *Murder Party*. It was also directed by Kusuda. The well-regarded Japanese actress Keiko Kishi played Mabuchi Junko, a stand-in for Miss Marple, in all three. These were remade a decade later as part of a deal with TV Asahi.

See also: *Agasa Kurisutī no Meitantei Powaro to Māpuru* and *Meitantei Akafuji Takashi*; **TV Asahi Adaptations**

"Nursery Rhyme of Nimrud" (poem)

The last poem Christie wrote in Nimrud ca. 1959, "Nursery Rhyme of Nimrud" is darker and more somber than her other "Nimrud Odes." It was written in the context of the Iraqi revolution of 1958. A short, four-line verse evoking a nursery rhyme, it makes clear that Christie's use of such rhymes in her crime fiction is strategic and not sentimental. Another theme that also appears in her novels is the use of a house to reflect broader troubles. The poem depicts a house in Iraq about to face a storm: it is still standing but "cannot last"; the poem closes with: "And that is the end, RIP, of you all" (qtd. in Morgan 281). The poem is unpublished but is quoted in Janet Morgan's *Agatha Christie: A Biography*.

See also: **Archaeology**; **"The Last Days of Nimrud"**

Nursery Rhymes

As Dana Perec and Loredana Pungă reflect in their 2019 article, "They Do It with Nursery Rhymes," "the universe of childhood" was constantly on Christie's mind, something evidenced in her letters and autobiography (249). The link to childhood runs throughout her fiction, too. Famously, Christie tended to use nursery rhymes to in her crime novels, often using the structure of the rhyme or song for her own plot, and frequently using them for titles:

> In some of the cases when Agatha Christie's novels have titles which are taken from easily recognizable nursery rhymes or games for children, the connection between the title and the plot is that a keyword can be identified as being part of the clue that solves the murder mystery. In other cases, the title works more like an overall metaphor, a commentary on the moral of the story [249].

The use of a nursery rhyme or counting song provides an obvious contrast between childish innocence and the violence of murder. However, it also draws attention to what Suzanne van der Beek calls "sinister potential in nursery rhymes" (23)—and more generally in childhood—and thereby the artificiality of the concept of childhood innocence. After all, the action of *And Then There Were None* is simply a literal rendition of the contents of "Ten Little Indians." To this end also, in *Crooked House*, the murderer is actually a child, destroying notions of childhood purity.

Novels and short stories which take their titles from children's rhymes include *And Then There Were None; Crooked House; Five Little Pigs;* "Four and Twenty Blackbirds"; *Hickory Dickory Dock;* "How Does Your Garden Grow?"; *Mrs. McGinty's Dead; One, Two, Buckle My Shoe; A Pocket Full of Rye;* "Sing a Song of Sixpence"; and "Three Blind Mice." Several subsequent authors have tried to emulate Christie's use of nursery rhymes as structuring principles, more often than not using the "One for Sorrow" rhyme. H.R.F. Keating's pastiche of a Sven Hjerson story is titled "Jack Fell Down" from the nursery rhyme "Jack and Jill."

See also: ***And Then There Were None* (novel);** *Five Little Pigs;* **"How Does Your Garden Grow?";** *Mrs. McGinty's Dead; A Pocket Full of Rye; The Mousetrap; One, Two, Buckle My Shoe*

Nye, Sir Stafford

Sir Stafford Nye is an English diplomat who is the protagonist of *Passenger to Frankfurt*. He is eccentric with a sometimes unprofessional sense of humor, and the characterization is frequently compared to that of Sir Rupert Croft-Lee in *They Came to Baghdad*, another diplomat who also wears an exuberant cloak.

Ober, Harold (1881–1959)

Christie's American agent from 1929 until his death, Harold Ober also represented such authors as William Faulkner, J.D. Salinger, H.G. Wells, Jack London, and F. Scott Fitzgerald. Following Ober's death, his agency, Harold Ober Associates, continued to handle Christie's work. Christie had more dealings with her British agent, Edmund Cork, than with Ober.

See also: **Cork, Edmund**

Obolovich, Prince Nicholas. See **Cade, Anthony**

"Ode to Christopher Columbus" (poem)

This poem was written shortly after the death of Agatha Miller's father, Frederick, and has not been published. The author was age 11 at the time. It is not about her father directly but about her cat, "a little kittiwinks, / whose name (for short) was Cris" (qtd. in L. Thompson 41). Many of the family pets were named after historic American figures such as George Washington (a dog), a nod to Frederick's nationality.

See also: **Dogs; Odes to Friends**

Odes to Friends

Like most couples, Christie and her second husband, Max Mallowan, shared small creative in-jokes. Among these was the authorship of comical "odes" to their various friends and one another on digs in the 1950s. Many of these are reprinted in Mallowan's 1977 memoir, whereas "To M.E.L.M.," Christie's ode to her husband, was included in *Poems* (1973).

The poems tend to be loose pastiches of Lewis Carroll's nonsense verse and narrative poems, especially "The Walrus and the Carpenter." Much of Christie's breezy verse with Mallowan is in this vein: see also "The Saga of the Keeper, the Architect, and the Young Epigraphist" and "A-Sitting on a Tell," both of which open with apologies to Carroll.

The odes by Christie printed in *Mallowan's Memoirs* include two to his secretary, Barbara Peters (1908–93), whom he would go on to marry: these praise her work ethic, sardonically: she is "Saint Barbara the Martyr" and "the Nun of Nimrud" (271–72). Another is addressed to the well-known Assyriologist Donald Wiseman (1918–2010), mocking his intellectualism and verbosity; it culminates with him being awarded "a D.M.," translated as "Doctor of Mystification" (274).

Epigraphist Peter Hulin was interested in buses and timetables, and his ode has him being bored transcribing ancient tablets, his mind drifting to buses. "To J.L." is for Jørgen Læssøe (1924–93), a Danish epigraphist whom Mallowan considered "highly strung" and never able to finish his work but nonetheless popular (276). This verse is peppered with omissions, question marks, parentheses, and capital letters—creating a process whereby it is harder to read than it needs to be. Mallowan also includes a second Christie verse for Læssøe, marking the arrival of his colleagues from Denmark: "There came three Danes a'sailing, a'sailing on the sea…" (277).

These are affectionate but quite waspish rhymes. Mallowan's memoir also include odes to academics Joan Oates (nee Lines, 1928–) and her husband David Oates (1927–2004). The former catalogs Joan's physical attractiveness but in mathematical terms, comparing her to one of the pots she was studying—this has echoes of the disapproval expressed about attractive young women devoting themselves to research in "The Capture of Cerberus" (1947) and *Curtain* (1975). David Oates's ode refers to him as "Sheikh Daoud" (279).

A four-liner evoking "Baba Black Sheep" takes aim at Nicholas Kindersley's (1939–2015) large appetite. Artist Marjorie Howard (1898–1983) is mocked for her vagueness and her fame, having created a sculpture of Sir Mortimer Wheeler. Architect John Reid (1926–2004), who found himself inexplicably building a kiln for the archaeologists, has an ode as well: each verse ends with a variation on: "Well, I was surprised" (283–84).

There is also an ode to Tariq el-Madhlum, the Iraqi representative of the Antiquities Department, with whom Christie struck up a close friendship. This one takes aim at his interest in beautiful women and praises his ability to concentrate on work when his mind is elsewhere. Finally, Mallowan includes an ode to him: not the serious, romantic one published in *Poems* but a comic two-verser. It has Mallowan sighing at his colorful colleagues.

Mallowan also includes in his volume an ode he wrote to mark his wife's 80th birthday on 15 September 1970. Two pages of affectionate rhyming couplets, it is highly unlike Christie's odes, even if the jocular spirit is shared.

It is a reminder, perhaps that he was the archaeologist and she the writer.

See also: **Mallowan, Sir Max**; *Poems*

Oglander Family

There are two John Oglanders in "The King of Clubs"—a father and son who live in the property owned by the victim, impresario Henry Reedburn, and who are responsible for his accidental death. Also involved are the mother, Mrs. Oglander, and a daughter, Miss Oglander. Poirot helps cover up their guilt. There is another daughter who is estranged and is later revealed to be dancer Valerie Saintclair.

Ohlsson, Greta

Greta Ohlsson is a shy Swedish missionary with selectively poor English in *Murder on the Orient Express*. Secretly, she has a history as a nurse to the Armstrong family, which was destroyed in a kidnapping/murder and its aftermath. In 1974, Ingrid Bergman won an Academy Award for portraying Greta Ohlsson.

Oliver, Ariadne

Christie encouraged readers to see Ariadne Oliver as a fictional self-portrait. This comic character who assists Hercule Poirot and a select few other men with their investigations is a popular crime writer with

David Suchet as Hercule Poirot and Zoë Wanamaker as Ariadne Oliver. Courtesy (C) ITV Studios for *Masterpiece*.

regular gripes about the industry and the tedium of writing. It is a common perception that Christie is "having fun with her fame" through the character (Gill 93) and that "when Mrs. Oliver speaks we are listening to Agatha Christie" (Curran, *Secret Notebooks* 73).

The character's evolution, however, is slightly more complicated. She first appears as a ten-a-penny sensational novelist working for J. Parker Pyne in "The Case of the Discontented Soldier" (1932). Here, beyond a taste for apples, there is nothing to link her to Christie personally. By 1936, she is a friend of Poirot and one of the four central detectives in *Cards on the Table*. Here, she is "one of the foremost writers of detective and other sensational stories" and the author of *The Body in the Library* (COT 12). Christie had not yet written a book of that name—it was at the time a cliché of the genre, so the point here is not that Mrs. Oliver is Christie but that Mrs. Oliver writes clichéd fiction. Unlike Christie at this point, Mrs. Oliver is "a hot-headed feminist" (9) and "an earnest believer in woman's intuition," lobbying for a woman to head Scotland Yard (9). This character that talks glibly about throwing in an extra murder to break up the dialogue is a parody of popular conceptions about successful female novelists.

Christie evolved the character into a strategic self-portrait in 1952 in *Mrs. McGinty's Dead*, which includes some transparently autobiographical diatribes about stage dramatists interfering with a novelist's work. Mrs. Oliver goes on to work with Poirot throughout the 1950s, 1960s, and 1970s in *Dead Man's Folly*, *Third Girl*, *Hallowe'en Party*, and *Elephants Can Remember* and works with Mark Easterbrook in *The Pale Horse*. She is discussed extensively in *The Clocks*. What is most interesting about the character is her choice words about her own creations. Mrs. Oliver is an author of mysteries such as *The Lotus Murder, Death of a Debutante*, and *The Dying Goldfish*, which feature the idiosyncratic Finnish detective Sven Hjerson. Her rants about being saddled with Hjerson are obviously Christie's thoughts on being saddled with her own quirky European creation. "Why a Finn when I know nothing about Finland? Why a

vegetarian? Why all the idiotic mannerisms he's got? These things just happen," Mrs. Oliver complains—interestingly enough, to Poirot—in *Cards on the Table*. "You try something—and people seem to like it—and then you go on—and before you know where you are you've got someone like that maddening Sven Hjerson tied to you for life" (68).

Olivier, Madame

Madame Olivier is a formidable French scientist who seems to be modeled on Marie Curie, in *The Big Four*. She is "Number Three" in a shadowy criminal empire.

O'Malley, Louisa

Louisa O'Malley is a crime writer who uses the Cavendish Secretarial Bureau in *The Clocks*. Detection Club authority Martin Edwards ("Clocks" n.p.) has suggested that she may be based on U.S. mystery writer Elizabeth Daly.

"On the Orient Express." See **"Have You Got Everything You Want?"**

"Once a Thief." See **"The Pearl of Price"**

"One Hour with Thee" (waltz)

"One Hour with Thee" is a waltz written by Christie at age 17. It was published under the name A.M.C. Miller but is difficult to find. The waltz is often played in Christie's holiday home, Greenway, where there is a piano, and where a copy exists. It consists of a short introduction in 4/4 time followed by three waltz melodies and an interlude in Bb minor, which Greenway's house pianist Dawn Fallon calls "unusual" with "some dark mysteriousness about it" (n.p.). Pianist Yi-Chih Lu uploaded a recording of him playing the piece to YouTube in 2019 (Lu).

See also: **Music**

One, Two, Buckle My Shoe (novel; alternative titles: *An Overdose of Death*; *The Patriotic Murders*)

Published ahead of schedule in 1940, *One, Two, Buckle My Shoe* engages deliberately with the reality of World War II. It is very much a novel written at the war's outset and combines Golden Age light-heartedness with dark concern over the state of global politics. It begins with a typically character-focused scenario:

Hercule Poirot visits his dentist in Harley Street, and readers learn (or remember, from *Death in the Clouds*) that he is terrified of the dentist. However, the dentist, Mr. Morley, has timely small-talk about dictators and democracies. Soon enough, of course, Morley is murdered, and it emerges that he seems to have killed one of his patients earlier that day. Poirot investigates.

The investigation leads him to the politically significant financier Alistair Blunt, and it becomes apparent that this and other murders are connected with attempts on Blunt's life. Poirot speaks to the financier's family and to his agitators, especially the young revolutionary Howard Raikes, who is romantically involved with Blunt's niece. There are three murders in all: the dentist, a blackmailer, and a failed actress. Poirot eventually identifies Blunt and his secret wife as the murderers who killed to avoid the relationship becoming public knowledge—Blunt is a bigamist, who married his first wife for love and his second for political capital. Although Blunt tries to justify his actions—if he is disgraced, Britain's standing will fall at this sensitive political moment—Poirot refuses to let him go free. Poirot's duty, after all, is not to nations but to innocent people.

Christie's research for this novel was less concerned with the political scene—an ever-present backdrop to 1930s life—than with Harley Street dentistry. Prior to drafting the first notes for the plot, she sent her secretary Carlo Fisher to her own dentist to make an appointment where Christie would interview him in exchange for his usual fee. The research mainly informs the opening chapters, especially the dentist's bedside manner, where key clues as to why he will be killed are introduced via what appears to be comic scene-setting.

One, Two, Buckle My Shoe verges on jingoism, especially at the end when Poirot rouses the young characters with talk of "[t]he New Heaven and the New Earth" and the promise of life after war (249–50). In fact, Christie was not pleased with the result and felt pressured by her publishers into including this element—which she described in unflattering terms. The bulk of the novel develops the unthinking nationalism of,

say, "The Kidnapped Prime Minister." In that story, the prime minister, who explicitly represents England, is under threat from an external enemy who turns out to be in his inner circle. This time, Blunt, who is presented as "needed in the world" and "necessary to the continued peace and well-being of this country" (244, 246), is himself the enemy against politically insignificant individuals, of whom Poirot declares himself the agent. This is also the first Christie text in which "The Reds ... and our Blackshirted friends" (55)—the left and the right—are presented as equally sinister.

The use of a nursery rhyme to structure chapters puts the novel in a similar category to *And Then There Were None*, published in 1939. Again, a childish rhyme structures a story about mass murder. Although this technique is often evoked to imply escapism in Christie's work, it also draws attention to the brutality of nursery rhymes and throws into question the idea of childish innocence. More pertinently in the context of war, it highlights the insidious violence of narratives we are taught from birth. Although Christie never dwelled particularly on gore, it is certainly there in the books, and this one contains the only instance of a character—a policeman, in fact—vomiting at the sight of a corpse.

Christie's agents and publishers were cautious about *One, Two, Buckle My Shoe*, with its explicit war focus, and decided to publish it quickly, while the war was still fresh, with more escapist titles such as *Evil under the Sun* pushed back to the 1940s, when times would be harder. In this vein, Collins asked Christie to make some changes, including a lengthy and explicit discussion of the dangers of war toward the end of the manuscript. Christie was not comfortable but complied—and Poirot's observations about no human life being more important than any other are still widely quoted.

The novel was dramatized as an episode of *Agatha Christie's Poirot*, starring David Suchet and broadcast on ITV on 19 January 1992. On 30 August 2004, BBC Radio 4 broadcast its own version starring John Moffatt.

Characters: Amberiotis, Mr.; Arnholdt, Rebecca; Barnes, Mr.; Biggs, Alfred;

Blunt, Alistair; Blunt, Gerda; Carter, Frank; Chapman, Albert; Chapman, Mrs.; Fletcher, Agnes; George(s); Japp, Chief Inspector James; Montressor, Helen; Morley, Georgina; Morley, Henry; Neville, Gladys; Olivera, Jane; Olivera, Julia; Poirot, Hercule; Raikes, Howard; Reilly, Mr.; Sainsbury-Seale, Mabelle

See also: *Agatha Christie's Poirot*; *Hercule Poirot* (BBC radio series); Nursery Rhymes; War

Only for Dons (novel-writing competition)

This whimsical name was given to a novel-writing competition run by Collins, "to encourage new crime writing talent" (Curran, *Hooded* 222). It opened in spring 1959, to academic university staff in the United Kingdom and Ireland, with a first prize of £2,000 and publication. Judges were Nicholas Blake (aka Cecil Day-Lewis), Julian Symons, and Agatha Christie. The competition received 50 manuscripts. Christie nominated newcomer D.M. Devine's first book, *My Brother's Killer*, but this title was disqualified because Devine was a university administrator and not a "don." Nonetheless, the competition sparked interest in Devine, and the book was published as a Collins Crime Club title in 1961, followed by 12 others. Devine enjoyed a more distinguished career than the two winners.

The competition was won by Cecil Jenkins with *Message from Sirius* and R.J. White with *The Smartest Grave*, which were both published as Crime Club titles in January 1961. Christie presented them with cheese at the Savoy Hotel on 15 June 1960 at an event to mark the Crime Club's 30th anniversary.

See also: Collins Crime Club; *The Times Anthology of Detective Stories*

Opzet of Ongeluk (Accident or Planned; television adaptation)

Opzet of Ongeluk (Accident or Planned) is a Dutch television adaptation of the one-act play *The Patient*, expanding the plot to fill 90 minutes. This production was filmed in late 1982 but was consistently withdrawn from broadcast before airing in the Netherlands on 12 May 1986.

See also: *Rule of Three* (play-set)

"The Oracle at Delphi" (story)

In the closing installment of *Parker Pyne Investigates*, the statistician-turned-detective travels incognito to Delphi, Greece, where a wealthy woman's son is kidnapped. The twist to this story is that the woman who consults J. Parker Pyne is given an extraordinary set of instructions, tantamount to criminal orders. In the end, a tangential character, Mr. Thompson, unmasks this man as an imposter. Thompson is the real Pyne.

The story was first published in the United States in the April 1933 *Cosmopolitan* as part of Pyne stories under the title of *Have You Got Everything You Want? If Not, Consult Mr. Parker Pyne*. In the United Kingdom, it appeared with two other stories in *Nash's Pall Mall Magazine* in July 1933, under the title *More Arabian Nights of Parker Pyne*. It was collected in 1934, in *Parker Pyne Investigates*.

Characters: Aristopoulous; Parker Pyne, J.; Peters, Mrs.; Peters, Willard; Peters, Willard J.; Thompson, Mr.

See also: *Parker Pyne Investigates*

Ordeal by Innocence (film). See Cannon Group Films

Ordeal by Innocence (novel; alternative title: *The Innocent*)

Along with *Crooked House*, Christie named *Ordeal by Innocence* as one of the two novels "that satisfy me best" (*AA* 520). Both titles are about families, and neither features a recurring detective; indeed, in both works, the hero who is stepping into the family stumbles upon the truth. The family in *Ordeal by Innocence* is more modern than that in *Crooked House*, as it includes adopted members, and is more focused on the young adult generation than on intergenerational relationships. Combined with the family theme, the novel uses the eminently Christian conceit of re-examining a closed case from the past.

Geophysicist Arthur Calgary returns from an Antarctic expedition and learns that a convicted murderer has died in prison. However, Calgary knows that, had he been in England, he could have testified in the trial of this man, Jacko Argyle, and accounted for Jacko's whereabouts at the time of the murder two years ago. He travels to Devon to visit the Argyle family and tell them. The family is not relieved to learn of the black sheep's innocence, because, having come to terms with such matters, they are now living with fear, suspicion, and uncertainty. The investigation into the murder of Jacko's adoptive mother, Rachel Argyle, is reopened, and soon there is another death.

Although there is talk of psychoanalysis, and "moral range" (*OBI* 111) is medicalized in the text, it is essentially a romantic drama and mystery. The key personalities that emerge are those of people who are dead when the action begins: Rachel and Jacko Argyle. Rachel appears to have had distinct but highly plausible personas. There is a public one, of a public-spirited woman "determined to make [her five adopted children] feel wanted, to give them a real home, be a real mother to them" (181). The sentiments, however, have not translated into good parenting, which several characters blame on the lack of a "blood tie" (182). Her daughter, Hester, describes the effect as toxic: "it made me feel so ineffectual, so stupid. Everything I did went wrong" (196). It is not a black-and-white, Jekyll-and-Hyde characterization but an illustration of personalities, ideals, and practicalities in conflict.

Jacko undergoes several transformations in the eyes of Calgary who at first wants to redeem him and prove his innocence. He emerges as a villain. Although he did not directly murder his mother, he was instrumental in her death. He is revealed to have been fatally charming and to have seduced and manipulated several older women, including the Argyle family's quiet housekeeper, Kirsten Lindstrom. It is Kirsten who killed Rachel for Jacko, who wanted money, and whom she believed she would marry. In the end, then, Calgary has proved Jacko's technical innocence of murder but a more complex and complicated measure of culpability.

Adoption in this novel goes against the message in *They Do It with Mirrors*, published 16 years earlier, although it similarly raises the question of "how much there is in heredity" (180). In both novels, characters resent their adoption—as did Christie's mother, Clarissa "Clara" Miller. However, in *Mirrors*, new models of family relationships based on love and respect are formed, as blood relatives and relatives by adoption learn to live together and use familial terms. In *Ordeal by Innocence*, an emphasis on "blood ties" is upheld by several characters, and one happy romance that closes the book with the promise of marriage is between adoptive siblings.

The novel was adapted into a BBC Radio 4 drama in 1983 and a poorly received Canon Group film in 1985, starring Donald Sutherland and Faye Dunaway. In 2006, a French graphic novel adapted by Chandre appeared; this was translated into English two years later. An episode of *Agatha Christie's Marple*, inserting Miss Marple into the story, was broadcast in 2007. The same year, a play version by Mary Jane Hansen premiered in New York, and a 2009 episode of *Les Petits Meurtres d'Agatha Christie* was also inspired by the novel. In 2018, the BBC broadcast a controversial three-part adaptation by Sarah Phelps.

Characters: **Argyle, Christina (Tina)**; Argyle, Hester; **Argyle, Jack (Jacko)**; Argyle, Leo; Argyle, Michael (Mickey); **Argyle, Rachel**; **Calgary, Arthur**; Clegg, Joe; Clegg, Maureen; Craig, Dr. Donald; Durrant, Mary; Durrant, Philip; Hush, Superintendent; **Lindstrom, Kirsten**; MacMaster, Dr. (Mac); Marshall, Andrew; Porch; Vaughan, Gwenda; Warborough, Mr.

See also: **Agatha Christie's Marple**; **BBC Radio Adaptations**; **BBC Television Adaptations since 2015**; **Canon Group Films**; **Crooked House** (novel); **Miller, Clarissa ("Clara")**; **Les Petits Meurtres d'Agatha Christie**; **Ordeal by Innocence** (play); **They Do It with Mirrors**

Ordeal by Innocence (play)

In 2004, the New York State Theatre Institute was authorized by Agatha Christie Ltd. to adapt *Ordeal by Innocence* (1958) as a stage play. This followed a request in 2003 to adapt *Murder on the Orient Express*. Rights were not available for that novel, but Mathew Prichard, Christie's grandson, suggested four possible titles, all relatively obscure: *The Man in the Brown Suit*, *The Sittaford Mystery*, *Postern of Fate*, and *Ordeal by Innocence*. The fourth of these was officially requested in December that year, and three versions were submitted by different playwrights to Agatha Christie Ltd. in July 2005. The company approved one by Mary Jane Hansen a year later.

In February 2007, a production was mounted by the New York State Theatre Institute. The play was written with input from the Christie estate and included music by Will Severin. The 90-page script calls for two sets, representing multiple scenes; although the plot invites a one-scene country-house setting, the action goes from a tomb to a police station to a country garden and various liminal spaces like staircases. It was directed by Elizabeth Swain, with set design by Richard Finkelstein. Agatha Christie Ltd. owns the rights to this script, which has yet to be published or restaged.

See also: *Ordeal by Innocence* (novel)

Ordeal by Innocence (television adaptation). See **BBC Television Adaptations since 2015**

Oriento Kyuukou Satsujin-Jiken. See **Fuji TV Adaptations**

Osborne, Charles (1927–2017)

An Australian theater critic and journalist, Charles Osborne wrote an early critical companion to Christie's work, *The Life and Crimes of Agatha Christie* (1982, rev. 2000). In the late 1990s, he was permitted by the Christie estate to "novelize" three of her plays: *Black Coffee* (1998), *The Unexpected Guest* (1999), and *Spider's Web* (2000). Osborne's novelizations tend toward translating the dialogue and the stage directions into prose with respect for the original work but also highlighting the distinct skills she drew on as a novelist and playwright.

See also: *Black Coffee* (play and novel); *Spider's Web* (play and novel); *The Unexpected Guest* (play and novel)

Osborne, Zachariah

A small, plump, insignificant-seeming pharmacist in *The Pale Horse*, Zachariah is gossipy and keen to discuss the case. He turns out to be a criminal mastermind, running a faceless organization that specializes in killing people for money. Despite Osborne's apparent unpretentiousness, his Achilles heel is his vanity. He is ultimately an egoist, and detectives succeed in drawing out a confession by questioning his intelligence.

Otterbourne, Rosalie, and Salome

An author of tawdry romances in *Death on the Nile* (1937), Salome Otterbourne allows Christie to mock the kind of writer she could have become. The character's path has been very different than her creator's: although Christie was a teetotaler, Otterbourne is a secret alcoholic who terrorizes her adult daughter. Nonetheless, Rosalie Otterbourne bears some resemblance to Rosalind Christie/Hicks. Rosalie is quiet and resentful. She ultimately finds happiness in love with Tim Allerton, who is equally under his mother's thumb.

The Outraged Heart. See *The Hollow* (novel)

An Overdose of Death. See *One, Two, Buckle My Shoe*

Owen, U.N.

U.N. Owen is the name used in letters of invitation to lure guests to Soldier Island, where they will be killed in sequence as punishment for past conduct in *And Then There Were None*. The signatures on invitations are deliberately misleading, but two legible signatures read "Una Nancy Owen" and "Ulrik Norman Owen." The name, as characters realize, translates to "Unknown." Throughout the novel, the unknown murderer is referred to as "Mr. Owen" and is first thought to be an outsider until the guests realize that nobody else is on the island—Owen is one of them.

The Pale Horse (novel)

A remarkable novel, *The Pale Horse* manages something Christie had tried and arguably failed to achieve in several early short stories: it marries the occult and the whodunit genres. In it, a dying woman gives a priest a list of names, and the priest is murdered. Young historian Mark Easterbrook learns that these names all belong to people who have died unexpectedly but apparently naturally and who seem otherwise unconnected.

Mark's interest in the deaths costs him the affections of his girlfriend, Hermia Redcliffe, but he finds allies in the eccentric novelist Ariadne Oliver and an unpretentious local woman, Ginger Corrigan, who plays an active role in the investigation. Before long, Mark learns of an underground organization, the Pale Horse, which arranges for people to die in exchange for a fee. "The Pale Horse" is the name of a converted inn from which three "witches" operate. It is also, of course, Death, the fourth horse of the apocalypse in the Book of Revelation. Mark meets a shady disbarred lawyer, Mr. Bradley, who explains the venture in mysterious terms, and then meets three self-proclaimed witches—Sybil Stamfordis, Bella Webb, and Thyrza Grey—who insist that they can use black magic to arrange anyone's death. Ginger poses as Mark's wife in a test of the process—and soon she starts to become seriously ill.

Finally, Mark learns what is really occurring. The witchcraft is a smokescreen, and the deaths are not supernaturally caused, although at least one of the "witches" truly believes that they possess malevolent powers. Instead, the Pale Horse organization runs a business in customer relations, sending women door-to-door to collect information about the targets' cosmetic products. These products are later laced with thallium, which slowly poisons the victim, mimicking a variety of natural ailments. Mark and Inspector Lejeune, an investigating officer, unmask an unassuming pharmacist as the murderer. Mr. Osborne cannot be coerced into confession, however, until Lejeune successfully bruises his ego by calling him stupid. In the end, Mark and Ginger agree to marry for real.

The Pale Horse is an unusual novel for Christie, confronting changing times by appealing to metanarratives both old (religion and superstition, with the witches described in Shakespearean terms) and new (consumerism, medicalization, and mass communication). Early on, Mark observes that "the superstition of today is the science of tomorrow" (20), setting a tone for the novel. With the mechanics of the central organization, the novel also contains an uncharacteristically stark critique of the workings of capitalism (see Mills). The presence of familiar characters from Poirot's and Miss Marple's universes acts to reassure readers that it is still a Christie. To this end, Major and Rhoda Despard return from *Cards on the Table* and Rev. Caleb and Maud Dane-Calthrop return from *The Moving Finger*. Another recurring character is Christie's fictional alter-ego, Ariadne Oliver, in her only appearance without Poirot or Parker Pyne.

Oliver shares traits here with Christie as well as Dorothy L. Sayers. In *The Pale Horse*, Oliver recalls having measles, which made her hair fall out, as a teenager—something that happened to Sayers. There are, according to Chris Willis, several tributes to Sayers in *The Pale Horse*. Willis relates the references to "an organisation that specialises in Removals—Human" (*Pale Horse* 107) to Sayers's story "The Leopard Lady," which features such a group and states that "Dr. Corrigan's theory that criminal behaviour stems from a chemical imbalance echoes the theories of Dr. Pemberthy in Sayers' novel *The Unpleasantness at the Bellona Club*" (Willis 12). These may well be coincidences, as neither point is particularly unique. However, Sayers's death in 1957 had necessarily affected Christie, not least handing her the presidency of the Detection Club.

Since its publication in 1961, *The Pale Horse* has had a stronger link than most Christie novels to real murder cases (see **True Crime**). There have been three radio adaptations: a Russian version in 1991 and British versions in 1993 and 2018. In addition, there have been four television adaptations: A modernized British version in 1997, an episode of *Agatha Christie's Marple*, inserting Miss Marple into the action, in 2010, an episode of the French series *Les Petits Meurtres d'Agatha Christie* in 2016, and a two-part BBC television adaptation in 2020.

Characters: Ardingley, David; Bradley, Mr.; Brandon, Eileen; Brent, Michael; Brokbank, Lady; Coppins, Mr.; Coppins, Mrs.; Corrigan, Dr. James (Jim); **Corrigan, Katherine (Ginger)**; Cripps, Mrs.; Curtis, Tom; **Dane-Calthrop, Maud, and Rev. Caleb**; Davis, Mrs.; **Delafontaine,**

Mary; **Despard, Major John, and Rhoda**; **Easterbrook, Mark**; Ellis, Lou; Gerahrty, Mrs.; Gorman, Father; **Grey, Thyrza**; Hesketh-Dubois, Lady; **Lancaster, Mrs.**; Lee, Detective Sergeant; Lejeune, Inspector; Luigi; Macalastair, Miss; O'Flynn, Father; **Oliver, Ariadne**; **Osborne, Zachariah**; Parker, Mrs.; Potter, Mike; Redcliffe, Hermia; **Stamfordis, Sybil**; Stirling, Pamela (Poppy); Tuckerton, Mrs.; Tuckerton, Thomasina; **Venables, Mr.**; **Webb, Sybil**

See also: *Agatha Christie's Marple*; BBC Radio Adaptations; BBC Television Adaptations since 2015; Christianity; Curses; *The Pale Horse* (1997 television adaptation); *Les Petits Meurtres d'Agatha Christie*; Russian Radio Adaptations; True Crime

The Pale Horse (1997 television adaptation)

The first screen adaptation of *The Pale Horse* was made by Anglia Television and broadcast on ITV on 23 December 1997. This low-budget adaptation was set in the 1990s, more likely for budgetary reasons than stylistic ones, although ITV did attempt a more expensive modern Christie six years later with *Sparkling Cyanide* (2003). The telemovie stars Colin Buchanan, most famous as one half of TV detective duo Dalziel and Pascoe, as Mark Easterbrook—a sculptor rather than a scholar as in the book. Like the two other screen adaptations of *The Pale Horse*, this one omits the character Ariadne Oliver. It gives Mark a more central role, making him the prime suspect in one of the murders. The production, directed by Charles Beeson, makes some questionable decisions, including a cheap subplot where a disabled man is faking his disability, which only show the superiority of the source material—which anticipates and undermines such ideas.

See also: *The Pale Horse* (novel); *Sparkling Cyanide* (2003 television adaptation)

The Pale Horse (2020 television adaptation). See BBC Television Adaptations since 2015

Palgrave, Major

Major Palgrave is a pompous, elderly man with a glass eye who dies in *A Caribbean Mystery* after recognizing a murderer he had described in an anecdote. The problem is that nobody listened to his stories, so nobody can identify the murderer.

Palk, Constable

St. Mary Mead village constable Palk features in "Tape-Measure Murder" and *The Body in the Library*. There is another Constable (George) Palk in the future (the year 2000) in "Promotion in the Highest."

"A Palm Tree in Egypt" (poem; alternative title: "A Palm Tree in the Desert"). See *The Road of Dreams* (poetry collection)

Papopolous, Dmitri

A Greek antiquarian dealer and diamond-cutter in *The Mystery of the Blue Train*, Dmitri Papopolous is "[a] receiver of stolen goods" who "deals with the highest in Europe and with the lowest of the riff-raff of the underworld" (173).

Pardoem, Reuben

In *Endless Night*, he is "a big burly man" (190), cousin to Ellie Rogers who represents the veneer of civility, as his condolences on her death quickly descend into money talk.

Parker Pyne Investigates (story collection; alternative title: *Mr. Parker Pyne, Detective*)

The year 1934 was firmly in Christie's heyday. By the time Collins published *Parker Pyne Investigates* in November (published in America by Dodd, Mead as *Mr. Parker Pyne, Detective*), she had already released four titles that year: *Murder on the Orient Express*, *The Listerdale Mystery*, *Unfinished Portrait*, and *Why Didn't They Ask Evans?*.

The twelve stories collected had previously been published in magazines. The book changes tone sharply around the half-way point, which reflects the two original series. American magazine *Cosmopolitan* published five stories as a "novel" in August 1932, under the banner *Are You Happy? If Not, Consult Mr. Parker Pyne*: **"The Case of the Discontented Soldier," "The Case of the Distressed Lady," "The Case of the City Clerk," "The Case of the Discontented Husband,"** and **"The Case of the Rich Woman."** Along with **"The Case of the Middle-Aged Wife,"** which ended up opening the volume, these were later published in U.K. magazines.

From the seventh story, *Parker Pyne Investigates* changes tone, becoming more conventionally mysterious and in some cases abandoning the Parker Pyne premise—a statistical approach and an imaginative outlook helping unhappy people recapture lost joy—altogether. In these stories, the detective is traveling around the world and encountering crimes and puzzles en route. Four stories—"**Have You Got Everything You Want?**," "**The House at Shiraz**," "**Death on the Nile**," and "**The Oracle at Delphi**"—were published in *Cosmopolitan* again as a novel in April 1933. This time, the title was: *Have You Got Everything You Want? If Not, Consult Mr. Parker Pyne*. In the United Kingdom, they appeared, alongside "**The Pearl of Price**" and "**The Gate of Baghdad**," in *Nash's Pall Mall* magazine, in two sets of three: as *The Arabian Nights of Parker Pyne* and *More Arabian Nights of Parker Pyne*.

There are two other Parker Pyne stories, "The Regatta Mystery" and "Problem at Pollensa Bay," which are occasionally appended to modern editions of *Parker Pyne Investigates*.

Parker Pyne, J. ("Christopher")

A statistician and former civil servant, J. Parker Pyne's Christian name (or Christian initial) is inconsistent in the 14 stories that feature him. The first 12 of these are collected in *Parker Pyne Investigates*, and the other two, "The Regatta Mystery" and "Problem at Pollensa Bay," have been collected variously elsewhere and in some editions of the first book.

Pyne is an unusual detective, particularly in his early cases. He runs a kind of agency and advertises in the *Times*: anyone who is unhappy is urged to consult him. In this way, he encounters a range of problems from the domestic to the emotional to the criminal. He tackles them by sending his employees—such as the vampish Madeleine de Sara—into manufactured adventures that will lead the client to a happy resolution. The later stories are more conventional mysteries, involving theft, murder, or criminal impersonation.

What unites the stories—whether they are set in London or on Pyne's tour of Western Asia—is the character's approach to psychology. As a statistician, he believes that there are only six types of people, and therefore estimates which extraordinary circumstances will give his clients what they seek based on probability. This explanation is a mathematical costume for the methodology employed by Jane Marple—what she calls "human nature," he calls "statistics."

The other notable point about Pyne is that two of his colleagues would go on to work—as more fleshed-out characters—with or for Hercule Poirot. Both Felicity Lemon and Ariadne Oliver are underdeveloped caricatures when they work for Parker Pyne, in each case some years before making their first appearances with Poirot.

Christie was not as attached to Pyne as to her other creations ,and he is one of the few characters that she was happy to offer to dramatists. However, the relevant producers were less attached still, and Pyne has only enjoyed a few radio and television appearances (including in *Murder Clinic*, *The Agatha Christie Hour*, and some BBC radio plays). The character has never had his own series.

Parrotti, Signor

Signore Parrotti is a pseudonym adopted by Hercule Poirot in *Dumb Witness* and *After the Funeral*.

Parsons, Mr.

A gossipy neighbor in "Behind the Screen," not dissimilar to Mr. Pye in *The Moving Finger*, Mr. Parsons is a "little mottled" man who barges into the crime scene, "stammering with excitement" (*SBS* 162).

Partners in Crime (film). See *Associés Contre le Crime*

Partners in Crime (radio series)

The BBC produced a 12-part radio series based on Christie's 1929 short story collection *Partners in Crime* in 1954. Much of the publicity capitalized on the fact that its married stars, Richard Attenborough and Sheila Sim, were well known as the West End stars of *The Mousetrap* (1952). Attenborough and Sim played Tommy and Tuppence Beresford, Christie's married detectives, and worked closely with Christie for the characterization. The stories were adapted by Rex Reinits with additional dialogue by Colin Willock and broadcast live from 13 April to 13 July.

Episodes include (with adapted story/ stories, if different, in brackets): *Meet the Beresfords* ("A Fairy in the Flat" and "A Pot of Tea"), *The Mysterious Stranger* ("The Adventure of the Sinister Stranger"), *The House of Lurking Death, The Man in the Fog* ("The Man in the Mist"), *The Ambassador's Boots, The Thin Woman* ("The Sunningdale Mystery"), *A Stab in the Back* ("The House of Lurking Death"), *The Man with the Gold Tooth* ("The Clergyman's Daughter" and "The Red House"), *In Camera* ("The Affair of the Pink Pearl"), *Finessing the King, The Crackler, The Unbreakable Alibi*, and *The Man Who Was Number Sixteen*.

Music for the program was composed by Alan Paul, and it attracted some high-profile guest stars, including Cecile Chevreau, Lockwood West, Marjorie Westbury, Derrick Guyler, and Maurice Denham (who would play Poirot on BBC radio in 1987's *The Mystery of the Blue Train*). No copies of the series have survived.

See also: **BBC Radio Adaptations**; *The Mousetrap*; *Partners in Crime* **(story collection)**.

Partners in Crime (story collection)

Published in 1929, *Partners in Crime* collects 14 short stories featuring Agatha Christie's married detectives, Tommy and Tuppence Beresford. Although the book is typically considered a short story collection because most of the narratives are self-contained, these stories are sufficiently reordered and rewritten, stretched into 23 "chapters," to make it as much a novel as *The Big Four*. For this reason, as well as to appreciate the overall scope of the work, *Partners in Crime* is considered here as a single entity.

Christie had created the Beresfords in her second novel, *The Secret Adversary* (1922), which ends with news that they will marry. She would return to them sporadically throughout her career, allowing them to age as Hercule Poirot and Miss Marple do not. The stories collected in this book were mostly written in 1924 in a series of

12 for the *Sketch*, following the success of two Poirot series, most recently *The Man Who Was No. 4*, and they show that Christie was trying to create more than a series detective. The Tommy and Tuppence stories are light-hearted and, crucially, parodies of other detective stories. Unfortunately, no correspondence survives between author and magazine about these stories or the level of satisfaction of each party. However, they were popular enough with readers to be collected at the end of the decade when a significant number of uncollected Poirot stories could also have been anthologized.

In the book, the premise is that the Beresfords have set up practice as private detectives but are bored with the few cases they receive. They receive an offer from the Secret Service to set up shop as a higher-end detective agency in exchange for helping the service unmask a Bolshevik conspiracy. This framing device has little to do with most of the stories, but the final case ties it together. In the meantime, the energetic couple decides to solve each case in the manner of a famous detective from literature, usually to comical effect. Accordingly, the kinds of cases they encounter are also styled after those Christie's peers would create.

The first published Tommy and Tuppence story, "The First Wish," appeared in the *Grand Magazine* in December 1923. This became "The Clergyman's Daughter" (chapter 20) and "The Red House" (chapter 21). In it, the Beresfords investigate apparent poltergeist activity in the style of one of the most popular detectives of the day, Anthony Berkeley's Roger Sheringham, a mercurial and egocentric crime writer.

The first story in the *Sketch*, "Publicity" (24 September 1924) sets much of the groundwork, as do chapters 1 and 2 ("A Fairy in the Flat" and "A Pot of Tea"), which it became in the book. In this, the couple is warned to be on the lookout for the number 16, which is one of many names given to a Russian spy the Secret Service is hunting. "The Affair of the Pink Pearl" (1 October 1924) became chapters 3 and 4, under the same title. In it, Tommy determines to imitate Dr. John Thorndyke, the forensic, physical clue-oriented creation of R. Austin

Freeman. He also tries—and fails—to make deductions, a la Sherlock Holmes, about his client.

"Finessing the King" followed on 8 October 1924 and became chapter 8, "Finessing the King," and chapter 9, "The Gentleman Dressed in Newspaper." The Christian name of Isabel Ostrander's policeman Tommy McCarty, who solved mysteries in *Argosy* and its predecessor magazines with fireman Dennis Riordan, may have suggested the pair for parody. As do many of Ostrander's stories, Christie's concerns playing-cards and human vice. "The Case of the Missing Lady" (15 October 1924) became chapter 9, and Sir Arthur Conan Doyle's Sherlock Holmes is the parody of choice. It is obvious that readers are expected to have a detailed knowledge of Holmes, as the character in addition to the investigative technique and story structure is riffed upon here—for instance, Tuppence offers Tommy cocaine but begs him to leave the violin alone. The case involves a bride-to-be who has gone missing, and the solution is comically trivial.

Next up was "The Case of the Sinister Stranger" (22 October 1924), which became "The Adventure of the Sinister Stranger" (chapters 5 and 6). This story parodies another detective pair that is now little-known: the Okewood Brothers, created by Douglas Williams, a pen-name for the jingoistic (George) Valentine Williams. Williams's forgettable stories tend to involve one brother getting into difficult situations only to be saved by the other. In this parody, the Beresfords end up on a high-stakes goose chase pursuing a sinister foreign doctor.

"The Sunninghill Mystery" (27 October 1924) became chapters 15 and 16, "The Sunningdale Mystery." It is often given special scrutiny because it is the most Christie-ish story in the set, with its straightforward whodunit style and elaborate solution. It is, in fact, a parody of Baroness Emmuska Orczy's Old Man in the Corner series about a detective who solves cases in newspapers from the corner of a teashop and relates them to young journalist. Set on a golf course, the story certainly evokes Christie's circumstances at the time of writing, living in Sunningdale as her first husband pursued a passion for golf.

"The House of Lurking Death" (5 November 1924) became chapters 17 and 18 under the same name. The detectives visit a gothic house and investigate suitably clichéd poisoned chocolates, which turn out not to be poisoned, in the manner of A.E.W. Mason's Inspector Hanaud. "The Matter of the Ambassador's Boots" (12 November 1924) became chapter 22, "The Ambassador's Boots," and is a character-driven parody of H.C. Bailey's Reggie Fortune series. The key mystery—why a U.S. ambassador's luggage was taken and returned—and the sleight-of-hand solution are typically Christie-like.

"The Affair of the Forged Notes" (19 November 1924) became chapters 13 and 14 with the much more pulpish title "The Crackler"; this refers to someone who forges banknotes. It is a parody of Edgar Wallace's popular stories. Christie and many of her middlebrow peers were extremely snobbish about Edgar Wallace, especially the volume and perceived low quality of his work. "Blindman's Buff" (26 November 1924) became chapter 10. Suitably, it parodies the blind detective, Thornley Colton, created by Clinton Holland Stagg. "The Man in the Mist" (3 December 1924) became chapters 11 and 12, and Tommy takes the role of G.K. Chesterton's reticent Father Brown. Because Chesterton's stories are so basic, they are hard to parody, and most of the comedy here involves Tommy dressing up in clerical accouterments while acting unclerically. The puzzle, involving a glamorous actress, is more complex than a usual Father Brown one.

The final story in the *Sketch* series, "The Man Who was Number Sixteen" (10 December 1924), also closes the volume as chapter 23. This is where the Beresfords confront their largely-absent arch-nemesis, Number 16. They do this in the style of Hercule Poirot himself. However, it is less a parody of Poirot stories in general, despite repeated references to "little grey cells" and Tuppence's insistence that this time Captain Hastings will be triumphant, than a parody of *The Man Who Was Number Four* (which became *The Big Four*), which had been published in the same magazine earlier in the year.

The remaining story, "The Unbreakable Alibi," was written around the time the book was collected, and appears as chapter 19. It was published in the *Illustrated London News*'s Christmas edition, *Holly Leaves*, on 1 December 1928 and as "Alibi" in *Tit-Bits*' "Christmas Extra" in 1929. The title is perhaps strategic, as the play *Alibi*, based on *The Murder of Roger Ackroyd*, was then running. The story is especially light-hearted, parodying Freeman Wills Croft's Inspector French tales and breaking one of the cardinal rules of detective fiction by using the plot device of identical twins.

Although original publicity for *Partners in Crime* emphasized the parodic nature of the stories—even erroneously stating on the dust jacket that Sapper's Bulldog Drummond is given the treatment—as time has advanced, Christie's name has eclipsed those of her subjects. By the time of her death, paperback editions merely referred to the Beresfords "assuming the methods and even the personalities of such great fictional detectives as Sherlock Holmes—and Hercule Poirot!," and Christie acknowledged in her autobiography that she herself could not remember all the original sleuths. At the time of this writing, Christie's official website makes no reference to parodies on the book's main dedicated page.

Most of the stories collected have been dramatized in some form. A CBS adaptation of "The Case of the Missing Lady" aired in the United States on 7 December 1950, under the title "The Disappearance of Mrs. Gordon Davison." Part of *Nash Airflyte Theatre*, it starred future President Ronald Reagan in his television debut as Tommy. In 1953, the BBC aired a radio series, *Partners in Crime*, based on the stories, with *The Mousetrap* stars Sheila Sim and Richard Attenborough in the leads. An LWT series adapted 10 of the stories aired on ITV in 1983, starring Francesca Annis and James Warwick, who had previously headed an adaptation of *The Secret Adversary*. A 2012 French movie, *Associés contre le crime: L'oeuf d'Ambroise* (released in English as *Partners in Crime*), directed by

Pascal Thomas, is an eccentric retelling of "The Case of the Missing Lady."

Characters: **Alice**; Barnard, Major; Barton, Lady Laura; **Batt, Albert; Beresford, Prudence ("Tuppence"); Beresford, Thomas ("Tommy")**; Bett, Hamilton; Blairgowrie, Duke of; Blunt, Theodore; Bower, Dr. Carl; Burton, Dr.; Carroway, Earl of; **Carter, Mr.**; Cheriton, Earl of; Chilcott, Mary; Clonray, Lady Susan; Coggins, Mr.; Crockett, Mrs.; Cumings, Alice; Deane, Monica and parents; **Drake, Una, and Vera**; Dymchurch, Detective Inspector; Estcourt, Marvyn; Evans, Doris; **Faulkener, Captain Jimmy**; Feodorsky, Gregor; Ganges, Miss; Gerald; Glen, Gilda; Gregory; Hale, Captain; **Hannah; Hargreaves, Lois**; Harker, Captain; **Hill, Gladys**; Hollaby, Mr.; Hollaby, Mr.; Holloway, Mrs.; Honeycott, Mrs.; Kingston-Bruce, Beatrice; Kingston-Bruce, Colonel Charles; Laidlaw, Major; Laidlaw, Marguerite; Lanchester, Lord; Leconbury, Lord; Lecky, Mr.; Leicester, Marjory; Leigh-Gordon, Hermione; Le Marchant, Jimmy; March, Cicely; **Marriot, Detective Inspector**; Merivale, Lady Vere; Merivale, Sir Arthur; Montgomery Jones, Mr.; Montgomery Jones, Lady Aileen; Oglander, Mrs.; O'Hara, Eileen; Partridge, Mr.; Quant, Esther; Radclyffe, Lady Lucy; Reilly, James; Rice, Dicky; Ryder, Hank; Sessle, Captain Anthony; Sessle, Mrs.; Smith, Janet; Stavanson, Gabriel; **St Vincent, Lawrence; Van Dusen, Mrs.**; Vassilly; Westerham, Ralph; Wilmott, Randolph

See also: *Bélisaire et Prudence Beresford*; **Bright Young Things; CBS television adaptations;** *Partners in Crime* **(1983 television series);** *Partners in Crime* **(BBC radio series); Pastiche and Parody**

Partners in Crime (1983 television series)

The first detective series for television based on Christie's work, *Partners in Crime* followed *The Agatha Christie Hour* in LWT's bid for Christie supremacy. With a budget of £2 million, it focused on "authenticity" with stagey Art Deco 1920s sets and an earnest faithfulness to the light mystery novel and stories that were its source. The series starred Francesca Annis and James Warwick, who had previously appeared in *Why Didn't They Ask Evans?*, as Tuppence and Tommy Beresford.

The series opened with a two-hour special, an adaptation of *The Secret Adversary*, in which the detectives meet. As with previous LWT efforts, this was dramatized by Pat Sandys. It aired on ITV on 9 October 1983 and introduced the central couple, other recurring characters such as Albert the lift-boy (Reece Dinsdale), and their situation.

Subsequent one-hour episodes were based on the short stories collected in *Partners in Crime* (1929), excluding "The Adventure of the Sinister Stranger," "Blind Man's Buff," and "The Man Who Was Number Sixteen." Elements of parody were removed from these adaptations, to make them standalone mysteries. Also removed was a connecting subplot about Russian espionage, making the series (with the exception of *The Secret Adversary*) more domestic than its source material.

The shorter episodes are as follows: "The Affair of the Pink Pearl" (16 October 1983), "The House of Lurking Death" (23 October 1983), "The Sunningdale Mystery" (30 October 1983), "The Clergyman's Daughter" (6 November 1983), "Finessing the King" (27 November 1983), "The Ambassador's Boots" (4 December 1983), "The Man in the Mist" (11 December 1983), "The Unbreakable Alibi" (18 December 1983), "The Case of the Missing Lady" (1 January 1984), and "The Crackler" (14 January 1984). Although the series received mixed-to-poor reviews, it has fared better in export to America and as a focus of nostalgia with fans wary of more recent adaptations. It also served to reassure the Christie estate that a series of Poirot adaptations would be faithful to the spirit of Christie's work, leading to the commissioning of *Agatha Christie's Poirot* (1989–2013).

See also: ***Bélisaire et Prudence Beresford***; **Beresford, Prudence (Tuppence)**; **Beresford, Thomas (Tommy)**; **LWT adaptations**; *Partners in Crime* **(story collection)**; *Partners in Crime* **(2015 television series)**; *The Secret Adversary* **(novel)**.

Partners in Crime (2015 television series)

As part of a rebranding effort, Agatha Christie Ltd. sold television rights to the BBC following the conclusion of ITV's *Agatha Christie's Poirot* (1989–2013) and *Agatha Christie's Marple* (2004–14). The BBC announced that its first new Christie series, *Partners in Crime*, and standalone miniseries, *And Then There Were None*, would air in 2015.

Partners in Crime is the second major British television series about Tommy and Tuppence Beresford, following LWT's effort of the same name in 1983. If LWT's version was a critical success but a ratings failure, the opposite can be said of the BBC's attempt. The buzz around this series—especially the introduction of what were essentially "new" Christie detectives for most audiences—was considerable. The producers attempted to follow the formula that had worked so well for *Marple*: they chose a blanket 1950s setting and adopted a tone of mainstream (i.e., straight) camp. One producer was David Walliams, a middle-aged comedian who took on the lead role of Tommy alongside a young and glamorous Jessica Chastain as Tuppence.

This move to a more conventional detective partnership—a middle-aged inept man and young, beautiful woman as opposed to the equally matched pair of Christie's books—sacrificed a great deal of the Beresfords' symbiosis. Efforts to relocate various contexts (from the Russian Revolution to World War II) to a vague 1950s Cold War backdrop played out as confusing, and Christie fans and relatives were offended by tongue-in-cheek references to the author's mental breakdown in 1926.

The first season aired in six parts—three based on *The Secret Adversary* and three based on *N or M?*—from 26 July 2015. By the last episode, broadcast on 30 August 2015, ratings had dropped from 8.78 million to 4.46 million. Although Agatha Christie Ltd. and the BBC had signed a contract for a second season, this was quietly unsigned before it could be announced.

See also: **BBC Television Adaptations since 2015**; **Beresford, Prudence (Tuppence)**; **Beresford, Thomas (Tommy)**; *N or M?*; *The Secret Adversary* **(novel)**; **War**

Passenger to Frankfurt

Subtitled "An Extravaganza," *Passenger to Frankfurt* (1970) is generally regarded as Christie's failure. The ever-pithy Robert Barnard, for example, calls it "an incomprehensible muddle" (193). However, there is evidence that it is the book that its 80-year-old author had always wanted to write. For one thing, she insisted on its publication despite protests from family and publishers. For another, it draws on ideas littered throughout her notebooks and published work over previous decades. Finally, Christie was proud of it: according to some sources, she suggested, after the success of Sidney Lumet's *Murder on the Orient Express* (1974), that *Passenger to Frankfurt* would make a good film.

The novel is ambitious. Much of the hostility to it comes from the fact that it is not in any real sense a mystery novel—although a trusted character is unmasked toward the end—and that it has a paranoid, repetitive tone. To address this discrepancy, Christie uniquely opens her 1980 novel with a lengthy introduction, in which she explains that her job as a writer is to "[h]old up a mirror to 1970 in England" (13). This is not the typical view of her novels, but it tallies with her stated ambitions in creating the village of St Mary Mead, so often regarded as "a museum of nostalgia" (Bargainnier 171), as an effort to reflect "everyday" life (Christie 1953e, 6). If Christie's attempt is to write about real life, there is some method to the repetition and the paranoia.

The introduction outlines a series of catastrophic events happening not on a global stage but to people: "A girl strangled.... Young men and boys—attacked or attacking.... Children missing and children's murdered bodies found not far from their homes" (*PTF* 13). This is not, she writes, happening "yet, *but it could be*" (13, emphasis original). "Fear," she writes, "is awakening—fear of what may be" (13), going on to describe globalization and terrorism. She then talks about understanding this fear, by quoting Elizabethan poetry, suggesting that while times change and become more unknown, the humanity that orchestrates these changes is itself unchanging and knowable.

The plot concerns Sir Stafford Nye, a diplomat, who stumbles into a global conspiracy. Through clues slipped to him during a Wagnerian opera, he learns of a secret plot to establish a new, fascist world order. The figurehead for this movement is to be the secret son of Adolf Hitler, who, unbeknownst to many, survived World War II. The story is likely untrue but it is nonetheless fueling a new fascist movement. Sir Stafford encounters several conspirators and influential persons mobilizing youth movements so that they themselves can achieve singular goals; these include a particularly grotesquely-drawn hedonistic woman who worships youth and beauty. He also learns of a new mind control drug—Project B—which aims to increase altruism in human subjects. The novel's precarious conclusion includes the promise that the young revolutionaries will be drugged with Project B, as Sir Stafford arranges to marry the attractive agent who started him on his adventure.

Themes that appear repeatedly in late Christie are global conspiracies serving personal ends for those at the top, the timeless pull of beauty, the mobilization of youth, and music as a structuring principle—action and character development loosely follows structures in Wagner's *Ring* cycle. There is one recurring character in this book: the mysterious financier, Mr. Robinson, who first appeared in *The Mystery of the Blue Train* (1928) but features extensively in the late books, and is the only character to have interacted directly with all Christie's major recurring detectives: Poirot, Miss Marple, and the Beresfords.

The novel was published in 1970. Christie received several Hollywood requests to film it, and declined them, although she rethought this after the success of *Murder on the Orient Express* on screen in 1974. However, the book has never been dramatized in any medium.

Characters: Altamount, Lord Edward; Andrews, Squadron Leader; Blunt, Admiral Philip; Brent, Clifford; Brewster, James ("Jim"); Chetwynd, Gordon; Cleckheaton, Lady Matilda; Coin, Monsieur; Cortman, Mildred ("Milly Jean"); Cortman, Sam; Eckstein, Professor; Franz Joseph; Gottlieb, Professor John; Grosjean, Monsieur; Horsham, Henry; Juanita; Kettely, Roderick; Kleek, Sir James; Lazenby, Cedric;

Leatheran, Nurse Amy; McCulloch, Dr.; Munro, Colonel; Neumann, Lisa; **Nye, Sir Stafford;** Packham, Sir George; **Pikeaway, Colonel Ephraim;** Pugh, Eric; **Reichardt, Dr.; Robinson, Mr.;** Shoreham, Professor Robert ("Robbie"); Spiess, Heinrich; Vitelly, Signor; **von Waldsausen, Countess Charlotte ("Big Charlotte"); Zerkowski, Countess Renata**

See also: **Anti-Semitism; "The Capture of Cerberus" (1940 short story);** *They Came to Baghdad;* War

The Passing of Mr. Quinn (film and novel)

The first British movie based on a Christie story, *The Passing of Mr. Quinn,* transforms its source material beyond the point of recognition. So great was the deviation that Christie ultimately changed the name of Mr. Quinn to Mr. Harley Quin, and the title of the story on which this film was based to "The Coming of Mr. Quin."

This 1928 silent film was directed by Leslie S. Hiscott and starred Stewart Rome as Alec Portal with Trilby Clark as his love interest, Eleanor. In this film, Eleanor is married to a mad professor who is murdered by one of her admirers, in disguise as the mysterious Mr. Quinn (or, as he was in early drafts and the pulp novel published to promote the film, "Quinny").

A book of the film, following the script fairly closely, was published in 1928 by the London Book Company as part of its cheap Novel Library. The novelization was credited to "G. Roy McRae," certainly a pseudonym and most likely an anagram for somebody working at the studios. The picture was released internationally by British Argosy with a blaze of publicity capitalizing on the Christie name.

Many years later, Rome indicated that the plan had been for a series of films about Quinn (Haining, *Murder* 40). However, despite good box-office receipts, the film was a critical failure and nothing materialized. Hiscott went on to make some Poirot "talkies" with Twickenham Studios.

See also: **"The Coming of Mr. Quin"; Twickenham Studios Films**

"The Passing of Mr. Quinn" (story). See "The Coming of Mr. Quin"

Pastiche and Parody

Pastiche and parody are at the heart of Christie. From his introduction in *The Mysterious Affair at Styles,* Hercule Poirot is presented as a comical disappointment to anyone who was expecting Sherlock Holmes. His relationships are also parodic. Not only is Captain Hastings so phenomenally stupid as an assistant that he makes Nigel Bruce's Dr. Watson look like a savant, but Poirot has at one point a twin brother called Achille who is, like Holmes's brother Mycroft, brought up without any notice only to disappear just as suddenly. He also has his version of Holmes's "*The* woman," Irene Adler—the flamboyant, oversized Countess Vera Rossakoff. The idea of this big, brash woman and the neat, precise Poirot together is thoroughly mined for comic effect.

In the *Partners in Crime* stories, Tommy and Tuppence Beresford are amusing themselves by solving each case in the manner of a famous literary detective. In the final case, "The Man Who Was Number 16," Tommy decides he will be Poirot. His way of being Poirot will involve "[n]o moustaches, but lots of grey cells," to which Tuppence responds that "this particular adventure will be called the 'Triumph of Hastings'" (PIC 329). The parody that follows consists mainly of Tommy and Tuppence calling each other "mon ami" at regular intervals. Tommy gets frustrated at one point that talking about his "little grey cells" does not actually get results: "It's easier to use your little grey cells in fiction than it is in fact," he says (342).

Literary. As Christie moved away from parody in her books, other crime writers embraced it. The 1933 novel *Ask a Policeman,* written by members of the Detective Club, had many of its authors parodying one another by writing about each other's detectives. Gladys Mitchell, Anthony Berkeley, and Dorothy L. Sayers took part but not Agatha Christie. A 1936 publication, *Parody Party,* featured such luminaries as E.C. Bentley and Edmund Crispin sending up the likes of John Buchan and Dorothy L. Sayers.

Christie may not have participated actively, but she was not immune to parodies by others. Leo Bruce (aka Rupert Croft-Cooke) published *The Case for Three Detectives*, which introduced his series character, Sergeant Beef, in 1937. The novel sees Beef in competition with three suspiciously familiar detectives: an impossibly out-of-touch aristocrat called Lord Simon Plimsoll (Lord Peter Wimsey), a diminutive Catholic priest who makes cryptic abstract allusions, Monsignor Smith (Father Brown), and a bombastic Belgian know-it-all called Amer Picon. *Amer picon* is a bitter French aperitif not unlike Poirot's beloved *crème de casis*. After a murder is committed, these three men arrive apparently from nowhere and no one bats an eyelid: of course, if a rich person dies in a country house, the amateur sleuths will appear.

Picon is just a little more extreme than Poirot. He asks left-of-center questions, the only difference being we never hear why the answer was relevant. He mangles English proverbs. He gets mistaken for a commercial traveler just as Poirot gets taken for a hairdresser. The difference is that while Poirot gets offended, Picon fails to notice and speaks, extensively, at cross purposes with someone who thinks he is trying to sell them something. And he peppers his vocabulary with excessive disconnected French noises.

Murder in Pastiche, or Nine Detectives All at Sea, by Marion Mainwaring, came almost 20 years later, in 1955. Again, multiple sleuths appear together, this time on a ship where a murder is expected to occur—mainly because there are nine detectives on board. A certain Atlas Poireau is on board, alongside such figures as Jerry Pason, Mallory King, and Lord Simon Quinsey. This character is obsessive about order and method. In the chapter where he is introduced, nearly every one of his observations revolves around the word *disorder*. He sees everything in shape, reflecting Poirot's obsession with angles and order.

Danish author Tage la Cour, who translated and introduced several Poirot short stories, wrote a Poirot parody story in Swedish, "Mord til Jul," in 1952. This was later translated to "The Murder of Santa Claus" and published in *Ellery Queen's Mystery Magazine* (EQMM) alongside reprint of Christie's Poirot story "Triangle at Rhodes" (as "Before It's Too Late"). The detective in Cour's story is "Hercules Poire." Cour would go on to parody several detectives under many names and collect his efforts in the 1975 volume *Kaleidoskop*. Norma Schier, who later collected her own parodies as *The Anagram Detectives* (1979), published "The Telecomshire Fen" in EQMM in 1967 as part of a series written under many pseudonyms. This time, the author was credited as "Cathie Haig Star" (an anagram of Agatha Christie), and various characters appear in the text, with new anagrammed names. The game for the reader is to guess whose style is being mimicked and to spot and decipher the anagrams.

EQMM published several Christie parodies in her lifetime, as well as tributary crosswords and verses that were often by illustrious people—the kind of things often reserved for the recently deceased. It is testament to the author's high status that she was already considered far enough removed from the rest of the industry to be a known benchmark for parody, even in the outlets reprinting her work. The Christmas 1974 edition featured, alongside Christie's "Strange Jest" and a Christie-themed crossword, "Murder in the Pantry," a Miss Marple parody by Michele Spirn.

Since Christie's death, several novels have been explicit pastiches or parodies of her work. A French mystery, now known in English as *The Eleventh Little Indian*, by long-term duo Yves Jacquemard and Jean-Michele Sénécal, appeared in 1979. Set during a stage production of *And Then There Were None*, in which nearly all the actors are killed backstage, it invokes several of Christie's specific and most theatrical plot twists. The mystery is solved with reference to passages from Christie, whose books are treated as a kind of scripture. In 1990, to mark Christie's centenary, Tim Heald published *A Classic English Crime*, a collection of 13 new stories from members of the Crime Writers' Association to mark the event. Each contribution is its own form of tribute to Christie, whether parodic (such as Julian Symons's "Holocaust at Mayhem Parva"), straight (Catherine Aird's "Cause and Effect"), or outright pastiche (H.R.F. Keating's "Jack Fell Down").

Cozy novelist Carolyn G. Hart's 1991 novel *The Christie Caper* is set during an Christie centenary celebration and does not reflect Christie's fiction so much as popular stereotypes about it. More connected to the novels is Gilbert Adair's postmodern "Evadne Mount" trilogy—*The Act of Roger Murgatroyd* (2006), *A Mysterious Affair of Style* (2007), and *And Then There Was No One* (2009), which plays metatextually with both the clichés of the genres and the specifics of the books to make a point about form and language.

With a resurgence of interest in Golden Age crime fiction, the 2010s and 2020s have seen several novelists marketed as "perfect for fans of Agatha Christie," with products ranging from straightforward whodunits to examples of domestic noir and even science fiction. It is notable that only some of instances where Christie appears as a detective in a fictional narrative pastiche her style, while most take a different direction (see **Fictional Portrayals of Agatha Christie**).

On Stage and Screen. The 1972 stage musical *Something's Afoot* by James McDonald, David Vos, and Robert Gerlach, spoofs golden age crime fiction, especially Christie, and specifically key elements of *And Then There Were None* (1939). The closing number of the show is "I Owe It All to Agatha Christie." It opened on Broadway in 1976, four months after Christie's death, and closed after 61 performances. A more successful London run in 1977 garnered an Olivier Award nomination. The musical is rarely revived. More successful has been the slapstick comedy stage show *The Play That Goes Wrong* (2012), in which a Christie-style murder mystery is being performed by hopeless actors who stumble over furniture, mix up lines, and move when their characters are dead. On stage, comedic takes on the Christie formula have moved beyond engaging with the genre itself and toward using it as an "establishment" backdrop for other forms of comedy.

Film parody has maintained an engaging-with-the-tropes format, although this has broadened from the specific to the general in the most commercial productions. Neil Simon's 1976 film *Murder by Death* follows a familiar format: five great detectives are called to an old house for "dinner and a murder." They are each challenged to solve the case, and by the end they each offer a solution only to be told they are wrong. There are two Christie tributes here: a Miss Jessica Marbles from Sussex and a Monsieur Milo Perrier from Brussels. There is no Lord Peter Wimsey or Roderick Alleyn substitute. Instead, Perrier is sharing his limelight with parodies of famous *filmed* detectives: Nick Charles (aka The Thin Man), Sam Spade, and Charlie Chan.

By contrast, the Netflix production *Murder Mystery* (2019), in which obnoxious American tourists stumble across a Golden Age–style mystery, name-checks Christie multiple times, although engagement is with general clichés rather than specific novels or films. Similarly, Rhian Johnson's 2019 hit *Knives Out*, although name-checking several Golden Age novelists including John Dickson Carr and building on some elements of famous plots, is more concerned with contemporary impressions of Golden Age crime fiction than with the fiction itself.

Since the 1974 movie *Murder on the Orient Express*, Poirot—and to a lesser extent Miss Marple—have been well-known enough to be parodied on mainstream television in sketch shows starting with a poorly aged sketch from Jack Benny in 1976, titled "Murder on the Oregon Express." Ronnie Barker and Ronnie Corbett's long-running sketch-show *The Two Ronnies* included two sketches in the 1980s that have better stood the test of time, "Murder Is Served" and "The Teddy Bear Who Knew Too Much." Ronnie Barker, who had played Poirot straight in a stage production of *Peril at End House*, here played the character as a kind of accented Sherlock Holmes, alongside Ronnie Corbett's acerbic Miss Marple.

"The Teddy Bear Who Knew Too Much" combines the two jokes most used in Poirot parodies on television. First, Poirot and Miss Marple are presented as a couple living together in a cottage. This idea is repeated in, for example, a 2000 sketch in *The Peter Serafinowicz Show* in the 2000s, where the pair finds numerous excuses to end up in bed on the pretext of looking for clues. The other common joke is the idea that Poirot is the one committing all the murders. It is, after all, the most logical way to explain why so many people die around him. The joke reemerges in *Poirot Comes to Dinner*, a 2014 web sketch from double act PistolShrimps. Other parodies such as an occasional set on the BBC program *That Mitchell and Webb Look* derive humor from specific elements of recent television broadcasts.

A German television series, *Agathe Kann's Nicht Lassen* (Agathe Can't Help It, 2005–07), is vaguely based on the Miss Marple novels, and each episode directly builds on the premise of one. The detective character, named Agathe, is a kind of elevated version of Miss Marple, played by Ruth Drexel to comic effect. At the same time in the United Kingdom, a more general parody/pastiche name-checking Christie's titles but drawing on clichés around her work rather than anything in the texts appeared in the long-running *Doctor Who* in the episode "The Unicorn and the Wasp." An example of this approach is the presence of a giant wasp, based on the cover art for *Death in the Clouds* but totally unrelated to the content of that book.

See also: **Continuation Fiction**; **Fictional Portrayals of Agatha Christie**; *Partners in Crime* (story collection)

The Patient. See *Rule of Three*

Paton, Captain Ralph

Stepson and adopted son to Roger Ackroyd in *The Murder of Roger Ackroyd*, Ralph Paton is the prime suspect because he has fled the crime scene. In an arranged engagement with his cousin, Flora Ackroyd, he is secretly married to Ursula Bourne and has been hidden away by Dr. Sheppard, who is trying to frame him for the murder. Paton is a handsome, underdeveloped character.

The Patriotic Murders. See *One, Two, Buckle My Shoe*

Paul Lamond Games. See **Games**

Pauncefort-Jones, Dr.

Dr. Pauncefort-Jones is a highly distinguished and absent-minded archaeologist in *They Came to Baghdad*, who blithely accepts Victoria Jones as his (fictitious) niece without needing any convincing. This is a playful reflection on archaeologists with whom Christie worked: brilliant in their fields but focused on work at the expense of everything else.

"The Pearl." See **"The Pearl of Price"**

"The Pearl of Price" (story; alternative titles: "Once a Thief"; "The Pearl")

One of the J. Parker Pyne travel stories, "The Pearl of Price" takes its title from Jesus's parable of the pearl in Matthew 13:45–46, where he speaks of a "pearl of great price." On holiday, Pyne helps recover a missing pearl earring. He unmasks an archaeologist who has taken the earring so he can fund a new exhibition, hiding it in piece of plasticine. A similar device is used in both versions of "The Regatta Mystery."

This story is notable for the small talk in it, encompassing dominant topics of the day, from "Middle Eastern" politics to gender roles, mystical writings, and psychoanalysis. None of these relate to the central mystery. It was published as "The Pearl" along with two other stories under the title *More Arabian Nights of Parker Pyne* in the July 1933 *Nash's Pall Mall Magazine*. In 1934, it appeared in the collection *Parker Pyne Investigates*.

Characters: Blundell, Caleb; Blundell, Carol; **Carver, Dr.**; Dubosc, Colonel; Hurst, Jim; Marvel, Sir Donald; **Parker Pyne, J.**

See also: *Parker Pyne Investigates*; **"The Regatta Mystery"**

Pearson, James ("Jim")

In *The Sittaford Mystery*, Jim Pearson is a generally inadequate young man, arrested for the murder of Captain Trevelyan. His much more competent fiancée, Emily Trefusis, sets out to clear his name and, against the judgment of most people around her, sticks with him. There is an optimistic note, suggesting that he can be reformed.

Pearson, Mrs.

Mrs. Pearson is Hercule Poirot's landlady at 14 Farraway Street in *The Big Four*, who is praised for her "motherly supervision" in "A Letter to My Publisher" (2). She appears to be Poirot's version of Sherlock Holmes's landlady, Mrs. Hudson. Her name may be a combination of that of Hudson and Mrs. Pearce, the similarly no-nonsense housekeeper in George Bernard Shaw's *Pygmalion*.

Pebmarsh, Millicent

Millicent Pebmarsh is a former schoolmistress who, since she lost her sight, has become an invaluable ambassador for blind children and upstanding community figure. She is revealed to be the head of a Soviet spy-ring. The character started out as Miss Leadbetter in "The Clock Stop."

Pedlar, Sir Eustace

Sir Eustace Pedlar is a boorish, egocentric, bullying, and completely enchanting Member of Parliament in *The Man in the Brown Suit*, who is revealed to be a criminal mastermind known as the Colonel. Sir Eustace is based on a real person, Major Ernest Belcher, CBE (1871–1949), who encouraged Christie to write him into the novel as the villain. Like Pedlar, Belcher was well known for his outlandish anecdotes of dubious verisimilitude. Major Belcher joined the round-the-empire tour on which Agatha and Archie Christie were fellow travelers in 1922 and curated the subsequent British Empire Exhibition in 1924–25.

Peel Edgerton, Sir James

Sir James Peel Edgerton is an intelligent, highly respected parliamentarian and criminal defense attorney in *The Secret Adversary*. He represents the Conservative (and conservative) political establishment in a sea of espionage and intrigue. However, it is revealed that Sir James has organized the criminal activities himself in an attempt to seize power.

Pender, Dr.

Dr. Pender is an elderly clergyman in *The Thirteen Problems*, who relates "The Idol House of Astarte."

See *The Thirteen Problems*

Penguin Books

Penguin Books, known for its distinctive two-tone paperbacks, was founded by Allen Lane in 1935. Lane—the nephew of John Lane, Christie's first publisher at The Bodley Head—reportedly had the idea for "good books at a price everybody could afford" at Exeter St. Davids train station, on the way home from a meeting with Christie ("Celebrating Sir Allen"). The first Penguin books were published in 1935 and sold 1 million copies within 10 months. They were launched with a set of 10 that were color-coded: green for crime, orange for general fiction, and blue for biography—with other colors and categories added later. So successful was the enterprise that Penguin later introduced a vending machine system for people to buy the books at busy train stations. The two "green" titles in the initial run were Christie's *The Mysterious Affair at Styles* and Sayers's *The Unpleasantness at the Bellona Club*.

In 1948, Penguin launched a set of 10 Christie titles, selected for variety, and all originally published by Collins. It printed 100,000 of each. The series was composed of *Appointment with Death*, *The ABC Murders*, *Lord Edgware Dies*, *(The) Murder at the Vicarage*, *The Murder of Roger Ackroyd*, *The Seven Dials Mystery*, *Peril at End House*, *Murder on the Orient Express*, *The Mystery of the Blue Train*, and *The Sittaford Mystery*. For these, Christie provided a rare smiling photograph and a biography, which appeared on the back covers.

In her biographical note, Christie describes her childhood as happy and cites her second-favorite origin story for her first novel, claiming that she wrote it at her mother's suggestion while ill, having run out of things to read. She talks about her likes ("I enjoy my food [and] adore flowers") and her dislikes ("I … hate the taste of any kind of alcohol, have tried and tried to like smoking, but can't manage it"), as well as describes her pleasure in traveling. This series quickly sold out.

The second set of 10 Christies was produced in 1953 and consisted of Christie's own choices. Some were titles that had appeared in the previous set—*The Murder of Roger Ackroyd*, *Parker Pyne Investigates*, *Death Comes as the End*, and *The Mysterious Mr. Quin*—but the other six were titles previously unpublished by Penguin: *The Body in the Library*, *Death on the Nile*, *The Labours of Hercules*, *(Miss Marple and) the Thirteen Problems*, *The Moving Finger*, and *Crooked House*. For these 10, Christie wrote new forewords; some have been reprinted in

Fontana, HarperCollins, or Harper editions in subsequent decades.

See also: **Forewords to Penguin Editions**; **"Sir Allen Lane: A Flair for Success"**

Pennefather, Canon Ambrose

The worldly, gregarious, and middle-aged Canon Ambrose Pennefather acts as detective in Christie's play *Murder on the Nile* (1943).

Pennington, Andrew

In *Death on the Nile*, Andrew Pennington is Linnet Doyle's U.S. solicitor, who has established a kind of artificial bonhomie with her as "Uncle Andrew" and who has been embezzling her money. He tries, impulsively, to kill her shortly before her 21st birthday.

Pennyfather, Canon

In *At Bertram's Hotel* (1965), the elderly and absent-minded Canon Pennyfather is kidnapped and impersonated by a criminal gang as part of a train robbery.

"The Perfect Maid." See **"The Case of the Perfect Maid"**

***Peril at End House* (novel)**

Published in 1932, *Peril at End House* revives the old Hercule Poirot formula. Like the early novels and stories, the book features Captain Hastings and Inspector Japp. It has a typical Cornish setting, with a crumbling country house, and includes several themes and plot devices that were quickly becoming classically Christie. Christie acknowledges a tonal shift in the more recent Poirot novels obliquely: early on, Poirot tells Hastings he was much missed during *The Mystery of the Blue Train*: "Your experience would have been invaluable to me.... My valet, Georges, ... has no imagination whatsoever" (2). The pair's banter is back, especially in the early chapters when Poirot and Hastings are on holiday in St. Loo, Cornwall, refusing to get drawn into any investigations. Within a few pages, Poirot praises Hastings's lack of imagination, calls him "the faithful dog" (5), and responds to "I have been thinking" with "[a]n admirable exercise, my friend. Continue it" (15). He later repeats the dog line (105) and, when offering Hastings up to lead a séance, says: "I feel the conditions are propitious. You feel the same, Hastings" (214). There is no mention of Hastings's wife in this book.

Noticing a pretty woman—frequently called "impish" (7)—who has apparently narrowly missed a bullet, Poirot and Hastings spend some time in her family home, End House. They learn that this Magdala "Nick" Buckley has had several recent escapes from death and believe someone is trying to kill her. Neither Nick nor her rich, artistic friends who party hard take the danger seriously. Poirot encourages Nick to invite her cousin, Maggie, for a few days to keep watch. At a fireworks party, where Nick and Maggie are dressed similarly, Maggie is shot dead. As Nick begins to take seriously the idea that someone is trying to kill her, she reveals that she was engaged to marry a missing-declared-dead pilot, Michael Seton, whose fortune will now pass to her under his will. Poirot stages Nick's death and then, once this has forced some secrets out, has the living Nick materialize at a séance. He then reveals the truth: that the whole plan was staged by Nick as a way to murder her cousin. Both Nick and Maggie are called Magdala, and it was Maggie who was engaged to Seton. With her cousin dead, Nick would be able to claim Seton's money, since the will benefits "Magdala Buckley."

Nick's motive is an obsessive love for End House, which she fears she will be forced to sell. Claiming Seton's millions allows her to continue living in and maintaining her family home. Nick is the last of a long line of Buckleys at End House, and she speaks regularly of her love for it, which is clearly unhealthy. The family home, indeed, exerts a stronger tie than the bonds of blood, as she happily murders her cousin to achieve her ends. Maggie's mother says there is "an evil feeling about that house," whereas the servant Ellen complains of "an atmosphere of evil.... Bad thoughts bad deeds ... in the air" (133, 169). More than once, it is suggested that the house itself is behind the many tragedies of the novel. An unsustainable ancestral pile, much of its sinister atmosphere is tied up in a former occupant: Nick's grandfather, who was known as "Old Nick" and is the model for the "impish" behavior of "Young Nick." In the murderer as well as the wider plot, there is a tension between gothic degeneracy, tied up with property, ancestry, and the modern destruction of pleasure-seeking.

One subplot concerns one of the drug-addled Bright Young Things: Nick's emaciated friend Frederica "Freddie" Rice. She has, readers learn, a no-good husband in the background. This character only appears at the very end, where he fires a bullet at Freddie. At this point, Nick has been exposed as her cousin's murderer and her story of dodging a bullet proved bogus. There have been subtle parallels throughout between Nick and Freddie, despite their superficial differences. Nick has copied Freddie's fashion choices, her adoption of a masculine name, and even her sex life, as it is revealed that the man currently in love with Nick is Freddie's former boyfriend. The two women have shared a cocaine habit but to a different extent. At the end, Poirot sees Freddie as a woman whose life can be redeemed, but Nick is an outright villain. Freddie is a product of her time: a young flapper whose decadence leads to degeneracy. Nick, however, is a gothic survival from a "cursed" house who makes only gestures to change with the times. Her lies throughout—including the fairy-tale romance with Michael and the black dress copied from her cousin—are modeled on other people's experiences, and as an antagonist she is marked by an inauthenticity in the face of changing times.

With a straightforward plot, memorable recurring characters, and a typical Christie twist, *Peril at End House* has been adapted numerous times. Arnold Ridley's stage adaptation debuted at the Vaudeville Theatre on 1 May 1940 with Francis L. Sullivan returning to the role of Poirot. A film version, *Zagadka Endkhauza* (Endhouse Riddle), was released in Russia in 1989. The next year, a British adaptation formed the first feature-length episode of *Agatha Christie's Poirot* on ITV. In 2000, BBC Radio 4 broadcast a five-part radio adaptation. Four years later, a three-part animation formed episodes 16–19 of *Agasa Kurisutī no Meitantei Powaro to Māpuru* on NHK. A modern French version followed as the fourth

episode of *Les Petits Meurtres d'Agatha Christie* on France 2 in 2009. In addition, there has been a hidden-object computer game adaptation by Floodlight Games (in 2007) and a French graphic novel by Thierry Jollet with illustrations by Didier Quella-Guyot (2009; the English translation appeared a year earlier).

Characters: Buckley, extended family members (Gerald, Giles, Jean, and Nicholas); **Buckley, Magdala ("Maggie"), and Magdala ("Nick")**; **Challenger, Commander George**; **Croft, Bert and Mildred**; **Ellen**; **Graham, Dr.**; **Hastings, Captain Arthur**; Hood; **Japp, Inspector James**; Lazarus, James ("Jim"); MacAllister, Dr.; **Poirot, Hercule**; **Rice, Frederica (Freddie)**; Rice, Mr.; Seton, Matthew; Seton, Michael; Vyse, Charles; **Weston, Colonel**; Whitfield, Mr.; Wilson, William

See also: *Agasa Kurisutī no Meitantei Powaro to Māpuru*; *Agatha Christie's Poirot*; Bright Young Things; Games; *Hercule Poirot* (BBC radio series); Houses; *Peril at End House* (play); *Les Petits Meurtres d'Agatha Christie*; *Zagadka Endkhauza*

Peril at End House (play)

In 1938, Christie granted Arnold Ridley permission to adapt her 1932 novel *Peril at End House* for the stage. Ridley was at this time best known for his 1925 stage thriller *The Ghost Train*, although his turn as an actor in sitcom *Dad's Army* has since eclipsed his writing achievements. The script was written in a few months. A production materialized in 1940: following a short run in Richmond, it opened at the Vaudeville Theatre in the West End, on 1 May. The star was Francis L. Sullivan, reprising the role of Poirot, which he had played in *Black Coffee* (1930) on stage and *The Wasp's Nest* (1937) on television. Sullivan certainly felt ownership over the role and he himself took charge of casting the production. The West End cast also included the artist Olga Davenport (then Olga Edwardes) as Nick Buckley.

There have been few amateur productions or revivals—although one in 1952 featured comedian Ronnie Barker as Poirot—and a planned American run never materialized.

On 29 May 1948, the BBC broadcast a production starring Austin Trevor, the original screen Poirot, over the radio. This was the last official play to feature Poirot until Ken Ludwig's *Murder on the Orient Express* (2017).

See also: *Back Coffee* (play); *Peril at End House* (novel).

Perry, Alice, and Amos

In *By the Pricking of My Thumbs*, Alice Perry is described as a friendly witch. She and her husband, Amos, live in a house that piqued Tuppence Beresford's interest when she saw it in a mysterious painting. Locals in her village really believe she is a witch, showing the survival of an old rural way of life well into the 1960s.

Personal Call

In the 30-minute radio play *Personal Call*, a man is haunted by telephone calls from his first wife, who died beneath a train some years ago. His current wife also receives a call. In the end, it transpires that the wife's sister was making the calls, correctly suspecting that he killed her. However, nobody admits to having called the new wife. This is one of Christie's most concise pieces of dramatic writing and is modeled on the kinds of thirty-minute plays being broadcast in the United States in series such as *Suspense!* However, it was written for and broadcast as the *BBC Radio Light Programme*.

The first BBC production aired on 31 May 1954. It was rerecorded on 29 November 1960. Both broadcasts were thought lost for decades, but the 1960 version was released as part of the BBC's *Agatha Christie: The Lost Plays* in 2015. In 2009, National Public Radio in the United States broadcast a new version, along with three other Christie scripts, in a special series, *Mystery Series Live—On the Air*. The script has been performed a few times on stage, usually as part of *Murder in the Studio*, which also includes *The Yellow Iris* and *Butter in a Lordly Dish*. That set-up started life as *Murder on Air*, performed by Bill Kenwright Ltd.'s Agatha Christie Theatre Company in 2008. A similar staged reading of these radio scripts and *Three Blind Mice* ran in 2012 and 2013 in and around Florida, as *The BBC Murders*. This, too, is occasionally revived.

Characters: Brent, James; Brent, Pam; Curries, Evan; Curtis, Mary; Enderby, Mr.; Fay; Lamb, Mrs.; **Narracott, Inspector**

See also: *The BBC Murders*; *Butter in a Lordly Dish*; *Murder in the Studio*

Peters, Andrew ("Andy")

Andrew Peters is a young American research chemist, part of a utopian political movement, who falls in love with Hilary Craven in *Destination Unknown*. It transpires that he is an FBI agent working undercover; in fact, "Andy Peters" is a false identity for Major Boris Glydr, a Polish cousin to Elsa Mannheim/Betterton who is investigating her death.

Peters, Willard

Willard Peters is the weedy and dyspeptic son of Willard J. and Mrs. Peters in "The Oracle at Delphi." He is kidnapped on holiday in a plot to acquire his mother's diamond necklace.

Petherick, Mr., and Mr.

There are two Mr. Pethericks, a father and son, who are colorless solicitors in St. Mary Mead. The elder Mr. Petherick is part of the Tuesday Night Club in *The Thirteen Problems*. His son has taken over the firm in "Miss Marple Tells a Story."

***Petits Meurters d'Agatha Christie Les* (TV series; alternative titles: *Agatha Christie's Criminal Games*; *Agatha Christie's Little Murders*)**

The detectives introduced in *Petits Meurtres en Famille* returned in the first series of *Les Petits Meurtres d'Agatha Christie* in 2009. This French comedy mystery series uses its own characters in episodes loosely inspired by Christie's plots.

Episodes are broadcast in short runs, retrospectively collated into seasons. Season 1 is set in the 1930s and was broadcast between 2009 and 2012 on France 2. It features Antoine Duléry as Commissaire Jean Larosière and Marius Colucci as Inspector Émile Lampion. It is composed of 11 episodes based on *The ABC Murders* (9 January 2009), *Ordeal by Innocence* (16 January 2009), *The Moving Finger* (11 September 2009), *Peril at End House* (6 November 2009), *Cat Among the Pigeons* (8 September 2010), *Sad Cypress* (15 September 2010), *Five*

Little Pigs (8 April 2011), *Taken at the Flood* (15 April 2011), *The Body in the Library* (28 October 2011), *Sleeping Murder* (17 February 2012), and *Lord Edgware Dies* (14 September 2012).

Season 2 is set in the 1950s and was broadcast between 2013 and 2020. It features Samuel Labarthe as Commissaire Swan Laurenc, Blandine Ballavoir as journalist Alice Avril, and Élodie French as Marlene Leroy, secretary to the commissioner. Twenty-five of the twenty-seven episodes are based on Christie texts, and two are original stories. The first original story, *Le Crime de Noel* ("The Christmas Crime"), was first broadcast in Switzerland, on RTS One on 19 December 2017, and five days later in France on France 2. It concerns the murder of a Santa Claus and remains (at the time of this writing) the most-viewed episode of the series. The second original story, *Un Cadavre au Petit Déjeuner* ("A Corpse at Breakfast") is an extremely camp musical season finale, broadcast on 16 October 2020.

Other episodes in the season are based on *They Do It with Mirrors* (29 March 2013), *Sparkling Cyanide* (5 April 2013), *Dumb Witness* (22 November 2013), *Why Didn't They Ask Evans?* (27 December 2013), *Hallowe'en Party* (26 September 2014), *Cards on the Table* (3 October 2014), *The Murder on the Links* (10 October 2014), *Hickory Dickory Dock* (28 August 2015), *Murder Is Easy* (4 September 2015), *Mrs. McGinty's Dead* (11 September 2015), *A Murder Is Announced* (18 September 2015), "The Adventure of Johnnie Waverly" (26 August 2016), *The Pale Horse* (2 September 2016), *The Murder at the Vicarage* (9 September 2016), *The Mysterious Affair at Styles* (16 September 2016), *A Caribbean Mystery* (23 September 2016), *The Man in the Brown Suit* (1 September 2017), *The Mirror Crack'd from Side to Side* (8 September 2017), *Third Girl* (15 September 2017), *Three Act Tragedy* (31 August 2018), *Hercule Poirot's Christmas* (7 September 2018), *The Sittaford Mystery* (28 September 2018), *Evil Under the Sun* (6 September 2019), *Towards Zero* (13 September 2019), and *Appointment with Death* (20 September 2019).

Season Three, set in the 1970s, stars Emilie Gavois-Kahn as curator Annie Gréco, Arthur Dupont as Inspector Max Beretta, and Chloé Chaudoye as psychologist Rose Bellecour. It began airing in 2021, with a mix of adaptations and original stories: *La Nuit qui Ne Finit Pas* (The Night That Doesn't End; *Endless Night*; 29 January 2021), *La Chamber Noir* (The Black Room; original, 5 February 2021), *Le Vallon* (The Valley; *The Hollow*), *Quand Les Souris Dansent* (When the Mice Dance; original), *Mourir sur Scène* (Death on Stage; original), and *Jusqu'à ce que la Mort Nous Sépare* ('Til Death Do Us Part; original).

The series has never been broadcast or sold in the United Kingdom, although some episodes are available in the United States (as *Agatha Christie's Little Murders*) and Australia (as *Agatha Christie's Criminal Games*). It has some high-profile admirers among English-speaking Christie fans, who tend to react with hostility to any deviations from source texts that do not conform to their preconceptions (i.e., any Poirot that is not David Suchet). Screen scholar Mark Aldridge admires the series because it does not claim fidelity to the source material. It is likely that simply being in another language gives it some legitimacy for certain fans that English or American adaptations can never possess.

See also: *Petits Meurtres en Famille*

Petits Meurtres en Famille (alternative titles: *A Family Murder Party*; *Little Murders in the Family*; television adaptation)

This 2006 French miniseries is based on *Hercule Poirot's Christmas* but introduces new detective characters: Captain Larosière (Antoine Duléry) and his young assistant, Emile Lampion (Marius Colucci). Taking its nod from Pascal Thomas's irreverent film adaptations, it is essentially a farce inspired by the novel's premise. The four-part, six-hour production was highly successful and spawned a series, *Les Petits Meurtres d'Agatha Christie*. In international export, it has been released as the first season of the subsequent series, although the latter includes its own adaptation of *Hercule Poirot's Christmas*.

See also: **Hercule Poirot's Christmas**; **Les Petits Meurtres d'Agatha Christie**

Petter, Florrie

In *Butter in a Lordly Dish*, Florrie Petter is a working-class, true crime fan who lives with her mother in the latter's boarding house. Her chatty dialogue tends to begin with "Well."

Phillpotts, Eden (1862–1960)

A prolific novelist, poet, and playwright based in Devon, Eden Phillpotts was a close friend of the Miller family. Christie credited him with encouraging her to write her first novel, *The Mysterious Affair at Styles*. Specifically, Christie credits Phillpotts in her autobiography for encouraging her to focus on her strength for writing "gay, natural dialogue" and "to cut all moralisations out" (*AA* 165): the speech-like dialogue presented without obvious showmanship has been highlighted several times as one reason for Christie's near universal appeal. Christie dedicated her 1932 novel *Peril at End House* to Phillpotts and wrote his obituary for the *Sunday Times* in 1960.

Phillpotts published multiple titles annually up until his death at age 98. Many of his novels are rural in tone and set on or around Dartmoor. He also wrote at least 26 crime novels, critically admired in his lifetime but now largely forgotten. In 1976, his daughter, Adelaide, who had been a childhood friend of Christie, revealed that her father had sexually abused her (Dayananda).

See also: *Akhnaton; An Autobiography*

"Philomel Cottage" (story; alternative title: "A Stranger Walked In")

This story is best known as the inspiration for Frank Vosper's highly significant play, *Love from a Stranger,* although that is more largely drawn from Christie's own adaptation, *The Stranger*. It is the story of Alix Martin, a woman in her thirties, who marries the handsome Gerald Martin and comes to suspect that he is a serial killer who is planning to murder her. Waiting for help to arrive, she slips him a slow-acting poison and keeps him in place by telling stories—Scheherazade style—of imaginary murders committed by her.

"Philomel Cottage" is unlike Christie's other fiction—it is, in fact, an early example of domestic noir, although it bears many of the author's trademarks. For instance, a love triangle is central, and the metatextuality is also present: Alix muses on what would happen "had this been a story" (*TLM* 33).

Another typical Christie theme is a minor focus on the couple's residence as a symbol of dysfunction despite appearances in their marriage. Gerald chooses the house without consulting Alix, and he names it, dismissing her objections as working-class ignorance. Comparisons could be drawn to Christie's first marriage when her husband used her money to buy a home near the Sunningdale golf course and insisted on calling it "Styles" after the tragic house in her first novel.

The story was first published in the *Grand Magazine* in November 1924 and was collected in *The Listerdale Mystery* in 1934. By this point, Christie had already adapted it into *The Stranger*, a three-act-play that would inspire Vosper's 1936 stage hit, *Love from a Stranger*. Besides the many screen and radio adaptations of *Love from a Stranger*, "Philomel Cottage" has been adapted several times. In the United States, CBS aired three productions as part of *Suspense!* In Russia, a radio adaptation aired in 1990. In the United Kingdom, a BBC radio version aired in 2002.

Characters: Ames, Mr.; **George**; Hexworthy, Mr.; Lamaitre, Charles; **Martin, Alix, and Gerald**; Windyford, Dick

See also: **BBC Radio Adaptations**; **CBS Radio Adaptations**; *Love from a Stranger* **(play)**; **Russian Radio Adaptations**; *The Stranger*; **True Crime**

"Picnic 1960." See *Poems*

Pierce, Mrs.

This name belongs to two characters: an unreliable cleaner in "Murder in the Mews" and a gossipy tobacconist in *Murder Is Easy*.

"Pierette Dancing on the Moon." See *A Masque from Italy*

"Pierrot Grown Old" (alternative title: "Pierrot Grows Old."). See *A Masque from Italy*

"Pierrot's Song by the Hearth." See *A Masque from Italy*

"Pierrot's Song to the Moon." See *A Masque from Italy*

Pikeaway, Colonel Ephraim

Colonel Ephraim Pikeaway is a pipe-smoking senior figure in the Special Branch and other areas of British Intelligence. He first appears in *Cat Among the Pigeons* and later in *Passenger to Frankfurt* and *Postern of Fate*.

Pinkerton, Lavinia

The elderly Lavinia Pinkerton suspects a serial killer in her sleepy village/town of Wychford-under-Ashe in *Murder Is Easy*. Her surname (reflecting that of a famous detective agency) indicates an inquisitive nature and that her ideas should probably not be discounted, although she appears in U.S. editions as "Lavinia Fullerton." She is murdered early on, prompting an investigation by Luke Fitzwilliam, whom she met en route to Scotland Yard.

"Playing the Innocent." See "The Golden Ball" (story)

"Plots" (nonfiction work)

An extract from Christie's autobiography was published as "Plots" in the HarperCollins anthology *Howdunit: A Masterclass in Crime Writing by Members of the Detection Club* (2020), edited by Martin Edwards. In it, Christie describes the mundane circumstances under which plots come to her, the process of recording them in notebooks, and the inspiration for the character Carlotta Adams in *Lord Edgware Dies* (1933).

See also *An Autobiography*

"The Plymouth Express" (story; alternative titles: "The Girl in Electric Blue"; "The Mystery of the Plymouth Express"; "The Plymouth Express Affair")

"The Plymouth Express" is an early Hercule Poirot story, in which the Hon. Florence Carrington is discovered dead beneath her seat on a train. Her father, steel magnate Ebenezer Halliday, asks Poirot to investigate the case. With Inspector Japp's help, Poirot uncovers both an affair and a jewel theft, unmasking the victim's maid, Jane Mason, as a member of a criminal gang that orchestrated the theft and murder. West Country railway timetables form key plot points but are not as dryly presented as they are in the work of Freeman Wills Croft.

"The Plymouth Express" was published as "The Mystery of the Plymouth Express" in the *Sketch* on 4 April 1923 and in the United States as "The Plymouth Express Affair" in the January 1924 edition of *The Blue Book Magazine*. It appeared in the U.S. collection *The Under Dog* (1951) and in the U.K. collection *Poirot's Early Cases* (1974). The basic story was reworked and expanded into *The Mystery of the Blue Train* (1928), when Christie struggled to devise a new plot following a traumatic experience.

"The Plymouth Express" was filmed as the fourth episode of the third series of *Agatha Christie's Poirot*, starring David Suchet and broadcast on ITV on 20 January 1991. A two-part animated version, part of the series *Agasa Kurisutī no Meitantei Powaro to Māpuru*, was broadcast on Japanese network NHK on 6 and 13 February 2005, with Kōtarō Satomi as Poirot. The story has also inspired an interactive dinner party game, *A First Class Murder*, produced by Paul Lamond Games under its "Murder à la Carte" banner in 2004.

Characters: Carrington, Hon. Florence (Flossie); Carrington, Richard; de la Rochefour, Count Armand; Halliday, Ebenezer; **Hastings, Captain Arthur**; **Japp, Inspector James**; Mason, Jane; Narky, Red; **Poirot, Hercule**; Simpson, Lieutenant Alec

See also: *Agasa Kurisutī no Meitantei Powaro to Māpuru*; **Agatha Christie's Poirot**; **Games**; **Poirot's Early Cases**; *The Under Dog* (story collection)

"The Plymouth Express Affair." See "The Plymouth Express"

A Pocket Full of Rye (novel)

In 1953, when *A Pocket Full of Rye* was published, Christie wrote that Miss Marple had become a potential rival to Hercule Poirot (Foreword, *Miss Marple and the Thirteen Problems* 5). This was also the second year in a row in which Christie published both Poirot and Miss Marple books and, by this stage, the 1950s had seen more novels featuring the latter. *A Pocket Full of Rye* puts Miss Marple into comfortable Christie territory: there is a country house, a village, a dysfunctional family, and crimes linked by a nursery rhyme.

As in her short stories "Sing a Song of Sixpence" and "Four and Twenty Blackbirds," Christie uses "Sing a Song of Six-pence" here. This time, the murderer is consciously following the order of the rhyme, specifically:

> The king was in his counting house,
> Counting out his money;
> The queen was in the parlor,
> Eating bread and honey.
> The maid was in the garden,
> Hanging out the clothes,
> When down came a blackbird
> And pecked off her nose.

The first victim is a wealthy financier named Rex (i.e., King) Fortescue, the second is his wife, and the third is a maid, Gladys, whose humiliation in death—"pecked on the nose" with a clothespin—causes Miss Marple, who once trained her, to vow vengeance. An extremely formulaic novel, *A Pocket Full of Rye* garnered polite, if sometimes slightly patronizing, reviews: Maurice Richardson in the *Observer* commented, "How well she nearly always writes, the dear, decadent old death trafficker" (10), whereas *New York Times* critic Anthony Boucher said the book "represents Christie in top form.... you aren't apt to find a better job of professional craftsmanship this year" ("Report" BR23). Although the label of "cozy crime" is slowly dropping from Christie's shoulders, *A Pocket Full of Rye* could easily be used to justify it.

Much of the action takes place in Fortescue's suburban mansion, Yew Tree Lodge. Although often compared by scholars to the house in *Crooked House*, Yew Tree Lodge has the opposite role. The Three Gables is a collapsing ancestral pile that has been made monstrous by attempts to change with the times without addressing any of its problems, something symbolized by bindweed. Yew Tree Lodge—inaccurately named as it is not surrounded by Yew Trees—represents new money seeking to re-create a vision of lost English decadence. The house has regularly been compared to Christie's marital home Sunningdale, where her first husband played golf (Osborne 263).

Christie had a broken wrist when she composed *A Pocket Full of Rye*. Therefore, the bulk of it was dictated. In later years, this would become the norm for Christie, but until this point she had chiefly used the technique for short stories. Following abridged serializations in the *Daily Express* and the *Chicago Tribune*, the novel was published by Collins in the United Kingdom and Dodd, Mead in the United States in 1953. It has been dramatized on several occasions: first as a Russian movie, *Tayna Chyornykj Drozdov*, in 1983, then as a BBC television adaptation, part of *Miss Marple*, in 1985. Ten years later, BBC Radio 4 aired an audio adaptation, and the relevant episode of *Agatha Christie's Marple* aired on ITV in 2009.

Characters: Ansell, Mr.; Anstice, Lord Frederick (Freddie); Bates, Marion; Bell, Miss; Bernsdorff, Professor' Billingsley, Mr.; Chase, Miss; **Clithering, Sir Henry**; Crospie, Dr.; Crump, Mr.; Crump, Mrs.; Curtis, Ellen; **Dove, Mary**; Dubois, Vivian; Ellis; Emmett, Mr.; Emmett, Mrs.; Fortescue, Elaine; Fortescue, Elvira; **Fortescue, Lancelot (Lance)**; **Fortescue, Patricia (Pat)**; **Fortescue, Percival ("Percy/Val"), and Jennifer**; **Fortescue, Rex, and Adele**; Griffith, Miss; Grosvenor, Irene; Hardcastle, Mrs.; Hay, Sergeant; Isaacs, Dr.; **Jackson, Fred**; Kitty; Latimer, Mrs.; MacKenzie, Donald; MacKenzie, Helen; MacKenzie, Mr.; **Marple, Jane**; **Martin, Gladys**; **Neele, Inspector**; Ramsbottom, Miss; Sandeman, Sir Edwin; Somers, Miss; Sparrow, Mrs.; Trefusis James, Miss; Waite, Detective Constable; Wright, Gerald

See also: *Agatha Christie's Marple*; *Miss Marple* (radio series); *Miss Marple* (television series); Nursery Rhymes; *Tayna Chyornyki Drozdov*

Poems (poetry collection)

Published in 1973, *Poems* includes Christie's complete first volume of poetry, *The Road of Dreams* (1925) with 27 later poems. *The Road of Dreams* itself had combined one complete manuscript with a selection of other verses, so this is very much a piecemeal volume. Many of the latter poems appear to have been written in the 1960s. After the early poems, there are poems subdivided into "Places," "Things," "Love Poems and Others," and "Verses of Nowadays."

They are light, rhyming verses, not so much about language as about ideas and observations. For instance, "From a Grown-up to a Child" rejects on the kindness of "fairies" to "little girls" of all ages; i.e., the consist power of imagination (121). "Racial Musings" argues against racism, dismissing "a gulf between Black and White" as "A BORE. A BORE. A BORE" (123). "Picnic 1960" contrasts the grant high teas of Bertram's Hotel by describing the simple pleasures of a light lunch aside a busy road (124). "I Wore My New Canary Suit," which starts off as a jaunty sketch, evolves in a very few lines into a reflection on grief and trauma. One entry in the second half of the volume, "Jenny by the Sky," is taken from the 1965 collection *Star Over Bethlehem*. Two of the late poems, "My Flower Garden" and "Remembrance" were published as booklets by Souvenir Press in 1988, with illustrations by Richard Allen.

Volume 1 is *The Road of Dreams,* with some differences. It has a slightly revised order and includes one poem not in the original pamphlet: "Islot of Brittany." Despite some scholarly suggestions to the contrary, which seem to stem from Wikipedia, both the reprint and the original include "Dark Sheila."

Volume 2 is composed of "Beauty," "The Water Flows," "The Sculptor," and "A Wandering Tune" under the heading *Things*; "Ctesiphon," "In Baghdad," "An Island," "The Nile," "Dartmoor," "To a Cedar Tree," and "Calvary" under the heading *Places*; "Count Ferson to the Queen," "Beatrice Passes," "Undine," "Hawthorn Trees," "Lament of the Tortured Lover," "What is Love?," "To M.E.L.M. in Absence," "Remembrance," "A Choice," "My Flower Garden," "Enchantment," and "Jenny by the Sky" under the heading *Love Poems and Others*; and "From a Grown-up to a Child," "I Wore My New Canary Suit," "Racial Musings," and "Picnic 1960" under the heading *Verses of Nowadays*.

Two of these newer poems, "Remembrance" and "My Flower Garden," were published by Souvenir Press as standalone hardbacks, illustrated by Richard Allen, in 1988.

See also: *A Masque from Italy*; *The Road of Dreams* (poetry collection)

Poirot, Achille

In *The Big Four*, Hercule Poirot mentions in passing that he has a twin brother, Achille. Captain Hastings is surprised. Achille, says Hercule, is as intelligent as his brother but not so proactive. The narrative allusion to Mycroft Holmes, brother of Sherlock, is clear. Indeed, in the much later *The Labours of Hercules*, a friend of Poirot's wonders about Mycroft and Achille and their respective mothers' choices in Christian names.

Unlike Hercule, Achille wears no moustache and has a distinctive scar on his upper lip. Toward the end of *The Big Four*, he appears in disguise as Hercule, in a false moustache—but in fact, this *is* Hercule Poirot, who has shaved and scarred his own face, to convince his captors that he is his twin. Achille Poirot, he confesses, never existed.

"Poirot and the Crime in Cabin 66" (story; alternative titles: "Crime in Cabin 66"; "The Quickness of the Hand")

The original version of "Problem at Sea," "Poirot and the Crime in Cabin 66" is slightly longer than the better-known version. It was published in *The Strand* on 19 February 1936 and later in numerous U.K./U.S. pulp editions: *Crime in Cabin 66* (Vallencey Press, 1943), *Poirot on Holiday* (Vallencey Press, 1943), and *Poirot Knows the Murderer* (Polybooks, 1946). The shorter version, "Problem at Sea," which appears in U.K. and U.S. Christie anthologies, first appeared in the 12 January 1936 *This Week*, a magazine supplement of the [Washington, D.C.] *Sunday Star*.

Characters: **Clappterton, Adeline, and John**; Cregan, Pamela ("Pam"); Forbes, General; **Henderson, Ellie**; Mooney, Kitty; **Poirot, Hercule**

See also: *Poirot Knows the Murderer*; *Poirot on Holiday*; **"Problem at Sea"**

"Poirot and the Regatta Mystery" (story)

Received wisdom states that Christie wrote "Poirot and the Regatta Mystery," which was published in *The Strand* in June 1936 before changing her mind and rewriting the story with J. Parker Pyne for book publication in 1939. However, a close-reading of both texts suggests it is more likely

Christie wrote the story with Pyne and was obliged to change it for commercial reasons to a Poirot case for the magazine market. The *Strand* had published a Pyne story, "Problem at Pollensa Bay," in November 1935 and was now publishing a loose Poirot series. A sentence-by-sentence comparison of the two stories shows some signs:

- The detectives speak differently ("Very uncertain animal, the horse," says Pyne [*PPB* 147], whereas Poirot says, "An animal a little uncertain, the horse" [*PRM* 878])—in an *original* Poirot story, he would have picked a more euphonic image.
- The Poirot version shows signs of padding. Sentences are arbitrarily expanded in a manner one also sees, for instance, in the anthologized version of "The Under Dog." When shortening texts, Christie tended not to cut down sentences but to remove entire paragraphs. There are parts missing from the Pyne version, but these are all references to categorizing human behavior and are generally replaced with something else.
- Poirot discusses his fee toward the end, something Pyne tends to do (and does in his version of the story)—but not something Poirot would do if he happened to solve a case on holiday.

Nonetheless, the official line is that the stories were written in order of publication. After its appearance in *The Strand* (preceded by a U.S. appearance in the *Chicago Tribune*), "Poirot and the Regatta Mystery" appeared in three pulp paperbacks in New York and London: as a single-story booklet, *Poirot and the Regatta Mystery* (Todd, 1943), with "The Crime in Cabin 66" in *Poirot on Holiday* (Todd, 1943), and with two other stories in *Poirot Lends a Hand* (Polybooks, 1946). It remained uncollected until 2008, when it was published by Harper as a postscript to a "complete" collection of Poirot short stories.

Characters: Leathern, Eve; Leathern, Samuel; Llewelyn, Evan; Marroway, Lady Pamela; Marroway, Sir George; Pointz, Isaac; **Poirot, Hercule**; Rustington, Janet; Stein, Leo

See also: ***Poirot Lends a Hand***; ***Poirot on Holiday***; "The Regatta Mystery" (story)

"Poirot and the Regular Customer." See "Four and Twenty Blackbirds"

"Poirot and the Triangle at Rhodes." See "Triangle at Rhodes"

Poirot Award. See **Agatha Awards**

Poirot, Hercule
Hercule Poirot's biography is relatively straightforward. He was born in the mid-nineteenth century somewhere in Belgium. Poirot had some siblings including a sister, Yvonne, and later "many nieces and grand-nieces" (*COT* 193). An identical twin brother, Achille, proves in *The Big Four* to be Poirot in disguise, although he is referred to by another character in *The Labours of Hercules*. Poirot became "one of the most celebrated members of the Belgian police" (*MAS* 35) before retiring at an undisclosed time. In spring 1916, he was smuggled from Belgium to France and arrived in Essex, England, as a refugee. Here he became reacquainted with an old friend, Captain Hastings, and from there established a career in London—and around the world—as a private detective. Poirot died, aged around 130, in the early 1970s.

Poirot stands at five feet, four inches tall. He has an egg-shaped head, suspiciously black hair (revealed in *The ABC Murders* to be dyed and in *Curtain* to be a wig), and an elaborate moustache of which he is immensely proud. His ruling passions are order and method, and he frequently professes himself to have "a bourgeois attitude to murder" (*COT* 68). As a detective, Christie created him to be as unlike Sherlock Holmes as possible, and he has set the template for the quirky outsider or misunderstood sleuth in fiction.

However, the difference from Holmes is less in the trappings of characterization than in the detection method. Although by 1944, Howard Haycraft noted that Poirot "spurns the aid of science," making him old-fashioned (132), this "champion[ing] of theory over matter" (132) was itself an innovation when Christie created the character. Whereas Holmes and his imitators occupy themselves with the latest technologies to interpret physical clues, Poirot consistently mocks fingerprints and footprints—because, although he never says it directly, only a logical problem can really play fair with the reader. His version of "the psychology" and "the little grey cells" is about finding the truth logically: "If the facts will not fit the theory," he says in his debut, "let the theory go" (*MAS* 120). "Arrange your facts," he elaborates in the second novel. "Arrange your ideas. And if some little fact will not fit in—do not reject it, but consider it closely. Though its significance escapes you, be sure that it is significant" (*MOL* 153). In several texts, he builds houses out of cards to aid in ordering his thoughts.

Some efforts have been made to find the individual Belgian refugee on whom Christie based Poirot—and, indeed, she claimed to have seen two different men who might have been Poirot in real life—but this rather misses the point. Working in the Voluntary Aid Detachment (VAD) during World War I, she certainly came into contact with many Belgian men, and they certainly gave her the idea to make her detective Belgian—but there is no evidence that the character himself is based on one person. The name was, she always maintained, pure invention, although some have linked it with Jules Poiret and/or Hercules Popeau, French detectives created by Frank Howell Evans and Marie Belloc Lowndes respectively.

But—as Poirot consistently reminds people—he is not French but Belgian. The use of Belgium as a country of origin is strategic: of course, it allows for comedy when people talk about France, and artistically it makes him doubly an outsider—even his otherness is consistently mischaracterized (including beyond the page, by critics discussing him). However, it also makes him completely unthreatening: as Heather Worthington points out, British readers in the 1920s were unlikely to have strong opinions about Belgium or Belgian people (29). The nationality lets Poirot be generically European with minimal baggage, allowing him to reflect English or British prejudice as an "other" rather than a specific national identity in his own right. Colin Watson wrote that Poirot is not really Belgian but "an altogether English creation—as English

as a Moorish cinema foyer or hotel curry or comic yodelers. He personified English ideas about foreigners and was therefore immediately familiar to readers and acceptable by them" (*Snobbery* 167).

More than "acceptable," Poirot was quickly embraced by the reading public. Christie famously came to regret being tied to Poirot, proclaiming him a "detestable, bombastic tiresome little creature" (FGD 8) and seething inwardly when fans said she must love him: such exchanges are parodied effectively in *Cards on the Table*, when Ariadne Oliver regrets having created a quirky European detective character who has become inexplicably popular—she complains to her dear friend Poirot. Nonetheless, as she wrote to a fan who complained in the 1960s that Poirot was getting too old, as long as he earned her good money, she was tied to him.

Sir Arthur Conan Doyle notoriously grew frustrated with Holmes and killed him off in "The Final Problem" (1893), only to respond to public pressure—and the allure of royalties—by returning Holmes to print in *The Hound of the Baskervilles* (1901–02). Christie made a similar but more strategic move, writing Poirot's death in *Curtain: Poirot's Last Case* around 1940. This manuscript was sent to both her U.K. and U.S. publishers with instructions that it not be published until after her death (although, entertainingly, several parties misread the covering letters, grew worried that the golden goose was being eliminated, and suggested all kinds of ruses for avoiding Poirot's death). Christie likely thought she might die during World War II, although there must also have been a catharsis in killing off Poirot. Nonetheless, she continued to write about him throughout and beyond the war—although now with the confidence to introduce him on her terms, not his; he tends in postwar novels to arrive late in the course of things, often halfway or two-thirds into the book.

Throughout his career, Poirot is a modernist, and he remains frozen in time, although the world around him changes. This description introducing him and his flat in *After the Funeral* could have come in any post–1930 novel:

There were no curves in the room. Everything was square. Almost the only exception was Hercule Poirot himself, who was full of curves. His stomach was pleasantly rounded, his head resembled an egg in shape, and his moustaches curved upwards in a flamboyant flourish [*ATF* 99].

He clashes with youth culture regularly but most significantly in *Hickory Dickory Dock* and "The Adventure of the Christmas Pudding," where students and teenagers indulge him as an amusing relic at their peril, and *Third Girl*, where the world of drugs and bohemianism is clearly beyond him. He is spurred to action in that case by a potential client running out on him because he is "too old" (*TG* 9).

Curtain: Poirot's Last Case was published in 1975, a few months before Christie's death. The news of Poirot's death was significant as the character and his creator had come to typify the Golden Age of detective fiction, already viewed as an historical movement. Poirot became the only fictional character in history to receive an obituary in the *New York Times*: on the front page, no less. The obituary garnered praise from several figures, including diplomat Patricia Roberts Harris, whose letter to the editor deemed it "delightful that The Times took Mr. Poirot as seriously as both he and I did," going on to discuss her own relationship with Poirot, reading about him on various holidays (30). This shows Christie's sheer reach and respectability at this point, as the first African American member of the U.S. cabinet advertised herself as a fan. Several other newspapers and magazines around the world followed that paper's lead, with their own tributes to the Belgian detective.

Although *Curtain* was supposed to stop anyone interfering with Poirot after Christie's death, the character has not remained undisturbed. In addition to an extensive afterlife on the stage, screen, and radio, Poirot has been resurrected by several authors, officially and unofficially. Officially licensed fiction featuring Poirot includes Julian Symons's *The Great Detectives* (1981); Carlo Fruttero and Franco Lucentini's *La Verità Sul Caso D* (1989); and Sophie Hannah's series of novels, beginning with *The Monogram Murders* (2013).

"Poirot Indulges a Whim." See "The Adventure of the Cheap Flat"

Poirot Investigates (short story collection)

By 1923, Christie was keen to end her contract with The Bodley Head, which she considered exploitative. She had been contracted to produce six books for the firm, which had published three. She submitted two manuscripts it was unlikely to accept— *Poirot Investigates* and *Vision*, a supernatural novella written many years before. The publisher rejected both, because the stories in *Poirot Investigates* had all been published in the *Sketch* (as *The Grey Cells of M. Poirot*), and the latter because it was not publishable.

Christie had by now acquired an agent, Edmund Cork, who negotiated the publication of *Poirot Investigates* in 1924, leaving Christie with just two more books to produce, including the almost-finished *The Man in the Brown Suit*. The first edition is much sought-after by collectors, partly because of the cover art—an illustration of Poirot, looking very aristocratic, by W. Smithson Broadhead, which had appeared in the *Sketch* in March 1923. Christie described this idea of Poirot as not unlike her own, and it is known that Ian Holm modeled his performance in *Murder by the Book* (1986) on the image.

The following 11 stories appear in the U.K. edition: **"The Adventure of the 'Western Star,'" "The Tragedy at Marsdon Manor," "The Adventure of the Cheap Flat," "The Mystery of Hunter's Lodge," "The Million Dollar Bond Robbery," "The Adventure of the Egyptian Tomb," "The Jewel Robbery at the 'Grand Metropolitan,'" "The Kidnapped Prime Minister," "The Disappearance of Mr. Davenheim," "The Adventure of the Italian Nobleman,"** and **"The Case of the Missing Will."** The U.S. version, published by Dodd, Mead in 1925, includes a further three stories, also taken from the *Sketch*: **"The Chocolate Box," "The Veiled Lady,"** and **"The Lost Mine"**—in the United Kingdom, these would appear five decades later in *Poirot's Early Cases*.

Poirot Knows the Murderer (booklet)

Poirot Knows the Murderer is a pulp booklet produced by Polybooks in London and New York in March 1946. It is composed of "**The Mystery of the Baghdad Chest**," "The Crime in Cabin 66" (now titled "**Problem at Sea**"), and "**Christmas Adventure**."

Poirot Lends a Hand (booklet)

Poirot Lends a Hand is a pulp booklet produced by Polybooks in London and New York in March 1946. It is composed of "**Problem at Pollensa Bay**," the Poirot version of "**The Regatta Mystery**," and "**The Veiled Lady**."

Poirot Loses a Client. See Dumb Witness

"Poirot Makes an Investment." See "The Lost Mine"

Poirot on Holiday (booklet)

Poirot on Holiday is a pulp booklet produced by Todd Publishing in London and New York in November 1943. It is composed of the Hercule Poirot version of "**The Regatta Mystery**" and "**The Crime in Cabin 66**" (now called "**Problem at Sea**").

"Poirot Puts a Finger in the Pie." See "The Adventure of the 'Western Star'"

Poirot, Yvonne

Yvonne Poirot is Hercule Poirot's younger sister, mentioned in the original (magazine) version of "The Chocolate Box" but omitted from anthologized versions.

Poirot's Early Cases (short story collection)

By 1974, Christie was no longer capable of producing a novel. Her 1973 effort, *Postern of Fate*, had been kindly reviewed but, according to her husband, the effort had almost killed her. Although it was not yet time to publish Hercule Poirot's prewritten last case, *Curtain*, William Collins collected some 18 magazine stories—most written around 1923—and published them as *Poirot's Early Cases*. These had previously been collected in U.S. anthologies: *Poirot Investigates* (1925), *The Regatta Mystery and Other Stories* (1939), *Three Blind Mice and Other Stories* (1950), *The Under Dog and Other Stories* (1951), and *Double Sin and Other Stories* (1961).

Christie may not have been happy with the finished product. Her idea of a collection was a highly unsuitable one including a confusing array of novels and stories.

Moreover, previously, she had rewritten stories for U.K. collections, sometimes updating the action as in *The Adventure of the Christmas Pudding* in 1960. However, here, the stories appeared as they had done in the U.S. editions. Other versions of "The Under Dog" and "Problem at Sea" do exist, but these are ones that were expanded for publication elsewhere. "The Affair at the Victory Ball" was certainly taken from a magazine print rather than any typescript submitted, as the text Christie submitted to the *Sketch* was heavily altered by its editors, and it is the altered version that appears here.

The cover art was a source of contention. The famously difficult Christie had become more accommodating in her old age but absolutely hated Collins's proposal to show Poirot's pinstriped legs standing over a suitcase with a label bearing his name. In the end, an uneasy compromise was reached, as the image was cropped so that Poirot would not look too tall and brightened. However, the result is strikingly generic and not particularly Christie-ish or festive (this book was 1974's "Christie for Christmas").

The volume is composed of "**The Affair at the Victory Ball**," "**The Adventure of the Clapham Cook**," "**The Cornish Mystery**," "**The Adventure of Johnnie Waverly**," "**The Double Clue**," "**The King of Clubs**," "**The Lemesurier Inheritance**," "**The Lost Mine**," "**The Plymouth Express**," "**The Chocolate Box**," "**The Submarine Plans**," "**The Third Floor Flat**," "**Double Sin**," "**The Market Basing Mystery**," "**Wasps' Nest**," "**The Veiled Lady**," "**Problem at Sea**," and "**How Does Your Garden Grow?**"

"The Poison Cup." See "The Apples of Hesperides"

Portal, Alec, and Eleanor

Alec and Eleanor Portal are husband and wife in "The Coming of Mr. Quin." Eleanor was tried and acquitted for the murder of her abusive first husband 10 years previously. In fact, he was killed by Eleanor's lover, Derek Capel, who committed suicide; Eleanor thought he did so because he suspected her. On the 10th anniversary of the event, Eleanor plans to commit suicide, but Mr. Satterthwaite's ability to provide an explanation for events saves her life.

Porter, Major

Major Porter is a tedious old man, described as typical of the species, in *Taken at the Flood*. Only Hercule Poirot listens to his extensive stories. However, when embellishing the truth has significant legal and life-or-death consequences, he cannot stand the guilt and takes his own life.

There is also a Major John Porter (D.S.O.) in "The Shadow on the Glass." A quiet, impassive man, he is horrified to find himself at a house party with his old friend Richard Scott and a married woman with whom they were both in love many years ago.

Postern of Fate (novel)

It is rare to find critical praise—or attention—for *Postern of Fate*, the last novel written by Christie. John Curran summarizes the general view, calling it "a challenge" (*Making* 397) and "a sad end to a wonderful career" (407). Nonetheless, despite the lack of plotting and readability (the book is clearly heavily edited), there is much of interest to scholars tracing themes and their development, and to biographers.

The novel has the elderly Tommy and Tuppence Beresford living in a new home, The Laurels. Tuppence finds several children's books in the house and sorts through these. Among them are her favorite titles, especially the works of Robert Louis Stevenson, and inside a copy of *The Black Arrow,* she finds a secret code. Translated, it reads: "Mary Jordan did not die naturally. It was one of us. I think I know which" (*POF* 22). Tuppence launches into an investigation, which does not interest Tommy, until their staff member Beatrice tells them that Mary Jordan once lived at The Laurels. As the couple investigates matters, they encounter British Intelligence officers, who reveal that Mary's death may have its roots in World War I. Tuppence also realizes that military operations may relate to children's toys, including a wooden horse with a hollowed-out stomach.

As the investigation progresses, a key witness, "Old Isaac" Bodlicott, is killed. Isaac is a local man who encapsulates the difficulty of their investigation: most of their evidence comes from him, and his authenticity is uncertain. He "claimed to be ninety (not generally believed)" (62) and is the font of all memories and anecdotes that may or may not be embellished: they are "flights of fancy, claimed usually as flights of memory" (62). Toward the end, Mr. Robinson solves the mystery, identifying spies and murderers, and thanks Tommy and Tuppence for their help. Instead of offering them imperial honors, he offers them a toast "in acknowledgement of the service they have rendered to their country," despite their small role. Hannibal, their dog, who has merely threatened to bite people, is made "a Count of this Realm" (254).

In many ways, the novel is a retrospective of Christie's life and career. One should remember that Tommy and Tuppence are idealized portraits of Christie and her first husband, Archie Christie, who age with happy parity. Of course, the books Tuppence spends so long devouring are Christie's own childhood favorites. Tuppence's opinions on film adaptations—"it never seems right" (18)—are likely the author's own. Similar interpretations can be applied to complaints about postmen and service people. There is a monkey puzzle—a key feature of Christie's upbringing—and Hannibal, the Beresfords' dog, is a direct portrait of Christie's own dog at the time—a positively aggressive terrier also called Hannibal, whose photograph appears on the back of the first edition in an echo of the marketing for *Dumb Witness*. Occasionally, somebody suggests that *Postern of Fate* must have been written by Max Mallowan or someone else, because it is so much less focused than anything else Christie wrote: the line "[Hannibal] only pretends he's going to … bite you" (46) could only have come from her.

Common Christie themes are covered—memory, the lie of childhood innocence, the incomprehensibility of house names that do not suit the houses, wordplay and phonetic clues, and so on—and several characters from older works return. These include Albert Batt, a steady presence in the Beresfords' stories, who has transformed over the years from a lift boy to an "experienced butler" (223); the intelligence officer Colonel Pikeaway, who has featured in *Cat Among the Pigeons* (1959) and *Passenger to Frankfurt* (1970); and most notably Mr. Robinson, the enigmatically well-connected financier who has crossed paths with all Christie's major detectives. Mr. Robinson discusses serious political matters relating to the case, and introduces, anecdotally, a key and rarely acknowledged theme of late Christie: the story of a man whose terrifying political power arose from his ability to "[blow] the fascist trumpet without calling it fascism" (112). Later, in a distillment of an ongoing theme, a would-be-dictator or cult leader is dismissed as a "Confidence Trick[ster]" (253).

A working title for this book was "Death's Caravan," which comes from the same place as *Postern of Fate*: "Gates of Damascus," a poem by James Elroy Flecker, which is also quoted in "The Gate of Baghdad" (1933). Christie's notebooks show that she used material that had previously been written for *The Secret Adversary* (1922)—namely, a conversation about house names. Although Christie would not write another novel, by the time *Postern of Fate* was published, she had made fairly detailed plans for the next one, which would have involved a *Rope*-style exploration of committing murder out of curiosity to see if it changes someone's personality. However, Christie was, by 1973, no longer capable of writing a novel. The high frequency of "Oh" at the beginning of dialogue and the repetitiveness indicate that Christie almost certainly dictated this one. It was highly edited by Mallowan and his secretary, Barbara, prior to submission to Collins, after which it was edited again. Nonetheless, the published version contains some embarrassing moments; for example, there is confusion twice about who is speaking.

The book was published in the United Kingdom by Collins and the United States by Dodd, Mead in 1973. It received a positive review in the *Observer* from the loyal Maurice Richardson and muted praise elsewhere. Reviews in the *New York Times* and the *Literary Journal*, among others, were excoriating. However, it made the bestseller lists on both sides of the Atlantic. It has never been dramatized in any form.

Characters: Andrew; Atkinson, Colonel; Barber, Miss; **Batt, Albert**; **Beatrice**; Beddingfield family; **Beresford, Betty**; **Beresford, Deborah**; **Beresford, Prudence ("Tuppence")**; **Beresford, Thomas ("Tommy")**; Bodlicott, Henry; **Bodlicott, Isaac (Old Isaac)**; Bodlicott, Mrs.; Bolland, Miss; Coates, Major; Clarence; **Collodon, Miss**; **Crispin, Angus**; Faggett, Mrs.; Griffin, Winifred; Gwenda; **Hannibal**; Janet; Jordan, Mary; **Little, Dorothy (Dotty)**; Lupton, Mrs.; **Mutton Chop**; **Mullins, Iris ("Dodo")**; Parkinson family; **Pikeaway, Colonel Ephraim**; Price-Ridley, Miss; **Robinson, Mr.**; Rosalie

See also: **Dogs**; *N or M?*; *Passenger to Frankfurt*; *The Secret Adversary*; War

"A Pot of Tea" (story; alternative title: "Publicity"). See *Partners in Crime* (story collection)

Poultny, Annie. See **Annie**

Pratt, Dorothy ("Jane")

A housemaid in "A Fruitful Sunday," Dorothy Pratt is known by her employer as "Jane" because that—her middle-name—is deemed more suitable for servants. As discussed under entries for "Edna" and "Gladys," that was a common practice in historical times, but Christie only reflects upon it in this story.

Prentice, Ann

The central figure in the Mary Westmacott novel *A Daughter's a Daughter*, Ann is a middle-aged woman who has a tense relationship with her daughter. A widow, she has fallen hard for a new, charming rogue who has just returned to England from Burma. She eventually reconciles with his daughter, after much personal drama, and is happy to see Sarah go out and pursue her own life. She resigns herself to living with Edith and in "the peace of God which passeth all understanding" (200).

Prentice, Sarah

In the Mary Westmacott novel *A Daughter's a Daughter*, Sarah is Ann Prentice's adult daughter. The two have a sometimes strained relationship with many of their anxieties and insecurities bound up in men. Sarah is bitterly resentful of her mother's new, young fiancé—in scenes that likely echo those between Christie and her own daughter, Rosalind, when she announced her engagement to the young Max Mallowan—and, after an unsuitable marriage, falls into a life of addiction and misery until she is rescued by her old love, Gerry Lloyd.

Preston, Hailey

In *The Mirror Crack'd from Side to Side*, Hailey Preston is "a willowy young man with long wavy hair," with a "tender" manner (49)—one of two apparently homosexual men. The other is Margot Bence's unnamed "pansy partner" (199) who calls Craddock "my dear" (166), revels in kitsch, and is "almost as willowy as Hailey Preston" (164–65).

Price, Lily

Lily Price is a prospective homeowner with a boyfriend called Harry in *The Mirror Crack'd from Side to Side*. In a sign of changing times, the couple is not married.

Price-Ridley, Martha

Martha Price-Ridley is a recurring background character, a villager in St. Mary Mead who lives next door to the vicarage. An inveterate gossip, she appears in *The Body in the Library*, "The Case of the Perfect Maid," and *The Murder at the Vicarage*.

Prichard, James (1970–)

The son of Mathew Prichard and only great-grandson of Agatha Christie, James Prichard has, since 2016, served as chairman and chief executive officer of Agatha Christie Ltd.

See also: **Agatha Christie Ltd.; Prichard, Mathew**

Prichard, Mathew (1943–)

The only child of Rosalind Hicks and only grandchild of Agatha Christie, Mathew Prichard ran Agatha Christie Ltd. from 2004 to 2014. He actively promotes and protects his grandmother's legacy in various media and has generally been more open than his mother to reaching new audiences with less traditional approaches to the source material. In 2012, he edited Christie's 1922 letters from the British Empire Exhibition, publishing them as *The Grand Tour*. Prichard was appointed a Commander of the British Empire (CBE) in 1994 and received the Prince of Wales Medal for Philanthropy in 2012.

Christie was extremely fond of her grandson and famously gifted him all future royalties from *The Mousetrap* when he was a boy. He believes she based the character of Michael Rogers in *Endless Night* on him.

See also: **Agatha Christie Ltd.; Christie, Colonel Archibald; Hicks, Rosalind**

Prichard, Rosalind. See **Hicks, Rosalind**

"The Princess Sings." See *The Road of Dreams* (poetry collection)

"Problem at Pollensa Bay" (story; alternative title: "Siren Business")

This story features J. Parker Pyne. It was first published in the United Kingdom in the November 1935 *Strand* that also featured Winston Churchill's article "The Truth about Hitler"—making the holiday setting particularly valuable escapism.

The brief tale offers an amusing take on English people abroad, as Pyne is on holiday in Mallorca and immediately notices all the other English people seeking out their fellow countrymen from behind the *Continental Daily Mail*, ready to make "some pleasant non-committal remark" (*PPI* 6). He is not averse to "hotel manners" (6) but fears being accosted by an English mother and unable to escape the boredom of polite conversation. He is indeed confronted by the unhappy Mrs. Chester and her "likeable" adult son Basil Chester (8). When it emerges that Pyne can "give … you the most amazing thrilling adventures" if "you've lost interest in life" (10), Mrs. Chester begs him to help prevent her son marrying the modish Betty Gregg who drinks, likes make-up, and might even wear trousers. Pyne introduces Basil to an even less desirable vamp, played by his assistant Madeleine de Sara, and his mother becomes convinced that Betty was right for Basil all along.

Christie visited Mallorca a few times, first in 1932 and reportedly enjoyed walking along the Port de Pollença, which inspired the choice of setting. In 2008, the Balearic government's Institute for Tourism Strategy and Marketing and Pollensa Council decided to use Christie's likeness in marketing materials, particularly citing "Problem at Pollensa Bay." It had failed to make the most of the living Christie during one of her visits in 1964, when dignitaries and a full band were sent to greet the 1 millionth passengers to arrive at Palma Airport: the couple standing behind Christie, who embarrassingly thought the fanfare was for her benefit.

The story appeared in the United States in the 5 September 1936 *Liberty Magazine* as "Siren Business." It was anthologized as "Problem at Pollensa Bay" in the U.S. collection *The Regatta Mystery* (1939) and later was reprinted alongside "Christmas Adventure" in a two-story volume from Todd Press (1943) and as part of the pulp trilogy *Poirot Lends a Hand* (Polybooks, 1946). It also appeared in the U.K. collection *Problem at Pollensa Bay* (1991).

Characters: Chester, Adela; Chester, Basil; **de Sara, Madeleine**; Gregg, Betty; Hans; **Parker Pyne, J.**; Stella; Wycherley, Nina

See also: *Parker Pyne Investigates; Poirot Lends a Hand*; *Problem at Pollensa Bay* (story collection)

***Problem at Pollensa Bay* (story collection; alternative title: *Problem at Pollensa Bay and Other Stories*)**

Problem at Pollensa Bay is a posthumous collection of generally early magazine stories, published in the United Kingdom in 1991 by HarperCollins. Some of the stories had already appeared in U.S. anthologies, and some would not be published in book form in the United States until *The Harlequin Tea Set* in 1997. *Problem at Pollensa Bay* includes two Parker Pyne stories: "**Problem at Pollensa Bay**" and "**The Regatta Mystery.**" Although notes in the first edition claim both started life as Poirot stories in *The Strand*, only "The Regatta Mystery" did so. There are two Poirot stories: "**The Second Gong**" and "**Yellow Iris.**" There are two Harley Quin stories: "**The Harlequin Tea Set**" and "**The Love Detectives.**" Finally, there are two standalone stories: "**Next to a Dog**" and "**Magnolia Blossom.**"

"Problem at Sea" (story; alternative titles: "Poirot and the Crime in Cabin 66"; "Crime in Cabin 66"; "The Quickness of the Hand")

A relatively late Poirot story, "Problem at Sea" is a locked-room mystery with a gimmicky twist that could easily have been developed into a novel. Hercule Poirot is on a cruise in Egypt, with a typically colorful collection of fellow passengers. An unpopular woman, Mrs. Clapperton, is murdered in her cabin while the steamer is docked at Alexandria. Poirot teams up with two enthusiastic young women to discover the killer: her husband, who faked an alibi by drawing on his skills as a ventriloquist and who believed without cause that he might marry one of the younger women. The story closes with one of Poirot's most memorable lines: "I do not approve of murder" (*PEC* 236), which Christie would expand on in *Cards on the Table*.

"Problem at Sea" is a slightly shorter version of "Poirot and the Crime in Cabin 66," which appeared in *The Strand* and various pulp booklets. This version of the story was first published in *This Week*, a magazine supplement of the [Washington, D.C.] *Sunday Star,* on 12 January 1936 and later appeared in the U.S. anthology *The Regatta Mystery and Other Stories* (1939) and in the U.K. collection *Poirot's Early Cases* (1974). It was dramatized for television in the first series of ITV's *Agatha Christie's Poirot*, broadcast on 19 February 1989. There have been two radio versions: an American one, part of Harold Huber's *Mystery of the Week* (CBS, 1946–47) and a German one, part of SWR's *Krimi-Sommer mit Hercule Poirot*, broadcast on 12 July 2006.

Characters: **Clappterton, Adeline, and John**; Cregan, Pamela (Pam) Forbes, Genera; **Henderson, Ellie**; Mooney, Kitty; **Poirot, Hercule**

See also: *Agatha Christie's Poirot; Krimi-Sommer mit Hercule Poirot; Mystery of the Week*; "**Poirot and the Crime in Cabin 66**"; Poirot, Hercule; *Poirot's Early Cases; The Regatta Mystery* (story collection); Theatricality

"Progression." See *The Road of Dreams* (poetry collection)

"Promotion in the Highest." See *Star Over Bethlehem* (story/poetry collection)

Protheroe, Anne

The glamorous, unhappy wife of Colonel Protheroe in *The Murder at the Vicarage*,

Anne Protheroe confesses to her husband's murder but withdraws her confession when her lover, Lawrence Redding, is exonerated. However, Miss Marple proves that the couple collaborated to kill the colonel, then confessed in obviously false ways so they would not be suspected. Anne successfully navigates village gossip, judging that the scandal of adultery will act as a smoke screen so that people cannot see past to the mechanics of the crime. She also judges that an elderly witness will notice her skintight dress, which cannot conceal a gun, on the day of the murder. However, her selection of Miss Marple as this witness backfires.

Protheroe, Colonel Lucius

Colonel Lucius Protheroe is the father of Lettice Protheroe and the objectionable victim in *The Murder at the Vicarage*, who makes enemies as easily as he breathes. A magistrate and patriarch, he is highly conservative and tiresome—more irritating than evil, and a fairly typical victim in Golden Age crime fiction.

Protheroe, Lettice

Lettice Protheroe is the young daughter of Colonel Protheroe and stepdaughter of Anne Protheroe in *The Murder at the Vicarage*. Tall and vague, she resents her father and stepmother. She is denied the typical romantic subplot—that goes to the vicar's wife, Griselda Clement, and Lettice's lover turns out to be the murderer who is also romancing her stepmother. Instead, her arc involves reuniting with her biological mother, Mrs. Lestrange, and taking responsibility, becoming her mother's travel companion and caregiver.

Pryce, Miss

Two very different characters share the name of Miss Pryce. The first, in "The Gate of Baghdad," is "a stern aunt with the suspicion of a beard and a thirst for Biblical knowledge" (*PPI* 129). The second, in the play version of *Appointment with Death*, is a version of Miss Price from the novel: a twee, talkative, and highly suggestible middle-aged lady. Both are traveling in Western Asia.

Pseudonyms

Known pseudonyms of Christie, nearly all used before she was published, include Daniel Miller, Mac Miller, Martin West, Mary Westmacott, Monosyllaba, Mostyn Grey, Nathaniel Miller, and Sydney West.

These names have obvious roots in Christie's extended family. West was her maternal grandmother's maiden name. Miller was her own name, and the Christian names are easily traceable as first or middle names of close relatives. Nathaniel Miller was the name of her paternal grandfather. Her mother and sister also employed pseudonyms such as Callis Miller (for Clara, her mother) and Mostyn Miller (for Madge, her sister). The latter presumably inspired the name Mostyn Grey. Only Mary Westmacott made it onto a book cover, although poetry was published as "A. M. Christie" and two books were published under the name Agatha Christie Mallowan, so she was not only published under the name by which she was best known. The names Daniel Miller and Nathaniel Miller were resurrected in some contracts with Collins, including for the heavily autobiographical Westmacott novel, *Unfinished Portrait* (1934). Christie also published one letter as Hercule Poirot in 1944.

The name Raymond West, given to Miss Marple's bestselling and highly arrogant nephew, likely has a similar derivation and may even be a private joke about the pen-name "Martin West." Christie had originally submitted *The Mysterious Affair at Styles,* her first novel, under various male pseudonyms including West, convinced that a masculine name would help her sell—but had been told that the gothic connotations of "Agatha" would do even better. She later exploited femininity to commercial ends throughout her career, presenting her books and herself as comforting domestic staples, and even poked fun at women writing under male pseudonyms in *Three Act Tragedy*, where a worldly macho playwright, Anthony Astor, turns out to be a meek diminutive woman called Muriel Wills.

See also: **Westmacott, Mary**

Psychoanalysis

Among Christie's high-profile admirers in her lifetime was Sigmund Freud, who enjoyed reading "detective stories" when bedridden: "Agatha Christie and Dorothy L. Sayers were special favourites" (Paul Roazen, qtd. in Osborne 400). Although the populist and the intellectual might seem poles apart at first glance, scholars such as Dewi Evans have compared Hercule Poirot's investigative technique to Freud's: "Freud's revelation of a conscious self whose actions are frequently at the mercy of apparently repressed impulses has, in the murder plot, its social equivalent" (n.p.). Indeed, as Susan Rowland points out, both detective fiction and psychoanalysis involve "looking for clues to previously unsolved traumas," whereas the detective and the psychoanalyst share "methodology [and] tropes of analysis, plotting and deciphering" (86).

The main aim of psychoanalysis is to discover and explain the mysteries of the unconscious mind. As a practice, it developed with its popularizer, Sigmund Freud, in the 1890s and became a much-discussed, and much misunderstood, staple of early-twentieth-century life across Europe and America. When Christie started writing in the wake of the major trauma of World War I, psychoanalysis was at its most popular. Her early crime novels reflect this fashion in casual offhand remarks: in *The Man in the Brown Suit*, for instance, the narrator's comically interfering friend who "goes in rather for psycho-analysis" tries to diagnose the criminal with "a 'fear complex'" (309): there is no other way she can understand the solution to the crime. The tone is, typically for popular fiction of the time, gently satiric about the search for meaning through medical means.

In Golden Age crime fiction, psychoanalysis is normally called "psychology" (something distinct from Poirot's and Miss Marple's understandings of "psychology," which Robert Barnard has stated amount to "folk wisdom" [45]). Psychoanalysts, typically comic figures or red herrings because they are so sinister in Christie, are generally called "psychologists" (such as Gladys Mitchell's detective Mrs. Bradley) or sometimes the more fashionable "alienists" (such as Dr. Neumann in the original version of "The Capture of Cerberus"). The plots

rarely link with psychoanalysis directly—for example, in *Sleeping Murder*, a visit to a mental specialist leaves the protagonist wondering if being mad oneself is a prerequisite for such employment, but this is simply comedy and has no direct bearing on the plot.

However, as indicated above, the techniques of Christie's detective and those of psychoanalysts have been compared. They are not, though, identical, and sometimes conclusions are in conflict. Samantha Walton points out that, in *The ABC Murders*, "Christie portrays a discord between Poirot's method and police work inflected with psychoanalytic understanding, and offers an ambivalent critique of the value of psychology in detection" (61). In this novel, the serial killer is able to evade the police because he ticks all their modern boxes for a pathological madman, and they look for clues to the killer's character rather than cold, logical clues as to who could have done it. Poirot looks for motives for specific crimes and at physical clues rather than delving into a psyche.

Christie's characters are interested in human nature and in categorizing individuals within psychological "types." Miss Marple does this with her village parallels, correctly anticipating actions and motives by comparing people she meets with those from her village of whom they remind her. Parker Pyne does it, too, with his statistical approach grounded in the idea that there are only six types of person. However, none of Christie's heroes label the categories or seek to explain them exhaustively, with the authority of science. The idea of complexes, which can be named, labeled, and fully explained, is frequently mocked.

However, this is very much an aspect of Christie's detective fiction. It is perhaps to do with the genre's interaction with the notion of truth. Her early short stories show a more open fascination with psychoanalysis. In the stories collected in *The Hound of Death*, in particular, it is frequently infused with the paranormal. For instance, the central character in "The Strange Case of Sir Arthur Carmichael," while depicted as a psychoanalyst, is described not as a doctor of the mind but as a doctor of the soul. He is called in to explain another character's inexplicable behavior, and he determines that it is the result of transfiguration, following a curse. Psychoanalysis is seen here as something supposed to unlock the inexplicable, in all its forms.

See also: *The Man in the Brown Suit* (novel); "The Mystery of Hunter's Lodge"; Poirot, Hercule; "The Strange Case of Sir Arthur Carmichael"

"Publicity." See **"A Fairy in the Flat" and "A Pot of Tea"**

"Pulcinella." See *A Masque from Italy*

Puriyaadha Pudhir. See **Indian-Language Adaptations**

Pye, Mr.
In LGBTQ⁺ scholarship, Mr. Pye is one of the most widely cited examples of a gay man in Christie. A small, effeminate man with an interest in antiques in *The Moving Finger*, he ticks many of the boxes for homosexual (or gender inversion) coding in popular culture of the 1930s and 1940s. As Anthony Slide writes, Pye "is what used to be termed euphemistically a confirmed bachelor and there seems to be little reason to doubt that Agatha Christie intended he should be regarded as a harmless gay character" (41). He is referred to by one of the investigators as a "spinster" (*TMF* 195).

The Pyramids of Giza. See **Games**

Quain, Cyril
Cyril Quain is a popular, but tedious, novelist who uses the Cavendish Secretarial Bureau in *The Clocks*. Detection Club authority Martin Edwards ("The Clocks" n.p.) has suggested that he may be based on Freeman Wills Crofts.

Queen of Crime
The title "Queen of Crime" has become, in some contexts, shorthand for Christie but surprisingly little research has been done into its origin beyond a widespread and generalized attribution to reviewer Maurice Richardson at the *Observer*. Richardson seems to have first used the term referring to "Agatha [Christie], Dorothy [L. Sayers] and Ellery [Queen]" as the "three queens of crime," with Josephine Bell a potential successor, in 1937 (Dobkins).

Ellery Queen, of course, was a pseudonym for the male cousins Frederic Dannay and Manfred B. Lee, and Richardson was joking, to an extent. In a 1956 interview ("Genteel Queen of Crime"), Nigel Dennis noted that it was already an established moniker for Christie by 1926, when *The Murder of Roger Ackroyd* was published (Dennis 92).

Although Christie is generally considered the supreme writer of detective fiction, there are widespread references to "Queens of Crime." The term tends to include Christie and contemporaries such as Margery Allingham, Dorothy L. Sayers, and Ngaio Marsh, but increasingly Gladys Mitchell and/or Josephine Tey (the latter not strictly Golden Age) are added to the set.

The idea of "Queens of Crime" reflects a common critical presumption that Golden Age crime fiction is inherently feminine. It is a traditional distinction in scholarship, "between an effete and feminized English tradition of classic crime fiction and a masculine and muscular American [hardboiled] tradition" (Gulddal, King, and Rolls, Introduction 3). Contemporary scholarship is doing much to undermine this distinction.

See also: **Golden Age Crime Fiction**

"'Queen of Crime' Is a Gentlewoman" (interview)
An interview with Marcelle Bernstein was published in the *Los Angeles Times* on Sunday, 8 March 1970, to mark the U.S. paperback publication of *Hallowe'en Party*. The two-page spread is mostly Christie in her own words, set-up with remarks from her agent, that she is "an old-fashioned gentlewoman" (Bernstein 60) and peppered with Bernstein's observations, normally to provide structure and context. Christie begins by stating that it is "embarrassing" to be famous, and for readers to feel that they know her (60). She goes on to discuss her "vitality" in old age, attributing it to a leisurely youth without formal education, and takes care to present herself as an old-fashioned Edwardian gentleman who has stumbled into success by "pure luck" (60).

Christie states that times have changed and become more violent, especially for young people. Although there is an element of noting that boys have become more violent, the remarks are generally about how unsafe boys and girls are in the modern world—something reflected in the increased number of child deaths and child criminals in her latter works. Christie suggests that "[m]urder stories are mainly done for entertainment with a dash of the old morality play behind them; you defend the innocent and pin down the guilty," thus affirming as she often would that hers was not the world of hardboiled socially relevant crime; indeed, she claims to dislike "violence" and "messy deaths" (60).

Turning to her own life, Christie talks about the influence of her grandmother and great-aunt on the development of Miss Marple and discusses her first marriage with remarkable candor: "I married at 24. We were very happy for 22 years. Then my mother died a very painful death and my husband found a young woman. Well, you can't write your fate. Your fate comes to you. But you can do what you like with the characters you create" (61). Writing crime fiction, that "old morality tale," was demonstrably not a release for Christie in the aftermath of her mother's death and her husband's infidelity; she went on to fictionalize events pseudonymously in the Mary Westmacott novel *Unfinished Portrait*, which deals with the complex emotions rather than following a tight plot. Neither Bernstein nor Christie mentions this or expands on the above confession, but Bernstein describes Christie's 1926 disappearance. Presumably, this will have caused concern among the Christie camp as she, her daughter, and her agents tended to take swift action if anyone tried to raise the event publicly.

The conversation becomes jaunty once more, as Christie describes irritating Stephen Glanville with research questions for *Death Comes as the End* and checking the positions of light switches on the Orient Express for *Murder on the Orient Express*. She compares the process of creating a character for a book to that of "auditioning an actor" (Bernstein 61). She opines that writing can be "boring"; that she is more interested in writing dialogue than "describing people or places," and that detective novels do not need to be more than 45,000 words long, despite pressure on her to produce 60,000–70,000 words (61). Nowadays, this would likely be doubled.

See also: "Genteel Queen of Crime"; "An Interview with Agatha Christie" (1970)

"The Quickness of the Hand." See **"Poirot and the Crime in Cabin 66"**

Quimper, Dr.
Physician to elderly hypochondriac Luther Crackenthorpe in *4.50 from Paddington*, Dr. Quimper proves to have murdered his wife in the heat of a midlife crisis, wanting to marry another woman. He is dismissed as a suspect early on, partly due to his social position and partly because he is a "regular old woman," incapable of violence (99). This is the inverse of the trick played by Christie in her first novel, *The Mysterious Affair at Styles* (see **Howard, Evelyn**).

Quin, Harley
This character's name alone gives a clue to his character: he is "Harlequin the Invisible," the figure from the Harlequinade. Earl F. Bargainnier describes him as "Christie's only completely omniscient detective" (92). In the 14 short stories in which he appears, he works with Mr. Satterthwaite, a shy looker-on at life. Quin, who normally appears in circumstances where some trick of the light gives the impression that he is dressed in Harlequin's motley, acts as a catalyst for Satterthwaite to realize that he sees and understands more than he knew.

"You make me see things," says Satterthwaite in "The Dead Harlequin," "things I ought to have seen all along—that I actually have seen—but without knowing I saw them" (*MMQ* 227). Quin replies that human beings tend to be "not content to just see things" but inevitably "tack the wrong interpretation on" (227). Quin is a semi-supernatural figure: his exits are more often than not into the sea or into space at the end of the story. He simply comes in at key moments and helps Satterthwaite realize his own useful role in things. Quin was one of Christie's favorite of her own creations and, after the first film in 1928, refused further permission to dramatize these stories.

Quin appears in the 12 stories collected in *The Mysterious Mr. Quin* as well as in "The Love Detectives" and "The Harlequin Tea Set."

Race, Colonel Johnny

Colonel Race is a central character in two standalone novels (*The Man in the Brown Suit* and *Sparkling Cyanide*) and two Hercule Poirot cases (*Cards on the Table* and *Death on the Nile*), and authors a letter of introduction for Poirot in *Appointment with Death*. A member of the British Secret Service, he is first introduced as a dashing potential love interest for the narrator Anne Beddingfeld in *The Man in the Brown Suit* but later becomes a more conventional part of Poirot's professional network. More down to earth and conversational than most of Christie's spies, he is a suave ex-military gentleman of independent means. Several actors have played him on screen, most notably David Niven in *Death on the Nile* (1978), but the character is often changed in or omitted from adaptations.

"Racial Musings." See *Poems*

"The Radium Thieves." See *The Big Four* (novel)

Radnor, Jacob

Jacob Radnor is a weak but charming young man who woos both the young Freda Stanton and her older aunt, Mrs. Pengelly, in "The Cornish Mystery." This is a typical ne'er-do-well, albeit one whose true nature, including his weaknesses, is hidden until the end of the story.

Radzky, Countess

The histrionic Countess Radzky is among the guests at Chimneys in *The Seven Dials Mystery* and is later revealed to be a benevolent spy for the Seven Dials organization. In reality, she is Babe St. Maur, a talented and aspiring actress from New York. She is spotted because the two women have the same mole on their necks.

Rafiel, Jason

Jason Rafiel is an extremely wealthy and cantankerous man befriended by Miss Marple while she is on vacation in *A Caribbean Mystery*. He is generally antisocial but always surrounded by attendants, and he respects Miss Marple because she has "got brains" (*ACM* 162). By the end of the novel, he has revealed, beneath the exterior, unexpected swellings of generosity, taking care of his distraught secretary, Esther Walters, to whom he is generally rude. He likens Miss Marple to Nemesis, the goddess of revenge, when she catches the murderer.

In *Nemesis*, published seven years later, Rafiel is dead, and his solicitors contact Miss Marple with news of a generous bequest and a mission. Rafiel commissions Miss Marple to clear his son's name: Michael Rafiel was falsely imprisoned for murdering a girlfriend many years ago. In his letter, Jason Rafiel reminds Miss Marple of the vision of "Nemesis," surrounded by pink knitting.

Rafiel, Michael

The late Jason Rafiel's son in *Nemesis*, Michael Rafiel is considered a black sheep and a bad lot, because of his flippant way with women, but his father is convinced that he was wrongly convicted for murder. Investigating to clear his name, Miss Marple determines that Michael's chief qualities are loyalty and kindness, things obscured by his bad-boy history, and his freedom from prison represents a second chance.

Ragg, Gordon. See **Whitfield, Lord**

"The Rajah's Emerald" (story)

This 1926 short story is now best-known for introducing a character named James Bond (not the spy). Bond, a holidaymaker, accidentally puts on the wrong trousers in a holiday villa, and discovers in their pocket a gigantic emerald. This proves to be a priceless jewel belonging to the Rajah of Maraputna, and its theft is in all the newspapers. When he returns to the scene, he is stopped by a policeman, Inspector Merrilees, who accuses him of stealing the emerald, and arrests him. As the two men head toward Bond's lodgings to recover the stone, they pass a police station, where Bond cries out that Inspector Merrilees has picked his pocket. Other policemen arrive, search the inspector, and discover the stone that Bond has hidden in the other man's pocket. Wealthy landowner Lord Edward Campion arrives and identifies the inspector as an imposter—his dishonest valet in disguise. Bond is commended for his quick thinking and enjoys a rise in social standing.

Besides its plot, "The Rajah's Emerald" is interesting for its discussion of socialism. Bond becomes an angry socialist due to disgruntlement at rude treatment by wealthy women and a "little yellow book" of political maxims. However, once he has won the favor of a kindly Lord, he decides that capitalism is the finest course.

The story was first published in *Red Magazine* on 30 July 1926 and appeared in the U.K. collection *The Listerdale Mystery* (1934) and in the U.S. anthology *The Golden Ball* (1971). It has never been dramatized, but some elements of the plot and setting were recycled for Christie's 1962 one-act play, *Afternoon at the Seaside*.

Characters: Bond, James; Campion, Lord Edward; Grace; Jones; Maraputna, Rajah of; Merrilees, Detective Inspector; Sopworth, Claud and sisters

See also: *Afternoon at the Seaside*; *The Golden Ball* (story collection); *The Listerdale Mystery* (story collection)

Ralston, Giles, and Mollie
Called Giles and Molly Davis in both versions of "Three Blind Mice," the Ralstons run Monkswell Manor as a guesthouse in *The Mousetrap*. They are a young, energetic couple struggling to make a life for themselves in the aftermath of World War II. Over the course of the play, it becomes clear that they do not really know each other at all: they married shortly after meeting and, although everything winds up happily for them, they realize that they are unaware of one another's backgrounds or even their movements on a given day.

Ramona, Dolores. See **de Sara, Madeleine**

Randolph, Myrna
Myrna Randolph is the woman with whom Rodney Scudamore is rumored to be having or to want an affair in the Mary Westmacott novel *Absent in the Spring*.

Raphion
Raphion is the name given by Alan Grierson to a malformed creature he befriends,

which turns out to be God, in "In the Cool of the Evening."

"Rare Interview with Agatha Christie." See **"Entrevista a Agatha Christie"**

Ratchett, Samuel ("Cassetti")
Potentially the most evil victim in the Christie canon, "Samuel Ratchett" is an alias for Signor Cassetti, an Italian-American gangster who masterminded the kidnap and murder of the young Daisy Armstrong. He is killed in *Murder on the Orient Express* by a makeshift international jury of 12 people affected by the previous case. Ratchett assumes that his money means he can buy anything or anyone, and one of the great evils unveiled in the novel is that he is generally right: one of his underlings has taken the fall in the Armstrong case. However, Poirot refuses to act as his bodyguard, stating simply, "I do not like your face" (*MOE* 36).

Rathbone, Dr.
In *They Came to Baghdad*, Dr. Rathbone runs the Olive Branch, a front business that claims to be pursuing world peace. It is used by Rathbone for money laundering, but there is another, more sinister purpose applied by Edward Goring.

The Rats. See ***Rule of Three***

Ravenscroft, Celia
Celia Ravenscroft is Ariadne Oliver's goddaughter, whose prospective marriage to Desmond Burton-Cox prompts a reinvestigation into her parents' deaths in *Elephants Can Remember*. She was away at boarding school when the murder-suicide occurred so is unable to provide information. She represents a sane and rational counterpart to her prospective mother-in-law, who is hung up on heredity.

Ravenscroft, General Sir Alistair, and Lady Margaret ("Molly")
Alistair and Margaret Ravenscroft are the deceased parents of Celia Ravenscroft in *Elephants Can Remember*. In an echo of a device used in *A Murder Is Announced*, Molly has died and been replaced by her mentally unstable twin sister, Dolly Jarrow, whose dangerous behavior spurred Sir Alistair to take desperate measures.

Rayburn, Harry

Harry Rayburn is the stern, handsome stranger Anne Beddingfeld longs for, finds, grows to fear, and then falls in love with in *The Man in the Brown Suit*. With a complicated backstory that amounts to a secret fortune and title, he represents the heroic love interest of mass-produced popular culture to which this novel pays parodic tribute.

"The Red House" (story; alternative title: "The First Wish"). See *Partners in Crime* (story collection)

"The Red Signal" (story)

Like *The Sittaford Mystery*, "The Red Signal" involves a warning at a séance followed by a murder. In this earlier story, however, there is a focus on psychology. Sir Alington West, an eminent alienist, attends a séance with an obviously fake medium to discreetly observe a member of the party with suspected psychological issues. After talking about subconscious secrets, Sir Alington is shot to death following the séance. His nephew, Dermot West, is the prime suspect, because Sir Alington knew that Dermot was in love with the married hostess, Claire Trent. However, it turns out that Claire's husband is insane and trying to frame her. In the end, Jack commits suicide, and Dermot plans to marry Claire.

There is much talk in this story of séances accessing the subconscious. There are also discussions of hereditary traits such as color-blindness, which would later feature in "The Harlequin Tea Set." "The Red Signal" was first published in June 1924 in the *Grand Magazine*. In 1933, it appeared in the U.K. collection *The Hound of Death*. It appeared in the United States in *The Witness for the Prosecution* in 1948. It has been dramatized for television twice. A live version appeared as part of *Suspense* on CBS on 22 January 1952. A second adaptation, part of *The Agatha Christie Hour*, aired on ITV on 2 November 1982.

Characters: Eversleigh, Violet; Johnson; Milson; Thompson, Mrs.; Trent, Claire; Trent, Jack; Verall, Inspector; West, Sir Alington; West, Dermot

See also: ***The Agatha Christie Hour***; **CBS Television Adaptation**; ***The Hound of Death*** (story collection); **Psychoanalysis**; ***The Sittaford Mystery***

The Red Signal (television adaptation). See **CBS Television Adaptations**

Redding, Lawrence

Lawrence Redding is an attractive, bohemian artist in *The Murder at the Vicarage*, who is having an affair with Anne Protheroe and a cover-affair with her stepdaughter, Lettice. Unlike, for example, Basil Blake in *The Body in the Library*, he is an example of an attractive, dangerous-seeming cad who turns out to be even worse than he seems.

Redfern, Christine, and Patrick

Christine and Patrick Redfern are the murderers in *Evil under the Sun*. They live under a false name—she is Jane Martindale, and he is Edward Corrigan. Compounding their criminality, they are probably not really married. Patrick is a charming, sexually attractive Irishman, and Christine is a faded English rose type who seems heartbroken by Patrick's dalliances with Arlena Stewart. She mentions that she used to be a teacher—in fact, she was a gym mistress and is extremely strong. They have a history of conspiring to murder women for money.

Reed, Giles, and Gwenda

Giles and Gwenda Reed are young newlyweds in *Sleeping Murder*. Giles is British and is absent for much of the novel, whereas Gwenda, who was raised in New Zealand, feels instantly at home in her new house in England. She experiences uncanny sensations around the house, as she starts to remember things about it. When she remembers a murder, she calls in Miss Marple for help. It turns out that she lived there when very young before she was sent to New Zealand, and it is repressed memories that are resurfacing. Gwenda's mission to find out what happened to her missing stepmother, Helen, is equally a mission to reclaim Helen's name from gossip and rumors. *Sleeping Murder* is about Gwenda returning home: to England, to her childhood, and to womanhood.

Reeves, Pamela

In *The Body in the Library*, the 16-year-old Pamela Reeves is lured away from school by two people claiming to be from Hollywood. They promise to transform her into a superstar overnight, like Vivien Leigh (or Clara Bow), and give her a "makeover." In fact, they are changing her appearance so that she will resemble Ruby Keene; they kill her, and her body ends up in Colonel Bantry's library. She was killed so that Mark Jefferson and Josie Turner could confuse Ruby's time of death—but her bitten finger nails help identify her.

The Regatta Mystery (short story collection)

A U.S. collection of short stories, published in 1939, *The Regatta Mystery* includes a rewritten version of "Poirot and the Regatta Mystery" featuring J. Parker Pyne ("**The Regatta Mystery**"). Other stories collected include "**The Mystery of the Baghdad Chest**," "**How Does Your Garden Grow?**," "**Problem at Pollensa Bay**," "**Yellow Iris**," "**Miss Marple Tells a Story**," "**The Dream**," "**In a Glass Darkly**," and "**Problem at Sea**." All these would be collected in subsequent U.K. volumes.

"The Regatta Mystery" (story)

This J. Parker Pyne short story may have started out as an Hercule Poirot story (see "Poirot and the Regatta Mystery"). This version, however, was published in the U.S. anthology of the same name in 1939 and appeared in the U.K. collection *Problem at Pollensa Bay* (1991). On holiday, the statistician learns that a party trick involving a priceless diamond, the Morning Star, has gone horribly wrong. He solves the mystery, however, identifying a sleight of hand by which the diamond was attached to a plate with a piece of chewing gum.

Characters: Leathern, Eve; Leathern, Samuel; Llewellyn, Evan; Marroway, Lady Pamela; Marroway, Sir George; **Parker Pyne, J.**; Pointz, Isaac; Rustington, Janet; Stein, Leo

See also: "**Poirot and the Regatta Mystery**"; *Problem at Pollensa Bay* (story collection); *The Regatta Mystery* (story collection)

"The Regent's Court Murder." See "The Adventure of the Italian Nobleman"

Reichardt, Dr.

A large, expressive German psychiatrist in *Passenger to Frankfurt*, Dr. Reichardt tells extensive stories about patients he has treated for megalomania and the belief that they are Adolf Hitler. In this, he is an equivalent character to Dr. Neumann in the 1940 version of "The Capture of Cerberus."

Reid, Major

Major Reid is a character whose affair with the protagonist's daughter Barbara Wray in the Mary Westmacott novel *Absent in the Spring* is never discussed outright, leading to repression and misery. Lascivious, off-page love interests for married women in Christie tend to be majors.

Reilly, Dr. Giles, and Sheila

The level-headed Dr. Giles Reilly in *Murder in Mesopotamia* calls in Hercule Poirot when there is a murder on a dig; Sheila is his outspoken daughter. Sheila is described as a fashionable person—with "the usual lip-sticked mouth … and a sarcastic way of talking" (27) that frustrates the no-nonsense narrator Amy Leatheran. However, men such as Bill Coleman and David Emmott see her as a woman growing into her personality.

Reilly, Mr.

In *One, Two, Buckle My Shoe*, he is a dentist working in the same practice as the late Mr. Morley. He is an angry Irish alcoholic, drawn along rather stereotypical lines. In *They Do It with Mirrors*, a potentially different dentist called Mr. Reilly appears in a village parallel; he practiced next door to dentist Leonard Wylie and took in all Wylie's patients when the latter was suspected of alcoholism.

Remember, Remember. See **Games**

Remembered Death. See *Sparkling Cyanide*

"Remembrance." See *Poems*

Renauld, Eloise, and Paul

Eloise and Paul Renauld are a married couple in *The Murder on the Links*; Paul is the murder victim, whose letter asking Hercule Poirot for help arrives after his death. A wealthy couple, they met in South America and are living under assumed names. Twenty-two years before the novel's events, Paul (real name Georges Conneau) was involved in a murder case involving a faked burglary. To stave off blackmail, he has planned to fake his own death, working with Eloise to stage a murder—although the plan goes awry, and Paul is killed. Poirot initially suspects Madame Renauld because her grief appears manufactured, but when she identifies the body (seeing for the first time that it really is Paul's), she falls apart, and he becomes convinced that she was not involved.

Renauld, Jack

Jack Renauld is Paul Renauld's son in *The Murder on the Links*, born in South Africa and experiencing both money problems and a love triangle; he is French detective Giraud's prime suspect in the murder.

Restarick, Norma

In *Third Girl*, Norma Restarick nearly consults Hercule Poirot "about a murder she might have committed" but withdraws because he is "too old" (7, 13). Aged 19 or 20, she moves in artistic circles and represents the modern young woman of the 1960s.

"The Resurrection of Amy Durrant." See "The Companion"

Revel, Virginia

The young, fun-loving widow of a diplomat in *The Secret of Chimneys*, Virginia Revel is being blackmailed over a misunderstanding but, as she is bored, finds it amusing. She ends up marrying Anthony Cade and becoming queen of a small Baltic kingdom.

Reynolds, Joyce, and Leopold

Joyce Reynolds is a 13-year-old girl who is drowned in *Hallowe'en Party* after claiming to have witnessed a murder. She is a notorious liar and self-publicist. Leopold is her younger brother, who tries to blackmail her killer and ends up drowned as well.

Rice, Frederica ("Freddie")

Nick Buckley's closest friend in *Peril at End House*, Freddie Rice is presented as a hard, self-absorbed woman, but Hercule Poirot admires her honesty, and she emerges as a complex, conflicted character. A survivor of domestic violence, she is addicted to cocaine and used by her friends—including Nick, who frames her for murder. In fact, she is the kind of well-put-together person that Nick attempts to emulate. From her clothes and her drug habit to her masculine nickname, Nick is a walking impersonation of Freddie.

Rice, Inspector

Christie created three characters with the name of Inspector Rice, all by-the-books investigators. In "The Third-Floor Flat," Inspector Rice is based in London. In "Behind the Screen," he is based in the countryside. In *The ABC Murders*, he is based in Doncaster.

Rich, Eileen

Eileen Rich is a teacher at Meadowbank School in *Cat Among the Pigeons* who is not afraid to take risks; for this reason, she is chosen to succeed Honoria Bulstrode as headmistress. This is a modern move, since she has recently taken a leave of absence due to pregnancy, although she is unmarried.

"The Rich Woman Who Wanted Only to be Happy." See "The Case of the Rich Woman"

Richards, Anne, and James

In *Death in the Clouds*, Anne Richards is the secret daughter of Madame Giselle, traveling on the plane as her maid, and the secret wife of James Richards, the latter traveling as Norman Gale. She is murdered in a taxi to prevent her claiming her inheritance and impeding his plans to marry another woman.

Ridgeway, Linnet/Kay. See Doyle, Linnet

Rival, Merlina

A self-described actress, Merlina Rival (real name Flossie Gapp) is an unsavory woman of questionable ethics in *The Clocks*. She (mis)identifies the murdered man as her husband, Harry Castleton, and is soon murdered in the London Underground to prevent her revealing who paid her to do so.

"The Road of Dreams" (poem). See *The Road of Dreams* (poetry collection)

The Road of Dreams (poetry collection)

Often referred to as a self-published pamphlet, Christie's first volume of poetry was published by Geoffrey Bles, whose publishing house was eventually bought by William Collins. This is how, 48 years later, *The*

Road of Dreams could be included in the Collins volume *Poems* (1973).

Bles established his publishing house in 1923 and published *The Road of Dreams* in January 1925. It contains a broad range of poems and ballads—many of which had music, now lost, written for them—in four sections. The bulk of these were written before Christie was a published crime writer, and some were published in magazines. The first section, "A Masque from Italy," is a lyric drama, composed of nine poems or "songs" and likely performed by Agatha Miller and her friends as teenagers (see **"A Masque from Italy"**). The second section, "Ballads," seems highly performative as well. For example, "Elizabeth of England," a poem about Queen Elizabeth I confronting her childlessness and viewing her nation as her child, is clearly an interaction between two voices.

"Dreams and Fantasies" moves from discussions of love to discussions of God and religion. Notable are the title poem, "The Road of Dreams," in which religious mysteries are presented almost like a whodunit, and "Down in the Wood," which Christie included in full in her autobiography many years later. This poem plays with words more than is usual in the volume. Christie's poetry tends to be about ideas, not language, but lines such as "Skirling and whirling, the leaves are alive! / Driven by Death in a devilish dance!" (*P* 53) demonstrate experimentation with lexis.

The final section, "Other Poems," retains the religiosity but tends to be about loss. Inevitably, World War I features, and Christie may have been inspired by William Blake in choosing how to arrange them. As with Blake's *Songs of Innocence and Experience*, she juxtaposes distinct viewpoints on common themes. For example. "World Hymn 1914" (originally, "World Hymn") (which cries, "The God of War is nigh!," 71) is paired with "Easter 1918" (which observes the "valiant passing" of the faithful, 73). One poem omitted from the 1973 reprint is "In a Dispensary," perhaps the most widely-quoted verse from the piece, which describes working with poisons and being attracted to the primary colors of toxic substances.

As well as "A Masque from Italy," *The Road of Dreams* includes the following:

Ballads—"The Ballad of the Flint," "Elizabeth of England," "The Bells of Brittany," "Dark Sheila," "Ballad of the Maytime," "The Princess Sings"

Dreams and Fantasies—"The Dream Spinners," "Down in the Wood," "The Road of Dreams," "Beatrice Passes," "Heritage," "The Wanderer," "The Dream City," "A Passing"

Other Poems—"Spring," "Young Morning," "Hymn to Ra," "A Palm Tree in Egypt" (alternative title: "A Palm Tree in the Desert"), "World Hymn, 1914" (alternative title: "World Hymn"), "Easter, 1918," "In a Dispensary," "To a Beautiful Old Lady," "Wild Roses," "Love Passes," "Progression," "There Where My Lover Lies," and "Pierrot Grows Old."

Of these, three had been published in 1919. "Dark Sheila" and "A Passing" appeared in *Poetry Today*, and "World Hymn 1914" appeared (as "World Hymn") in *The Poetry Review*.

See also: ***A Masque from Italy***; *Poems*

Roads of Memory (play)

Roads of Memory is a one-act play by W.E. Fuller (aka actor, playwright, bookseller, and broadcaster William Edwin Fuller) that was based on a short story by Christie and performed by the Hobart Repertory Theatre Society in Hobart, Tasmania, Australia, on 31 August 1932. A review of the manuscript "A Play in One Act" in the Fuller Collection at the University of Tasmania reveals that the play is based on Christie's "The Jewel Robbery at the Grand Metropolitan" (1923). It is unclear whether such an adaptation was authorized. The play was performed alongside four original pieces, with titles such as "Smith and the Devil."

See also: **"The Jewel Robbery at the Grand Metropolitan"**

Roberts, Dr. Geoffrey

A likable Harley Street physician, Geoffrey Roberts is one of four suspects in *Cards on the Table* and is revealed as the murderer. Like the other three suspects, he has been called to a bridge party by Mr. Shaitana, who is displaying his "collection" of murderers who were unpunished for their crimes to Hercule Poirot; Roberts stabs Shaitana during a bridge game to stop him from talking. Roberts is responsible for at least four deaths: he kills Mr. and Mrs. Craddock, out of lust for the latter; then Shaitana, as described; and finally Mrs. Lorrimer, who knows too much. When Poirot confronts Roberts with (manufactured) evidence, Roberts acknowledges that he "over-played [his] hand" and praises Poirot for playing the game so well (257).

Roberts, Gladys. See **Gladys**

Robinson, John

John Robinson is a soubriquet adopted by Norman Gale in a semi-comic routine in *Death in the Clouds.*

Robinson, Mr.

A monumental man of uncertain nationality and an unclear job description, Mr. Robinson operates at a high level in finance. He has worked with Hercule Poirot (*Cat Among the Pigeons*), Miss Marple (*At Bertram's Hotel*), Tommy and Tuppence Beresford (*Postern of Fate*), and in a standalone novel (*Passenger to Frankfurt*). These are all late novels, published between 1959 and 1973, although Christie's presentation of the character does shift over time. He starts off as one of many establishment shadow-faces from whom the detectives draw intelligence, but by the last novel, he is a benevolent authority figure who tidies up loose ends for the detectives and assures them that they are doing a good job. Increasingly, he is positioned as "a prominent figure in certain circles," which are never specified but are integral to "our modern world" (*CATP* 247). Robinson is a name often supplied by Christie when a character needed a pseudonym (for example, in *Partners in Crime*), Tuppence uses the name Miss Robinson; in *Death in the Clouds*, Norman Gale disguises himself as John Robinson; and in "The Adventure of the Cheap Flat," smugglers use the name Robinson for property rental.

Robson, Cornelia

Cornelia Robson is a timid poor relation to Marie Van Schuyler, who travels with her in *Death on the Nile* and *Murder on the Nile.*

She is selected by the criminals to witness a fake shooting that will give them an alibi because of her naïveté. However, despite her unworldliness, she possesses a moral backbone. Unlike Simon Doyle, she turns down the opportunity to marry for money.

Rogers, Eleanor ("Ellie")

Eleanor Rogers is the victim in *Endless Night*; she is, like Linnet Doyle in *Death on the Nile*, a young American heiress killed by her young, charming new husband for her money. A more developed character than Linnet—although both are referred to as "poor little rich girls"—she is extremely unworldly, not because of her wealth but because of her trust. All her life, she has been used by relatives, guardians, and hangers-on, and has never known real care.

Rogers, Ethel, and Thomas

In *And Then There Were None*, Thomas and Ethel Rogers are introduced as the butler and cook-housekeeper on Soldier Island. However, like the eight guests, they have only just arrived; they were hired for the purpose. The couple is present because, in the past, they allowed a wealthy employer, Jennifer Brady, to die, so they could inherit her money. Mrs. Rogers tends toward the hysterical, whereas her husband is snide and judgmental. Like everyone else on the island, they die over the course of a weekend.

Rogers, Michael ("Mike")

The young, working-class Michael Rogers is the narrator of *Endless Night*; he is intent on bettering himself, culturally and financially. Although he presents himself as the hero of the story, it transpires that he is its villain, with a record of killing several people since boyhood for material gain. He finally breaks down when he learns to feel compassion for one victim. Whereas Simon Doyle, his equivalent character in *Death on the Nile*, dies an easier death than he deserves, Mike ends up imprisoned, both literally and within his own mind, trying to tell his story.

"Romance and a Red Runabout." See "The Manhood of Edward Robinson"

Ronnie. See **Goodman, Adam**

The Rose and the Yew Tree (novel)

The fourth novel published under the name Mary Westmacott, *The Rose and the Yew Tree* was also the first under contract with Heinemann, after Collins declined it, and the last before a journalist revealed the author's true identity. It contains the most obvious clue to its author for readers unacquainted with Christie's biography, as it is set in the fictional seaside town of St. Loo—part of Cornwall with elements of Torquay—which also features in *Peril at End House* and other Christie mysteries. The title comes from Christie's favorite poet T.S. Eliot's *Four Quartets*: "The moment of the rose and the moment of the yew tree are of equal duration" (qtd. in *RYT* 2).

The Rose and the Yew Tree is narrated by Hugh Norreys, an injured man recovering at St. Loo. He has fallen in love at first sight with the beautiful Isabella Charteris but so, too, has the ugly and unpleasant John Gabriel who is irresistible to women, which Hugh cannot understand. Gabriel becomes a Member of Parliament on a Conservative party ticket, proclaiming ardent convictions but secretly admitting that he has no strong political feelings. He soon resigns his seat and runs away with Isabella. When an attempt is made on Gabriel's life, Isabella steps in front of him and takes the bullet. Her death is a Damascus moment for the worldly Gabriel, who devotes his remaining years to spiritual matters, becoming the saintly Father Clement.

As the book was written with a presumption of anonymity, it contains franker descriptions of sexuality and domestic violence as well as more forthright comments on politics than do Christie's mystery novels. It is a decidedly conservative but politically cynical novel. It received mixed reviews, with critics praising the characterization and expressing concerns about the plotting—the polar opposite of reviews for Christie's detective novels. Notably, verdicts on subsequent Westmacott books, published when the truth about Westmacott was known, would follow the crime review pattern, indicating that preconceptions about an author can spill into the review process. In 2020, a dramatization was broadcast on BBC Radio 4.

Characters: **Burt, Dr. James, and Milly**; Carslake, Captain; Carslake, Mrs.; **Charteris, Isabella**; Bigham Charteris, Mrs.; **Gabriel, Major John Merryweather;** Langley, Anne; Mordaunt, Anne; **Norreys, Hugh;** Norreys, Jennifer; Norreys, Robert; **Norreys, Teresa**; Parfitt; St. Loo, Lady; St. Loo, Lord Rupert; Tregellis, Amy; Trenchard, Anne; **Tresillian, Lady Camilla**; **Yougoubian, Catherine**

See also: BBC Radio Adaptations; War; Westmacott, Mary

Rossakoff, Countess Vera

A large, flamboyant woman whose title is a matter of some debate, Countess Vera Rossakoff is a jewel thief and involved at a low level with various criminal enterprises. She enjoys living and forcefully expresses her opinion that women should dress up and make themselves attractive. Hercule Poirot is completely enchanted with her and occasionally wonders about marrying her. A larger-than-life figure, she is described with language similar to that used of contemporary drag queens (Bernthal, *Queering* 132). The comic potential of attraction between the prim, dainty detective and the large, outrageous countess is fully exploited in the texts. It is both a parody of commercial pressures to have the detective fall in love and an overt satire on Sherlock Holmes's relationship with Irene Adler. Rossakoff appears in "The Double Clue" (a riff on "A Scandal in Bohemia") and reappears in *The Big Four* and both versions of "The Capture of Cerberus." She is also referenced in "The Mystery of the Spanish Chest" and *Curtain*. Dramatists struggle with this character, as bombastic as the Poirot of the page. In the series *Agatha Christie's Poirot,* for example, she is played on two different occasions as a demure and conventional love interest in "The Double Clue" and as a degenerate wreck of a woman in *The Labours of Hercules.*

Rouselle, Mademoiselle ("Maddie")

Before Zélie Meauhourat, Mademoiselle Rouselle was a governess or au pair for Celia Ravenscroft in *Elephants Can Remember.* The nicknames of the two au pairs—Maddie and Zellie—evoke "Mademoiselle," because they are French.

Rowe, Janet ("Nannie")

Governess to Josephine Leonides in *Crooked House*, Janet Rowe is referred to mainly as "Nannie." A homely, reassuring woman, she instantly makes the 35-year-old narrator feel "like a reassured little boy of four" (97). Not an intelligent woman, she even blames the family murder on communists, and her solution to most problems is a nice cup of cocoa.

Royde, Adrian, and Thomas

Adrian Royde is the deceased lover of Audrey Strange in *Towards Zero*. His death in a car crash may have had something to do with her ex-husband, Nevile Strange. His brother, Thomas, is a generally wordless guest at Gull's Point, who only has the use of one arm.

Rudd, Jason

Director Jason Rudd is the fifth husband of actress Marina Gregg in *The Mirror Crack'd from Side to Side*. He wants this marriage to last and protect his unworldly wife from the realities of life and from herself.

Rule of Three (play-set)

Three one-act plays were performed together as *Rule of Three* in the Duchess Theatre, London, from 20 December 1962. The plays—*The Rats*, *The Patient*, and *Afternoon at the Seaside*—are occasionally staged individually as well as together. They are standalone pieces, but designed to share a cast.

Christie's earliest notes for this project, from 1955, suggest that she was thinking about adapting three short stories, provisionally "Accident," "The Rajah's Emerald," and "S.O.S." Only "The Rajah's Emerald" seems to have inspired, in a roundabout way, one of the pieces.

Director Hubert Gregg read *The Rats* first and considered it "a good enough melodrama. Acceptable" (Gregg 144)— his version of high praise. This is a dark, explicitly homophobic piece, in which two young adulterers are cornered by the man's depraved gay admirer. It was on the basis of this that Gregg and Peter Saunders, the producer, agreed to stage *Rule of Three*.

The best-known installment is *Afternoon at the Seaside*, a light-hearted comedy about a missing emerald necklace. This was the hit of the trio, with critics praising the observational comedy. Nonetheless, Gregg insisted that it was his decision to insert some *Carry On* style slapstick routines, including one involving a bathing dress, that made it a hit. BBC television took the rare promotional step of broadcasting a performance of *Afternoon at the Seaside* on 9 February 1963.

The final act is *The Patient*, a thriller in which a paralyzed woman finds out, in the most dramatic way, who caused her injuries. In this, Christie insisted upon a device that she had first attempted in print, back in "The Affair at the Victory Ball" in 1923. It had been denied then but was allowed for the initial performances of *Rule of Three*, having been employed in the Ellery Queen stories and radio plays since the 1940s. Just before the culprit's revelation, Christie's recorded voice played out to the auditorium, giving them one minute to consider the facts and come up with a name. Later, this became a strange, short recorded poem. *The Patient* was filmed in 1982 (broadcast in 1986) for Dutch television, as *Opzet of Ongeluk*.

Characters: Brice, Jennifer; Cray, Inspector; Crum, George; Crum, Mrs.; Foley, Inspector; Forrester, David; Ginssbery, Dr.; Grey, Sandra; Gunner, Mrs.; Gunner, Percy; Hanbury, Alec; Jackson, Brenda; Lansen; Ross, Emmeline; Ross, William; Somers, Arthur; Somers, Noreen; Wheeler, Bob; Wingfield, Bryan

See also: **Gregg, Hubert**; **Homosexuality**; ***Opzet of Ongeluk***; **"The Rajah's Emerald"**; ***Rule of Three*** **(television adaptation)**

Rule of Three (television adaptation)

Rule of Three was a special broadcast on the BBC to promote *Rule of Three*, Christie's struggling set of one-act plays that had opened in the West End to mixed reviews. This broadcast presented just *Afternoon at the Seaside*, the light-hearted first act/play, performed by the London cast but with some alterations for television. It aired on 3 February 1962, three months into *Rule of Three*'s run.

See also: ***Rule of Three*** **(play-set)**

Russian Radio Adaptations

In 1966, the Soviet Union broadcast an ambitious, or-chestrally-scored version of *Murder on the Orient Express,* starring Vsevolod Yakut as Hercule Poirot and Anatoly Ktorov as Monsieur Buch. In 1988, it broadcast a version of *The Mousetrap,* starring Vera Glagoleva as Molly Ralston. *Teatr u mikrofona* (The-atre at the Microphone) is a long-running Russian radio series broadcast on Russian stations All-Union Radio and, later, Radio 1, from Moscow, until 2000. It fea-tured several multi-part adaptations of Christie nov-els, short story collections, and plays. The choice of fod-der is eclectic. Miss Marple was memorably played as an extremely worldly woman by Olga Areseva.

These include versions of the following (with the year of broadcast, if known, in parentheses): "Philo-mel Cottage" (1990), "The Witness for the Prosecu-tion" (1990), "The Gipsy" (1990), "Tape-Measure Mur-der" (1991), *The Pale Horse* (1991), "Jane in Search of a Job" (1992), "The Case of the Missing Lady" (1993), "The Blue Geranium" (1994), "The Idol House of Astarte" (1994), "A Christmas Trag-edy" (1994), "The Bloodstained Pavement" (1994), "Mr. Eastwood's Adventure" (1994), "Wireless" (1995), *Five Little Pigs* (2000), *The Body in the Library,* "The Last Séance," "The Mystery of the Blue Jar," "Murder in the Mews," "The Four Suspects," and "The House at Shiraz."

Publicity still from *Murder Most Foul* with Margaret Ruth-erford as Miss Marple and Charles Tingwell as Inspector Craddock. MGM, 1964.

Rutherford, Dame Margaret (1892–1972)

Best known for playing the eccentric Madame Arcati in the 1945 film *Blithe Spirit,* Margaret Rutherford is most notable to Christie aficionados as the first person to play Miss Marple on the silver screen. She starred in four films for MGM from 1961 to 1964, making an additional cameo in the role in *The Alphabet Murders* (1965). Ruth-erford's larger-than-life, bumbling persona was not suited to the character created by Christie, and Christie despaired of viewers who thought the screen persona was true to Christie's conception of the character.

Nonetheless, the author greatly respected Dame Margaret, as she would become, and, in 1962, Christie dedicated *The Mir-ror Crack'd from Side to Side,* which inci-dentally features moviemaking spelling tragedy, to her. Still, by 1964, she was suf-ficiently riled to include on the title page of *A Caribbean Mystery* the disclaimer that it featured "the original character as created by Agatha Christie."

Dame Margaret's family was wealthy and troubled. At the time of her birth, her father, William Rutherford Benn, was certified insane for killing her grandfather. As a girl, she believed he was dead, but she later found out that he was living at Broadmoor. The fear of becoming psychopathic haunted her and led to a serious dilemma about accepting roles in any films or plays concerning murder. Dame Margaret married Stringer Davies, who was written into the Miss Marple films as "Mr. Stringer." The couple unofficially adopted Dawn Langley Simmons, then known as Gordon Langley Hall.

See also: **MGM Films**

Ryland, Abe

Thought to be the richest man in the world, Abe Ryland is an American tycoon in *The Big Four*. Early on, he is revealed to be "Number Two" in a criminal organization intent for world domination. His enormous wealth grants the group access to enormous power.

Rymer, Amelia

Amelia Rymer is the title character in "The Case of the Rich Woman," who has more money than she knows what to do with and comes to learn the value of living humbly. Christie often claimed that her characters were based on strangers she had glimpsed and built stories around, but this one was based on a stranger who spoke to her outside a shop window.

Sad Cypress (novel)

Published in 1940, *Sad Cypress* pre-empts several stylistic changes that Christie would make in the coming decade. Among these are a prioritization of psychology that was a source of experimentation in *And Then There Were None* and further distinguished in such titles as *Five Little Pigs*, *Towards Zero*, and *The Hollow*. Although psychology can be said to be key to much of Christie's writing, the plots of these titles are directly structured around it. The novel also marks a change in the presentation of Hercule Poirot, who had previously appeared in the first chapters of his cases but does not enter *Sad Cypress* until its eighth chapter. This also became a theme of the 1940s novels, including *Five Little Pigs*, *The Hollow*, and *Taken at the Flood*. Miss Marple, too, makes a late appearance in *The Moving Finger* (1943). A third change that would

become a Christie staple is a focus on reliving a past tragedy; this is hardly surprising in the context of a world war at a time when most adults could remember another. As in *Towards Zero*, *Sparkling Cyanide*, and *Five Little Pigs* (and the later *Nemesis* and *Elephants Can Remember*, and *Sleeping Murder*), the older tragedy that is revisited has its roots even further back: in childhood and a family home.

These shifts in tone and style represent commercial awareness as well as a writer maturing. With the coming of World War II, there were questions around the sustainability of an escapist genre where evil can be neatly explained in a clever solution and everything can return to normal. Indeed, Dorothy L. Sayers had famously moved away from detective fiction with her final Lord Peter Wimsey novel, *Busman's Honeymoon* (1937), sold as "a love story with detective interruptions." Christie herself had already written a novel that might be said to exhaust and expose the limits of the Golden Age/interwar format: *And Then There Were None* (1939) in which the 10 protagonists blur the lines among victim, suspect, killer, and investigator. *Sad Cypress* is, then, an experimental novel that works well as a fairly-clued whodunit with a typically dramatic twist but also takes the format in a new psychological, emotional direction with a focus on characters and ideas formerly more prominent in the Mary Westmacott books.

A prologue shows the young Elinor Carlisle on trial for murdering the young Mary Gerrard. Part 1 covers the build-up to and immediate aftermath of Mary's death, part 2 features the investigation, and part 3 consists of Elinor's court case that is the scene for Poirot's identification of the guilty party.

Much of the plot centers on the ethereal victim, Mary, who has blossomed from an ungainly girl into a beautiful young woman and seems to have captured the affections of Laura Welman, a rich, dying woman for whom her father works as groundskeeper. After receiving an anonymous warning that Mary has designs on the family fortune, Elinor, Laura's niece, visits the family home with her cousin-cum-fiancé, Roddy

Welman. During the stay, Laura dies without making a will; Roddy announces that he does not love with Elinor and is in love with Mary; Mary's father dies, and she discovers that she is illegitimate; and, surrounded by death, she decides to leave her money to a mysterious aunt in New Zealand. Elinor fantasizes about killing Mary but maintains a pretense of hospitality. After consuming sandwiches and tea with Elinor and Nurse Jessie Hopkins, who looked after Laura, Mary dies.

Elinor is arrested for murder, under suspicion of poisoning the sandwich paste. However, Peter Lord, a family doctor who is in love with her, enlists Poirot to prove her innocence. After much investigation, Poirot determines that Jessie murdered Mary and framed Elinor: she is the mystery aunt in New Zealand, and Mary—actually Laura's illegitimate daughter—was killed for what proves to be a large inheritance. Rather than poisoning the sandwich paste, the nurse poisoned the tea that only she and the victim drank, injecting herself with apomorphine so she would vomit the poison. Poirot suspects her when he sees a mark on her wrist, and she says she caught it on a rose; however, the roses on the property are thornless. Poirot absolves Elinor, who hated Mary, of guilt, because "thinking murder [is not] the same thing as *planning* murder" (241; emphasis in original). She agrees to marry Peter.

Many wartime concerns are reflected in the text. From Poirot prising information out of a xenophobic Englishwoman by namedropping Princess Elizabeth (later Queen Elizabeth II) to Elinor's guilt over wishing death on an enemy who subsequently dies, *Sad Cypress* is grounded in the emotional introspection of Britain at war. Even the rose that provides the vital clue frequently reminds Elinor of an old conflict: the War of the Roses (102). One of the most striking examples, however, is the suspicion raised around sandwich paste. Frequently, characters express suspicion about paste—"there's a lot of poisoning with fish paste" (219)—reflecting a more general hostility to processed and preserved food that was becoming increasingly common with the rise of tinned goods in the age of wartime rationing. But no one—including the implied reader—suspects the tea, a traditional symbol of British imperialism and domestic stability. Elinor's ability to move beyond her childhood—including marriage outside of the family—reflects an ability to move on from attendant trauma. In this, Elinor serves as an interesting contrast to the heroine of the later *Taken at the Flood*, who returns from the war bored with her cousin-fiancé but, after a fling with an outsider who turns out to be a murderer, returns to him because of the comfort of the familiar.

There was some disagreement between Christie and her publishers, Collins, over the dustjacket. Christie hated the proposed cover, describing it as "awful" and "common," and pressing for a "striking" black-and-white design (Aldridge, *Poirot* 150), even doodling a cypress tree and coffin in her notebook (Curran, *Secret Notebooks* 375). Although the publishers were wary about reprinting multiple jackets in a time of paper shortage, Christie held her ground, and a minimalist blue, black, and yellow design featuring a cypress tree in silhouette was produced.

Sad Cypress was serialized in the United States in *Collier's Weekly* from 25 November 1939 to 13 April 1940. It was published by Collins in the United Kingdom and Dodd, Mead in the United States in March 1940, before being serialized in the United Kingdom in the *Daily Express* from 23 March to 13 April 1940. The first dramatization came in 1940, when Lionjel Gamlin played Poirot in extracts for the radio program *Crime Magazine*. The full novel was dramatized for BBC Radio 4 in 1992. It was filmed for television as part of *Agatha Christie's Poirot* in 2003. In 2010, a French adaptation formed part of *Les Petits Meurtres d'Agatha Christie*.

Characters: Abbot, Mr.; Attenbury, Sir Samuel; Bigland, Ted; Bishop, Mrs.; Brill, Inspector; Bulmer, Sir Edwin; **Carlisle, Elinor**; **Draper, Mary**; Garcia, Dr. Alan; Gerrard, Eliza; Gerrard, Ephraim; **Gerrard, Mary**; **Hopkins, Nurse Jessie**; Horlick; Littledale, James; **Lord, Dr. Peter**; Marsden, Chief Inspector; Marshall, Edward James; O'Brien, Nurse; **Poirot, Hercule**; Rycroft,

Sir Lewis; Seddon, Mr.; Sedley, Amelia; Slattery, Mrs.; Wargrave, Alfred; Welman, Laura; **Welman, Roderick (Roddy)**

See also: *Agatha Christie's Poirot*; *Hercule Poirot* (BBC radio series); *Les Petits Meurtres d'Agatha Christie*; Shakespeare, William; War

"The Saga of the Keeper, the Architect, and the Young Epigraphist" (poem)

The long poem "The Saga of the Keeper, the Architect, and the Young Epigraphist" was written in 1952. Like "A-Sitting on a Tell," it is a comic reflection on experiences on an archaeological dig and pastiches the style of Lewis Carroll. As with the much earlier "The Chemists and the Pharmacists," this one parodies "The Walrus and the Carpenter." The opening stanza makes the source material and general tone clear:

> The Keeper and the Architect
> Were looking at mud brick.
> They pondered how, and why, and if,
> And how much? And how thick?
> And what degrees in Centigrade
> Were best to do the trick [Mallowan 282].

The "Keeper" is Professor Cyril Gadd, keeper of the Department of Western Asiatic Antiquities at the British Museum. He was, according to Max Mallowan, so "pessimistic" that, despite the team making major discoveries in 1952, his colleagues believed from his manner that they had found nothing "of surpassing interest" (281–82). The poem has the Keeper preparing a fire to bake ancient tablets (the first step of cleaning and restoring them). However, the tablets object, "[t]urning a little pink" and insisting that they should not like to enter the fire (282), in the manner of the oysters in "The Walrus and the Carpenter." The tablets are nonetheless committed to the fire, and "the Young Epigraphist"—probably Peter Hulin—sorts through them and the cuneiform becomes legible.

The poem was not intended for publication. It appeared in *Mallowan's Memoirs* (1977) along with several of Christie's "odes" to friends.

See also: "**A-Sitting on a Tell**"; **Mallowan, Sir Max**; **Odes to Friends**

Sainsbury-Seale, Mabelle

Mabelle Sainsbury-Seale is an eccentric, middle-aged actress in *One, Two, Buckle My Shoe,* who is murdered in a particularly cruel manner. She is bludgeoned to death after remembering the bigamous Alistair Blunt's secret first marriage, but another woman impersonates her to obscure the time of death. The imposter, Gerda Blunt, is able to convince people that she is Mabelle by copying her clothes, mannerisms, and verbal eccentricities: this woman exists to people around her as no more than a collection of quirks and signifiers.

St. John, Daphne, and Gerald

Daphne St. John is a young woman who appears lost and confused; she tries to manipulate J. Parker Pyne into abetting a jewel robbery in "The Case of the Distressed Lady." She overuses the word *frightful.* "Daphne St John" is probably a pseudonym. Her husband, Gerald, may or may not be imaginary. He is significantly older than his wife and "gets so annoyed" at her "frightfully extravagant" ways (*PPI* 43).

St. Maur, Babe. See Radzky, Countess

St. Mary Mead

Miss Marple's village has become synonymous with what Colin Watson called "Mayhem Parva": that is, "a museum of nostalgia" populated by spinsters and vicars living in a long Edwardian afternoon (Watson, "Mayhem"; Watson, *Snobbery* 171). It is often evoked on television as an escapist, chocolate-box village, where the concerns of reality do not exist. However, Christie used the village to reflect social change brushing up against nostalgic worldview consistently throughout her career.

St. Mary Mead was first introduced as a village in Kent in *The Mystery of the Blue Train,* a Poirot novel, in 1928. Creating Miss Marple in the same year, in "The Tuesday Night Club," she placed her in the same village but situated it in the fictional county of Downshire in *The Murder at the Vicarage* (1930). In the second Miss Marple novel, *The Body in the Library* (1942), the location has become Radfordshire. Wherever it is, it is somewhere in the South of England (normally the South West, as it is accessible via the 4:50 from Paddington Station), near the fictional towns of Market Basing and Danemouth.

The village was never supposed to be unrealistic. In 1953, Christie wrote that the "cozy village atmosphere" was deliberate—but not for escapist reasons: "For a crime to be interesting it should occur amongst people you yourself might meet any day" (Foreword, *Moving Finger* 6). It reflected a kind of behind-the-terms pocket of Middle England very much in existence when Christie was writing. This is partly evidenced in *The Murder at the Vicarage*, when an inquest is held in the local pub (inevitably called the Blue Boar). Holding inquests in pubs or inns was common practice in the eighteenth and nineteenth centuries, because they had to be held within 48 hours of suspicious deaths, and it was difficult to find public spaces that could accommodate sufficient numbers at such short notice. By the twentieth century, with better transport and technology, this was largely moot and London stopped the practice in 1901, with most places following within a few years. St Mary Mead, then, was created as a place that is behind the times.

The prevalence of maps and diagrams in the early novels reinforces this idea that it is a real place. So, too, do recurring characters. Christie evidently mapped out key neighbors in St. Mary Mead prior to writing the first novel, and she draws on this colorful cast all the way through to *Nemesis* (1971). Some characters die over the years—not necessarily by murder, often because of old age (such as Miss Weatherby)—and some breed (Griselda Clement), while young people grow up (Leonard Clement Jr.) and old people retire (Dr. Haydock) or move (Mrs. Price-Ridley).

Although attitudes to newcomers like the arty Basil Blake in *The Body in the Library* tend to be hostile, St. Mary Mead does change. It faces modernity most notably in *The Mirror Crack'd from Side to Side* (1962), with the addition of a council estate. Miss Marple initially shares her fellow villagers' concerns about the novelty but comes to accept that "the Development" is its own self-contained world within the microcosm of the village and notes that, fundamentally, people are the same however and wherever they were raised. At the same time, as Anne Hart points out in her biography of Jane Marple, "to revisit [St. Mary Mead] in the fifties, sixties, and seventies was to find many of its inhabitants and institutions older but reassuringly unchanged" (*Miss Marple* 20–21).

See also: *The Body in the Library*; Market Basing; Mayhem Parva; *The Mirror Crack'd from Side to Side*; *The Murder at the Vicarage* (novel); *The Thirteen Problems* (story collection); Nostalgia

St. Vincent, Lawrence

Lawrence St. Vincent is an upper-class twit, next in line to the earldom of Cheriton, who becomes Tommy and Tuppence Beresford's first client in "A Fairy in the Flat"/"A Pot of Tea," and recommends them to new clients in "The Affair of the Pink Pearl" and "The Crackler."

Saintclair, Valerie

Valerie Saintclair is the stage name for the estranged daughter of the Oglanders in "The King of Clubs." Saintclair is a glamorous dancer who is due to marry Prince Paul of Maurania, whose origins are shrouded in mystery. Like many celebrities of the 1920s, she appears to have capitalized on a sense of mystery, being described as a woman who "seemed to exhale an atmosphere of romance," her elaborate clothing "invested … with an exotic flavour" by force of personality alone (84).

"The Saints of God." See *Star Over Bethlehem* (story/poetry collection)

Sampson, Mr.

Like Old Isaac in *Postern of Fate*, Mr. Sampson is considered to be the oldest person in his village—in this case, St. Mary Mead, in *The Mirror Crack'd from Side to Side*. As with Isaac, his claimed age—98—is not widely believed.

"Sanctuary" (story; alternative titles: "The Man on the Chancel Steps"; "Murder at the Vicarage")

"Sanctuary," a late Miss Marple short story, revisits the village setting as well as some characters from *A Murder Is Announced* (1950). The protagonist is Diana "Bunch" Harmon, the amiable wife of a vicar. A man collapses on the steps of Bunch's church, gasping the word *sanctuary*; something that sounds like her husband's name, Julian; and "please" (9). No one at the vicarage can explain the death or the last words, so Bunch calls in a "sweet old lady, Miss Jane Marple" (17). Miss Marple digs into family histories and exotic backstories to unravel the mystery, which is partially based on similar sounding names and words.

"Sanctuary" was serialized in *This Week*, a magazine supplement of the [Washington, D.C.] *Sunday Star* (12–19 September), under the confusing title "Murder at the Vicarage." It was published again in *Woman's Journal* the next month, where it was a last-minute replacement for *Hercule Poirot and the Greensbore Folly* (2015) to raise funds for the Westminster Abbey restoration appeal. It appeared in the U.S. anthology *Double Sin and Other Stories* (Dodd, Mead, 1961) and the U.K. anthology *Miss Marple's Final Cases* (Collins, 1979). It was dramatized for BBC Radio 4 as part of *Miss Marple's Final Cases*—the last outing for June Whitfield as Miss Marple—and broadcast on 30 September 2015.

Characters: Abel, Constable; Burt, Mrs.; **Craddock, Inspector Dermot**; Eccles, Mr.; Eccles, Mrs.; Ernie; **George**; **Gladys**; Griffiths, Dr.; **Harmon, Diana (Bunch), and Rev. Julian**; Harper; Hayes, Sergeant; Jacobs, Mrs.; Jones; **Marple, Jane**; Moss, Edwin; Mundy, Mr.; Mundy, Mrs.; St John, Jewel; St John, Walter; **Tiglath Pilesar**; **West, Joan, and Raymond**; Zobeida

See also: *Double Sin* (story collection); *Miss Marple's Final Cases* (radio series); *Miss Marple's Final Cases* (story collection); *A Murder Is Announced* (novel)

Sanders, Gladys. See **Gladys**

Santonix, Rudolf

Rudolf Santonix is a brilliant, troubled architect and friend of Mike Rogers in *Endless Night*. Suffering from an incurable disease, he resolves to live through his creations, which burst with vitality. His vision is entirely individual, not following but setting trends—because he does not have time to follow others.

Satipy

Married to Yahmose in *Death Comes as the End*, Satipy is "a tall, energetic, loud-tongued woman, handsome in a hard,

commanding kind of way" (8). Her domineering nature leads him to kill her. The use of the masculine "handsome" to describe her at the outset establishes an inversion of gender roles in the marriage.

Satterthwaite, Mr.

A looker-on at life, Mr. Satterthwaite is a shy, diminutive, elderly man who is uncertain of his place in the world. He normally appears in Harley Quin stories, where the semi-supernatural Quin appears at opportune moments to help him realize he knows more than he thinks he does. However, he also works with Hercule Poirot. Satterthwaite is a snob who has authored a pamphlet on his famous friends and their decors. He is an outsider, in the sense that he does not believe romance or emotional relationships are for him. However, as a looker-on, people talk to him and confide in him. In particular, women take him into their confidence, because, as one character puts it, "you are half a woman. You know what we feel—what we think—the queer, queer things we do" (*MMQ* 141).

Satterthwaite is, for Dennis Sanders and Len Lovallo, "like the observer-character found so often in Henry James: the man who fills the vacuum of his own empty life with an intense interest in observing the lives of others" (67). However, for some, the character is one who lacks the confidence to *find* his own place in the world; who needs to understand social codes and formulae by watching others. He is, as Sanders and Lovallo point out, "the prototypical cultured bachelor house-guest" (67) who fulfills—and sets great store by—social requirements. However, he occupies an artificial world, which he sees as performative, and his role within it is that of the outsider. He brings couples together and understands people, but he never seems to think that the stories he observes are part of him.

Satterthwaite has been read as a homosexual or queer character. It is certainly true that he has no business falling in love with women. Like Hercule Poirot, he admires beauty, but he does so for purely artistic reasons. For example, in "The Face of Helen," a beautiful woman makes him breathless:

There were, he knew, such faces in the world—faces that made history. ... Beauty! ... There is such a thing.... The shape of a face, the line of an eyebrow, the curve of a jaw. He quoted softly under his breath: "*The face that launched a thousand ships.*" [*MMQ* 187; emphasis in original]

In the first "queer" reading of Christie, published in 2009, Dennis Altman argued that

Sattherwaite [sic] cries out for a queer reading: what is [one] to make of a man who "is an admirer of Kew Gardens and was once in love in his youth," gave "definitely 'queer' parties" and "had a large share of femininity"[?] [n.p.]

In fact, the second of these quotes is a remark made about Mr. Shaitana in *Cards on the Table*, which explains Altman's otherwise puzzling next statement that "Sattherwaite [sic] is killed off in 1936 ... meeting the fate of almost all homosexual characters of his era" (n.p.). The analysis is an example of lazy stereotyping that has traditionally pervaded crime fiction scholarship and the urge to make Christie fit a certain thesis about social conservatism. In fact, the sensitivity with which Satterthwaite's otherness is handled certainly warrants further scholarship.

He appears in the stories collected in *The Mysterious Mr. Quin* as well as "The Harlequin Tea Set," "The Love Detectives," "Dead Man's Mirror," and *Three Act Tragedy*.

Saunders, Sir Peter (1911–2003)

Theatrical producer Peter Saunders was, for more than half his life, best known for producing and promoting *The Mousetrap* from its first production in 1952 until his retirement in 1993. World War II interrupted a career in moviemaking, and Saunders started producing for the theater in 1947, following military service. He first worked with Christie on *Murder at the Vicarage* (1949), producing nearly every title of hers for the West End and some tours subsequently. Few would deny that *The Mousetrap* owed its success, before that success became self-fulfilling, at least in part to Saunders's insistent and imaginative publicity efforts. So associated with the production did he become that his 1972 autobiography was titled *The*

Mousetrap Man, and Christie contributed an introduction.

See also: **Gregg, Hubert**; *The Mousetrap* **(play)**

Savaranoff, Dmitri

A world-famous Russian chess master, Dmitri Savaranoff has become a recluse but steps out of retirement to play against Gilmour Wilson in *The Big Four*. After Wilson dies during the match, Hercule Poirot investigates and determines that Savaranoff is, in fact, master criminal Claud Darrell (aka "Number Four") in disguise.

Savernake, Henrietta

Henrietta Savernake is a modernist sculptor in *The Hollow* who is working on a new piece, "The Worshipper," taking as inspiration the wife of her lover, John Christow, who murders him in a fit of passion. Henrietta is a bright and capable young woman, but she tunes out of conversations to think about her work and its Greek archetypal origins. Christie, of course, has often been criticized for using stereotypes or archetypes in her fiction, and the presence of a creative modernist who draws on archetypes goes some way toward challenging distinctions between high and low art.

Sayers, Maggie. See **de Sara, Madeleine**

Scheele, Ana

Secretary to Otto Morganthal in *They Came to Baghdad*, Ana Scheele is a hardworking woman who is very good at covering her tracks. She seems to be trailing people during the novel and is presented as a suspicious, almost sinister presence—although she is on the side of good, working to undermine extensive political agitation. She and Victoria Jones resemble one another, despite their very different personalities.

Scherz, Rudi

Rudi Scherz is a Swiss waiter and small-time con artist who is killed in *A Murder Is Announced* after recognizing Charlotte Blacklock. In some ways, this character is typical of working-class victims in Christie's work, in that he is conned into participating in an elaborate murder scheme with the promise of easy money.

The Scoop **(computer game).** See **Games**

"The Scoop" (novella)

Following the success of "Behind the Screen," the BBC requested a second round-robin murder mystery from members of the Detection Club for broadcast in 1931. This time, the lineup was slightly different, including Dorothy L. Sayers, Agatha Christie, E.C. Bentley, Anthony Berkeley (Cox), Freeman Wills Crofts, and Clemence Dane—six very different types of crime writer. Each contributed two chapters, once again reading them on the airwaves, and the text of their contributions was published weekly in *The Listener* to accompany the broadcasts. Christie's contributions to "The Scoop" were chapter 2 ("At the Inquest") and chapter 4 ("The Weapon").

The project was coordinated by Sayers, who wrote the opening and closing chapters. The authors sketched the plot out together, then shared sketch-outlines of their own chapters before writing individually as the series progressed. This was a change in approach from that employed for *Behind the Screen*, and a different approach again would be taken for *The Floating Admiral*. It was not entirely successful: in Sayers's opening chapter, she sets up journalist Mr. Oliver as a kind of everyman protagonist, but other contributors tired of him, and he disappears halfway through the novella, only to reappear in Sayers's closing chapter.

For inspiration, the authors drew on a real criminal case. Two infamous "Crumbles murders" took place within four years on a shingle beach near Eastbourne, known as the Crumbles. The latter of these, in 1924, was that of 38-year-old typist Emily Kaye by notorious womanizer Patrick Mahon, who tried to hide her bloody effects in railway luggage. It has inspired several books and television productions in subsequent years. With surprising levity, *The Scoop* refers to "the Jumbles case"—the Jumbles being the (fictional) site of a cottage in Sussex.

Nerves meant that Christie read her installments too quickly, and she would only make one more extended live broadcast on the BBC, reading "Miss Marple Tells a Story" in 1934. It is nonetheless interesting to imagine Christie grappling with a cockney accent and conveying Gladys Sharp's "vulgar wink" (*SBS* 23). Chapter 2 has Christie in her comfort zone, describing an inquest and introducing characters with brief, biting strokes, whereas chapter 4 is not written with any élan. "The ungloved murderer," the hero announces, "is becoming as extinct as the dodo" (46)—the first of many clichés that pepper that chapter.

Following the broadcast and publication from January to April 1931, "The Scoop" was dormant until it was published in book form, alongside "Behind the Screen," in 1983. It has inspired a computer game by Telarium, released for Apple II in 1986 and MS-DOS in 1989.

Characters introduced by Agatha Christie: **Araby, Mr.**; Catsby, Mrs.; Evans, Mary; Maria; **Sharp, Gladys**

Other characters: Blackwood, Beryl; Bradford, Chief Inspector; Hemingway, Mr.; Hemingway, Mrs.; Johnson; Kent, Mrs.; Mainwaring, Amethyst; Oates, Inspector C.F.S.; Oliver, Mr.; Potts, Arthur; Potts, Geraldine; Redman; Smallpiece, Mr.; Timmins, Irene; Tracey, Geraldine; Vaughn Fisher, Henry

See also: **"Behind the Screen"; The Detection Club; *The Floating Admiral*; Games.**

The Scoop (VHS game). See **Games**

Scudamore, Joan

The Mary Westmacott novel *Absent in the Spring* is told from Joan Scudamore's perspective. An outwardly successful, prim and proper middle-aged woman, she realizes when stranded that her life is not perfect because of her emotional distance from those she loves. Wife of Rodney Scudamore, she is mother to Tony Scudamore, Barbara Wray, and Averil.

Scudamore, Rodney

In the Mary Westmacott novel *Absent in the Spring*, Joan Scudamore's husband is a quiet, hen-pecked man. His wife has browbeaten him into a distinguished legal career instead of letting him pursue his passion for farming and simple living.

"The Sculptor." See *Poems*

"The Second Gong" (story)

Christie was winding down Hercule Poirot short stories when she wrote "The

Second Gong." It was published in *Ladies' Home Journal* in June 1932 and *The Strand* in July 1932 before it was expanded and reimagined into "Dead Man's Mirror."

Wealthy eccentric Hubert Lytcham-Roche calls Poirot to his stately home, Lytcham Close, to investigate suspected fraud. When Poirot arrives, he learns that Hubert is uncharacteristically late to dinner and finds him dead, apparently of suicide, in a locked room. The resultant plot and the trick by which the murder was committed (here indicated in the title) are identical to those in "Dead Man's Mirror," although the murderer's identity and role in the story are different.

Despite the appearance of "Dead Man's Mirror" in the volume of that name in 1937, "The Second Gong" was anthologized in the United States in *Witness for the Prosecution* (1948). It would not appear in a U.K. collection until *Problem at Pollensa Bay* (1991).

Characters: Ashby, Joan; Barling, Gregory ("Greg"); Cleves, Diana; Dalehouse, Harry; Digby; Keene, Geoffrey; Lytcham-Roche, Hubert; Lytcham-Roche, Mrs.; Marshall, Captain John; **Poirot, Hercule**; Reeves, Inspector

See also: **"Dead Man's Mirror" (novella)**; ***Problem at Pollensa Bay* (story collection)**; ***The Witness for the Prosecution* (story collection)**

The Secret Adversary (novel)

Early working titles for *The Secret Adversary* were *The Joyful Venture* and *The Young Adventurers*. The general version of how Christie came to write it stems from her autobiography, and—despite the heavy role of politics in the novel—is distinctly apolitical. The story goes that Christie wrote it, buoyed more by a contract with The Bodley Head than the early commercial success of *The Mysterious Affair at Styles*, to help with the costs of maintaining her family home, Ashfield. Struggling to find inspiration, she visited a café and overheard a conversation about a woman called Jane Fish. The name sounded so funny and therefore memorable that she ran with the idea and ended up writing about a similar conversation, out of which spun an adventure story.

The account is disingenuous, as the novel is steeped in the political mood of the immediate post–World War I period. A prologue details the sinking of the RMS *Lusitania* in 1915, where a British agent, expecting to drown, entrusts a young American woman with diplomatic secrets. The rest of the action takes place in the early 1920s. A chance encounter brings together young friends Thomas Beresford ("Tommy") and Prudence Cowley ("Tuppence"), who have not seen each other since the war. Struggling to make ends meet, they agree to advertise themselves as "young adventurers for hire" (22). As part of light conversation, Tommy describes a chat he overheard about a woman called Jane Finn, remembering the unusual name. When Tuppence is approached by a shifty-looking Mr. Whittington, she gives a false name, improvising "Jane Finn." The man is astonished and thinks she has secret knowledge. He gives her £50 and disappears without a trace. After stumbling upon a mystery, Tommy and Tuppence advertise in the *Times* for anyone with knowledge of Jane.

They are approached by three people, including Jane's wealthy American cousin, Julius P. Hersheimmer, who wants to know where she is, and a representative of the British intelligence agency, who tasks them with uncovering an international Bolshevik conspiracy that is also looking for Jane, the girl on the *Lusitania*. Tommy and Tuppence set off in search of the conspiracy and its leader, an elusive figure known only as "Mr. Brown." After several adventures in a variety of exotic and squalid locations, they discover that Mr. Brown is in fact Sir James Peel Edgerton, a leading barrister and Member of Parliament who seems to be on the path to become a future (Conservative) prime minister. His motivation is absolute power. He eventually confesses a desire to be "[a]n autocrat! A dictator! And such power could only be obtained by working outside the law" (305). The egos of individuals transcend the strengths or weaknesses of given political doctrines. The novel ends with Tommy and Tuppence agreeing to set up a detective agency for "fun" and to pursue the greater adventure of marriage (312).

As the first of the largely-neglected Tommy and Tuppence series, *The Secret*

Adversary has received only limited critical attention. Biographers talk about it chiefly as an early indication that Christie did not wish to be yoked to the character of Hercule Poirot (this was her second novel). It is not uncommon for biographers to point out that Tommy and Tuppence form here—and arguably in later texts—an idealized portrait of Agatha and Archie Christie, a partnership of equals who go on to age collegially throughout the next four books. The novel's political overtones have been covered in some depth. Danny Nicol has identified "a startling degree of anti-Labour [Party] bias" in the novel, claiming that Christie presents left-wing activism the product of "misunderstandings" from foolish working-class people who "are being manipulated" and are "mere pawns" in one man's grab for power (3). It is true that the novel never really questions the idea that a left-wing political landscape would be bad for the country's economy, whereas there is never any question of sharing the fabulous wealth that belongs to a very few mostly positive characters. Mr. Carter, the paternal representative of British intelligence, insists that "[a] Labour Government at this juncture would ... be a grave disability for British trade" (*TSA* 49).

The book was written within a few years of World War I, when several European countries were pivoting to the left, and Britain, although staunchly conservative, was also seeing some change, including the establishment of the Communist Party of Great Britain in 1920. Bill Peschel points out that the threat to British security is not specific but "a rogue's gallery" of German nationalism, Russian communism Irish separatism, and petty criminals (373–74). Peschel sees this as a paranoid but of-its-time idea of threats to Britishness, although it could also be understood as a less developed version of something Christie achieves much more successfully in *They Came to Baghdad* (1953) and *Destination Unknown* (1954), where communists and fascists find out they are working for the same people: political movements in Christie are never, at their roots, about political convictions but about the success and power of a few bad men. Gillian Gill points out that politics informs the mechanics of the plot in *The Secret Adversary*:

> Christie relies on the fact that, at least for her own generation of readers, an outstanding member of the Tory establishment, a Member of Parliament and King's Counsel, a man touted as the next Prime Minister, is one person who will never be suspected of being a criminal mastermind [172].

For Gill, this serves as both clever structuring and a cynicism about established politics; a "congenital ... suspicio[n] of all political structures and arguments" (172).

Early reviews tended to praise the novel as a "jaunty" thriller that ticked all the conventional boxes (Sanders and Lovallo 13), but later critical responses judge it against the standard and tone of a 55-year career marked by whodunits: Charles Osborne in 1981 called it "good clean reactionary fun" (22), whereas Robert Barnard in 1980 called it "[t]he first and best (no extravagant complement this) of the Tommy and Tuppence stories," also describing it as "[g]ood reactionary fun" (195). There are elements here of sheer disappointment that this is not a classical whodunit but a thriller with whodunit elements. Notwithstanding a brief appearance from Inspector Japp, who also is featured in *Styles*, the novel is strikingly dissimilar to its predecessor. There is also the unavoidable fact that these responses were written in a decade marked by the normalization of right-wing establishment politics in both the United Kingdom and the United States; the idea highlighted by Gill that a bastion of the establishment could pull the strings on left-wing agitations for personal gain would not have been popular. Notably, screen adaptations have all played down this aspect of the text, instead presenting personal corruption as an isolated phenomenon that is unique to the corrupt individuals.

The Secret Adversary was published in the United Kingdom by The Bodley Head and in the United States by Dodd, Mead, in 1922. It has been adapted into multiple formats. A 1929 German silent film, *Die Abenteurer GmbH* (Adventures Inc.), was the first Christie screen adaptation. A more nostalgic screen adaptation for London Weekend

Television, broadcast on ITV on 9 October 1983, launched the television series *Partners in Crime* starring Francesca Annis and James Warwick. There was a French graphic novel by François Rivière, *Mister Brown*, illustrated by Frank Leclercq, in 2003, later translated into English as *The Secret Adversary* in 2008. A campy stage version by Johan Hari and Sara Punshon premiered on a British tour in 2015, and the same year, the BBC launched its doomed series *Partners in Crime*, starring Jessica Raine and David Walliams, with a three-part adaptation of *The Secret Adversary*. In the United States, where the text is out of copyright, school drama departments have been known to dramatize the text. A notable youth theater version is a 2016 effort from David Hansen, which largely transposes the text to the stage.

Characters: Adams, Dr.; Annette; **Annie**; **Batt, Albert**; Beresford, Sir William; **Beresford, Thomas ("Tommy")**; Bond, Sister; **Carter, Mr.**; Clymes; Colombier, Madame; Cowley, Archdeacon; **Cowley, Prudence ("Tuppence")**; Danvers; Dufferin, Miss; Edith; Felix; Finn, Amos; **Finn, Jane**; Flossie; Greenbank, Sister; Grieber, Ivan; Hall, Dr.; Hersheimmer, Hiram; **Hersheimmer, Julius P.**; Ivanovich, Boris; **Japp, Inspector James**; Keith, Edgar; Keith, Eleanor; Kramenin; Lewis, Mabel; **Peel Edgerton, Sir James**; Potter, Mr.; Roylance, Dr.; Rysdale, Peter; Sadie, Marjorie; Stepanov, Count; Sweeney, Mrs.; **Vandemeyer, Marguerite ("Rita")**; Westhaven, Sister; Westway; **Whittington, Edward**

See also: *Abentuerer GmbH, Die*; *Partners in Crime* (1983 television series); *Partners in Crime* (2015 television series); *The Secret Adversary* (play); War

The Secret Adversary (play)

In 2015, a plethora of new Christie products appeared as part of a major rebranding move for the 125th anniversary of the author's birth. Among these was a new play by Sarah Punshon and Johan Hari, two media commentators who are notably less conservative than the traditional voices of Christie in the media. This two-hour version of the early novel *The Secret Adversary* toured the United Kingdom from March to May. A play for seven and later eight actors, it takes much of its inspiration from Patrick Barlow's wildly successful 2005 dramatization of John Buchan's *The Thirty-Nine Steps* and, like its predecessor, mines the basic premise of the plot for physical and situational comedy.

Advertising itself as "nifty, old-fashioned fun," the production by the Watermill Theatre in association with Eleanor Lloyd Productions featured minimal sets and musical numbers. It was directed by coauthor Sarah Punshon and starred Garmon Rhys as Tommy and Emerald O'Hanrahan as Tuppence.

See also: **Beresford, Prudence ("Tuppence")**; **Beresford, Thomas ("Tommy")**; *The Secret Adversary* (novel)

The Secret of Chimneys (novel)

Christie's 1925 novel *The Secret of Chimneys* was her last for The Bodley Head. A light-hearted thriller with an espionage backdrop, it is set in a country house, Chimneys, and features an array of characters who might have come from the pages of P.G. Wodehouse. Many of these, like the setting, would return in *The Seven Dials Mystery* (1929), and Superintendent Battle, introduced here, would become a regular character.

The novel features a group of communist agitators called "the Red Hand." The name seems to come from the Black Hand, a Serbian secret military society, founded in 1901 with the aim of overturning various regimes to unite Serbian territories. It has often been credited with helping bring about World War I. Likewise, real-life hotels appear thinly veiled to comic effect. For example, characters meet at Harridge's (Claridge's) and the Blitz (the Ritz).

A century on, *The Secret of Chimneys* is arguably Christie's most dated novel. It contains casual racism—"God in heaven!" cries one character. "He has married a black woman in Africa!" (294)—and paints a surprisingly uncritical picture of eugenics as a topic of interest for the well-bred. The Balkan kingdom of Hezoslovakia (which in later books becomes Herzoslovenia) is very clearly based on Russia, which had lost its monarchy to a communist uprising in

1918. The Obolovitch dynasty is, transparently, the Romanov dynasty, and the slain king of the novel (Nicholas IV) is obviously the slain tsar of real life (Nicholas II). The solution, in which the slightly left-wing Anthony Cade decides to embrace his new role as an absolute monarch over people in which he has no interest, is extremely of its time.

Christie adapted the novel into a play, *Chimneys* (now called *The Secret of Chimneys*), which was likely performed in the 1940s, but there is no full account of a performance before 2003. A graphic novel by François Rivière was released in France in 2002 and translated into English in 2007. The novel has been generally ignored by dramatists but was the very loose inspiration for an episode of *Agatha Christie's Marple* in 2010.

Characters: Anchokoff, Boris; Andrassy, Captain; Badgworthy, Inspector; **Battle, Superintendent**; **Brent, Lady Eileen ("Bundle")**; **Brent, Sir Clement**; **Brun, Genevieve**; **Cade, Anthony (Gentleman Joe)**; Cartwright, Dr.; Dutch Pedro; Edgbaston, Lord; **Eversleigh, William ("Bill")**; Fish, Hiram P.; Isaacstein, Herman ("Fat Ikey"); Johnson, Constable; **King Victor**; **Lemoine, Inspector**; Lolopretjzyl, Baron; **Lomax, Hon. George ("Codders")**; Manuelli, Guiseppi; McGrath, James ("Jimmy"); **Melrose, Colonel**; **Mory, Angèle**; Obolovich, Prince Michael; **Obolovich, Prince Nicholas**; Revel, Hon. Timothy; **Revel, Virginia**; Stylptitch, Count; Taylor, Miss; **Tredwell**; **Varaga, Queen**; Wynwood, Professor

See also: *Agatha Christie's Marple*; Herzoslovakia; Market Basing; *The Seven Dials Mystery*; *The Secret of Chimneys* (play)

The Secret of Chimneys (play; alternative title: *Chimneys*)

The play *Chimneys* has been published and licensed by Samuel French, Ltd as *The Secret of Chimneys*, although it was written and first performed under the former title. The play was written around 1928, and the consensus among archivists and theatrical scholars is that it was never performed until it was "rediscovered" and staged in Calgary, Canada in October 2003. In fact, archival correspondence between Christie and her agent, Edmund Cork, indicates that it was at least tried out in the 1940s with talk of a production, which never occurred, in the early 1950s.

The play is a fairly straightforward and rather dull adaptation of the 1925 comedy thriller *The Secret of Chimneys*. For the most part, Christie has picked out dramatic moments from the novel and summarized other action in long explanative dialogue. The play keeps the novel's light comic tone with some new dialogue along the same lines thrown in ("It's just as exciting," Virginia remarks, "to buy a new experience as it is to buy an evening frock" [*SOC-P*, 31]), whereas some of the jokes, for instance about the "foreign baron" and his "unpronounceable name" (18), are lost without the written word. It can most charitably be considered a failed experiment in self-adaptation. Certainly, it precedes Christie's strongest work dramatizing her own novels and short stories by at least a decade.

The play includes two sets and 14 characters, although only 13 appeared in the first production.

Characters: Andrassy, Boris; Banks, Herman; **Battle, Superintendent**; **Brent, Lady Eileen ("Bundle")**; **Cade, Anthony**; **Caterham, Marquis of**; **Eversleigh, William ("Bill")**; **Lemoine, Inspector**; **Lomax, Hon. George ("Codders")**; **Revel, Virginia**; **Tredwell**; **X, Monsieur**.

See also: *The Secret of Chimneys* (novel)

Sedgwick, Lady Bess

An extremely high-living adventuress in *At Bertram's Hotel*, Lady Bess Sedgwick turns out to be involved in large-scale criminal activity, apparently taking part for the pleasure of living on the edge. Toward the end of the novel, she surprises many observers by displaying a conscience, confessing to murder and committing suicide, so that her daughter, the real killer, can escape punishment. Coming after a difficult relationship between the two women, this demonstrates the unorthodox strength of the mother-daughter bond.

Serrocold, Carrie Louise

The elderly matriarch of Stoneygates and

younger sister to Ruth van Rydock in *They Do It with Mirrors*, Carrie Louise Serrocold is generally viewed as an unworldly, naïve figure who "sees no evil, hears no evil, and speaks no evil" (103). Neither her extended family nor the police listen to her when she says she cannot believe anyone would want to kill her, but Miss Marple does—and determines that Carrie Louise is in fact the only person who sees things as they really are. Her unworldliness is in fact a disconnect from the performativity of everyday life: she sees straight to the truth.

The one point of continuity in Stoneygates, which houses a mishmashed, multigenerational family from various bloodlines and a modern reformatory, Carrie Louise is different things to different people. This is reflected in the fact different characters call her different things: "Carrie Louise," "Grandam," "Caroline," or "Mrs. Serrocold" (57).

Serrocold, Lewis

In *They Do It with Mirrors*, Lewis Serrocold is Carrie Louise's third husband and the father to Edgar Lawson, "who always put causes before people" (32).

"The Servant Problem." See "The Case of the Perfect Maid"

Seton, Edward

Edward Seton is a charming murderer, convicted and executed after Justice Sir Laurence Wargrave summed up against him in the past in *And Then There Were None*. According to rumor, Seton was innocent, and Wargrave had a vendetta against him. However, he really was guilty, according to evidence that could not be admitted in court, and Wargrave could see that he was making a favorable impression on the jury. Seton's guilt proves that Wargrave was, unlike everyone else on the island, not responsible for an innocent person's death. Paradoxically, this proves that he must be the murderer, exacting revenge on his fellow guests, as the only person without a real reason to be there.

The Seven Dials Mystery (novel)

With a setting and supporting cast that had previously appeared in *The Secret of Chimneys* four years earlier, *The Seven Dials Mystery* is as close as Christie came to a sequel. As in the previous book, the action takes place in the country estate of Chimneys, where Bright Young Things become embroiled in an international conspiracy and Wodehouse-like personal drama, which intersect. It was Christie's first substantial novel written after her 1926 disappearance—although *The Big Four* and *The Mystery of the Blue Train*, both largely planned before the upheavals and written without enthusiasm and with help, had also been published in the interim. It represents a return to the lighthearted frivolity of the country-house thriller. Christie famously enjoyed writing thrillers because they were easier than mysteries and required less plotting. When writing in 1928–29, she also had just completed *Chimneys*, the play adaptation of the former novel, so its characters and details were fresh in her mind. Of course, *The Seven Dials Mystery* is as much a whodunit as it is a conspiracy thriller and a comedy of manners.

A group of young house guests at Chimneys decides to play a joke on Gerry Wade, who always oversleeps. They place a set of alarm clocks around his bed to go off at regular intervals. When he does not emerge, even after the alarms have sounded, the butler Tredwell investigates and finds Wade dead. Before long, somebody has changed the clocks so that Wade is surrounded by seven. Shortly afterward, Lady Eileen "Bundle" Brent is driving recklessly when she finds a young man dying from a gunshot wound. He gasps some last words about "Seven Dials" and "Jimmy Thesiger." Thesiger is one of Bundle's houseguests, who was involved with the alarm-clock joke. She teams up with him to investigate the sinister Seven Dials.

The Seven Dials Club in Soho is a real place now—a jazz bar—but in Christie's day, it was a fictional location, based on various fashionably sordid nightclubs such as the 43 Club on Gerrard Street. The owner of that club was jailed for five years after several scandalous parties involving London's upper set in the 1920s. In the novel, the Seven Dials is headquarters to a secret society with seven members, all of whom are known by a number. In a set-up reminiscent of events in *The Secret Adversary*, Bundle spies on them and learns that they have plans involving a secret formula and a coming weekend at Chimneys. There follows a dramatic nighttime sequence at Chimneys, in which Thesiger is shot at and the formula is recovered by Superintendent Battle, who also appeared in the previous book and who seems oddly set on discouraging Bundle from interfering with the Seven Dials. The novel closes with an equally dramatic showdown among Bundle; Thesiger; and "Number Seven," the mysterious leader of the Seven Dials, who turns out to be Battle. In the end, it transpires that the Seven Dials is an organization for law and order, preventing criminal activities with undercover civilians. Thesiger was, in fact, that villain all along. Bundle and her love interest, Bill Eversleigh, agree to marry, and Bundle is admitted into the Seven Dials, of which Bill is already a member.

This would be Christie's last jaunty thriller for some years. The transparency of the genre formula—especially similarities to *The Secret Adversary*—and the increased presence of clues and tricks—including one that would be recycled in *Death on the Nile*—show Christie's increased comfort writing full murder mysteries and that light-hearted thrillers had for now served their term. Despite evidence of exhausting a theme, the book was a fresh enough return to form to top sales of *The Mystery of the Blue Train* with an initial U.K. print run exceeding 8,000. An LWT television adaptation aired on ITV on 8 March 1981.

Characters: Alfred; Andras, Count; Bateman, Rupert; **Battle, Superintendent; Brent, Lady Eileen ("Bundle"); Brent, Sir Clement**; Brent, Lady Marcia; Cassell, Dr.; Coote, Lady Maria; Coote, Sir Oswald; Daventry, Vera ("Socks"); Devereux, Ronald ("Ronny"); Digby, Sir Stanley; Eberhard, Herr; **Eversleigh, William ("Bill")**; Howell, Mrs.; **Lomax, Hon. George ("Codders"); Macatta, Mrs.; Melrose, Colonel**; Mosgorovsky, Mr.; Murgatroyd, Mr.; Phelps, Hayward; **Radzky, Countess; St. Maur, Babe**; St. Maur, Gerald; Stevens; Stevens, Mrs.; **Thesiger; James (Jimmy); Tredwell**; Wade, Gerald ("Gerry"); Wade, Lorraine

See also: **Bright Young Things; Market** Basing; *The Secret of Chimneys* (novel); **LWT Adaptations**

The Seven Dials Mystery (television adaptation). See **LWT Adaptations**

Shaista, Princess

The cousin of the late Prince Ali Yusuf of Ramat, Princess Shaista is a pupil at Meadowbank School in *Cat Among the Pigeons* and has a highly superior manner. However, Hercule Poirot notices that she is much older than she claims and is really an imposter: the actual Shaista has been kidnapped.

Shaitana, Mr.

The victim in *Cards on the Table*, Mr. Shaitana mocks what he calls the "bourgeois" British polite society (5). He is a collector, whose prize collection is of people: individuals who got away with murder. When he invites four of his exhibits and four detectives to a bridge party, he is killed. Shaitana likes to shock and is extensively queer-coded: he dresses flamboyantly, calls men "my dear," and takes pleasure in mocking convention. His surname derives from an Arabic word for Satan or "devil," and British characters view him uneasily as a threat—because he is emphatically not one of them.

"The Shadow in the Night." See "The Submarine Plans"

"The Shadow on the Glass" (story; alternative title: "Jealousy Is the Devil")

The short story "The Shadow on the Glass" concerns a potentially haunted property called Greenways House. This is likely nothing to do with Christie's real-life holiday home, Greenway House: she acquired that property in 1928, and "The Shadow on the Glass" was first published (in the *Grand Magazine*) in 1924. In 1930, the story appeared as part of the collection *The Mysterious Mr. Quin*.

Attending a house party hosted by Mr. and Mrs. Unkerton, Mr. Satterthwaite notices a conflagration of love triangles among the middle-aged guests. He also hears about a ghost that appears in one of the windows—a stain that resembles a cavalier and has been the source of legends. Several arguments are overheard on the grounds of Greenways, and eventually two of the guests—Moira Scott and Captain Jimmy Allenson—are found shot dead in the gardens. Like the others, Satterthwaite is unable to explain much to Inspector Winkfield when he arrives the scene.

Apparently from nowhere, Harley Quin arrives and helps Satterthwaite remember small details he thought he had forgotten. Satterthwaite realizes that his preconceptions about the crime were wrong and works out that the two victims must have been embracing at the time of their deaths. This makes Richard Scott, Moira's husband, the obvious suspect, and an examination of a window reveals how the shots were fired.

To execute the crime, Scott relies on nobody seeing him through a window, because they expect to see the shadow of a ghost there. This is a case of relying on superstition to hide in plain sight. It is a version of one of the oldest stories—Edgar Allan Poe's "The Purloined Letter" (1844), of much interest to psychoanalysts and semioticians, involves a letter that cannot be found being hidden in a letter rack. Here, the sleight-of-hand is given a typically semi-supernatural twist characteristic of 1920s Christie.

Characters: Allenson, Captain Jimmy; Drage, Lady Cynthia; **Porter, Major John; Quin, Harley; Satterthwaite, Mr.;** Scott, Moira; Scott, Richard; **Staverton, Iris;** Thompson; Unkerton, Mrs.; Unkerton, Ned; **Winkfield, Inspector**

Shakespeare, William (1564–1616)

Christie believed that Shakespeare should be enjoyed, not studied. She made great efforts, detailed in her autobiography, to take her child and grandchild to see Shakespeare on stage in vibrant productions, believing the writing to contain the best heights and depths of human psychology and emotion.

Shakespeare provides a constant presence to Christie's work, including lending titles to *Sad Cypress* (from *Twelfth Night*), *Taken at the Flood* (from *Julius Caesar*), *By the Pricking of My Thumbs* (from *Macbeth*), and *The Mousetrap* (from *Hamlet*—and so successful that the line about calling a play

"The Mousetrap" reportedly gets a laugh during performances of *Hamlet*). Quotations appear regularly, too, sometimes providing, in cryptic ways, clues. This is the case, for instance, with the line, "Who would have thought the old man to have so much blood in him?" (*Macbeth*), quoted in *Hercule Poirot's Christmas*, and with "Who is Julia? What is she?" (*Two Gentlemen of Verona*), quoted in both *One, Two, Buckle My Shoe* and *A Murder Is Announced*.

Shakespeare's presence in Christie's work extends beyond quotations from *Curtain* (written around 1940) onward. In that novel, Poirot, who dies, leaves Captain Hastings a copy of *Othello* as a clue to the villain's identity. The figure of Iago, Othello's manipulative adviser, hovers over much of the book's action and ultimately provides the clue to the villain's identity: he is a manipulator who does not kill himself but enjoys inciting people to the extent that they commit desperate deeds. Elsewhere, women are compared to *Hamlet*'s Ophelia (for instance, in *Appointment with Death*, *Third Girl*, and *Nemesis*) to imply intense, possibly underacknowledged, unhappiness.

A theme that often appears in the later books is that of three witches. The witches in *Macbeth* provide a template for several "triples" (and lone witches)—for example, in *Endless Night, By the Pricking of My Thumbs, Nemesis*, and, most notably, *The Pale Horse* (the latter almost begins with a performance of *Macbeth* and an analysis of the witches' scene). One character, presented as insightful, suggests after watching the show that the witches should not be played as "supernatural" but as "very ordinary … sly quiet old women"; not as "frightening" but as "an ordinary trio of old women" so mundane each one "just draw you in" (*TPH* 45).

This is exactly how Christie presents the three self-proclaimed witches in the rest of that book. However, it also provides an overview of Christie's approach to characterization and its roots in Shakespeare. Reducing power to the level of the personal, Christie's characters evoke common stereotypes and ideas about "types" of people. This draws readers into a certain way of reading and understanding them, making the impact of any deviation from expected behavior more striking and the spread of an idea more subtle and insidious.

See also: **By the Pricking of My Thumbs**; **The Pale Horse** (novel); Theatricality

Shane, Michael, and Rosamund

Rosamund Shane (née Abernethie) is an actress and niece to the late Richard Abernethie in *After the Funeral*. Not conventionally intelligent, she plays a vital role in this highly theatrical novel, identifying performances and impersonations—she is the only member of the family to notice that "Monsieur Pontarlier" is not a real person but Hercule Poirot in disguise. Her husband Michael is an aspiring actor with a fabricated alibi.

Shapland, Ann

Ann Shapland is an efficient secretary at Meadowbank School in *Cat Among the Pigeons*. She turns out to be a secret agent and serial murderer known as Angelica de Toredo.

Sharpe, Inspector

Inspector Sharpe is the investigating officer in *Hickory Dickory Dock*. This name was later used for a character based on Inspector Japp in the Japanese anime series *Agasa Kurisutī no Meitantei Powaro to Māpuru*.

The Shepherd's Warning

The first appearance of Tommy and Tuppence Beresford on stage was also the first authorized U.K. interactive dinner theater experience based on the work of Christie. Dramatized by Ben Muir from short stories in *Partners in Crime*, the play toured U.K. venues in September 2014, in a production by After Dark Productions, which had already created several Christie-themed dinner theater experiences.

Sheppard, Caroline

In *The Murder of Roger Ackroyd*, Dr. Sheppard's sister Caroline is a gossipy spinster, with a keen and wicked insight into human nature. Her vast network of wives and servants ensures her ready access to all the secrets and scandals in King's Abbott. This was a particularly special character for Christie, who was heartbroken to see Caroline replaced in the stage adaptation, *Alibi*, with the cold and pretty Caryl as an object for Poirot's love. She later acknowledged that Caroline had helped inspire the sleuth Miss Marple, created in 1928.

In 1999, critic Pierre Bayard published an alternative take on *The Murder of Roger Ackroyd*, claiming that the text shows Caroline and not her brother is the murderer. Bayard proposes that Caroline fooled both Poirot and her creator.

Sheppard, Dr. James

James Sheppard is a jovial village doctor who narrates *The Murder of Roger Ackroyd*. When he is identified as the murderer, the shock value lies beyond the novelty of a narrator-as-murderer. Shepherd has also presented himself to the reader as the most conventional, trustworthy of narrators and a potential long-serving replacement for Captain Arthur Hastings, who had been nominally written out of the Poirot books at the end of *The Murder on the Links*. As a doctor, he is more like the traditional Dr. Watson than Hastings ever was, and as a village doctor, he represents a domestic, safe presence. He also proclaims himself "Watson" more than once, although a rereading shows that Poirot never actually confides in him. This is also the first in a string of Christie murderers who are physicians named James.

Sherston, Captain Charles, and Leslie

Charles and Leslie Sherston are husband and wife in the Mary Westmacott novel *Absent in the Spring*. Charles is in prison for embezzlement, and Joan Scudamore is surprised by Leslie's devotion when there is no social advantage and by her own husband's praise for Leslie and grief when she dies of cancer.

Shitonoyakusoku. See **Fuji TV Adaptations**

Shoreham, Professor Robert (Robbie)

Paralyzed on his left side, Professor Robert Shoreham is "[o]ne of the greatest geniuses of our age" in *Passenger to Frankfurt* (228). He has gone quiet in the scientific world in recent years and retreated to listening to music—which proves useful.

Shubho Mahurat. See **Indian-Language Adaptations**

Silence and Circumstance (Dimond). See **Fictional Portrayals of Agatha Christie**

"The Sign in the Sky" (story; alternative title: "A Sign in the Sky")

The Quin and Satterthwaite story "The Sign in the Sky" is a courtroom mystery. The central trick, which would later form an element of *Taken at the Flood*, involves steam from a train seeming to make a question mark in the sky. While the witness discusses this (after the event) as a kind of omen of tragedy to come, it actually helps fix a warped timeline and prove when certain events occurred. The story was first published in *The Grand Magazine* in July 1925, and later collected in *The Mysterious Mr. Quin* (1930).

Characters: Barnaby, Lady Vivien; Barnaby, Sir George; Bullard, Louise; Dale, Sylvia; **Quin, Harley**; **Satterthwaite, Mr.**; Wylde, Martin.

See also: *The Mysterious Mr. Quin*; *Taken at the Flood*

Simmons, Julia, and Patrick

Apparently brother and sister, Julia and Patrick Simmons are young layabouts living with "Aunt Letty"—a distant cousin, Miss Blacklock—in *A Murder Is Announced*. Patrick is a student of engineering, and Julia was a voluntary dispenser during World War II. Secretly, Julia is not who she claims to be: she is Emma Stamfordis, a distant connection who is in line to inherit some money destined for Letty Blacklock. The real Julia has run away to be an actress, and Emma has taken her place. The reader is encouraged to suspect this young pair of nefarious doings; they are the obvious suspects in a village inhabited by respectable middle-aged and elderly people. However, while they have secrets, they are innocent of murder.

Sims, Inspector

Inspector Sims is a "big, burly man with a hearty manner" in "How Does Your Garden Grow?" (*PEC* 244). A typical kindly police inspector, he lacks any form of prejudice and is happy to be helped by Hercule Poirot.

"Sing a Song of Sixpence" (story)

One of three Christie narratives taking its title from the nursery rhyme of the same name, "Sing a Song of Sixpence" was first published in *Holly Leaves*, the Christmas supplement of the *Illustrated Sporting and Dramatic News*, in 1929. In 1934, it appeared in the U.K. volume *The Listerdale Mystery*, and in 1948, it was published in the U.S. volume *The Witness for the Prosecution*.

Sir Edward Palliser, a retired barrister who feels out of place in the modern world, is visited by the 30-year-old Magdalen Vaughan. Many years ago, he made love to her on a cruise, with an idle promise that if she ever needed anything, she need only ask. She tells him that her great-aunt, Mrs. Crabtree, has been murdered—apparently by one of the family. She thinks he can help because his experience in court will tell him if someone is guilty or innocent. Arriving at the property, Sir Edward goes through the dead woman's effects and notices the significance of a missing sixpence, which helps him identify the killer.

Characters: Ben; Crabtree, Emily; **Crabtree, Lily**; Crabtree, William; Lucy; Martha; Palliser, Ethel; Palliser, Sir Edward; Vaughan, Magdalene; Vaughan, Matthew

See also: *The Listerdale Mystery* (story collection); **Nursery Rhymes**; *The Witness for the Prosecution* (story)

"Sir Allen Lane: A Flair for Success" (obituary; alternative title: "Enter Allen Lane and the Penguins")

When Sir Allen Lane, founder of Penguin Books, died on 7 July 1970, the *Spectator* commissioned Christie to write a tribute. This was published on 18 July. In the essay, Christie, nearing her 80th birthday, reflects on her long "friendship" with Lane—a strong word for Christie who tended to distinguish professional and personal relationships but borne out by her correspondence with Lane housed in the University of Bristol's Penguin archive. Christie describes meeting John Lane, Allen Lane's uncle and the proprietor of The Bodley Head, in the 1910s when he accepted her debut, *The Mysterious Affair at Styles*, for publication. She describes meeting Allen Lane, who took over the company, in 1923 when she had a complaint about the cover art for *The Murder on the Links*.

The impression she conveys is one of vitality: "an impression of vigorous youth and a kind of attractive eagerness—someone very much alive, stretching out towards life and exhibiting a gaiety and friendliness that was immediately endearing" (7). There are personal reflections about his family, and Christie praises his business acumen. Finally, she commends his positivity in the face of serious illness. Allen Lane himself had written and read a similarly warm professional tribute to Christie in 1955 as part of the BBC program *Close-Up*.

See also: *Close-Up*; Penguin Books

"Siren Business." See "Problem at Pollensa Bay" (story)

The Sister-in-Law. See *The Lie*

The Sittaford Mystery (novel; alternative title: *The Murder at Hazelmoor*)

Although it features no recurring detective, *The Sittaford Mystery* is perhaps Christie's most archetypically Golden Age mystery novel, combining a West Country setting; an amateur detective in a love triangle; an apparently impossible crime with an outlandish, choreographed solution; and a novel, dramatic premise. It is also her most obviously Sherlock Holmes-inspired novel since 1923's *The Murder on the Links*. As Sir Arthur Conan Doyle died in 1930, it is possible that *The Sittaford Mystery* is Christie's tribute to him.

The action takes place over the Christmas period, where snow is making travel and communication difficult around Dartmoor. A group of friends gather in the village of Sittaford and pass the time with a séance. However, during a round of table-turning, a spirit apparently tells them that their friend, Captain Trevelyan, is dead. His oldest friend, Major Burnaby, is so shaken by the message that he walks across the snowy moor to Burnaby's house and discovers him murdered. Burnaby was a popular man and a wealthy one, so his dissolute nephew, Jim Pearson, is promptly arrested for his murder. However, Jim's fiancée, Emily Trefusis, knows that he lacks "the guts" to "murder people" (85, 86) and teams up with a journalist to find the real killer.

What is clear is that the murderer entered Burnaby's property through a window in heavy snow and that, barring any supernatural interference, someone in the village knew that he was being murdered at that time, because the news was communicated.

In the end, Emily realizes that Major Burnaby committed the crime. He spelled out the message during the séance to set the plot in motion. A healthy, retired athlete, he took skis to Burnaby's property, entered through the window, and killed Burnaby before skiing back and completing the journey on foot. This made it appear impossible that he had time to commit the murder. The motive was money: Trevelyan had won a large sum of money in a newspaper competition but had entered under his friend's name. After acquitting her rather useless fiancée, Emily celebrates with the journalist who proposes marriage—but she turns him down, preferring to stay with Jim. He is a "frightful idiot" (85) and is not "worth as much as" the journalist (249), but she loves him, so that is that.

The Dartmoor setting, a subplot involving an escaped convict and a mysterious couple with a secret relationship to him, and the significance of a pair of missing boots (in this case, ski boots) all mirror elements of Conan Doyle's *The Hound of the Baskervilles*. Mr. Rycroft, a twittering bachelor who helps Emily, mirrors Jack Stapleton in the same novel, although while Stapleton is interested in butterflies, Rycroft is interested in bird-watching, true crime, and the supernatural. Another tangential figure, the no-nonsense Miss Percehouse who never leaves her house but gets the outside world to come to her, evokes Major Sholto in *The Sign of Four*, although again the characters are very different. Finally, the central presence of séances ("table-turning") reflects a key interest of Conan Doyle's in later life. Conan Doyle was an ardent spiritualist, although he never let these interests influence his crime narrative. In *Sittaford*, one character proposes getting an opinion on the matter from Conan Doyle, indicating that he was alive when it was written or set—or that news does indeed travel slow in Sittaford. As Michael Cook has noted, this indicates "the memory of the genre," already configuring its roots in Sherlock Holmes and the gothic, by 1931 (10).

Other elements of the novel find parallels elsewhere in Christie's own canon. The execution of the crime is not unlike those in

The Murder of Roger Ackroyd and *Evil Under the Sun*: the murderer manufactures a pretext to reach the scene of the crime, which also enables him to obscure the time of death, destroy evidence, and give himself an alibi. The snowbound house and the killer's arrival on skis would later become elements of "Three Blind Mice" and *The Mousetrap*. It is also possible that the book inspired *Why Didn't They Ask Evans?* two years later. In a foreword to *Passenger to Frankfurt*, Christie recalled that *Evans* was inspired by a friend flinging down a mystery novel with the words, "Not bad, but why on earth didn't they ask Evans?" (*Frankfurt* 11). Evans in *Sittaford*, as in *Evans*, is a servant who holds key information. Notably, in this novel, nobody ever asks her about her master's activities that probably would have revealed the killer's motive.

Emily, who solves the case, is an example of Christie's young, entrepreneurial, no-nonsense, and business-minded heroine that calls to mind Anne Beddingfeld in *The Man in the Brown Suit*, Victoria Jones in *They Came to Baghdad*, and—to a lesser extent—Lady Frances Derwent in *Why Didn't They Ask Evans?* These women combine initiative, an interest in—but no romantic illusions about—men, and no conscience about lying. They are also good-looking, which is an important part of their skill set: like Anne Beddingfeld before her, Emily notes that she is able "to have her own way and boss … everybody she can" by virtue of being "rather good-looking," whereas other people have to do it "by force of character" (135). There is also an element of Caroline Shepherd and Miss Marple in Anne, who obtains much of her information from gossip via servants and shopkeepers.

The book was first published in the United States as *The Murder at Hazelmoor*, following a serialization in *Good Housekeeping*, in 1931. It was published in the United Kingdom under its British title the same year. There have been two screen adaptations, both of which changed the main detectives: an episode of *Agatha Christie's Marple* in 2006 and an episode of *Les Petits Meurtres d'Agatha Christie* in 2018. BBC Radio 4 broadcast a five-part adaptation in 1990.

Characters: **Abdul**; **Amy**; **Beatrice**; Belling, Mrs.; Belinda, Aunt; **Burnaby, Major John**; Carruthers; Curtis, Amelia; Curtis, Mr.; Davis, Miss; Dering, Martin; Dering, Sylvia; Dering, William; Duke, Mr.; Elmer; **Enderby, Charles**; Evans, Rebecca; Evans, Robert; Forder; **Freemantle Freddie**; Gardner, Jennifer; Gardner, Robert; Garfield, Ronald (Ronnie); Graves, Constable; Hibbert, Mary; Kirkwood, Frederick; Klarpent, Miss; Maxwell, Superintendent; **Narracott, Inspector**; Parker, Amos; Pearson, Brian; **Pearson, James (Jim)**; Percehouse, Caroline; Plunket, George; Pollock, Sergeant; Rosenkraun, Edgar; Rycroft, Martha; Rycroft, Mr.; **Tom**; **Trefusis, Emily**; **Trevelyan, Captain Joseph**; Warren, Dr.; Willett, Mrs.; Willett, Violet; Wyatt, Captain

See also: ***Agatha Christie's Marple***; **BBC Radio Adaptations**; **Conan Doyle, Sir Arthur**; ***The Mousetrap***; ***Les Petits Meurtres d'Agatha Christie***; **"The Red Signal"**

"The Six China Figures." See **"The Affair at the Victory Ball"**

Slack, Inspector

Inspector Slack is a St. Mary Mead policeman who appears in *The Body in the Library*, "The Case of the Perfect Maid," and *The Murder at the Vicarage*. Contrary to his name—and in a comic inversion of Dickensian naming practice—he is an intensely proactive individual who moves too fast to get anything done properly.

Sleeping Murder (novel)

Sleeping Murder has a typically Christiean premise—what crime writer Sophie Hannah has called a "How Is This Happening?" moment. Gwenda Reed, a newlywed from New Zealand, sees the house of her dreams in England and buys it. Looking around, she finds that she can anticipate various house elements such as the pattern of wallpaper that has been covered up and a door that has been painted over. At a performance of John Webster's *The Duchess of Malfi*, the line "Cover her face, mine eyes dazzle. She died young" (31) causes her to scream. She has a flashback of seeing a woman, strangled, at the foot of her new house's staircase.

Miss Marple, who is with her, suggests that this is a memory rather than a vision.

Sure enough, it turns out that Gwenda lived at that house as a child and that her young stepmother, Helen, went missing. Miss Marple and Gwenda join up with Helen's half-brother, Dr. James Kennedy, to investigate and learn that Helen was a nymphomaniac with several boyfriends. They investigate these men. In the end, Miss Marple determines that Helen was, like Arlena in *Evil under the Sun*, not "[m]an mad" (99) at all. Instead, "she was a perfectly normal young girl" with a "normal and harmless" desire to marry and move away from her half-brother's control (217).

Some confusion surrounds when and how Christie wrote *Sleeping Murder*. A popular story goes that she wrote it alongside *Curtain* around 1940. The two novels were then placed in a vault, with the plan that they would be published after her death, providing swan songs for Hercule Poirot and Miss Marple. However, archival research shows that *Curtain* was written and submitted first. There is less of a paper-trail for Miss Marple, which would eventually be subtitled *Miss Marple's Last Case*. It seems likely that Christie wrote it in the 1940s—or, according to archivist John Curran, the 1950s. Her notebooks and correspondence suggest that she edited the manuscript several times, up to 1962, when P.D. James published *Cover Her Face*: that was the original title of *Sleeping Murder*.

The quotation is one that had long-appealed to Christie. Its inclusion is slightly strange: Dr. Kennedy quoted the lines over his half-sister's corpse, which is why they trigger Gwenda's memory. The BBC screen adaptation makes this more plausible—he says, "I can't see your face; my eyes are dazzled"—thus avoiding an unnecessary question of implausibility. However, the device seems to have been considered carefully. Earlier, Christie had contemplated having David Hunter say the line ritualistically over his own sister's body in *Taken at the Flood*, which also had *Cover Her Face* as a working title, albeit briefly. Certainly, it is appropriate: in Webster's Jacobean tragedy, the line is said by a cardinal gazing at his beautiful sister's dead body.

The mystery plot, unlike its trappings, is similar to that in *Nemesis*, published in 1971. It is likely that Christie wrote both intending them to be Miss Marple's last cases. Both look back in time at a woman who has been murdered and libeled by an obsessive guardian. In both, Miss Marple catches the killer not in her usual manner—roping in a third party to lure them—but by acting as the bait herself. Christie used one scene, which may have been drawn from life, as a central tenet for another late novel, *By the Pricking of My Thumbs*: an old lady in a nursing home asks, out of the blue: "Is it your poor child [... b]ehind the fireplace[?]" (84). A similar scene also features in *The Pale Horse*.

Sleeping Murder was the first Christie title published after her death in 1976. Screen adaptations include an episode of the BBC's *Miss Marple*, broadcast in January 1987; a Syrian miniseries, *Jarimat fi Aldhdhakira* (Crime in Memory), which aired in 1992; a four-part animation as part of *Agasa Kurisutī no Meitantei Powaro to Māpuru,* which aired in March and April 2005; an episode of *Agatha Christie's Marple*, broadcast in February 2006; and the 10th installment of *Les Petits Meurtres d'Agatha Christie*, which aired in 2012. In December 2001, BBC Radio 4 broadcast a 90-minute dramatization, the last in its series of Miss Marple adaptations until *Miss Marple's Final Problems* in 2015.

Characters: **Afflick, Dorothy, and Jackie**; **Bantry, Colonel Arthur, and Dolly**; **Beatrice**; Danby, Aliso; Danby, Megan; **Erskine, Janet, and Major Richard**; Esther; **Fane, Walter, and family**; **Halliday, Major Kelvin**; **Haydock, Dr.**; Hengrave, Majo; Hengrave, Mrs.; **Kennedy, Dr. James**; **Kennedy, Helen Spenlove**; Kimble, Lily; **Lancaster, Mrs.**; Last, Inspector; Laws, Johnnie; Lazenby, Dr.; **Marple, Jane; Melrose; Colonel**; Paget, Edith; Penrose, Dr.; Primer, Detective Inspector; **Reed, Giles, and Gwenda**; Watchman, Mr.; **West, Joan, and Raymond**; Yarde, Dorothy

See also: *Agasa Kurisutī no Meitantei Powaro to Māpuru*; *Agatha Christie's Marple*; Houses; *Jarimat fi Aldhdhakira*; *Miss Marple* (radio series); *Miss Marple* (television series); *Nemesis*; *Les Petits Meurtres d'Agatha Christie*

Small, Florence

A school friend of Pamela Reeves in *The Body in the Library*, Florence Small tells Miss Marple information she would not reveal to the police.

Snow upon the Desert (novel)

Perhaps because it is a novel and perhaps because it is obliquely referenced in *Death on the Nile*, *Snow upon the Desert* is the most readily identified of Christie's unpublished works. It was her first novel, written under the pseudonym Monosylaba, and was, in one biographer's words, her attempt "at a worldly novel" (Morgan 50). A romantic novel set in Cairo, Christie started working on it around 1909 at age 19. She was inspired by time spent with her mother at the Gezirah Hotel—specifically, watching the people who would form the characters in her novel.

What is clear to the contemporary reader is that Christie was a character-based author; however, this and the gift for dialogue were not what she was going for in the manuscript, and as a result it is a poor novel. Several publishers rejected it and, eventually, she showed it to family friend—and successful novelist—Eden Philpotts. He advised her to "stick to gay, natural dialogue" and "cut all moralisations out" (qtd. in Morgan 51). The author also set herself unnecessary technical challenges: for instance, making the heroine half-deaf.

Christie later joked at her own expense through the character of the tawdry novelist Salome Otterbourne in *Death on the Nile* (1937). Otterbourne refers in the text to her novel, *Snow on the Desert's Face*, an in-joke referencing *Snow upon the Desert*, which was a lackluster romance. This reading is borne out by Christie's notes for the character, which refer to her as "Mrs. Pooper—cheap novelist"; Christie and her husband referred to one another as "Mr. and Mrs. Puper" (Green 198). The manuscript exists in the Christie Family Archive and, at the time of this writing, it has not been published—although it is not without the bounds of possibility that something will be done with it.

See also: **Death on the Nile** (novel), **Pseudonyms, Philpotts, Eden**

So Many Steps to Death. See **Destination Unknown**

Sobek

Sobek is the "handsome gay" (*DCE* 8) second son of Imhotep and brother to Renisenb in *Death Comes as the End*, characterized by a general lack of ambition or imagination. He also has violent tendencies and "likes killing" animals such as snakes (65)—something encouraged because it showcases his masculinity but seen as dangerous by Renisenb.

"The Solving Six." See **"The Tuesday Night Club"**

"The Solving Six and the Evil Hour." See **"The Idol House of Astarte"**

"The Solving Six and the Golden Grave." See **"Ingots of Gold"**

"Some Day They Will Get Me." See **"The Four Suspects"**

Someone at the Window (play)

The undated two-act play *Someone at the Window* is based on Christie's 1929 short story, "The Dead Harlequin." The play has 1934 as its present, with an extended flashback in 1919, so it is reasonable to assume it was written in 1933 or 1934. Notably, Christie's playwriting in-laws, Dorothy and Campbell Christie, had a comedy mystery, *Someone at the Door*, staged in 1935. Agatha was on good terms with them, often seeing their productions, so there may have been some discussions during the writing of both plays. Dorothy and Campbell's script is also set in a country-house and makes (albeit brief) references to ghosts and the supernatural, although the two scripts have very different plots.

In Christie's more dramatic story, discovering a past crime cures a rather brainless young protagonist of his nostalgia for Victoriana. This is an ambitious and detailed script which appears to have been hand corrected and professionally typed, although there do not seem to have been any ambitions to stage it. When she wrote it, Christie was not an established playwright and had not yet dared mount anything without the crowd-pleasing presence of Hercule Poirot. Its large cast of 16 and substantial scene changes may have discouraged potential players or publishers. The Christie family archive houses two copies of this script, although at the time of writing there are no plans for publication or performance. As this is a substantial and well-executed piece of drama, however, it may be a matter of time.

See also: "The Dead Harlequin"

"Something Is Missing." See "Behind the Screen" (novella)

"S.O.S." (story)

A semi-supernatural story, "S.O.S." is laced with gothic atmosphere and a typical 1920s interest in the mysteries of psychoanalysis. Mortimer Cleveland, "an authority on mental science" who is "peculiarly susceptible to atmosphere" (*HOD* 229–30) arrives at the Dinsmead family home after his car has broken down during a storm. He stays the night and, waking, finds "S.O.S." written in dust. Mr. and Mrs. Dinsmead are monstrous characters—one huge and the other tiny, and both apparently unpleasant—with two daughters, Magdalen and Charlotte, and a son, Johnnie. None of them admit to having written "S.O.S.," although Charlotte says she "easily might have done" because the house has an uncanny, haunted feeling (236). Mortimer believes that Charlotte's subconscious may have picked up on the house's residual trauma from past tragedies.

Magdalene admits to having written "S.O.S." because she has an uncanny sense of fear: everybody in the family apart from her brother seems to be drained and dispirited. Mortimer learns that Charlotte is not a biological Dinsmead but the daughter of "one of those rich Jewish gentlemen" (240) and that her adoptive parents are trying to kill her. With arsenic, they are poisoning the whole family but giving her a higher dose (a similar idea resurfaces in *4.50 from Paddington*, 1957). The son has built up a chemical resistance to arsenic.

This is essentially a murder mystery with supernatural trappings until the "S.O.S." is explained. Mortimer suggests that it would never have occurred to the Dinsmeads to poison their adopted daughter if the house had not been "cursed"—but that those same

spirits should be thanked for guiding Magdalene to write in the dust (247). Overall, it is one of Christie's most compact and direct attempts to reconcile the rational world of detective fiction with the irrationality of the supernatural—something couched in the vocabulary (if not the methodology) of psychoanalysis.

"S.O.S." was published in *The Grand Magazine* in February 1926, followed by publication in *The Hound of Death* (1933) in the United Kingdom and in *The Witness for the Prosecution* (1948) in the United States. Christie toyed with adapting it into a one-act play, as part of *Rule of Three* in 1962, but ultimately dismissed this idea.

Characters: Cleveland, Mortimer; Dinsmead, Charlotte; Dinsmead, Magdalen; Dinsmead, Maggie; Dinsmead, Mr.; Johnnie

See also **Anti-Semitism**; **Curses**; *The Hound of Death* (story collection); **Psychoanalysis**

Soshite Daremo Inakunatta. See *And Then There Were None*, **Screen Adaptations of**

"The Soul of the Croupier" (story)

A Harley Quin story, "The Soul of the Croupier" concerns a love triangle in a Monte Carlo casino, where Mr. Satterthwaite is on holiday. A croupier mistakenly gives Satterthwaite's roulette winnings to the Countess Czarina, another punter at the casino. Satterthwaite is greatly embarrassed and, with Mr. Quin's help, learns the emotional background to the croupier's actions. In the United States, the story was first published in *Flynn's Weekly* on 13 November 1926. In January 1927, it appeared in the United Kingdom in *The Story-Teller Magazine*. It was collected in *The Mysterious Mr. Quin* (1930).

See also: **Czarnova, Countess**; Martin, Elizabeth; **Quin, Harley**; Rudge, Franklin; **Satterthwaite, Mr.**; **Vaucher, Jeanne**; Vaucher, Pierre

See also: *The Mysterious Mr. Quin*

Sparkling Cyanide **(novel; alternative title:** *Remembered Death***)**

An expansion of the short story and radio play "Yellow Iris," *Sparkling Cyanide* dispenses with Hercule Poirot, making Colonel Johnny Race the central detective.

The novel is set two years after the death of Rosemary Barton, who was thought to have committed suicide at a birthday party. Unconvinced, her husband George gathers everyone who was present at the same table at the same restaurant. Shortly after toasting his wife's memory, George dies. Race uncovers numerous secrets and entanglements, and identifies a murder conspiracy (not the same as the solution to "Yellow Iris") bound up in lust for sex and money.

Stephen Farraday, with whom Rosemary had an affair, represents the ethically bankrupt world of careerism: he has switched political allegiance from Labour to the Conservative Party to make progress and has married to further his career. However, he ends up falling in love with his wife and settling for a happy family life. There is a broader trajectory at work here in which conservatism—seeking to re-create or uphold the past—has superficial appeal but does not hold up. George Barton's attempt to re-create the scene of his wife's death ends in his own death; the whole event falls on All Souls' Day, described as a day that ought to be "un–Christian" but is itself a key part of Christianity (180); what sparkles in high society is cyanide. At the heart of the murder plot, inevitably, is an inheritance.

The need to cling to Rosemary's ghost keeps many characters stuck within their memories of a world only two years old but vanished nonetheless. Language like "the ghost of a grin" (229) is used throughout. George is, of course, obsessed with grief, which kills him, but characters such as the Farradays and Iris are able to move on. However, the characters who represent clean breaks from the past and uncomplicated forward-driving are the villains. Victor Drake boasts of living in the moment: "I've sailed before the mast in a tramp steamer. I've been in the running for President in a South American Republic. I've been in prison!" (41): in this, he represents "the strength of the Devil" and cold allure that "could make evil seem amusing" (42). His accomplice, Ruth Lessing—whose name is the clue to her main characteristic—fails only because of other people's mistakes. She could have gotten away with it. Evil in this novel is powerful and is focused on going forward without looking back. If *Sparkling Cyanide* indicates a model for living, it veers toward ethically tempered ambition and remembrance without nostalgia.

Trauma and memory are key themes of *Sparkling Cyanide*, something encapsulated by its working title (and the title under which it was published in the United States), *Remembered Death*. The British publishers changed the title because World War II and remembered trauma were so fresh in public minds that such a somber title would lack the escapist appeal being marketed. For this reason, only two of Christie's 1940s U.K. titles directly refer to corpses: *The Body in the Library*—its title a recognizable genre cliché—and *Death Comes as the End*—a novel very clearly marketed as being about ancient Egypt. This is a far cry from trends only a decade previously, when *The ABC Murders, Murder in the Mews*, and *Murder in Mesopotamia* were published in a single year, following *Death in the Clouds* and preceding *Death on the Nile*. The American publication went to print in February 1945, taking the original title, under which it had appeared in a *Saturday Evening Post* serialization the previous year, and the title was only changed for the U.K. edition. Christie hated *Sparkling Cyanide* as a title, considering it too flippant.

The plot of *Sparkling Cyanide* centers both an authorial sleight of hand and a thematic focus on love, loss, and remembrance. These two features are intimately tied to the novel's postwar context, but they also tap into the universal appeal of the puzzle-based whodunit and the universality of human emotion. For this reason, it is less surprising that it might appear that both television adaptations of the novel have relocated the action to contemporary settings. In the United States, CBS aired an Emmy-nominated dramatization on 5 November 1983 with a screenplay by Robert Malcolm Young, mystery author Sue Grafton, and Steven Humphrey, and with stars Anthony Andrews and Deborah Raffin. This production, set in 1980s California, tapped into Reagan-era nostalgia and performative liberal objections to it.

Britain's ITV aired a dramatization

on 5 October 2003, starring Oliver Ford Davis and Pauline Quirk, set in the world of football management, to tackle contemporary celebrity culture. A three-part period-faithful radio adaptation by Joy Wilkinson was broadcast on BBC Radio 4 from 30 January 2012. A French adaptation relocating the action to 1950s France appeared as season 2, episode 2 of *Les Petits Meurtres d'Agatha Christie* in 2013.

Characters: Atwell, Maisie; **Barton, George**; **Barton, Rosemary**; Bennett, Paul; Bolsano, Giuseppe; Brice-Woodworth, Patricia; **Brown, Anthony ("Tony")**; Cranford, Mr.; Dewsbury, Lord; Drake, Caleb; **Drake, Lucilla, and Victor**; Farraday, Lady Sandra; **Farraday, Stephen**; Gaskell, Dr.; Kemp, Chief Inspector; Kidderminster, Lady; Kidderminster, Lord; King, Gloria; **Lessing, Ruth**; Marle, Hector; **Marle, Iris**; Marle, Viola; Morales, Pedro; **Morelli, Tony**; Pierre; **Race, Colonel Johnny**; Raymond, Jean; Shannon, Christine; Tollington, Gerald; West, Chloe; Wylie, Dr.

See also: **BBC Radio Adaptations; CBS Television Adaptations; *Les Petits Meurtres d'Agatha Christie*; *Sparkling Cyanide* (2003 television adaptation); "Yellow Iris"; *The Yellow Iris***

Sparkling Cyanide (1983 television adaptation). See **CBS Television Adaptations**

Sparkling Cyanide (2003 television adaptation)

This ITV adaptation of Christie's 1945 novel was broadcast in the United Kingdom on 5 October 2003. It is set in the twenty-first century and was intended to be the first in a series, but poor ratings put paid to that plan. Oliver Ford-Davies and Pauline Collins star as married spies—vaguely based on the character of Colonel Race in the book—and the production is typical of ITV mysteries in the early-twenty-first century.

Although the novel is set in prewar high society and the 1983 adaptation for CBS had transposed the action to California, this one was set in a London football club. The decision, touted in publicity materials (and certainly not in reviews) as "fun," likely has much to do with the phenomenal success, at the time, of ITV's enthusiastically low-brow

Footballers' Wives. A more general aim was to bring Christie to new, younger audiences, which was not an immediate success. The same drive saw an introduction of computer games from the Adventure Company and, eventually, the ITV series *Agatha Christie's Marple.* Indeed, a modern-day setting was briefly considered for that program.

See also: **CBS Television Adaptations**; *Sparkling Cyanide*

Spence, Superintendent Bert

Superintendent Bert Spence is a senior Scotland Yard figure who consistently postpones his retirement. He seems to be an established friend of Hercule Poirot's when he first appears in *Taken at the Flood* in 1948. He is a central investigator in *Mrs. McGinty's Dead,* which finds him living with his sister, Elspeth McKay. He is retired by 1969, in *Hallowe'en Party,* and helps Poirot gaze long into the past in *Elephants Can Remember.* He may be Colin Lamb's father in *The Clocks,* but this is more likely Superintendent Battle.

The Spider's Web (film)

The first Christie film in Technicolor, *The Spider's Web* is as conscious of the technology as James Cameron's *Avatar* is of its 3D effects. The sets, props, and costumes are full of bright—often clashing—colors. For example, chairs are bright yellow, walls and tables are bright blue and green, and the very proper housekeeper wears a garish red blouse. Even candles and crockery are colorful.

The film was partly a vehicle for its star, Glynis Johns, who was beginning the transition from Hollywood bombshell to British character actor. Similarly, her part (Clarissa) in the original play had been written for Margaret Lockwood, who had wanted a comedic role after her typical roles as a *femme fatale.* It also starred John Justin as Henry, Jack Hulbert as Sir Rowland Delahaye, Cicely Cortneidge as Miss Peake, and Ronald Howard as Jeremy, alongside a range of well-known British character actors. Although the publicity emphasized Christie's name, and the tagline ran, "DON'T TELL YOUR FRIENDS THE ENDING ... THEY WON'T BELIEVE

IT!," the key point of the film is certainly its comedy, with every joke from the stage script intact and additional physical comedy added.

The story's stage origins are evident not so much in the dialogue—although it is mostly lifted from the play—as in the flimsy-looking scenery. United Artists released the film in November 1960. Coming on the heels of the extremely well-received *Witness for the Prosecution* (1956), the film did not make a positive impression on cinema-goers, and it does not seem to have been released in the United States, except in an edited televised broadcast.

See also: **Spider's Web (play and novel)**; **Witness for the Prosecution, Screen Adaptations of**

Spider's Web (play and novel)

Christie became friendly with actress Margaret Lockwood in the 1940s. In 1953, Lockwood inquired through her agent whether Christie might write a play for her. The pair met and discussed what the play should be like. Lockwood wanted a comedy role, as she was tired of playing *femmes fatales*. She also asked Christie to write a part for veteran character actor Wilfrid Hyde-White. Christie wrote the play, which also included a part for Lockwood's daughter (who did not play it), during the rehearsals for *Witness for the Prosecution*.

Lockwood's character, Clarissa, is the bored wife of diplomat Henry Hailsham-Brown, who daydreams about extraordinary situations such as finding a dead man in the library. Toward the end of act 1, her perspicacious daughter, 12-year-old Pippa, finds a man's corpse. Comedy ensues as Clarissa and her houseguests seek to hide the body from the police to avoid a diplomatic scandal as her husband is due to host important guests. Meanwhile, there are mysteries to solve: who was the dead man, what was the valuable antique he was trying to steal, and who killed him?

The story is character-driven and was written with certain actors in mind. This shows, in that the plot is cobbled together from older Christie pieces. For example, one mystery and solution—the Hailsham-Browns obtaining their house at a bargain rate because the owners were criminals who needed someone called "Brown" to live there—started in "The Adventure of the Cheap Flat." Pippa believes she has killed the victim because she has taken a childish interest in voodoo and black magic, like Linda in *Evil under the Sun*. Attempts to hide the crime from the police involve a game of bridge in a direct replication of a plot device in "The King of Clubs." Finally, one twist at the end—the value of a letter lying not in its contents but in the stamp on its envelope—had previously appeared in "Strange Jest." *Spider's Web* (or *The Spider's Web*) had also been Christie's working title for several novels, most notably *The Moving Finger*. Audiences, of course, would not have known this; nor were they likely to have read or remembered stories published decades earlier and not yet anthologized, so the production would have been completely fresh to them.

The play had a short national tour before opening at the Savoy Theatre in the West End on 13 December 1954. At this time, *The Mousetrap* and *Witness for the Prosecution* were still running, making Christie the first female playwright to have three West End productions at the same time. It had 774 performances, with an additional performance of excerpts before an invited audience televised in 1955. It was published for amateur players in 1957.

Besides the 1955 broadcast, there have been several screen adaptations: the first was a German television version, *Das Spinnennetz* (The Spider Web), in 1956. The second was the British movie *The Spider's Web* (1960). A Portuguese version, *Teia de Aranha* (Cobweb), aired on television in 1961. There was a televised production, part of *Au Théâtre ce Soir,* broadcast in France in 1969, and BBC 2 remade the 1960 film for television in a production broadcast on 26 December 1982. In 2000, Charles Osborne's novelization of the script was published by HarperCollins. This third and final effort of Osborne's once again makes only minimal creative interventions.

Characters: Birch, Hugo; Costello, Oliver; Delehave, Sir Rowland; Elgin; Hailsham-

Brown, Clarissa; Hailsham-Brown, Henry; Hailsham-Brown, Pippa; Jones, Constable; Lord, Inspector; Peake, Mildred; Warrander, Jeremy

See also: **Osborne, Charles**; *The Spider's Web* (film); *Spider's Web* (1982 television adaptation); *Das Spinnennetz*; *A Théaâtre ce Soiru*

Spider's Web (television adaptation)

Often considered a remake of the 1960 film, this adaptation of *Spider's Web* was broadcast on BBC 2 on 26 December 1982. Director Basil Coleman did not interfere much with Christie's comedy-thriller script, making it a strikingly stagey production in an era when television plays tended toward the stage-like. The BBC was not yet known for its Christie screen adaptations, as the *Miss Marple* series was two years off, so *Spider's Web* did not have to face expectations resulting from a track record of productions.

Penelope Keith, fresh from *To the Manor Born* (1979–81), starred as Clarissa Hailsham-Brown, who dreams of becoming embroiled in a murder only find it happening. Noted character actors such as Thorley Walters, Elizabeth Spriggs, and David Yelland (later to play Poirot's valet George in *Agatha Christie's Poirot* and the detective on stage in *Witness for the Prosecution*) played supporting roles.

See also: *Spider's Web* (play and novel); *The Spider's Web* (film)

Das Spinnennetz (Spider Web, television adaptation)

Das Spinnennetz (Spider Web) is a West German television adaptation of Christie's *Spider's Web*, broadcast on 19 August 1956. It was directed by Fritz Umgelter and starred Marlies Schönau as Clarissa Hailsham-Brown. The program was well-received and was followed by *Ein Fremder kam ins Haus* (A Stranger Came into the House), the first of two West German versions of *Love from a Stranger*.

See also: *Spider's Web* (play and novel)

"Sporting Challenge." See "The Case of the Missing Will"

Spragg, Eurydice

Eurydice Spragg is a tacky medium in

"Motive vs. Opportunity" who preys on a grief-stricken man by claiming to communicate with his late granddaughter.

"Spring." See *The Road of Dreams* (poetry collection)

Springer, Grace

Grace Springer is the new games mistress at Meadowbank School, who is impaled with a javelin in the sports pavilion, in *Cat Among the Pigeons*. Her death causes more excitement than upset among the staff and students.

Sprot, Betty, and Millicent

A typical English mother on holiday in *N or M?*. Mrs. Millicent Sprot, for all her adenoidal mundanity, turns out to be a fascist double agent. Her cover is flawless, and the toddler daughter, Betty, who refers to herself in the third person, is part of her armor, which she happily discards when in danger. After the events of *N or M?*, Tommy and Tuppence Beresford adopt Betty, who becomes Betty Beresford and is mentioned in *By the Pricking of My Thumbs* and *Postern of Fate*.

Stamfordis, Sybil

One of the three self-proclaimed witches in *The Pale Horse*, Sybil Stamfordis is the acknowledged leader. In business terms—and the Pale Horse organization *is* a business—she is a middle-manager who has to successfully navigate the witchcraft and business angles. To this end, she convinces Bella Webb, her cook and fellow witch, that they are performing real magic while working through money matters with disbarred solicitor Mr. Bradley.

"Star Over Bethlehem" (story). See *Star Over Bethlehem* (story/poetry collection)

Star Over Bethlehem (story/poetry collection; alternative title: Star Over Bethlehem and Other Stories)

Christie spent much of 1965 compiling a special volume for publication in addition to her expected annual crime novel. *Star Over Bethlehem* is a collection of short stories and poetry with a religious feel that surprised many when it was published on 1 November 1965. An illustrated volume, with story titles such as "The Naughty

Donkey," many commentators assume that *Star Over Bethlehem* is a book for children, but most sections could easily be anthologized for adults. Christie's husband, Max Mallowan, described the book as a set of "Holy Detective Stories" (204). Some, however, clearly have their origins in stories told to children. Like *Come, Tell Me How You Live*, the book was published under the name Agatha Christie Mallowan, so readers would not be misled about its contents: as Christie wrote in her autobiography, concluded the year this *Star Over Bethlehem* was published, "one always wants to do something that isn't quite one's work" (*AA* 470).

Writing about Christianity, Christie was free to explore new devices and her own personality, as she had done when writing as Mary Westmacott. The book features an eclectic cast of characters. The Virgin Mary, Lucifer, saints, and angels appear alongside mundane widows and country constables. Action takes place in the past, present, and future (there are bleak predictions for the year 2000). Familiar themes from Christie's detective fiction seep through—the power of gossip is central to "The Island," whereas the difficulty of interpretation is at the heart of "Jenny by the Sky." But other areas, like mental illness, are explored more frankly than anywhere else. It is tempting to agree with the Charles Osborne that book was written, not for adults or for children, but chiefly for "Agatha Christie ... herself" (321).

If the whole thing has the ring of childhood, that is not a coincidence. For Christie, traditional Church of England Christianity went hand in hand with nostalgia for her youth. She had been raised, the youngest of three siblings, in late-nineteenth and early-twentieth century England and France. As an upper-middle class child, her religious faith had been very important to her. As a child, convicted in her religious principles, she had been terrified that her father would go to hell because he played croquet on Sundays. Her mother sampled every fashionable belief system but always reverted to Anglicanism, whereas her governess was, in Christie's words, "a Bible Christian" (*AA* 25). Throughout her life,

Christie remained unobtrusively devout, keeping a copy of Thomas à Kempis's *The Imitation of Christ* by her bedside until the end. For her, religion offered a sense of structure and moral framework that transcended the moods of the moment. *Star Over Bethlehem*, then, was an indulgence.

The title story had been published two decades before in *Woman's Journal* in December 1946. The volume also is composed of five poems and five stories not previously published: Poems include: **"A Greeting," "A Wreath for Christmas," "Gold, Frankincense and Myrrh," "Jenny by the Sky,"** and **"The Saints of God."** Stories include (in addition to **"Star Over Bethlehem"**): **"The Naughty Donkey," "The Water Bus," "In the Cool of the Evening," "Promotion in the Highest,"** and **"The Island."** Eight years later, "Jenny by the Sky" would be reprinted, with minor alterations to the layout, in *Poems*.

Characters: **Badstock, Mrs.;** Barbara, Saint; camel, the; Catherine, Saint; Chubb, Mrs.; Cristina, Saint; **Donkey, the;** Elizabeth of Hungary, Saint; Gabriel, Archangel; Gertrude; **Grierson, Alan;** Grierson, Janet; Grierson, Major Rodney; **Hargreaves, Mrs.;** Jesus; **John;** Joseph; Lamphrey, Edward; Lamphrey, Mrs.; Lawrence, Saint; **Mary;** Narracott, Jacob; **Palk, Constable George;** Peter, Saint; Raphion; Scoithín, Saint; Stewart, Johnnie; Stewart, Mrs.

See also: **Agatha Christie Indult,** *An Autobiography;* **Christianity;** *Come, Tell Me How You Live; Poems*

Starke, Lady Julia. See **Lancaster, Mrs.**

Starke, Sir Philip

Sir Philip Starke is a country squire in *By the Pricking of My Thumbs*, married to Lady Julia Starke and helping cover up her mental illness and criminal activities.

Starr, Raymond

Raymond Starr—aka Ramon Thomas Starr—is an exotic tennis instructor and dancer at the Majestic Hotel in Danemouth, who has anglicized his name to escape prejudice in *The Body in the Library*. He is generally considered a gigolo.

Staverton, Iris

Iris Staverton is an unlikely siren in "The

Shadow on the Glass" whose hold over men is powerful because it is slow-acting; she is not obviously beautiful or sexy but is inevitably the center of attention.

Steene, Lawrence
In the Mary Westmacott novel *A Daughter's a Daughter*, Lawrence Steene is Sarah Prentice's aristocrat boyfriend, later husband, with a highly unsavory reputation. He is louche and drug-addled, and almost breaks his wife, inducting her into his degenerate lifestyle.

Stewart, Arlena
Arlena Stewart is a fashionable actress in *Evil under the Sun*, considered the height of magazine-culture style because of her suntan, strong physique, revealing bathing attire, and multiple marriages and love affairs. Fundamentally, Arlena is misunderstood: she is not fatally attractive to men but fatally drawn to them. When Hercule Poirot reveals that an apparently weak, pathetic woman has used a fake tan and a bathing dress to impersonate her, Christie shows the tendency in popular culture for women to be little observed.

Stillingfleet, Dr. John
John Stillingfleet is a medic who is a friend of Hercule Poirot; he appears in "The Dream," *Sad Cypress*, and *Third Girl*.

Stoddart-West, Lady. See **Dubois, Martine**

"The Stolen Ghost." See "The Last Séance" (story)

"Stories That Thrill" (interview)
This early interview for the Melbourne *Herald* is an example of Christie's early willingness to engage with the press. It was granted while Christie was staying in Melbourne, with her husband, as part of their 1922 Empire tour, and a rare photograph of a smiling Christie accompanies it. The editor goes to lengths to present Christie as "a pioneer," partly because the column, *Women's World*, emphasized women's achievements and changing times. "Policewomen are no longer a novelty," the interview begins, disingenuously, "the sight of a woman lawyer excites no comment, but a woman writer of detective stories is still somewhat of a pioneer" (10).

In the interview, Christie suggests that she will never return to writing poetry because "[d]etective stories pay so much better"—the editor praises her "frankness" as "particularly charming" (10). Christie also suggests that she will not write about her experiences on tour until she is home, so she can gain some "distance" (10): in fact, she had already started sketching out *The Man in the Brown Suit*, inspired by experiences and characters she encountered in this time, but essentially it was true that she wrote about specific locales when she was not herself present.

See also: **Feminism**; *The Man in the Brown Suit*

Strange, Audrey
"A queer girl in many ways" (*TZ* 37), Audrey is the ex-wife of Nevile Strange, who divorced him to marry another man and became the subject of his psychopathic obsession in *Towards Zero*.

"The Strange Case of Sir Arthur Carmichael" (short story)
Purporting to be "from the notes of [an] eminent psychologist" (*HOD* 164), "The Strange Case of Sir Arthur Carmichael" is a supernatural short story. It shows the influence of Sir Arthur Conan Doyle on Christie: they both wrote supernatural stories alongside their crime fiction, and this one is certainly late-Victorian/Edwardian in tone. Dr. Edward Carstairs is called to look into "something uncanny" (166) in the home of Sir Arthur Carmichael, a young man whose personality has suddenly changed. When he visits, Carstairs learns that Sir Arthur has become obsessed with the sound and sight of "a fierce cat" (176), which nobody else has observed.

However, Carstairs hears it as well; he becomes convinced that it is some malevolent force targeting Sir Arthur. Before long, Sir Arthur's stepmother is attached and almost killed by a ghostly form, which turns out to have been, in some way, Sir Arthur himself. Both the Carmichaels recover. Carstairs realizes, but does not disclose, that Lady Carmichael had been experimenting with rituals to transport Sir Arthur's soul into the body of a cat, which she then killed, so that her son—his stepbrother—would inherit the estate. Events are officially explained as temporary illusions or dreams, and the matter rests without really being resolved.

This story combines early-twentieth-century interests in "psychology"—a catch-all term for the mysteries of the human brain, encompassing psychoanalysis and parapsychology—and heredity, with the central baronetcy inevitably evoking *The Hound of the Baskervilles* (even down to the corrupt first baronet's Christian name). It was first published in the United Kingdom in *The Hound of Death* (1933) and in the United States in *The Golden Ball* (1971).

Characters: Carmichael, Lady; **Carmichael, Sir Arthur;** Carmichael, Sir William; Carstairs, Dr. Edward; Patterson, Phyllis; Settle, Dr.

See also: **Curses; Conan Doyle, Sir Arthur;** *The Golden Ball* (story collection); *The Hound of Death* (story collection).

"Strange Jest" (story; alternative title: "A Case of Buried Treasure")

"Strange Jest" is quintessentially Miss Marple: it has her assisting a young couple with a matter of inheritance by drawing parallels with the people and places she knows, remembering old idioms, and using feminine domestic items. Jane Helier introduces Miss Marple to her friends Edward Rossiter and Charmian Stroud, a young couple. Charmian's mischievous uncle, Mathew Stroud, has died and left his fortune to them—but they cannot locate it. All they have to go on is Mathew's last gesture as he died: tapping his right eye and smiling.

Miss Marple compares Uncle Mathew to her own Uncle Henry who was "fond of practical jokes," leading Edward to think "she's gaga" (37). Visiting Uncle Mathew's house, Miss Marple uses a hairpin to discover a secret compartment within a secret drawer in a desk. However, it contains nothing but love letters and a recipe for gammon and spinach in old envelopes. The letters are signed "Betty Martin." Recalling that "all my eye and Betty Martin" and the expression "gammon and spinach" both mean "nonsense," Miss Marple realizes that the contents of the envelopes are valueless.

The stamps on the envelopes are extremely valuable and are actually the form of Uncle Mathew's fortune. Edward is so impressed that he promises to raise a glass to Uncle Henry (44).

The first magazine publication was in *This Week,* a magazine supplement of the [Washington, D.C.] *Sunday Star,* on 2 November 1941. The story appeared in the U.S. collection *Three Blind Mice* (1950) and the U.K. collection *Miss Marple's Final Cases* (1979). It was dramatized as an episode of *Agasa Kurisutī no Meitantei Powaro to Māpuru* in 2004.

Characters: Eldritch, Mrs.; **Helier, Jane; Henry, Uncle; Marple, Jane;** Stroud, Charmian; Stroud, Mathew; Rossiter, Edward; West, Lionel

Strange, Kay

The second wife of Nevile Strange in *Towards Zero,* Kay Strange is young and independently wealthy. Presented as spoilt and entitled, she is ultimately the victim of a man who married her for money, reflecting how women are blamed for men's dysfunction.

Strange, Nevile

Nevile Strange is a well-known and well-loved tennis player, caught between his ex-wife and his current wife in *Towards Zero.* A handsome, charming man, he is revealed to be a psychopath, with persistent homicidal childish tendencies, like Sergeant Trotter in *The Mousetrap.*

The Stranger (play)

In 1932, Christie adapted "Philomel Cottage" (1924) into a three-act play, *The Stranger,* but does not seem to have pursued performance seriously. Some years later, Frank Vosper would use this script as the basis for his own play, *Love from a Stranger.* In later life, Christie would remember this, incorrectly, as a one-act play, which had formed the third act of the later, more famous script. Christie's version would not be published—or indeed licensed for performance—until 2019, thanks to the archival work of producer Julius Green. Green considers the original to be "arguably the better play" (114). With a cast of six, the script is focused on character development, as Christie worked to flesh out the original story. By contrast, Vosper's version is more focused on plot and suspense.

Characters: Bradshaw, Enid; Birch, Mrs.; Huggins, Mrs.; Lane, Dick; Strange, Gerald; West, Doris

See also: *Love from a Stranger* (play); "Philomel Cottage" (story)

A Stranger Walked In (film). See *Love from a Stranger,* Screen Adaptations of

"A Stranger Walked in" (story). See "Philomel Cottage"

Stravinska, Anna

Anna Stravinska is the assumed name of a dead woman in *4.50 from Paddington,* whose body remains unidentified for a long time. Stravinska was a Russian dancer about whom little is known. She turns out to be the secret wife of Dr. Quimper, who kills her so he can woo and marry Emma Crackenthorpe.

Strete, Mildred

The biological daughter of Carrie Louise Serrocold (then Gulbrandsen) and Eric Gulbrandsen in *They Do It with Mirrors,* Mildred Strete has grown into a "respectable and slightly dull" "Canon's widow" (33). She is fiercely resentful of her adopted sister, Pippa, who she feels has taken all their parents' attention, and believes she is entitled, by blood, to more. However, she later mellows and becomes known to Pippa's chidden as "Aunt Mildred."

"Stronger than Death" (story)

An unpublished early supernatural short story, "Stronger than Death" is housed in the Christie Family Archive.

See also **"The Green Gate"**

Stubbs, Lady Harriet ("Hattie")

The real Hattie Stubbs is dead, and Sir George's insalubrious girlfriend has taken her place. She goes missing in "Hercule Poirot and the Greenshore Folly" and its expansion, *Dead Man's Folly,* when the real Hattie's cousin arrives on the scene, to avoid being identified. The pseudo-Hattie is remarkably dim-witted and pretty, unlike the real Hattie.

Stubbs, Sir George

Sir George Stubbs is a large, red-faced squire who owns Nasse House in *Dead Man's Folly* and Greenshore House in its

source novella, "Hercule Poirot and the Greenshore Folly." Married to Lady Hattie Stubbs, he is secretly James Folliat, an unsavory member of the family that built and traditionally owned the property, who has been proclaimed dead.

Styles House

In *The Mysterious Affair at Styles,* Christie's debut, the murders take place at a fictional Essex property, Styles Court. When Christie used her earnings to buy a property in Sunningdale in the early 1920s, her husband Archie suggested they call it Styles House. Like Styles in the book, the house proved a backdrop for great unhappiness. In fact, it was already, in Christie's words, "an unlucky house" with a history of tragedy: "The first [owner] lost all his money; the second his wife," and the third set of owners "separated" and "departed" (*AA* 345). Archie retained the house after the couple divorced and sold it in 1928.

See also: **Christie, Colonel Archibald (Archie)**; **Greenway House**; *The Mysterious Affair at Styles*; **Winterbrook House**

"The Stymphalean Birds" (alternative titles: "The Case of the Vulture Women"; "The Vulture Women"). See *The Labours of Hercules*

"The Submarine Plans" (story; alternative title: "The Shadow in the Night")

A short story that was later expanded into "The Incredible Theft," "The Submarine Plans" has a roughly similar plot. It was first published in *The Sketch* in 1923 and later appeared in the U.S. collection *The Under Dog* (1961) and the U.K. collection *Poirot's Early Cases* (1974). This story is perhaps Christie's take on Sir Arthur Conan Doyle's "The Adventure of the Naval Treaty" (1893), just as "The Veiled Lady" is a version of "The Illustrious Client."

Characters: Alloway, Lord; Carson, Mrs.; Fitzroy; **Hastings, Captain Arthur**; **Poirot, Hercule**; Weardale, Sir Henry (Harry); Weardale, Lady Juliet; Weardale, Leonard

See also: **Conan Doyle, Sir Arthur**; **"The Incredible Theft"**; *Poirot's Early Cases*; *The Under Dog* (story collection)

Suchet, Sir David (1946–)

David Suchet is an actor, best-known as

"the definitive Hercule Poirot" (Sova 318), having played the character in television adaptations of nearly every Poirot novel and short story. Suchet, who was knighted in 2020, feels a strong attachment to the character. In his memoir, *Poirot and Me*, he claims to be "the custodian of Dame Agatha's creation" (Suchet and Wansell 91). His first brush with Christie was playing Inspector Japp to Peter Ustinov's Poirot in *Thirteen at Dinner* (1985).

See also ***Agatha Christie's Poirot***

Sugden, Superintendent

Superintendent Sugden is the investigating officer in *Hercule Poirot's Christmas*, who turns out to be an illegitimate son of the victim. He murdered Simeon Lee in an act of revenge with childlike venom and resourcefulness. The character, and his spectacular breakdown upon being identified as the murderer, are drawn similarly to Sergeant Trotter in *The Mousetrap*.

Suicide

It is an open secret that Christie was suicidal in 1926. During the breakdown of her marriage, she thought more than once about "ending it all" (HOS 11), and rumors persisted that she had at one point tried to fling herself from a balcony—something that she discusses in the pseudonymous *Unfinished Portrait*. Perhaps for this reason, suicide is not treated lightly in her fiction. It is, in fact, treated far less lightly than murder.

Overall, characters who commit suicide in her fiction are rare. They are normally penitent (or cornered) murderers, as in *The Murder of Roger Ackroyd*, *Death on the Nile*, *And Then There Were None*, *Crooked House*, and the play version of *Appointment with Death*. Christie's fiction makes occasional use of the ploy whereby an apparent suicide turns out to be murder (*Why Didn't They Ask Evans?*, *Cards on the Table*, "Dead Man's Mirror," *The Moving Finger*, *Sparkling Cyanide*, and *Taken at the Flood*). In these cases, when characters speak lightly of suicide, it reflects poorly on them—these are presented as idle gossip with accompanying aphorisms and truisms such as "[t]hose people who threaten suicide never do it" (*SpC* 25).

The ultimate act of self-sabotage is treated more heavily by the author. The murder-looking-like-suicide trick is inverted in "The Market Basing Mystery" and "Murder in the Mews," two versions of the same plot in which a woman has been driven to kill herself. In both stories, a loyal friend stages the scene to look like murder so that the man who is morally responsible for the death can be implicated. It also appears in "Wasp's Nest," where a man plans his own suicide to set up a rival as murderer. Even within the superficial parameters of short genre fiction, this is a considered reflection on the psychology of guilt and accountability.

Murder on the Orient Express includes a rare example of the murderers going unpunished—because they are seen to be serving justice on Samuel Ratchett (aka Cassetti), who epitomizes evil. Among his many crimes, he is responsible for a number of suicides: people who killed themselves after the trauma he inflicted by masterminding the kidnap and murder of a child. Those victims' loved ones have joined with others to exert revenge, which Poirot sees as justifiable.

Towards Zero begins with a man contemplating throwing himself into the sea: it takes the course of the novel for him to discover a reason to live: not happiness but utility, as he helps to solve the case and restore justice. A more intense version of the same dynamic is at the heart of *Destination Unknown*. There are no easy, pat solutions to suicidal tendencies in Christie, but ways of learning to live with them.

See also: ***Destination Unknown***; **Disappearance of Agatha Christie**; **"The Man from the Sea"**; ***Towards Zero***; ***Unfinished Portrait***

Summerhayes, Maureen

An attractive, disorganized woman, Maureen Summerhayes runs a guesthouse in Broadhinny with her husband, Major Johnnie Summerhayes, in *Mrs. McGinty's Dead*. Her cooking is not to Poirot's taste, but he teaches her how to cook omelets. She is mentioned in *Cat Among the Pigeons* as a friend of Julia and Mrs. Upjohn.

"The Sunningdale Mystery" (story; alternative title: "The Sunninghill Mystery").

See ***Partners in Crime*** (story collection)

The Sunningdale Mystery (story collection)

In 1933, Collins published chapters 11 to 23 of *Partners in Crime* as *The Sunningdale Mystery*, a cheap volume preceding the first paperback. The collection is composed of the following short stories: "**The Sunningdale Mystery**," "**The House of Lurking Death**," "**The Unbreakable Alibi**," "**The Clergyman's Daughter**," "**The Red House**," "**The Ambassador's Boots**," and "**The Man Who Was No. 16.**"

"The Sunninghill Mystery." See "**The Sunningdale Mystery**" (story)

"The 'Supernatural' Murder." See "**The Idol House of Astarte**"

The Suspects. See *The Hollow* (play)

Sutcliffe, Jennifer

Jennifer Sutcliffe is niece to Bob Rawlinson and a schoolgirl who lacks imagination in *Cat Among the Pigeons*. Her tennis racket hides valuable jewels, unbeknownst to her; she swaps it with Julia Upjohn because the grip is awkward.

"Swan Song" (story)

An uncharacteristically dark story that closes *The Listerdale Mystery*, "Swan Song" concerns a mercurial opera singer's last performance. Portraying Tosca, Paula Nazorkoff stabs the man who wronged her lover during her performance. First published in the *Grand Magazine* in September 1926, the story draws on Christie's interest in opera as a potential career prior to writing; it is likely that she wrote another version in her teens or twenties. "Swan Song" appears in the U.K. anthology *The Listerdale Mystery* (1934) and the U.S. anthology *The Golden Ball* (1971). BBC Radio 4 broadcast a 30-minute modernized adaptation, including lesbians in what was perhaps a test of the waters before greater liberties along these lines were authorized for ITV's *Agatha Christie's Marple* from 2004.

Characters: Amery, Blanche; Bréon, Edouard; Calthorp, Donald; Capelli, Bianca; Cowan, Mr.; Elise; Leconmere, Lord; **Nazorkoff, Paula**; Read, Vera; Rustonbury, Lady; Rustonbury, Lord; Roscari, Signor

See also: **BBC Radio Adaptations**; *The Golden Ball* (story collection); *The Listerdale Mystery* (story collection); **Music**

Symmington, Mona, and Richard ("Dick")

Mona Symmington is the first victim in *The Moving Finger* (1943), whose reputation as a hypochondriac convinces people that her death was suicide, and Richard Symmington is her husband who kills her. Although, as several characters point out, the husband is normally the most likely suspect in murder cases, Symmington exploits local prejudice about rumors in anonymous letters and the assumption that a woman must be behind such spiteful actions to evade the police.

Taken at the Flood (novel; alternative title: *There Is a Tide*)

A strikingly complex novel with a three-book structure, *Taken at the Flood* represents Christie's negotiation of changing times and changing requirements for crime fiction following World War II. The plot concerns the wealthy Cloade family in the aftermath of patriarch Gordon Cloade's death in a wartime bombing. They have been sheltered from the wider world, never needing to work or make much effort because Gordon provided each with a stable income, but his new young wife, Rosaleen, is poised to inherit all his money.

The arrival of Rosaleen, whom none of the Cloades have met, causes some discomfort. Although she is easily swayed and seems happy to write checks for any family petitioners, her protective brother, David Hunter, insists that she should keep all the money. Soon, a man arrives in the village, implying that he is Robert Underhay, Rosaleen's presumed-dead first husband (thus making her marriage to and inheritance from Gordon invalid), although there is some evidence that he is an actor, hired by the Cloades. Before long, he turns up dead, and Hercule Poirot becomes involved. Major Porter, a mutual friend of Poirot and Underhay, identifies the body as Underhay's but soon commits suicide, out of guilt for lying to the police. The dead man was not Underhay but rather a distant relative of the Cloades.

Rosaleen grows more and more fearful of the ill will surrounding her, becoming agitated. She is found dead of apparent suicide, but Poirot reveals that it was murder. Poirot identifies Hunter as Rosaleen's killer, suggesting that she was never his sister. Rosaleen died by the same bomb as Gordon, and Hunter convinced an impressionable housemaid to pose as his sister so that he could claim the Cloade inheritance; he killed her to prevent her from confessing to Poirot. Poirot attributes the death of the stranger to nervous cousin Rowley Cloade, who accidentally knocked him against a fender in a fit of rage upon discovering that he was playing an unethical trick on Rosaleen. Poirot agrees to pin the crime on Hunter and advises Rowley to settle down with his cousin, Lynn Marchmont.

Lynn is a central figure in this novel. Returning from active duty as a WREN, she is frustrated to find that, although the war changed her life fundamentally, nothing at home has changed. She grows frustrated with her cousin/fiancé Rowley, who did not serve in the war, and who is just the same as ever, and is briefly attracted to the dangerous Hunter. However, the ever-changed Lynn and the ever-the-same Rowley end up happily preparing for marriage when Rowley reveals an unexpected violent streak, and they look forward to striking a balance between continuity and adventure.

Several features of earlier works are recycled in Taken at the Flood. As in "While the Light Lasts," a man calling himself Enoch Arden appears to be a deceased first husband. As in "The Sign in the Sky," steam from a train forms a question mark in the sky, noted by a lovesick woman as an omen but in fact providing a clue about times and timing. As in The Floating Admiral, a man poses as a woman to evade detection. As in Murder in Mesopotamia, Poirot tells a young woman that she is lucky to have a man who might strike her, because it shows he cares. As in "The King of Clubs," an accidental killing is staged to look like a murder.

The working title was Cover Her Face, a quotation from John Webster's The Duchess of Malfi that became the working title for Sleeping Murder. In the latter text, a man recites the relevant passage—lamenting the death of a sister—over his sister's corpse after he has killed her. Christie's notebooks show that she originally planned to have Hunter deliver the same lines, ritualistically (Curran, Secret Notebooks 398). Presumably, this would not have connected with the death of his imposter sister but would have occurred earlier to provide an opaque clue that the real Rosaleen was dead. However, with the Tennyson quotation and the Shakespeare quotation, there were likely already enough allusions in the text. Either way, Christie went on to use the "cover her face" idea effectively in Sleeping Murder.

The novel was submitted for publication as There Is a Tide—a quote from William Shakespeare's The Tempest that appears in the book. However, Collins, Christie's U.K. publisher, feared a mix-up with another novel in bookshops, There Is a Time, so the book became Taken at the Flood, another part of the same quotation. However, this change was made too late for the U.S. edition so, as with Sparkling Cyanide/Remembered Death, the U.S. version carries Christie's specified title.

Christie was asked by a magazine to abridge the manuscript for serialization, and the surprisingly explicit demands included removing Hercule Poirot. Angry but obliging, Christie made the changes, but the magazine decided not to publish that version. There was, then, no magazine serialization, and the book was published in the United States in March 1948 (Dodd, Mead) and the United Kingdom in November 1948 (Collins).

A BBC Radio 4 dramatization, featuring John Moffatt aired in 2003 and the relevant episode of Agatha Christie's Poirot, starring David Suchet, was broadcast in 2006.

Characters: **Arden, Enoch**; Cloade, Frances; Cloade, Gordon; Cloade, Jeremy; Cloade, Katherine ("Kathy"); **Cloade, Roland ("Rowley")**; **Cloade, Rosaleen**; **Corrigan, Eileen**; **Edna**; Elvary, Madame; **George(s)**; Graves, Sergeant; **Hunter, David**; **Leadbetter, Mrs.**; Lippencott, Beatrice; **Marchmont, Adela**; **Marchmont, Lynn**; Mellon, Mr.; **Poirot, Hercule**; **Porter, Major**; **Spence, Superintendent Bert**; Underhay, Robert; Vavasour, Johnnie

See also: **Agatha Christie's Poirot;**

Feminism; *Hercule Poirot* (BBC radio series); "The King of Clubs"; Shakespeare, William; "The Sign in the Sky"; War; "While the Light Lasts" (story)

A Talent for Murder (Wilson). See **Fictional Portrayals of Agatha Christie**

Tanios, Arabella ("Bella")

Arabella Tanios is the overlooked niece of Emily Arundell and cousin of the more extroverted Charles and Theresa Arundell in *Dumb Witness*. She is considered a tragic figure by the family, particularly Theresa, whose style she copies at a fraction of the price. As a murderer, she uses this and prejudice against her Greek husband to her advantage, cultivating the impression that she is an abused wife and stirring suspicion against him. The novel is inconsistent about whether her maiden name was "Winter" or "Biggs" (although, as her father was Professor Biggs, the latter is most likely).

Tanios, Dr. Jacob

Dr. Jacob Tanios is the Greek husband of Bella Tanios in *Dumb Witness*. Prejudice against him is rife in the village, although he is a blameless man. His wife, who is a murderer, uses this prejudice to frame him for her crimes.

"Tape-Measure Murder" (story; alternative titles: "The Case of the Retired Jeweller"; "Village Murder")

A St. Mary Mead mystery, "Tape-Measure Murder" has a woman with newfound orthodox Christian fervor found murdered when a dressmaker arrives at her door. Her remarkably stoic husband is suspected. However, Miss Marple proves that the killer was the dressmaker, afraid that the victim would confess their past as robbers/jewel thieves to a charismatic evangelist. The story is a typical example of a familiar, everyday village setting and characters enabling Christie to deal with the extremes of human behavior, as she considers the psychology of religious mania. This extends beyond the highly strung victim, Mrs. Spenlow, and the charming evangelist, Ted Gerard. Mr. Spenlow, whose silence is so suspicious, sees his "fortitude" as noble, because he once read about a Chinese philosopher who was admired for carrying on as normal when his wife died. Miss Marple points out: "the people of St Mary Mead react rather differently. Chinese philosophy does not appeal to them" (*MMFC* 57). Nor does it appeal to Mr. Spenlow, who has merely read about a philosopher. Miss Marple's Uncle Henry, "a man of unusual self-control" (57), makes an appearance in the form of an anecdote.

"Tape-Measure Murder" was published in *This Week,* a magazine supplement of the [Washington, D.C.] *Sunday Star,* on 16 November 1941 and in *The Strand* the following year. It appeared in the U.S. anthology *Three Blind Mice* (1950) and in the UK anthology *Miss Marple's Final Cases* (1979). On 3 October 2004, an animated version was broadcast on NHK as part of *Agasa Kurisutī no Meitantei Powaro to Māpuru.* On 16 September 2015, a radio adaptation, part of *Miss Marple's Final Cases,* was broadcast on BBC Radio 4.

Characters: Abercrombie, Jim; Abercrombie, Sir Robert; Antony; Gerard, Ted; Gordon; **Hartnell, Amanda; Henry, Uncle; Marple, Jane; Melchett, Colonel; Palk, Constable;** Pollit, Miss; **Slack, Inspector;** Spenlow, Mr.; Spenlow, Mrs.; Young Fred

See also: ***Agasa Kurisutī no Meitantei Powaro to Māpuru***; ***Miss Marple's Final Cases*** (radio series); ***Miss Marple's Final Cases*** (story collection); **St. Mary Mead**

Tarka. See **Indian-Language Adaptations**

Tatiana, Grand Duchess

Mentioned in *Appointment with Death,* the Grand Duchess Tatiana is the daughter of a tsar, believed killed in a revolution but rumored to be alive and living in New York. This is Christie's latest of several evocations of the story of the Grand Duchess Anastasia of Russia, who was killed in the 1918 revolution but rumored to have survived. By 1938 when *Appointment with Death* was published, Anna Anderson, the most famous imposter claiming to be Anastasia, had become extremely well-known, and she and several others had operated from New York. Christie also references the Anastasia case obliquely in "The Girl in the Train" and "Jane in Search of a Job."

Taylor, Beatrice

Beatrice Taylor is a teenage girl who

committed suicide in the past in *And Then There Were None*. In service to Emily Brent, she became pregnant, and her employer turned her out and condemned her with fanatical religiosity, leading to her suicide. As her own death approaches, Brent begins to feel guilt and believes that Beatrice is haunting her, exacting revenge.

Tayna Chyornykj Drozdov (The Secret of the Blackbirds, film)

The first Russian-language movie based on a Christie novel, *Tayna Chyornykj Drozdov* (The Secret of the Blackbirds) was released in the Soviet Union on 21 November 1983. This was based on *A Pocket Full of Rye*. It was directed by Vadim Derbenyov and starred Estonian veteran Ita Ever as Miss Marple. With a rich color palette, the film follows the novel's plot closely while emphasizing the grotesqueness of the murder victim's vast wealth.

See also: *A Pocket Full of Rye*

Tea for Three (play)

Tea for Three, the one-act adaptation of the short story "Accident," was penned in 1939 by Margery Vosper, sister of Frank Vosper, who had adapted Christie's "Philomel Cottage" as *Love from a Stranger*. It is unclear why the play was written or if it was performed at the time, but it was published in an anthology, *Nelson's Theatre Craft Series No. 2*, with works by five other authors. It has certainly been staged by amateur and repertory companies in the United Kingdom and the United States over the years. The 10-page script follows Christie's plot fairly closely, and all the action takes place in a country house's lounge-drawing room.

See also: "**Accident**"; *Love from a Stranger* (play)

Teddy Bear (play)

Described by theater producer Julius Green as "endearing and performable" (41), *Teddy Bear* is a one-act play that has never been published or produced. It exists only in the Christie Family Archive. Green places its composition in the 1910s (41–43), but it may be even older. A comedy for two men and two women, it was written under the name George Miller. It concerns Virginia, who resolves to become a juvenile

criminal to interest a philanthropist who seemingly gives all his attention to worthy causes. In the end, she gives up and settles for a poor but eager suitor. The basic set-up is used to more sinister effect in *Hickory Dickory Dock* (1955).

See also: **Hickory Dickory Dock**

Teia de Aranha (Cobweb, television adaptation)

A 1961 television adaptation of *Spider's Web*, *Teia de Aranha* (Cobweb) was a filmed stage performance, airing on Portuguese television on 2 December 1961. Among the cast was the noted Ruy de Carvalho, fresh from a successful run in the Portuguese version of *The Mousetrap*. De Carvalho soon left the stage to focus on film and television but in 2020 agreed to return to *The Mousetrap*, aged 93, although the COVID-19 pandemic and a hernia operation thwarted these plans.

See also: **Spider's Web** (play and novel)

Teledrama. See And Then There Were None, Screen Adaptations of; The Mousetrap, Screen Adaptations of

Temple, Dr. Elizabeth

A retired headmistress in *Nemesis* who was acquainted with the dead Verity Hunt, Dr. Elizabeth Temple is too intelligent to be happy. This manifests in strange, esoteric conversations with Miss Marple, in which Dr. Temple declares that people who die young avoid a lot of pain.

Ten Little Indians. See And Then There Were None (novel); And Then There Were None (1943 play); And Then There Were None, Screen Adaptations of

Ten Little Ni---rs. See And Then There Were None (novel); And Then There Were None (1943 play); And Then There Were None, Screen Adaptations of

"The £10 Adventure." See "The Case of the City Clerk"

Ten Years (play)

An unpublished, unperformed one-act play, *Ten Years* exists only in the Christie Family Archive. According to Julius Green, it was likely inspired by George Bernard Shaw's plays. Specifically, Green suggests that it and three other short plays (*Teddy*

Bear, *Marmalade Moon*, and *Eugenia and Eugenics*) may have been intended as "comic interludes" in Grand Guignol performances (53). At the center of the script is a couple, Elliot and Désirée, who have agreed to a trial of married life for 10 years. Toward the end of the period, Elliot believes it has been a great success and that it has cured him of a disdain for orthodoxy. Désirée, however, declares that she is looking forward to being free again: "I want to *live*—to live *my* life—not yours" (Green 51; emphasis in original). The play ends with the couple agreeing to stay together for the sake of their child. Presuming Christie wrote this in the early years of a marriage that lasted longer than it could have for the sake of her daughter, it is not difficult to infer, as Green does (50), that there is an autobiographical influence at work.

See also: *Eugenia and Eugenics*; **Marmalade Moon**; *Teddy Bear*

"The Terrible Catastrophe." See **The Big Four** (novel)

"Test for Murder." See **"Accident"**

A *Théâtre ce Soiru* (Theater Tonight, television series)

The French television series *Théâtre ce Soir* (Theater Tonight) was broadcast from 1966 to 1986 on France 1. It consisted of filmed productions of live stage shows. Among these were two Christie plays: *Spider's Web* ("La Toile d'Araignée") on 3 January 1969 and *And Then There Were None* ("Dix Petits Nègres") on 1 October 1970.

See also *And Then There Were None*, **Screen Adaptations of**

The *Theatre Guild on the Air* (radio series)

The WKNA radio series *The Theatre Guild on the Air* was broadcast in the United States from 1945 to 1953. On 16 March 1952, it featured a 60-minute adaptation of the play *Love from a Stranger*, starring Ray Milland and Edna Best.

See also: *Love from a Stranger* (play)

Theatricality

A growing body of criticism agrees that "Christie's world is a world of theatricality and secrecy" (York 6). Her oft-criticized use of character stereotypes is being re-evaluated as strategic: she shows characters *pretending* to be extremely conventional "types" to hide their secrets, which could be almost anything, and the fact that readers might not necessarily see depth on the page just means it is not being shown: not that it is absent. Moreover, Christie's crimes themselves, with complicated mechanisms involved, are often highly theatrical.

This is not just the case in narratives with theatrical settings such as *Three Act Tragedy*, where the murderer is an actor who is always playing an onstage or offstage part, or *Lord Edgware Dies*, in which identities are routinely swapped between a variety of people connected with theatrical circles. It is also the case in, for example, *Death on the Nile* and *They Do It with Mirrors*, where colluding murderers perform violent scenes to distract witnesses from something happening elsewhere. Identity and behavior in Christie, then, are presented as artificial and performative.

See also: **Death on the Nile** (novel); **Lord Edgware Dies** (novel); *They Do It with Mirrors*; *Three-Act Tragedy*

"The Theft of the Opalsen Pearls." See **"The Jewel Robbery at the Grand Metropolitan"**

"The Theft of the Royal Ruby." See **"The Adventure of the Christmas Pudding"**

There Is a Tide. See *Taken at the Flood*

"There Where My Lover Lies." See *The Road of Dreams* (poetry collection)

"There's Nothing Like Love." See **"Yellow Iris"** (story)

Thesiger, James ("Jimmy")

James Thesiger is a Bright Young Thing in *The Seven Dials Mystery* who becomes involved in Bundle Brent's investigation but turns out to be the murderer. His motive is unusual: he seems to be committing murder chiefly out of boredom. The idea of young aristocrats lacking any purpose or role in life and turning destructive was widespread in 1920s popular culture. Thesiger is a specifically Christian reflection on the nightclub phenomenon in that he is not actually connected with the nightclub in the novel but still typifies some of the problems discussed arising from it.

They Came to Baghdad (novel)

Published in 1951, *They Came to Baghdad* was Christie's first thriller since *N or M?* a decade earlier. It is a spy story with comic elements—indeed, it was marketed as "Her gayest novel yet"—with the action taking place in London and Baghdad. The book was not well-received by Christie's publishers, which even asked her agent, Edmund Cork, if it had been submitted as a joke. However, Christie pushed for it to be published quickly before the political situation in Western Asia overtook the events of the novel. Despite the publishers' reservations and only modest success in the United Kingdom, the book was so well received in the United States that it was immediately adapted for television.

The heroine, Victoria Jones, is very much in the mold of Anne Beddingfeld in *The Man in the Brown Suit*: young and restless with a vast imagination and appetite who is a good and enthusiastic liar. Whereas Anne eats ice cream, Victoria eats sandwiches. Sacked from her job as a typist because of a joke at her employer's expense, she wonders what to do and meets a cherubically good-looking man, Edward Goring, on a park bench. Edward tells her he is flying out to Baghdad to work for Dr. Rathbone, a translator, and Victoria decides, on a whim, to meet him there. On the journey to Baghdad, she observes several colorful characters and invents extravagant lies about her own background. In Baghdad, she is flung into a wild adventure, when a man stumbles into her hotel room, begging her to hide him, and dies (another parallel to Anne).

Investigating his cryptic last words, she joins an archaeological dig where, miraculously, the leader Dr. Pauncefoot Jones accepts her as a niece he has forgotten. She comes to learn of a secret meeting between world superpowers in Baghdad to discuss the development of a new type of weapon. With the help of the British Secret Service, Victoria traces attempts to sabotage the meeting to an organization apparently seeking world peace: the Olive Branch.

The book may be escapist, but it is also thoroughly engaged in the changing state of the world, and there are elements of Christie's own experiences in Baghdad in it. The spy/victim Henry Carmichael, known as Fakir, is a fairly obvious portrait of T.E. Lawrence (aka Lawrence of Arabia). Real assassinations are mentioned, and themes from Christie's bleak "Lullaby of Nimrud" are repeated. The book is dedicated "to all my friends in Baghdad," and its ending is optimistic. There are hints that peace could be on the horizons for these nations. It is implied that a war that was brewing in Korea can now be avoided (as Christie's eagerness to publish shows, she was likely aware that the Korea War and the Cold War would pan out differently). Adding to the optimism, Victoria grows out of her infatuation with a beautiful man about whom she only knows his name.

Prior to its book publication on 5 March 1951, *They Came to Baghdad* was published in an abridged eight-part serial in *John Bull* magazine in the United Kingdom. Later that year, the same abridged serial appeared in the *Star* newspaper in Canada. The novel was filmed as a live episode of *Studio One* in the United States in 1952. In 1983, CBS acquired the rights for a modernized television version, and, despite a script appearing in the late 1980s, this did not materialize. The idea of a modernized film version was proposed in the early 2000s but also went nowhere. In 2018, Entertainment One acquired the rights for a television miniseries, to air in 2022.

Characters: **Abdul**; Baker, Richard; Best, Mr.; Cardew Trench, Mrs.; Carmichael, Harry; Catherine; Clayton, Gerald; Clayton, Rosa; **Crofton-Lee, Sir Rupert**; Crosbie, Captain; Dakin; **Goring, Edward**; Hamilton-Clipp, Mr.; Hamilton-Clipp, Mrs.; Harold; Hassan, Salah; **Jones, Victoria**; Morganthal, Otto; **Pauncefort-Jones, Dr.**; Pauncefort-Jones, Elsie; Rakounian, Michael; **Rathbone, Dr.**; **Scheele, Anna**; Shrivenham, Lionel; Tio, Marcus; Wygate, Miss

See also: **Archaeology; CBS Television Adaptations;** *Destination Unknown;* *They Came to Baghdad* **(2022 television adaptation)**

They Came to Baghdad (1952 television adaptation). See **CBS Television Adaptations**

They Came to Baghdad (2023 television adaptation)

Entertainment One acquired the rights to adapt *They Came to Baghdad* (1951) for television in 2018. The studio announced plans to film a miniseries for release in the 2020s, with production overseen by Carolyn Newman and Polly Williams. Plans to option the novel had previously come up in the early 2000s, when Entertainment One was discussing modernized versions of this, *Witness for the Prosecution*, and *Death on the Nile*.

See also: *They Came to Baghdad* (novel)

They Do It with Mirrors (novel; alternative title: *Murder with Mirrors*)

In this novel, Miss Marple stays with an old friend, Carrie Louise Serrocold, who is troubled by something indefinable. Carrie Louise lives with her third husband, Lewis, and an extended family from various marriages at Stoneygates, a crumbling gothic estate that is partly used as a rehabilitation facility for juvenile delinquents.

Christian Gulbrandsen, Carrie Louise's stepson from a previous marriage, visits and appears troubled. He asks Lewis about the state of Carrie Louise's heart. One of the delinquents, Edgar Lawson, who works as a kind of secretary to Lewis, has a strange habit of claiming famous men are secretly his father. One day, he explodes in front of everyone and locks himself in a room with Lewis, shouting that Lewis is his real father. As this is going on, distant gunshots are heard, and Gulbrandsen later is found dead.

Inevitably, secrets emerge, and there are more deaths. Lewis confides in Miss Marple and the police that Carrie Louise is being poisoned; he says this is what Gulbrandsen found out. Carrie Louise refuses to believe that anyone is trying to kill her, a perspective that is widely dismissed as naïve. Finally, Miss Marple reveals that Lewis is the murderer, and Edgar really is his son. The argument behind a closed door was staged to give Lewis time to run around the property and fire the shot. Carrie Louise was never being poisoned; Gulbrandsen had discovered financial irregularities in the running of Stoneygates. All of this is secondary to the emotional story lines in this complicated family, where half-siblings and adopted siblings resent one another, and, like the building itself, this ever-growing family is unsustainable.

At the heart of *They Do It with Mirrors* are theatricality and showmanship. There is, of course, the use of theater as therapy for young criminals and the extremely theatrical set-up of the crime itself. The U.K. title alludes to a magician's trick—that is to say, an act performed for an audience. Miss Marple only solves the case when she thinks "in terms of theatre," considering everyone who heard the argument between Lewis and Edgar as "the audience" (*TDM* 187). But the theatricality runs to the setting and characters themselves as well. Stoneygates is not what it appears—it is a crumbling gothic manor, no longer fit for a purpose, playing the part of a stable country family home at the same time as it plays the part of a modern, state-of-the-art reform family for young offenders. Edgar is similarly too mad to be real. The character is deliberately presented as theatrical so that nobody—including the reader—will believe him when he tells the truth: that he is Lewis's son.

Of all the characters, Carrie Louise is the one who appears most "out of touch with reality" (209); the one who has spent a glamorous life thinking the best of people, slipping in and out of marriages, and making herself look younger than she is. However, as Miss Marple points out, she is the only one *in touch* with reality, and easy assumptions about what is and is not natural are themselves illusions.

The other key theme in this novel, bound up with its staginess, is a discussion, widespread in the 1950s, of nature versus nurture. This key theme, bound up in the presentation of family homes and juvenile delinquency, is also present in many of Christie's contemporary works: *Crooked House* (1949), *Mrs. McGinty's Dead* (1952), and *Ordeal by Innocence* (1958), for example. The attempt to maintain a Victorian family home on the same grounds as a modern rehabilitation center for young offenders is doomed to overlap in a mutually destructive way. Indeed, the man trying to tie together the incompatible ideas of rehabilitating juvenile delinquents while maintaining a (mostly reconstructed) nuclear family is the murderer, and one of his "cases"—his accomplice—is his son. Moreover, a central dynamic in the novel is the resentment that Mildred Strete, Carrie-Louise's only biological daughter, feels for another line of the family: the one descended from her adopted sister, Pippa. Her insistence that blood ties are important reaches its zenith when she discovers that her sister's biological father was a murderer and therefore accuses her niece of murder. She undergoes a change of heart by the end of the novel, as the family branches out, and she becomes a real, caring aunt.

Following abridged serializations in *Cosmopolitan* and *John Bull*, the novel was published by Dodd, Mead in the United States, then Collins in the United Kingdom, in 1952. It has been filmed for television four times: first, as the second and last outing for Helen Hayes as Miss Marple in CBS's *Murder with Mirrors* (1985); next as a 1991 episode of the BBC's *Miss Marple* with Joan Hickson; then as a 2010 episode of ITV's *Agatha Christie's Marple* with Julia McKenzie; and, in 2013, a French version, part of *Les Petits Meurtres d'Agatha Christie*, which dispenses with Christie's series detectives. There has also been a BBC Radio 4 adaptation, staring June Whitfield, broadcast in 2001.

Characters: Backhouse, Johnnie; Baumgarten, Mr.; Bellever, Juliet ("Jolly"); Curry, Inspector; Galbraith, Dr.; Gilfoy, Mr.; Gregg, Ernie; Gulbrandsen, Christian; Gulbrandsen, Eric; **Hudd, Georgina ("Gina")**; Hudd, Walter; Jenkins, Arthur; Lake, Detective Sergeant; **Lawson, Edgar**; **Marple, Jane**; Maverick, Dr.; Moncrieff, Miss; **Reilly, Mr.**; Restarick, Alexis ("Alex"); Restarick, Johnnie; Restarick, Stephen; San Severiano, Guido; San Severiano, Philippa ("Pippa"); **Serrocold, Carrie Louise**; **Serrocold, Lewis**; Strete, Canon; **Strete, Mildred**; **Van Rydock, Ruth**; Wylie, Leonard

See also: *Agatha Christie's Marple*; **CBS Television Adaptations**; *Miss Marple* **(radio series)**; *Miss Marple* **(television series)**; **Theatricality**

"The Third-Floor Flat" (story; alternative title: "In the Third Floor Flat")

In the early short story "The Third-Floor Flat," Hercule Poirot investigates a murder in the flat two floors beneath his own. It is very much in the Sherlock Holmes vein, with Poirot receiving respect and recognition from his published cases, just as Holmes does in Sir Arthur Conan Doyle's short stories. The story has proven problematic for Christie scholars trying to locate Poirot's living quarters, as he is said here to live on the fifth floor of Friar Mansions and not Whitehaven Mansions, his better-known address.

The story has Poirot becoming acquainted with four young people who are in and out of romantic entanglements and who stumble upon a body when one of them enters the wrong flat after a night out. This was, of course, no accident but a scheme by one to kill his secret wife.

"The Third-Floor Flat" was published in January 1929 in the United Kingdom in *Hutchinson's Magazine* and in the United States in *Detective Story Magazine*. It appeared in the U.S. collection *Three Blind Mice* (1950) and the U.K. collection *Poirot's Early Cases* (1974). A BBC radio adaptation was broadcast in 1954. A television adaptation, part of *Agatha Christie's Poirot*, was broadcast on ITV on 5 February 1989. On 26 August 2006, German radio station SWR broadcast its own version as part of *Krimi-Sommer mit Hercule Poirot* (Crime Summer with Hercule Poirot).

Characters: Bailey, Donovan; **Faulkener, Jimmy**; Garnett, Patricia ("Pat"); Grant, Ernestine; Hope, Mildred; **Poirot, Hercule**; **Rice, Inspector**

See also: *Agatha Christie's Poirot*; **BBC Radio Adaptations**; *Krimi-Sommer mit Hercule Poirot*; *Poirot's Early Cases*; *Three Blind Mice* **(story collection)**

Third Girl (novel)

The 1966 "Christie for Christmas" shows efforts to accommodate contemporary culture, typical of the author's work in that decade. *Third Girl* is largely from the perspective of Christie's fictional alter ego, Ariadne Oliver, allowing her to comment on how times, fashions, and people have changed over time. This is done with wry humor rather than with any real attempt to understand change: for example, Mrs. Oliver reflects at one point that "LSD" should refer to pounds, shillings, and pence. "Long-haired fellows, beatniks, Beatles, all sorts" are dismissed as "silly" (43), albeit by an unsympathetic character, but Christie makes a genuine attempt to insert Hercule Poirot and Mrs. Oliver into their world.

In 1966, the year of publication of *Third Girl,* Christie gave a rare and therefore highly-quoted interview with Francis Wyndham in the *Sunday Times* (reprinted in the *Washington Post*). In it, she notes that:

> [m]odern taste has changed very largely from detective stories to crime stories … just a series of violent episodes succeeding each other…. I'm afraid Poirot gets more and more unreal as time goes by. A private detective who takes cases just doesn't exist these days, so it becomes more difficult to involve him and make him convincing in so doing [E5].

This idea that Poirot is a detective out of his own time provides the novel's premise. Poirot is at breakfast considering the monograph he has written. This is itself a self-consciously fictional move, because Sherlock Holmes famous wrote monographs. It also links back to *The Clocks,* where the project is first mentioned. Poirot's "*Magnum Opus*" is a critical survey not of detectives but of detective fiction through history, finding fault with Edgar Allan Poe but praising Wilkie Collins and some U.S. authors (*TG* 5)—the book therefore interacts on the first page with its own status as an unfashionable branch of genre fiction and shows the central character agreeing with changing tastes. Poirot's manservant George tells him "a young person" wishes to consult him "about a murder she might have committed" (6–7). However, when this woman appears, she refuses to see him because he is "too old" (9). The brief first chapter, then, shows clear authorial awareness of how Poirot novels are perceived and commits to address the issue.

Poirot works with Mrs. Oliver to identify his visitor and learns that she is Norma Restarick, a "Third Girl" (that is, a member of a modern flat-share who responded to a newspaper notice). Their next step is to find out the person whom Norma might have murdered. They learn that she is addicted to drugs, and Poirot's old friend Dr. Stillingfleet looks after her. Meanwhile, Mrs. Oliver ends up shadowing the mercurial David Baker, Norma's artistic boyfriend, and is knocked unconscious. The detectives enter two worlds: that of Norma's middle-class, extended family and that of young, hedonistic artists. The solution finally reached by Poirot is an astonishing mix of old-school double-identities in Swinging Sixties trappings. He reveals that Norma's stepmother and her roommate are one and the same and that her father is an imposter and that they had been plotting a series of murders to gain the family fortune, pumping Norma with drugs to set her up to believe that she had committed the crimes.

Christie was informed that her editor was "amazed at the way you have 'got' young people" in the novel (qtd. in L. Thompson 467), although critics over the years have been less kind. Robert Barnard, for example, calls it "embarrassing" (197). The general consensus is that Christie shows an elderly hostility to the extravagances of youth and is scathing about young women's fashions but more accommodating of young men. Certainly, Poirot—like his author in interviews and letters—despairs of how women are dressed. He describes his almost-client as "[a]n Ophelia devoid of physical attraction" (15), and words such as "sloppy," "skimpy," and "doubtful cleanliness" (8) are applied to her. It is frequently observed that one can never be quite sure of a young person's sex, and it is true that male fashion receives a kinder, still cynical write-up: "He was … representative of the youth of today. He wore a black coat, an elaborate velvet waistcoat, skin tight pants, and rich curls of chestnut hair hung down on his neck. He looked exotic and rather beautiful, and it needed a few moments to be certain of his sex" (38).

This is David, whom Mrs. Oliver christens "the Peacock." When the imposter stepmother calls David a "[h]orrible creature … dreadful. Effeminate, exotic," Poirot protests these descriptions and says David is beautiful, "not unlike a Vandyke portrait" (39). Consistently throughout his career, Poirot has admired male beauty—from *Lord Edgware Dies* (1933) and *The Labours of Hercules* (1947) to *Third Girl*—and he will again in *Hallowe'en Party* (1969). Some commentators such as Charles Osborne have sought to explain this as signs that he was a creation of a female author whose mind sometimes wandered (326–27), although the focus on paintings is clearly a deliberate theme of the novel, used in a manner that harkens back to Sir Arthur Conan Doyle's *The Hound of the Baskervilles*. Others have argued that Poirot's love of male beauty is part of his rejection of brutish masculinity in crime fiction (Bernthal *Ageless* 89). Mark Aldridge has pointed out that this novel and *The Clocks* reveal Christie's appreciation of young men's "tight trousers" (*Poirot* 204). There is also a reference along these lines with the caveat that they "emphasise knock knees" in "The Adventure of the Christmas Pudding" (*ACP* 29).

Christie often reused characters and locations, but the frequency of this increased significantly in her later works. *Third Girl* sees the return of the omnipotent Mr. Goby, an information agent who appeared in *The Mystery of the Blue Train* and *After the Funeral*, and would return in *Elephants Can Remember*. Dr. Stillingfleet, who ends up marrying Norma, previously appeared in "The Dream" and was mentioned in *Sad Cypress*. Poirot's staff members George and Miss Lemon also are in play. The investigating officer, Chief Inspector Neele, may or may not be Inspector Neele of *A Pocket Full of Rye*.

The novel was dramatized for television as part of *Agatha Christie's Poirot* with the action awkwardly shifted to 1936. The episode was broadcast on ITV on 28 September 2008.

Characters: **Baker, David**; Cary, Frances; Conolly, Sergeant; **George(s)**; **Goby, Mr.**; Horsfield, Sir Roderick; Jacobs, Miss; **Lemon, Felicity**; **Neele, Chief Inspector**; **Oliver, Ariadne**; **Poirot, Hercule**; Reece-Holland, Claudia; Restarick, Andrew; **Restarick, Norma**; Restarick, Mary; Sonia; **Stillingfleet, Dr. John**

See also: *Agatha Christie's Poirot*; "The Algebra of Agatha Christie"; *The Clocks*

Thirteen at Dinner (novel). See *Lord Edgware Dies*

Thirteen at Dinner (television adaptation). See **CBS Television Adaptations**

13 for Luck! (story collection)

Although Christie has been marketed aggressively to young readers since her death, the idea of a volume designed to appeal to youth appalled her. "I *hate* this silly teenager business," she wrote to her agent Edmund Cork when her U.S. publisher, Dodd, Mead, announced *13 for Luck!* "My books are written for adults and always have been" (qtd. in Morgan 324; emphasis in original). Nonetheless, Dodd, Mead published the anthology in hardback in 1961 and a Dell paperback edition without an exclamation mark or subtitle followed in 1974. The British edition, published by Collins, appeared in hardback in 1966.

The publication is notable as the first to feature six Christie detectives (Hercule Poirot, Jane Marple, J. Parker Pyne, Harley Quin, and Tommy and Tuppence Beresford), albeit in individual stories. The aim was clearly to introduce young readers to the range of Christie's writing and to inspire purchases of the books from which the stories were taken—something made clear by the advertisements for those titles in the back of the volume, and the blurb, which implies that there is a plot-driven something for every taste: "Do you like thrillers, baffling mysteries, spine-chilling perils, secret codes, surprise endings? Agatha Christie has all of these." Christie objected to publishers mentioning a seventh detective, "Inspector Evans," in the blurb, as he is not a series character and only appears in the short story "Accident."

There are differences between the U.S. and U.K. editions, because *13 for Luck!* is a collection of previously anthologized short stories. Four titles that were published in the U.S. edition had at that time not been anthologized in the United Kingdom, so they were replaced. The collected stories are as follows, with previous publications in parentheses:

"The Veiled Lady" (U.S. version of *Poirot Investigates*, 1925)—U.S. only, "**The Nemean Lion**" (*The Labours of Hercules*,

1947)—U.S. & U.K., **"The Girdle of Hippolyta"** (*The Labours of Hercules*, 1947)—U.S. & U.K., **"The Market Basing Mystery"** (*The Under Dog and Other Stories*, 1951)—U.S. & U.K., **"Tape-Measure Murder"** (*Three Blind Mice and Other Stories*, 1950)—U.S. only, **"The Blue Geranium"** (*The Thirteen Problems*, 1932)—U.S. & U.K., **"The Four Suspects"** (*The Thirteen Problems*, 1932)—U.S. & U.K., **"Greenshaw's Folly"** (*The Adventure of the Christmas Pudding and a Selection of Entrées*, 1960)—U.K. only, **"The Face of Helen"** (*The Mysterious Mr. Quin*, 1930)—U.S. & U.K., **"The Bird with the Broken Wing"** (*The Mysterious Mr. Quin*, 1930)—U.S. & U.K., **"The Regatta Mystery"** (*The Regatta Mystery and Other Stories*, 1939)—U.S. only, **"Problem at Pollensa Bay"** (*The Regatta Mystery and Other Stories*, 1939)—U.S. only, **"The Unbreakable Alibi"** (*Partners in Crime*, 1929)—U.S. & U.K., **"The Witness for the Prosecution"** (*The Hound of Death*, 1933)—U.K. only, **"Where There's a Will"** (*The Hound of Death*, 1933)—U.K. only, "The Mystery of the Spanish Shawl" [see **Mr. Eastwood's Adventure"**] (*The Listerdale Mystery*, 1934)—U.K. only, and **"Accident"** (*The Listerdale Mystery*, 1934)—U.S. & U.K.

"The Veiled Lady," "Problem at Pollensa Bay," and an alternative version of "The Regatta Mystery" had in fact appeared in both countries in the obscure 1946 volume *Poirot Lends a Hand*, published by Polybooks, but it is likely that even Christie and Cork had forgotten this, and this was an out-of-print pulp volume not published by Collins. "The Market Basing Mystery" had not been anthologized in the United Kingdom before, so its inclusion in both editions probably can be attributed to an oversight.

The Thirteen Problems (story collection; alternative titles: *Miss Marple and the Thirteen Problems*; *The Tuesday Club Murders*)

A short story collection published in 1932, *The Thirteen Problems* appeared in the United States as *The Tuesday Club Murders*. The first six stories were published in *The Royal Magazine* in 1928 under the title *The Solving Six* and the subsequent seven in various outlets between 1930 and 1931. Christie started this series with an idea of "six people whom I thought might meet once a week in a small village and describe some unsolved crime," and the first character she created was Miss Jane Marple whom, she explains in her autobiography, is based in part on her grandmother's "Ealing cronies" (*AA* 436). From Miss Marple sprung the other five characters, all of whom provide something of a contrast to her and therefore serve to highlight her own superior powers of deduction. The most significant—and enduring—of these is her "modern novelist" nephew, Raymond West, "who deals with strong meat in his book" (436) and chides his aunt as unworldly while she gently undermines him. In the second set of six stories, written two years later, the members of the Tuesday Night Club have altered somewhat. The final story in the collection, "Death by Drowning," is not a Tuesday Night Club case.

Fictional references to crime-solving "clubs" in the late 1920s are not uncommon. They reflect the common perception of mystery fiction as a game to be played, akin to a crossword puzzle, and the presence of "Crime Clubs" in both the United Kingdom and the United States (the former being a literary imprint and the latter an actual book club). However, as in Anthony Berkeley (Cox)'s *The Poisoned Chocolate Case*, Christie's creation of a fictional "criminology" circle also evokes the Detection Club, a new organization of crime writers of which Christie was a founding member. She would later become its president. As well as discussing crime fiction, this group regularly met to talk about real murders and engaged in a great many games, rituals, and collaborations.

The second entry to *The Thirteen Problems*, "The Idol House of Astarte," is a whodunit with the trappings of a ghost story. A clergyman, Dr. Pender, relates an incident from his past in which a group of spirited friends decide to hold "a wild orgy" in an apparently haunted house. When pagan rituals and a Roman goddess are invoked, a man collapses and is declared dead. Despite a visible stab-wound, no weapon can be found. Hearing the story, Miss Marple is able easily to consider "the facts and disregard all that atmosphere of heathen goddesses" (41) to name the killer.

There are three hints that "The Idol House of Astarte" may have started life as another story in the late 1910s or early 1920s: the supernatural theme is a hallmark of Christie's early efforts; stylistic touches such as "said he" instead of "he said" betray Christie's debt to older writers such as Sir Arthur Conan Doyle and are common in her late 1910s but not late 1920s stories; and the twist in the tale is both simplistic and poorly camouflaged before its revelation, something already mastered by Christie by 1928.

Another representative example from the volume, "The Bloodstained Pavement," is the fourth of the "problems" and is recounted by artist Joyce Lemprière. It is set in a Cornish village, where a tourist's wife is drowned. Joyce, painting a picture of a pub, overhears a conversation among three people: Denis; his plain wife, Margery; and an old friend, Carol. The three make an appointment to meet at a cave. Later, Joyce returns to paint the pub, which now has two dripping bathing suits outside it, when she is distracted by a bearded man who talks about local history. She realizes that she has apparently painted bloodstains into her work and looks up to see that the bloodstains are suddenly there on the pavement. Denis emerges from the pub and asks if anyone has seen Carol. Two days later, Joyce reads in the newspaper that Margery has died in a swimming accident.

Back in the Tuesday Night Club, the consensus is that there is not enough of a story to grasp, let alone solve, the mystery, but Miss Marple points out that the bloodstains must have come from one of the bathing suits. Joyce confirms that she later discovered Denis and Carol were really married and that it had been an elaborate plot to kill Margery, his new, bigamous wife, for her money. The blood had been on Carol's red bathing suit. Elements of this plot, combined with elements of "Triangle at Rhodes" (1936), would go on to inform *Evil under the Sun* (1941).

"The Affair at the Bungalow" is related by actress Jane Helier, who describes a case of a woman masquerading as Jane who slips a playwright a doctored drink; he later is accused of taking jewels from a bungalow. Miss Marple is the only member of the club who cottons on to the circumstances behind the story.

The final story in the collection, "Death by Drowning," is not part of the series, and, although the others had appeared under the "Solving Six" banner in the *Royal Magazine* (December 1927–May 1928) and *The Story-Teller Magazine* (December 1929–May 1930), this was published later, in *Nash's Pall Mall* in November 1931 as "Village Tragedy." In it, characters who would become fixtures in St, Mary Mead and the Marpleverse, Sir Henry Clithering and Dolly Bantry, discuss the death of a local girl who drowned after becoming pregnant. Miss Marple, who has knowledge of the case, makes some cryptic comments and is able to identify the killer in a rather elaborate manner.

The Thirteen Problems is composed of the following stories (with year of first publication in parentheses): "The Tuesday Night Club" (1927), "The Idol House of Astarte" (1928), "Ingots of Gold" (1928), "The Bloodstained Pavement" (1928), "Motive v. Opportunity" (1928), "The Thumb Mark of St. Peter" (1928), "The Blue Geranium" (1929), "The Companion" (1930), "The Four Suspects" (1930), "A Christmas Tragedy" (1930), "The Herb of Death" (1930), "The Affair at the Bungalow" (1930), and "Death by Drowning" (1931).

Several of the stories have been adapted for television or radio. A string of Russian radio adaptations in 1994 included versions of "The Blue Geranium," "The Idol House of Astarte," "A Christmas Tragedy," "The Four Suspects," and "The Bloodstained Pavement." The Japanese anime series *Agasa Kurisutī no Meitantei Powaro to Māpuru* (2004–05) included versions of "Tape-Measure Murder," "Ingots of Gold," "The Blue Geranium," and "Motive vs. Opportunity." "The Blue Geranium" has had two further adaptations: on American radio in *Murder Clinic* (1942) and on British television in *Agatha Christie's Marple* (2013).

Characters: **Ashley, Diana**; Averbury, Claud; Badger, Mr.; Badgworth, Inspector;

Bantry, Colonel Arthur, and Dolly; Bartlett, Mrs.; Barton, Mary; Bercy, Martin; Bercy, Sir Ambrose; Brewster, Nurse; Brown, Jimmy; Carpenter, Adelaide; Carruthers, Mrs.; Carstairs, Nurse; **Clara**; Clark, Milly; **Clithering, Sir Henry**; Clode, Christobel ("Chris"); Clode, George; Clode, Mary; **Clode, Simon**; Copling, Nurse; Dacres, Captain Denis; Dacres, Margery; David, Lucy; Davis, Carol Harding; Davis, Joan; Denman, Audrey; Denman, Geoffrey; Denman, Mabel; Denman, Mr.; Dobbs; Dorothy; Drewitt, Inspector; Durrant, Amy; Elizabeth; Ellis, Joe; Emmott, Rose; Emmott, Tom; Footit, Henry; Garrod, Grace; Garrod, Philip; Gaunt, Emma; Greene, Netta; Hargraves, Mr.; Hargraves, Mrs.; **Haydock, Dr.**; Haydon, Elliot; Haydon, Richard; **Helier, Jane**; Higgins, Bill; Instow, Jean; Jones, Albert; Jones, Mrs.; Keene, Sylvia; Kelvin, Mr.; Lamb, Miss; **Lemprière, Joyce**; **Linch, Gladys**; Longman, Professor; Lorimer, Jerry; Lloyd, Dr.; Mannering, Lady; Mannering, Violet; **Marple, Jane**; **Melchett, Colonel**; Newman, John; Pebmarsh, Mrs.; **Pender, Dr.**; **Petherick, Mr.**; Pleasegood, Mr.; **Poultny, Annie**; Pritchard, George; Pritchard, Mary; Rawlinson, Dr.; Rogers, Captain; Rosen, Dr.; Rosen, Greta; Salmon, Sir Joseph; **Sanders, Gladys**; Sanders, Jack; Sandford, Rex; Sims, Mrs.; **Spragg, Eurydice**; Spragg, Mr.; Swatz, Gertrud; Symonds, Dr.; Trent, Mrs.; Trout, Mrs.; **West, Raymond**; Wye, Maud

See also: *Agasa Kurisuti no Meitantei Powaro to Māpuru*; *Agatha Christie's Marple*; "Does Woman's Instinct Make Her a Good Detective?"; *Murder Clinic*; Russian Radio Adaptations; St. Mary Mead

Thompson, Mr.

Mr. Thompson is a pseudonym for J. Parker Pyne, traveling incognito in "The Oracle at Delphi."

Three Act Tragedy (novel; alternative title: *Murder in Three Acts*)

At a dinner party in Cornwall, a clergyman selects a martini at random from a tray, drinks, and dies of an apparent heart attack. Although there are no signs of foul play, the host—retired actor Sir Charles Cartwright—suspects that the Rev. Stephen Babbington was murdered. A man who "is always acting" (5), Sir Charles decides "to play the part of the great detective" (35), to the distaste of his acquaintances Mr. Satterthwaite and Hercule Poirot, who appear together for the first time here. While the three men holiday in France, psychoanalyst Sir Bartholomew Strange hosts a London sherry party with many of the same guests who appeared at the event in Cornwall. He dies as the table, and coroners confirm that both men were poisoned with nicotine. Suspicion immediately falls on Sir Bartholomew's new butler, Ellis, who has disappeared without a trace and who seemed oddly familiar with the victim. However, evidence is uncovered suggesting that Ellis may also have been killed.

Although Satterthwaite plays a generally supporting role, Poirot encourages Sir Charles and the young Lady Hermione "Egg" Lytton-Gore to do his legwork. They interview most of the suspects and report back to him. Sir Charles, facing a midlife crisis, is passionately in love with Egg, who has "hero-worship" for him (36, 42, 253, 259). The suspects under scrutiny are more high-class than usual: they include Cynthia and Captain Dacres, a fashion designer and her gambler husband; the aristocratic Lady Lytton-Gore, Egg's mother; a well-known actress, Angela Sutcliffe, who once had an affair with Sir Charles; Oliver Manders, an angry socialist from a prosperous background; and Muriel Wills, a painfully forgettable woman who is better known as Anthony Astor, an author of manly plays.

Theatricality is everywhere in this story, especially melodrama in the third death. The victim is Margaret de Rushbridger, a patient mentioned in passing by Sir Bartholomew at dinner. The name is so unusual that servants recall it later. Poirot is summoned to see her in Sir Bartholomew's sanitarium, only to learn that she was poisoned by a box of chocolates. This was delivered to the sanatorium by a dirty-looking man who says a woman dropped it to him along with two crowns from a top window. More theatricality appears when Poirot has Sir Charles mime his death so the mechanics of switching a glass can be tested. Moreover, Christie opens the novel with the kind of creative credits that would appear in a play: "Directed by Sir Charles Cartwright," "Illumination by Hercule Poirot," and so on (i). Poirot, too, is theatrical, revealing for the first and only time that his broken English is largely applied for effect (although this is undermined by the way he says it): "I can speak the exact, the idiomatic English. But, my friend, to speak the broken English is an enormous asset....I invite [English people's] gentle ridicule [so they are] off their guard" (259). Finally, the twist of the novel relies on the realization that the first murder—the motive for which has been puzzling—was "a dress rehearsal" (255).

Sir Charles, the murderer, is incredibly theatrical. Even without the pre-text admission that he has "directed" events, he is presented as a natural actor from the first page, who treats each phase of life as a new role. Poirot reveals that Sir Charles had planned to murder Sir Bartholomew, who knew incriminating evidence about his past. The murder of Stephen Babbington was merely a dress-rehearsal, to see if he could switch the poisoned glass for an unpoisoned one after the event. Sir Charles disguised himself as Ellis the butler to murder Sir Bartholomew. Mrs. de Rushbridger was killed purely as a decoy. The motive was a desire to marry Egg. The novel ends with Sir Charles planning to "choose his exit" (258), Egg falling into Oliver's arms, and Poirot musing on the "terrible possibility" that he himself could have drank the poison at the first party (260).

In the U.K. publication and the original serial, Sir Charles is already married to a certain Gladys Mugg, who is in a sanatorium. Under British law at the time, a man could not divorce his wife on the grounds of insanity, so Sir Charles kills the psychoanalyst who knows about the marriage to leave the path clear for Egg. The U.S. edition contains a different solution, written by Christie but often attributed by scholars to her editors. Presumably because divorce laws differed in the United States, this version has Sir Charles trying to hide the fact that he is insane, and Egg is given a foreshadowing sense of danger when she is with him (explained as "Woman's intuition" [Christie, *Murder in Three Acts* 172]). Confronted with police officers

and brain specialists, Sir Charles becomes "shrill" and paranoid (173), and he is taken away to "be taken care of" (173).

The novel was first published as *Murder in Three Acts* in the *Saturday Evening Post* (9 June to 14 July 1934). The U.S. edition was published by Dodd, Mead in 1934, and the U.K. version was issued by Collins early the next year. The last of Peter Ustinov's television appearances as Poirot, *Murder in Three Acts* was broadcast on CBS on 30 September 1986. A U.K. television adaptation starring David Suchet was broadcast as part of *Agatha Christie's Poirot* on ITV1 on 1 January 2010. A French version, part of *les petits meurtres d'Agatha Christie,* aired on France 2 on 25 August 2018. A five-part BBC Radio 4 version starring John Moffatt aired 8 July to 5 August 2002.

Characters: Babbington, Margaret; **Babbington, Rev. Stephen**; Babbington sons (Edward, Lloyd, Robin, and Stephen Jr.); Baker; Ball, Victoria; Bassington, Violet; **Cartwright, Sir Charles**; Church, Beatrice; Coker, Doris; Crossfield, Superintendent; Dacres, Captain; Dacres, Cynthia; **de Rushbridger, Margaret**; Eden, Lady; Eden, Lord; **Ellis, John**; See Cartwright, Sir Charles. **Johnson, Colonel**; Leckie, Martha; **Lyndon, Gladys**; **Lytton Gore, Hermione ("Egg")**; Lytton Gore, Lady Mary; MacDougal, Dr.; **Manders, Oliver**; Marcelle; Millray, Violet; **Poirot, Hercule; Satterthwaite, Mr.;** Sims, Doris; Strange, Sir Bartholomew; Sutcliffe, Angela; Temple; West, Alice; **Wills, Muriel**

See also: *Agatha Christie's Poirot*; CBS Television Adaptations; *Hercule Poirot* (BBC radio series); *Petits Meurtres d'Agatha Christie*; Theatricality

"Three Blind Mice" (novella)

A novella based on the radio and television play of the same name, "Three Blind Mice" was published in *Cosmopolitan* in May 1948 and later appeared in the United States in *Three Blind Mice and Other Stories* (1950). It is the basis of *The Mousetrap* and has never been published in the United Kingdom. This is because of a written request from Christie that the story not be published in the United Kingdom until the play's run had concluded.

The story is roughly identical to that of *Three Blind Mice* but with more psychological exploration, especially interior monologues from Molly Davis, one of the newlywed owners of Monkswell Manor. The cast of major characters is still one short of that in *The Mousetrap*: the mannish Miss Casewell does not appear.

Prior to its dramatization as *The Mousetrap*, "Three Blind Mice" was adapted for U.S. television, as an episode of CBS's *Sure as Fate*, broadcast on 31 October 1950. A Brazilian television play based on the novella was broadcast on 21 January 1956, and a Bengali movie, *Chupi Chupi Aashey* (Silently He Comes), was released in 1960. Other screen versions of the story are based on the play.

Characters: **Boyle, Mrs.; Davis, Giles, and Molly**; Gregg, Maureen; Lyon, Mrs.; Metcalf, Major; Paravicini, Mr.; **Trotter, Sergeant**; **Wren, Christopher**

See also: **CBS Television Adaptations; Homosexuality; Indian-Language Adaptations; *The Mousetrap*; Nursery Rhymes; *Three Blind Mice* (radio play)**

Three Blind Mice (radio play)

In 1947, Queen Mary, the widow of King George V, turned 80. To mark the occasion, the BBC committed to a special radio broadcast, for which she requested a new story by Christie. The BBC approached Christie who, despite a tendency to be cautious about her relationship with the corporation, agreed. *Three Blind Mice*, a 16-page, 30-minute play, was broadcast on 26 May. Elements of the plot had already appeared in *The Sittaford Mystery* and *Hercule Poirot's Christmas*. However, the chief inspiration was a real crime case: the death of Dennis O'Neill.

Shortly after its broadcast as part of the *Light Programme*, the BBC turned it, with minimal tweaks, into a 30-minute television drama, broadcast on 21 October 1947, with direction by Barrie Edgar. In 2009, National Public Radio in the United States broadcast the first production since 1947, along with three other Christie scripts, in a special series, *Mystery Series Live—On the Air*. In 2012, a staged reading became part of the line-up of *The BBC Murders* at the

Capitol Theatre, Florida, which toured in 2013.

Christie expanded the radio play into a novella of the same name, published in 1948—so likely already in progress when Christie was first approached—and that in turn became the record-breaking stage play *The Mousetrap*.

See also: ***The BBC Murders***; ***The Mousetrap***; **"Three Blind Mice" (story)**; **True Crime**

Three Blind Mice (story collection; alternative title: *Three Blind Mice and Other Stories*)

The title novella, which became the basis of *The Mousetrap* in 1952, dominates this U.S. short story collection and is the only installment that has not been published in the United Kingdom. This is because Christie stipulated that the story should not be published in the United Kingdom until the play had closed in London. British readers, however, can access the script of *The Mousetrap* in a mainstream Harper edition.

Three Blind Mice and Other Stories was published by Dodd, Mead in 1950. Beside "**Three Blind Mice**," entries include (U.K. book appearances in parentheses): "**Strange Jest**" (*Miss Marple's Final Cases*, 1979), "**Tape-Measure Murder**" (*Miss Marple's Final Cases*), "**The Case of the Perfect Maid**" (*Miss Marple's Final Cases*), "**The Case of the Caretaker**" (*Miss Marple's Final Cases*), "**The Third-Floor Flat**" (*Poirot's Early Cases*, 1974), "**The Adventure of Johnnie Waverly**," "**Four and Twenty Blackbirds**" (*Poirot's Early Cases*). and "**The Love Detectives**" (*Problem at Pollensa Bay*, 1991). It is the first volume to feature Hercule Poirot, Miss Marple, and Harley Quin at the same time.

"Three Blind Mice," Screen Adaptations of. See *The Mousetrap*, Screen Adaptations of

"The Three Strange Points." See "The Dream"

"The Thumb Mark of St. Peter" (story; alternative title: "Ask and You Shall Receive"). See *The Thirteen Problems*

Tiglath Pilesar

Tiglath Pilesar is a cat belonging to

Bunch and Rev. Julian Harmon; he gets into mischief in *A Murder Is Announced* and appears in "Sanctuary."

"The Time Hercule Poirot Failed." See "The Chocolate Box"

The Times Anthology of Detective Stories (story collection)

In spring 1972, Christie was one of five judges in a competition run by the *Times* of London. The other judges were playwright Tom Stoppard, Lord Butler (president of the Royal Society of Literature), John Higgins of the *Times*, and Tom Maschler of Jonathan Cape (the publishing house that sponsored the competition). The competition called for a short story in the traditional detective mold, a kind of response to the rise of U.S. psychological crime fiction and the decline of the British whodunit. The winner received £500 and a £500 contract for a detective novel.

That year, Jonathan Cape published the winning entry, those that placed second and third, and seven runners-up in *The Times Anthology of Detective Stories*. John Sladek (1937–2010), a New Waver, won with "By an Unknown Hand"; he is now best known as a science fiction writer, although he did produce a detective novel, *Black Aura*, which Cape published in 1974.

Other authors in the volume include Nigel Abercrombie (1908–86), who subsequently published mainly on French classicism; Ida Shewan (1922–2006), who does not seem to have published since; Michael Freeman (b. 1951), now a professor of history; Alex Josey (1910–86), who became a political journalist focused especially on Malaysia; John Garforth (1934–2014), who became best known for writing novels based on popular television shows such as *The Avengers*; Kenneth Strongman (1940–2019), a New Zealand psychologist; Don Carleton, an Irish American who became a local historian in Bristol; Monica Lee (b. 1926), who had fled Czechoslovakia for political reasons; and Sean Stiles (b. 1939), a South African journalist. The competition may not have resulted in finding new takes on British crime fiction, partly because the winning entries are all highly traditional.

"To a Beautiful Old Lady." See *The Road of Dreams* (poetry collection)

"To a Cedar Tree." See *Poems*

"To M.E.L.M. in Absence." See *Poems*

"Toile d'Araignée, La." See *Théâtre ce Soir, Au*

Tom

In *The Sittaford Mystery*, Tom works at the Three Crowns and is "a one for noticing" (223). He is therefore an important resource overlooked by the police but embraced by the amateur detective Emily Trefusis.

Torquay

The seaside town where Christie was born and raised, Torquay is located on the coast of Devon, England. Christie is now the town's most famous export, and it holds an annual International Agatha Christie Festival around her birthday (15 September), as well as advertising an "Agatha Christie Mile" and an "Agatha Christie Literary Trail." It is also home to a Christie museum. Known as the English Riviera, Torquay has been a popular holiday destination since the nineteenth century, when naval officers found it a peaceful place to relax during the Napoleonic wars.

Torquay is eminently present in Christie's fiction, but she only mentions it directly in "The Unbreakable Alibi." The town and its landmarks appear more commonly in fictional form such as Danemouth in *The Body in the Library*. The Grand Hotel, where Agatha and Archie Christie spent their one-night honeymoon, is re-created in various novels as the Majestic Hotel. Christie's childhood home, Ashfield, was in Torquay, and her holiday home, Greenway, was just outside it.

See also: Ashfield; Nostalgia

Towards Zero (film). See *L'Heure Zero*

Towards Zero (novel; alternative title: *Come and Be Hanged!*)

One of Christie's more experimental novels, *Towards Zero* is an early psychological thriller and a police procedural as much as it is a Golden Age mystery. Superintendent Battle investigates the crimes, taking center stage for the first time as the novel's primary sleuth. This is the final Battle book.

It is dedicated to Robert Graves, with a note that it is not intended as "a candidate for Mr. Graves' literary pillory." Graves himself was not quite the fan Christie believed him: he later complained of his embarrassment at having this novel dedicated to him and stated of Christie: "her English is schoolgirlish, her situations for the most part artificial, her detail faulty" (qtd. in Lask 16).

Gull's Point, a home off the coast of Devon, is the setting, where Lady Camilla Tressilian invites her extended family for an awkward summer fortnight. Tensions that arise center around her nephew, Nevile Strange, a famous tennis player, and the two Mrs. Stranges. His ex-wife, Audrey, who is depressed, is present, as is his new wife, the highly resentful Kay. So, too, are both those women's lovers. A visitor to the house is Mr. Treves, a retired solicitor, who reminisces about a child he knew who committed murder and got away with it. This was many years ago, and, Treves says, he would recognize that child anywhere because of a peculiar characteristic. Every young adult present has a peculiar characteristic.

Mr. Treves dies, but his death is explained as a heart attack. Shortly later, however, Lady Tressilian is beaten to death with a golf club. All clues seem to point to Audrey. However, Battle finally reveals that Nevile was the child murderer and is quite unstable. When Audrey left him, he sought revenge by murdering his aunt and framing Audrey for the crime.

Unusually, the novel opens with a glimpse of Battle's private life: readers learn that he has a daughter who is in trouble at school—she has confessed to stealing. However, she did not do it. This is not mere character background; it also informs the plot and gives Battle the psychological key to the whodunit element. He catches the murderer psychologically, too, goading Nevile with taunts that he was stupid and did not think the crime through. This serves a pragmatic purpose: so often in Christie, evidence against a killer is circumstantial. This often leads Hercule Poirot to manufacture evidence in a trap (e.g., *Death in the Clouds*) or Miss Marple to set a trap with human bait (e.g., *The Moving Finger*). Battle's approach, it seems, is psychological.

Towards Zero was serialized as *Come and Be Hanged!* in three parts in *Collier's Weekly*, in May 1944. It was published the same year by Collins in the United Kingdom and Dodd, Mead in the United States to glowing reviews. The first play adaptation, by Christie herself, was written and staged in 1945. The second adaptation, by Christie in collaboration with Gerald Verner, was first staged in 1956. An Italian television adaptation, *Verso L'ora Zero*, aired in 1980. In the early 1990s, a British movie version was in production, but the Christie estate withdrew the rights over the inclusion of incest, and the film ended up as *Innocent Lies* (1995).

There were two screen adaptations in 2007: an episode of *Agatha Christie's Marple*, with Miss Marple inserted into the action, and a French movie, *L'Heure Zéro* (Zero Hour), which heralded a wave of French cinematic Christies. In 2010, BBC Radio 4 broadcast a three-part adaptation by Joy Wilkinson. Another French screen adaptation, an episode of *Les Petits Meurtres d'Agatha Christie*, aired in 2019.

Characters: Aldin, Mary; Amphrey, Miss; Antonelli, Guiseppe; Barrett; Battle, Sylvia; Battle, Mrs.; **Battle, Superintendent**; Bentham, Alice; Brinton, Diana; Cornelly, Lord; Daniels, Mr.; Darlington, Mr.; Darlington, Mrs.; Depleach; Don; Drake, Allen; Hudson, Walter; Hurstall; Joe; Jones, Detective Sergeant; Lamorne; Lazenby, Dr.; **Latimer, Ted**; Leach, Inspector James ("Jim"); Lewis, Mr.; Lord, Rufus; **MacWhirter, Angus**; MacWhirter, Mona; Merrick; Mitchell, Major; Parsons, Olive; Rogers, Mrs.; **Royde, Adrian, and Thomas**; Royd, Mrs.; Spicer, Mrs.; **Strange, Audrey; Strange, Kay; Strange, Nevile**; Trelawny; **Tressilian, Lady Camilla**; Tressilian, Matthew; **Treves, Mr.**; Williams

See also: *Agatha Christie's Marple*; **BBC Radio Adaptations; Greenway House;** *L'Heure Zero; Les Petits Meurtres d'Agatha Christie; The Mousetrap;* **Suicide;** *Towards Zero* **(1945 play);** *Towards Zero* **(1956 play)**

Towards Zero (1945 play)

In 1944, the Shubert brothers, notable Broadway producers, commissioned Christie to dramatize her new bestseller, *Towards*

Zero, for the stage. She did so, delivering the script that December. The play had a one-week tryout in Martha's Vineyard, MA, but it was not a success. Audiences complained of a hasty third-act reveal and an implausible final sequence.

The play was almost entirely forgotten and certainly overshadowed by the 1956 stage adaptation of the same name until 2015, when Julius Green published *Curtain Up*, his examination of Christie's theater career. Green unearthed a script by Christie in the Shubert Family Archive. It was promptly made available for license by Samuel French Ltd. and is now known as the "outdoor version" of *Towards Zero*. In 2019, it received its U.K. premier in a performance by the Maddermarket Theatre, an amateur company with its own venue in Norwich.

Characters: Collier, Janet (Collie); da Costa, Peter; Harvey, Sergeant; Leach, Sergeant; MacGregor; O'Donnell; **Royde, Thomas**; **Strange, Audrey**; **Strange, Kay**; **Strange, Nevile**; Wilson, Dr.

See also: *Towards Zero* **(1956 play)**; *Towards Zero* (novel)

Towards Zero (1956 play)

The second stage adaptation of *Towards Zero* (a 1944 novel) is generally published under Christie's name, but it was mostly written by Gerald Verner, with Christie's assistance. In fact, it was commissioned and initially promoted in 1951 as an adaptation entirely by Verner, following several failed attempts to get script "deemed to be workable" based on the novel (Green 419). By 1952, the play was being promoted as forthcoming, but now Christie's name dominated all publicity.

For various reasons, the play was not staged until 1956, by which point Christie had been somewhat involved in script revisions. It is odd that she is generally taken to be a coauthor, main author, or even sole author of this play, since she made more alterations to the script for *Murder at the Vicarage*, for which she is never credited.

The three-act play takes place entirely in a drawing room in Cornwall and is, like the novel, as much a study of jealousy as it is a murder mystery. Recurring character

Superintendent Battle of the C.I.D. makes his first stage appearance since *Chimneys* (1930) and his last in his creator's lifetime, although he would be revived by Leslie Darbon in *Cards on the Table* (1979). *Towards Zero* ran in Nottingham prior to its West End opening on 4 September 1956 at St. James's Theatre. It was not a critical success.

Characters: Aldin, Mary; **Battle, Superintendent**; Benson, Police Constable; **Latimer, Ted**; Leach, Inspector; Royde, Thomas; **Strange, Audrey**; **Strange, Kay**; **Strange, Nevile**; Treves, Mathew.

See also: *Towards Zero* **(1945 play)**; *Towards Zero* (novel)

"The Tragedy at Marsdon Manor" (story; alternative titles: "Hercule Poirot, Insurance Investigator"; "The Marsdon Manor Tragedy"; "The Mystery at Marsdon Manor")

In this early short story, Poirot and Hastings investigate the apparently accidental death of Mr. Maltravers at Marsdon Manor, which occurred shortly after he took out a substantial life insurance policy. Poirot proves murder and catches the criminal—Mrs. Maltravers—via a psychological trap. Like several of Christie's 1920s short stories, this once blurs an interest with psychology—Poirot plays a game of word association—with one in parapsychology and the paranormal.

The story was published in *The Sketch* on 18 May 1923 and *Blue Book* on 5 March 1924. It was collected in *Poirot Investigates* (1924–25). On 6 October 1942, a radio version was broadcast in the United States as part of *Murder Clinic*. On 3 February 1991, a British television adaptation aired as an episode of *Agatha Christie's Poirot*.

Characters: Bernard, Dr. Ralph; Black, Captain; Everett, Mr.; **Hastings, Captain Arthur**; **Japp, Inspector James**; Maltravers, Mr.; Maltravers, Mrs.; **Poirot, Hercule**; Wright, Alfred

See also: *Agatha Christie's Poirot*; *Murder Clinic*; *Poirot Investigates*

"The Tragic Family of Croydon" (article)

Christie wrote this column for the 11 August 1929 *Sunday Chronicle*. In it, she discusses a sensational poisoning case that was then dominating the newspapers and public gossip, and calls for "sympathy and kindly feeling" toward the people involved (298). The case involved the Sydney family in Surrey and remains unsolved. Three people in the Sydney and Duff families died of arsenic poisoning between 1928 and 1928, leading to widespread suspicion of poisoning by relatives.

Christie's article considers the case a "fascinating and baffling" one (TFC 295), the "truth" of which may never come "to light" but insists that it "HAS a solution. It is known the one person—the murderer" (294; emphasis in original). She holds that the case "is essentially a family drama" and considers the players in turn, speculating on motives—in much the same way she would later do for Charles Bravo (see **"A Letter from Agatha Christie"**). She concludes by stating the need for "earnest sympathy and pity for the innocent" but concedes that "public interest is natural" (297, 298). Finally, she condemns "obscene and disgusting anonymous letters" sent to the family (298).

The article caused no kind of stir when it was published, but in 2013 it was published in a reissue of the Detection Club's *Six Against the Yard* (1936), where Christie's name appears bigger than anyone else's on the cover despite that act that she did not contribute anything to the book itself. Although editor Martin Edwards seeks to frame it as an essay about a "perfect crime," because that is broadly the book's theme, it is of interest to the scholar because—as Edwards also points out—many themes of the Croydon case would feature in Christie's fiction in subsequent decades.

See also: **The Detection Club**; **True Crime**

"Traitor Hands." See **"The Witness for the Prosecution"** (story)

"The Trams" (poem)

Christie's first publication was a four-stanza poem in an Ealing newspaper in July 1901. An electric tramline had opened, passing through Ealing on the Uxbridge Road on 10 July, and Agatha Miller, then aged 10, had written about it. Many years later, she recalled that it opened:

When first the electric trams did run
In all their scarlet glory,
'Twas well, but ere the day was done,
It was another story [*AA* 127].

The poem goes on to lament a "shoe that was pinched"—referring to a fault in a transmission line, or "shoe" (127), and evoking an American idiom for trouble or difficulty. This is a remarkable piece of wordplay for a 10 year old. Encouraged by her great-aunt, the young poet took it to a local newspaper office, and it was duly printed. The poem has proven impossible for researchers to trace, and the title given to this entry is arbitrary.

See also: *An Autobiography*

"A Trap for the Unwary." See **"The Actress"**

Tredwell

Tredwell is the quintessential name for an immaculate, faintly pompous butler in Christie's 1920s works. There are Tredwells in both versions of *The Secret of Chimneys* as well as "The Adventure of Johnnie Waverly," *The Seven Dials Mystery* (this is the same character as in *Chimneys*), and *Black Coffee*. Each one treads well and is "a stately, white-haired butler" (*SOC-P* 7).

Trefusis, Emily

Emily Trefusis is an extremely resourceful and "very accomplished young woman" in *The Sittaford Mystery* (95) who teams up with a journalist to save her fiancé from a murder conviction. Emily is one of Christie's young no-nonsense heroines but not a wealthy Bright Young Thing and is closer in outlook and methodology to Miss Marple than to Tuppence Beresford.

Três Ratinhos Cegos. See *The Mousetrap,* **Adaptations of**

Tresillian, Lady Camilla

A murder victim in *Towards Zero*, Lady Tressillian owns the property at Gull's Point, off St. Loo, and is killed for her money. She is also the only character to cross between the Agatha Christie and Mary Westmacott universes, as she appears in *The Rose and the Yew Tree* (published after *Towards Zero* but set earlier). In that book, she is one of the "three old ladies with their erect bearing, their dowdy clothing, their diamonds in old fashioned settings" who are widely associated in people's minds with St. Loo Castle (13).

Trevelyan, Captain Joseph

The owner of Sittaford House and the victim in *The Sittaford Mystery*, Captain Joseph Trevelyan is a sporting military man whose sportsmanship is his undoing. He trusts his oldest friend, Major Burnaby, to share the pair's winnings from a crossword competition. The result is that Burnaby murders him.

Treves, Mr./Mathew

In *Towards Zero*, Mr. Treves is an elderly solicitor who recognizes among the house party at Gull's Point someone who committed murder as a child. He dies after a heart attack, brought on by a rigged elevator in a hotel. Lacking a Christian name in the novel, he is called "Mathew" in the 1956 play version.

"Triangle at Rhodes" (story; alternative titles: "Before It's Too Late"; "Double Alibi"; "Poirot and the Triangle at Rhodes")

A long short story, "Triangle at Rhodes" is often considered a prototype for *Evil under the Sun* (1941). Like that novel, it has Hercule Poirot holidaying at a beach destination where a mature beauty, caught up in a love triangle with a younger man, is murdered by a pair of unlikely lovers. Poirot is visiting Rhodes and watching people when he is caught up in the drama surrounding Valentine Chantry, a 39-year-old woman who has been famous for her beauty since she was 16. Witnessing scenes between Valentine, her overly devoted husband Tony, the attentive young man Douglas Gold, and his shy wife Marjorie, Poirot remarks on a love triangle. He later advises Marjorie to leave the island "*if you value your life*" (*MITM* 269; emphasis in original). Shortly afterward, Valentine is murdered via her signature pink gin cocktail, and poison is found in Douglas's pocket. However, Poirot quickly reveals that the murderers are Tony and Marjorie, who are secret lovers and who have set up the whole triangle to frame Douglas. Earlier, Poirot was warning Marjorie that she ought to rethink her priorities to avoid the hangman.

The story was first published in issue 545 of *The Strand Magazine* in May 1936, under the title "Poirot and the Triangle at Rhodes." It appeared in the U.K. anthology *Murder in the Mews: 4 Poirot Stories* (Collins, 1937) and the U.S. collection *Dead Man's Mirror* (Dodd, Mead, 1937). In the 1940s, Christie considered adapting it for the stage, possibly with music, as another vehicle for Francis L. Sullivan who had previously played Poirot; this did not occur. An adaptation by Stephen Wakelam, starring David Suchet as Poirot, was broadcast on 12 February 1989 as series 1, episode 6 of *Agatha Christie's Poirot*. A German radio adaptation was broadcast on 12 August 2006, as part of SWR's *Krimi-Sommer mit Hercule Poirot* (Crime Summer with Hercule Poirot).

Given that some of the Poirot stories published in the mid–1930s were intended to be J. Parker Pyne stories and given the focus in this one on observing human nature on holiday, it is not without the bounds of possibility that an alternative version featuring that detective exists somewhere, undiscovered.

Characters: Barnes, General; Blake, Sarah; Chantry, Commander Tony; **Chanty, Valentine**; Gold, Douglas; Gold, Marjorie; Lyall, Pamela; **Poirot, Hercule**

See also: ***Agatha Christie's Poirot***; ***Krimi-Sommer mit Hercule Poirot***; ***Murder in the Mews*** (story collection)

Tripp, Isabel, and Julia

Isabel and Julia Tripp are elderly sisters and self-proclaimed mediums in *Dumb Witness*. They are considered strange by the villagers, who note their vegetarianism and amateur photography as examples of eccentricity. They appear to be Christian Scientists.

Trotter, (Detective) Sergeant

Apparently the detective in "Three Blind Mice" and *The Mousetrap*, Sergeant Trotter turns out to be a survivor of child abuse, suffering from a form of homicidal arrested development. He is seeking revenge on adults who could have stopped his older brother dying of neglect many years ago. The character's ability to infiltrate and control a household simply by claiming to be a policeman speaks to paranoia and uncertainty in the post–World War II period.

True Crime

Real murder cases provided considerable creative fodder for Christie and her peers. It has been suggested that her debut crime novel, *The Mysterious Affair at Styles*, was influenced by the crimes of the "Rugeley Poisoner," William Palmer, who was hanged in 1856. Palmer used strychnine in a similar manner to the murderers in *Styles*, and the case reportedly inspired Charles Dickens's *Bleak House* (one of Christie's favorite novels), but links between Palmer's case and *Styles* remain hypothetical. Other cases also have been linked to the book, often in attempts to attract tourists to the relevant locations.

The Murder on the Links was based on a real case, although, as discussed in the entry for that novel, its influence has been overstated. The infamous "Crumbles murders" of 1924 inspired "The Scoop," a collaborative novella. Most famously, *Murder on the Orient Express* draws on the particularly evil kidnapping and killing of Charles Lindbergh Jr., offering readers a fantasy of resolution and vengeance: when Christie wrote and published the novel, no one had been arrested, although, as anticipated in the book, a minor player in the conspiracy was later executed. This is the only example of Christie writing a fictional work about an ongoing case, but it is not a detail-by-detail account of the real-life case.

Another of her most recognizable successes, *The Mousetrap*, was also inspired by a real, relatively recent case of child murder. Twelve-year-old Dennis O'Neill and his brother were abused and starved by their foster parents on a remote farm in the 1940s, and Dennis died in 1945. The public outcry led to manslaughter charges for the caregivers and hefty reforms of Britain's child welfare laws. In Christie's play (and the two versions of "Three Blind Mice"), a version of the younger brother presents himself as a functional member of society but is really in arrested development, pursuing revenge on all the adults who are complicit by implication—that is, those who saw or ought to have seen what was occurring but did nothing.

Toward the end of her life, Christie contemplated writing something inspired by the Leopold and Loeb case. In 1924, two American students, Nathan Leopold and Richard Loeb, who had become fascinated by the Nietzschean concept of the superman, decided to kill a young relative of Loeb to see if they could get away with it. The case inspired Patrick Hamilton's 1928 play *Rope*, later filmed by Alfred Hitchcock. Christie considered the idea of "experiments in murder" (qtd. in Curran, *Making* 404) in the 1970s but was by then beyond writing a new novel.

Christie's fiction is full of direct references to famous historic cases, with Lizzie Borden, Constance Kent, Dr. Crippen, and the unsolved murder of Charles Bravo being mentioned several times throughout the canon. "Remember the long continued success of Jack the Ripper," warns Poirot in *The ABC Murders* (64). Outside of her fiction, Christie sometimes commented publicly on famous cases—"The Tragic Family of Croydon" is her only published piece explicitly dealing with an ongoing case, and she was more comfortable hypothesizing about the Bravo case (see **"A Letter from Agatha Christie"**).

A ghoulish interest in true crime is presented in her fiction as a distinctly working-class phenomenon, and connected with magazine culture: it is satirized extensively to this extent in *Butter in a Lordly Dish* and *Mrs. McGinty's Dead*. Even more highbrow accounts of real crimes, like the ever-evolving play about Constance Kent in *Crooked House*, are presented as tacky. In interviews such as "Genteel Queen of Crime" and "'Queen of Crime' Is a Gentlewoman," she emphasized that her murders were deliberate retreats from real crime and real violence. However, it is evident from examples above that real crimes steered many of her plots, and she believed that it was her duty as a writer to "hold up a mirror" to the world around her (*PTF* 13).

The Pale Horse has the strongest post-publication links with true crime. At least three cases in the 1970s were solved after people involved read or recalled the novel and recognized the symptoms of thallium poisoning. The most famous case concerned mass poisoner Graham Young, whose victims' deaths were being blamed on a mystery contagion. In 1971, a medic conferring with Scotland Yard recognized the symptoms, not from training but from reading *The Pale Horse*. Four years later, a Latin American woman wrote to Christie, explaining that she had been able to prevent a woman's death at her husband's hands after recognizing the symptoms of thallium poisoning from this novel. A case of thallium poisoning in Qatar was thwarted by a nurse who had read the novel. It also may have inspired a murderer, George Trepal, who poisoned his neighbors with thallium after reading *The Pale Horse* in 1988. Other Christie titles that inspired real murderers include "The Tuesday Club Murders." In 1977, in Créances, France, Roland Roussell acknowledged that the story had inspired him to poison a woman with atropine in an act of revenge. His intended victim never drank the wine he poisoned, but his uncle and various relatives did. In 2009, in Qazvin, Iran, Mahin Qadri, who has been dubbed Iran's first female serial killer, claimed that her crimes were inspired by reading Farsi translations of Christie's books. She poisoned and robbed elderly women.

See also: "Genteel Queen of Crime"; "A Letter from Agatha Christie"; *The Murder on the Links, Mousetrap; The; Murder on the Orient Express* (novel); *The Pale Horse* (novel); "'Queen of Crime' is a Gentlewoman"; "The Scoop" (novella); "The Tragic Family of Croydon"

Tucker, Marlene

Marlene Tucker is a teenaged girl guide with lurid tastes in *Dead Man's Folly* and its source novella, "Hercule Poirot and the Greenshore Folly." During a village fete, she plays the part of a victim in a "murder hunt," where she is really killed.

"The Tuesday Club Murders" (story). See "The Tuesday Night Club"

The Tuesday Club Murders (story collection). See *The Thirteen Problems*

"The Tuesday Night Club" (story; alternative titles: "The Solving Six"; "The Tuesday Club Murders"). See *The Thirteen Problems*

Turner, Josephine ("Josie")

In *The Body of the Library*, Josie Turner is Ruby Keene's cousin, who (mis)identifies the body as hers. A dancer and bridge hostess at the Majestic Hotel, she has, contrary to appearances, been trying to infiltrate the wealthy Jefferson family and killed her cousin who accomplished this on her own. Josie is secretly married to Mark Jefferson and is his accomplice in a murder-for-inheritance plot.

Twentieth Century Studios Films

Murder on the Orient Express (2017) was the first English-language cinematic film based on a Christie novel since *Appointment with Death* (1988). Its realization followed lengthy discussion with Ridley Scott, who was originally set to direct a Christie film and later became a producer. The plan was always to bring Hercule Poirot to the silver screen for a twenty-first-century audience, with more action and sex appeal than in previous films. Early rumors were of modern-day settings, with Poirot to be played by Johnny Depp. However, by the time *Murder on the Orient Express* was announced, Depp was to play the victim, and Kenneth Branagh had signed on to direct and star.

The film has a script by Michael Green and, although the script is entirely new (and, if anything, influenced by the 2001 telemovie), it is self-consciously an attempt to recapture the success and impact of the 1974 version. This is reflected in the cast, with several illustrious names connected with the production at various points. Some such as Angelina Jolie ended up dropping out, but the final cast—including Judi Dench, Daisy Ridley, Michelle Pfeiffer, Penelope Cruz, and more—is highly star-studded. The film includes several action sequences and embraces Branagh's trademark style-over-substance approach to direction. Although several reviewers noted that the movie was designed to gather Supporting Actor Academy Award nominations, it received none, unlike its predecessor.

However, as the final line of the script makes clear, further outings were planned, and before long a remake of *Death on the Nile* (which had followed *Orient*

Express in the 1970s) was announced. It was filmed in 2019 for release in 2020, although the COVID-19 pandemic moved the release date back several times. By the end of 2020, it was rumored that the film would be released for streaming on Disney Plus—since Twentieth Century–Fox had been acquired by Disney—but in the end, a new release date of February 2022 was announced. Following the pattern of the EMI films, *Death on the Nile* features an all-star cast, but the stars are not quite as lustrous as those in its predecessor. Although the caliber of actors in *Murder on the Orient Express* was so high that future Oscar-winner Olivia Colman did not even feature on the poster, *Death on the Nile* features movie stars like Gal Godot, Armie Hammer, and Annette Benning alongside internationally successful television stars like Dawn French, Russell Brand, and Sophie Okonedo.

Green's screenplay reprises the character of M. Bouc from *Murder on the Orient Express* to act as Poirot's sidekick, replacing Colonel Race in *Death on the Nile*. The character dies, inviting a series-wide focus on Poirot's relationships and grief. As in the previous film, the set was built at a studio in Surrey: a giant to-scale replica steamer was built from Thomas Cook's 1930s fleet and placed on the railway track used in *Orient Express* at Longcross Studios. The casts' reactions to seeing the ship for the first time were caught on camera and used in the film. One highly publicized element of the movie is the 128-carat Tiffany diamond worn by Gadot, who plays Linnet. In the book, the character wears pearls, but in the film, it is this large South African diamond, famously worn by Audrey Hepburn in publicity for *Breakfast at Tiffany's* and by others rarely since then.

Industry rumors suggest that the next film in the franchise will be *Hallowe'en Party*, with action relocated to post–World War II Venice. Branagh has acquired the rights to direct at least four Christie novels.

See also: ***Death on the Nile*** (novel); **EMI films; *Murder on the Orient Express* (novel); Poirot, Hercule**

Twickenham Studios Films

From 1931 to 1934, Twickenham Studios produced three films featuring Austin Trevor as Hercule Poirot. These are the first screen Poirot adaptations and the first Christie "talkies." The same studios would go on to produce the long-running television series *Agatha Christie's Poirot* in 1989. Producer Julius Hagen had previously produced *The Passing of Mr. Quinn* (1929), which had been a critical failure, and this was his second attempt at spawning a Christie series.

The first two films, *Alibi* (1931) and *Black Coffee* (1931), are both based on plays and offer fairly straightforward translations of the script from stage to screen. The third, *Lord Edgware Dies* (1934), is the only one that survives today and is an adaptation of the previous year's novel. Remarkably, it contains almost every element of the plot in just 80 minutes, even allowing three minutes for Jane Carr, who plays Lady Edgware as a kind of Mae West tribute act, to sing at a piano.

Trevor, a matinee idol, was an unexpected choice for Poirot; he once claimed that he only had the role because he could speak with a French accent. He gives a competent performance, capturing the detective's idiosyncrasies in a way that subsequent commentators have claimed he did not. Because *Lord Edgware Dies* is difficult to obtain, some commentators may have assumed a certain performance based on the actor's looks. Many years later, Trevor would play Poirot twice more on BBC Radio. His final film role would be a butler in the MGM's *The Alphabet Murders* (1965), to Tony Randall's Poirot.

See also: ***Alibi; Black Coffee; Lord Edgware Dies*** (novel); ***Agatha Christie's Poirot***

TV Asahi Adaptations

As part of an effort to expand Christie's international reach during a rebrand in the 2010s, Agatha Christie Ltd. struck deals with two Japanese television production companies, TV Asahi and Fuji TV. TV Asahi was commissioned to make three modern-day adaptations of Miss Marple novels, all of which had been filmed in Japanese a decade earlier by NTV. As in the NTV versions, these scripts replaced Miss Marple with another character, now a policewoman, Too Amano (played by Yuki Amami), with Police Chief Shokokuji (Ikki Sawamura) acting as her stooge.

The first two aired on consecutive days— 24 and 25 March 2018, in an Agatha Christie Special Weekend, followed by a repeat of NTV's adaptation of *And Then There Were None* from the previous year. *Hindai Tokkyū Satsujin-jiken* (Night Express Train to Murder, based on *4.50 from Paddington*) aired first, followed by *Daijoyu Satsujin-jiken* (Murder of a Great Actress, based on *The Mirror Crack'd from Side to Side*). There was a 13-month wait for the next installment, *Yokoku Satsujin* (Notice of Murder, based on *A Murder Is Announced*), which aired on 14 April 2019.

See also: *4.50 from Paddington* (novel); *The Mirror Crack'd from Side to Side*; *A Murder Is Announced* (novel); **NTV Adaptations**

"The Unbreakable Alibi" (story; alternative title: "Alibi"). See *Partners in Crime* (story collection)

"The Uncrossed Path." See **"Accident"**

"The Under Dog" (story)

Unusually, Poirot's client in this story correctly identifies the murderer within the first few paragraphs. Poirot is called to investigate the death of Sir Reuben Astwell. The baronet's nephew has been arrested, but Poirot's client, Lady Astwell, is convinced that it was the secretary, Owen Trefusis. After uncovering a string of family scandals, Poirot reveals exactly how and why Trefusis did it.

The story was first published in the United States in the 1 April 1926 *Mystery Magazine* as a "novelette." It appeared in the *London Magazine* in October 1926. An expanded version was published alongside E. Phillips Oppenheim's "Blackman's Wood" in a 1929 volume, *Two New Crime Stories,* by the Reader's Library (reprinted as *Two Thrillers,* part of the Daily Express Fiction Library in 1936). The expansion took the form of inserted chapter breaks and fleshed-out sentences. For example, "Poirot looked at him sadly" (*ACP* 115)

became "Poirot looked at him sadly, shaking his head" ("The Under Dog" 24).

The original (shorter) story was collected in the 1951 U.S. collection *The Under Dog* and the 1960 collection *The Adventure of the Christmas Pudding*, introduced by the author as an "entrée." The story was filmed as series 5, episode 2 of ITV's *Agatha Christie's Poirot*, starring David Suchet and broadcast on 24 January 1993.

Characters: Astwell, Lady Nancy; Astwell, Sir Reuben; Astwell, Victor; Benson, Mr.; Blyunt, Major; Cazalet, Dr.; Cole, Miss; Elkins, Mr.; England, Captain; **George(s)**; **Gladys**; Langddon, Miss; Leverson, Charles; Margrave, Lily; **Mayhew, Mr.**; **Miller, Inspector**; Naylor, Captain Humphrey; Parsons; **Poirot, Hercule**; Swann, Captain; Trefusis, Owen

See also: ***The Adventure of the Christmas Pudding*** (story collection); *Agatha Christie's Poirot*; ***The Under Dog*** (story collection)

The Under Dog (story collection; alternative title: ***The Under Dog and Other Stories***)

The 1951 short story collection *The Under Dog* was published by Dodd, Mead in the United States. It contains nine stories, all previously published in 1920s magazines (in all but one case, in *The Sketch*), and was the first anthology publication of each. U.K. readers would have to wait until 1960's *The Adventure of the Christmas Pudding* to read the title story in a revised form and until *Poirot's Early Cases* (1974) to read the remaining eight.

The volume contains "**The Adventure of the Clapham Cook**," "**The Affair at the Victory Ball**," "**The Cornish Mystery**," "**The King of Clubs**," "**The Lemesurier Inheritance**," "**The Market Basing Mystery**," "**The Plymouth Express**," "**The Submarine Plans**," and "**The Under Dog**."

"Undine." See *Poems*

The Unexpected Guest (play and novel)

Christie's reputation as a playwright was, to a degree, riding on *The Unexpected Guest* when it opened at the Duchess Theatre in London's West End on 12 August 1958. Her previous play, *Verdict*, had been a flop. However, the critical consensus was one of relief and pleasure, as the play returns to familiar territory. It is set in a country house in Wales and opens with Laura standing over her much older husband's corpse, holding a gun. A stranger, Michael Starkwedder, enters through the French windows, and from there a murder mystery unfolds. The solution is typically surprising. The play enjoyed a good run, including a royal performance—at which the youngest cast member fell ill and had to be replaced—and *The Unexpected Guest* enjoyed a theatrical run in the United States, with Hollywood star Joan Fontaine playing Laura. Despite high hopes, it did not achieve a Broadway run.

The play is notable for including a mentally ill character, 19-year-old Jan Warwick, whose condition is handled sensitively. By contrast, the wheelchair-bound victim, Richard Warwick, is presented as completely cruel and dangerous—malignancy is a human, not a medical, trait. This part is not a popular one with actors, as Warwick has no lines and has to spend the whole first scene playing dead. The unusual name Michael Starkwedder was chosen for the stranger/murderer precisely because it is unusual: Christie once commented that nobody would suspect such a strange name of being a false identity.

The Unexpected Guest has been filmed several times, first as a 1973 Indian film, *Dhund,* which has been remade under different titles in 1988, 1990, 1997, and 2012. An Italian television movie, *L'ospite inatteso,* followed in 1980, and a Japanese version, *Manekarezaru kyaku: Fujisanroku renzoku satsujin jiken,* in 2001. In 1982, BBC Radio 4 aired a dramatization by Michael Bakewell. Charles Osborne turned the script into a novel in 2000.

Characters: Angell, Henry; Bennett, Miss; Cadwallader, Sergeant; Farrar, Julian; Starkwedder, Michael; Thomas, Inspector; Warwick, Jan; Warwick, Laura; Warwick, Richard

See also: **BBC Radio Adaptations**; *Fuji-sanroku Renzoku Satsujin-jiken*; **Indian-Language Adaptations**; *Kirifuri-sanso Satsujin-jiken*; **Osborne, Charles**

"The Unexpected Guest" (story). See *The Big Four* (novel)

Unfinished Portrait (novel)

In the *Bloomsbury Handbook to Agatha Christie,* Merja Makinen warns against reading the Mary Westmacott novels as strictly autobiographical. This is an important point to make, as biographers in particular have tended to treat them as thinly veiled memoirs. However, the autobiographical nature of *Unfinished Portrait* cannot be overstated. It is, emotionally, entirely true, and most events that take place in it have direct parallels in Christie's autobiography: what Gillian Gill calls "repeating scenes" (101), with an underlying emotional honesty entirely from the perspective of Celia, the protagonist. Indeed, Christie is said to have told a relative: "If you want to know what I'm like read *Unfinished Portrait*" (qtd. in Cade 182). The "true" story is framed by an entirely fictional narrator who meets Celia and hears her story, falls in love with her, and leaves her to find herself.

It is a novel about a marriage breaking down. Celia, on the verge of suicide, meets a familiar-seeming stranger and tells him all about her life to date. This starts with a happy but unearthly childhood, where the content young Celia has nightmares about a stranger ("the Gunman") entering the family home, develops through marriage to a dashing military man (Dermot), and culminates with his leaving her for another woman (Marjorie). At the end of the novel, Celia identifies the stranger she has spoken to as the Gunman of her dreams and realizes that she can now live openly—the threat was never from without but from within. The Gunman story also appears in Christie's autobiography, albeit without resolution.

Just as Christie's husband Archie left her, shortly after her mother's death, for a secretary, Nancy Neele, so, too, does Dermot leave Celia, who is mourning the death of her mother, for Marjorie. Christie never commented publicly on Neele, despite using the surname in Harrogate during her highly publicized disappearance. However, she gives her alter ego some forceful words, giving an ethical core to her anger, when Dermot asks Celia for a quiet, no-fault divorce:

> I think that's disgusting! If I loved a man I'd go away with him even if it was wrong. I might take a man from his wife—I don't think I would take a man from his child—still, one never knows. But I'd do it *honestly*. I'd not skulk in the shadow and let someone else do the dirty work and play safe myself. I think both of you are disgusting—disgusting. If you really loved each other and couldn't live without each other I would at least resect you. I'd divorce you if you wanted—although I think divorce is wrong. But I won't have anything to do with lying and pretending and making a put-up job of it [569–70; emphasis in original].

From here, Celia recounts Dermot "bullying" her (570) into agreeing a divorce, and her subsequent mental breakdown. Gill calls this a presentation of "the pressure to divorce … amount[ing] to psychological battering" (107). Barely mentioned is the toll of all this on Judy, Celia's young daughter who is, like Rosalind Christie in 1926, seven years old. Judy—like, one suspects, Rosalind—becomes an emotional pawn in exchanges between her parents, loved by Celia but slightly resented for not understanding.

Significant attention has been given by biographers to *Unfinished Portrait*, although it is probably the least academically analyzed of the Westmacott novels. Approaches vary: Gill looks at marriage and relationships, finding evidence of "serious problems between" Christie and her daughter (102), concluding that the novel is really about the inability of any subsequent relationship to replace the love of Christie's own mother, who had died at such a difficult time (103). Like Gill's, Andrew Norman's book is psychoanalytically informed. It is chiefly about the disappearance and is subtitled *The Finished Portrait*; Norman is particularly interested in the Gun Man. Laura Thompson looks at events and, especially, the presentation of childhood, and concludes that "*Unfinished Portrait* was written by somebody unable to stop themselves, heedless of pain or shame or damage" (159). Regardless of approach, the biographers agree that it is raw and strikingly truthful novel.

Characters: Aubrey; Banks, Miss; Barre, Monsieur; Beauge, Madame; Beauge, Jeanne; Bennett, Miss; **Celia**; **Connell, Marjorie**; **Cyril**; Deburgh, Major Johnnie; Denman, Mary; **Dermot**; Fanny; **Gladys**; Graham, Ralph; Grannie; Grant, Mrs.; Grant, Bernard; **Grant, Jim**; Gregg; Hayes, Mary; Hood, Miss; **Judy**; Kate; Kochter, Monsieur; Larraby, J.; Leadbetter, Miss; Lebrun, Madame; Lestrange, Miss; Lottie; Luke, Mrs.; MacRae, Margaret; Mackintosh, Miss; Maitland, Janet; Maitland, Captain Peter; Mauhourat, Miss; **Miriam**; Patterson, Janet; Payne, Maisie; Priestman, Margaret; Raynes, Roger; Rouncewell, Mrs.; Rumbolt, Mr.; Rumbolt, Mrs.; Steadman, Mrs.; Susan; Swinton, Sybil; Tenterden, Miss; West, Bessie

See also: **Christie, Colonel Archibald ("Archie")**; **Disappearance of Agatha Christie**; **The Gunman**; **Hicks, Rosalind**; **Westmacott, Mary**

The Unicorn and the Wasp. See **Fictional Portrayals of Agatha Christie**

"The Unsinkable Agatha Christie" (interview; alternative title: "Dame Agatha Tells Whodunit")
Antony Armstrong Jones, First Earl of Snowdon (1930–2017), was a photographer and filmmaker who owed his title and notoriety to an 18-year marriage to Princess Margaret, sister of Queen Elizabeth II. Lord Snowdon capitalized on his celebrity to obtain work, one example of which was a photoshoot with an elderly Christie in 1974. The shoot took place in June of that year, at Winterbrook, Wallingford. The photographs are informal and uncommonly human, highlighting the author's frailty, and even include photos of Christie and her husband, Max Mallowan, saying goodbye at the garden gate.

During the session, Snowdon and Christie chatted. They reflected on the new film of *Murder on the Orient Express* and Christie's cautious optimism about it. They also discussed her health and her legacy: she stated that she would like to be remembered as no more nor less than an entertainer. What Christie did not know was that her guest was recording the conversation via Dictaphone. In December 1974, the conversation was published as a syndicated interview in several newspapers around the world—which infuriated Christie, who considered it a private conversation between friends. It is possible that, given Christie's poor health, Snowdon had been holding back the "interview" until a time when she would be unable to mount a serious protest.

Snowdon went on to work closely with Agatha Christie Ltd. In 1982, he held a photoshoot with the cast of *Evil under the Sun* for the *Sunday Times*: these photos have become iconic collector's items. He also did a shoot for *Partners in Crime* in 1983.

See also: *Murder on the Orient Express* (1974 film); Winterbrook House

Upjohn, Julia, and Mrs. Upjohn

In *Cat Among the Pigeons*, Julia Upjohn is a rather awkward schoolgirl who has one real friend, Jennifer Sutcliffe. She and Hercule Poirot, of whom she has heard through family friend Maureen Summerhayes, get along well, and Poirot gives her some of Prince Ali Yusuf's recovered jewels at the end of the book. Her mother, Mrs. Upjohn, is a highly eccentric agent for military intelligence.

Upward, Robin

Robin Upward is a young theatrical impresario in *Mrs. McGinty's Dead*, who is working with Ariadne Oliver to bring her creation Sven Hjerson to the stage. Christie has this character express many of the frustrating things Michael Morton expressed to her when dramatizing *The Murder of Roger Ackroyd* and trying to turn Hercule Poirot into a suave French ladies' man. A camp and sexually ambiguous man who lives with his (adoptive) mother, he has a unisex name which itself turns out to be false. In reality, he is Evelyn Hope, the mysterious child—widely assumed to be a daughter—of murderer Eva Kane, whose family history is covered in Sunday magazines.

Uso o Tsuku Shitai. See NTV Adaptations

Van Aldin, Rufus

Rufus Van Aldin is a tasteless American millionaire devoted to his daughter, Ruth Kettering, in *The Mystery of the Blue Train*. He recommends Hercule Poirot to Dr. Reilly in *Murder in Mesopotamia*.

Van Dusen, Mrs.

Mrs. Van Dusen is a pseudonym used by a detective in "The House of Lurking Death" and by a murderer in *Lord Edgware Dies*.

Van Rydock, Ruth

An old friend of Miss Marple in *They Do It with Mirrors*, Ruth Van Rydock is a glamorous American who has been married three times and consistently touched up her appearance. Exactly the same age as Miss Marple, she looks and lives very differently.

Van Schuyler, Marie

"A kind of period piece" (*DOTN* 89), a bejeweled American aristocrat "with an expression of reptilian contempt" (81), Marie Van Schuyler travels in *Death on the Nile* "in glorious isolation" (90), although flanked by two assistants. A snob, she provides comic relief in the novel, and enables a satire on class preoccupations and their hypocrisies. She was memorably played (as Mrs. Van Schyler) by Bette Davis in the 1978 film. The equivalent character in the play, *Murder on the Nile*, is Mrs. ffolliat-ffolkes.

Vandemeyer, Marguerite ("Rita")

A glamorous older woman in *The Secret Adversary*, Marguerite Vandemeyer is one of the only characters who knows the identity of "Mr. Brown," the master criminal under investigation. She believes that she is safe and part of his scheme but, inevitably, she is killed for what she knows.

"Vanishing Lady." See "The Arcadian Deer"

Vanishing Point. See Fictional Portrayals of Agatha Christie

Vansittart, Eleanor

Eleanor Vansittart is an efficient, perfectly put-together teacher at Meadowbank School in *Cat Among the Pigeons*. Inspiring envy in some of her colleagues, she is killed with a sandbag in the sports pavilion.

Varaga, Queen. See Brun, Genevieve

Vaucher, Jeanne. See Czarnova, Countess

"The Veiled Lady" (story; alternative titles: "The Case of the Veiled Lady"; "The Chinese Puzzle Box")

The early Hercule Poirot story "The Veiled Lady" bears more than a passing resemblance to Sir Arthur Conan Doyle's "The Adventure of Charles Augustus Milverton" (1904). In Conan Doyle's story, Sherlock Holmes and Dr. Watson are approached by a society beauty who says she is being blackmailed. Holmes sympathizes and breaks into the blackmailer's house. He discovers the papers, but he and Watson are observed leaving the blackmailer's residence. He later learns that the blackmailer was murdered and realizes that he was killed by a victim. Siding with the murderer, Holmes lets the case rest.

In Christie's story, Poirot and Hastings are approached by a veiled lady who introduces herself as Lady Millicent Castle Vaughn and says she is being blackmailed by Charles Lavington. Outraged, Poirot and Hastings break into Lavington's house, where they are discovered, and find the letter inside a Chinese box. Poirot later learns that Lavington has been killed. Here, the stories veer apart. Poirot reveals that Lady Millicent is not who she claims to be but is actually part of a criminal gang. Knowing that Lavington had possession of some stolen jewelry, also hidden in the Chinese box, she hired Poirot to retrieve it. The story has comic framing, as it opens with Poirot lamenting that criminals have become too lazy and/or have not heard of him, and closes with him rejoicing that they are so aware of him that they use him in their schemes.

The story was published in *The Sketch* on 3 October 1923 and collected in the U.S. version of *Poirot Investigates* (1925). The first U.K. book publication was in *Poirot Lends a Hand* (1946), followed by *Poirot's Early Cases* (1974). A dramatization, part of *Agatha Christie's Poirot*, aired on ITV on 14 January 1990. A jigsaw puzzle based on the story was released by Paul Lamond Games in 2002.

Characters: Castle Vaughan, Lady Millicent; Croker; Gertie; **Hastings, Captain Arthur**; **Japp, Inspector James**; Lavington, Mr.; **Poirot, Hercule**; Reed; Southshire, Duke of

See also: ***Agatha Christie's Poirot***; **Conan Doyle, Sir Arthur**; **Games**; *Poirot Investigates*; *Poirot's Early Cases*

Venables, Mr.

Mr. Venables is a fabulously wealthy man in *The Pale Horse*, who is physically interesting: he has a prominent Adam's apple and pronounced facial features, which make him memorable, and no discernible backstory, which makes him suspicious. Indeed, after seeing him in a car, Mr. Osborne decided to frame him for murder—but failed to realize that he could not have seen Venables walking around because Venables uses a wheelchair.

Verdict (play)

Christie's theatrical offering for 1955, on the heels of *The Mousetrap*, *Witness for the Prosecution,* and *Spider's Web*, was supposed to be *No Fields of Amaranth.* However, her agent Edmund Cork and producer Peter Saunders were not happy with it, and productions of *A Daughter's a Daughter* and *Towards Zero* were mounted in the next few years instead. The play was not a murder mystery, so there was little confidence in its commercial potential. Nonetheless, Christie believed it "the best play I have written, with the exception of *Witness for the Prosecution*" (*AA* 520), and she continued to work on it over the next three years.

When it was mounted in 1958, it was given a new title, *Verdict*, which Christie hated. In part, she thought the original title more suitable, and she was also likely concerned that such a crime-themed title could mislead and therefore disgruntle audiences. This proved the case. Christie's autobiography summarizes the play as less "a detective story or a thriller" than a play, which happens to feature murder, but the point of which is "that an idealist is always dangerous, a possible destroyer of those who love him" (*AA* 520). The play, Christie writes, "poses the question of how far you can sacrifice, not yourself, but those you love, to what they believe in, even though they do not" (*TMT* 520). These are themes in late Christie, although usually they are given a mystery spin, as in *They Came to Baghdad* and *Hallowe'en Party*.

Professor Karl Hendryk lives with his disabled wife and her cousin, his secretary. They are refugees from an unnamed political force in Europe. A young woman, becoming obsessed with Hendryk, kills his wife. The professor's crime is such intense idealistic interest in his work that he fails to notice the world around it or to reconcile his idealistic principles with reality. The original title, *No Fields of Amaranth*, makes it into the script, with a twice-quoted passage from Walter Savage Landor's *Imaginary Conversation* between Aesop and Rhode: "There are no fields of Amaranth on this side of the grave" and so on. The original program—and original acting edition—included notes explaining that amaranth is the plant also known as love lies bleeding. Christie also draws on this idea in the Mary Westmacott novel *A Daughter's a Daughter*, revised around the same time she wrote *Verdict*.

The play was difficult to mount and cast, but, after a premier in Wolverhampton, it opened at the Strand Theatre, London, on 22 May 1958. It was a critical disaster and not a box office success. Matters were further complicated by the curtain falling one minute before the end of the first performance, so first-night reviewers had an extremely confused idea about how it was supposed to end. Christie's ambitious treatment of psychological themes was not necessarily what the public wanted, and—like *Passenger to Frankfurt*—*Verdict* was considered a failure despite its author's high opinion of it.

Characters: Cole, Lester; Hendryk, Anna; Hendryk, Professor Karl; Koletzy, Lisa; Ogden, Detective Inspector; Pearce, Police Sergeant; Rollander, Helen; Rollander, Sir William; Roper, Mrs.

See also: *A Daughter's a Daughter* (novel)

Vereeker, Nell

As a girl in the Mary Westmacott novel *Giant's Bread*, Neil Vereeker is an awkward friend to Vernon Deyre. As a woman, she pursues the finer things in life, marrying and separating from Vernon and later marrying into money, but she never finds happiness.

Verso L'ora Zero (Toward Zero Hour)

Verso L'ora Zero (Toward Zero Hour) is an Italian television adaptation of *Towards Zero*, marking that novel's first appearance on the screen. Broadcast on Rai 1 on 13 May 1980 (exactly one week after *L'ospite Inatesso*, based on *The Unexpected Guest*), it is set in 1935 and features a cast of notable Italian actors, including Sergio Rossie, Guiseppe Pambieri, Angela Goodwin, and Renato Montalbano.

See also: *L'ospite Inatesso*; *Towards Zero* (novel)

"Village Murder." See **"Tape-Measure Murder"**

"Village Tragedy." See **"Death by Drowning"**

"Vision" (novella)

"Vision" is an unpublished novella, probably written as a short story in Christie's late teens and set aside. A meandering fantasy story, it is interesting for showing the author finding a distinctive voice as she combines the influences of the day's magazine writers. Christie made use of "Vision" in 1923, expanding the narrative half-heartedly and submitting it to The Bodley Head along with the collection of short stories that compose *Poirot Investigates* (1924). Although Christie did not expect this to be accepted for publication—which was the case—she used it to fulfill the terms of her contract, which called for six books. The Bodley Head refused to consider *Vision* a book under the terms of the contract and initially refused to consider *Poirot Investigates* on the grounds that the stories had already been published in *The Sketch*. However, Christie obtained an agent—Edmund Cork, who would stay with her to the rest of her life—and eventually the short story collection was counted, although the fantasy novella was not. This meant she had two novels due before she could conclude her contract and find a new publisher with more favorable terms. *Vision* is in the Christie Family Archive but has never been published.

See also: Cork, Edmund; *Poirot Investigates*

"The Voice in the Dark" (story)

Harley Quin is more than usually in the background in the short story "The Voice in the Dark." Mr. Satterthwaite meets an old friend, Lady Stranleigh, who has survived extensive tragedy and pursued a life of hedonism. She is concerned about her daughter who apparently been hearing a ghost. Satterthwaite visits the daughter, Margery Gale, who is reluctantly consulting a medium. The voice of her aunt, Beatrice, who died in a shipwreck, comes through, and through non-mystic means they receive news that Lady Stranleigh has been poisoned. With prompting from Quin, Satterthwaite realizes that Beatrice survived the shipwreck but lost her memory and has been living as her own maid, Alice Clayton. That is who Lady Stranleigh told her she was, so Lady Stranleigh could inherit Beatrice's fortune for herself. Beatrice has recovered her memory and is extracting revenge. This story was published in *The Story-Teller* in March 1927 and appeared in the collection in *The Mysterious Mr. Quin* in 1930.

Characters: Casson, Mrs.; Clayton, Alice; Gale, Margery; Keane, Marcia; Lloyd, Mrs.; **Quin, Harley; Satterthwaite, Mr.;** Stranleigh, Lady Barbara; Vavasour, Roley

See also: *The Mysterious Mr. Quin*

Vole, Leonard, and Romaine

In "The Witness for the Prosecution" and *The Witness for the Prosecution*, Leonard Vole is the man in the dock. Romaine Heilger is his common-law wife, a Viennese former actress who goes to extraordinary lengths to get him acquitted. A charmer, Leonard has manipulated an old lady, Emily French, into leaving him all her money, then killed her. He has manipulated Romaine into giving him a very dramatic alibi, decimating her own reputation in the process. The 1925 short story presents him as a clever man who gets away with it. In the 1953 play, he double-crosses Romaine with another woman, so she kills him in the courthouse.

Von Deinim, Carl

A German refugee in *N or M?*, who is arrested on suspicion of being a spy after suspicious documents are found in his possession. A talented chemist, von Denim is presented as a victim of xenophobia, in contrast to the typically English, understated Mrs. Sprot who is in fact a German spy.

Von Waldsausen, Countess Charlotte ("Big Charlotte")

An immensely wealthy and powerful woman, Countess Charlotte von Waldsausen is morbidly obese, rarely moves, and is based in Bavaria in *Passenger to Frankfurt*. Obsessed with youth and beauty, she surrounds herself with Aryan youths as courtesans. Compared to Brunhild in Wagner's *Siegfried*, she is an enthusiastic Nazi who wants to bring about a new world order. She is presented as an utterly grotesque character who is only allowed to go on unchallenged because she is so very rich.

Vosper, Frank (1899–1937). See *Love from a Stranger* (play)

"The Vulture Women" See "The Stymphalean Birds"

Wade, Reginald ("Reggie")

Reginald Wade is a young idiot "with all the pathos of a dumb animal" (*PPI* 55) in "The Case of the Discontented Husband." Trying to make his wife jealous, he stages an affair with Madeleine de Sara, but then believes he is in love with Madeleine, causing a chaotic resolution.

Waite, Josephine ("Joe")

Josephine Waite is Vernon Deyre's tomboy friend growing up in the Mary Westmacott novel *Giant's Bread*. She ends up in a sordid elopement with a married artist.

Walters, Esther

A practical and efficient secretary to Jason Rafiel in *A Caribbean Mystery*, the widowed Esther Walters develops in a most extraordinary manner. She is described as "intelligent, good-tempered, understand[ing]" (165) but with "nothing outstanding about her" (166). However, she later is exposed as being in love with hotelier Tim Kendal and as his unwitting accomplice in a string of murders. She is emotionally distraught by the end of the book.

She returns as Esther Anderson, a happily remarried woman, in *Nemesis*. Although she had been vowing undying hatred by the end of *A Caribbean Mystery*, here she is the picture of civility when she runs into Miss Marple. She now "look[s] well, and very gay" (*N* 43).

"A Wandering Tune." See *Poems*

War

Christie's novels are traditionally considered timeless, socially disengaged upper-middle-class fantasies, but the thread of war ran through her life, career, and fiction. The shadow of war molded her childhood: her brother fought in the Boer War (1899–1902). Later, World War I (1914–18), in which her first husband served, and World War II (1939–45), in which her second husband served, had profound impacts on her life and work.

As Rebecca Mills and J.C. Bernthal write in *Agatha Christie Goes to War*:

Christie's first novel, *The Mysterious Affair at Styles* (1920), written and set during World War I, introduced Hercule Poirot as a Belgian refugee and his companion Captain Hastings as a soldier. The Poirot canon and the broader Christie canon are bookended by war. It is not simply that the last novel published in Christie's lifetime, *Curtain: Poirot's Last Case* (1975), was written during World War II and, while intended to appear timeless, is clearly set in a landscape indelibly marked by the conflict. There is also Christie's posthumously published autobiography, in which she devotes whole chapters to "War," "The Second War," and her adventures with her archaeologist husband unearthing evidence of ancient conflicts [2].

The household in *Styles* is "a war household" (*Styles* 18), and, from the start, Christie negotiates the anxieties and ambivalences around women taking on the active share of civilian work while men are away. Writing the book, Christie drew on her own experience as a volunteer nurse and apothecary's apprentice under the Voluntary Aid Detachment (VAD) in Torquay, where she tended to wounded soldiers, encountered Belgian refugees who inspired Hercule Poirot, and learned about poisons. The war is endlessly discussed in future novels and, by *And Then There Were None* and *One, Two, Buckle My Shoe* (both written around 1938), the imminence of another world war is palpable.

Although Christie's written response to World War II has been little studied, there are two types of novel and therefore two types of critical response. The books published during the war tend to be more than usually escapist: there is the holiday setting of *Evil under the Sun* (1941), the metatextual comedy of *The Body in the Library* (1942), and the fantasy of a wounded pilot recovering in a prewar village in *The Moving Finger* (1943). These respond to a public need, for escape in a "high-speeding and unstable world," which socialist publisher and intellectual Cecil Palmer noted was a necessary "mental drug" (479). On the other hand, there are sadder texts, generally written directly before or after the war that directly confront the problems of rationing (*Sad Cypress*, 1940; *A Murder Is Announced*, 1950) or bombing (*Taken at the Flood*, 1948). During the war, Christie only referenced it directly in one published novel—*N or M?*, published in 1941.

In *N or M?*, the now middle-aged Tommy and Tuppence Beresford hunt down Nazi spies among middle-class tourists on an island retreat. This novel is not at all heavy, but it was investigated by MI5, because of a minor character, the boorish Major Bletchley. It was later established that Christie was not referring to the top-secret Bletchley Park. The adventure makes sense for the Beresfords, who had first appeared in 1922's *The Secret Adversary*, negotiating the "red threat" and considering the rise of communism as a capitalistic plot. Still, Christie was not allowed to change the ending of *N or M?*, as she intended, to have the London flat of the Beresfords bombed: that was considered too close to reality. Similarly, she was not able to publish the original version of "The Capture of Cerberus" in 1940, because it directly concerns Adolf Hitler and the Nazis. The most intensely personal response to the war seems to be in *Taken at the Flood*, published three years after V.E. Day. As Mills points out, the devastation at the heart of the novel—a bombing that destroyed a home and the household within it—is described with language and anecdotes reflecting Christie's own experience with a bombed property at Sheffield Terrace in London ("Blitz" 144).

As one of the most popular writers in the world, Christie was involved in the war effort. She returned to volunteer work with University College London; allowed the

U.S. Department of Defense to use Greenway house for convalescing soldiers; and even contributed a recipe, "Agatha Christie's Mystery Potatoes," to a wartime cookery book. However, when contacted to write propaganda for the British—as she would later be contacted by the Russians during the Cold War—she refused.

Even less studied is Christie's response to the Cold War (ca. 1947–91). This may be because, unlike the two world wars, it is rarely reflected in television adaptations of her work. The BBC's unsuccessful 2015 series, *Partners in Crime*, is an exception—but this makes a show of inserting the war into the plots rather than building on anything in the texts. Nonetheless, texts such as *They Came to Baghdad* (1952), *Destination Unknown* (1954), and even *The Clocks* (1963) engage directly with the conflict, specifically its outshoots for British people: anxiety, helplessness, and fear. There is, in many of the later novels, reflected fears about a cult of youth, being mobilized via political ideologies. Gill Plain points out that "Cold War despair" is always presented in relation "to the generic *Zeitgeist*" ("'Tale Engineering'" 192) and that these novels do not minimize the importance or impact of war. The heroes do not overcome the backdrop of conflict, but learn to live with it: "They are adaptive realists rather than idealists" (192). The point of reference in these war texts, however, is World War II, the conflict that Christie and her readers knew best. Hitler is referenced increasingly, and with increasing concern, in the later texts—and in *Passenger to Frankfurt* (1970), there is talk of Hitler's son returning to continue his work. Plain attributes Christie's continued popularity and relevancy—"even as the clue-puzzle formula entered its twilight years"—in part to her engagement with the Cold War (195).

"The War Bride" (story)

An unpublished early short story, "The War Bride" is housed in the Christie Family Archive. It was likely written during or immediately after World War I. The concepts of hasty marriages and not really knowing one's husband are themes that Christie would come to revisit many times, most notably in *Murder in Mesopotamia* (1936), the central drama of which is predicated on a hasty wartime marriage.

See also: **Murder in Mesopotamia**; **"While the Light Lasts" (short story); War**

Wargrave, Sir Laurence

Sir Laurence Wargrave is a toad-like retired judge among the guests on Soldier Island in *And Then There Were None*. Known as a "hanging judge" who sent several people to their deaths, Wargrave is a prime suspect in the ritualistic killings until he appears to be murdered half-way through the novel. However, he is the killer, punishing people who have killed in the past but could not be punished by law. Wargrave leaves a childish written confession in a bottle, thrown out to sea, before taking his own life at the end of the novel.

The letter reveals a complex personality, marked by two conflicting tendencies: to cause pain and to uphold justice. The choreographed murders in *And Then There Were None* fulfill his wish to commit "murder on a grand scale" (*ATTWN* 202) while satisfying his thirst for justice: none of his victims is innocent. This quote, like the judge's surname, evokes the context of impending war in which *And Then There Were None* was written: Joseph Conrad (72) famously used that expression to describe colonization.

Warren, Angela

In *Five Little Pigs*, Angela Warren is Caroline Crale's younger half-sister, who has, in the 16 years since her brother-in-law's murder, become a successful archaeologist. An example of a young, driven, professionally-minded woman, she has overcome a permanent disfigurement caused by Caroline in childhood. This had been a source of permanent guilt for Caroline, who confessed to a murder she believed was committed by Angela. However, just has the Crales' bohemian marriage had been misinterpreted by those around them, Caroline had misinterpreted a simple childish prank by Angela as an act of murder.

The Wasp's Nest (screenplay)

The first Christie television adaptation and her first piece of writing for the screen, was based on her 1928 short story "Wasps' Nest" and aired live on the BBC Television Service on 18 June 1937. The 20-minute production was part of a series, *Theatre Parade*, and a rare example of a unique-to-television performance rather than a filmed stage program.

In fact, the one-act play was written five years earlier as a short piece for a royal charity matinee in 1932. Francis L. Sullivan, who had played Hercule Poirot in *Black Coffee* in 1930, was granted the rights to stage it at London's Arts Theatre or as a music hall act, although—as Julius Green observes—it does not seem to have been performed in any of these contexts (108).

However, Sullivan took the role to the screen. He was joined by D.A. Clarke-Smith as Charles Harborough (based on John Harrison), Antoinette Cellier as Nina Bellamy (based on Molly Deane), and Wallace Douglas as Claude Langdon (based on Claude Langton). Two productions were aired on the same day: one at 3:35 p.m. and one at 9:40 p.m. The first broadcast was positively reviewed in the *Observer* two days later (E.H.R.).

Christie added touches of melodrama to the story such as having Poirot appear to drink poison to force a confession from the guilty party. Although it was a success, Christie—whose relationship with the BBC was professional but not fulsomely enthusiastic—had little to do with television adaptations of her work subsequently. In the 1940s, an American broadcast was discussed, but Christie and her agent agreed not to pursue this so as to avoid damaging Sullivan's ego, as he felt a degree of ownership over it.

Characters: Bellamy, Nina; Harborough, Charles; Langdon, Claude; **Poirot, Hercule**.

See also: *Black Coffee* (play); **Poirot, Hercule**; "Wasps' Nest" (short story).

"Wasps' Nest" (story; alternative title: "Worst of All")

In the brief tale "Wasps' Nest," Hercule Poirot surprises an old friend, John Harrison, with the announcement that he has arrived to prevent a murder. The reader is led to suspect that Harrison is the intended victim—to be killed by his fiancée's former lover, Claud Langton. However, Poirot reveals that Harrison is planning a suicide staged to look like murder, which will see his rival Langton hanged. Poirot manages to prevent the death, and Harrison weeps with gratitude.

The story was first published in the *Daily Mail* on 20 November 1928. It was anthologized in the United States in *Double Sin and Other Stories* (Dodd, Mead, 1961) and in the United Kingdom in *Poirot's Early Cases* (Collins, 1974). It was the dramatized as the first Christie television production, *The Wasp's Nest*, broadcast on the BBC Television Service on 18 June 1937, starring Francis L. Sullivan as Poirot. A new dramatization by David Renwick, with an expanded plot, was broadcast on ITV on 29 January 1991 as part of the series *Agatha Christie's Poirot*, starring David Suchet as Poirot.

Characters: Deane Molly; Langton, Claude; **Poirot, Hercule**; Sullivan, John

See also: *Agatha Christie's Poirot*; *Double Sin* (story collection); *Poirot's Early Cases*; **Suicide**; *The Wasp's Nest* (play)

"The Water Bus." See *Star Over Bethlehem* (story/poetry collection)

"The Water Flows." See *Poems*

Watts, Margaret ("Madge," 1879–1950)

The older sister of Christie, Madge Watts (née Miller) was known to friends and relatives as "Punkie" and was considered the writer in the family. A healthy amount of envy inspired many of her sister's early efforts in writing. Madge, unlike her sister, was educated at a boarding school. She had several stories published in magazines such as *Vanity Fair* under the name Callis Miller and was the first in the family to have a play staged in the West End. *The Claimant*, based on the Roger Tycheborne case, opened at the Queen's Theatre in September 1924, with Fay Compton in the cast. When news of this development arrived in May 1922, Christie wrote to her mother: "I shall be furious if [Madge] arrives 'on the film' before I do!" (*Grand Tour* 171). Madge married James Watts and had one son, Jack Watts, who became a Member of Parliament.

See also: *The Grand Tour*; Miller, Clarissa (Clara); *The Mysterious Affair at Styles*

Waverly, Ada, and Marcus

Ada and Marcus Waverly are the parents of the missing Johnnie Waverly in "The Adventure of Johnnie Waverly." Ada is the daughter of a self-made millionaire and has inherited his hardness. Marcus is a country squire of diminishing wealth.

Waynflete, Honoria

Honoria Waynflete is an elderly church warden in *Murder Is Easy*, who turns out to be a serial murderer. Her crimes are motivated by a desire to destroy Lord Whitfield, who broke off an engagement to her many years before, by making it look like he is a deranged killer. The things that make her an unlikely murderer are those that make her an unlikely madwoman: social position, age, gender, and an ability to play the social game.

"The Weapon." See "The Scoop" (novella)

Webb, Bella

One of the three self-proclaimed witches in *The Pale Horse*, Bella Webb is Thyrza Grey's cook, and embraces the ceremonial side of black magic. She gleefully kills a chicken and performs a ritual with its insides in front of narrator Mark Easterbrook. She seems to actually believe that she, Thyrza, and Sybil Stamfordis, are real witches with powers over life and death.

Webb, Sheila

Sheila Webb is the female protagonist, chief suspect, and the narrator's romantic interest in *The Clocks*. Sheila Rosemary Webb is a young stenographer who is tricked into attending a crime scene in the novel's prologue. In the course of the novel, she learns that she is in the secret daughter of spymaster Millicent Pebmarsh. Although she does not play any proactive role in investigating the crimes, Webb complicates conventional morality in the novel by tampering with the crime scene for selfish reasons and still being narratively rewarded with marriage. The character started out as Nancy Holloran in "The Clock Stopped."

"Weird Monster." See "The Flock of Geryon"

Weldon's Ladies' Journal

A short story by Christie was published in *Weldon's Ladies' Journal* in July 1932 and advertised as its key feature. However, no surviving copies of the issue or records of the story are known to exist. The magazine targeted women and was known for offering knitting pattern supplements.

Welman, Roderick ("Roddy")

In *Sad Cypress*, Roderick Welman is Laura Welman's nephew and is engaged to his cousin, Elinor Carlisle, chiefly because Roderick and Elinor are best friends and because he wishes to please his aunt. The engagement starts to sour after Elinor inherits money and gives him a share—he feels he is living on her charity and wants to be the dominant partner in a marriage. Ultimately, Elinor moves on from Roddy.

West, Magda

Magda West is the stage name of Magda Leonides in *Crooked House*. She is the mother of Sophia, Eustace, and Josephine Leonides, and is an extraordinarily self-absorbed stage actress-producer. Magda is introduced "smoking a cigarette in a long holder and … wearing a peach satin negligee," her "cascade of Titian hair ripp[ling] down her back" (29–30). This extremely theatrical first impression shows how she greets the police and prepares readers for a deliberately artificial character.

West, Raymond, and Joan/Joyce

Miss Marple's nephew, Raymond West, is a well-known novelist and poet, allowing Christie to poke fun at "clever young men who went to Oxford" (*ACM* 6) and at popular authors—sometimes he is presented as a pompous modernist and sometimes as a crowd-pleasing bestseller. The word *self-conscious* is used repeatedly of him in "The Tuesday Night Club" (9). West invariably underestimates his aunt, referring to her as "a perfect period piece" (*SM* 27); she tends to indulge his self-importance and ignorance with a knowing smile or a twinkle. The surname West is a family name from Christie's maternal side.

Joan West is Raymond's wife, although she is introduced in *The Thirteen Problems* as Joyce Lemprière. She is a modernist artist who is slightly more respectful of Miss

Marple than is her husband. The Wests appear or are significantly discussed in *At Bertram's Hotel*, *The Body in the Library*, *A Caribbean Mystery*, *4.50 from Paddington*, *The Mirror Crack'd from Side to Side*, *A Murder Is Announced*, *Sleeping Murder*, and in the short stories collected in *The Thirteen Problems*, as well as in "Greenshaw's Folly," "Miss Marple Tells a Story," and "Sanctuary."

Westholme, Lady

Lady Westholme is a career-oriented British politician married to a simple peer in *Appointment with Death*, in which she murders a former prison warden to stop her unsavory past escaping. An ardent feminist, she annoys the other characters and the implied reader by talking incessantly and rhetorically about social inequalities. She is a very early example of a female politician in crime fiction and, although she is not presented as a sympathetic character but as a semi-comic one, she is afforded the narrative dignity of criminal agency. When Christie turned *Appointment with Death* into a play in 1945, the character became a more straightforward, snobbish, comedy character, reflecting that times had changed and a female Member of Parliament was no longer notable in the same way.

Westmacott, Mary

Under the pseudonym of Mary Westmacott, Christie published six novels between 1930 and 1956. These books are not, as is often claimed, slushy romances. Christie's daughter Rosalind Hicks called them "bitter-sweet stories about love" (Hicks 50), and her grandson Mathew Prichard claimed that they "gave my grandmother the chance to better explore the human psychology she was so intrigued by, freed from the expectations of her mystery fans" ("The Mary Westmacotts"). Commentators outside the family tend to emphasize the novels' autobiographical elements. For example, Laura Thompson suggests that these books gave Christie "absolute freedom": "She could go wherever she wanted, … even into the recesses of her own past" (366).

The name is a combination of family names: Mary was Christie's first middle name and Westmacott was the surname of distant relatives. The use of a female pseudonym, for an author who had previously tried to publish under a string of male ones, is telling: Christie was finally confident of success writing as a woman. Moreover, as Sarah E. Whitney (44, 48) points out, it allowed her to explore gendered issues—especially related to emotional violence—that she would not emphasize in her crime fiction until later in her career.

The first Westmacott book, published in 1930, was *Giant's Bread*, and only one relative guessed the author's true identity. It was followed in 1934 by *Absent in the Spring*, the most intensely personal of the novels, which directly dramatizes incidents from Christie's childhood and first marriage. *Absent in the Spring* (1944), often considered Christie's masterpiece, was written in three days, with the author in a feverish state. *The Rose and the Yew Tree* was published in 1947. This novel, less autobiographical but more overtly concerned with politics than Christie's crime fiction, is set in St. Loo, a fictional town that recurs in Christie's crime fiction. However, readers did not apparently notice until a journalist identified Christie as Westmacott in 1949 after checking the copyright records (a similar incident happened to Robert Galbraith, aka J.K. Rowling, in 2013).

Christie wrote to her agent: "The people I really minded about knowing were my friends. Cramping to one's subject matter. It's really all washed up" (Gill 156). Nonetheless, she went on to publish two more novels as Westmacott: *A Daughter's a Daughter* (1952), based on the then-unperformed 1930 play of the same name, and *The Burden* (1956), the first Westmacott title fully planned and written with the secret identity exposed. For these two books, Christie insisted on marketing them separately from her crime books, with no reference to her other fiction on the title page, although both were published with author photographs and references to "Agatha Christie" on the back covers.

See also: ***Absent in the Spring***; ***The Burden***; ***A Daughter's a Daughter*** (novel); ***Giant's Bread***; **Pseudonyms**; ***The Rose and the Yew Tree***; ***Unfinished Portrait***

Weston, Colonel

Colonel Weston heads the investigations from St. Loo in *Evil under the Sun* and *Peril at End House.*

Wetherby, Caroline

A neighbor of Miss Marple in St. Mary Mead, Caroline Wetherby is introduced as "a mixture of vinegar and gush" in *The Murder at the Vicarage* (13)—the narrator then points out that, despite Miss Wetherby's bile and Miss Marple's serenity, the latter is "the more dangerous of the two" (13). Miss Wetherby reappears in *The Body in the Library* and "The Case of the Perfect Maid." She is long-dead by 1962's *The Mirror Crack'd from Side to Side.*

Weyman, Michael

Michael Weyman is a disgruntled socialistic architect in "Hercule Poirot and the Greenshore Folly" and its expansion, *Dead Man's Folly.*

"What I Would Do if I Were Starving" (article)

Why Christie was commissioned to write this article is unclear, but she was an occasional contributor to *Britannia and Eve*, and presumably the money was good. It seems clear that Christie did not choose the subject herself, as she writes with typical lightness, but some mental gymnastics are required to make the content fit the title. It was published in *Britannia and Eve* in July 1931.

The short answer to the title's implied question is "I should cook!" Christie, writing with a love of food and cookery, suggests that dieting is one of the great inconvenience of modern times and that cookery is an essential skill. She claims that women will always be able to find work as cooks, and that cooking is easy, simply a matter of following recipes: "excellent plain cooking can be done by an amateur who reads the rules and sticks to them" (11).

In the context of impending rations and food shortages throughout the 1930s in the build-up to World War II, the article may appear oblivious. Once war and food shortages were realities, Christie became fully engaged. For instance, she contributed a recipe for using old potatoes and cheap, preserved ingredients to a wartime cookbook ("Agatha Christie's Mystery Potatoes"). Her fiction, too, offers examples of rationing, tins, and making do: *And Then There Were None*, *Sad Cypress*, *A Murder is Announced*, and *The Mousetrap* are key examples, covering prewar, wartime, and postwar rationing and mindsets.

See also: **"The Crime Passionnel"**; *Sad Cypress*

"What Is Love?" See *Poems*

What Mrs. McGillicuddy Saw! See *4.50 from Paddington*

What We Did in the Great War (booklet)

A self-produced booklet by Christie and Eileen Morris, with whom she worked closely during World War I. *What We Did in the Great War* includes 60 pages with illustrations and card covers. It includes items by both women, individually and collectively (such as a comic Agony Aunt column and a comic guide to etiquette). Christie's contributions include a fully-scored operetta, *The Young Students*, and a poem, "The Chemists and the Pharmacists" which—like the much later "The Saga of the Keeper, the Architect, and the Young Epigraphist"—parodies Lewis Carroll's "The Walrus and the Carpenter."

The style and the project are relatively juvenile, although Christie was in her mid-twenties and Morris around thirty when it was compiled. Morris (1887–1945) was one of Christie's closest friends at this time, and it is largely due to that friendship that Christie worked as a VAD and took up writing. In her autobiography, Christie describes her friend's "remarkable mind" and aptness for poetry: "She was the first person I had come across with whom I could discuss *ideas*" (190; emphasis in original). Christie notes that Morris and she never discussed their private lives or personal, emotional matters—although the friendship was one on which Christie drew considerably after her divorce.

Anthony Morris, Eileen's brother, was second master at Horris Hill School. Knowledge of this world helped his sister help Christie find a school for her daughter, Rosalind, in 1928. Christie describes the siblings as very alike in her autobiography, and regrets that "I knew her for many years and yet I often wonder in what her private life consisted" (190). There is evidence from accounts of Horris Hill pupils that neither sibling was heterosexual.

See also: **War**

"Where There's a Will" (1923). See **"The Case of the Missing Will"**

"Where There's a Will" (1925). See **"Wireless"**

"Where's the Catch?" See **"Motive versus Opportunity"**

"While the Light Lasts" (story)

First published in *Novel Magazine* in 1924, the story "While the Light Lasts" was not anthologized in Christie's lifetime but appeared in 1997 in the U.K. collection *While The Light Lasts* and U.S. anthology *The Harlequin Tea Set*. It has a plot that would inform Christie's first pseudonymous novel, *Giant's Bread*. There is also a character referred to as Enoch Arden, recognizable as the man from the sea in Alfred, Lord Tennyson's narrative poem of that name. Christie would go on to use this name and device in *Taken at the Flood* and elements of the situation in *Murder in Mesopotamia*.

The title comes from a quotation: "While the light lasts I shall remember, and in the darkness I shall not forget," which was inscribed on the tombstones of several soldiers in World War I. It is often attributed to Tennyson, but its origins are obscure. The story feels Edwardian-colonial in tone, but it is fundamentally about the upheaving tragedy of war and the difficulty of moving on.

On a tobacco plantation in Rhodesia, George Crozier notices that his wife, Diedre, has something on her mind. She is thinking about her first husband, Tim Nugent, who was killed during World War I. A stranger calling himself Enoch Arden appears, and he turns out to be Tim. There is brief hope that everything that has happened since the war can be undone, but before long, Tim shoots himself, and Diedre returns to her life with George in the oppressive heat.

Characters: **Arden, Enoch**; Crozier, Diedre; Crozier, George; Nugent, Tim; Walters, Mr.

See also: ***Taken at the Flood; Murder in Mesopotamia; While the Light Lasts* (story collection)**

While the Light Lasts (story collection; alternative title: *While the Light Lasts and Other Stories*)

Published in 1997, *While the Light Lasts* is a collection of nine short stories previously published in magazines or newspapers but not collected in Christie's lifetime. The stories were collected by archivist Tony Medawar, and in the original publication, each was accompanied by research notes. It is, necessarily, a hotchpotch collection, including two Hercule Poirot mysteries—both of which were later expanded under different titles for the 1960 volume *The Adventure of the Christmas Pudding*. Others tend to be brief psychological stories, some of which were initially written before the author started writing mysteries.

The volume did not appear in the United States, but one with a similar line-up, *The Harlequin Tea Set*, did. Stories collected in *While the Light Lasts* include **"The House of Dreams," "The Actress," "The Edge," "Christmas Adventure," "The Lonely God," "Manx Gold," "Within a Wall," "The Mystery of the Baghdad Chest,"** and **"While the Light Lasts."**

Whitfield, Lord

Born Gordon Ragg, Lord Whitfield is a self-made millionaire who has risen through the newspaper industry and never ceases reminding people of the fact in *Murder Is Easy*. Although he is the prime suspect in a string of murders and believes that God or destiny is striking down his enemies, he turns out to be the central figure in an elaborate revenge plot. This character provides a classist look at new money in a typically conservative setting, and that the character is a figure of ridicule—down to having a gold-digging fiancée—indicates an overall middlebrow conservatism at this point of Christie's career. However, the character is interesting in that most *nouveau riche* characters in golden age crime fiction are murderers or victims, not innocent bystanders.

Whitstable, Dame Laura

Dame Laura Whitstable is a kind of

matriarch in the Mary Westmacott novel *A Daughter's a Daughter*, although she is a family friend/godmother to Sarah Prentice. A popular psychologist, she helps her friends subtly and observes the Prentices' emotional entanglements with the detachment of a woman who has really lived.

Whittington, Edward

The shadowy Edward Whittington belongs to a secret international conspiracy, and his attempt to enlist Prudence Cowley (later Tuppence Beresford) in the cause sparks the action that leads to its downfall in *The Secret Adversary*. He is "a big man, clean shaven, with a heavy jowl" (17).

Who Killed Ackroyd? See *The Murder of Roger Ackroyd*

Why Didn't They Ask Evans? (novel; alternative title: *The Boomerang Clue*)

Why Didn't They Ask Evans? begins with Bobby Jones, a vicar's son in his twenties who shares a name with an U.S. golf master but cannot play golf. After hitting a golf-ball wildly off course on a cliff-edge, he discovers a dying man at the foot of the cliff, who gasps the final words, "Why didn't they ask Evans?" The man is identified, and his death ruled an accident, but suspicions are aroused when an attempt is made on Bobby's life. As Bobby and his friend, Lady Frances "Frankie" Derwent, try to work out the meaning of the words, they end up infiltrating the Bassington-ffrench household, located near a sanitorium, and several dramatic events follow. Although there is a strong whodunit element, the novel is predominantly a thriller, and its light-handed treatment of murder, psychoanalysis, and espionage is a hangover from Christie's 1920s thrillers. Her later thrillers such as *Destination Unknown* are more somber in tone.

The idea of dying words is one Christie had previously lampooned as a tired cliché in *Partners in Crime* and only used seriously in short stories such as "The Unexpected Guest" (and the later "Sanctuary"). The words seem to have come from Christie visiting a friend, whose brother flung a detective novel—very possibly Christie's own *The Sittaford Mystery*—aside, lamenting that the whole matter could have been resolved

sooner: "Not bad, but why on earth didn't they ask Evans?" (*PTF* 12). The same remark may have inspired a scene in *Lord Edgware Dies*, in which Hercule Poirot overhears a theatergoer say the play would have been over sooner "if they'd just had the sense to ask Ellis" and realizes that speaking to a servant of that name will give him valuable information (*LED* 172). The eponymous Evans also turns out to be a servant.

Why Didn't They Ask Evans? is the last of Christie's novels with "Bright Young Things" and is typically rife with parody and metatextuality: for example, when trapped in a sealed room, Frankie notes, "In books there's always an eleventh-hour rescue," shortly before a minor character falls in through the skylight and rescues her (240). Bobby's mind is similarly "nourished on *The Third Bloodstain*, *The Case of the Murdered Archduke* and *The Strange Adventure of the Florentine Dagger*"; he rejects other reading matter as "lack[ing] pep" (54). The most sinister character, who inevitably turns out to be not only innocent of all crimes but an active force for good in society, is a Canadian psychiatrist, Dr. Nicholson, who owns a sanatorium nearby, where his beautiful young wife is apparently terrified of him. Nicholson has no social skills and asks awkward questions, in addition to a generally sinister physicality that even extends to his ears. In his confession, the murderer, a member of the respectable Bassington-ffrench family, describes framing Nicholson as "rather fun" and states that the doctor is "a harmless old ass, but he does look exactly like a scientific super-criminal on the films" (252).

Christie's own legacy "on the films" had launched in 1928 with a loose and poorly-received adaptation of a short story, *The Passing of Mr. Quinn*, in which the villain had been exactly this kind of man—the sinister Professor Appleby of the film is "subtle in his cruelty," apparently "omniscien[t]," "cruel and sinister," "disconcerting," "fastidious," and constantly skirting "the line between genius and insanity" (McRae 1, 3)—precisely how Nicholson is presented. Mocking this trope, Christie asserts her fiction's value not only to surprise but also to resist the clichés associated with her genre and even her name.

The cliché of the least likely suspect being the criminal was still relatively new when Christie wrote *Why Didn't They Ask Evans?*, but already it is undermined. Roger Bassington-ffrench, the self-described "bold, bad villain of the piece" (288), is the investigators' prime suspect for almost half the novel, and only Frankie directly refuses to suspect him at any point. Meanwhile, his accomplice, Moira Nicholson, is presented as supremely virginal and weak—something commented on several times by both protagonists—making her the least likely suspect in the world of the novel and therefore the most likely suspect to most readers. As in *The Seven Dials Mystery*, once the young investigators discover that their rival romantic interests are international criminals, they decide to marry one another. *Why Didn't They Ask Evans?* offers the final example in Christie of marriage as a happy ending in and of itself, although it features in a more sophisticated form in resolutions in later novels such as *Crooked House*.

An abridged version of *Why Didn't They Ask Evans?* was published as *The Boomerang Clue* in the November 1933 *Redbook*. The first book publication was of the magazine version in the McCall Company's *Six Redbook Novels* (1933/4), which also featured *The Thin Man* by Dashiell Hammett and other titles. The full Collins edition in the United Kingdom (under the main title) came out in 1934, and the U.S. edition (also titled *The Boomerang Clue*) was issued by Dodd, Mead in 1935.

Scenes from *Why Didn't They Ask Evans?* were dramatized by the BBC as part of its series *Crime Writers*, airing on 12 November 1978: these featured Patricia Hodge and Christopher Scoular reciting lines directly from the text. A landmark LWT adaptation—then widely and correctly understood as launching the Christie brand in earnest for television—was broadcast on ITV on 29 March 1980, starring Francesca Annis and James Warwick, who would go on to play Tommy and Tuppence Beresford. An unrecognizable adaptation, with action moved to the 1950s and Miss Marple (Julia McKenzie) written in, was filmed in 2008 as part of ITV's *Agatha Christie's Marple*. It was broadcast in the United States on 26 July 2009 and the United Kingdom on 15 June 2011. A French adaptation, part of *Les Petits Meurtres d'Agatha Christie*, aired in 2013. In 2021, Hugh Laurie announced that he would write and star in a miniseries version.

Characters: Arbuthnot, George; Bassington-ffrench, Henry; **Bassington-ffrench, Roger**; Bassington-ffrench, Sylvia; Bassington-ffrench, Thomas; **Beadon, Badger**; Carstairs, Alan; Cayman, Amelia; Cayman, Leo; **Derwent, Lady Frances (Frankie)**; **Jones, Robert (Bobby)**; King, Donald; Maltravers, Dolly; Mere, Albert; **Nicholson, Dr., and Moira**; Pratt, Rose; Pritchard, Alex; Rivington, Colonel; Rivington, Mrs.; **Roberts, Gladys**; Savage, John; Thomas, Dr.; Williams, Inspector

See also: *Agatha Christie's Marple*; **Bright Young Things; LWT Adaptations;** *Les Petits Meurtres d'Agatha Christie*

Why Didn't They Ask Evans? (1981 television adaptation). See **LWT Adaptations**

Why Didn't They Ask Evans? (2022 television adaptation). See **BBC Television Adaptations since 2015**

"The Wife of the Kenite" (story)

The early short story "The Wife of the Kenite" pre-empts Christie's later interest in the human cost of war and ideology, as well as her use of Bible stories as structuring narratives, which comes to the fore in late novels such as *By the Pricking of My Thumbs* and *Hallowe'en Party*. Stylistically, it is unmistakably early Christie: brief, emotional, to the point, and with tension mounting toward a twist ending in the form of a single line of dialogue, as in "The Witness for the Prosecution."

A German soldier, Conrad Schaefer, arrives in Johannesburg, South Africa, where he is involved in smuggling weapons under the guise of agriculture. He arrives in the home of Mr. Henshel and is immediately struck by his wife, Mrs. Henshel. When Schaefer is left alone with Mrs. Henshel, she drugs him and announces that he, while stationed in Belgium, cut off her first husband's hand. She will, she says, exact vengeance as Jael, wife of Heber the Kenite, did in the Bible.

The protagonist, Schaefer, is clearly unsympathetic and wholly immersed in a racist ideology. When he is attracted to Mrs. Schaefer, he is shocked and disgusted to find that she is Flemish. It is notable that Schaefer's understanding of Englishmen as brainwashed, ratlike creatures is similar to a much-criticized description provided by Christie of a Jewish man in *The Mystery of the Blue Train*.

Written on commission for *Home Magazine* in Australia, "The Wife of the Kenite" was published in 1922 and quickly forgotten. For decades, it existed in various unlicensed printings either translated into Italian or translated back from Italian into English. Sometimes, it was known as "The Kenite's Wife." The original manuscript was finally anthologized with stories by other Golden Age authors in Tony Medawar's anthology *Bodies from the Library* (2018). The next year, it appeared for the first time in a Christie anthology, *The Last Séance: Tales of the Supernatural*.

Characters: Henshel, Mr.; Henshel, Mrs.; Schaefer, Conrad

See also: **Anti-Semitism**; **Christianity**; *The Last Séance* **(story collection)**; **War**

Wilbraham, Major Charles

Major Charles Wilbraham is a bored military man in "The Case of the Discontented Soldier," who is helped by J. Parker Pyne without realizing it. He recovers his zest for life when he believes he is saving a pretty girl from certain death.

"Wild Roses." See *The Road of Dreams* (poetry collection)

Wilkinson, Jane

Jane Wilkinson is a husky American actress who kills her husband for social advantage in *Lord Edgware Dies*. Twenty years after *Edgware*, Poirot comments on this character in *After the Funeral* (1953), remarking that he "was nearly defeated ... by the extremely simple cunning of a vacant brain" (103). Jane does not exist beyond her performed personality. Her lack of substance as a character is not a disguise but an identity, so there is nothing to find beneath the surface. A product of twentieth-century consumer culture, she is all surface and therefore holds power.

Williams, Cecilia

A loyal, observant governess in *Five Little Pigs*, Cecilia Williams is the "little piggy [who] had none." Keeping her employers' secrets, she accidentally obstructs justice.

Williams, Maude

In *Mrs. McGinty's Dead*, Hercule Poirot considers it a strange trick of nature that a woman as smart, beautiful, and generally attractive as Maude Williams should be interested in her hideous, awkward colleague James Bentley. The two work at an estate agency.

Williamson, Ted

Ted Williamson is a beautiful young mechanic in "The Arcadian Deer," whom Poirot helps in a Satterthwaite-style way to find Williamson's long-lost love.

Wills, Muriel

Muriel Wills is a shy, nervous, and very perceptive playwright in *Three Act Tragedy*. Resembling "an inefficient nursery governess" (19), she is always a surprise to people who meet her: her pen-name, Anthony Astor, suggests a man of the world, but she is the antithesis. Crime writer Josephine Tey (aka Elizabeth MacKintosh), who wrote stage plays as Gordon Daviot, was reportedly offended by this character.

Wilson, Gilmour

A rising star in chess, the U.S. world champion Gilmour Wilson is murdered during a game, via an electrocuted chess piece, in *The Big Four*.

Winkfield, Inspector

Inspector Winkfield is the investigating officer in "The Shadow on the Glass" and "The Bird with the Broken Wing." He is a quiet, efficient, and underdeveloped character, although by the latter he is "an old acquaintance" of Quin and Satterthwaite (*MMQ* 252).

Winterbrook House

Christie and her second husband, Max Mallowan, bought Winterbrook House, just outside of Wallingford, in 1934. The couple did not make extensive use of it at first, but from 1961 until Christie's death in 1976, it was their primary residence, and she died in the home. The property became a Grade

II listed building in 1986, which means it is considered an important property.

See also: **Ashfield, Greenway House, Styles House**

"Wireless" (story; alternative title: "Where There's a Will")

"Wireless" is a short story in which Charles Ridgeway decides to scare his elderly aunt to death by imitating the voice of her dead husband in a broadcast over her new wireless radio. His trick succeeds, and the aunt dies of a heart attack. However, in the process, her will, which names Charles as her heir, falls into the fireplace and becomes invalid. In a final twist, Charles learns that his aunt was expected to die shortly.

The story reflects early hostility to and superstition surrounding new inventions. Mary Harter, the aunt, initially worries about "[t]he waves, you know—the electric waves" (98), which could come from anywhere and connect to anything. It was first published in the United Kingdom in the *Sunday Chronicle Annual 1925–6* in December 1925 and then in the United States in *Mystery Magazine* in March 1926. The story appeared in the U.K. anthology *The Hound of Death* (1933) and as "Where There's a Will" in the U.S. collection *The Witness for the Prosecution* (1948).

"Wireless" was dramatized (as "Where There's a Will") with James Mason sinister as Charles, in a 1949 episode of the long-running CBS radio series *Suspense!*.

Characters: Elizabeth; Harter, Mary; Harter, Miriam; Harter, Patrick; Meynell, Dr.; Ridgeway, Charles

See also: **CBS Radio Adaptations**; *The Hound of Death* (story collection); *The Witness for the Prosecution* (story collection)

"Witch Hazel" (story)

A supernatural short story written in the early 1950s, "Witch Hazel" was never intended for publication. It concerns a girl, Hazel, who has been gifted with second sight. During an enforced retreat with her aunt, Hazel's gifts are exploited by an unscrupulous businessman. The story was partly inspired by the experiences of Christie's mother, Clara Miller. In 1955, Christie tried and failed to expand the story into a novel. However, elements of it inspired the Mary Westmacott novel *The Burden* (1956).

See also: *The Burden*; **Miller, Clara**; **Westmacott, Mary**

"Within a Wall" (story)

The short story "Within a Wall" was first published in *Royal Magazine* in October 1925. It concerns a modernist artist who realizes, upon examining his own artwork, that he does not love his wife, and she does not understand his art. He falls in love with another, more artistic woman, who dies, and ends up trapped in his present marriage. The psychological dynamic at play here is in greater evidence in Christie's first pseudonymous novel, *Giant's Bread*. It shows an early experimentation with modernism and an interest in artist temperaments and human passions. The story was collected in 1997 in the U.K. anthology *While the Light Lasts* and the U.S. anthology *The Harlequin Tea Set*.

Characters: Everard, Alan; Haworth, Jane; Loring, Isabel; Winnie

See also: *Giant's Bread*; *The Harlequin Tea Set and Other Stories*; *While the Light Lasts* (story collection)

Witness for the Prosecution (play)

A brief short story with a striking last-line twist, "The Witness for the Prosecution" attracted little to no attention when it was first published in 1925 and remained relatively unknown following its appearance in *The Hound of Death* (1933). However, after its publication in a 1948 American collection named after it, the story caused a sensation in the entertainment industry, inspiring multiple radio and television adaptations and several requests to adapt it for the stage or silver screen.

Peter Saunders, Christie's main producer, suggested that the story would make a good courtroom drama in 1951. Christie was not impressed and told him that if he wanted a play, "he should write it himself" (Green 334). He did exactly that and, when he showed Christie the script, she was horrified enough to write one of her own. The work involved heavy research at the Old Bailey and with her theatrical people's legal teams. The result was a mammoth play with a huge cast—even with actors doubling their roles, as the script suggests, it requires at least 15 players. Christie updated the setting, too, to the 1950s, making Leonard Vole—the man in the dock—a World War II veteran struggling to adjust to civilian life.

Unlike the short story, the play has a double twist. The story ends with the shocking Vole, who had been acquitted thanks to the protagonist's efforts, was guilty after all. The play, however, goes further. Vole's wife, who lied on the stand for him, learns that he has been unfaithful and stabs him. She vows to be tried not for perjury but for murder. This powerful twist adds drama and is significantly more sophisticated than its source material—showing an evolved attitude toward charming, immoral men.

The play is generally considered the author's best. So successful was this new ending on stage that multiple people have claimed credit for it, most notably Hubert Gregg, the director, in his rather vituperative memoir. The play opened at the Winter Garden Theatre, London on 28 October 1953 with a fabulous Old Bailey set, which was the subject of much publicity. It opened to rave reviews and ran for nearly three years, so that when *Spider's Web* opened in 1954, Christie became the first female playwright in history to have three West End productions running simultaneously.

A Broadway production was mounted in December 1954. The play was the basis of Billy Wilder's highly successful 1957 movie starring Charles Laughton and Marlene Dietrich and of a 1982 television movie with Ralph Richardson and Diana Rigg. Another movie, produced by and starring Ben Affleck, is expected in the early 2020s. A West End revival opened in 2017 at the London County Hall and was a surprise critical success; its run has been extended to at least 2022.

Characters: Carter; Clegg, Mr.; Greta; Hearne, Inspector; McKenzie, Janet; **Mayhew, Mr.**; Myers, Mr.; Wainwright, Justice Mr.; Robarts, Sir Wilfred; **Vole, Leonard and Romaine**; Wyatt, Dr.

See also: *Witness for the Prosecution*, Screen Adaptations of; "The Witness for the Prosecution" (short story)

Witness for the Prosecution, Screen Adaptations of

Even before the play version, the short story "The Witness for the Prosecution" had proven popular with radio and television dramatists because of its dramatic courtroom setting and neat twist. Once Christie's play came along, with a relatively quick film adaptation starring Marlene Dietrich, the story was cemented as a desirable property. The play has the advantage of a double twist, and the title alone is attention-grabbing, so *Witness for the Prosecution* was destined to be among Christie's more adaptable works.

The BBC aired the first screen adaptation on 10 June 1949, starring John Sale, Dale Rogers, and Mary Kerridge. The 40-minute drama expanded the brief story with flashbacks and character development, rather than focusing all action on the court case. On 31 October the same year, NBC in the United States aired its own version with Walter Abel, Nicholas Saunders, and Felicia Montealegre. This would herald an era of Christie television adaptations in the United States; Christie, who disliked the medium, was not inclined to grant requests from the United Kingdom but seems to have minded less about versions she would never have to see or discuss.

CBS aired the next version on 7 November 1950 as part of the series *Danger*. This one featured Prime Minister Winston Churchill's daughter, Sarah Churchill, as Romaine. CBS also aired the next attempt as part of *Lux Video Theatre* on 17 September 1953, starring Edward G. Robinson. The West End play adaptation opened less than six weeks later. This play formed the basis for the next two major productions.

Naturally, there were numerous requests to film *Witness for the Prosecution* for the big screen—including one in Cuba, which the author had dismissed without ceremony. With the success of the stage run, these proposals only intensified. Christie finally agreed to a production directed by Billy Wilder, which became a 1957 hit movie. It starred Charles Laughton, a former stage Poirot whom Christie had considered for the role in the West End, with his wife Elsa Lanchester as his long-suffering

Publicity still from *Witness for the Prosecution* with Charles Laughton (front, standing) as Sir Wilfrid Robarts, Tyrone Power (in dock) as Leonard Vole, and Henry Daniell (seated, front) as Mayhew. United Artists, 1957.

assistant. Tyrone Power played Leonard Vole, whereas the role of his devious wife went to Marlene Dietrich. Film scholar Mark Aldridge reports that "Hollywood legend (and publicity) has it that a $90,000 scene was inserted merely to show off Dietrich's legs" (*Screen* 87), and indeed publicity materials make a great deal of the star's sex symbol status. The film was a runaway success.

It was remade in 1982 as a Hallmark television production, starring the equally sultry Diana Rigg in the Dietrich role. Ralph Richardson played Sir Wilfred; like Laughton, he had been considered by Christie for the role on stage. Broadcast on CBS on 4 December 1982, the adaptation was a hit in the ratings but a critical failure. The production had been beleaguered, perhaps hastened so it would be broadcast in the same year as Rigg's other Christie outing, *Evil under the Sun*, was released in cinemas. The

next version of the play was a filmed stage production in India, in 2004, under the title *Khara Sangayach Tar*.

For Christmas 2016, the BBC aired Sarah Phelps's three-part adaptation of the short story. This interpretation sees the criminal couple getting away with murder, destroying the solicitor Mayhew (Toby Jones) in the process, as they celebrate their culture of youth. A sexualized production with a dull color palette, it was set in 1923, on the day Adolf Hitler first gained political power in Germany. It was not received as well as Phelps's *And Then There Were None* from the previous year.

Several cinematic remakes have been mooted in the twenty-first century, but the most developed is one announced in 2016, directed by and starring Ben Affleck. As of 2021, it is classified by producer Basi Akpabio as "in production."

See also: ***Witness for the Prosecution***

(play); "The Witness for the Prosecution" (story)

"The Witness for the Prosecution" (story; alternative title: "Traitor Hands")

The brief short story "The Witness for the Prosecution" concerns a solicitor's efforts to achieve acquittal for his client, Leonard Vole, for the murder of an elderly woman who left him her money. Mayherne, the solicitor, believes in Vole's innocence, although Vole's wife, Romaine, suddenly reveals that she is not technically married to him and gives evidence implying his guilt. However, a mysterious woman with a disfigured face meets Mayherne and gives him some love letters, which reveal Romaine to be lying for her own reasons.

When these are revealed in court, Romaine confesses to lying, and Vole is acquitted. Later, speaking to Romaine, Mayherne realizes that she, an actress, was the woman he met: she fabricated the evidence against herself. There was no other way to convince jurors that Vole was innocent in the face of evidence against him. There is a final twist:

"[Y]ou *thought* he was innocent—"
"And you *knew* it? I see," said little Mr. Mayherne.
"My dear Mr. Mayherne," said Romaine, "you do not see at all. I knew—he was guilty!" [*HOD* 140; emphasis in original]

Prior to the breakdown of her marriage in 1926, Christie wrote several short stories and novels praising the cleverness of men who might be on the wrong side of the law—this story is one example, and another is *The Secret of Chimneys*. However, things quickly changed, and immoral men—especially those who are magnetic to women, like Vole—tended to become victims (such as in *The Hollow*) or, if criminals, to receive their comeuppance (such as in *Death on the Nile*). When Christie adapted the story for the stage in the 1950s, she added an extra twist, in which Vole reveals he has been having an affair with a younger woman, and his wife kills him shortly before the curtain falls.

This is a brief story, first appearing in *Flynn's Weekly* to little fanfare. In the United Kingdom, it appeared—out of place as the only non-supernatural story—in *The Hound of Death and Other Stories* (1933) and later in the United States in *The Witness for the Prosecution and Other Stories* (1948). It might well have been forgotten after that. However, the rise of radio and then television saw a plethora of dramatic interest. Even before Christie's play, which opened in 1953, there had been at least three radio versions and four television versions in the United Kingdom and the United States alone. The play would inspire two large-scale screen adaptations, in 1957 and 1982, but the short story is the basis of all radio adaptations, including one from Russia (1990), one from Germany (1995), and one from the United Kingdom (2002). The three-part 2016 BBC television adaptation is also based on the short story. A forthcoming movie produced by and starring Ben Affleck is likely to be based on the play.

Characters: French, Emily; Harvey, George; **Heilger, Romaine**; MacKenzie, Janet; Mayherne, John; Mogson, Mrs.; **Vole, Leonard, and Romaine**

See also: **BBC Radio Adaptations; CBS Radio Adaptations; German Radio Adaptations; *The Hound of Death* (story collection); NBC Radio Adaptations; Russian Radio Adaptations; *Witness for the Prosecution*, Screen Adaptations of; *Witness for the Prosecution* (play)**

The Witness for the Prosecution (story collection)

A U.S.-only collection published by Dodd, Mead in 1948, *The Witness for the Prosecution and Other Stories* collects stories that had previously appeared in U.K.-only collections (*The Hound of Death* and *The Listerdale Mystery*) or had not been in anthology. It brought the title story to broad attention and can be viewed as directly responsible for numerous radio and television adaptations in the late 1940s and early 1950s, preceding the stage version.

Christie was miffed with the original dust-jacket blurb—which did not make it to print—for its indication that the stories feature beloved heroes such as Sir Edward Palliser. Sir Edward appears in "Sing a Song of Sixpence" (and nowhere else) and, by 1948, Christie had forgotten him. Contents previously published in *The Listerdale Mystery* include "**Accident,**" "**The Mystery of the Spanish Shawl**" (U.K. title "Mr. Eastwood's Adventure"), "**Sing a Song of Sixpence,**" and "**Philomel Cottage.**" Stories that had appeared in *The Hound of Death* include "**The Fourth Man,**" "**The Mystery of the Blue Jar,**" and "**The Red Signal.**" "**The Second Gong**" would be collected posthumously in *Problem at Pollensa Bay*.

"**The Woman Concerned.**" See "**The Case of the Middle-Aged Wife**"

The Woman on the Orient Express (Ashford). See **Fictional Portrayals of Agatha Christie**

"**The Woman Who Stole a Ghost.**" See "**The Last Séance**" (story)

Woolley, Katharine (1888–1945). See **Leidner, Louise**

"**World Hymn, 1914**" (poem; alternative title: "**World Hymn**"). See *The Road of Dreams* (poetry collection)

World War I. See **War**

World War II. See **War**

"**The World's End**" (story; alternative title: "**World's End**")
"The World's End" is a Harley Quin story first published in *Flynn's Weekly* on 20 November 1926 and is included in the anthology *The Mysterious Mr. Quin* (1930). "The World's End" is set on the island of Corsica, where Mr. Satterthwaite is holidaying with his pompous friend, the Duchess of Leith. He meets an unhappy artist, Naomi Carlton-Smith; a theatrical troupe with a famous, absent-minded actress, Rosina Nunn; and, of course, the mysterious Mr. Quin who happens to be on the island.

Rosina talks about a priceless opal that was stolen from her by a playwright a year previously. Although the stone was never found, she ensured that the playwright, Alec Gerard, went to prison. Mr. Quin takes an interest in a small wooden box—like a Chinese puzzle box—owned by Rosina. As the party examines it, they notice a secret compartment containing the opal. Rosina realizes that she accused Alec falsely.

In the end, with Alec's name to be cleared,

Naomi is happy: she has, it emerges, been engaged to him. There are hints that she had been planning to end her life on the island but will no longer do so. Quin disappears, apparently into the sea, as Naomi says goodbye to Satterthwaite. She has painted Quin—in full harlequin regalia.

One feature of Christie's early work that was generally but not entirely erased by the 1930s is prominent in "The World's End": discussions of artistry. Naomi is a modernist abstract artist, and although the duchess sees her work as rather silly, Satterthwaite understands emotional depth and careful technique of it. Christie developed this theme in *Giant's Bread* (1930) and to a lesser extent in *The Hollow* (1946) but generally chose to promote herself as a writer who happened to produce what people wanted to read almost by chance. This made her paradoxically critic-proof.

Characters: Carlton-Smith, Naomi; Gerard, Alec; Judd, Henry; **Leith, Duchess of (Maria)**; Nunn, Rosina; **Quin, Harley**; **Satterthwaite, Mr.**; Tomlinson, Mr.; Vyse, Mr.

See also: *Giant's Bread*; *The Hollow* (novel); *The Mysterious Mr. Quin*

"**Worst of All.**" See "**Wasps' Nest**" (story)

Wray, Barbara, and William
In the Mary Westmacott novel *Absent in the Spring*, it is widely speculated that Barbara Scudamore rushed into the marriage with boring William Wray to escape her domineering mother, Joan Scudamore. The couple works to rebuild their relationship.

"**A Wreath for Christmas.**" See *Star Over Bethlehem* (story/poetry collection)

Yahmose
Yahmose is Renisenb's gentle brother, who is considered "a dear ... kind to everybody—and as gentle as a woman" in *Death Comes as the End* (119). Because of his weakness, he is consistently overlooked and considered a victim rather than a killer. This is a convincing portrait of toxic masculinity.

"**Yellow Iris**" (story; alternative title: "**Hercule Poirot and the Sixth Chair**"; "**There's Nothing Like Love**")
Popularly considered to be "*Sparkling Cyanide* in embryonic form" (Osborne 177),

"Yellow Iris" is in fact the second iteration of its plot. It started life as a radio play, *The Yellow Iris*, although the story appeared in the July 1937 edition of *The Strand Magazine*, four months before the broadcast. The dialogue is largely identical to that in the script, although some of Hercule Poirot's vocal quirks, notably the word *hein*, are absent. As in the radio play, Poirot is summoned to a London nightclub, the Jardin des Cygnes, on the anniversary of a surprising death. When history repeats itself and another woman appears to choke on her drink, Poirot unmasks the murderer.

Like the radio play, the story features song lyrics written by Christie, although two as opposed to five, and these are not the same songs that feature in the script. Several biographers have speculated that Christie may well have written music to accompany the lyrics in "Yellow Iris." Much more sophisticated than the ephemeral background music for "The Yellow Iris," the songs in "Yellow Iris" reflect on love and loss with lyrics such as "I've forgotten you / I never think of you / Oh, what a lie" (74) and "There's nothing like Love / For getting you down" (81).

There have been two new radio adaptations of the story. The first, an episode of NBC's *Murder Clinic*, aired on 25 July 1942. The second, part of SWR's German series *Krimi-Sommer mit Hercule Poirot*, was broadcast on 19 August 2006. A heavily expanded television adaptation by Anthony Horowitz was broadcast as part of ITV's *Agatha Christie's Poirot* on 31 January 1991, starring David Suchet. This preceded its U.K. publication in an anthology, *Problem at Pollensa Bay* (HarperCollins, 1991), by eight months. It had previously appeared in the U.S. collection *The Regatta Mystery* (1939).

Characters: Carter, Stephen; Chapell, Anthony; **Louise**; Luigi; **Poirot, Hercule**; Russell, Barton; Russell, Iris; Valdez, Lola

See also: ***Agatha Christie's Poirot***; ***Krimi-Sommer mit Hercule Poirot***; ***Murder Clinic***; ***The Regatta Mystery*** (story collection); ***Problem at Pollensa Bay*** (story collection); ***Sparkling Cyanide***; ***The Yellow Iris*** (radio play)

The Yellow Iris (radio play; alternative title: Yellow Iris)

Although consensus has it that *The Yellow Iris*, Christie's first self-penned radio play, was an adaptation of the story "Yellow Iris," archival evidence and the texts themselves show that the radio play came first. Christie wrote this script at the request of the BBC and, at about the same time, adapted it as a short story. A live production starring Anthony Holles as Hercule Poirot was transmitted on 29 October 1937.

The script is very brief and stretches to fill 45 minutes only by virtue of five songs, with lyrics by Christopher Hassall and music by Jack Beaver, occurring throughout. The action is set in a cabaret-style nightclub, and the songs are designed to be varied, typical contemporary background-style music. These songs include "You're God for My Bad Habits" (*MITS* 44), "You Live in My Heart" (46–47, 62–63), "Your Heart Was in My Hands" (49–50), "There's Danger in the Tango Band" (52), and "Interrupted Rhythm" (57).

The short story, with virtually identical dialogue, includes two original songs by Christie, clearly inspired by two of the above: "There's Nothing Like Love" is based on "You Live in my Heart" and "I've Forgotten You" is based on "Your Heart Was in My Hands."

An experimental piece, *The Yellow Iris* was poorly received. Joyce Grenfell, reviewing it for the *Observer*, remarked that it "turned out to be a ten-minute sketch padded with cabaret and dance music, and made to spread over forty minutes…. Much better to have treated the piece as the short sketch it really was" (27). The broadcast was repeated two days later, but the experiment was not.

In the twenty-first century, the radio play has been rediscovered and staged or broadcast several times, including as part of *The BBC Murders* and *Murder in the Studio*.

Characters: Carter, Stephen; Chappell, Anthony; **Poirot, Hercule**; Russell, Barton; Valdez, Lola; Weatherby, Pauline

See also: ***The BBC Murders***; ***Murder in the Studio***; "Yellow Iris" (story)

"The Yellow Jasmine Mystery." See ***The Big Four*** (novel)

Yokoku Satsujin (2007). See **NTV Adaptations**

Yokoku Satsujin (2019). See **TV Asahi Adaptations**

Yougoubian, Catherine

A minor but extremely colorful character in the Mary Westmacott novel *The Rose and the Yew Tree*, Catherine Yougoubian "has the persistence of a sledgehammer and the monotony of an oxyacetylene blowpipe: combined with the wearing effect of water dropping on a stone" (4). She introduces Hugh in the prologue to the dying John Gabriel, before the narrative goes back in time.

Young Agatha. See **Fictional Portrayals of Agatha Christie**

"Young Morning." See *The Road of Dreams* (poetry collection)

The Young Students. See *What We Did in the Great War*

Yusuf, Ali

There are two Ali Yusufs, both connected with jewels. The first is an Iraqi accomplice of the antiquities forger Raoul Menier in *Murder in Mesopotamia*. He is a jeweler who makes fabulous paste imitations from wax impressions. The second Ali Yusuf is a prince. The hereditary Sheikh of Ramat, his death in a plane crash has created an international incident in *Cat Among the Pigeons*.

Zagadka Endhauza (The Riddle of End House)

A Russian version of *Peril at End House* and the last Christie movie of the twentieth century (excluding unofficial adaptations), *Zagadka Endhauza* (The Riddle of End House) was released in 1990. It was directed by Vadim Derbenyov, who had also directed *Tanya Chyornykj Drozdov* in 1983. That had been a Miss Marple film; this was a Poirot one. Antoliy Ravikovich stars as a dandy Hercule Poirot. Once again, the plot follows that of the novel closely, this time presenting 1930s England as an extravagant, gilded place with a lot of gold on show.

See also: *Peril at End House* **(novel)**

Zara

Zara is a medium with surprisingly accurate powers of perception in "The King of Clubs." She also seems to appear as "Zara the Crystal Gazer" in "Accident."

Zehn Kleine Negerlein. See *And Then There Were None*, **Screen Adaptations of**

Zerkowski, Countess Renata

Also known as Daphne Theodofanous and Mary Ann, Countess Renata Zerkowski is a young political operative from international aristocratic stock, seeking to undermine that Youth Movement with its Nazi ideology, in *Passenger to Frankfurt*. "Mary Ann" is a codename, given by the British secret service; it is deliberately unexotic to reflect that her loyalties are with the British. She ends up as Sir Stafford Nye's romantic interest.

Zielinsky, Ella

Secretary to Jason Rudd in *The Mirror Crack'd from Side to Side*, Ella Zielinsky is in love with her employer. She dies in a particularly vicious way after trying to blackmail the murderer.

Annotated Bibliography

Adams, Tom, and John Curran. *Tom Adams Uncovered: The Art of Agatha Christie and Beyond.* HarperCollins, 2015. Curran provides commentary on Adams's cover paintings, and examples of his other work are presented.

Adams, Tom, and Julian Symons. *Agatha Christie: The Art of Her Crimes,* Everest House, 1981. A coffee-table book of Adams's Christie cover art with commentary by Symons.

"Agatha Christie." "Who Pays the Cost?" *The Herald,* 20 Mar. 1929, p. 6. A joke letter purporting to be by Christie.

Aldridge, Mark. *Agatha Christie on Screen.* Palgrave, 2016, doi: https://doi.org/10.1057/978-1-137-37292-5. An archivally informed examination of Christie in U.K. and U.S. screen adaptations.

_____. *Poirot: The Greatest Detective in the World.* HarperCollins, 2020. Archivally rich scholarship, detailing the background behind Poirot books and adaptations.

Allingham, Margery. "Mysterious Fun for Millions of Innocent Escapists." *New York Times Book Review,* 4 June 1950: BR2. Allingham pays tribute to Christie at the time of the publication of Christie's 50th whodunit (*A Murder Is Announced*), calling her "a woman of extraordinary ability."

Altman, Dennis. "Reading Agatha Christie." *Inside Story,* 5 Jan. 2009, insidestory.org.au/reading-agatha-christie. Altman considers the fate of "gay characters" in Christie's work but with mis-remembered examples only.

Anderson, Isaac. "New Mystery Stories." *New York Times Book Review,* 28 Feb. 1937, p. 23. Anderson has a less than favorable opinion of Christie's *Cards on the Table.*

"Archeologist Husband." *Herald and Review from Decauter,* 14 Jan. 1952, p. 8. A gossip column attributing a famous quote to Christie.

Arnold, Jane. "Detecting Social History: Jews in the Works of Agatha Christie." *Jewish Social Studies,* vol. 49, nos. 3–4, 1987, pp. 275–82. Arnold catalogs Jews in Christie's work and interrogates charges of antisemitism.

Baldock, Nick. "The Christian World of Agatha Christie." *First Things,* 4 Aug. 2009, www.firstthings.com/web-exclusives/2009/08/the-christian-world-of-agatha-christie. Baldock explores Christian theology in Christie's mid-career.

Bargainnier, Earl F. *The Gentle Art of Murder: The Detective Fiction of Agatha Christie.* Popular Press, 1980. An early example of Christie scholarship, making the case for thematic analysis.

Barnard, Robert. *A Talent to Deceive: An Appreciation of Agatha Christie.* Collins, 1980. Popular scholarship, which examines key themes and summarizes the major novels.

Barzun, Jacques, and Wendell Hertig Taylor. *A Catalogue of Crime: Being a Reader's Guide to the Literature of Mystery, Detection, & Related Genres.* Harper, 1971. An encyclopedic look at Anglo-American detective fiction; necessarily, it is not exhaustive and entries are highly subjective, providing an insight into the (puzzle-focused) critical priorities of the day. A second edition was produced in 1989.

Bayard, Pierre. *Who Killed Roger Ackroyd? The Murderer Who Eluded Hercule Poirot and Deceived Agatha Christie,* trans. Carol Cosman. Fourth Estate, 2000. Bayard uses Christie's novel to question authorial authority and the nature of language, arguing that the narrator of *The Murder of Roger Ackroyd* hid a major secret from Poirot and his creator. Bayard later wrote a similar analysis of *And Then There Were None.*

BBC Sounds Archive. www.bbc.co.uk/archive. Contains clips of and relating to Christie.

Bernstein, Marcelle. "Agatha Christie: 'Queen of Crime' Is a Gentlewoman." *Los Angeles Times,* 8 Mar. 1970, pp. 60–61. An interview with Christie, in her 80th year, in which Christie cultivates a domestic persona.

Bernthal, J. C., ed. *The Ageless Agatha Christie: Essays on the Mysteries and the Legacy* McFarland, 2016. Essay collection with new readings and discussions of aspects of Christie's life, career, and legacy.

_____. "'A Dangerous World': The Hermeneutics of Agatha Christie's Later Novels." Blyth and Jack, pp. 167–82. Bernthal argues that Christie's later novels use biblical narratives and archetypes to scope the social relevance of crime writing in a changing world.

_____. *Queering Agatha Christie: Revisiting the Golden Age of Detective Fiction.* Palgrave, 2016. An analysis of "queer potential" in Christie's detective fiction before 1953, arguing that Christie's texts destabilize concepts of normality.

"Best of the Year." *Sight and Sound,* vol. 21, no. 3, Jan–Mar 1952, p. 102. A magazine feature in which Christie and others discuss their favorite films of 1951.

Birns, Margaret Boe. "Agatha Christie's Portrait of the Artist." *Clues: A Journal of Detection,* vol. 1, no. 2, 1980, pp. 31–34. Birns reads *The Hollow* as an emotional self-portrait recalling the collapse of Christie's first marriage.

Birns, Nicholas, and Margaret Boe Birns. "Detective Fiction and the Prose of Everyday Life: Agatha Christie, Margery Allingham, Ngaio Marsh and Gladys Mitchell in the 1950s." *The 1950s: A Decade of Modern British Fiction,* Bloomsbury, 2018, pp. 205–34.

Blyth, Caroline, and Alison Jack, eds. *The Bible in Crime Fiction and Drama: Murderous Texts.* Clark, 2019. Essay collection that discusses connections between biblical and crime texts.

Board of Deputies of British Jews. "Jews in Britain Timeline." *Board of Deputies of British Jews: Advocacy for the Community,* n.d., www.bod.org.uk/jewish-facts-info/jews-in-britain-timeline. A timeline of key dates in British Jewish history.

Bolin, Alice. "Miss Marple vs. the Mansplainers: Agatha Christie's Feminist Detective Hero." *Electric Literature,* 15 May 2015, electricliterature.com/miss-marple-vs-the-mansplainers-agatha-christies-feminist-detective-hero. A blog post pointing out that Miss Jane Marple is a woman who is often underestimated.

Boucher, Anthony [William Anthony Parker White]. "Criminals at Large." *New York Times,* 25 Sept. 1966: BR61. Boucher states that Christie's *At Bertram's Hotel* is "a joy to read from beginning to end," singling out its "acute sensitivity to the contrasts between this era and that of Miss Marple's youth."

———. "Report on Criminals at Large." *New York Times,* 18 Apr. 1954, p. BR23. Complimentary review of Christie's *A Pocket Full of Rye.*

———. "A Roundup of Criminals at Large." *New York Times,* 4 Oct 1964, p. BR28. Boucher lauds Christie's *The Clocks,* calling it "remarkable for intricacies and niceties of construction that should dazzle any younger competitors."

Brodbeck, Catherine, and Kemper Donovan. "And Then There Were 31: Sparkling Cyanide by Agatha Christie." *All About Agatha (Christie),* 23 June 2019, soundcloud.com/user-269339596/and-then-there-were-31-sparkling-cyanide-by-agatha-christie. This podcast explores Christie's detective novels in chronological order, with diversions for short story discussions and interviews. Brodbeck and Donovan are American millennials, bringing this slant to the texts.

Brown, Shane. "'Scoring Off a Foreigner?' Xenophobia, Antisemitism, and Racism in the Works of Agatha Christie." *Clues: A Journal of Detection,* vol. 38, no. 1, 2020, pp. 70–80. In the context of Brexit and press outrage at Christie adaptations tackling social issues, Brown explores Christie's own presentation of xenophobia, antisemitism, and racism.

Bruce, Leo [Rupert Croft-Cooke]. *Case for Three Detectives.* 1937. Academy Chicago Publishers, 2005. Bruce parodies three well-known fictional detectives in this debut of Sergeant Beef, including Hercule Poirot.

Buchan, John [Baron Tweedsmuir]. "Ourselves and the Jews." *The Graphic,* 5 Apr. 1930, p. 12. In this article, Buchan defends Zionism, claiming that it is in Britain's fiscal interest to espouse numerous negative stereotypes about Jews.

Cade, Jared. *Agatha Christie and the Eleven Missing Days.* 1998. Owen, 2000. Cade's unauthorized biography examines Christie's disappearance in 1926 and includes interviews with her in-laws' descendants; Cade argues that Christie staged her disappearance.

Cardullo, R. J. "Westward Faux." *Journal of the West,* vol. 58, no. 2, 2019, pp. 3–11. Cardullo points out that elements of Christie's *Murder on the Orient Express* appear in the 1975 Western film *Breakheart Pass.*

Carson, Paul. "An Interview with Agatha Christie." *Gastonia Gazette,* 1 May 1966, p. 42. An interview to promote the film *Ten Little Indians* (1965).

Chandler, Raymond. "The Simple Art of Murder." *Atlantic Monthly,* Dec. 1944, pp. 53–59. An influential example of detective fiction analysis, arguing that the American hard-boiled genre is a necessary antidote to genteel British crime writing.

Charteris, Charlotte. "A Strange Night in a Strange House: The Country House as a Queer Space in Interwar Mystery Fiction." *Clues: A Journal of Detection,* vol. 35, no. 2, 2017, pp. 89–99. Charteris examines one of the most heavily stereotyped themes in the work of Christie and her peers, arguing that the country house can be read as gothic and destabilizing rather than nostalgic and wistful.

Christie, Agatha. *The ABC Murders.* Collins, 1936.

———. *The Adventure of the Christmas Pudding and a Selection of Entrées.* Collins, 1960.

———. *After the Funeral.* Collins, 1953.

———. Agatha Christie Family Archive, Agatha Christie Archive Trust, Torquay, UK. Contains numerous photographs, letters, and ephemera as well as manuscripts, both published and unpublished.

———. *The Agatha Christie Hour.* Collins, 1982.

———. *And Then There Were None.* 1939. HarperCollins, 2012.

———. *Appointment with Death.* 1938. Harper, 2016.

———. *At Bertram's Hotel.* Collins, 1965.

———. *An Autobiography.* Collins, 1977.

———. *The Big Four.* 1927. HarperCollins, 1994.

———. *Black Coffee.* 1934. Samuel French, 2014.

———. *The Body in the Library.* Collins, 1942.

_____. Business Correspondence Archive, U of Exeter. Contains letters between Christie and her British agent, Edmund Cork.

_____. *By the Pricking of My Thumbs.* 1968. Harper, 2015.

_____. *Cards on the Table.* 1936. Harper, 2016.

_____. *A Caribbean Mystery.* Collins, 1964.

_____. "The Case of the Caretaker's Wife." Curran, *Murder in the Making,* pp. 240–58.

_____. *Cat Among the Pigeons.* Collins, 1959.

_____. "Cleopatra as the Dark Lady." *The Times* [London], 3 Feb. 1973, p. 15.

_____. "The Clock Stopped." *Yorkshire Magazine,* Autumn 1949, p. 24.

_____. *The Clocks.* Collins, 1963.

_____. *Crooked House.* Dodd, 1949.

_____. *Curtain: Poirot's Last Case.* Collins, 1975.

_____. *Dead Man's Folly.* Collins, 1956.

_____. *Death Comes as the End.* 1945. Harper, 2017.

_____. *Death in the Clouds.* Collins, 1935.

_____. *Death on the Nile.* 1937. HarperCollins, 2012.

_____. *Destination Unknown.* 1954. HarperCollins, 2001.

_____. "Detective Writers in England." *CADS: Crime and Detective Stories,* no. 55, Dec. 2008, pp. 3–6.

_____. "Does a Woman's Instinct Make Her a Good Detective?" 1928. *Murder, She Said: The Quotable Miss Marple,* ed. Tony Medawar, HarperCollins, 2019, pp. 149–54.

_____. "Drugs and Detective Stories." 1941. Christie, *Styles: Hercule Poirot's First,* pp. xiii–xvi.

_____. *Dumb Witness.* Collins, 1937.

_____. *Elephants Can Remember.* Collins, 1972.

_____. *Endless Night.* Collins, 1967.

_____. *Five Little Pigs.* Collins, 1943.

_____. Foreword. *Crime Collection 1,* by Christie, Hamlyn, 1969, front matter. A brief foreword to a collection of omnibus editions

_____. Foreword. *Crooked House,* by Christie, Penguin, 1953, p. 5. One of several forewords written by Christie for a set of Penguin books in 1953.

_____. Foreword. *Death Comes as the End,* by Christie, Penguin, 1953, p. 5. One of several forewords written by Christie for a set of Penguin books in 1953.

_____. Foreword. *Miss Marple and the Thirteen Problems,* by Christie, Penguin, 1953, p. 5. One of several forewords written by Christie for a set of Penguin books in 1953.

_____. Foreword. *Parker Pyne Investigates,* by Christie, Penguin, 1953, p. 7. One of several forewords written by Christie for a set of Penguin books in 1953.

_____. Foreword. *The Body in the Library,* by Christie, Penguin, 1953, p. 5. One of several forewords written by Christie for a set of Penguin books in 1953.

_____. Foreword. *The Labours of Hercules,* by Christie, Penguin, 1953, p. 3. One of several forewords written by Christie for a set of Penguin books in 1953.

_____. Foreword. *The Moving Finger,* by Christie, Penguin, 1953, p. 6. One of several forewords written by Christie for a set of Penguin books in 1953.

_____. *4.50 from Paddington.* Collins, 1957.

_____. *The Grand Tour: Letters and Photographs from the British Empire Expedition.* HarperCollins, 2012.

_____. *Hallowe'en Party.* 1969. Harper, 2015.

_____. *Hercule Poirot and the Greenshore Folly.* HarperCollins, 2014.

_____. "Hercule Poirot—Fiction's Greatest Detective." *Daily Mail,* 15 Jan. 1938, p. 8.

_____. *Hercule Poirot: The Complete Short Stories.* Harper, 2008.

_____. *Hercule Poirot's Christmas.* Collins, 1938.

_____. *Hickory Dickory Dock.* Collins, 1955.

_____. *The Hollow.* Collins, 1946.

_____. *The Hound of Death and Other Stories.* Odhams, 1933.

_____. Introduction. *The Mousetrap Man,* by Peter Saunders, Collins, 1972, pp. 7–9. A late offering, Christie introduces the stage producer's autobiography with recollections about her own theatrical career.

_____. *The Labours of Hercules.* Collins, 1947.

_____. *The Last Séance: Tales of the Supernatural.* HarperCollins, 2019.

_____. "A Letter from Agatha Christie." *Sunday Times Magazine,* 20 Oct. 1968, p. 23. Part of a feature on true crime, Christie discusses here the unsolved murder of Charles Bravo.

_____. "A Letter to My Publisher." 1936. Pamphlet suppl. to Christie, *Styles: Hercule Poirot's First,* n.p.

_____. "Letter to *Woman's Day.*" 1971. Spec. collections, U of Exeter.

_____. *The Listerdale Mystery.* 1934. Harper, 2016.

_____. *Lord Edgware Dies.* Collins, 1933.

_____. *The Man in the Brown Suit.* Bodley Head, 1924.

_____. "Margery Allingham—A Tribute." 1968. *The Allingham Minibus: With a Tribute by Agatha Christie.* By Margery Allingham. Agora, 2019, ebook.

_____. *The Mary Westmacott Collection.* Vols. 1 and 2. HarperCollins, 2005.

_____. *The Mirror Crack'd from Side to Side.* Collins, 1962.

_____. *Miss Marple's 6 Final Cases and 2 Other Stories.* Collins, 1979.

_____. *The Mousetrap and Other Plays.* Harper, 2011.

_____. *The Moving Finger.* Collins, 1943.

_____. "Mrs. Agatha Christie: Her Own Story of Her Disappearance." *Daily Mail,* 16 Feb. 1928, p. 11.

_____. *Mrs. McGinty's Dead.* 1952. Harper, 2014.

_____. *The Murder at the Vicarage.* 1930. Harper, 2016.

_____. *Murder in Mesopotamia.* Collins, 1936b.

_____. *Murder in the Mews*. Collins, 1937.

_____. *Murder in the Studio*. Samuel French, 2019.

_____. *Murder in Three Acts*. 1934. Popular Lib., 1977. The American version of *Three Act Tragedy* includes an altered ending, which Christie herself wrote.

_____. *A Murder Is Announced*. Collins, 1950.

_____. *Murder Is Easy*. 1939. Harper, 2017.

_____. *The Murder of Roger Ackroyd*. Collins, 1926.

_____. *The Murder on the Links*. Bodley Head, 1923.

_____. *Murder on the Nile*. 1948. Samuel French, 2011.

_____. *Murder on the Orient Express*. Collins, 1934.

_____. *The Mysterious Affair at Styles*. Bodley Head, 1921.

_____. *The Mysterious Mr. Quin*. 1930. Harper, 2017.

_____. *The Mystery of the Blue Train*. Collins, 1928.

_____. *N or M?* Dodd, 1941.

_____. *Nemesis*. Collins, 1971.

_____. *One, Two, Buckle My Shoe*. Collins, 1940.

_____. *Ordeal by Innocence*. Collins, 1958.

_____. *The Pale Horse*. Collins, 1961.

_____. *Parker Pyne Investigates*. 1934. HarperCollins, 2017.

_____. *Partners in Crime*. Collins, 1929.

_____. *Passenger to Frankfurt: An Extravaganza*. Collins, 1970.

_____. *Peril at End House*. 1932. Harper, 2015.

_____. *A Pocket Full of Rye*. Collins, 1953.

_____. *Poems*. Collins, 1973.

_____. "Poirot and the Regatta Mystery." 1936. Christie, *Poirot: Complete Short Stories*, pp. 865–76.

_____. *Poirot Investigates*. Bodley Head, 1924.

_____. *Poirot's Early Cases*. Collins, 1974.

_____. *Postern of Fate*. Collins, 1973.

_____. *Problem at Pollensa Bay and Other Stories*. HarperCollins, 1991.

_____. *Sad Cypress*. 1941. Collins, 1951.

_____. *The Secret Adversary*. Bodley Head, 1922.

_____. *The Secret of Chimneys*. Bodley Head, 1925.

_____. *The Secret of Chimneys*. Samuel French, 2018.

_____. "Sir Allen Lane: A Flair for Success." *The Spectator*, 18 July 1970, pp. 7–8.

_____. *The Sittaford Mystery*. Collins, 1931.

_____. *Sleeping Murder*. Collins, 1976.

_____. *Sparkling Cyanide*. Collins, 1944.

_____. *Spider's Web*. 1954. Samuel French, 2001.

_____. *Styles: Hercule Poirot's First and Last Cases*. HarperCollins, 2016.

_____. *Taken at the Flood*. Collins, 1948.

_____. *They Came to Baghdad*. Collins, 1951.

_____. *They Do It with Mirrors*. 1952. HarperCollins, 2016.

_____. *Third Girl*. Collins, 1966.

_____. *The Thirteen Problems*. Collins, 1932.

_____. *Three Act Tragedy*. 1935. Harper, 2016.

_____. *Three Blind Mice and Other Stories*. Dodd, 1950.

_____. *Towards Zero*. 1944. HarperCollins, 2017.

_____. *Towards Zero*. 1944. Penguin, 1978. This edition reproduces the original text, censored in modern editions due to racist language.

_____. "The Tragedy Family of Croydon." Detection Club, *Six*, pp. 293–99.

_____. "The Under Dog." *Two New Crime Stories*, by Agatha Christie and E. Phillips Oppenheim, Reader's Library, 1929, pp. 9–142. An expanded version of the 1925 short story, produced with an original Oppenheim novella as part of a cheap subscription series, later republished as a *Daily Express* promotion.

_____. "What I Would Do if I Were Starving." *Britannia and Eve*, vol. 3, no. 7, 1931, pp. 10–11, 94.

_____. *While the Light Lasts and Other Stories*. 1997. HarperCollins, 1998.

_____. *Why Didn't They Ask Evans?* 1934. Harper-Collins, 2017.

Christie, Agatha, and Charles Osborne. *Black Coffee*. HarperCollins, 1998. Osborne, an actor and author of *The Life and Crimes of Agatha Christie*, turned three Christie plays into novels, starting with *Black Coffee*. The others were *The Unexpected Guest* (1999) and *Spider's Web* (2000).

Christie, Agatha, Dorothy L. Sayers, Hugh Walpole, E. C. Bentley, Anthony Berkeley, Clemence Dane, Ronald Knox, and Freeman Wills Crofts. *The Scoop & Behind the Screen*. Berkley, 1986.

Cohen, Claire. "Surfing, Single Motherhood and Sexual Betrayal: Agatha Christie Should Be a Feminist Icon." *Daily Telegraph*, 13 June 2015, www.telegraph.co.uk/women/womens-life/11672325/Agatha-Christie-Feminist-icon-surfer-and-single-mother.html. A newspaper editorial viewing Christie as a modern woman.

Conrad, Joseph. *Heart of Darkness*. 1899. Broadview, 2003. An influential novella critiquing imperialism and racist topographies.

Cook, Michael. *Detective Fiction and the Ghost Story*. Palgrave, 2014. A set of case studies, examining the relationship between detective fiction and the supernatural. As well as Christie, Cook focuses on Arthur Conan Doyle. M. R. James, and Tony Hillerman.

Crescentini, Federica. "'There Are Things One Doesn't Forget': The Second World War in 'Three Blind Mice' and *The Mousetrap*." Mills and Bernthal, *War*, pp. 109–23. An exploration of war and memory in Christie's novella and play.

Curran, John. "Agatha Christie's Black Coffee: A Mystery within a Mystery." *CADS: Crime and Detective Stories*, no. 67, Mar. 2014, pp. 41–43. Curran hypothesizes that *Black Coffee* was written earlier than is commonly thought.

_____. *Agatha Christie's Murder in the Making: More Stories and Secrets from her Archives*. HarperCollins, 2011. A second publication of material from Christie's notebooks, with an emphasis on unused plot ideas, which also features unpublished draft short stories.

_____. *Agatha Christie's Secret Notebooks: Fifty Years of Mysteries in the Making*. HarperCollins, 2009. A significant publication of material from Christie's notebooks, including plot outlines and previously unpublished draft short stories.

_____. *The Hooded Gunman*. HarperCollins, 2019.

A photographic history of the Collins Crime Club.

Darbon, Leslie. *Cards on the Table*. Samuel French, 1982. A stage adaptation of Christie's 1936 novel.

Dayananda, James Y. "Phillpotts [married name Ross] (Mary) Adelaide Eden." 1976. *Oxford Dictionary of National Biography*, October 2012, doi: https://doi.org/10.1093/ref:odnb/49176. An interview with Adelaide Phillpotts Ross, daughter of Christie mentor Eden Phillpotts and a childhood friend of Christie, reveals sexual abuse by Phillpotts of his daughter.

Dennis, Nigel. "Genteel Queen of Crime: Agatha Christie Puts Her Zest for Life into Murder." *Life*, 14 May 1956, pp. 87–102. A rare interview in which Christie presents a domestic, unthreatening image.

Derleth, August. "Outstanding 1968 Books, Selected by August Derleth." *Capital Times* [Madison, WI], 5 Dec. 1968, p. 62. Author-publisher-critic Derleth selects Christie's *Endless Night* as an outstanding book of 1968.

_____. "Outstanding 1969 Books, Selected by August Derleth." *Capital Times* [Madison, WI], 4 Dec 1969, p. 62. Author-publisher-critic Derleth selects Christie's *By the Pricking of My Thumbs* as an outstanding book of 1969.

The Detection Club. *The Floating Admiral*, Doubleday, 1932.

_____. *Six against the Yard*. 1929. HarperCollins, 2013.

Dobkins, Michael. "This Tickled My Curiosity, So…" *Twitter*, 13 Apr. 2020, www.twitter.com/MichaelDobkins/status/1249630330044076032. A tweet demonstrating archival research into the term *Queen of Crime*.

"Editorial." *Manchester Evening Chronicle*, 19 Apr. 1905, p. 2. An antisemitic newspaper editorial.

Edwards, Martin. "Agatha Christie's Poirot: The Clocks—Review." *Do You Write Under Your Own Name?*, 27 Dec. 2011, doyouwriteunderyourownname.blogspot.com/2011/12/agatha-christies-poirot-clocks-review.html. A review of Christie's novel on Edwards's blog.

_____. *The Golden Age of Murder*. HarperCollins, 2015. The definitive account of how the Detection Club was established, with background information about key members. Edwards, president of the Detection Club and former chair of the Crime Writers' Association, is an authority on Golden Age crime fiction.

_____. "Plotting." *The Routledge Companion to Crime Fiction*, ed. Janice M. Allan et al., Routledge, 2020, pp. 185–93. An analysis of plotting techniques, drawing on Christie as a Golden Age exemplar.

Edwards, Owen Dudley. "Agatha Christie's 'The Hollow.'" *The Drouth*, n.d. www.thedrouth.org/agatha-christies-the-hollow-by-owen-dudley-edwards. An analysis of *The Hollow* in the style of popular literary criticism.

E.H.R. "Television." *The Observer*, 20 June 1937, p.

14. Includes a positive review of the first Christie television production.

Erman, Adolf. *The Literature of the Ancient Egyptians*. 1927. Translated by Aylward M. Blackman, Blom, 1971. Erman explains the source of a quotation that appears in Christie's *Death Comes at the End*.

"Eugene, Eugenia and Little Eugenics." *Life*, June 1913, p. 931. A satiric cartoon reflecting on the rise of eugenics in pre–World War I popular culture.

Evans, Curtis. "A Is for Adenoids: The Adenoidal Agatha Christie." *The Passing Tramp*, 6 Nov. 2019, thepassingtramp.blogspot.com/2019/11/a-is-for-for-adenoids-adenoidal-agatha.html. A blog post about maids and stereotypes in Christie's fiction. Evans is a prominent publisher and Golden Age enthusiast, whose blog demonstrates the forensic detail of fan scholarship.

Evans, Dewi Llyr. "A Drop of Water from a Stagnant Pool: Agatha Christie's Parapractic Murders." *CrimeCulture*, Summer 2007, www.crimeculture.com/Contents/ArticlesSummer07/Christie.html. Evans links Hercule Poirot's detection methods to the analytic techniques of Sigmund Freud.

Fallon, Dawn. "'One Hour with Thee'—Notes on Waltz Composed by Agatha Christie." *Facebook*, 5 Mar. 2013, www.facebook.com/notes/dawn-fallon-pianist/one-hour-with-thee-notes-on-waltz-composed-by-agatha-christie/300654216728558. Fallon, then-in-house pianist at the Christie holiday home Greenway, describes Christie's only published waltz.

Federal Bureau of Investigation [FBI]. "Lindbergh Kidnapping." n.d. www.fbi.gov/history/famous-cases/lindbergh-kidnapping. A history of the March 1932 kidnapping case of Charles Lindbergh, Jr., that was a strong influence on Christie's *Murder on the Orient Express*.

"Film Guide." *Radio Times*, Christmas/New Year 2004, p. 56. Television listings pithily summarizing *The Mirror Crack'd* (1980).

Fowles, John. Introduction. Adams and Symons, pp. 7–8. Tom Adams illustrated the work of the well-known Fowles, who here introduces Adams's photo-book of Christie covers.

Fuller, William Edwin. "A Play in One Act." 1932. Fuller Collection, Private Deposit Collection, Spec. and Rare Collections, U of Tasmania, Australia. UTAS SPARC F6–15c. Ms. of a play, also known as *Roads of Memory*, that is an adaptation of Christie's "The Jewel Robbery at the Grand Metropolitan."

Gatiss, Mark. "No, It's a Loose Adaptation…." *Twitter*, 23 Oct. 2013, www.twitter.com/Markgatiss/status/393119242931163136. In this tweet, dramatist/actor Mark Gatiss dismisses Christie's *The Big Four*, which he adapted, as "unadaptable."

Gill, Gillian. *Agatha Christie: The Woman and Her Mysteries*. Robson, 1991. An unauthorized feminist biography, drawing heavily on novels written as Mary Westmacott for psychological insights.

Gordon-Smith, Dolores. "Captain Arthur Hastings, O.B.E." *CADS: Crime and Detective Stories,* no. 84, Dec. 2020, pp. 21–23. A brief biography of Captain Hastings.

Green, Julius. *Curtain Up—Agatha Christie: A Life in Theatre.* HarperCollins, 2015. An extensive history of Christie's contributions to the theater, including analyses of unpublished and previously unknown scripts.

Gregg, Hubert. *Agatha Christie and All That Mousetrap.* Kimber, 1980. Gregg directed many of Christie's plays and presents her as an unfriendly, business-minded individual in this memoir.

Grenfell, Joyce. "Broadcasting the Old Contemptibles." *The Observer,* 7 Nov. 1937, p. 27. Grenfell, later well known as an actress and comedian, reviews Christie's first radio play.

Gulddal, Jesper, Stewart King, and Alistair Rolls, eds. *Criminal Moves: Modes of Mobility in Crime Fiction,* Liverpool UP, 2019. This edited collection seeks to challenge distinctions between popular and literary fiction, examining crime fiction in dialogue with "processes of appropriation and transculturation" (19).

———. "Introduction—Criminal Moves: Towards a Theory of Crime Fiction Mobility." Gulddal, King, and Rolls, *Criminal Moves,* pp. 1–26. The editors of this volume discusses its purpose as "challeng[ing] the distinction between literary and popular fiction" (1).

Haining, Peter. *Agatha Christie: Murder in Four Acts,* Virgin, 1990. A glossy history of stage, film, radio, and television adaptations in the United Kingdom and the United States to the point of publication.

———. *Agatha Christie's Poirot: A Celebration of the Great Detective.* Boxtree/LWT, 1995. A promotional coffee-table book to promote the ITV television series, featuring cast interviews and overviews of the main characters.

Harris, Patricia Roberts. "On the Death of Poirot." *New York Times,* 14 Aug. 1975, p. 30. A letter to the editor that praises Christie and Poirot in anticipation of *Curtain.*

Hart, Anne. *The Life and Times of Hercule Poirot.* Sphere, 1990. A biography of Poirot, based on material in published fiction. It is occasionally updated, even after the author's death, with details of new English-language screen adaptations.

———. *The Life and Times of Miss Marple.* 1985. Sphere, 1991. A biography of Miss Marple, based on material in published fiction. It is occasionally updated, even after the author's death, with details of new English-language screen adaptations.

Haycraft, Howard. *Murder for Pleasure: The Life and Times of the Detective Story.* Appleton-Century, 1941. Important early discussion of the evolution of the detective genre, including coverage of Christie's Hercule Poirot.

Hellman, Geoffrey. "The Mallowans." *The New Yorker,* 29 Oct. 1966, p. 51. A rare interview with Christie and her second husband, offering a glimpse of them at home and in dialogue.

Hesford, Walter. "The Detective as Prophet: Arnaldur Indridason's Inspector Erlendur." *Christianity and the Detective Story,* ed. Anya Morlan and Walter Raubicheck, Cambridge Scholars Publishing, 2013, pp. 167–79. Using Indridason's detective as a case study, Hesford considers fictional detectives as secular substitutes for priests.

Hicks, Rosalind. "The Secret of Mary Westmacott." Underwood, *Centenary,* pp. 50–51. Christie's daughter introduces the novels written by Christie under the pseudonym Mary Westmacott, emphasizing that they are about love but are not romances.

Hughes, Dorothy B. "The Christie Nobody Knew." Keating, *First Lady,* pp. 121–30. A distinguished noir novelist and critic, Hughes was a well-documented Christie fan; in this contribution to Keating's elegiac retrospective, she examines the Mary Westmacott novels.

"In the Best Tradition: Mystification and Art." *Times Literary Supplement,* 25 Feb. 1955, p. 124. A mid-century editorial claiming that crime fiction can be psychologically nuanced and, unusually, using Christie as an example.

Jones, Julia. *The Adventures of Margery Allingham.* Golden Duck, 2009. A biography of Christie's fellow Detection Club member Allingham.

Keating, H. R. F., ed. *Agatha Christie: First Lady of Crime.* Weidenfeld, 1977. Essay collection edited by Inspector Ghote creator Keating that explores Christie's life, technique, and reasons for her success.

———. "Jack Fell Down." *A Classic English Crime,* ed. Tim Heald, Pavillion, 1990, pp. 95–111. A short story that offers a pastiche of Hercule Poirot but features Sven Hjerson, the detective created by Ariadne Oliver in the Christie universe.

Klein, Roberta S. "Agatha Christie: A Feminist Reassessment." PhD diss., U of Pennsylvania, 1999. Klein argues with textual analysis that Christie can be read in the context of late-twentieth-century feminism.

Knepper, Marty S. "Agatha Christie—Feminist." *The Armchair Detective,* vol. 16, 1983, pp. 398–406. The first article to consider Christie as a feminist writer.

———. "Agatha Christie's *The Mystery of the Blue Train*: 'Easily the Worst Book'?." *Clues: A Journal of Detection,* vol. 22, no. 1, 2001, pp. 33–39. Knepper challenges Christie's own assessment of her novel, suggesting that it is innovative, perhaps because it was difficult to write.

———. "Reading Agatha Christie's Miss Marple Series: The Thirteen Problems." *In the Beginning: First Novels in Mystery Series,* ed. Mary Jane DeMarr, Popular Press, 1995, pp. 33–59. An early example of detailed analysis of a Marple text, part of a wave of scholarship between the popular, stereotype-based scholarship of the 1980s and the analytic, text-based or theorized contributions of the 2000s.

Kyzlinkova, Lidia. "Social Issues in Agatha Christie's Mysteries: Country, Class, Crime, Clothes and Children." *BRNO Studies in English,* vol. 23, 1997, pp. 115–27. Kyzlinkova examines Christie's presentation of working-class stereotypes, asking whether they reflect her views or her context.

Laing, Jennifer, and Warwick Frost. *Explorer Travellers and Adventure Tourism.* Channel View, 2014. An analysis of travel in popular culture, considering the interrelationship of tourism and exploration, including examples from Christie's *Murder in Mesopotamia.*

Lask, Thomas. "Hercule Poirot Is Dead: Famed Belgian Detective." *New York Times,* 6 Aug. 1975, pp. 1, 16. The most famous obituary for a fictional character, this appeared on the paper's front page and was widely emulated. It is, in reality, a retrospective of Christie's career, anticipating *Curtain,* the last Poirot novel, which was soon to be published.

Lawson, Mark. "Being Hercule Poirot." *Radio Times,* 1–7 Dec. 2018, pp. 12–15. Promotional interviews for the BBC's *The ABC Murders,* focusing on John Malkovich's interpretation of Poirot.

Light, Alison. *Forever England: Femininity, Literature and Conservatism between the Wars.* Routledge, 1991. A game-changing monograph, the first chapter of which positions Christie as a "conservative modernist"—that is, a popular writer whose work can nonetheless be formally studied. Light inspired much of the middlebrow studies movement.

Lu Yi-Chih. "Agatha Christie: One Hour with Thee." *YouTube,* 6 Jan. 2019, www.youtube.com/watch?v=vdwn7qjNWk0. Web. A recording of Christie's only published waltz.

Ludwig, Ken. *Agatha Christie's Murder on the Orient Express.* Samuel French, 2019. A stage adaptation of the 1934 novel.

Lukas, J. Anthony. "Censorship Rises in South Africa." *New York Times,* 25 Nov. 1964, p. 6. Lukas notes that Christie's *A Caribbean Mystery* was barred from sale in South Africa as the government moved against what it considered "'undesirable' literature."

Makinen, Merja. *Agatha Christie: Investigating Femininity.* Palgrave, 2006. The first sustained single-theme analysis of Christie, examining gender in Christie's crime fiction.

———. "Contradicting the Golden Age: Reading Agatha Christie in the Twenty-First Century." Gulddal, King, and Rolls, *Criminal Moves,* pp. 77–94. Makinen argues that interpretations of classic crime fiction can grow and evolve alongside the genre itself.

———. "Hidden in Plain Sight: The Mary Westmacott Novels." *The Bloomsbury Handbook to Agatha Christie,* ed. J. C. Bernthal and Mary Anna Evans, Bloomsbury, forthcoming. An examination of the Westmacott novels, which insists on textual analysis rather than reading them as autobiography

Mallowan, Agatha Christie. *Come, Tell Me How You Live.* 1946. HarperCollins, 1999.

———. *Star Over Bethlehem and Other Stories.* Collins, 1965.

Mallowan, Max. *Mallowan's Memoirs: Agatha and the Archaeologist.* 1977. HarperCollins, 2001. Chiefly a professional memoir, Mallowan also discusses the later years of his marriage to Christie in human terms.

Maloney, Alison. *Bright Young Things: Life in the Roaring Twenties.* Virgin Press, 2012. An overview of fashionable society in 1920s London.

Margolis, Ruth. "Agatha Christie: Four Heroines that Make her an Unlikely Feminist Icon." *BBC America, Anglophena,* Sept. 2015, www.bbcamerica.com/anglophenia/2015/09/agatha-christie-four-heroines-that-make-her-an-unlikely-feminist-icon. A tabloid-style discussion of strong women in Christie.

Martin, Sarah, and Sally West. "Mapping War, Planning Peace: Miss Marple and the Evolving Village Space, 1930–1962." Mills and Bernthal, *War,* 11–27. A psychogeographic exploration of the Miss Marple novels reflecting the impact of conflict between and after the world wars.

"The Mary Westmacotts." *Agatha Christie,* n.d., www.agathachristie.com/en/about-christie/family-memories/the-mary-westmacotts. The official Christie website introduces her pseudonymous novels, drawing on remarks by her daughter and grandson.

McRae, G. Roy. *The Passing of Mr. Quinn.* HarperCollins, 2017. Novelization of the 1928 silent film that was based on the Christie short story of the same name.

Mills, Rebecca. "Detecting the Blitz: Memory and Trauma in Christie's Postwar Writings." Mills and Bernthal, *War,* pp. 137–54. An examination of echoes of war and memories of trauma in Christie's postwar novels, drawing also on autobiographical descriptions of the Blitz.

———. "England's Pockets: Objects of Anxiety in Agatha Christie's Post-War Novels." Bernthal, *Ageless,* pp. 29–44. Mills examines some of Christie's late novels and discusses their negation of cultural anxieties.

Mills, Rebecca, and J. C. Bernthal, eds. *Agatha Christie Goes to War.* Routledge, 2020.

———. Introduction. Mills and Bernthal, *War,* pp. 1–10. Mills and Bernthal present an edited collection that introduces the importance of historical context, positioning Christie as a war writer, especially evoking World War II.

Mr. London. "A Penalty of Realism." *Portsmouth Evening News,* 20 Aug. 1926, p. 6. Society gossip in a newspaper, reporting that Christie had suffered a nervous breakdown and blaming the stress of prolific publication.

Morgan, Janet. *Agatha Christie: A Biography.* 1984. HarperCollins, 1997. The first authorized biography of Christie, Morgan tows a respectful line, drawing on letters in the family archive.

"*The Moving Finger*: Behind the Scenes." *The*

Moving Finger, by Agatha Christie, Harper, 2004, pp. 301–19. Reproduced press-pack for a television adaptation.

"*The Murder at the Vicarage*: Behind the Scenes." *The Murder at the Vicarage,* by Agatha Christie, Harper, 2004, pp. 385–415. Reproduced press-pack for a television adaptation.

"Mystery at Magpie Manor." *Out of the Ark Music,* n.d., www.outoftheark.co.uk/mystery-at-magpie-manor.html. Details about a play for American schools, inspired by Christie.

Nicol, Danny. "'Bad Business': Capitalism and Criminality in Agatha Christie's Novels." *Entertainment and Sports Law Journal,* vol. 17, no. 6, 2019, art. 6, pp. 1–11, doi: doi.org/10.16997/eslj.230. Nicol considers criticisms of capitalism in Christie's war-conscious fiction.

Norman, Andrew. *Agatha Christie: The Finished Portrait.* History Press, 2007. A semi-psychanalytic look at Christie's 1926 disappearance, claiming that she lapsed into a "fugue state" (106).

Oram, Alison. *Her Husband Was a Woman! Women's Gender-Crossing in Modern British Popular Culture.* Routledge, 2007. Extensive archival research and analysis of British mid-twentieth century moral panic around women cohabiting.

Osborne, Charles. *The Life and Crimes of Agatha Christie.* 1981. HarperCollins, 2000. A reader's companion to the major novels, plays, and story collections, providing details about Christie's life and summaries of the texts.

Palmer, Cecil. "On Behalf of the Thriller." *Times Literary Supplement,* 16 July 1938, p. 479. A short editorial on the verge of World War II, defending reading "thrillers" (i.e., detective fiction) as providing much-needed escapism.

Parkinson, Michael. Extract from *Michael Parkinson's Confession Album—1973.* Underwood, *Centenary,* p. 23. In this publication, broadcaster Parkinson compiled likes and dislikes of well-known people, which included Christie.

Penguin Books Archive, U of Bristol. Contains correspondence between Christie and Sir Allen Lane, relating to social plans and plans for Penguin Books.

Perec, Dana, and Loredana Pungă. "They Do It with Nursery Rhymes: The Mystery of Intertextuality in Agatha Christie's Detective Fiction from a Literary Critic's and a Translator's Perspective." *B.A.S.: British and American Studies,* vol. 25, 2019, pp. 247–56. An analysis of the incorporation of nursery rhymes into Christie's texts and the challenges that these present to linguists and translators.

Peschel, Bill. "Revolutionaries, Saboteurs, and Spies." *The Deluxe Complete, Annotated Secret Adversary.* Peschel Press, 2013, pp. 372–81. One of many supplementary essays in Peschel's footnoted edition of an early Christie novel. Peschel publishes these as and when the texts enter public domain in the United States.

Plain, Gill. "'Tale Engineering': Agatha Christie and the Aftermath of World War II." *Literature & History,* vol. 29, no. 2, 2020, pp. 179–99, doi: doi.org/10.1177%2F0306197320945945. Examining three postwar Christies, Plain argues that she renegotiated the puzzle format, incorporating grief, gender, and contemporary anxieties.

———. *Twentieth Century Crime Fiction: Gender, Sexuality and the Body.* Edinburgh UP, 2001. Exploring gender and sexuality in UK and US mid-century fiction, Plain challenges critical notions that position the plot as the most important part of the genre.

Poulter, Chrissie. "Wasn't It Wonderful!. .. Her Very. ." *Twitter,* 29 Aug. 2020, twitter.com/ChrissiePoulter/status/1299724211984969728. A tweet comparing Christie to Henrik Ibsen.

Prichard, Mathew. Foreword. Christie and Osborne, pp. i–ii. Prichard is Agatha Christie's only grandson; his foreword to *Black Coffee* introduces it to fans as canon.

Pronzini, Bill. *Gun in Cheek: An Affectionate Guide to the "Worst" in Mystery Fiction.* 1982. Dover Publications, 2017. Pronzini discusses *The Invisible Host* by Gwen Bristow and Bruce Manning, a novel that precedes Christie's *And Then There Were None* and has a similar plot line.

Pujolràs-Noguer, Esther. "'She Was Such an Exotic Creature': Feeding the Orientalist Machine in Agatha Christie's *Murder in Mesopotamia.*" *Crime Fiction Studies,* vol. 3, no. 1, forthcoming. Pujolràs-Noguer considers the relationship between gender and racial constructions, arguing that the victim in Christie's novel is "Orientalized" in part via sexualization, and blamed for her own downfall.

Queen, Ellery [Frederic Dannay and Manfred B. Lee]. Ellery Queen Papers, Beinecke Rare Book and Manuscript Lib., Yale U. Contains correspondence relating to *Ellery Queen's Mystery Magazine,* which published Christie's short stories extensively.

Richardson, Maurice. Rev. of *A Pocket Full of Rye,* by Agatha Christie. *The Observer,* 15 Nov. 1953, p. 10. Patronizing review of Christie's *A Pocket Full of Rye.*

Rowland, Susan. *From Agatha Christie to Ruth Rendell: British Women Writers in Detective and Crime Fiction,* Palgrave, 2001. In one of the first monographs to contextualize Christie, Rowland studies selected novels alongside those of other women, either contemporary or later (Margery Allingham, Dorothy L. Sayers, Ngaio Marsh, P. D. James, and Ruth Rendell/Barbara Vine).

Rowse, A. L. *Memories of Men and Women, American and British.* UP of America, 1983. The historian's acerbic memoir includes a chapter on his friendship with Max Mallowan and includes extensive gossip about Agatha Christie, presenting her as naïve and sexless.

RTP Arquivos. "Entrevista a Agatha Christie," 6 Apr. 1984, arquivos.rtp.pt/conteudos/entrevista-a-agatha-christie. Web. An interview ca. 1960 for Portuguese television.

St. John Stott, Graham, and Aysar Yaseen. "The Balkan Theme in *The Secret of Chimneys*." *SIC: Journal of Literature, Culture and Literary Translation*, vol. 6. no. 2, 2016, pp. 1–19, www.sic-journal.org/Article/Index/406. An exploration of the use of "Balkan stereotypes" in Christie's 1925 thriller.

Sanders, Dennis, and Len Lovallo. *The Agatha Christie Companion*. Allen, 1984. Overviews of the novels and short story collections, with summaries of contemporary reviews.

Saunders, Peter. *The Mousetrap Man*. Collins, 1972. Theatrical memoirs of the man who produced most of Christie's plays, including *The Mousetrap*.

Sayers, Dorothy L. Introduction. *Great Short Stories of Detection, Mystery and Horror*, Gollancz, 1928, pp. 9–47. Often anthologized as "An Omnibus of Crime," this lengthy introduction is a dissertation on detective fiction, making an early case for it to be taken seriously and upholding its roots as Aristotelean.

_____. *Strong Poison*. 1929. New English Lib., 2012. An influential detective novel featuring Lord Peter Wimsey and Harriet Vane.

Schwartz, Hillel. *The Culture of the Copy*. 1996. Zone, 2014. A sustained analysis of Western depictions of doubles and doubling.

Scowcroft, P. L. "Agatha Christie and Music, British and Other." *Classical Music on the Web*, n.d., www.musicweb-international.com/agatha_christie.htm. English musician Scowcroft summarizes Christie's ambitions for a career in music.

Shaw, Marion, and Sabine Vanacker. *Reflecting on Miss Marple*. 1991. Routledge, 2018. This first book-length academic study of Miss Marple contextualizes her as a creation to exploit and challenge stereotypes about women.

Slide, Anthony. *Gay and Lesbian Characters and Themes in Mystery Novels: A Critical Guide to Over 500 Works in English*. McFarland, 1993. The first and most extensive catalog of gay and lesbian references in Anglo-American crime fiction, which looks at mainstream fiction rather than specifically LGBTQ+ subgenres.

Smith, Michael. *Bletchley Park: The Code-Breakers of Station X*. Shire, 2013. A popular history of British codebreaking during World War II.

Snowdon, Lord [Antony Armstrong-Jones]. "The Unsinkable Agatha Christie." *Toronto Star*, 14 Dec. 1974, p. G1. Published as an interview with an 84-year-old Christie, this was a covertly-recorded conversation, discussing matters such as the *Murder on the Orient Express* film.

Sova, Dawn B. *Agatha Christie A to Z: The Essential Reference to Her Life & Writings*. 1996. Checkmark, 2000. An encyclopedic overview of most Christie novels, stories, and characters.

Spenser, Edmund. *The Faerie Queene*, Book 1, Macmillan, 1893. This epic poem provides the quotation on Christie's gravestone.

Stine, Whitney. *"I'd Love to Kiss You...": Conversations with Bette Davis*. Thorndike, ME: Thorndike Press, 1990. Davis comments on filming *Murder with Mirrors* (based on Christie's *They Do It with Mirrors*) with Helen Hayes.

Street, Sarah. "Autobiography in *Agatha* (1979): 'An Imaginary Solution to an Authentic Mystery.'" Bernthal, *Ageless,* pp. 161–75. A behind-the-scenes look at the production problems plaguing the biographical movie.

Strømmen, Hannah M. "Poirot, the Bourgeois Prophet: Agatha Christie's Biblical Adaptations." Blyth and Jack, pp. 149–66. Strømmen considers Poirot as a prophetic character and biblical authority.

Suchet, David, and Geoffrey Wansell. *Poirot and Me*. Headline, 2013. Suchet's memoir, which in early drafts was a photo-book, focuses on his experiences starring in *Agatha Christie's Poirot*.

Symons, Julian. *The Great Detectives: Seven Original Investigations*. Orbis, 1981. Symons, author of *Bloody Murder*, a key text in crime fiction scholarship, here provides pastiches/biographies of seven major detectives from fiction, including Christie's Poirot and Miss Marple. This is technically the first authorized Christie continuation fiction.

_____. "Hercule Poirot, il est mort." *New York Times*, 12 Oct. 1975, p. 289. Symons reviews the final Hercule Poirot novel and reflects on Christie's achievements.

Symons, Julian, and Edmund Crispin [Robert Bruce Montgomery]. "Is the Detective Story Dead?." *Times Literary Supplement*, 23 June 1961, 392–93. A "recorded dialogue," curated by Anthony Lejeune, in which the two authors consider the need for crime fiction to adapt to changing times.

Tennenbaum, Michael. "And Then There Were Three." *The New Bedside, Bathtub & Armchair Companion to Agatha Christie*, ed. Dick Riley and Pam McAllister, Ungar, 1991, pp. 146–48. A survey of the 1945, 1965, and 1974 screen adaptations of *And Then There Were None*, with a table comparing character "types."

Tennyson, Alfred Lord. *The Works of Alfred, Lord Tennyson*. Grosset, 1892. Tennyson, Christie's favorite poet, is heavily referenced in her work.

Thompson, Howard. "Quiet Murders Suit Miss Christie." *New York Times*, 27 Oct. 1966, p. 57. Thompson interviews Christie and her second husband, Max Mallowan, while they were in the United States for Mallowan's lecture tour.

Thompson, Laura. *Agatha Christie: An English Mystery*. 2007. Headline, 2008. In the second authorized Christie biography, Thompson seeks the "real woman" behind Christie's persona, drawing on archived materials, personal interviews, and the Westmacott novels.

Thomson, H. Douglas. *Masters of Mystery*. Collins, 1931. A very early example of book-length popular scholarship, this summarizes British crime fiction and popular interpretations of it in the middle of the Golden Age.

Torquemada [Edward Powys Mather]. Rev. of *The Hound of Death*. *The Observer*, 18 Apr. 1937, p. 7. The crossword creator, to whom Christie was often compared, offered a lukewarm review of *The Hound of Death* but was more positive elsewhere in reviews of her mystery fiction.

Trent, Paul. "The Strain on Mrs. Christie." *Daily Mail*, 10 Dec. 1926, p. 8. The crime writer was one of many who wrote columns speculating on Christie's fate during her 1926 disappearance. He suggested a mental health crisis.

Tynan, Kathleen. *Agatha: The Agatha Christie Mystery*, Star, 1978. A novel imagining Christie's actions during her 1926 disappearance, filmed in 1979 as *Agatha*.

Underwood, Lynn, ed. *The Agatha Christie Centenary*. HarperCollins, 1990. This centenary booklet, with considerable input from the Christie family, reproduces "lost" material by Christie (a story, an interview, an article, and a poem) alongside new essays.

_____. "The Gentle but Determined Character." Underwood, *Centenary*, pp. 44–46. A brief overview of Miss Marple and her inspirations.

"Unsolved Mystery." *Dunstan Times*, 15 Oct. 1934, p. 6. A newspaper report on a murder case involving anonymous letters.

Van der Beek, Suzanne. "Agatha Christie and the Fantastic Detective Story." *Clues: A Journal of Detection*, vol. 34, no. 1, 2016, pp. 22–30. Analyzing *And Then There Were None*, Van der Beek argues that Christie problematizes distinctions between the natural and the supernatural.

Wallace, [Richard Horatio] Edgar. "My Theory of Mrs. Christie: Either Dead or in London." *Daily Mail*, 11 Dec. 1926, p. 9. The thriller writer was one of many who wrote columns speculating on Christie's fate during her 1926 disappearance. He suggested it was a stunt.

Walton, Samantha. *Guilty but Insane: Mind and Law in Golden Age Detective Fiction*. Oxford UP, 2015. An examination of psychiatry, criminality, and madness in interwar fiction by Christie, Ngaio Marsh, Dorothy L. Sayers, and Gladys Mitchell.

Watson, Colin. "Mayhem Parva and Wicked Belgravia." *Crime Writers*, ed. H. R. F. Keating, BBC, 1978, pp. 48–63. Watson summarizes his concept of "Mayhem Parva," as introduced in *Snobbery with Violence*.

_____. *Snobbery with Violence: English Crime Stories and Their Audiences*. 1971. Methuen, 1987. Popular criticism typifying a view of Christie and her peers as conservative, nostalgic, and socially disengaged.

Weaver, William. "Music and Mystery." Keating, *First Lady* 183–92. A chapter outlining Christie's early interest in opera and the role of music in her 1920s and 1930s fiction.

Westmacott, Mary [Agatha Christie]. *Absent in the Spring*. 1944. Christie, *Westmacott Collection 1*, pp. 593–755.

_____. *The Burden*. 1956. Christie, *Westmacott Collection 2*, pp. 385–575.

_____. *A Daughter's a Daughter*. Heinemann, 1952.

_____. *Giant's Bread*. 1930. Christie, *Westmacott Collection 1*, pp. 1–330.

_____. *The Rose and the Yew Tree*. 1947. Christie, *Westmacott Collection 2*, pp. 1–190.

_____. *Unfinished Portrait*. 1944. Christie, *Westmacott Collection 1*, pp. 331–592.

Whitney, Sarah E. "A Hidden Body in the Library: Mary Westmacott, Agatha Christie, and Emotional Violence." *Clues: A Journal of Detection*, vol. 29, no. 1, 2011, pp. 37–50. An exploration of emotional violence in the Westmacott novels, also considering their impact on Christie's crime writing.

Wilkinson, Joy. "Killing Miss Marple." *BBC Writers Room*, 10 Dec. 2015, www.bbc.co.uk/blogs/writersroom/entries/984036e3-ebff-4d2c-90f1-4aab15ee9d9a. A blog post in which Wilkinson discusses her adaptations of three Miss Marple stories for radio.

Williams, Emlyn. *Emlyn: An Early Autobiography, 1927–1935*. Viking, 1974. A memoir describing, among other things, Frank Vosper's account of writing the screenplay for *Love from a Stranger*.

Willis, Chris. "The Witching Hour." *The Agatha Christie Collection*, vol. 44, 2003, pp. 9–15. An entry from a magazine that ran 2002–05. Published fortnightly, each issue came with a hardback book.

Wilson, Edmund. "Who Cares Who Killed Roger Ackroyd? A Second Report on Detective Fiction." *New Yorker*, 20 Jan. 1945, p. 59. Wilson's article does not name Christie but uses her then-most-famous title to evoke her brand of fiction. He dismisses British crime writing as banal and socially irrelevant.

"With the Detectives." *Auckland* [NZ] *Star*, 24 Dec. 1936, Supplement, p. 8. A short, positive review of Christie's *Cards on the Table*.

"Woman's World: Stories That Thrill." *The Herald*, Saturday evening ed., 20 May 1922, p. 10. An early interview with Christie, emphasizing her gender and demonstrating that she was once happy to talk to the press; contains themes developed in *The Man in the Brown Suit*.

Worthington, Heather. *Key Concepts in Crime Fiction*. Routledge, 2011. A primer for undergraduate students introducing major debates in Anglo-American crime fiction studies.

Wyndham, Francis. "Agatha Christie's Algebra." *Washington Post*, 19 June 1966, p. E5. A widely published, oft-cited interview, in which Wyndham coins the phrase *animated algebra*, suggesting that Christie's fiction typifies a form of diversion in which the puzzle is paramount.

York, R. A. *Agatha Christie: Power and Illusion*. Palgrave, 2007. York challenges conventional ideas of "cozy" crime fiction, arguing that Christie is writing about a performative world where polite society, and the stereotypes she draws on, are masquerades and truth is always hidden.

Index